Volume C
Since 1900

Out of Many

A History of the American People

Third Edition

John Mack Faragher
Yale University

Mari Jo Buhle
Brown University

Daniel Czitrom
Mount Holyoke College

Susan H. Armitage
Washington State University

Prentice Hall, Upper Saddle River, New Jersey 07458

Library of Congress Cataloging–in–Publication Data
Out of many: a history of the American people / John Mack Faragher
. . . [et al.]. — 3rd ed., Combined ed.
p. cm.
Includes bibliographical references and index.
ISBN 0-13-949760-9
1. United States—History. I. Faragher, John Mack
E178.1.0935 2000 98–34110
973—dc21 CIP

Editorial Director: Charlyce Jones Owen
Executive Editor: Todd R. Armstrong
Development Editor: David Chodoff
Production Editor: Louise Rothman
Creative Director: Leslie Osher
Art Director: Anne Bonanno Nieglos
Editor-in-Chief of Development: Susanna Lesan
Marketing Manager: Sheryl Adams
Interior and Cover Designer: Thomas Nery
Cover Art: Ralph Fasanella, *Sunday Afternoon—Stickball Game,* 1953
AVP, Director of Production and Manufacturing: Barbara Kittle
Manufacturing Manager: Nick Sklitsis
Manufacturing Buyer: Lynn Pearlman
Photo Researcher: Barbara Salz
Photo Editor: Lorinda Morris-Nantz
Copy Editor: Sylvia Moore
Editorial Assistant: Holly Jo Brown
Line Art Coordinator: Guy Ruggiero
Cartographers: Alice and William Thiede/
CARTO-GRAPHICS
Electronic Page Layout: Scott Garrison and Rosemary Ross

Credits and acknowledgments for materials borrowed from other sources and reproduced, with permission, in this textbook appear on pages C–1 – C–3.

This book was set in 11/12 Weiss by the HSS in-house formatting and production services groups and was printed and bound by RR Donnelley & Sons Company. The cover was printed by Phoenix Color Corp.

Printed in the United States of America
10 9 8 7 6 5 4 3 2 1

ISBN 0-13-010033-1

Prentice-Hall International (UK) Limited, *London*
Prentice-Hall of Australia Pty. Limited, *Sydney*
Prentice-Hall Canada Inc., *Toronto*
Prentice-Hall Hispanoamericana, S.A., *Mexico*
Prentice-Hall of India Private Limited, *New Delhi*
Prentice-Hall of Japan, Inc., *Tokyo*
Pearson Education Asia Pte. Ltd., *Singapore*
Editora Prentice-Hall do Brasil, Ltda., *Rio de Janeiro*

To our students,
our sisters,
and our brothers

BRIEF CONTENTS

Contents

22 World War I, 1914–1920 642

23 The Twenties, 1920–1929 673

24 The Great Depression and the New Deal, 1929–1940 714

25 World War II, 1941–1945 748

26 The Cold War, 1945–1952 785

27 America at Midcentury, 1952–1963 817

28 The Civil Rights Movement, 1945–1966 848

29 War Abroad, War at Home, 1965–1974 878

31 The Conservative Ascendancy, since 1980 945

Maps

Charts, Graphs, and Tables

PREFACE

Out of Many, A History of the American People, third edition, offers a distinctive and timely approach to American history, highlighting the experiences of diverse communities of Americans in the unfolding story of our country. These communities offer a way of examining the complex historical forces shaping people's lives at various moments in our past. The debates and conflicts surrounding the most momentous issues in our national life—independence, emerging democracy, slavery, westward settlement, imperial expansion, economic depression, war, technological change—were largely worked out in the context of local communities. Through communities we focus on the persistent tensions between everyday life and those larger decisions and events that continually reshape the circumstances of local life. Each chapter opens with a description of a representative community. Some of these portraits feature American communities struggling with one another: African slaves and English masters on the rice plantations of colonial Georgia, or Tejanos and Americans during the Texas war of independence. Other chapters feature portraits of communities facing social change: the feminists of Seneca Falls, New York, in 1848; the sitdown strikers of Flint, Michigan, in 1934; and the African Americans of Montgomery, Alabama, in 1955. As the story unfolds we find communities growing to include ever larger groups of Americans: The soldiers from every colony who forged the Continental Army into a patriotic national force at Valley Forge during the American Revolution; the movie-goers who dreamed a collective dream of material prosperity and upward mobility during the 1920s; and the Americans linked in ever-growing numbers in the virtual communities of cyberspace as the twenty-first century begins.

Out of Many is also the only American history text with a truly continental perspective. With community vignettes from New England to the South, the Midwest to the far West, we encourage students to appreciate the great expanse of our nation. For example, a vignette of seventeenth-century Santa Fé, New Mexico illustrates the founding of the first European settlements in the New World. We present territorial expansion into the American West from the point of view of the Mandan villagers of the upper Missouri River of North Dakota. We introduce the policies of the Reconstruction era through the experience of African Americans in the Sea Island of South Carolina. This continental perspective drives home to students that American history has never been the preserve of any particular region.

In these ways *Out of Many* breaks new ground, but without compromising its coverage of the traditional turning points that we believe are critically important to an understanding of the American past. Among these watershed events are the Revolution and the struggle over the Constitution, the Civil War and Reconstruction, and the Great Depression and World War II. In *Out of Many*, however, we seek to *integrate* the narrative of national history with the story of the nation's many diverse communities. The Revolutionary and Constitutional period tried the ability of local communities to forge a new unity, and success depended on their ability to build a nation without compromising local identity. The Civil War and Reconstruction formed a second great test of the balance between the national ideas of the revolution and the power of local and sectional communities. The Depression and the New Deal demonstrated the impotence of local communities and the growing power of national institutions during the greatest economic challenge in our history. *Out of Many* also looks back in a new and comprehensive way—from the vantage point of the beginning of a new century and the end of the Cold War—at the salient events of the last fifty years and their impact on American communities. The community focus of *Out of Many* weaves the stories of the people and of the nation into a single compelling narrative.

SPECIAL FEATURES

With each edition of *Out of Many* we have sought to strengthen its unique integration of the best of traditional American history with its innovative community-based focus and strong continental perspective. A wealth of special features and pedagogical aids reinforces our narrative and helps students grasp key issues.

- **Community and Diversity.** *Out of Many*, third edition, opens with an introduction, titled "Community and Diversity," that acquaints students with the major themes of the book, providing them with a framework for understanding American history.
- **Immigration and Community: The Changing Face of Ethnicity in America.** This feature, new to this edition, highlights

the impact of the immigrant experience on the formation of American communities. There are four Immigration and Community features in the book. The first covers the colonial period through 1800, the second covers from 1800 to 1860, the third covers from 1860 to 1930, and the last covers the period since 1930. Each is six pages long and opens with an overview of the character of immigration during the period in question. This overview is followed by a section called "In Their Own Words" that consists of extracts from primary sources written by immigrants themselves and by native-born Americans in response to the new arrivals. Study questions at the end of each Immigration and Community feature ask students to relate issues raised in the overview and documents to broader issues in American history.

- **History and the Land.** These features focus on the geographical dimension of historical change to give students an appreciation of the relationship between geography and history. Each elucidates an important historical trend or process with a map and a brief explanatory essay.
- **American Communities.** Each chapter opens with an American Communities vignette that relates the experience of a particular community to the broader issues discussed in the chapter.
- **Maps.** *Out of Many*, third edition, has more maps than any other American history textbook. Many maps include topographical detail that helps students appreciate the impact of geography on history.
- **Overview tables.** Overview tables, also new to this edition, provide students with a summary of complex issues.
- **Graphs, charts and tables.** Every chapter includes one or more graphs, charts, or tables that help students understand important events and trends.
- **Photos and illustrations.** The abundant illustrations in *Out of Many*, third edition, include many images that have never before been used in an American history text. None of the images is anachronistic—each one dates from the historical period under discussion. Extensive captions treat the images as visual primary source documents from the American past, describing their source and explaining their significance.
- **Chapter-opening outlines and key topics lists.** These pedagogical aids provide students with a succinct preview of the material covered in each chapter.
- **Chronologies.** A chronology at the end of each chapter helps students build a framework of key events.
- **Review Questions.** Review questions help students review, reinforce, and retain the material in each chapter and encourage them to relate the material to broader issues in American history.
- **Recommended Reading and Additional Bibliography.** The works on the short, annotated Recommended Reading list at the end of each chapter have been selected with the interested introductory student in mind. The extensive Additional Bibliography provides a comprehensive overview of current scholarship on the subject of the chapter.

CLASSROOM ASSISTANCE PACKAGE

In classrooms across the country, many instructors encounter students who perceive history as merely a jumble of names, dates, and events. *Out of Many*, third edition, brings our dynamic past alive for these students with a text and accompanying print and multimedia classroom assistance package that combine sound scholarship, engaging narrative, and a rich array of pedagogical tools.

PRINT SUPPLEMENTS

Instructor's Resource Manual

A true time-saver in developing and preparing lecture presentations, the *Instructor's Resource Manual* contains chapter outlines, detailed chapter overviews, lecture topics, discussion questions, readings, and information on audio-visual resources.

Test Item File

Prepared by Gisela Ables, Mike McCormick, and David Aldstadt, Houston Community College

The *Test Item File* offers a menu of more than 1,500 multiple-choice, identification, matching, true-false, and essay test questions and 10–15 questions per chapter on maps found in each chapter. The guide includes a collection of blank maps that can be photocopied and used for map testing purposes or for other class exercises.

Prentice Hall Custom Test

This commercial-quality computerized test management program, available for Windows, DOS, and Macintosh environments, allows instructors to select items from the Test Item File and design their own exams.

Transparency Pack

Prepared by Robert Tomes, St. John's University

This collection of more than 160 full-color transparency acetates provides instructors with all the maps, charts, and graphs in the text for use in the classroom. Each transparency is accompanied by a page of descriptive material and discussion questions.

Study Guide, Volumes I and II

Prepared by Elizabeth Neumeyer, Kellogg Community College, and S. Ross Doughty, Ursinus College

Each chapter in the *Study Guide* includes a chapter commentary and outline, identification terms, multiple-choice questions, short essay questions, map questions, and questions based on primary source extracts.

Documents Set, Volumes I and II

Prepared by John Mack Faragher, Yale University, and Daniel Czitrom, Mount Holyoke College

The authors have selected and carefully edited more than 300 documents that relate directly to the themes and content of the text and organized them into five general categories: community, social history, government, culture, and politics. Each document is approximately two pages long and includes a brief introduction and study questions intended to encourage students to analyze the document critically and relate it to the content of the text. The Documents Set is available at a substantial discount when packaged with *Out of Many*.

Retrieving the American Past: A Customized U.S. History Reader

Written and developed by leading historians and educators, this reader is an on-demand history database that offers 52 compelling modules on topics in American History, such as: Women on the Frontier, The Salem Witchcraft Scare, The Age of Industrial Violence, and Native American Societies, 1870–1995. Approximately 35 pages in length, each module includes an introduction, several primary documents and secondary sources, follow-up questions, and recommendations for further reading. By deciding which modules to include and the order in which they will appear, instructors can compile the reader they want to use. Instructor-originated material—other readings, exercises—can be included. Contact your local Prentice Hall Representative for more information about this exciting custom publishing option.

Understanding and Answering Essay Questions

Prepared by Mary L. Kelley, San Antonio College

This brief guide suggests helpful study techniques as well as specific analytical tools for understanding different types of essay questions and provides precise guidelines for preparing well-crafted essay answers. The guide is available free to students when packaged with *Out of Many*.

Reading Critically About History

Prepared by Rose Wassman and Lee Rinsky, both of DeAnza College

This brief guide provides students with helpful strategies for reading a history textbook. It is available free when packaged with *Out of Many*.

Themes of the Times

Themes of the Times is a newspaper supplement prepared jointly by Prentice Hall and the premier news publication, *The New York Times*. Issued twice a year, it contains recent articles pertinent to American history. These articles connect the classroom to the world. For information about a reduced-rate subscription to *The New York Times*, call toll-free: (800) 631–1222.

MULTIMEDIA SUPPLEMENTS

History on the Internet

This brief guide introduces students to the origin and innovations behind the Internet and World Wide Web and provides clear strategies for navigating the web to find historical materials. Exercises within and at the end of the chapters allow students to practice searching the wealth of resources available to the student of history. This 48-page supplementary book is free to students when packaged with *Out of Many*.

Out of Many CD-ROM

This innovative electronic supplement takes advantage of the interactive capabilities of multimedia technology to enrich students' understanding of the geographic dimension of history with animated maps, timelines, and related on-screen activities tied to key issues in each chapter of *Out of Many*.

Out of Many Companion Website

Address: http://www.prenhall.com/faragher

With the *Out of Many* Companion Website, students can now take full advantage of the World Wide Web and use it in tandem with the text to enrich their study of American history. The Companion Website ties the text to related material available on the Internet. Its instructional features include chapter objectives, study questions, news updates, and labeling exercises.

The American History CD-ROM

This vast library of more than 2500 images was compiled by Instructional Resources Corporation for instructors for creating slide shows and supplementing lectures. Among its resources are 68 film sequences, 200 works of art, and more than 100 maps. It also includes an overview of historical periods narrated by Charles Kuralt.

ACKNOWLEDGMENTS

In the years it has taken to bring *Out of Many* from idea to reality and to improve it in successive editions, we have often been reminded that although writing history sometimes feels like isolated work, it actually involves a collective effort. We want to thank the dozens of people whose efforts have made the publication of this book possible.

At Prentice Hall, Todd Armstrong, Executive Editor, gave us his full support and oversaw the entire publication process. David Chodoff, Senior Development Editor, greatly helped to strengthen the book's most distinctive features with his careful attention to detail and clarity. Susanna Lesan, now Editor-in-Chief of Development, worked with us on the first edition of the text; without her efforts this book would never have been published. Louise Rothman, Production Editor, oversaw the entire complicated production process in an exemplary fashion. Barbara Salz, our photo researcher, expertly tracked down the many pertinent new images that appear in this edition.

Among our many other friends at Prentice Hall we also want to thank: Phil Miller, President; Charlyce Jones Owen, Editorial Director; Sheryl Adams, Marketing Manager; Leslie Osher, Creative Design Director; Anne Nieglos, Art Director; Patterson Lamb, Copy Editor; and Holly Jo Brown, Editorial Assistant.

Although we share joint responsibility for the entire book, the chapters were individually authored: John Mack Faragher wrote chapters 1–8; Mari Jo Buhle wrote chapters 18–20, 25–26, 29–30; Daniel Czitrom wrote chapters 17, 21–24, 27–28, 31; and Susan Armitage wrote chapters 9–16.

Historians around the country greatly assisted us by reading and commenting on our chapters for this and previous editions. We want to thank each of them for the commitment of their valuable time.

Donald Abbe, Texas Tech University, TX
Richard H. Abbott, Eastern Michigan University, MI
Guy Alchon, University of Delaware, DE
Don Barlow, Prestonsburg Community College, KY
William Barney, University of North Carolina, NC
Alwyn Barr, Texas Tech University, TX
Debra Barth, San Jose City College, CA
Peter V. Bergstrom, Illinois State University, IL
William C. Billingsley, South Plains College, TX
Peter H. Buckingham, Linfield College, OR
Bill Cecil-Fronsman, Washburn University of Topeka, KS
Victor W. Chen, Chabot College, CA
Jonathan M. Chu, University of Massachusetts, MA
P. Scott Corbett, Oxnard College, CA
Matther Coulter, Collin Country Community College, TX
Virginia Crane, University of Wisconsin, Oshkosh, WI
Jim Cullen, Harvard University, MA
Thomas J. Curran, St. John's University, NY
Richard V. Damms, Ohio State University, OH
Elizabeth Dunn, Baylor University, TX
Emmett G. Essin, Eastern Tennessee State Unversity, TN
Mark F. Fernandez, Loyola University, IL
Leon Fink, University of North Carolina, Chapel Hill, NC
Michael James Foret, University of Wisconsin, Stevens Point, WI
Joshua B. Freeman, Columbia University, NY
Glenda E. Gilmore, Yale University, CT
Don C. Glenn, Diablo Valley College, CA
Lawrence Glickman, University of South Carolina, SC
Kenneth Goings, Florida Atlantic University, FL
Mark Goldman, Tallahassee Community College, FL
Gregory L. Goodwin, Bakersfield College, CA
Gretchen Green, University of Missouri, Kansas City, MO
Emily Greenwald, University of Nebraska at Lincoln, NE
Mark W. T. Harvey, North Dakota State University, ND
James A. Hijiya, University of Massachusetts at Dartmouth, MA
Raymond M. Hyser, James Madison University, VA
John Inscoe, University of Georgia, GA

John C. Kesler, Lakeland Community College, OH
Peter N. Kirstein, Saint Xavier University, IL
Frank Lambert, Purdue University, IN
Susan Rimby Leighow, Millersville University, PA
Janice M. Leone, Middle Tennessee University, TN
Glenn Linden, Southern Methodist University, Dallas, TX
George Lipsitz, University of California, San Diego, CA
Judy Barrett Litoff, Bryant College, RI
Jesus Luna, California State University, CA
Larry Madaras, Howard Community College, MD
Lynn Mapes, Grand Valley State University, MI
John F. Marszalek, Mississippi State University, MS
Scott C. Martin, Bowling Green State University, OH
Robert L. Matheny, Eastern New Mexico University, NM
Thomas Matijasic, Prestonsburg Community College, KY
M. Delores McBroome, Humboldt State University, CA
Gerald McFarland, University of Massachusetts, Amherst, MA
Sam McSeveney, Vanderbilt University, TN
Warren Metcalf, Arizona State University, AZ
M. Catherine Miller, Texas State University, TX
Norman H. Murdoch, University of Cincinnati, OH
Gregory H. Nobles, Georgia Institute of Technology, GA
Dale Odom, University of Texas at Denton, TX
Sean O'Neill, Grand Valley State University, MI
Edward Opper, Greenville Technical College, Greenville, SC
Charles K. Piehl, Mankato State University, MN
Carolyn Garrett Pool, University of Central Oklahoma, OK
Christie Farnham Pope, Iowa State University, IA
Susan Porter-Benson, University of Missouri, MO
Russell Posner, City College of San Francisco, CA
John Powell, Penn State University, Erie, PA
Sarah Purcell, Central Michigan University, MI
Joseph P. Reidy, Howard University, DC
Marilyn D. Rhinehart, North Harris College, TX
Leo P. Ribuffo, George Washington University, DC
Judy Ridner, California State University at Northridge, CA
Neal Salisbury, Smith College, MA
Roberto Salmon, University of Texas-Pan American, TX
Steven Schuster, Brookhaven Community College, TX
Megan Seaholm, University of Texas, Austin, TX
Nigel Sellars, University of Oklahoma, Norman, OK
John David Smith, North Carolina State University, NC
Patrick Smith, Broward Community College, FL
Mark W. Summers, University of Kentucky, KY
John D. Tanner, Jr., Palomar College, CA
Robert R. Tomes, St. John's University, NY
Michael Miller Topp, University of Texas at El Paso, TX
John Trickel, Richland Community College, IL
Steve Tripp, Grand Valley State University, MI
Fred R.Van Hartesveldt, Fort Valley State University, GA
Philip H. Vaughan, Rose State College, OK
Robert C. Vitz, Northern Kentucky University, KY
F. Michael Williams, Brevard Community College, FL
Charles Regan Wilson, University of Mississippi, MS
Harold Wilson, Old Dominion University, VA
William Woodward, Seattle Pacific University, WA
Loretta E. Zimmerman, University of Florida, FL

Each of us depended on a great deal of support and assistance with the research and writing that went into this book. We want to thank: Kathryn Abbott, Nan Boyd, Krista Comer, Crista DeLuzio, Keith Edgerton, Carol Frost, Jesse Hoffnung Garskof, Jane Gerhard, Todd Gernes, Melani McAlister, Cristiane Mitchell, J. C. Mutchler, Tricia Rose, Gina Rourke, and Jessica Shubow.

Our families and close friends have been supportive and ever so patient over the many years we have devoted to this project. But we want especially to thank Paul Buhle, Meryl Fingrutd, Bob Greene, and Michele Hoffnung.

ABOUT THE AUTHORS

Chris Freitag

JOHN MACK FARAGHER

John Mack Faragher is Arthur Unobskey Professor of American History at Yale University. Born in Arizona and raised in southern California, he received his B.A. at the University of California, Riverside, and his Ph.D. at Yale University. He is the author of *Women and Men on the Overland Trail* (1979), which won the Frederick Jackson Turner Award of the Organization of American Historians, *Sugar Creek: Life on the Illinois Prairie* (1986), and *Daniel Boone: The Life and Legend of an American Pioneer* (1992). He is also the editor of *The American Heritage Encyclopedia* (1988).

DANIEL CZITROM

Daniel Czitrom is Professor and Chair of History at Mount Holyoke College. He received his B.A. from the State University of New York at Binghamton and his M.A. and Ph.D. from the University of Wisconsin, Madison. He is the author of *Media and the American Mind: From Morse to McLuhan* (1982), which won the First Books Award of the American Historical Association. His scholarly articles and essays have appeared in the *Journal of American History, American Quarterly, The Massachusetts Review*, and *The Atlantic*. He is currently completing *Mysteries of the City: Culture, Politics, and the Underworld in New York, 1870–1920.*

MARI JO BUHLE

Mari Jo Buhle is Professor of American Civilization and History at Brown University, specializing in American women's history. She is the author of *Women and American Socialism, 1870–1920* (1981) and *Feminism and its Discontents: A Century of Struggle with Psychoanalysis* (1998). She is also coeditor of *Encyclopedia of the American Left*, second edition (1998). She currently serves as an editor of a series of books on women and American history for the University of Illinois Press. Professor Buhle held a fellowship (1991–1996) from the John D. and Catherine T. MacArthur Foundation.

SUSAN H. ARMITAGE

Susan H. Armitage is Professor of History at Washington State University. She earned her Ph.D. from the London School of Economics and Political Science. Among her many publications on western women's history are three coedited books, *The Women's West* (1987), *So Much To Be Done: Women on the Mining and Ranching Frontier* (1991), and *Writing the Range: Race, Class, and Culture in the Women's West* (1997). She is the editor of *Frontiers: A Journal of Women's Studies.*

COMMUNITY & DIVERSITY

One of the most characteristic features of our country has always been its astounding variety. The American people include the descendants of native Indians, colonial Europeans, Africans, and migrants from virtually every country and continent. Indeed, as we enter the new century the nation is absorbing a tide of immigrants from Latin America and Asia that rivals the great tide of immigrants from eastern and southern Europe that arrived at the beginning of the twentieth century. Moreover, the United States is one of the world's largest nations, incorporating more than 3.6 million square miles of territory. The struggle to make a nation out of our many communities is what much of American history is all about. That is the story told in this book.

Every human society is made up of communities. A community is a set of relationships that link men, women, and their families into a coherent social whole, more than the sum of its parts. In a community people develop the capacity for unified action. In a community people learn, often through trial and error, how to transform and adapt to their environment. The sentiment that binds the members of a community together is the origin of group identity and ethnic pride. In the making of history, communities are far more important than even the greatest of leaders, for the community is the institution most capable of passing a distinctive historical tradition to future generations.

Communities bind people together in multiple ways. They can be as small as the local neighborhood, in which people maintain face-to-face relations, or as large as the imagined entity of the nation. This book examines American history from the perspective of community life—an ever widening frame that has included larger and larger groups of Americans.

Networks of kinship and friendship, and connections across generations and among families, establish the bonds essential to community life. Shared feelings about values and history establish the basis for common identity. In communities, people find the power to act collectively in their own interest. But American communities frequently took shape as a result of serious conflicts among groups, and within communities there often has been significant fighting among competing groups or classes. Thus the term community,

John L. Krimmel, Election Day in Philadelphia (1815).

John L. Krimmel, Painting, (1786–1821), oil on canvas, H. 16⅜" x W. 25⅝". (AN:59.131) Courtesy, Winterthur Museum, *Election Day in Philadelphia* (1815).

as we employ it here, includes tension and discord as well as harmony and agreement.

For years there have been persistent laments about the "loss of community" in modern America. But community has not disappeared—it is continually being reinvented. Until the late eighteenth century, community was defined primarily by space and local geography. The closer one gets to the present, the more community is reshaped by new and powerful historical forces such as the nation state, the marketplace, industrialization, the corporation, mass immigration, and electronic media.

The American Communities vignettes that open each chapter of *Out of Many* reflect this shift. Most of the vignettes in the pre–Civil War chapters focus on geographically-defined communities, such as the ancient Indian city at Cahokia, or the experiment in industrial urban planning in early nineteenth-century Lowell, Massachusetts. In the post–Civil War chapters different and more modern kinds of communities make their appearance—the community of Hollywood movie audiences in the 1920s, or the "virtual communities" made possible by new computer technologies. Also, the nearer we get to the present, the more we find Americans struggling to balance their membership in several communities simultaneously. These are defined not simply by local spatial arrangements, but by categories as varied as racial and ethnic groups, occupations, political affiliations, and consumer preferences.

Ralph Fasanella, Sunday Afternoon—Stickball Game, 1953

The title for our book was suggested by the Latin phrase selected by John Adams, Benjamin Franklin, and Thomas Jefferson for the Great Seal of the United States: *E Pluribus Unum*—"Out of Many Comes Unity." These men understood that unity could not be imposed by a powerful central authority but had to develop out of mutual respect among Americans of different backgrounds. The revolutionary leadership expressed the hope that such respect could grow on the basis of a remarkable proposition: "We hold these truths to be self-evident, that all men are created equal; that they are endowed by their Creator with certain unalienable rights; that among these are life, liberty, and the pursuit of happiness." The national government of the United States would preserve local and state authority but would guarantee individual rights. The nation would be strengthened by guarantees of difference.

Out of Many—that is the promise of America, and the premise of this book. The underlying dialectic of American history, we believe, is that as a people

William Hahn, Market Scene, Sansome Street, San Francisco.

William Hahn, *Market Scene, Sansome Street, San Francisco.* Crocker Art Musuem, Sacramento, CA. E.B. Crocker Collection.

we need to locate our national *unity* in the celebration of the *differences* that exist among us; these differences can be our strength, as long as we affirm the promise of the Declaration. Protecting the "right to be different," in other words, is absolutely fundamental to the continued existence of democracy, and that right is best protected by the existence of strong and vital communities. We are bound together as a nation by the ideal of local and cultural differences protected by our common commitment to the values of our revolution.

Today—with the many social and cultural conflicts that abound in the United States—some Americans have lost faith in that vision. But our history shows that the promise of American unity has always been problematic. Centrifugal forces have been powerful in the American past, and at times the country has seemed about to fracture into its component parts. Our transformation from a collection of groups and regions into a nation has been marked by painful and often violent struggles. Our past is filled with conflicts between Indians and colonists, masters and slaves, Patriots and Loyalists, Northerners and Southerners, Easterners and Westerners, capitalists and workers, and sometimes the government and the people. Americans often appear to be little more than a contentious collection of peoples with conflicting interests, divided by region and background, race and class.

Our most influential leaders also sometimes suffered a crisis of faith in the American project of "liberty and justice for all." Thomas Jefferson not only believed in the inferiority of African Americans, but he feared that immigrants from outside the Anglo-American tradition might "warp and bias" the development of the nation "and render it a heterogeneous, incoherent, distracted mass." We have not always lived up to the American promise, and there is a dark side to our history. It took the bloodiest war in American history to secure the human rights of African Americans, and the struggle for full equality continues nearly a century and a half later. During the great influx of immigrants in the early twentieth century, fears much like Jefferson's led to movements to *Americanize* the foreign born by forcing them, in the words of one leader, "to give up the languages, customs, and methods of life which they have brought with them across the ocean, and adopt instead the language, habits, and customs of this country, and the general standards and ways of American living." Similar thinking motivated Congress at various times to bar the immigration of Asians and other ethnic groups into the country, and to force assimilation on American Indians by denying them the freedom to practice their religion or even to speak their own language. Such calls for restrictive unity resound in our own day.

But other Americans have argued for a more idealistic version of *Americanization*. "What is the American, this new man?" asked the French immigrant Michel Crévecoeur in 1782. "A strange mixture of blood which you will find in no other country," he answered; in America, "individuals of all nations are melted into a new race of men." A century later Crévecoeur was echoed by historian Frederick Jackson Turner, who believed that "in the crucible of the frontier, the immigrants were Americanized, liberated, and fused into a mixed race, English in neither nationality nor characteristics. The process has gone on from the early days to our own."

The process by which diverse communities have come to share a set of common American values is one of the most fundamental aspects of our history. It did not occur, however, because of compulsory *Americanization* programs, but because of free public education, popular participation in democratic politics, and the impact of popular culture. Contemporary America does have a common culture: we laugh at the same television sitcoms and share the same aspirations to own a home and send our children to college—all unique American traits.

To a degree that too few Americans appreciate, this common culture resulted from a complicated process of mutual discovery that took place when different ethnic and regional groups encountered one another. Consider just one small and unique aspect of our culture, the barbecue. Americans have been barbecuing since before the beginning of written history. Early settlers adopted this technique of cooking from the Indians—the word itself comes from a native term for a framework of sticks over a fire on which meat was slowly cooked. Colonists typically barbecued pork, fed on Indian corn. African slaves lent their own touch by introducing the use of hot sauces. Thus the ritual that is a part of nearly every American family's Fourth of July silently celebrates the heritage of diversity that went into making our common culture.

The American educator John Dewey recognized this diversity early in this century. "The genuine American, the typical American is himself a hyphenated character," he declared, "international and interracial in his make-up." The point about our "hyphenated character," Dewey believed, "is to see to it that the hyphen connects instead of separates." We, the authors of *Out of Many*, share Dewey's perspective on American history. "Creation comes from the impact of diversity," wrote the American philosopher Horace Kallen. We also endorse Kallen's vision of the American promise: "A democracy of nationalities, cooperating voluntarily and autonomously through common institutions, . . . a multiplicity in a unity, an orchestration of mankind." And now, let the music begin.

CHAPTER TWENTY-ONE

URBAN AMERICA AND THE PROGRESSIVE ERA

1900–1917

John Sloan (1871–1951), *Italian Procession, New York,* 1913–1925, oil on canvas, 24 x 28 inches. San Diego Museum of Art, gift of Mr. and Mrs. Appleton S. Bridges.

Chapter Outline

AMERICAN COMMUNITIES

The Henry Street Settlement House: Women Settlement House Workers Create a Community of Reform

A shy and frightened young girl appeared in the doorway of a weekly home-nursing class for women on Manhattan's Lower East Side. The teacher beckoned her to come forward. Tugging on the teacher's skirt, the girl pleaded in broken English for the teacher to come home with her. "Mother," "baby," "blood," she kept repeating. The teacher gathered up the sheets that were part of the interrupted lesson in bed making. The two hurried through narrow, garbage-strewn, foul-smelling streets, then groped their way up a pitch-dark, rickety staircase. They reached a cramped, two-room apartment, home to an immigrant family of seven and several boarders. There, in a vermin-infested bed, encrusted with dried blood, lay a mother and her newborn baby. The mother had been abandoned by a doctor because she could not afford his fee.

The teacher, Lillian Wald, was a twenty-five-year-old nurse at New York Hospital. Years later she recalled this scene as her baptism by fire and the turning point in her life. Born in 1867, Wald enjoyed a comfortable upbringing in a middle-class German Jewish family in Rochester. Despite her parents' objections, she moved to New York City to become a professional nurse. Resentful of the disdainful treatment nurses received from doctors and horrified by the inhumane conditions at a juvenile asylum she worked in, Wald determined to find a way of caring for the sick in their neighborhoods and homes. With nursing school classmate Mary Brewster, Wald rented a fifth-floor walk-up apartment on the Lower East Side and established a visiting nurse service. The two provided professional care in the home to hundreds of families for a nominal fee of ten to twenty-five cents. They also offered each family they visited information on basic health care, sanitation, and disease prevention. In 1895, philanthropist Jacob Schiff generously donated a red brick Georgian house on Henry Street as a new base of operation.

The Henry Street Settlement stood in the center of perhaps the most overcrowded neighborhood in the world, New York's Lower East Side. Roughly 500,000 people were packed into an area only as large as a midsized Kansas farm. Population density was about 500 per acre, roughly four times the figure for the rest of New York City and far more concentrated than even the worst slums of London or Calcutta. A single city block might have as many as 3,000 residents. Home for most Lower East Siders was a small tenement apartment that might include paying boarders squeezed in alongside the immediate family. Residents were mostly recent immigrants from southern and eastern Europe: Jews, Italians, Germans, Greeks, Hungarians, Slavs. Men, women, and children toiled in the garment shops, small factories, retail stores, breweries, and warehouses to be found on nearly every street. An Irish-dominated machine controlled local political affairs.

The Henry Street Settlement became a model for a new kind of reform community composed essentially of college-educated women who encouraged and supported one another in a wide variety of humanitarian, civic, political, and cultural activities. Settlement house living arrangements closely resembled those in the dormitories of such new women's colleges as Smith, Wellesley, and Vassar. Like these colleges, the settlement house was an "experiment," but one designed, in settlement house pioneer Jane Addams's words, "to aid in the solution of the social and industrial problems which are engendered by the modern conditions of urban life." Unlike earlier moral reformers who tried to impose their ideas from outside, settlement house residents lived in poor communities and worked for immediate improvements in the health and welfare of those communities. Yet as Addams and others repeatedly stressed, the college-educated women were beneficiaries as well. The settlement house allowed them to preserve a collegial spirit, satisfy the desire for service, and apply their academic training.

With its combined moral and social appeal, the settlement house movement attracted many educated young women and grew rapidly. There were six settlement houses in the United States in 1891,74 in 1897, more than 200 by 1900, and more than 400 by 1910. Few women made settlement work a career. The average stay was less than five years. Roughly half of those who worked in the movement eventually married. Those who did make a career of settlement house work, however, typically chose not to marry, and most lived together with female companions. As the movement flourished, settlement house residents called attention to the plight of the poor and fostered respect for different cultural heritages in countless articles and lectures. Leaders of the movement, including Jane Addams, Lillian Wald, and Florence Kelley, emerged as influential political figures during the progressive era.

Wald attracted a dedicated group of nurses, educators, and reformers to live at the Henry Street Settlement. By 1909 Henry Street had more than forty residents, supported by the donations of well-to-do New Yorkers. Wald and her allies convinced the New York Board of Health to assign a nurse to every public school in the city. They lobbied the Board of Education to create the first school lunch programs. They persuaded the city to set up municipal milk stations to ensure the purity of milk. Henry Street also pioneered tuberculosis treatment and prevention. Its leaders became powerful advocates for playground construction, improved street cleaning, and tougher housing inspection. The settlement's Neighborhood Playhouse became an internationally acclaimed center for innovative theater, music, and dance.

As settlement house workers expanded their influence from local neighborhoods to larger political and social circles, they became, in the phrase of one historian, spearheads for reform. Lillian Wald became a national figure—an outspoken advocate of child labor legislation and woman suffrage and a vigorous opponent of American involvement in World War I. She offered Henry Street as a meeting place to the National Negro Conference in 1909, out of which emerged the National Association for the Advancement of Colored People. It was no cliché for Wald to say, as she did on many occasions, "The whole world is my neighborhood."

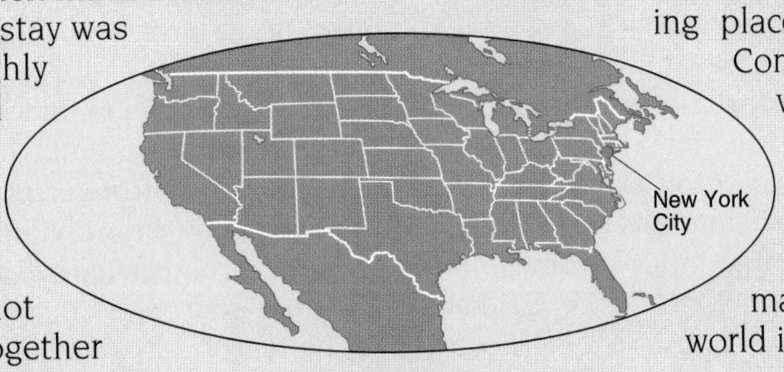

Key Topics

- The political, social, and intellectual roots of progressive reform
- Tensions between social justice and social control
- The urban scene and the impact of new immigration
- Political activism by the working class, women, and African Americans
- Progressivism in national politics

THE CURRENTS OF PROGRESSIVISM

Between the 1890s and World War I, a large and diverse number of Americans claimed the political label "progressive." Progressives could be found in all classes, regions, and races. They shared a fundamental ethos, or belief, that America needed a new social consciousness to cope with the problems brought on by the enormous rush of economic and social change in the post–Civil War decades. Yet progressivism was no unified movement with a single set of principles. It is best understood as a varied collection of reform communities, often fleeting, uniting citizens in a host of political, professional, and religious organizations, some of which were national in scope.

Progressivism drew from deep roots in hundreds of local American communities. At the state level it flowered in the soil of several key issues: ending political corruption, bringing more businesslike methods to governing, and offering a more compassionate legislative response to the excesses of industrialism. As a national movement, progressivism reached its peak in 1912, when the four major presidential candidates all ran on some version of a progressive platform. This last development was an important measure of the extent to which local reform movements like the Henry Street Settlement and new intellectual currents had captured the political imagination of the nation.

The many contradictions and disagreements surrounding the meaning of progressivism have led some historians to dismiss the term as hopelessly vague. Some progressives focused on expanding state and federal regulation of private interests for the public welfare. Others viewed the rapid influx of new immigrants and the explosive growth of large cities as requiring more stringent social controls. Another variant emphasized eliminating corruption in the political system as the key to righting society's wrongs. In the South, progressivism was for white people only. Progressives could be forward looking in their vision or nostalgic for a nineteenth-century world rapidly disappearing. Self-styled progressives often found themselves facing each other from opposite sides of an issue.

Yet at the local, state, and finally national levels, reform rhetoric and energy shaped most of the political and cultural debates of the era. Understanding progressivism in all its complexity thus requires examining what key reform groups, thinkers, and political figures actually did and said under its ambiguous banner.

Unifying Themes

Three basic attitudes underlay the various crusades and movements that emerged in response to the fears gnawing at large segments of the population. The first was anger over the excesses of industrial capitalism and urban growth. At the same time, progressives shared an essential optimism about the ability of citizens to improve social and economic conditions. They were reformers, not revolutionaries. Second, progressives emphasized social cohesion and common bonds as a way of understanding how modern society and economics actually worked. They largely rejected the ideal of individualism that had informed nineteenth-century economic and political theory. For progressives, poverty and success hinged on more than simply individual character; the economy was more than merely a sum of individual calculations. Progressives thus opposed social Darwinism, with its claim that any effort to improve social conditions would prove fruitless because society is like a jungle in which only the "fittest" survive. Third, progressives believed in the need for citizens to intervene actively, both politically and morally, to improve social conditions. They pushed for a stronger government role in regulating the economy and solving the nation's social problems.

Progressive rhetoric and methods drew on two distinct sources of inspiration. One was evangelical Protestantism, particularly the late-nineteenth-century social gospel movement. Social gospelers rejected the idea of original sin as the cause of human suffering. They emphasized both the capacity and the duty of Christians to purge the world of poverty, inequality, and economic greed. A second strain of progressive

Currents of Progressivism

	Key Figures	Issues	Institutions/Achievements
Local Communities	Jane Addams, Lillian Wald, Florence Kelley, Frederic C. Howe, Samuel Jones	• Improving health, education, welfare in urban immigrant neighborhoods • Child labor, eight-hour day • Celebrating immigrant cultures • Reforming urban politics • Municipal ownership/regulation of utilities	• Hull House Settlement • Henry Street Settlement • National Consumers League • New York Child Labor Committee • Bureau of Municipal Research
State	Robert M. LaFollette, Hiram Johnson, Al Smith	• Limiting power of railroads, other corporations • Improving civil service • Direct democracy • Applying academic scholarship to human needs	• "Wisconsin Idea" • State Workmen's Compensation • Unemployment Insurance • Public utility regulation
	James K. Vardaman, Hoke Smith	• Disfranchisement of African Americans	• Legalized segregation
National	Theodore Roosevelt	• Trustbusting • Conservation and Western development • National regulation of corporate and financial excesses	• Reclamation Bureau (1902) • U.S. Forest Service (1905) • Food and Drug Administration (1906) • Meat Inspection Act (1906) • Hepburn Act–ICC (1906)
	Woodrow Wilson	• National regulation of corporate and financial excesses • Reform of national banking	• Graduated Income Tax (1913) • Federal Reserve Act (1913) • Clayton Antitrust Act (1914) • Federal Trade Commission (1914)
Intellectual/ Cultural	Jacob Riis	• Muckraking	• *How the Other Half Lives* (1890)
	Lincoln Steffens, Ida Tarbell, Upton Sinclair, S.S. McClure		• *Shame of the Cities* (1902) • *History of Standard Oil* (1904) • *The Jungle* (1906) • *McClure's Magazine*
	John Dewey	• Education reform	• *Democracy and Education* (1916)
	Louis Brandeis	• Sociological jurisprudence	• *Muller v. Oregon* (1908)
	Edwin A. Ross	• Empowering "ethical elite"	• *Social Control* (1901)

Courtesy George Eastman House

Lewis Hine took this photo of a young girl working on a thread spinning frame in a North Carolina cotton mill. Between 1908 and 1918 Hine worked for the National Child Labor Committee, documenting the widespread abuse of child labor in the nation's mills, factories, mines, and canneries. "These pictures," Hine wrote, "speak for themselves and prove that the law is being violated."

thought looked to natural and social scientists to develop rational measures for improving the human condition, believing that experts trained in statistical analysis and engineering could make government and industry more efficient. Progressivism thus offered an uneasy combination of social justice and social control, a tension that would characterize American reform for the rest of the twentieth century.

Women Spearhead Reform

In the 1890s the settlement house movement had begun to provide an alternative to traditional concepts of private charity and humanitarian reform. Settlement workers found they could not transform their neighborhoods without confronting a host of broad social questions: chronic poverty, overcrowded tenement houses, child labor, industrial accidents, public health. As on Henry Street, college-educated, middle-class women constituted a key vanguard in the crusade for social justice. As reform communities, settlement houses soon discovered the need to engage the political and cultural life of the larger communities that surrounded them.

Jane Addams founded one of the first settlement houses, Hull House, in Chicago in 1889 after years of struggling to find work and a social identity equal to her talents. A member of one of the first generation of American women to attend college, Addams was a graduate of Rockford College. Many educated women were dissatisfied with the life choices conventionally available to them: early marriage or the traditional female professions of teaching, nursing, and library work. Settlement work provided these women with an attractive alternative. Hull House was located in a run-down slum area of Chicago. It had a day nursery, a dispensary for medicines and medical advice, a boardinghouse, an art gallery, and a music school. Addams often spoke of the "subjective necessity" of settlement houses. By this she meant that they gave young, educated women a way to satisfy their powerful desire to connect with the real world. "There is nothing after disease, indigence and guilt," she wrote, "so fatal to life itself as the want of a proper outlet for active faculties."

Social reformer Florence Kelley helped direct the support of the settlement house movement behind groundbreaking state and federal labor legislation. Arriving at Hull House in 1891, Kelley found what she described as a "colony of efficient and intelligent women." In 1893, she wrote a report detailing the dismal conditions in sweatshops and the effects of long hours on the women and children who worked in them. This report became the basis for landmark legislation in Illinois that limited women to an eight-hour workday, barred children under fourteen from working, and abolished tenement labor. Illinois governor John Peter Altgeld appointed Kelley as chief inspector for the new law. In 1895 Kelley published *Hull House Maps and Papers*, the first scientific study of urban poverty in America. Moving to Henry Street Settlement in 1898, Kelley served as general secretary of the new National Consumers' League. With Lillian Wald she established the New York Child Labor Committee and pushed for the creation of the U.S. Children's Bureau, established in 1912.

Kelley, Addams, Wald, and their circle consciously used their power as women to reshape politics in the progressive era. Electoral politics and the state were historically male preserves, but female social progressives turned their gender into an advantage. They built upon the tradition of female moral reform, where women had long operated outside male-dominated political institutions to agitate and organize. Activists like Kelley used their influence in civil society to create new state powers in the service of social justice. They left a legacy that simultaneously expanded the social welfare function of the state and increased women's public authority and influence.

The Urban Machine

Women had to work outside existing political institutions not just because they could not vote, but also because city politics had become a closed and often corrupt system. By the turn of the century Democratic Party machines, usually dominated by first- and second-generation Irish, controlled the political life of most large American cities. The keys to machine strength were disciplined organization and the delivery of essential services to both immigrant communities and business elites. The successful machine politician viewed his work as a business, and he accumulated his capital by serving people who needed assistance. For most urban dwellers, the city was a place of economic and social insecurity. Recent immigrants in particular faced frequent unemployment, sickness, and discrimination. In exchange for votes, machine politicians offered their constituents a variety of services. These included municipal jobs in the police and fire departments, work at city construction sites, intervention with legal problems, and food and coal during hard times.

For those who did business with the city—construction companies, road builders, realtors—staying on the machine's good side was simply another business expense. In exchange for valuable franchises and city contracts, businessmen routinely bribed machine politicians and contributed liberally to their campaign funds. George Washington Plunkitt, a stalwart of New York's Tammany Hall machine, good-naturedly defended what he called "honest graft": making money from inside information on public improvements. "It's just like lookin' ahead in Wall Street or in the coffee or cotton market. . . . I seen my opportunities and I took 'em."

The machines usually had close ties to a city's vice economy and commercial entertainments. Organized prostitution and gambling, patronized largely by visitors to the city, could flourish only when "protected" by politicians who shared in the profits. Many machine figures began as saloonkeepers, and liquor dealers and beer brewers provided important financial support for "the organization." Vaudeville and burlesque theaters, boxing, horse racing, and professional baseball were other urban enterprises with economic and political links to machines. Entertainment and spectacle made up a central element in the machine political style as well. Constituents looked forward to the colorful torchlight parades, free summer picnics, and riverboat excursions regularly sponsored by the machines.

This publicity photograph of neighborhood children taking an art class at the Henry Street Settlement, New York City, around 1910, suggested that cultural pursuits and learning could flourish in slum neighborhoods with the help of a settlement house.

On New York City's Lower East Side, where the Henry Street Settlement was located, Timothy D. "Big Tim" Sullivan embodied the popular machine style. Big Tim, who had risen from desperate poverty, remained enormously popular with his constituents until his death in 1913. "I believe in liberality," he declared. "I am a thorough New Yorker and have no narrow prejudices. I never ask a hungry man about his past; I feed him, not because he is good, but because he needs food. Help your neighbor but keep your nose out of his affairs." Critics charged that Sullivan controlled the city's gambling and made money from prostitution. But his real fortune came through his investments in vaudeville and the early movie business. Sullivan, whose district included the largest number of immigrants and transients in the city, provided shoe giveaways and free Christmas dinners to thousands every winter. To help pay for these and other charitable activities, he informally taxed the saloons, theaters, and restaurants in the district.

Progressive critics of machine politics routinely exaggerated the machine's power and influence. State legislatures, controlled by Republican rural and small-town elements, proved a formidable check on what city-based machines could accomplish. Reform campaigns that publicized excessive graft and corruption sometimes led voters to throw machine-backed mayors and aldermen out of office. And there were never enough patronage jobs for all the people clamoring for appointments. In the early twentieth century, to expand their base of support, political machines in the Northeast began concentrating more on passing welfare legislation beneficial to working-class and immigrant constituencies. In this way machine politicians often allied themselves with progressive reformers in state legislatures. In New York, for example, Tammany Hall figures such as Robert Wagner, Al Smith, and Big Tim Sullivan worked with middle-class progressive groups to pass child labor laws, factory safety regulations, worker compensation plans, and other efforts to make government more responsive to social needs. As Jewish and Catholic immigrants expanded in number and proportion in the city population, urban machines also began to champion cultural pluralism, opposing prohibition and immigration restrictions and defending the contributions made by new ethnic groups in the cities.

Political Progressives and Urban Reform

Political progressivism originated in the cities. It was both a challenge to the power of machine politics and a response to deteriorating urban conditions. City governments, especially in the Northeast and industrial Midwest, seemed hardly capable of providing the basic services needed to sustain large populations. For example, an impure water supply left Pittsburgh with one of the world's highest rates of death from typhoid, dysentery, and cholera. Most New York City neighborhoods rarely enjoyed street cleaning, and playgrounds were nonexistent. "The challenge of the city," Cleveland progressive Frederic C. Howe said in 1906, "has become one of decent human existence."

Reformers placed much of the blame for urban ills on the machines and looked for ways to restructure city government. The "good government" movement, led by the National Municipal League, fought to make city management a nonpartisan, even nonpolitical, process by bringing the administrative techniques of large corporations to cities. Reformers revised city charters in favor of stronger mayoral power and expanded use of appointed administrators and career civil servants. The New York Bureau of Municipal Research, founded in 1906, became a prototype for similar bureaus around the country. It drew up blueprints for model charters, ordinances, and zoning plans designed by experts trained in public administration.

Business and professional elites became the biggest boosters of structural reforms in urban government. In the summer of 1900 a hurricane in the Gulf of Mexico unleashed a tidal wave on Galveston, Texas. To cope with this disaster, leading businessmen convinced the state legislature to replace the mayor-council government with a small board of commissioners. Each commissioner was elected at large, and each was responsible for a different city department. Under this plan voters could more easily identify and hold accountable those responsible for city services. The city commission, enjoying both policy-making and administrative powers, proved very effective in rebuilding Galveston. By 1917 nearly 500 cities, including Houston, Oakland, Kansas City, Denver, and Buffalo, had adopted the commission form of government. Another approach, the city manager plan, gained popularity in small and midsized cities. In this system, a city council appointed a professional, nonpartisan city manager to handle the day-to-day operations of the community.

Progressive politicians who focused on the human problems of the industrial city championed a different kind of reform, one based on changing policies rather than the political structure. In Toledo, Samuel "Golden Rule" Jones served as mayor from 1897 to 1904. A capitalist who had made a fortune manufacturing oil well machinery, Jones created a strong base of working-class and ethnic voters around his reform program. He advocated municipal ownership of utilities, built new parks and schools, and established an eight-hour day and a minimum wage for city employees. In Cleveland, wealthy businessman Thomas L. Johnson served as mayor from 1901 to 1909. He emphasized both efficiency and social welfare. His popular program included lower streetcar fares, public baths, milk and meat inspection, and an expanded park and playground system.

Progressivism in the Statehouse

Their motives and achievements were mixed, but progressive politicians became a powerful force in many state capitals. In Wisconsin, Republican dissident Robert M. La Follette forged a coalition of angry farmers, small businessmen, and workers with his fiery attacks on railroads and other large corporations. Leader of the progressive faction of the state Republicans, "Fighting Bob" won three terms as governor (1900–1906), then served as a U.S. senator until his death in 1925. As governor he pushed through tougher corporate tax rates, a direct primary, an improved civil service code, and a railroad commission designed to regulate freight charges. La Follette used faculty experts at the University of Wisconsin to help research and write his bills. Other states began copying the "Wisconsin Idea"—the application of academic scholarship and theory to the needs of the people.

La Follette railed against "the interests" and invoked the power of the ordinary citizen. In practice, however, his railroad commission accomplished far less than progressive rhetoric claimed. It essentially represented special interests—commercial farmers and businessmen seeking reduced shipping rates. Ordinary consumers did not see lower passenger fares or reduced food prices. And as commissioners began to realize, the national reach of the railroads limited the effectiveness of state regulation. Although La Follette championed a more open political system, he also enrolled state employees in a tight political machine of his own. The La Follette family would dominate Wisconsin politics for forty years.

Western progressives displayed the greatest enthusiasm for institutional political reform. In the early 1900s, Oregon voters approved a series of constitutional amendments designed to strengthen direct democracy. The two most important were the initiative, which allowed a direct vote on specific measures put on the state ballot by petition, and the referendum, which allowed voters to decide on bills referred to them by the legislature. Other reforms included the direct primary, which allowed voters to cross party lines, and the recall, which gave voters the right to remove elected officials by popular vote. Widely copied throughout the West, all these measures intentionally weakened political parties.

Western progressives also targeted railroads, mining and timber companies, and public utilities for reform. Large corporations such as Pacific Gas and Electric and the Southern Pacific Railroad had amassed enormous wealth and political influence. They were able to corrupt state legislatures and charge consumers exorbitant rates. An alliance between middle-class progressives and working-class voters reflected growing disillusionment with the ideology of individualism that had helped pave the way for the rise of the big corporation. In California, attorney Hiram Johnson won a 1910 progressive campaign for governor on the slogan "Kick the Southern Pacific Railroad Out of Politics." In addition to winning political reforms, Johnson also put through laws regulating utilities and child labor, mandating an eight-hour day for working women, and providing a state worker compensation plan.

In the South, reform governors, such as James Vardaman of Mississippi and Hoke Smith of Georgia, often drew on the agrarian program and flamboyant oratory of populism. But southern progressives were typically city professionals or businessmen rather than farmers. Like their northern and western counterparts, they focused their attention on strengthening state regulation of railroads and public utilities, improving educational facilities, reforming city governments, and reining in the power of large corporations.

While southern populism had been based in part on a biracial politics of protest, southern progressivism was for white people only. A strident racism accompanied most reform campaigns against entrenched conservative Democratic machines, reinforcing racial discrimination and segregation. Southern progressives supported black disfranchisement as an electoral reform. With African Americans removed from political life, they argued, the direct primary system of nominating candidates would give white voters more influence. Between 1890 and 1910 southern states passed a welter of statutes specifying poll taxes, literacy tests, and property qualifications with the explicit goal of preventing voting by blacks. This systematic disfranchisement of African American voters stripped black communities of any political power. To prevent the disfranchisement of poor white voters under these laws, states established so-called understanding and grandfather clauses. Election officials had discretionary power to decide whether an illiterate person could understand and reasonably interpret the Constitution when read to him. Unqualified white men were also registered if they could show that their grandfathers had voted.

Southern progressives also supported the push toward a fully segregated public sphere. Between 1900 and 1910 southern states strengthened laws requiring separation of races in restaurants, streetcars, beaches, and theaters. Schools were separate but hardly equal. A 1916 Bureau of Education study found that per capita expenditures for education in southern states averaged $10.32 a year for white children and $2.89 for black children. And African American teachers received far lower salaries than their white counterparts. The legacy of southern progressivism was thus closely linked to the strengthening of the legal and institutional guarantees of white supremacy.

New Journalism: Muckraking

Changes in journalism helped fuel a new reform consciousness by drawing the attention of millions to urban poverty, political corruption, the plight of industrial workers, and immoral business practices. As early as 1890, journalist Jacob Riis had shocked the nation with his landmark book *How the Other Half Lives,* a portrait of New York City's poor. A Danish immigrant who arrived in New York City in 1871, Riis became a newspaper reporter, covering the police beat and learning about the city's desperate underside. Riis's book included a remarkable series of photographs he had taken in tenements, lodging houses, sweatshops, and saloons. These striking pictures, combined with Riis's analysis of slum housing patterns, had a powerful impact on a whole generation of urban reformers.

Within a few years, magazine journalists had turned to uncovering the seamier side of American life. The key innovator was S. S. McClure, a young Midwestern editor who in 1893 started America's first large-circulation magazine, *McClure's*. Charging only a dime for his monthly, McClure effectively combined popular fiction with articles on science, technology, travel, and recent history. He attracted a new readership among the urban middle class through aggressive subscription and promotional campaigns, as well as newsstand sales. By the turn of the century *McClure's* and several imitators—*Munsey's, Cosmopolitan, Collier's, Everybody's,* and the *Saturday Evening Post*—had circulations in the hundreds of thousands. Making extensive use of photographs and illustrations, these cheap upstarts soon far surpassed older, more staid and expensive magazines such as the *Atlantic Monthly* and *Harper's* in circulation.

In 1902 McClure began hiring talented reporters to write detailed accounts of the nation's social problems. Lincoln Steffens's series *The Shame of the Cities* (1902) revealed the widespread graft at the center of American urban politics. He showed how big-city bosses routinely worked hand in glove with businessmen seeking lucrative municipal contracts for gas, water, electricity, and mass transit. Ida Tarbell, in her *History of the Standard Oil Company* (1904), thoroughly documented how John D. Rockefeller ruthlessly squeezed out competitors with unfair business practices. Ray Stannard Baker wrote detailed portraits of life and labor in Pennsylvania coal towns.

McClure's and other magazines discovered that "exposure journalism" paid off handsomely in terms of increased circulation. The middle-class public responded to this new combination of factual reporting and moral exhortation. A series such as Steffens's fueled reform campaigns that swept individual communities. Between 1902 and 1908, magazines were full of articles exposing insurance scandals, patent medicine frauds, and stock market swindles. Upton Sinclair's 1906 novel *The Jungle,* a socialist tract set among Chicago packinghouse workers, exposed the filthy sanitation and abysmal working conditions in the stockyards and the meatpacking industry. In an effort to boost sales, Sinclair's publisher devoted an entire issue of a monthly magazine it owned, *World's Work,* to articles and photographs that substantiated Sinclair's devastating portrait.

In 1906, David Graham Phillips, in a series for *Cosmopolitan* called "The Treason of the Senate," argued that many conservative U.S. senators were no more than mouthpieces for big business. President Theodore Roosevelt, upset by Phillips's attack on several of his friends and supporters, coined a new term when he angrily denounced Phillips and his colleagues as "muckrakers" who "raked the mud of society and never looked up." Partly due to Roosevelt's outburst, the muckraking vogue began to wane. By 1907, S. S. McClure's original team of reporters had broken up.

Museum of the City of New York, Jacob A. Riis Collection. Photo by Jessie Tarbox Beals.

In his landmark book, How the Other Half Lives (1890), *Jacob* Riis *made innovative use of photographs and statistics to argue for housing reform. This photograph depicts an Italian immigrant family of seven living in a one-room apartment. Overcrowded and dilapidated tenements threatened the entire city "because they are the hot-beds of the epidemics that carry death to the rich and poor alike; the nurseries of pauperism and crime that fill our jails and police courts."*

But muckraking had demonstrated the powerful potential for mobilizing public opinion on a national scale. Reform campaigns need not be limited to the local community. Ultimately, they could engage a national community of informed citizens.

Intellectual Trends Promoting Reform

On a deeper level than muckraking, a host of early-twentieth-century thinkers challenged several of the core ideas in American intellectual life. Their new theories of education, law, economics, and society provided effective tools for reformers. The emergent fields of the social sciences—sociology, psychology, anthropology, and economics—emphasized empirical observation of how people actually lived and behaved in their communities. Progressive reformers linked the systematic analysis of society and the individual characteristic of these new fields of inquiry to the project of improving the material conditions of American society. In doing so they called on the academy for something it had never before been asked to provide—practical help in facing the unprecedented challenges of rapid industrialization and urbanization.

Sociologist Lester Frank Ward, in his pioneering work *Dynamic Sociology* (1883), offered an important critique of social Darwinism, the then orthodox theory that attributed social inequality to natural selection and the "survival of the fittest." Ward argued that the conservative social theorists responsible for social Darwinism, such as Herbert Spencer and William Graham Sumner, had wrongly applied evolutionary theory to human affairs. They had confused organic evolution with social evolution. Nature's method was genetic: unplanned, involuntary, automatic, and mechanical. An octopus had to lay 50,000 eggs to maintain itself; a codfish hatched a million young fish a year in order that two might survive. By contrast, civilization had been built on successful human intervention in the natural processes of organic evolution. The human method was telic: planned, voluntary, rational, dynamic. "Every implement or utensil," Ward argued, "every mechanical device, every object of design, skill, and labor, every artificial thing that serves a human purpose, is a triumph of mind over the physical forces of nature in ceaseless and aimless competition."

Philosopher John Dewey criticized the excessively rigid and formal approach to education found in most American schools. In books such as *The School and Society* (1899) and *Democracy and Education* (1916), Dewey advocated developing what he called "creative intelligence" in students, which could then be put to use in improving society. Schools ought to be "embryonic communities," miniatures of society, where children were encouraged to participate actively in different types of experiences. By cultivating imagination and openness to new experiences, schools could develop creativity and the habits required for systematic inquiry. Dewey placed excessive faith in the power of schools to promote community spirit and democratic values. But his belief that education was the "fundamental method of social progress and reform" inspired generations of progressive educators.

At the University of Wisconsin, John R. Commons founded the new field of industrial relations and organized a state industrial commission that became a model for other states. Working closely with Governor Robert M. La Follette, Commons and his students helped draft pioneering laws in worker compensation and public utility regulation. Another Wisconsin faculty member, economist Richard Ely, argued that the state was "an educational and ethical agency whose positive aim is an indispensable condition of human progress." Ely believed the state must directly intervene to help solve public problems. He rejected the doctrine of laissez faire as merely "a tool in the hands of the greedy." Like Commons, Ely worked with Wisconsin lawmakers, applying his expertise in economics to reforming the state's labor laws.

Progressive legal theorists began challenging the conservative view of constitutional law that had dominated American courts. Since the 1870s the Supreme Court had interpreted the Fourteenth Amendment (1868) as a guarantee of broad rights for corporations. That amendment, which prevented states from depriving "any person of life, liberty, or property, without due process of law," had been designed to protect the civil rights of African Americans against violations by the states. But the Court, led by Justice Stephen J. Field, used the due process clause to strike down state laws regulating business and labor conditions. The Supreme Court and state courts had thus made the Fourteenth Amendment a bulwark for big business and a foe of social welfare measures.

The most important dissenter from this view was Oliver Wendell Holmes Jr. A scholar and Massachusetts judge, Holmes believed the law had to take into account changing social conditions. And courts should take care not to invalidate social legislation enacted democratically. After his appointment to the Supreme Court in 1902, Holmes authored a number of notable dissents to conservative court decisions overturning progressive legislation. Criticizing the majority opinion in *Lochner v. New York* (1905), in which the Court struck down a state law setting a ten-hour day for bakers, Holmes insisted that the Constitution "is not intended to embody a particular theory."

Holmes's pragmatic views of the law seldom convinced a majority of the Supreme Court before the late 1930s. But his views influenced a generation of lawyers who began practicing what came to be called sociological jurisprudence. In *Muller v. Oregon* (1908), the Court upheld an Oregon law limiting the maximum hours for working women. Noting that "woman's physical structure and the performance of maternal functions place her at a disadvantage," the Court found that "the physical well-being of woman becomes an object of public interest and care." Louis Brandeis, the state's attorney, amassed statistical, sociological, and economic data, rather than traditional legal arguments, to support his arguments. The "Brandeis Brief" became a common strategy for lawyers defending the constitutionality of progressive legislation.

The new field of American sociology concentrated on the rapidly changing nature of community. German social theorist Ferdinand Tönnies developed an extremely influential model for describing the recent evolution of western society from *Gemeinschaft* to *Gesellschaft*: from a static, close-knit, morally unified community to a dynamic, impersonal, morally fragmented society. If the new urban-industrial order had weakened traditional sources of morality and values—the family, the church, the small community—then where would the mass of people now learn these values?

This question provided the focus for Edward A. Ross's landmark work *Social Control* (1901), a book whose title became a key phrase in progressive thought. Ross argued that society needed an "ethical elite" of citizens "who have at heart the general welfare and know what kinds of conduct will promote this welfare." The "surplus moral energy" of this elite—ministers, educators, professionals—would have to guide the new mechanisms of social control needed in America's *Gesellschaft* communities.

SOCIAL CONTROL AND ITS LIMITS

Many middle- and upper-class Protestant progressives feared that immigrants and large cities threatened the stability of American democracy. They worried that alien cultural practices were disrupting what they viewed as traditional American morality. Viewing themselves as part of what sociologist Edward Ross called the "ethical elite," progressives often believed they had a mission to frame laws and regulations for the social control of immigrants, industrial workers, and African Americans. This was the moralistic and frequently xenophobic side of progressivism, and it provided a powerful source of support for the regulation of drinking, prostitution, leisure activities, and schooling. Organizations devoted to social control constituted other versions of reform communities. But these attempts at moral reform met with mixed success amid the extraordinary cultural and ethnic diversity of America's cities.

The more extreme proponents of these views also embraced the new pseudo-science of eugenics, based on the biological theories of the English scientist Francis Galton. Eugenicists stressed the primacy of inherited traits over environmental conditions for understanding human abilities and deficiencies. They argued that human society could be bettered only by breeding from the best stock and limiting the offspring of the worst. By the 1920s, these theories had gained enough influence to contribute to the drastic curtailing of immigration to America (see Chapter 23).

The Prohibition Movement

During the last two decades of the nineteenth century, the Woman's Christian Temperance Union had grown into a powerful mass organization. The WCTU appealed especially to women angered by men who used alcohol and then abused their wives and children. It directed most of its work toward ending the production, sale, and consumption of alcohol. But local WCTU chapters put their energy into nontemperance activities as well, including homeless shelters, Sunday schools, prison reform, child nurseries, and woman suffrage. The WCTU thus provided women with a political forum in which they could fuse their traditional moral posture as guardians of the home with broader public concerns. By 1911 the WCTU, with a quarter million members, was the largest women's organization in American history.

Other temperance groups had a narrower focus. The Anti-Saloon League, founded in 1893, began by organizing local-option campaigns in which rural counties and small towns banned liquor within their geographical limits. It drew much of its financial support from local businessmen, who saw a link between closing a community's saloons and increasing the productivity of workers. The league was a one-issue pressure group that played effectively on anti-urban and anti-immigrant prejudice. League lobbyists targeted state legislatures, where big cities were usually underrepresented. They hammered away at the close connections among saloon culture, liquor dealers, brewers, and big-city political machines.

The prohibition movement found its core strength among Protestant, native-born, small-town, and rural Americans. But prohibition found support as well in the cities, where the battle to ban alcohol revealed deep ethnic and cultural divides within America's urban communities. Opponents of alcohol were generally "pietists" who viewed the world from a position of moral absolutism. These included native-born, middle-class Protestants associated with evangelical churches along with some old-stock Protestant immigrant denominations. Opponents of prohibition were generally "ritualists" with less arbitrary notions of personal morality. These were largely new-stock, working-class Catholic and Jewish immigrants, along with some Protestants, such as German Lutherans.

The Social Evil

Many of the same reformers who battled the saloon and drinking also engaged in efforts to eradicate prostitution. Crusades against "the social evil" had appeared at intervals throughout the nineteenth century. But they reached a new level of intensity between 1895 and 1920. In part, this new sense of urgency stemmed from the sheer growth of cities and the greater visibility of prostitution in red-light districts and neighborhoods. Antiprostitution campaigns epitomized the diverse makeup and mixed motives of so much progressive reform. Male business and civic leaders joined forces with feminists, social workers, and clergy to eradicate "commercialized vice."

Between 1908 and 1914 exposés of the "white slave traffic" became a national sensation. Dozens of books, articles, and motion pictures alleged an international conspiracy to seduce and sell girls into prostitution. Most of these materials exaggerated the practices they attacked. They also made foreigners, especially Jews and southern Europeans, scapegoats for the sexual anxieties of native-born whites. In 1910 Congress passed legislation that permitted the deportation of foreign-born prostitutes or any foreigner convicted of procuring or employing them. That same year, the Mann Act made it a federal offense to transport women across state lines for "immoral purposes."

But most antiprostitution activity took place at the local level. Between 1910 and 1915, thirty-five cities and states conducted thorough investigations of prostitution. The progressive bent for defining social problems through statistics was nowhere more evident than in these reports. Vice commission investigators combed red-light districts, tenement houses, hotels, and dance halls, drawing up detailed lists of places where prostitution took place. They interviewed prostitutes, pimps, and customers. These reports agreed that commercialized sex was a business run by and for the profit and pleasure of men. They also documented the dangers of venereal disease to the larger community. The highly publicized vice reports were effective in forcing police crackdowns in urban red-light districts.

Reformers had trouble believing that any woman would freely choose to be a prostitute; such a choice was antithetical to conventional notions of female purity and sexuality. But for wage-earning women, prostitution was a rational choice in a world of limited opportunities. Maimie Pinzer, a prostitute, summed up her feelings in a letter to a wealthy female reformer: "I don't propose to get up at 6:30 to be at work at 8 and work in a close, stuffy room with people I despise, until dark, for $6 or $7 a week! When I could, just by phoning, spend an afternoon with some congenial person and in the end have more than a week's work could pay me." The antivice crusades succeeded in closing down many urban red-light districts and larger brothels, but these were replaced by the streetwalker and call girl, who were more vulnerable to harassment and control by policemen and pimps. Rather than eliminating prostitution, reform efforts transformed the organization of the sex trade.

The Redemption of Leisure

Progressives faced a thorny issue in the growing popularity of commercial entertainment. For large numbers of working-class adults and children, leisure meant time and money spent at vaudeville and burlesque theaters, amusement parks, dance halls, and motion picture houses. These competed with municipal parks, libraries, museums, YMCAs, and school recreation centers. For many cultural traditionalists, the flood of new urban commercial amusements posed a grave threat. As with prostitution, urban progressives sponsored a host of recreation and amusement surveys detailing the situation in their individual cities. "Commercialized leisure," warned Frederic C. Howe in 1914, "must be controlled by the community, if it is to become an agency of civilization rather than the reverse."

By 1908 movies had become the most popular form of cheap entertainment in America. One survey estimated that 11,500 movie theaters attracted 5 million patrons each day. For five or ten cents "nickelodeon" theaters offered programs that might include a slapstick comedy, a Western, a travelogue, and a melodrama. Early movies were most popular in the tenement and immigrant districts of big cities, and with children. As the films themselves became more sophisticated and as "movie palaces" began to replace cheap storefront theaters, the new medium attracted a large middle-class clientele as well.

Progressive reformers seized the chance to help regulate the new medium as a way of improving the commercial recreation of the urban poor. Movies held out the promise of an alternative to the older entertainment traditions, such as concert saloons and burlesque theater, that had been closely allied with machine politics and the vice economy. In 1909, New York City movie producers and exhibitors joined with the reform-minded People's Institute to establish the voluntary National Board of Censorship (NBC). Movie entrepreneurs, most of whom were themselves immigrants, sought to shed the stigma of the slums, attract more middle-class patronage, and increase profits. A revolving group of civic activists reviewed new movies, passing them, suggesting changes, or condemning

John Sloan, *Movies*, 1913 oil painting. The Toledo Museum of Art.

Movies, *by John Sloan, 1913, the most talented artist among the so-called Ashcan realist school of painting. Active in socialist and bohemian circles, Sloan served as art editor for* The Masses *magazine for several years. His work celebrated the vitality and diversity of urban working-class life and leisure, including the new commercial culture represented by the motion picture.*

them. Local censoring committees all over the nation subscribed to the board's weekly bulletin. They aimed at achieving what John Collier of the NBC called "the redemption of leisure." By 1914 the NBC was reviewing 95 percent of the nation's film output.

Standardizing Education

Along with reading, writing, and mathematics, schools inculcated patriotism, piety, and respect for authority. Progressive educators looked to the public school primarily as an agent of "Americanization." Elwood Cubberley, a leading educational reformer, expressed the view that schools could be the vehicle by which immigrant children could break free of the parochial ethnic neighborhood. "Our task," he argued in *Changing Conceptions of Education* (1909), "is to break up these groups or settlements, to assimilate and amalgamate these people as a part of our American race, and to implant in their children, so far as can be done, the Anglo-Saxon conception of righteousness, law and order, and popular government."

The most important educational trends in these years were the expansion and bureaucratization of the nation's public school systems. In most cities centralization served to consolidate the power of older urban elites who felt threatened by the large influx of immigrants. Children began school earlier and stayed there longer. Kindergartens spread rapidly in large cities.

They presented, as one writer put it in 1903, "the earliest opportunity to catch the little Russian, the little Italian, the little German, Pole, Syrian, and the rest and begin to make good American citizens of them." By 1918 every state had some form of compulsory school attendance. High schools also multiplied, extending the school's influence beyond the traditional grammar school curriculum. In 1890 only 4 percent of the nation's youth between fourteen and seventeen were enrolled in school; by 1930 the figure was 47 percent.

High schools reflected a growing belief that schools be comprehensive, multifunctional institutions. In 1918 the National Education Association offered a report defining Cardinal Principles of Secondary Education. These included instruction in health, family life, citizenship, and ethical character. Academic programs prepared a small number of students for college. Vocational programs trained boys and girls for a niche in the new industrial order. Boys took shop courses in metal trades, carpentry, and machine tools. Girls learned typing, bookkeeping, sewing, cooking, and home economics. The Smith-Hughes Act of 1917 provided federal grants to support these programs and set up a Federal Board for Vocational Education.

Educational reformers also established national testing organizations such as the College Entrance Examination Board (founded in 1900) and helped standardize agencies for curriculum development and teacher training. In 1903 E. L. Thorndike published *Educational Psychology*, which laid the groundwork for education research based on experimental and statistical investigations. Progressives led in the development of specialized fields such as educational psychology, guidance counseling, and educational administration.

WORKING-CLASS COMMUNITIES AND PROTEST

The industrial revolution, which had begun transforming American life and labor in the nineteenth century, reached maturity in the early twentieth. In 1900, out of a total labor force of 28.5 million, 16 million people worked at industrial occupations and 11 million on farms. By 1920, in a labor force of nearly 42 million, almost 29 million were in industry, but farm labor had declined to 10.4 million. The world of the industrial worker included large manufacturing towns in New England; barren mining settlements in the West; primitive lumber and turpentine camps in the South; steelmaking and coal-mining cities in Pennsylvania and Ohio; and densely packed immigrant ghettos from New York to San Francisco, where workers toiled in garment trade sweatshops.

All these industrial workers shared the need to sell their labor for wages in order to survive. At the same time, differences in skill, ethnicity, and race proved powerful barriers to efforts at organizing trade unions that could bargain for improved wages and working conditions. So, too, did the economic and political power of the large corporations that dominated much of American industry. Yet there were also small, closely knit groups of skilled workers, such as printers and brewers, who exercised real control over their lives and labors. And these years saw many labor struggles that created effective trade unions or laid the groundwork for others. Industrial workers also became a force in local and national politics, adding a chorus of insistent voices to the calls for social justice.

The New Immigrants

On the eve of World War I, close to 60 percent of the industrial labor force was foreign-born. Most of these workers were among the roughly 9 million new immigrants from southern and eastern Europe who arrived in the United States between 1900 and 1914. In the nineteenth century, much of the overseas migration had come from the industrial districts of northern and western Europe. English, Welsh, and German artisans had brought with them skills critical for emerging industries such as steelmaking and coal mining. Unlike their predecessors, the new Italian, Polish, Hungarian, Jewish, and Greek immigrants nearly all lacked indus-

IMMIGRATION TO THE UNITED STATES (1901–1920)

Total: 14,532,000		% of Total
Italy	3,157,000	22%
Austria-Hungary	3,047,000	21
Russia and Poland	2,524,000	17
Canada	922,000	6
Great Britain	867,000	6
Scandinavia	709,000	5
Ireland	487,000	3
Germany	486,000	3
France and Low Countries (Belgium, Netherlands, Switz.)	361,000	2
Mexico	268,000	2
West Indies	231,000	2
Japan	213,000	2
China	41,000	*
Australia and New Zealand	23,000	*

*Less than 1% of total

Source: U.S. Bureau of the Census, *Historical Statistics of the United States from Colonial Times to 1970*, Washington, D.C., 1975.

trial skills. They thus entered the bottom ranks of factories, mines, mills, and sweatshops.

These new immigrants had been driven from their European farms and towns by several forces, including the undermining of subsistence farming by commercial agriculture; a falling death rate that brought a shortage of land; and religious and political persecution. American corporations also sent agents to recruit cheap labor. Except for Jewish immigrants, a majority of whom fled virulent anti-Semitism in Russia and Russian Poland, most newcomers planned on earning a stake and then returning home. Hard times in America forced many back to Europe. In the depression year of 1908, for example, more Austro-Hungarians and Italians left than entered the United States.

In 1892 *the federal government opened the immigration station on* Ellis Island, *located in* New York *City's harbor, where about* 80 *percent of the immigrants to the United* States *landed. As many as* 5,000 *passengers per day reported to federal immigration officers for questions about their background and for physical examinations, such as this eye exam. Only about* 1 *percent were quarantined or turned away for health problems.*

The decision to migrate usually occurred through social networks—people linked by kinship, personal acquaintance, and work experience. These "chains," extending from places of origin to specific destinations in the United States, helped migrants cope with the considerable risks entailed by the long and difficult journey. A study conducted by the U.S. Immigration Commission in 1909 found that about 60 percent of the new immigrants had their passage arranged by immigrants already in America. An Italian who joined his grandfather and cousins in Buffalo in 1906 recalled, "In western New York most of the first immigrants from Sicily went to Buffalo, so that from 1900 on, the thousands who followed them to this part of the state also landed in Buffalo."

Immigrant communities used ethnicity as a collective resource for gaining employment in factories, mills, and mines. One Polish steelworker recalled how the process operated in the Pittsburgh mills: "Now if a Russian got his job in a shear department, he's looking for a buddy, a Russian buddy. He's not going to look for a Croatian buddy. And if he sees the boss looking for a man he says, 'Look, I have a good man,' and he's picking out his friends. A Ukrainian department, a Russian department, a Polish department. And it was a beautiful thing in a way." Such specialization of work by ethnic origin was quite common throughout America's industrial communities.

The low-paid, backbreaking work in basic industry became nearly the exclusive preserve of the new immigrants. In 1907, of the 14,359 common laborers employed at Pittsburgh's U.S. Steel mills, 11,694 were eastern Europeans. For twelve-hour days and seven-day weeks, two-thirds of these workers made less than $12.50 a week, one-third less than $10.00. This was far less than the $15.00 that the Pittsburgh Associated Charities had estimated as the minimum for providing necessities for a family of five. Small wonder that the new immigration was disproportionately male. One-third of the immigrant steelworkers were single, and among married men who had been in the country less than five years, about two-thirds reported that their wives were still in Europe. Workers with families generally supplemented their incomes by taking in single men as boarders.

Not all the new immigrants came from Europe. Between 1898 and 1907 more than 80,000 Japanese entered the United States. The vast majority were young men working as contract laborers in the West, mainly in California. American law prevented Japanese immigrants (the Issei) from obtaining American citizenship, because they were not white. This legal discrimination, along with informal exclusion from many occupations, forced the Japanese to create niches for themselves within local economies. Most Japanese settled near Los Angeles, where they established small communities centered around fishing, truck farming, and the flower and nursery business. In 1920 Japanese farmers produced 10 percent of the dollar volume of California agriculture on 1 percent of the farm acreage. By 1930 over 35,000 Issei and their children (the Nisei) lived in Los Angeles.

Mexican immigration also grew in these years, providing a critical source of labor for the West's farms, railroads, and mines. Between 1900 and 1914, the number of people of Mexican descent living and working in the United States tripled, from roughly 100,000 to 300,000. Economic and political crises spurred tens of thousands of Mexico's rural and urban poor to emigrate north. Large numbers of seasonal agricultural workers regularly came up from Mexico to work in the expanding sugar beet industry and then returned. But a number of substantial resident Mexican communities also emerged in the early twentieth century.

Throughout Texas, California, New Mexico, Arizona, and Colorado, western cities developed barrios, distinct communities of Mexicans. Mexican immigrants attracted by jobs in the smelting industry made El Paso the most thoroughly Mexican city in the United States. In San Antonio, Mexicans worked at shelling pecans, becoming perhaps the most underpaid and exploited group of workers in the country. By 1910, San Antonio contained the largest number of Mexican immigrants of any city. In southern California, labor agents for railroads recruited Mexicans to work on building new interurban lines around Los Angeles. Overcrowding, poor sanitation, and deficient public services made many of these enclaves unhealthy places to live. Mexican barrios suffered much higher rates of disease and infant mortality than surrounding Anglo communities.

Urban Ghettos

In large cities, new immigrant communities took the form of densely packed ghettos. By 1920, immigrants and their children constituted almost 60 percent of the population of cities over 100,000. They were an even larger percentage in major industrial centers such as Chicago, Pittsburgh, Philadelphia, and New York. The sheer size and dynamism of these cities made the immigrant experience more complex than in smaller cities and more isolated communities. Workers in the urban garment trades toiled for low wages and suffered layoffs, unemployment, and poor health. But conditions in the small, labor-intensive shops of the clothing industry differed significantly from those in the large-scale, capital-intensive industries like steel.

New York City had become the center of both Jewish immigration and America's huge ready-to-wear clothing industry. The city's Jewish population was 1.4 million in 1915, almost 30 percent of its inhabitants. New York produced 70 percent of all women's clothing and 40 percent of all men's clothing made in the country. In small factories, lofts, and tenement apartments some 200,000 people, most of them Jews, some of them Italians, worked in the clothing trades. Most of the industry operated on the grueling piece-rate, or task, system, in which manufacturers and subcontractors paid individuals or teams of workers to complete a certain quota of labor within a specific time.

The garment industry was highly seasonal. A typical work week was sixty hours, with seventy common during busy season. But there were long stretches of unemployment in slack times. Even skilled cutters, all men, earned an average of only $16 per week. Unskilled workers, nearly all of them young single women, made only $6 or $7 a week. Perhaps a quarter of the work force, classified as "learners," earned only $3 to $6 a week. Often forced to work in cramped, dirty, and badly lit rooms, garment workers strained under a system in which time equaled money. Morris Rosenfeld, a presser of men's clothing who wrote Yiddish poetry, captured the feeling:

The tick of the clock is the boss in his anger
The face of the clock has the eye of a foe
The clock—I shudder—Dost hear how it draws me?
It calls me "Machine" and it cries to me "Sew!"

In November 1909 two New York garment manufacturers responded to strikes by unskilled women workers by hiring thugs and prostitutes to beat up pickets. The strikers won the support of the Women's Trade Union League, a group of sympathetic female reformers that included Lillian Wald, Mary Dreier, and prominent society figures. At a dramatic mass meeting in Cooper Union Hall, Clara Lemlich, a teenage working girl speaking in Yiddish, made an emotional plea for a general strike. She called for everyone in the crowd to take an old Jewish oath: "If I turn traitor to the cause I now pledge, may this hand wither from the arm I now raise." The Uprising of the 20,000, as it became known, swept through the city's garment district.

The strikers demanded union recognition, better wages, and safer and more sanitary conditions. They drew support from thousands of suffragists, trade unionists, and sympathetic middle-class women as well. Hundreds of strikers were arrested, and many were beaten by police. After three cold months on the picket line, the strikers returned to work without union recognition. But the International Ladies Garment Workers Union (ILGWU), founded in 1900, did gain strength and negotiated contracts with some of the city's shirt-

New York City Police set up this makeshift morgue to help identify victims of the disastrous Triangle Shirtwaist Company fire, March 25, 1911. Unable to open the locked doors of the sweatshop and desperate to escape from smoke and flames, many of the 146 who died had leaped eight stories to their death.

waist makers. The strike was an important breakthrough in the drive to organize unskilled workers into industrial unions. It opened the doors to women's involvement in the labor movement and created new leaders, such as Lemlich, Pauline Newman, and Rose Schneiderman.

On March 25, 1911, the issues raised by the strike took on new urgency when a fire raced through three floors of the Triangle Shirtwaist Company. As the flames spread, workers found themselves trapped by exit doors locked from the outside. Fire escapes were nonexistent. Within half an hour, 146 people, mostly young Jewish women, had been killed by smoke or had leaped to their death. In the bitter aftermath, women progressives led by Florence Kelley and Frances Perkins of the National Consumers' League joined with Tammany Hall leaders Al Smith, Robert Wagner, and Big Tim Sullivan to create a New York State Factory Investigation Commission. Under Perkins's vigorous leadership, the commission conducted an unprecedented round of public hearings and on-site inspections, leading to a series of state laws that dramatically improved safety conditions and limited the hours for working women and children.

Company Towns

Immigrant industrial workers and their families often established their communities in a company town, where a single large corporation was dominant. Cities such as Lawrence, Massachusetts; Gary, Indiana; and Butte, Montana, revolved around the industrial enterprises of Pacific Woolen, U.S. Steel, and Anaconda Copper. Workers had little or no influence over the economic and political institutions of these cities. In the more isolated company towns, residents often had no alternative but to buy their food, clothing, and supplies at company stores, usually for exorbitantly high prices. But they did maintain some community control in other ways. Family and kin networks, ethnic lodges, saloons, benefit societies, churches and synagogues, and musical groups affirmed traditional forms of community in a setting governed by individualism and private capital.

On the job, modern machinery and industrial discipline meant high rates of injury and death. In Gary, immigrant steelworkers suffered twice the accident rate of English-speaking employees, who could better understand safety instructions and warnings. A 1910 study of work accidents revealed that nearly a fourth of all new steelworkers were killed or injured each year. As one Polish worker described the immigrant's lot to his wife: "If he comes home sick then it is trouble, because everybody is looking only for money to get some of it, and during the sickness most will be spent." Mutual aid associations, organized around ethnic groups, offered some protection through cheap insurance and death benefits.

In steel and coal towns, women not only maintained the household and raised the children, they also boosted the family income by taking in boarders, sewing, and laundry. Many women also tended gardens and raised chickens, rabbits, and goats. Their produce and income helped reduce dependence on the company store. Working-class women felt the burdens of housework more heavily than their middle-class sisters. Pump water, indoor plumbing, and sewage disposal were often available only on a pay-as-you-go basis. The daily drudgery endured by working-class women far outlasted the "man-killing" shift worked by the husband. Many women struggled with the effects of their husbands' excessive drinking and faced early widowhood.

The adjustment for immigrant workers was not so much a process of assimilation as adaptation and resistance. Efficiency experts, such as Frederick Taylor (see Chapter 19), carefully observed and analyzed the time and energy needed for each job, then set standard methods for each worker. In theory, these standards would increase efficiency and give managers more control over their workers. But work habits and Old World cultural traditions did not always mesh with factory discipline or Taylor's "scientific management." A Polish wedding celebration might last three or four days. A drinking bout following a Sunday funeral might cause workers to celebrate "St. Monday" and not show up for work. Employers made much of the few Slavs allowed to work their way up into the ranks of skilled workers and foremen. But most immigrants were far more concerned with job security than with upward mobility. The newcomers learned from more skilled and experienced British and American workers that "slowing down" or "soldiering" spread out the work. As new immigrants became less transient and more permanently settled in company towns, they increased their involvement in local politics and union activity.

The power of large corporations in the life of company towns was most evident among the mining communities of the West, as was violent labor conflict. The Colorado Fuel and Iron Company (CFI) employed roughly half of the 8,000 coal miners who labored in that state's mines. In mining towns such as Ludlow and Trinidad, the CFI thoroughly dominated the lives of miners and their families. "The miner," one union official observed, "is in this land owned by the corporation that owns the homes, that owns the boarding houses, that owns every single thing there is there . . . not only the mines, but all the grounds, all the buildings, all the places of recreation, as well as the school and church buildings." By the early twentieth century, new immigrants, such as Italians, Greeks, Slavs, and Mexicans, composed a majority of the population in these western mining communities. About one-fifth of CFI miners spoke no English.

In September 1913, the United Mine Workers led a strike in the Colorado coalfields, calling for improved safety, higher wages, and recognition of the union. Thousands of miners' families moved out of company housing and into makeshift tent colonies provided by the union. In October, Governor Elias Ammons ordered the Colorado National Guard into the tense strike region to keep order. The troops, supposedly neutral, proceeded to ally themselves with the mine operators. By spring the strike had bankrupted the state, forcing the governor to remove most of the troops. The coal companies then brought in large numbers of private mine guards who were extremely hostile toward the strikers. On April 20, 1914, a combination of guardsmen and private guards surrounded the largest of the tent colonies at Ludlow, where more than a thousand mine families lived. A shot rang out (each side accused the other of firing), and a pitched battle ensued that lasted until the poorly armed miners ran out of ammunition. At dusk, the troops burned the tent village to the ground, routing the families and killing fourteen, eleven of them children. Enraged strikers attacked mines throughout southern Colorado in an armed rebellion that lasted ten days, until President Woodrow Wilson ordered the U.S. Army into the region. News of the Ludlow Massacre shocked millions and aroused widespread protests and demonstrations against the policies of Colorado Fuel and Iron and its owner, John D. Rockefeller Jr.

The AFL: "Unions, Pure and Simple"

Following the depression of the 1890s, the American Federation of Labor emerged as the strongest and most stable organization of workers. Samuel Gompers's strategy of recruiting skilled labor into unions organized by craft had paid off. Union membership climbed from under 500,000 in 1897 to 1.7 million by 1904. Most of this growth took place in AFL affiliates in coal mining, the building trades, transportation, and machine shops. The national unions—the United Mine Workers of America, the Brotherhood of Carpenters and Joiners, the International Association of Machinists—represented workers of specific occupations in collective bargaining. Trade autonomy and exclusive jurisdiction were the ruling principles within the AFL.

But the strength of craft organization also gave rise to weakness. In 1905 Gompers told a union gathering in Minneapolis that "caucasians" would not "let their standard of living be destroyed by negroes, Chinamen, Japs, or any others." Those "others" included the new immigrants from eastern and southern Europe, men and women, who labored in the steel mills and garment trades. Each trade looked mainly to the welfare of its own. Many explicitly barred women and African Americans from membership. There were some important exceptions. The United Mine Workers of America followed a more inclusive policy, recruiting both skilled underground pitmen and the unskilled aboveground workers. The UMWA even tried to recruit strikebreakers brought in by coal operators. With 260,000 members in 1904, the UMWA became the largest AFL affiliate.

AFL unions had a difficult time holding on to their gains. Economic slumps, technological changes, and aggressive counterattacks by employer organizations could be devastating. Trade associations using management-controlled efficiency drives fought union efforts to regulate output and shop practices. The National Association of Manufacturers, a group of smaller industrialists founded in 1903, launched an "open shop" campaign to eradicate unions altogether. "Open shop" was simply a new name for a workplace where unions were not allowed. The NAM supplied strikebreakers, private guards, and labor spies to employers. It also formed antiboycott associations to prevent unions in one trade from supporting walkouts in another.

Unfriendly judicial decisions also hurt organizing efforts. In 1906 a federal judge issued a permanent injunction against an iron molders strike at the Allis Chalmers Company of Milwaukee. In the so-called Danbury Hatters' Case (*Loewe v. Lawler*, 1908), a federal court ruled that secondary boycotts, aimed by strikers at other companies doing business with their employer, such as suppliers of materials, were illegal under the Sherman Antitrust Act. Long an effective labor tactic, secondary boycotts were now declared a conspiracy in restraint of trade. Not until the 1930s would unions be able to count on legal support for collective bargaining and the right to strike.

The IWW: "One Big Union"

Some workers developed more radical visions of labor organizing. In the harsh and isolated company towns of Idaho, Montana, and Colorado, miners suffered from low wages, poor food, and primitive sanitation, as well as injuries and death from frequent cave-ins and explosions. The Western Federation of Miners (WFM) had gained strength in the metal mining regions of the West by leading several strikes marred by violence. In 1899, during a strike in the silver mining district of Coeur d'Alene, Idaho, the Bunker Hill and Sullivan Mining Company had enraged the miners by hiring armed detectives and firing all union members. Desperate miners retaliated by destroying a company mill with dynamite. Idaho's governor declared martial law and obtained federal troops to enforce it. In a pattern that would become familiar in western labor relations, the soldiers served as strikebreakers, rounding up hundreds of miners and imprisoning them for months in makeshift bullpens.

In response to the brutal realities of labor organizing in the West, most WFM leaders embraced socialism and industrial unionism. In 1905, leaders of the WFM, the Socialist Party, and various radical groups gathered in Chicago to found the Industrial Workers of the World (IWW). The IWW charter proclaimed bluntly, "The working class and the employing class have nothing in common. . . . Between these two classes a struggle must go on until the workers of the world unite as a class, take possession of the earth and the machinery of production, and abolish the wage system."

William D. "Big Bill" Haywood, an imposing, one-eyed, hard-rock miner, emerged as the most influential and flamboyant spokesman for the IWW, or Wobblies, as they were called. Haywood, a charismatic speaker and effective organizer, regularly denounced the AFL for its conservative emphasis on organizing skilled workers by trade. He insisted that the IWW would exclude no one from its ranks. The Wobblies concentrated their efforts on miners, lumberjacks, sailors, "harvest stiffs," and other casual laborers. They glorified transient and unskilled workers in speeches and songs, aiming to counter their hopelessness and degradation. Openly contemptuous of bourgeois respectability, the IWW stressed the power of collective direct action on the job—strikes and, occasionally, sabotage.

The IWW briefly became a force among eastern industrial workers, tapping the rage and growing militance of the immigrants and unskilled. In 1909, an IWW-led steel strike at McKees Rocks, Pennsylvania, challenged the power of U.S. Steel. In the 1912 "Bread and Roses" strike in Lawrence, Massachusetts, IWW organizers turned a spontaneous walkout of textile workers into a successful struggle for union recognition. Wobbly leaders such as Haywood, Elizabeth Gurley Flynn, and Joseph Ettor used class-conscious rhetoric and multilingual appeals to forge unity among the ethnically diverse Lawrence work force of 25,000.

These battles gained the IWW a great deal of sympathy from radical intellectuals, along with public scorn from the AFL and employers' groups. The IWW failed to establish permanent organizations in the eastern cities, but it remained a force in the lumber camps, mines, and wheat fields of the West. In spite of its militant rhetoric, the IWW concerned itself with practical gains. "The final aim is revolution," said one Wobbly organizer, "but for the present let's see if we can get a bed to sleep in, water enough to take a bath in and decent food to eat."

The occasional use of violence by union organizers sometimes backfired against the labor movement. On October 1, 1910, two explosions destroyed the printing plant of the *Los Angeles Times*, killing twenty-one workmen. When John and James McNamara, two brothers active in the ironworkers' union, were charged with the bombing and indicted for murder, unionists of all political persuasions rallied to their defense. Leaders of the AFL, IWW, and Socialist Party joined in a massive campaign that stressed the labor-versus-capital aspects of the case. The *Los Angeles Times* and its influential owner Harrison Gray Otis, they noted, were strongly anti-union and had helped keep Los Angeles a largely nonunion city. Some even suggested that Otis himself, looking to give labor a black eye, was responsible for the bombs. On Labor Day 1911, as the trial approached, huge crowds in America's largest cities gathered to proclaim the McNamara brothers innocent. But they were guilty. In the middle of the trial, the McNamaras confessed to the dynamiting, shocking their many supporters. A Socialist candidate for mayor of Los Angeles, favored to win the election, was decisively defeated, and the city remained a nonunion stronghold.

Rebels in Bohemia

During the 1910s, a small but influential community of painters, journalists, poets, social workers, lawyers, and political activists coalesced in the New York City neighborhood of Greenwich Village. These cultural radicals, nearly all of middle-class background and hailing from provincial American towns, shared a deep sympathy toward the struggles of labor, a passion for modern art, and an openness to socialism and anarchism. "Village bohemians," especially the women among them, challenged the double standard of Victorian sexual morality, rejected traditional marriage and sex roles, advocated birth control, and experimented with homosexual relations. They became a powerful national symbol for rebellion and the merger of political and cultural radicalism.

The term "bohemian" referred to anyone who had artistic or intellectual aspirations and who lived with disregard for conventional rules of behavior. Other American cities, notably Chicago at the turn of the century, had supported bohemian communities. But the Village scene was unique, if fleeting. The neighborhood offered cheap rents, studio space, and good ethnic restaurants, and it was close to the exciting political and labor activism of Manhattan's Lower East Side. The world view of the Village's bohemian community found expression in *The Masses,* a monthly magazine founded in 1911 by socialist critic Max Eastman, who was also its editor. "The broad purpose of *The Masses,*" wrote John Reed, one of its leading writers, "is a social one—to everlastingly attack old systems, old morals, old prejudices—the whole weight of outworn thought that dead men have saddled upon us." Regular contributors included radical labor journalist Mary Heaton Vorse, artists John Sloan and George Bellows, and writers Floyd Dell and Sherwood Anderson.

At private parties and public events, the Village brought together a wide variety of men and women looking to combine politics, art, and support for the labor movement. Birth control activist Margaret Sanger found a sympathetic audience, as did IWW leader Big Bill Haywood. Journalist Walter Lippmann lectured on the new psychological theory of Sigmund Freud. Anarchist and feminist Emma Goldman wooed financial supporters for her magazine *Mother Earth*. Photographer Alfred Stieglitz welcomed artists to his gallery-studio "291."

For some, Greenwich Village offered a chance to experiment with sexual relationships or work arrangements. For others, it was an escape from small-town conformity or a haven for like-minded artists and activists. Yet the Village bohemians were united in their search for a new sense of community. Mary Heaton Vorse expressed their deeply pessimistic conviction that modern American society could no longer satisfy the elemental needs of community. "This is our weakness," she wrote. "Our strength does not multiply in our daily lives. There is a creative force in people doing things together." Intellectuals and artists, as well as workers, feeling alienated from the rest of society, sought shelter in the collective life and close-knit social relations of the Village community.

The Paterson, New Jersey, silk workers' strike of 1913 provided the most memorable fusion of bohemian sensibility and radical activism. After hearing Haywood speak about the strike at Mabel Dodge's apartment, John Reed offered to organize a pageant on the strikers' behalf at Madison Square Garden. The idea was to publicize the strike to the world and also raise money. The Villagers helped write a script, designed sets and scenery, and took care of publicity. A huge crowd watched more than a thousand workers reenact the silk workers' strike, complete with picket line songs, a funeral, and speeches by IWW organizers.

The spectacular production was an artistic triumph. One critic described the pageant as "a new art form, a form in which the workers would present their own story without artifice or theatricality, and therefore with a new kind of dramatic power." But the pageant was also a financial disaster. The Village bohemia lasted only a few years, a flame snuffed out by the chill political winds accompanying America's entry into World War I. Yet for decades Greenwich Village remained a mecca for young men and women searching for alternatives to conventional ways of living.

Publicity poster for the 1913 pageant, organized by John Reed and other Greenwich Village radicals, supporting the cause of striking silk workers in Paterson, New Jersey. This poster drew on aesthetic styles associated with the Industrial Workers of the World, typically including a heroic, larger than life image of a factory laborer.

WOMEN'S MOVEMENTS AND BLACK AWAKENING

Progressive era women were at the forefront of several reform campaigns, such as the settlement house movement, prohibition, suffrage, and birth control. Millions of others took an active role in new women's associations that combined self-help and social mission. These organizations gave women a place in public life, increased their influence in civic affairs, and nurtured a new generation of female leaders.

In fighting racial discrimination, African Americans had a more difficult task. As racism gained ground in the political and cultural spheres, black progressives fought defensively to prevent the rights they had secured during Reconstruction from being further undermined. Still, they managed to produce leaders, ideas, and organizations that would have a long-range impact on American race relations.

The New Woman

The settlement house movement discussed in the opening of this chapter was just one of the new avenues of opportunity that opened to progressive era women. A steady proliferation of women's organizations attracted growing numbers of educated, middle-class women in the early twentieth century. With more men working in offices, more children attending school, and family size declining, the middle-class home was emptier. At the same time, more middle-class women were graduating from high school and college. In 1900, only 7 percent of Americans went to high school, but 60 percent of those who graduated were women. Moreover, in 1870, only 1 percent of college-age Americans had attended college, about 20 percent of them women; by 1910 about 5 percent of college-age Americans attended college, but the proportion of women among them had doubled to 40 percent.

Single-sex clubs brought middle-class women into the public sphere by celebrating the distinctive strengths associated with women's culture: cooperation, uplift, service. The formation of the General Federation of Women's Clubs in 1890 brought together 200 local clubs representing 20,000 women. By 1900 the federation boasted 150,000 members, and by World War I it claimed to represent over a million women. The women's club movement combined an earlier focus on self-improvement and intellectual pursuits with newer benevolent efforts on behalf of working women and children. The Buffalo Union, for example, sponsored art lectures for housewives and classes in typing, stenography, and bookkeeping for young working women. It also maintained a library, set up a "noon rest" downtown where women could eat lunch, and ran a school for training domestics. In Chicago the Women's Club became a powerful ally for reformers, and club member Louise Bowen, a Hull House trustee, gave the settlement three-quarters of a million dollars.

For many middle-class women the club movement provided a new kind of female-centered community. As one member put it: "What college life is to the young woman, club life is to the woman of riper years, who amidst the responsibilities and cares of home life still wishes to keep abreast of the time, still longs for the companionship of those who, like herself, do not wish to cease to be students because they have left school." Club activity often led members to participate in other civic ventures, particularly "child-saving" reforms, such as child labor laws and mothers' pensions. Some took up the cause of working-class women, fighting for protective legislation and offering aid to trade unions. As wives and daughters of influential and well-off men in their communities, clubwomen had access to funds and could generate support for projects they undertook.

Other women's associations made even more explicit efforts to bridge class lines between middle-class homemakers and working-class women. The National Consumers' League (NCL), started in 1898 by Maud Nathan and Josephine Lowell, sponsored a "white label" campaign in which manufacturers who met safety and sanitary standards could put NCL labels on their food and clothing. Under the dynamic leadership of Florence Kelley, the NCL took an even more aggressive stance by publicizing labor abuses in department stores and lobbying for maximum-hour and minimum-wage laws in state legislatures. In its efforts to protect home and housewife, worker and consumer, the NCL embodied the ideal of "social housekeeping." "The home does not stop at the street door," said Marion Talbot, dean of women at the University of Chicago in 1911. "It is as wide as the world into which the individual steps forth."

Birth Control

The phrase "birth control," coined by Margaret Sanger around 1913, described her campaign to provide contraceptive information and devices for women. Sanger had seen her own mother die at age forty-nine after bearing eleven children. In 1910, Sanger was a thirty-year-old nurse and housewife living with her husband and three children in a New York City suburb. Excited by a socialist lecture she had attended, she convinced her husband to move to the city, where she threw herself into the bohemian milieu. She became an organizer for the IWW, and in 1912 she wrote a series of articles on female sexuality for a socialist newspaper.

When postal officials confiscated the paper for violating obscenity laws, Sanger left for Europe to learn more about contraception. She returned to New York determined to challenge the obscenity statutes with her own magazine, the *Woman Rebel*. Sanger's journal

Margaret Sanger (second from left) is shown outside the first birth control clinic, which she founded in Brooklyn, New York, in 1916. Sanger campaigned tirelessly to educate working-class women about contraception: she wrote and distributed pamphlets, lectured around the country, and invited arrest by publicly breaking obscenity laws. "Women cannot be on an equal footing with men," she wrote, "until they have full and complete control over their reproductive function."

celebrated female autonomy, including the right to sexual expression and control over one's body. When she distributed her pamphlet *Family Limitation*, postal inspectors confiscated copies and she found herself facing forty-five years in prison. In October 1914 she fled to Europe again. In her absence, anarchist agitator Emma Goldman and many women in the Socialist Party took up the cause.

An older generation of feminists had advocated "voluntary motherhood," or the right to say no to a husband's sexual demands. The new birth control advocates embraced contraception as a way of advancing sexual freedom for middle-class women as well as responding to the misery of those working-class women who bore numerous children while living in poverty. Sanger returned to the United States in October 1915. After the government dropped the obscenity charges, she embarked on a national speaking tour. In 1916 she again defied the law by opening a birth control clinic in a working-class neighborhood in Brooklyn and offering birth control information without a physician present. Arrested and jailed, she gained more publicity for her crusade. Within a few years, birth control leagues and clinics could be found in every major city and most large towns in the country.

Racism and Accommodation

At the turn of the century, four-fifths of the nation's 10 million African Americans still lived in the South, where most eked out a living working in agriculture. In the cities, most blacks were relegated to menial jobs, but a small African American middle class of entrepreneurs and professionals gained a foothold by selling services and products to the black community. They all confronted a racism that was growing in both intensity and influence in American politics and culture. White racism came in many variants and had evolved significantly since slavery days. The more virulent strains, influenced by Darwin's evolutionary theory, held that blacks were a "degenerate" race, genetically predisposed to vice, crime, and disease and destined to lose the struggle for existence with whites. By portraying blacks as incapable of improvement, racial Darwinism justified a policy of repression and neglect toward African Americans.

Southern progressives articulated a more moderate racial philosophy. They also assumed the innate inferiority of blacks, but they believed that black progress was necessary to achieve the economic and political progress associated with a vision of the New South. Their solution to the "race problem" stressed paternalist uplift. Edgar Gardner Murphy, an Episcopal clergyman and leading Alabama progressive, held that African Americans need not be terrorized. The black man, Murphy asserted, "will accept in the white man's country the place assigned him by the white man, will do his work, not by stress of rivalry, but by genial cooperation with the white man's interests."

African Americans also endured a deeply racist popular culture that made hateful stereotypes of black people a normal feature of political debate and everyday life. Benjamin Tillman, a U.S. senator from South Carolina, denounced the African American as "a fiend, a wild beast, seeking whom he may devour." Thomas Dixon's popular novel *The Clansman* (1905) described the typical African American as "half child, half animal, the sport of impulse, whim, and conceit . . . a being who, left to his will, roams at night and sleeps in the day, whose speech knows no word of love, whose passions, once aroused, are as the fury of a tiger." In northern cities "coon songs," based on gross caricatures of black life, were extremely popular in theaters and as sheet music. As in the antebellum minstrel shows, these songs reduced African Americans to creatures of pure appetite—for food, sex, alcohol, and violence. The minstrel tradition of white entertainers "blacking up"—using burnt cork makeup to pretend they were black—was still a widely accepted convention in American show business.

Amid this political and cultural climate, Booker T. Washington won recognition as the most influential black leader of the day. Born a slave in 1856, Washington was educated at Hampton Institute in Virginia, one of the first freedmen's schools devoted to industrial education. In 1881 he founded Tuskegee Institute, a black school in Alabama devoted to industrial and moral education. He became the leading spokesman for racial accommodation, urging blacks to focus on economic improvement and self-reliance, as opposed to political and civil rights. In an 1895 speech delivered at the Cotton States Exposition in Atlanta, Washington outlined the key themes of accommodationist philosophy. "Cast down your buckets where you are," Washington told black people, meaning they should focus on improving their vocational skills as industrial workers and farmers. "In all things that are purely social," he told attentive whites, "we can be as separate as the fingers, yet one as the hand in all things essential to mutual progress."

Washington's message won him the financial backing of leading white philanthropists and the respect of progressive whites. His widely read autobiography, *Up from Slavery* (1901), stands as a classic narrative of an American self-made man. Written with a shrewd eye toward cementing his support among white Americans, it stressed the importance of learning values such as frugality, cleanliness, and personal morality. But Washington also gained a large following among African Americans, especially those who aspired to business success. With the help of Andrew Carnegie he founded the National Negro Business League to preach the virtue of black business development in black communities.

Presidents Theodore Roosevelt and William Howard Taft consulted Washington on the few political patronage appointments given to African Americans. Washington also had a decisive influence on the flow of private funds to black schools in the South. Publicly he insisted that "agitation of questions of social equality is the extremest folly." But privately Washington also spent money and worked behind the scenes trying to halt disfranchisement and segregation. He offered secret financial support, for example, for court cases that challenged Louisiana's grandfather clause, the exclusion of blacks from Alabama juries, and railroad segregation in Tennessee and Georgia.

Racial Justice and the NAACP

Washington's focus on economic self-help remained deeply influential in African American communities long after his death in 1915. But alternative black voices challenged his racial philosophy while he lived. In the early 1900s, scholar and activist W. E. B. Du Bois created a significant alternative to Washington's leadership. A product of the black middle class, Du Bois had been educated at Fisk University and Harvard, where in 1895 he became the first African American to receive a Ph.D. His book *The Philadelphia Negro* (1899) was a pioneering work of social science that refuted racist stereotypes by, for example, discussing black contributions to that city's political life and describing the wide range of black business activity. In *The Souls of Black Folk* (1903), Du Bois declared prophetically that "the problem of the twentieth century is the problem of the color line." Through essays on black history, culture, education, and politics, Du Bois explored the concept of "double consciousness." Black people, he argued, would always feel the tension between an African heritage and their desire to assimilate as Americans.

Unlike Booker T. Washington, Du Bois did not fully accept the values of the dominant white society. He worried that "our material wants had developed much faster than our social and moral standards." *Souls*

Photographs and Print Division, Schomburg Center for Research in Black Culture, The New York Public Library, Astor, Lenox and Tilden Foundations.

In July 1905, a group of African American leaders met in Niagara Falls, Ontario, *to protest legal segregation and the denial of civil rights to the nation's black population. This portrait was taken against a studio backdrop of the falls. In* 1909, *the leader of the* Niagara movement, W.E.B. Du Bois *(second from right, middle row) founded and edited the* Crisis, *the influential monthly journal of the* National Association *for the* Advancement *of* Colored People.

represented the first effort to embrace African American culture as a source of collective black strength and something worth preserving. Spiritual striving, rooted in black folklore, religion, music, and history, were just as important as industrial education.

Du Bois criticized Booker T. Washington's philosophy for its acceptance of "the alleged inferiority of the Negro." The black community, he argued, must fight for the right to vote, for civic equality, and for higher education for the "talented tenth" of their youth. In 1905 Du Bois and editor William Monroe Trotter brought together a group of educated black men to oppose Washington's conciliatory views. Discrimination they encountered in Buffalo, New York, prompted the men to move their meeting to Niagara Falls, Ontario. "Any discrimination based simply on race or color is barbarous," they declared. "Persistent manly agitation is the way to liberty." The Niagara movement protested legal segregation, the exclusion of blacks from labor unions, and the curtailment of voting and other civil rights.

The Niagara movement failed to generate much change. But in 1909 many of its members, led by Du Bois, attended a National Negro Conference held at the Henry Street Settlement in New York. The group included a number of white progressives sympathetic to the idea of challenging Washington's philosophy. A new, interracial organization emerged from this conference, the National Association for the Advancement of Colored People. Du Bois, the only black officer of the original NAACP, founded and edited the *Crisis*, the influential NAACP monthly journal. For the next several decades the NAACP would lead struggles to overturn legal and economic barriers to equal opportunity.

NATIONAL PROGRESSIVISM

The progressive impulse had begun at local levels and percolated up. Progressive forces in both major political parties pushed older, entrenched elements to take a more aggressive stance on the reform issues of the day. Both Republican Theodore Roosevelt and Democrat Woodrow Wilson laid claim to the progressive mantle during their presidencies—a good example of how on the national level progressivism animated many perspectives. In their pursuit of reform agendas, both significantly reshaped the office of the president. As progressivism moved to Washington, nationally organized interest groups and public opinion began to rival the influence of the old political parties in shaping the political landscape.

Theodore Roosevelt and Presidential Activism

The assassination of William McKinley in 1901 made forty-two-year-old Theodore Roosevelt the youngest man to hold the office of president before or since. Born to a wealthy New York family in 1858, Roosevelt overcame a sickly childhood through strenuous physical exercise and rugged outdoor living. After graduating from Harvard he immediately threw himself into a career in the rough and tumble of New York politics. He won election to the state assembly, ran an unsuccessful campaign for mayor of New York, served as president of the New York City Board of Police Commissioners, and went to Washington as assistant secretary of the navy. During the Spanish-American War, he won national fame as leader of the Rough Rider regiment in Cuba. Upon his return, he was elected governor of New York and then in 1900 vice president. Roosevelt viewed the presidency as a "bully pulpit"—a platform from which he could exhort Americans to reform their society—and he aimed to make the most of it.

Roosevelt was a uniquely colorful figure, a shrewd publicist, and a creative politician. His three-year stint as a rancher in the Dakota Territory; his fondness for hunting and nature study; his passion for scholarship, which resulted in ten books before he became president—all these set "T.R." apart from most of his upper-class peers. Roosevelt preached the virtues of "the strenuous life," and he believed that educated and wealthy Americans had a special responsibility to serve, guide, and inspire those less fortunate.

In style, Roosevelt made key contributions to national progressivism. He knew how to inspire and guide public opinion. He stimulated discussion and aroused curiosity like no one before him. In 1902 Roosevelt demonstrated his unique style of activism when he personally intervened in a bitter strike by anthracite coal miners. Using public calls for conciliation, a series of White House bargaining sessions, and private pressure on the mineowners, Roosevelt secured a settlement that won better pay and working conditions for the miners, but without recognition of their union. Roosevelt also pushed for efficient government as the solution to social problems. Unlike most nineteenth-century Republicans, who had largely ignored economic and social inequalities, Roosevelt frankly acknowledged them. Administrative agencies run by experts, he believed, could find rational solutions that could satisfy everyone.

Trustbusting and Regulation

One of the first issues Roosevelt faced was growing public concern with the rapid business consolidations taking place in the American economy. In 1902 he directed the Justice Department to begin a series of prosecutions under the Sherman Antitrust Act. The first target was the Northern Securities Company, a huge merger of transcontinental railroads brought about by financier J. P. Morgan. The deal would have created a giant holding company controlling nearly all the long-distance rail lines from Chicago to California. The Justice Department fought the case all the way through a hearing before the Supreme Court. In *Northern Securities v. U.S.* (1904), the Court held that the stock transactions constituted an illegal combination in restraint of interstate commerce.

This case established Roosevelt's reputation as a "trustbuster." During his two terms, the Justice Department filed forty-three cases under the Sherman Antitrust Act to restrain or dissolve business monopolies. These included actions against the so-called tobacco and beef trusts and the Standard Oil Company. Roosevelt viewed these suits as necessary to publicize the issue and assert the federal government's ultimate authority over big business. But he did not really believe in the need to break up large corporations. Unlike many progressives, who were nostalgic for smaller companies and freer competition, Roosevelt accepted centralization as a fact of modern economic life.

Roosevelt considered government regulation the best way to deal with big business. After easily defeating Democrat Alton B. Parker in the 1904 election, Roosevelt felt more secure in pushing for regulatory legislation. In 1906 Roosevelt responded to public pressure for greater government intervention and, overcoming objections from a conservative Congress, signed three important measures into law. The Hepburn Act strengthened the Interstate Commerce Commission (ICC), established in 1887 as the first independent regulatory agency, by authorizing it to set maximum railroad rates and inspect financial records.

Two other laws passed in 1906 also expanded the regulatory power of the federal government. The battles surrounding these reforms demonstrate how progressive measures often attracted supporters with competing motives. The Pure Food and Drug Act established the Food and Drug Administration (FDA), which tested and approved drugs before they went on the market. The Meat Inspection Act empowered the Department of Agriculture to inspect and label meat products. In both cases, supporters hailed the new laws as providing consumer protection against adulterated or fraudulently labeled food and drugs. Sensational exposés by muckrakers, documenting the greed, corruption, and unhealthy practices in the meatpacking and patent medicine industries, contributed to public support for the measures. Upton Sinclair's best-selling novel *The Jungle,* depicting the horrible conditions in Chicago's packinghouses, was the most sensational and influential of these.

But regulatory legislation found advocates among American big business as well. Large meat packers such as Swift and Armour strongly supported stricter federal regulation as a way to drive out smaller companies that could not meet tougher standards. The new laws also helped American packers compete more profitably in the European export market by giving their meat the official seal of federal inspectors. Large pharmaceutical manufacturers similarly supported new regulations that would eliminate competitors and patent medicine suppliers. Thus these reforms won support from large corporate interests that viewed stronger federal regulation as a strategy for consolidating their economic power. Progressive era expansion of the nation-state had its champions among—and benefits for—big business as well as American consumers.

Conservation, Preservation, and the Environment

As a naturalist and outdoorsman, Theodore Roosevelt also believed in the need for government regulation of the natural environment. He worried about the destruction of forests, prairies, streams, and the wilderness. The conservation of forest and water resources, he argued, was a national problem of vital import. In 1905 he created the U.S. Forest Service and named conservationist Gifford Pinchot to head it. Pinchot recruited a force of forest rangers to manage the reserves. By 1909 total timber and forest reserves had increased from 45 to 195 million acres, and more than 80 million acres of mineral lands had been withdrawn from public sale. Roosevelt also sponsored a National Conservation Commission, which produced the first comprehensive study of the nation's mineral, water, forest, and soil resources.

On the broad issue of managing America's natural resources, the Roosevelt administration took the middle ground between preservation and unrestricted commercial development. Pinchot established the basic pattern of federal regulation based on a philosophy of what he called the "wise use" of forest reserves. "Wilderness is waste," Pinchot was fond of saying, reflecting an essentially utilitarian vision that balanced the demands of business with wilderness conservation. But other voices championed a more radical vision of conservation, emphasizing the preservation of wilderness lands against the encroachment of commercial exploitation.

The most influential and committed of these was John Muir, an essayist and founder of the modern environmentalist movement. Muir made a passionate and spiritual defense of the inherent value of the American wilderness. Wild country, he argued, had a mystical power to inspire and refresh. "Climb the mountains and get their good tidings," he advised. "Nature's peace will flow into you as the sunshine into the trees. The winds will blow their freshness into you, and the storms their energy, while cares will drop off like autumn leaves."

Muir had been a driving force behind the Yosemite Act of 1890. Yosemite Park, located in a

William Hahn (1829–1887), *Yosemite Valley from Glacier Point*, 1874. 27¼ x 46¼ inches. California Historical Society, gift of Albert M. Bender.

William Hahn, Yosemite Valley from Glacier Point (1874). *Congress established Yosemite as a national park in 1890. Paintings like this one, along with contemporary photographs, helped convince Congress of the uniqueness of Yosemite's natural beauty.*

valley amid California's majestic Sierra Nevada range, became the nation's first preserve consciously designed to protect wilderness. Muir served as first president of the Sierra Club, founded in 1892 to preserve and protect the mountain regions of the west coast as well as Yellowstone National Park in Wyoming, Montana, and Idaho. Muir was a tireless publicist, and his writings won wide popularity among Americans, who were increasingly drawn to explore and enjoy the outdoors. By the turn of the century, misgivings about the effects of "overcivilization" and the association of untamed lands with the nation's frontier and pioneer past had attracted many to his thinking.

A bitter, drawn-out struggle over new water sources for San Francisco revealed the deep conflicts between conservationists, represented by Pinchot, and preservationists, represented by Muir. After a devastating earthquake in 1906, San Francisco sought federal approval to dam and flood the spectacular Hetch Hetchy Valley, located 150 miles from the city in Yosemite National Park. The project promised to ease the city's chronic freshwater shortage and to generate hydroelectric power. Conservationists and their urban progressive allies argued that developing Hetch Hetchy would be a victory for the public good over greedy private developers, since the plan called for municipal control of the water supply. To John Muir and the Sierra Club, Hetch Hetchy was a "temple" threatened with destruction by the "devotees of ravaging commercialism."

Both sides lobbied furiously in Congress and wrote scores of articles in newspapers and magazines. Congress finally approved the reservoir plan in 1913; utility and public development triumphed over the preservation of nature. Although they lost the battle for Hetch Hetchy, the preservationists gained much ground in the larger campaign of alerting the nation to the dangers of a vanishing wilderness. A disappointed John Muir took some consolation from the fact that "the conscience of the whole country has been aroused from sleep." Defenders of national parks now realized that they could not make their case simply on scenic merit alone. They began to use their own utilitarian rationales, arguing that national parks would encourage economic growth through tourism and provide Americans with a healthy escape from urban and industrial areas. In 1916 the preservationists obtained their own bureaucracy in Washington with the creation of the National Park Service.

The Newlands Reclamation Act of 1902 represented another important victory for the conservation strategy of Roosevelt and Pinchot. With the goal of turning arid land into productive family farms through irrigation, the act established the Reclamation Bureau within the Department of the Interior and provided federal funding for dam and canal projects. But in practice, the bureau did more to encourage the growth of large-scale agribusiness and western cities than small farming. The Roosevelt Dam on Arizona's Salt River, along with the forty-mile Arizona Canal, helped develop the Phoenix area. The Imperial Dam on the Colorado River diverted water to California's Imperial and Coachella Valleys. The bureau soon became a key player in western life and politics, with large federally funded water projects providing flood control and the generation of electricity, as well as water for irrigation. The Newlands Act thus established a growing federal presence in managing water resources, the critical issue in twentieth-century western development.

Republican Split

When he won reelection in 1904, Roosevelt proclaimed his support for a "Square Deal" for all people. He was still essentially a conservative who supported progressive reform as the best way to head off the potential of class war. By the end of his second term, Roosevelt had moved beyond the idea of regulation to push for the most far-reaching federal economic and social programs ever proposed. He saw the central problem as "how to exercise . . . responsible control over the business use of vast wealth." To that end, he proposed restrictions on the use of court injunctions against labor strikes, as well as an eight-hour day for federal employees, a worker compensation law, and federal income and inheritance taxes.

In 1908, Roosevelt kept his promise to retire after a second term. He chose Secretary of War William Howard Taft as his successor. Taft easily defeated Democrat William Jennings Bryan in the 1908 election. During Taft's presidency, the gulf between "insurgent" progressives and the "stand pat" wing split the Republican Party wide open. To some degree, the battles were as much over style as substance. Compared with Roosevelt, the reflective and judicious Taft brought a much more restrained concept of the presidency to the White House. He supported some progressive measures, including the constitutional amendment legalizing a graduated income tax (ratified in 1913), safety codes for mines and railroads, and the creation of a federal Children's Bureau (1912). But in a series of bitter political fights involving tariff, antitrust, and conservation policies, Taft alienated Roosevelt and many other progressives.

After returning from an African safari and a triumphant European tour in 1910, Roosevelt threw himself back into national politics. He directly challenged Taft for the Republican Party leadership. In a dozen bitter state presidential primaries (the first ever held), Taft and Roosevelt fought for the nomination. Although Roosevelt won most of these contests, the old guard still controlled the national convention and renominated Taft in June 1912. Roosevelt's supporters stormed out, and in August the new Progressive Party nominated Roosevelt and Hiram Johnson of California as its presidential ticket. Roosevelt's "New Nationalism" presented a vision of a strong federal government, led by an activist president, regulating and protecting the various interests in American society. The platform called for woman suffrage, the eight-hour day, prohibition of child labor, minimum-wage standards for working women, and stricter regulation of large corporations.

The Election of 1912: A Four-Way Race

With the Republicans so badly divided, the Democrats sensed a chance for their first presidential victory in twenty years. They chose Governor Woodrow Wilson of New Jersey as their candidate. Although not nearly as well known nationally as Taft and Roosevelt, Wilson had

This political cartoon, drawn by Charles Jay Budd, appeared on the cover of Harper's Weekly, *September 28, 1912. It employed the imagery of autumn county fairs to depict voters as unhappy with their three choices for president. Note that the artist did not include the fourth candidate, Socialist Eugene Debs, who was often ignored by more conservative publications such as* Harper's.

built a strong reputation as a reformer. The son of a Virginia Presbyterian minister, Wilson spent most of his early career in academia. He studied law at the University of Virginia and then earned a Ph.D. in political science from Johns Hopkins. After teaching history and political science at several schools, he became president of Princeton University in 1902. In 1910, he won election as New Jersey's governor, running against the state Democratic machine. He won the Democratic nomination for president with the support of many of the party's progressives, including William Jennings Bryan.

Wilson declared himself and the Democratic Party to be the true progressives. Viewing Roosevelt rather than Taft as his main rival, Wilson contrasted his New Freedom campaign with Roosevelt's New Nationalism. Crafted largely by progressive lawyer Louis Brandeis, Wilson's platform was far more ambiguous than Roosevelt's. The New Freedom emphasized restoring conditions of free competition and equality of economic opportunity. Wilson did favor a variety of progressive reforms for workers, farmers, and consumers. But in sounding older, nineteenth-century Democratic themes of states' rights and small government, Wilson argued against allowing the federal government to become as large and paternalistic as Roosevelt advocated. "What this country needs above everything else," Wilson argued, "is a body of laws which will look after the men who are on the make rather than the men who are already made."

Socialist party nominee Eugene V. Debs offered the fourth and most radical choice to voters. The Socialists had more than doubled their membership since 1908, to more than 100,000. On election days Socialist strength was far greater than that, as the party's candidates attracted increasing numbers of voters. By 1912 more than a thousand Socialists held elective office in thirty-three states and 160 cities. Geographically, Socialist strength had shifted to the trans-Mississippi South and West.

Debs had been a national figure in American politics since the 1890s, and he had already run for president three times. An inspiring orator who drew large and sympathetic crowds wherever he spoke, Debs proved especially popular in areas with strong labor movements and populist traditions. He wrapped his socialist message in an apocalyptic vision. Socialists would "abolish this monstrous system and the misery and crime which flow from it." His movement would "tear up all privilege by the roots, and consecrate the earth and all its fullness to the joy and service of all humanity." Debs and the Socialists also took credit for pushing both Roosevelt and Wilson further toward the left. Both the Democratic and Progressive Party platforms contained proposals considered extremely radical only ten years earlier.

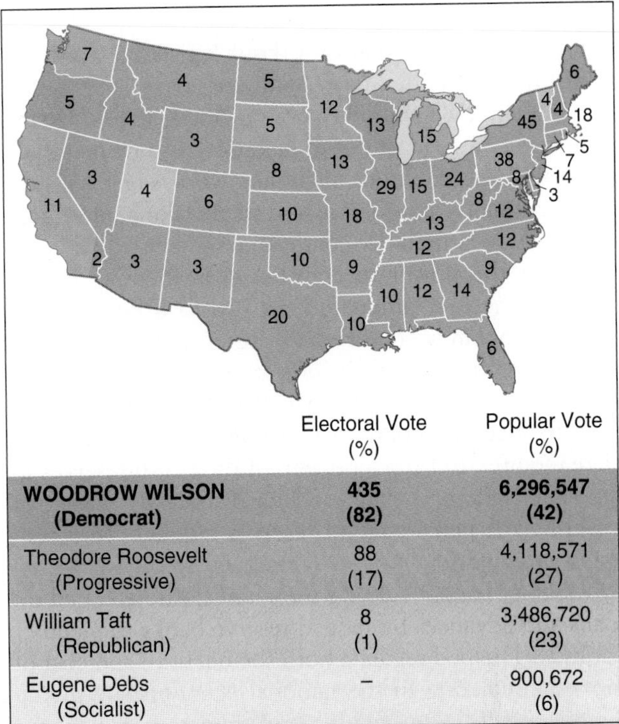

	Electoral Vote (%)	Popular Vote (%)
WOODROW WILSON (Democrat)	**435 (82)**	**6,296,547 (42)**
Theodore Roosevelt (Progressive)	88 (17)	4,118,571 (27)
William Taft (Republican)	8 (1)	3,486,720 (23)
Eugene Debs (Socialist)	–	900,672 (6)

The Election of 1912 *The split within the Republican Party allowed Woodrow Wilson to become only the second Democrat since the Civil War to be elected president. Eugene Debs's vote was the highest ever polled by a Socialist candidate.*

In the end, the divisions in the Republican Party gave the election to Wilson. He won easily, polling 6.3 million votes to Roosevelt's 4.1 million. Taft came in third with 3.5 million. Eugene Debs won 900,000 votes, 6 percent of the total, for the strongest Socialist showing in American history. Even though he won with only 42 percent of the popular vote, Wilson swept the electoral college with 435 votes to Roosevelt's 88 and Taft's 8, giving him the largest electoral majority ever to that time. In several respects, the election of 1912 was the first "modern" presidential race. It featured the first direct primaries, challenges to traditional party loyalties, an issue-oriented campaign, and a high degree of interest group activity.

Woodrow Wilson's First Term

As president, Wilson followed Roosevelt's lead in expanding the activist dimensions of the office. He became more responsive to pressure for a greater federal role in regulating business and the economy. This increase in direct lobbying—from hundreds of local and national reform groups, Washington-based organizations, and the new Progressive Party—was itself a new and defining feature of the era's political life. With the help of a Democratic-controlled Congress, Wilson pushed through a significant battery of reform proposals. By 1916 his reform program looked more like the New Nationalism that

Theodore Roosevelt had run on in 1912 than Wilson's own New Freedom platform. Four legislative achievements in Wilson's first term stand out.

The Underwood-Simmons Act of 1913 substantially reduced tariff duties on a variety of raw materials and manufactured goods, including wool, sugar, agricultural machinery, shoes, iron, and steel. Taking advantage of the newly ratified Sixteenth Amendment, which gave Congress the power to levy taxes on income, it also imposed the first graduated tax (up to 6 percent) on personal incomes. The Federal Reserve Act that same year restructured the nation's banking and currency system. It created twelve Federal Reserve Banks, regulated by a central board in Washington. Member banks were required to keep a portion of their cash reserves in the Federal Reserve Bank of their district. By raising or lowering the percentage of reserves required, "the Fed" could either discourage or encourage credit expansion by member banks. Varying the interest rate charged on loans and advances by federal reserve banks to member banks also helped regulate both the quantity and cost of money circulating in the national economy. By giving central direction to banking and monetary policy, the Federal Reserve Board diminished the power of large private banks.

Wilson also supported the Clayton Antitrust Act of 1914, which replaced the old Sherman Act of 1890 as the nation's basic antitrust law. Clayton reflected the growing political clout of the American Federation of Labor. It exempted unions from being construed as illegal combinations in restraint of trade, and it forbade federal courts to issue injunctions against strikers. But Wilson adopted the view that permanent federal regulation was necessary for checking the abuses of big business. The Federal Trade Commission (FTC), established in 1914, sought to give the federal government the same sort of regulatory control over corporations that the ICC had over railroads. Wilson believed a permanent federal body like the FTC would provide a method for corporate oversight superior to the erratic and time-consuming process of legal trustbusting. Wilson's hope that the FTC would usher in an era of harmony between government and business recalled the aims of Roosevelt and his big business backers in 1912.

On social issues, Wilson proved more cautious in his first two years. His initial failure to support federal child labor legislation and rural credits to farmers angered many progressives. A Southerner, Wilson also sanctioned the spread of racial segregation in federal offices. "I would say," he explained in 1913, "that I do approve of the segregation that is being attempted in several of the departments." As the reelection campaign of 1916 approached, Wilson worried about defections from the labor and social justice wings of his party. He proceeded to support a rural credits act providing government capital to federal farm banks, as well as federal aid to agricultural extension programs in schools. He also came out in favor of child labor reform and a worker compensation bill for federal employees. But by 1916 the dark cloud of war in Europe had already begun to cast its long shadow over progressive reform.

CONCLUSION

The American political and social landscape was significantly altered by progressivism, but these shifts reflected the tensions and ambiguities of progressivism itself. A review of changes in election laws offers a good perspective on the inconsistencies that characterized progressivism. Nearly every new election law had the effect of excluding some people from voting while including others. For African Americans, progressivism largely meant disfranchisement from voting altogether. Direct primary laws eliminated some of the most blatant abuses of big-city machines, but in cities and states dominated by one party, the majority party's primary effectively decided the general election. Stricter election laws made it more difficult for third parties to get on the ballot, another instance in which progressive reform had the effect of reducing political options available to voters. Voting itself steadily declined in these years.

Overall, party voting became a less important form of political participation. Interest group activity, congressional and statehouse lobbying, and direct appeals to public opinion gained currency as ways of influencing government. Business groups such as the National Association of Manufacturers and individual trade associations were among the most active groups pressing their demands on government. Political action often shifted from legislatures to the new administrative agencies and commissions created to deal with social and economic problems. Popular magazines and journals grew significantly in both number and circulation, becoming more influential in shaping and appealing to national public opinion.

Social progressives and their allies could point to significant improvements in the everyday lives of ordinary Americans. On the state level, real advances had been made through a range of social legislation covering working conditions, child labor, minimum wages, and worker compensation. Social progressives, too, had discovered the power of organizing into extraparty lobbying groups such as the National Consumers' League and the National American Woman Suffrage Association. Yet the tensions between fighting for social justice and the urge toward social control remained unresolved. The emphasis on efficiency, uplift, and rational administration often collided with humane impulses to aid the poor, the immigrant, the slum dweller. The large majority of African Americans, blue-collar workers, and urban poor remained untouched by federal assistance programs.

Progressives had tried to confront the new realities of urban and industrial society. What had begun as a discrete collection of local and state struggles had by 1912 come to reshape state and national politics. Politics itself had been transformed by the calls for social justice. Federal and state power would now play a more decisive role than ever in shaping work, play, and social life in local communities. That there was so much contention over the "true meaning" of progressivism is but one measure of its defining role in shaping early-twentieth-century America.

CHRONOLOGY

1889 Jane Addams founds Hull House in Chicago

1890 Jacob Riis publishes *How the Other Half Lives*

1895 Booker T. Washington addresses Cotton States Exposition in Atlanta, emphasizing an accommodationist philosophy

Lillian Wald establishes Henry Street Settlement in New York

1898 Florence Kelley becomes general secretary of the new National Consumers' League

1900 Robert M. La Follette elected governor of Wisconsin

1901 Theodore Roosevelt succeeds the assassinated William McKinley as president

1904 Lincoln Steffens publishes *The Shame of the Cities*

1905 President Roosevelt creates U.S. Forest Service and names Gifford Pinchot head

Industrial Workers of the World is founded in Chicago

1906 Upton Sinclair's *The Jungle* exposes conditions in the meatpacking industry

Congress passes Pure Food and Drug Act and Meat Inspection Act and establishes Food and Drug Administration

1908 In *Muller v. Oregon* the Supreme Court upholds a state law limiting maximum hours for working women

1909 Uprising of the 20,000 in New York City's garment industries helps organize unskilled workers into unions

National Association for the Advancement of Colored People (NAACP) is founded

1911 Triangle Shirtwaist Company fire kills 146 garment workers in New York City

Socialist critic Max Eastman begins publishing *The Masses*

1912 Democrat Woodrow Wilson wins presidency, defeating Republican William H. Taft, Progressive Theodore Roosevelt, and Socialist Eugene V. Debs

Bread and Roses strike involves 25,000 textile workers in Lawrence, Massachusetts

Margaret Sanger begins writing and speaking in support of birth control for women

1913 Sixteenth Amendment, legalizing a graduated income tax, is ratified

1914 Clayton Antitrust Act exempts unions from being construed as illegal combinations in restraint of trade

Federal Trade Commission is established

Ludlow Massacre occurs

1916 National Park Service is established

REVIEW QUESTIONS

1. Discuss the tensions within progressivism between the ideals of social justice and the urge for social control. What concrete achievements are associated with each wing of the movement? What were the driving forces behind them?
2. Describe the different manifestations of progressivism at the local, state, and national levels. To what extent did progressives redefine the role of the state in American politics?
3. What gains were made by working-class communities in the progressive era? What barriers did they face?
4. How did the era's new immigration reshape America's cities and workplaces? What connections can you draw between the new immigrant experience and progressive era politics?
5. Analyze the progressive era from the perspective of African Americans. What political and social developments were most crucial, and what legacies did they leave?
6. Evaluate the lasting impact of progressive reform. How do the goals, methods, and language of progressives still find voice in contemporary America?

RECOMMENDED READING

John D. Buenker, *Urban Liberalism and Progressive Reform* (1973). Explores the contributions of urban ethnic voters and machine-based politicians to the progressive movement.

Robert M. Crunden, *Ministers of Reform: The Progressives' Achievement in American Civilization, 1889–1920* (1982). Emphasizes the moral and religious traditions of middle-class Protestants as the core of the progressive ethos.

Alan Dawley, *Struggles for Justice: Social Responsibility and the Liberal State* (1991). Offers an important interpretation of progressivism that focuses on how the working class and women pushed the state toward a more activist role in confronting social problems.

Susan A. Glenn, *Daughters of the Shtetl: Life and Labor in the Immigrant Generation* (1990). A sensitive analysis of the experiences of immigrant Jewish women in the garment trades.

Dewey Grantham, *Southern Progressivism: The Reconciliation of Progress and Tradition* (1982). Examines the contradictions within the southern progressive tradition.

James R. Green, *The World of the Worker: Labor in Twentieth Century America* (1980). Includes a fine overview of life and work in company towns and urban ghettos in the early twentieth century.

Morton Keller, *Regulating a New Society: Public Policy and Social Change in America, 1900–1930* (1994). A comprehensive study of public policy making on local and national levels in early twentieth-century America.

Arthur Link and Richard L. McCormick, *Progressivism* (1983). The best recent overview of progressivism and electoral politics.

Kathryn Kish Sklar, *Florence Kelley and the Nation's Work* (1995). The first installment in a two-volume biography, this book brilliantly brings Florence Kelley alive within the rich context of late-nineteenth-century women's political culture.

Robert Wiebe, *The Search for Order, 1877–1920* (1967). A pathbreaking study of how the professional middle classes responded to the upheavals of industrialism and urbanization.

ADDITIONAL BIBLIOGRAPHY

The Currents of Progressivism

Walter M. Brasch, *Forerunners of Revolution: Muckrakers and the American Social Conscience* (1990)

John D. Buenker, John C. Burnham, and Robert M. Crunden, *Progressivism* (1977)

Mina Carson, *Settlement Folk: Social Thought and the American Settlement Movement, 1885–1930* (1990)

Allen F. Davis, *Spearheads for Reform: The Social Settlements and the Progressive Movement, 1890–1914* (1967)

Leon Fink, *Progressive Intellectuals and the Dilemmas of Democratic Commitment* (1997)

Richard Hofstadter, *The Age of Reform: From Bryan to FDR* (1955)

James T. Kloppenberg, *Uncertain Victory: Social Democracy and Progressivism in European and American Thought, 1870–1920* (1986)

William A. Link, *The Paradox of Southern Progressivism, 1880–1930* (1992)

Richard McCormick, *The Party Period and Public Policy* (1986)

Nell Irvin Painter, *Standing at Armageddon: The United States, 1877–1919* (1987)

Martin J. Schiesl, *The Politics of Efficiency: Municipal Administration and Reform in America* (1977)

Social Control and Its Limits

Paul M. Boyer, *Urban Masses and Moral Order in America, 1820–1920* (1978)

Mark T. Connelly, *The Response to Prostitution in the Progressive Era* (1980)

Eldon J. Eisenach, *The Lost Promise of Progressivism* (1994)

Alan M. Kraut, *Silent Travelers: Germs, Genes, and the "Immigrant Menace"* (1994)

W. J. Rorabaugh, *The Alcoholic Republic* (1979)

Ruth Rosen, *The Lost Sisterhood: Prostitutes in America, 1900–1918* (1982)

David Tyack and Elizabeth Hansot, *Managers of Virtue: Public School Leadership in America, 1820–1980* (1982)

Working-Class Communities and Protest

John Bodnar, *The Transplanted* (1985)

Melvyn Dubofsky, *We Shall Be All: A History of the Industrial Workers of the World* (1969)

Leslie Fishbein, *Rebels in Bohemia* (1982)

Alice Kessler-Harris, *Out to Work: A History of Wage Earning Women in the United States* (1969)

J. Anthony Lukas, *Big Trouble* (1997)

David Montgomery, *The Fall of the House of Labor* (1987)

Kathy Peiss, *Cheap Amusements: Working Women and Leisure in Turn of the Century New York* (1986)

Roy Rosenzweig, *Eight Hours for What We Will* (1983)

Ronald Takaki, *Strangers from a Different Shore: A History of Asian Americans* (1989)

Women's Movements and Black Awakening

Paula Baker, *The Moral Frameworks of Public Life* (1991)

Mari Jo Buhle, *Women and American Socialism* (1983)

Ellen Fitzpatrick, *Endless Crusade: Women Social Scientists and Progressive Reform* (1990)

Linda Gordon, *Woman's Body, Woman's Right: A Social History of Birth Control* (1976)

Louis R. Harlan, *Booker T. Washington: Wizard of Tuskegee, 1901–1915* (1983)

Charles F. Kellogg, *NAACP* (1967)

J. Morgan Kousser, *The Shaping of Southern Politics* (1974)

Molly Ladd-Taylor, *Mother Work: Women, Child Welfare, and the State, 1890–1930* (1994)

David Levering Lewis, *W.E.B. Du Bois: Biography of a Race, 1868–1919* (1993)

Elaine Tyler May, *Great Expectations: Marriage and Divorce in Post Victorian America* (1980)

National Progressivism

Kendrick A. Clements, *The Presidency of Woodrow Wilson* (1992)

John M. Cooper Jr., *The Warrior and the Priest: Theodore Roosevelt and Woodrow Wilson* (1983)

Stephen R. Fox, *The American Conservation Movement: John Muir and His Legacy* (1981)

Lewis L. Gould, *The Presidency of Theodore Roosevelt* (1991)

Thomas K. McCraw, *Prophets of Regulation* (1984)

Michael McGerr, *The Decline of Popular Politics* (1986)

Roderick Nash, *Wilderness and the American Mind* (1967)

Melvin I. Urofsky, *Louis D. Brandeis and the Progressive Tradition* (1981)

Biography

Ellen Chesler, *Woman of Valor: Margaret Sanger and the Birth Control Movement in America* (1992)

Allen F. Davis, *American Heroine: The Life and Legend of Jane Addams* (1973)

Helen L. Horowitz, *The Power and Passion of M. Carey Thomas* (1994)

J. Joseph Huthmacher, *Senator Robert F. Wagner and the Rise of Urban Liberalism* (1971)

Justin Kaplan, *Lincoln Steffens* (1974)

W. Manning Marable, *W.E.B. Du Bois* (1986)

Nick Salvatore, *Eugene V. Debs: Citizen and Socialist* (1982)

David P. Thelen, *Robert M. La Follette and the Insurgent Spirit* (1976)

Bernard A. Weisberger, *The LaFollettes of Wisconsin* (1994)

Robert Westbrook, *John Dewey and American Democracy* (1991)

CHAPTER TWENTY-TWO

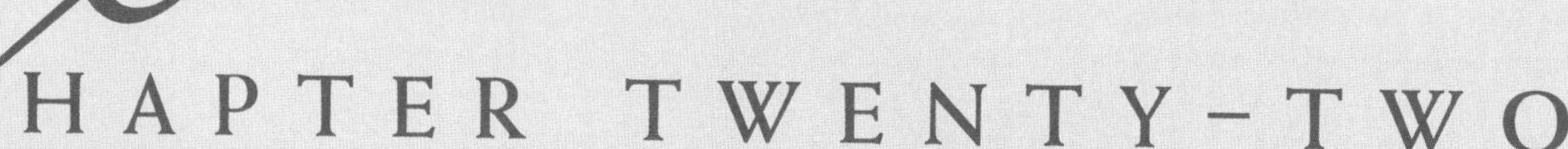

WORLD WAR I

1914–1920

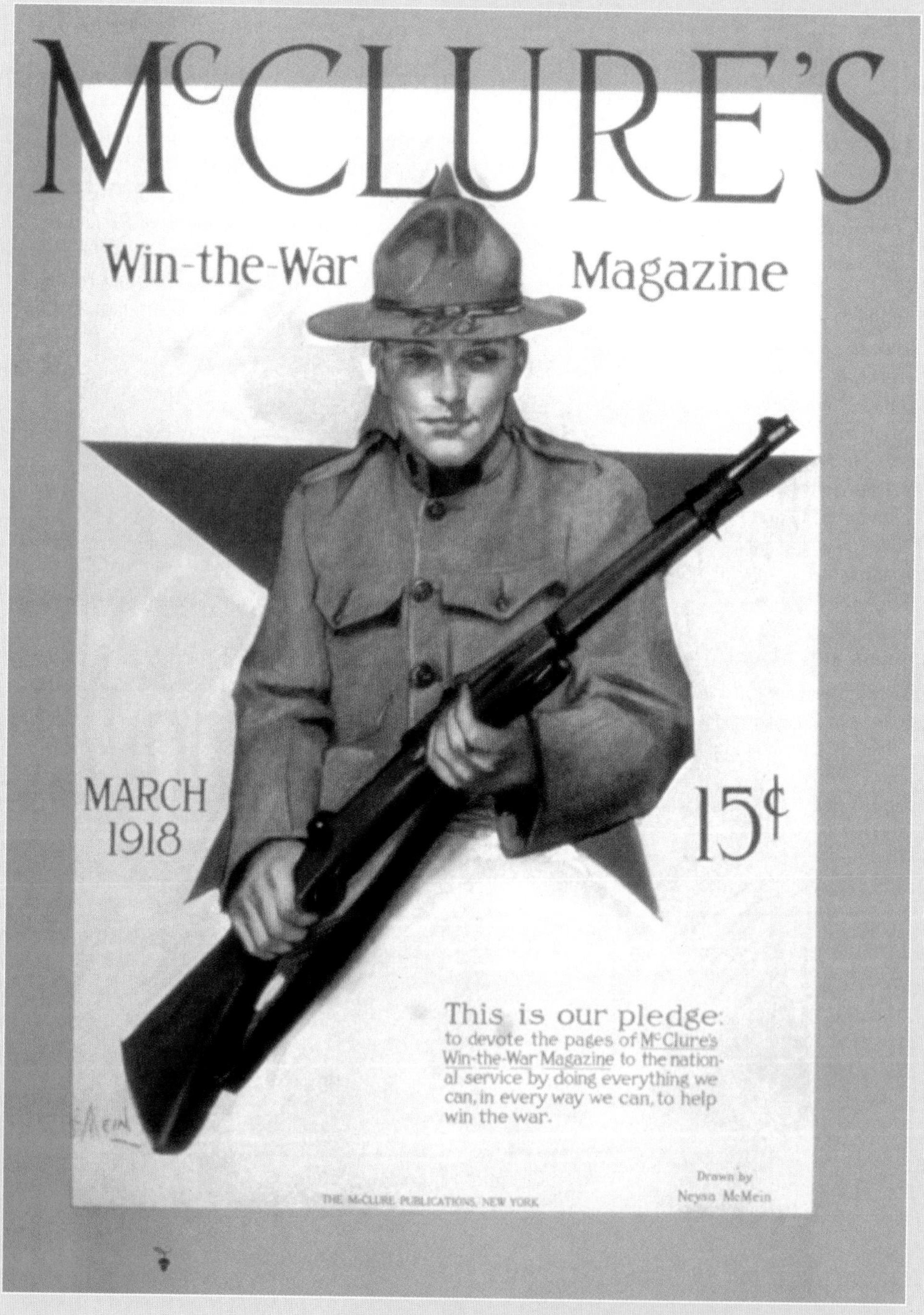

McCLURE'S
Win-the-War
Magazine
MARCH
1918
15¢
This is our pledge:
to devote the pages of McClure's Win-the-War Magazine to the national service by doing everything we can, in every way we can, to help win the war.
Drawn by
Neysa McMein
THE McCLURE PUBLICATIONS, NEW YORK

McClure's Win-the-War Cover, 1918.

Chapter Outline

AMERICAN COMMUNITIES

Vigilante Justice in Bisbee, Arizona

Early in the morning of July 12, 1917, two thousand armed vigilantes swept through Bisbee, Arizona, acting on behalf of the Phelps-Dodge mining company and Bisbee's leading businessmen to break a bitter strike that had crippled Bisbee's booming copper industry. The vigilantes seized miners in their homes, on the street, and in restaurants and stores. Any miner who wasn't working or willing to work was herded into Bisbee's downtown plaza, where two machine guns commanded the scene. From the Plaza more than 2,000 were marched to the local baseball park. There, mine managers gave them a last chance to return to work. Hundreds accepted and were released. The remaining 1,400 were forced at gunpoint onto a freight train, which took them 173 miles east to Columbus, New Mexico, where they were dumped in the desert.

The Bisbee deportation occurred against a complex backdrop. America had just entered World War I, corporations were seeking higher profits, and labor militancy was on the rise. Bisbee was only one of many American communities to suffer vigilantism during the war. Any number of offenses—not displaying a flag, failing to buy war bonds, criticizing the draft, alleged spying, any apparently "disloyal" behavior—could trigger vigilante action. In western communities like Bisbee, vigilantes used the superpatriotic mood to settle scores with labor organizers and radicals.

Arizona was the leading producer of copper in the United States. With a population of 8,000, Bisbee lay in the heart of the state's richest mining district. The giant Phelps-Dodge Company dominated Bisbee's political and social life. It owned the town's hospital, department store, newspaper, library, and largest hotel. With the introduction of new technology and open pit mining after 1900, unskilled laborers—most of them Slavic, Italian, Czech, and Mexican immigrants—had increasingly replaced skilled American and English-born miners in Bisbee's workforce.

America's entry into the war pushed the price of copper to an all-time high, prompting Phelps-Dodge to increase production. Miners viewed the increased demand for labor as an opportunity to flex their own muscle and improve wages and working conditions. Two rival union locals, one affiliated with the American Federation of Labor (AFL), the other with the more radical Industrial Workers of the World (IWW), or "Wobblies," sought to organize Bisbee's workers. On June 26, 1917, Bisbee's Wobblies went on strike. They demanded better mine safety, an end to discrimination against union workers, and a substantial pay increase. The IWW, making special efforts to attract lower-paid foreign-born workers to their cause, even hired two Mexican organizers. Although the IWW had only 300 or 400 members in Bisbee, more than half the town's 4,700 miners supported the strike.

The walkout was peaceful, but Walter Douglas, district manager for Phelps-Dodge, was unmoved. "There will be no compromise," he declared, "because you cannot compromise with a rattlesnake." Douglas, Cochise County Sheriff Harry Wheeler, and Bisbee's leading businessmen met secretly to plan the July 12 deportation. The approximately 2,000 men they deputized to carry it out were members of Bisbee's Citizens' Protective League and the Workers Loyalty League. These vigilantes included company officials, small businessmen, professionals, and anti-union workers. Local telephone and telegraph offices agreed to isolate Bisbee by censoring outgoing messages. The El Paso and Southwestern Railroad, a subsidiary of Phelps-Dodge, provided the waiting boxcars.

The participants in this illegal conspiracy defended themselves by exaggerating the threat of organized labor. They also appealed to patriotism and played on racial fears. The IWW opposed American involvement in the war, making it vulnerable to charges of disloyalty. A proclamation, posted in Bisbee the day of the deportation, claimed, "There is no labor trouble—we are sure of that—but a direct attempt to embarrass and injure the government of the United States." Sheriff Wheeler told a visiting journalist he worried that Mexicans "would take advantage of the disturbed conditions of the strike and start an uprising, destroying the mines and murdering American women and children."

An army census of the deportees, who had found temporary refuge at an army camp in Columbus, New Mexico, offered quite a different picture. Of the 1,400 men, 520 owned property in Bisbee. Nearly 500 had already registered for the draft, and more than 200 had purchased Liberty Bonds. More than 400 were married with children; only 400 were members of the IWW. Eighty percent were immigrants, including nearly 400 Mexicans. A presidential mediation committee concluded that "conditions in Bisbee were in fact peaceful and free from manifestations of disorder or violence." The deported miners nonetheless found it difficult to shake the accusations that their strike was anti-American and foreign inspired.

At their camp, the miners organized their own police force and elected an executive committee to seek relief. In a letter to President Wilson, they claimed "Common American citizens here are now convinced that they have no constitutional rights." They promised to return to digging copper if the federal government operated the nation's mines and smelters. IWW leader William D. "Big Bill" Haywood threatened a general strike of metal miners and harvest workers if the government did not return the deportees to their homes. The presidential mediation committee criticized the mine companies and declared the deportation illegal. But it also denied the federal government had any jurisdiction in the matter. Arizona's attorney general refused to offer protection for a return to Bisbee.

In September, the men began gradually to drift away from Columbus. Only a few ever returned to Bisbee. The events convinced President Wilson that the IWW was a subversive organization and a threat to national security. The Justice Department began planning an all-out legal assault that would soon cripple the Wobblies. But Wilson could not ignore protests against the Bisbee outrage from such prominent and patriotic Americans as Samuel Gompers, head of the American Federation of Labor. To demonstrate his administration's commitment to harmonious industrial relations, the president appointed a special commission to investigate and mediate wartime labor conflicts. But Arizona's mines would remain union free until the New Deal era of the 1930s.

America's entry into the war created a national sense of purpose and an unprecedented mobilization of resources. Unifying the country and winning the war now took precedence over progressive reforms. The war also aroused powerful political emotions and provided an excuse for some citizens to try to cleanse their communities of anyone who did not conform. In a 1918 speech, Arizona State Senator Fred Sutter hailed the benefits of vigilante justice. "And what are the results in Bisbee since the deportation?" he asked. "They are, sir, a practically 100 percent American camp; a foreigner to get a job there today had to give a pretty good account of himself. The mines are today producing more copper than ever before and we are a quiet, peaceful, law-abiding community and will continue so, so long as the IWWs or other enemies of the government let us alone."

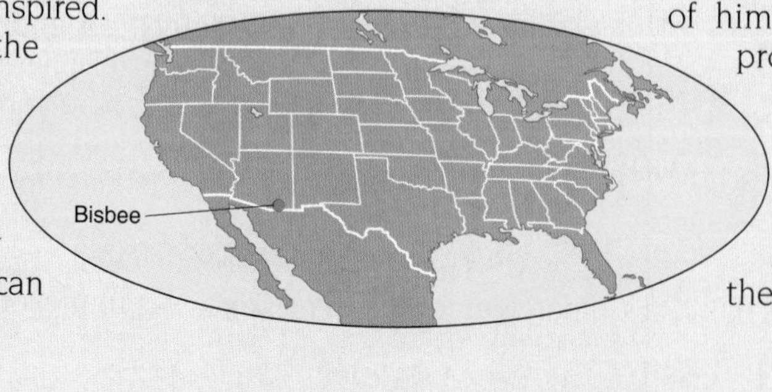

Bisbee

KEY TOPICS

- America's expanding international role
- From neutrality to participation in the Great War
- Mobilizing the society and the economy for war
- Dissent and its repression
- Woodrow Wilson's failure to win the peace

BECOMING A WORLD POWER

In the first years of the new century the United States pursued a more vigorous and aggressive foreign policy than it had in the past. Presidents Theodore Roosevelt, William Howard Taft, and Woodrow Wilson all contributed to "progressive diplomacy," in which commercial expansion was backed by a growing military presence in the Caribbean, Asia, and Mexico. This policy reflected a view of world affairs that stressed moralism, order, and a special, even God-given, role for the United States. By 1917, when the United States entered the Great War, this policy had already secured the country a place as a new world power.

Roosevelt: The Big Stick

Theodore Roosevelt left a strong imprint on the nation's foreign policy. Like many of his class and background, "T.R." took for granted the superiority of Protestant Anglo-American culture and the goal of spreading its values and influence. He believed that to maintain and increase its economic and political stature, America must be militarily strong. In 1900 Roosevelt summarized his activist views, declaring, "I have always been fond of the West African proverb, 'Speak softly and carry a big stick, you will go far.' "

Roosevelt brought the "big stick" approach to several disputes in the Caribbean region. Since the 1880s, several British, French, and American companies had pursued various plans for building a canal across the Isthmus of Panama, thereby connecting the Atlantic and Pacific Oceans. The canal was a top priority for Roosevelt, and he tried to negotiate a leasing agreement with Colombia, of which Panama was a province. But when the Colombian Senate rejected a final American offer in the fall of 1903, Roosevelt invented a new strategy. A combination of native forces and foreign promoters associated with the canal project plotted a revolt against Colombia. Roosevelt kept in touch with at least one leader of the revolt, Philippe Bunau-Varilla, an engineer and agent for the New Panama Canal Company, and the president let him know that U.S. warships were steaming toward Panama.

On November 3, 1903, just as the USS Nashville arrived in Colón harbor, the province of Panama declared itself independent of Colombia. The United States immediately recognized the new Republic of Panama. Less than two weeks later, Bunau-Varilla, serving as a minister from Panama, signed a treaty granting the United States full sovereignty in perpetuity over a ten-mile-wide canal zone. America guaranteed Panama's independence and agreed to pay it $10 million initially and an additional $250,000 a year for the canal zone. Years after the canal was completed, the U. S. Senate voted another $25 million to Colombia as compensation.

The Panama Canal was a triumph of modern engineering and gave the United States a tremendous strategic and commercial advantage in the Western Hemisphere. It took eight years to build and cost hundreds of poorly paid manual workers their lives. Several earlier attempts to build a canal in the region had failed. But with better equipment and a vigorous campaign against disease, the United States succeeded. In 1914, after $720 million in construction costs, the first merchant ships sailed through the canal.

"The inevitable effect of our building the Canal," wrote Secretary of State Elihu Root in 1905, "must be to require us to police the surrounding premises." Roosevelt agreed. He was especially concerned that European powers might step in if America did not. In 1903 Great Britain, Germany, and Italy had imposed a blockade on Venezuela in a dispute over debt payments owed to private investors. To prevent armed intervention by the Europeans, Roosevelt in 1904 proclaimed what became known as the Roosevelt Corollary to the Monroe Doctrine. "Chronic wrongdoing, or an impotence which results in a general loosening of the ties of civilized society," the statement read, justified "the exercise of an international police power" anywhere in the hemisphere. Roosevelt invoked the corollary to justify U.S. intervention in the region, beginning with the Dominican Republic in 1905. To counter the protests of European creditors (and the implied threat of armed intervention), Washington assumed management of the Dominican debt and customs services. Roosevelt and later presidents cited

This 1905 cartoon portraying President Theodore Roosevelt, The World's Constable, *appeared in* Judge *magazine. In depicting the president as a strong but benevolent policeman bringing order in a contentious world, the artist Louis Dalrymple drew on familiar imagery from Roosevelt's earlier days as a New York City police commissioner.*

the corollary to justify armed intervention in the internal affairs of Cuba, Haiti, Nicaragua, and Mexico.

American diplomacy in Asia reflected the Open Door policy formulated by Secretary of State John Hay in 1899. Japan and the western European powers had carved key areas of China into spheres of influence, in which individual nations enjoyed economic dominance. The United States was a relative latecomer to the potentially lucrative China market, and Hay sought guarantees of equal opportunity for its commercial interests there. In a series of diplomatic notes Hay won approval for the so-called Open Door approach, giving all nations equal access to trading and development rights in China. The outbreak of war between Japan and Russia in 1905 threatened this policy. Roosevelt worried that a total victory by Russia or Japan could upset the balance of power in East Asia and threaten American business enterprises. He became especially concerned after the Japanese scored a series of military victories over Russia and began to loom as a dominant power in East Asia.

Roosevelt mediated a settlement of the Russo-Japanese War at Portsmouth, New Hampshire, in 1905 (for which he was awarded the 1906 Nobel Peace Prize). In this settlement, Japan won recognition of its dominant position in Korea and consolidated its economic control over Manchuria. Yet repeated incidents of anti-Japanese racism in California kept American-Japanese relations strained. In 1906, for example, the San Francisco school board, responding to nativist fears of a "yellow peril," ordered the segregation of Japanese, Chinese, and Korean students. Japan angrily protested. In 1907, in the so-called gentlemen's agreement, Japan agreed not to issue passports to Japanese male laborers looking to emigrate to the United States and Roosevelt promised to fight anti-Japanese discrimination. He then persuaded the San Francisco school board to exempt Japanese students from the segregation ordinance.

But Roosevelt did not want these conciliatory moves to be interpreted as weakness. He thus built up American naval strength in the Pacific, and in 1908 he sent battleships to visit Japan in a muscle-flexing display of sea power. In that same year, the two burgeoning Pacific powers reached a reconciliation. The Root-Takahira Agreement affirmed the "existing status quo" in Asia, mutual respect for territorial possessions in the Pacific, and the Open Door trade policy in China. From the Japanese perspective, the agreement recognized Japan's colonial dominance in Korea and southern Manchuria.

Taft: Dollar Diplomacy

Roosevelt's successor, William Howard Taft, believed he could replace the militarism of the big stick with the more subtle and effective weapon of business investment. Taft and his secretary of state, corporate lawyer Philander C. Knox, followed a strategy (called "dollar diplomacy" by critics) in which they assumed that political influence would follow increased U.S. trade and investment. As Taft explained in 1910, he advocated "active intervention to secure for our merchandise and our capitalists opportunity for profitable investment." He hoped to substitute "dollars for bullets," but he was to discover limits to this approach in both the Caribbean and Asia.

Overall American investment in Central America grew rapidly, from $41 million in 1908 to $93 million by 1914. Most of this money went into railroad construction, mining, and plantations. The United Fruit Company alone owned about 160,000 acres of land in the Caribbean by 1913. But dollar diplomacy ended up requiring military support. The Taft administration sent the navy and the marines to intervene in political disputes in Honduras and Nicaragua, propping up factions pledged to protect American business interests. A contingent of U.S. Marines remained in Nicaragua until 1933. The economic and political structures of Honduras and Nicaragua were controlled by both the dollar and the bullet.

In China, Taft and Knox pressed for a greater share of the pie for U.S. investors. They gained a place for U.S. bankers in the European consortium building the massive new Hu-kuang Railways in southern and central China. But Knox blundered by attempting to "neutralize" the existing railroads in China. He tried to secure a huge international loan for the Chinese government that would allow it to buy up all the foreign railways and develop new ones. Both Russia and Japan, which had fought wars over their railroad interests in Manchuria, resisted this plan as a threat to the arrangements hammered out at Portsmouth with the help of Theodore Roosevelt. Knox's "neutralization" scheme, combined with U.S. support for the Chinese Nationalists in their 1911 revolt against the ruling Manchu dynasty, prompted Japan to sign a new friendship treaty with Russia. The Open Door to China was now effectively closed, and American relations with Japan began a slow deterioration that ended in war thirty years later.

The United States in the Caribbean, 1865–1933 *An overview of U.S. economic and military involvement in the Caribbean during the late nineteenth and early twentieth centuries. Victory in the Spanish-American War, the Panama Canal project, and rapid economic investment in Mexico and Cuba all contributed to a permanent and growing U.S. military presence in the region.*

Wilson: Moralism and Realism

Right after he took office in 1913, President Woodrow Wilson observed that "it would be the irony of fate if my administration had to deal chiefly with foreign affairs." His political life up to then had centered on achieving progressive reforms in the domestic arena. As it turned out, Wilson had to face international crises from his first day in office. These were of a scope and complexity unprecedented in U.S. history. Wilson had no experience in diplomacy, but he brought to foreign affairs a set of fundamental principles that combined a moralist's faith in American democracy with a realist's understanding of the power of international commerce. He believed that American economic expansion, accompanied by democratic principles and Christianity, was a civilizing force in the world. "Our industries," he told the Democratic National Convention in 1912, "have expanded to such a point that they will burst their jackets if they cannot find a free outlet to the markets of the world. . . . Our domestic markets no longer suffice. We need foreign markets."

Wilson, like most corporate and political leaders of the day, emphasized foreign investments and industrial exports as the keys to the nation's prosperity. He believed that the United States, with its superior industrial efficiency, could achieve supremacy in world commerce if artificial barriers to free trade were removed. He championed and extended the Open Door principles of John Hay, advocating strong diplomatic and military measures "for making ourselves supreme in the world from an economic point of view." Wilson often couched his vision of a dynamic, expansive American capitalism in terms of a moral crusade. As he put it in a speech to a congress of salesmen, "[Since] you are Americans and are meant to carry liberty and justice and the principles of humanity wherever you go, go out and sell goods that will make the world more comfortable and more happy, and convert them to the principles of America." Yet he quickly found that the complex realities of power politics could interfere with moral vision.

Wilson's policies toward Mexico, which foreshadowed the problems he would encounter in World War I, best illustrate his difficulties. The 1911 Mexican Revolution had overthrown the brutally corrupt dictatorship of Porfirio Díaz, and popular leader Francisco Madero had won wide support by promising democracy and economic reform for millions of landless peasants. U.S. businessmen, however, were nervous about the future of their investments, which totaled over $1 billion, an amount greater than Mexico's own investment and more than all other foreign investment in that country combined. Wilson at first gave his blessing to the revolutionary movement, expressed regret over the Mexican-American War of 1846–48, and disavowed any interest in another war. "I have constantly to remind myself," he told a friend, "that I am not the servant of those who wish to enhance the value of their Mexican investments."

But right before he took office, Wilson was stunned by the ousting and murder of Madero by his chief lieutenant, General Victoriano Huerta. Other nations, including Great Britain and Japan, recognized the Huerta regime, but Wilson refused. He announced that the United States would support only governments that rested on the rule of law. An armed faction opposed to Huerta known as the Constitutionalists and led by Venustiano Carranza emerged in northern Mexico. Both sides rejected an effort by Wilson to broker a compromise between them. Carranza, an ardent nationalist, pressed for the right to buy U.S. arms, which he won in 1914. Wilson also isolated Huerta diplomatically by persuading the British to withdraw their support in exchange for American guarantees of English property interests in Mexico.

But Huerta stubbornly remained in power. In April 1914 Wilson used a minor insult to U.S. sailors in Tampico as an excuse to invade. American naval forces bombarded and then occupied Veracruz, the main port through which Huerta received arms shipments. Nineteen Americans and 126 Mexicans died in the battle, which brought the United States and Mexico close to war and provoked anti-American demonstrations in Mexico and throughout Latin America. Wilson accepted the offer of the ABC Powers—Argentina, Brazil, and Chile—to mediate the dispute. Huerta rejected a plan for him to step aside in favor of a provisional government. But then in August Carranza managed to overthrow Huerta. Playing to nationalist sentiment, Carranza too denounced Wilson for his intervention.

As war loomed in Europe, Mexico's revolutionary politics continued to frustrate Wilson. For a brief period Wilson threw his support behind Francisco "Pancho" Villa, Carranza's former ally who now led a rebel army of his own in the North. But Carranza's forces dealt Villa a major setback in April, 1915, and in October, its attention focused on the war in Europe, the Wilson administration recognized Carranza as Mexico's *de facto* president. Meanwhile Pancho Villa, feeling betrayed, turned on the United States and tried to provoke a crisis that might draw Washington into war with Mexico. Villa led several raids in Mexico and across the border in early 1916 that killed a few dozen Americans. The man once viewed by Wilson as a fighter for democracy was now dismissed as a dangerous bandit.

In March 1916, enraged by Villa's defiance, Wilson dispatched General John J. Pershing and an army that eventually numbered 15,000 to capture him. For a year, Pershing's troops chased Villa in vain, penetrating 300 miles into Mexico. The invasion made Villa a

Mexican revolutionary leaders and sometime allies Francisco "Pancho" Villa (center) and Emiliano Zapata (right) are shown at the National Palace in Mexico City, ca. 1916. Zapata's army operated out of a base in the southern agricultural state of Morelos, while Villa's army controlled large portions of Mexico's North. In 1914 Villa captured the imagination of American reformers, journalists, and moviemakers with his military exploits against the oppressive Huerta regime. But in 1916, after several border clashes between his forces and U.S. military units, President Wilson dispatched a punitive expedition in pursuit of Villa.

symbol of national resistance in Mexico, and his army grew from 500 men to 10,000 by the end of 1916. Villa's effective hit-and-run guerrilla tactics kept the U.S. forces at bay. A frustrated General Pershing complained that he felt "just a little bit like a man looking for a needle in a haystack." He urged the U.S. government to occupy the northern Mexican state of Chihuahua and later called for the occupation of the entire country.

Pershing's invasion angered the Carranza government and the Mexican public. Skirmishes between American forces and Carranza's army brought the two nations to the brink of war again in June 1916. Wilson prepared a message to Congress asking permission for American troops to occupy all of northern Mexico. But he never delivered it. There was fierce opposition to war with Mexico throughout the country. Perhaps more important, mounting tensions with Germany caused Wilson to hesitate. He told an aide that "Germany is anxious to have us at war with Mexico, so that our minds and our energies will be taken off the great war across the sea." Wilson thus accepted negotiations by a face-saving international commission. In early 1917, with America moving toward direct involvement in the European war, Wilson began withdrawing American troops. Just a month before the United States entered World War I, Wilson officially recognized the Carranza regime.

Wilson's attempt to guide the course of Mexico's revolution and protect U.S. interests left a bitter legacy of suspicion and distrust in Mexico. It also suggested the limits of a foreign policy tied to a moral vision rooted in the idea of American exceptionalism. Militarism and imperialism, Wilson had believed, were hallmarks of the old European way. American liberal values—rooted in capitalist development, democracy, and free trade—were the wave of the future. Wilson believed the United States could lead the world in establishing a new international system based on peaceful commerce and political stability. In both the 1914 invasion and the 1916 punitive expedition, Wilson declared that he had no desire to interfere with Mexican sovereignty. But in both cases that is exactly what he did. The United States, he argued, must actively use its enormous moral and material power to create the new order. That principle would soon engage America in Europe's bloodiest war and its most momentous revolution.

THE GREAT WAR

World War I, or the Great War, as it was originally called, took an enormous human toll on an entire generation of Europeans. The unprecedented slaughter on the battlefields of Verdun, Ypres, Gallipoli, and scores of other places appalled the combatant nations. At the war's start in August 1914, both sides had confidently predicted a quick victory. Instead, the killing dragged on for more than four years and in the end transformed the old power relations and political map of Europe. The United States entered the war reluctantly, and American forces played a supportive rather than a central role in the military outcome. Yet the wartime experience left a sharp imprint on the nation's economy, politics, and cultural life, one that would last into the next decades.

The Guns of August

In August 1914 a relatively minor incident plunged the European continent into the most destructive war in its history until then. The last decades of the nineteenth century had seen the major European nations, especially Germany, enjoy a great rush of industrial development. During the same period, these nations acquired extensive colonial empires in Africa, Asia, and the Middle East. Only a complex and fragile system of alliances had kept the European powers at peace with each other since 1871. Two great competing camps had evolved by 1907: the Triple Alliance (also known as the Central Powers), which included Germany, Austria-Hungary, and Italy; and the Triple Entente (also known as the Allies), which included Great Britain, France, and Russia. At the heart of this division was the competition between Great Britain, long the world's dominant colonial and commercial power, and Germany, which had powerful aspirations for an empire of its own.

The alliance system managed to keep small conflicts from escalating into larger ones for most of the late nineteenth and early twentieth centuries. But its inclusiveness was also its weakness: the alliance system threatened to entangle many nations in any war that did erupt. On June 28, 1914, Archduke Franz Ferdinand, heir to the throne of the unstable Austro-Hungarian Empire, was assassinated in Sarajevo, Bosnia. The archduke's killer was a Serbian nationalist who believed the Austro-Hungarian province of Bosnia ought to be annexed to neighboring Serbia. Germany pushed Austria-Hungary to retaliate against Serbia, and the Serbians in turn asked Russia for help.

By early August both sides had exchanged declarations of war and begun mobilizing their forces. Germany invaded Belgium and prepared to move across the French border. But after the German armies were stopped at the River Marne in September, the war settled into a long, bloody stalemate. New and grimly efficient weapons, such as the machine gun and the tank, and the horrors of trench warfare meant unprecedented casualties for all involved. Centered in northern France, the fighting killed 5 million people over the next two and a half years.

American Neutrality

The outbreak of war in Europe shocked Americans. President Wilson issued a formal proclamation of neutrality and urged citizens to be "impartial in thought as well as in action." Most of the country shared the editorial view expressed that August in the New York Sun: "There is nothing reasonable in such a war, and it would be folly for the country to sacrifice itself to the frenzy of dynastic policies and the clash of ancient hatreds which is urging the Old World to destruction."

In practice, powerful cultural, political, and economic factors made the impartiality advocated by Wilson impossible. The U.S. population included many ethnic groups with close emotional ties to the Old World. Out of a total population of 92 million in 1914, about one-third were "hyphenated" Americans, either foreign-born or having one or both parents who were immigrants. Strong support for the Central Powers could be found among the 8 million German Americans, as well as the 4 million Irish Americans, who shared their ancestral homeland's historical hatred of English rule. On the other side, many Americans were at least mildly pro-Allies due to cultural and language bonds with Great Britain and the tradition of Franco-American friendship.

Both sides bombarded the United States with vigorous propaganda campaigns. The British effectively exploited their bonds of language and heritage with Americans. Reports of looting, raping, and the killing of innocent civilians by German troops circulated widely in the press. Many of these atrocity stories were exaggerated, but verified German actions—the invasion of neutral Belgium, submarine attacks on merchant ships, and the razing of towns—lent them credibility. German propagandists blamed the war on Russian expansionism and France's desire to avenge its defeat by Germany in 1870–71. It is difficult to measure the impact of war propaganda on American public opinion. As a whole, though, it highlighted the terrible human costs of the war and thus strengthened the conviction that America should stay out of it.

Economic ties between the United States and the Allies were perhaps the greatest barrier to true neutrality. Early in the war Britain imposed a blockade on all shipping to Germany. The United States, as a neutral country, might have insisted on the right of nonbelligerents to trade with both sides, as required by international law. But in practice, although Wilson protested the blockade, he wanted to avoid antagonizing Britain and disrupting trade between the United States and the Allies. Trade with Germany all but ended while trade with the Allies increased dramatically. As war orders poured in from Britain and France, the value of American trade with the Allies shot up from $824 million in 1914 to $3.2 billion in 1916. By 1917 loans to the Allies exceeded $2.5 billion compared to loans to the Central Powers of only $27 million. Increased trade with the Allies helped produce a great economic boom at home—transforming the economy in places like Bisbee, Arizona—and the United States became neutral in name only.

Preparedness and Peace

In February 1915, Germany declared the waters around the British Isles to be a war zone, a policy that it would enforce with unrestricted submarine warfare. All enemy shipping, despite the requirements of international law to the contrary, would be subject to surprise submarine attack. Neutral powers were warned that the problems of identification at sea put their ships at risk. The United States issued a sharp protest to this policy, calling it "an indefensible violation of neutral rights," and threatened to hold Germany accountable.

On May 7, 1915, a German U-boat sank the British liner Lusitania off the coast of Ireland. Among the 1,198 people who died were 128 American citizens. The Lusitania was in fact secretly carrying war materials, and passengers had been warned about a possible attack. Wilson nevertheless denounced the sinking as illegal and inhuman, and the American press loudly condemned the act as barbaric. An angry exchange of diplomatic notes led Secretary of State William Jennings Bryan to resign in protest against a policy he thought too warlike.

Tensions heated up again in March 1916 when a German U-boat torpedoed the Sussex, an unarmed French passenger ship, injuring four Americans. President Wilson threatened to break off diplomatic relations with Germany unless it abandoned its methods of submarine warfare. He won a temporary diplomatic victory when Germany promised that all vessels would be visited prior to attack. But the crisis also prompted Wilson to begin preparing for war. The National Security League, active in large eastern cities and bankrolled by conservative banking and commercial interests, helped push for a bigger army and navy and, most important, a system of universal military training. In June 1916 Congress passed the National Defense Act, which more than doubled the size of the regular army to 220,000 and integrated the state National Guards under federal control. In August, Congress passed a bill that dramatically increased spending for new battleships, cruisers, and destroyers.

Not all Americans supported these preparations for battle, and opposition to military buildup found expression in scores of American communities. As early as August 29, 1914, 1,500 women clad in black had marched down New York's Fifth Avenue in the Woman's Peace Parade. Out of this gathering evolved the American Union against Militarism, which lobbied against the preparedness campaign and against intervention in Mexico. Antiwar feeling was especially strong in the South and Midwest. Except for its vitally important cotton exports, the South generally had weaker economic ties to the Allies than other parts of the nation, as well as a historical suspicion of military power concentrated in Washington. The Midwest included communities with large German and socialist influences, both of which opposed U.S. aid to the Allies.

A group of thirty to fifty House Democrats, led by majority leader Claude Kitchin of North Carolina, stubbornly opposed Wilson's buildup. Jane Addams, Lillian D. Wald, and many other prominent progressive reformers spoke out for peace. A large reservoir of popular antiwar sentiment flowed through the culture in various ways. Movie director Thomas Ince won a huge audience for his 1916 film *Civilization*, which depicted Christ returning to reveal the horrors of war to world leaders. Two of the most popular songs of 1915 were "Don't Take My Darling Boy Away" and "I Didn't Raise My Boy to Be a Soldier."

Jane Addams (right), shown here in the late 1920s, remained active in the women's world peace movement until her death in 1935. In 1915 she had cofounded the Women's Peace Party, whose pacifist platform representing the views of the "mother half of humanity" attracted 25,000 members. But the American entry into World War I led to the Party's rapid demise.

To win reelection in 1916, Wilson had to acknowledge the active opposition to involvement in the war. In the presidential campaign, Democrats adopted the winning slogan "He Kept Us Out of War." Wilson made a strong showing in the West, where antiwar sentiment was vigorous, and he managed to draw hundreds of thousands of votes away from the antiwar Socialist Party as well. Wilson made a point of appealing to progressives of all kinds, stressing his support for the eight-hour day and his administration's efforts on behalf of farmers. The war-induced prosperity no doubt helped him to defeat conservative Republican Charles Evans Hughes in a very close election. But Wilson knew that the peace was as fragile as his victory.

Safe for Democracy

By the end of January 1917, Germany's leaders had decided against a negotiated peace settlement, placing their hopes instead in a final decisive offensive against the Allies. On February 1, 1917, Germany resumed its policy of unrestricted submarine warfare, with no warnings, against all neutral and belligerent shipping. (These attacks had been temporarily restrained in 1916, following U.S. protests.) This decision was made with full knowledge that it might bring America into the conflict. In effect, German leaders were gambling that they could destroy the ability of the Allies to fight before the United States would be able to effectively mobilize manpower and resources.

Howard Chandler Christy, *Fight or Buy Bonds*, poster, 1917. Museum of the City of New York, gift of John Campbell.

Halt the Hun. *This 1918 Liberty Loan poster used anti-German sentiment to encourage the purchase of war bonds. Its depiction of an American soldier as the protector of an innocent mother and child implied that the Germans were guilty of unspeakable war crimes.*

Wilson was indignant and disappointed. He still hoped for peace, but Germany had made it impossible for him to preserve his twin goals of U.S. neutrality and freedom of the seas. Reluctantly, Wilson broke off diplomatic relations with Germany and called on Congress to approve the arming of U.S. merchant ships. On March 1, the White House shocked the country when it made public a recently intercepted coded message, sent by German foreign secretary Arthur Zimmermann to the German ambassador in Mexico. The Zimmermann note proposed that an alliance be made between Germany and Mexico if the United States entered the war. Zimmermann suggested that Mexico take up arms against the United States and receive in return the "lost territory in New Mexico, Texas, and Arizona." The note caused a sensation and became a very effective propaganda tool for those who favored U.S. entry into the war. "As soon as I saw it," wrote Republican senator Henry Cabot Lodge of Massachusetts, an interventionist, "I knew it would arouse the country more than any other event." The specter of a German-Mexican alliance helped turn the tide of public opinion in the Southwest, where opposition to U.S. involvement in the war had been strong.

Revelation of the Zimmermann note stiffened Wilson's resolve. He issued an executive order in mid-March authorizing the arming of all merchant ships and allowing them to shoot at submarines. In that month, German U-boats sank seven U.S. merchant ships, leaving a heavy death toll. Anti-German feeling increased, and thousands took part in prowar demonstrations in New York, Boston, Philadelphia, and other cities. Wilson finally called a special session of Congress to ask for a declaration of war.

On April 2, on a rainy night before a packed and very quiet assembly, Wilson made his case. He reviewed the escalation of submarine warfare, which he called "warfare against mankind," and said that neutrality was no longer feasible or desirable. But the conflict was not merely about U.S. shipping rights, Wilson argued:

> The world must be made safe for democracy. Its peace must be planted upon the tested foundations of political liberty. We have no selfish ends to serve. . . . We shall fight for the things which we have always carried nearest our hearts,—for democracy, for the right of those who submit to authority to have a voice in their own Governments, for the rights and liberties of small nations.

This was a bold bid to give the United States a new role in international affairs. It asserted not just the right to protect U.S. interests but called also for change in basic international structures. Wilson's eloquent speech won over the Congress, most of the press, and even his bitterest political critics, such as

Theodore Roosevelt. The Senate adopted the war resolution 82 to 6, the House 373 to 50. On April 6, President Wilson signed the declaration of war. All that remained was to win over the American public.

AMERICAN MOBILIZATION

The overall public response to Wilson's war message was enthusiastic. Most newspapers, religious leaders, state legislatures, and prominent public figures endorsed the call to arms. But the Wilson administration was less certain about the feelings of ordinary Americans and their willingness to fight in Europe. It therefore took immediate steps to win over public support for the war effort, place a legal muzzle on antiwar dissenters, and establish a universal military draft. War mobilization was above all a campaign to unify the country.

Selling the War

Just a week after signing the war declaration, Wilson created the Committee on Public Information (CPI) to organize public opinion. It was dominated by its civilian chairman, the journalist and reformer George Creel. He had become a personal friend of Wilson's while handling publicity for the 1916 Democratic campaign. Creel quickly transformed the CPI from its original function as coordinator of government news into a sophisticated and aggressive agency for promoting the war. Creel remarked that his aim was to mold Americans into "one white-hot mass . . . with fraternity, devotion, courage, and deathless determination."

To sell the war, Creel raised the art of public relations to new heights. He enlisted more than 150,000 people to work on a score of CPI committees. They produced more than 100 million pieces of literature—pamphlets, articles, books—that explained the causes and meaning of the war. The CPI also created posters, slides, newspaper advertising, and films to promote the war. It called upon movie stars such as Charlie Chaplin, Mary Pickford, and Douglas Fairbanks to help sell war bonds at huge rallies. Famous journalists like the muckraker Ida Tarbell and well-known artists like Charles Dana Gibson were recruited. Across the nation, a volunteer army of 75,000 "Four Minute Men" gave brief patriotic speeches before stage and movie shows.

Three major themes dominated the materials disseminated by the CPI: America as a unified moral community; the war as an idealistic crusade for peace and freedom; and the image of a despicable enemy. The last of these featured an aggressively negative campaign against all things German. Posters and advertisements depicted the Germans as Huns, bestial monsters outside the civilized world. The CPI supported films such as *The Kaiser: The Beast of Berlin* and *The Prussian Cur*. German music and literature, indeed the German language itself, were suspect, and were banished from the concert halls, schools, and libraries of many communities. The CPI also urged ethnic Americans to abandon their Old World ties, to become "unhyphenated Americans." The CPI's push for conformity would soon encourage thousands of local, sometimes violent, campaigns of harassment against German Americans, radicals, and peace activists.

Founded by Clara Barton after the Civil War, the American Red Cross grew in both size and importance during World War I. Female volunteers, responding to humanitarian and patriotic appeals combined in posters like this one, provided most of the health and sanitary services to military and civilian casualties of the war.

Fading Opposition to War

By defining the call to war as a great moral crusade, President Wilson was able to win over many Americans who had been reluctant to go to war. In particular, many liberals and progressives were attracted to the possibilities of war as a positive force for social change. Many progressives identified with President Wilson's definition of the war as an idealistic crusade to defend democracy, spread liberal principles, and redeem European decadence and militarism. John Dewey, the influential philosopher, believed the war offered great "social possibilities" for developing the public good through science and greater efficiency.

Social welfare advocates, suffragists, tax reformers, even many socialists, now viewed war as a unique opportunity. War would require greater direct and coordinated involvement by the government in nearly every phase of American life. A group of prominent progressives quickly issued a statement of support for Wilson's war policy. They argued that "out of the sacrifice of war we may achieve broader democracy in Government, more equitable distribution of wealth, and greater national efficiency in raising the level of the general welfare."

The writer and cultural critic Randolph Bourne was an important, if lonely, voice of dissent among intellectuals. A former student of Dewey's at Columbia University, Bourne wrote a series of antiwar essays warning of the disastrous consequences for reform movements of all kinds. He was particularly critical of "war intellectuals" such as Dewey who were so eager to shift their energies to serving the war effort. "War is essentially the health of the State," Bourne wrote, and he accurately predicted sharp infringements on political and intellectual freedoms.

The Woman's Peace Party, founded in 1915 by feminists opposed to the preparedness campaign, dissolved. Most of its leading lights—Florence Kelley, Lillian D. Wald, and Carrie Chapman Catt—threw themselves into volunteer war work. Catt, leader of the huge National American Woman Suffrage Association (NAWSA), believed that supporting the war might help women win the right to vote. She joined the Women's Committee of the Council of National Defense and encouraged suffragists to mobilize women for war service of various kinds. A few lonely feminist voices, such as Jane Addams, continued steadfastly to oppose the war effort. But war work proved very popular among activist middle-class women. It gave them a leading role in their communities—selling bonds, coordinating food conservation drives, and working for hospitals and the Red Cross.

"You're in the Army Now"

The central military issue facing the administration was how to raise and deploy U.S. armed forces. When war was declared, there were only about 200,000 men in the army. Traditionally, the United States had relied on volunteer forces organized at the state level. But volunteer rates after April 6 were less than they had been for the Civil War or the Spanish-American War, reflecting the softness of prowar sentiment. The administration thus introduced the Selective Service Act, which provided for the registration and classification for military service of all men between ages twenty-one and thirty-five. Secretary of War Newton D. Baker was anxious to prevent the widespread, even violent, opposition to the draft that had occurred during the Civil War. Much of the anger over the Civil War draft stemmed from the unpopular provision that allowed draftees to buy their way out by paying $300 for a substitute. The new draft made no such allowances. Baker stressed the democratic procedures for registration and the active role of local draft boards in administering the process.

On June 5, 1917, nearly 10 million men registered for the draft. There was scattered organized resistance, but overall, registration records offered evidence of national support. A supplemental registration in August 1918 extended the age limits to eighteen and forty-five. By the end of the war some 24 million men had registered. Of the 2.8 million men eventually called up for service, about 340,000, or 12 percent, failed to show up. Another 2 million Americans volunteered for the various armed services.

U.S. soldiers leaving training camp, on their way to the European front, 1918. In just over a year national mobilization expanded the armed forces twentyfold, to nearly 5 million men and women. By November 1918, when the fighting ended, more than 2 million American troops were in Europe.

The vast, polyglot army posed unprecedented challenges of organization and control. But progressive elements within the administration also saw opportunities for pressing reform measures involving education, alcohol, and sex. Army psychologists gave the new Stanford-Binet intelligence test to all recruits and were shocked to find illiteracy rates as high as 25 percent. The low test scores among recent immigrants and rural African Americans undoubtedly reflected the cultural biases embedded in the tests and, for many test takers, their lack of proficiency in English. Most psychologists at the time, however, interpreted low scores in terms of racial theories of innate differences in intelligence. After the war, intelligence testing became a standard feature of America's educational system.

Ideally, the army provided a field for social reform and education, especially for the one-fifth of U.S. soldiers born in another country. "The military tent where they all sleep side by side," Theodore Roosevelt predicted, "will rank next to the public schools among the great agents of democratization." The recruits themselves took a more lighthearted view, while singing the army's praises:

Oh, the army, the army, the democratic army,
They clothe you and feed you because the army needs you
Hash for breakfast, beans for dinner, stew for suppertime,
Thirty dollars every month, deducting twenty-nine.
Oh, the army, the army, the democratic army,
The Jews, the Wops, and the Dutch and Irish Cops,
They're all in the army now!

The military reinforced old patterns of racism in American life by segregating African American troops and assigning most of them to menial and support tasks. Yet African Americans generally supported the war effort. The leading black newspaper of the day, the Chicago Defender, *predicted optimistically: "The colored soldier who fights side by side with the white American will hardly be begrudged a fair chance when the victorious armies return."*

Racism in the Military

But African Americans who served found severe limitations in the U.S. military. They were organized into totally segregated units, barred entirely from the marines and the Coast Guard, and largely relegated to working as cooks, laundrymen, stevedores, and the like in the army and navy. Thousands of black soldiers endured humiliating, sometimes violent treatment, particularly from southern white officers. African American servicemen faced hostility from white civilians as well, North and South, often being denied service in restaurants and admission to theaters near training camps. The ugliest incident occurred in Houston, Texas, in August 1917. Black infantrymen, incensed over continual insults and harassment by local whites, seized weapons from an armory and killed seventeen civilians. The army executed thirty black soldiers and imprisoned forty-one others for life, denying any of them a chance for appeal.

More than 200,000 African Americans eventually served in France, but only about one in five saw combat, as opposed to two out of three white soldiers. Black combat units served with distinction in various divisions of the French army. The all-black 369th U.S. Infantry, for example, saw the first and longest service of any American regiment deployed in a foreign army, serving in the trenches for 191 days. The French government awarded the *Croix de Guerre* to the entire regiment, and 171 officers and enlisted men were cited individually for exceptional bravery in action. African American soldiers by and large enjoyed a friendly reception from French civilians as well. The contrast with their treatment at home would remain a sore point with these troops upon their return to the United States.

Americans in Battle

Naively, many Americans had assumed that the nation's participation in the war could be limited to supplying economic aid and military hardware. At first, the main contribution came on the sea. German U-boats were sinking Allied ships at a rate of 900,000 tons each month; one of four British ships never returned to port. The United States began sending warships and destroyers to protect large convoys of merchant ships and to aid the British navy in assaulting U-boats. Within a year, shipping tonnage lost each month to submarine warfare had been reduced to 200,000; the flow of weapons, supplies, and troops continued. No American soldiers were lost on the way to Europe.

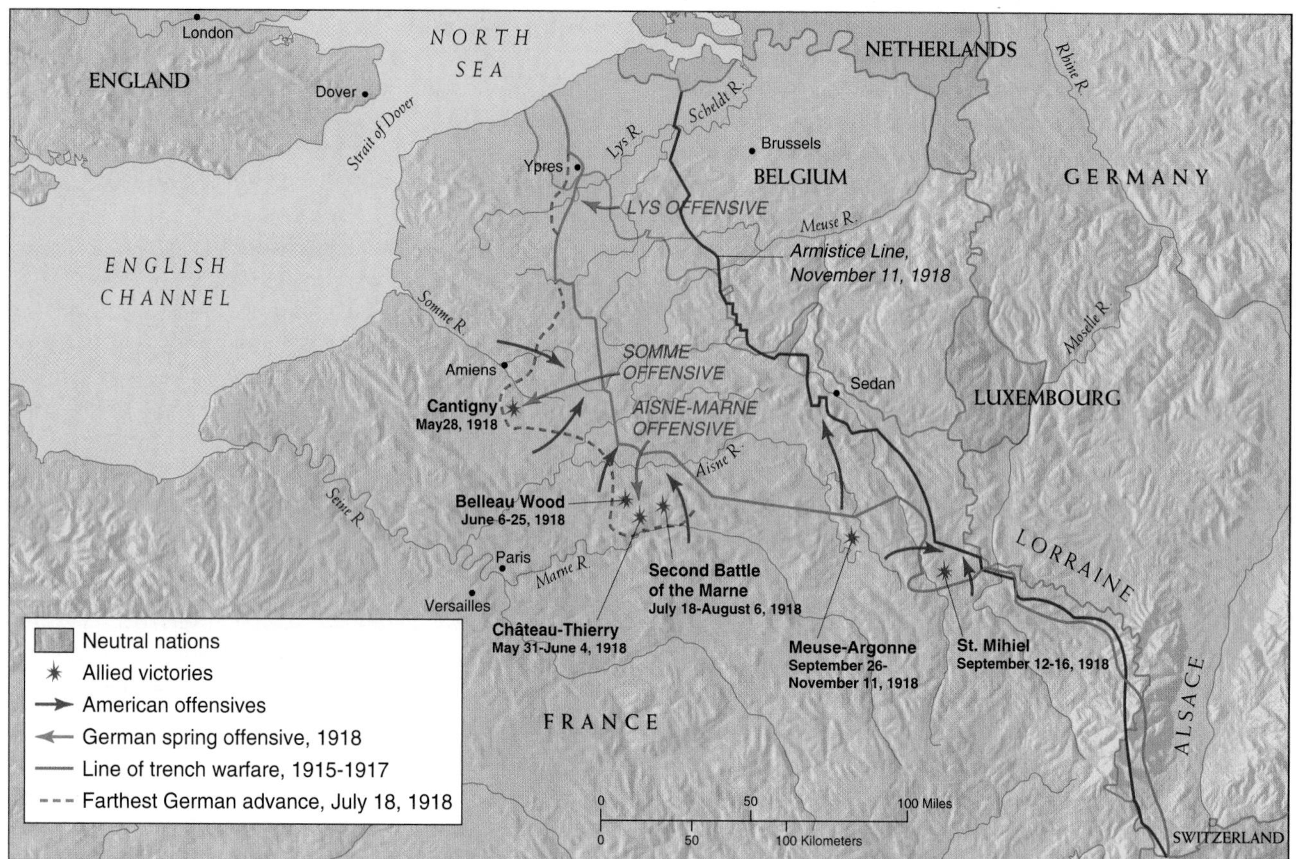

The Western Front, 1918 *American units saw their first substantial action in late May, helping to stop the German offensive at the battle of Cantigny. By September, more than 1 million American troops were fighting in a counteroffensive campaign at St. Mihiel, the largest single American engagement of the war.*

President Wilson appointed General John J. Pershing, recently returned from pursuing Pancho Villa in Mexico, as commander of the American Expeditionary Force (AEF). Pershing insisted that the AEF maintain its own identity, distinct from that of the French and British armies. He was also reluctant to send American troops into battle before they had received at least six months' training. The AEF's combat role would be brief but intense: not until early 1918 did AEF units reach the front in large numbers; eight months later the war was over.

Like Ulysses S. Grant, Pershing believed the object of war to be total destruction of the enemy's military power. He expressed contempt for the essentially defensive tactics of trench warfare pursued by both sides. But the brutal power of modern military technology had made trench warfare inevitable from 1914 to 1917. The awesome firepower of the machine gun and long-range artillery made the massed frontal confrontations of the Civil War era obsolete. The grim reality of life in the trenches—cold, wet, lice-ridden, with long periods of boredom and sleeplessness—also made a mockery of older notions about the glory of combat.

In the early spring of 1918 the Germans launched a major offensive that brought them within fifty miles of Paris. In early June about 70,000 AEF soldiers helped the French stop the Germans in the battles of Château-Thierry and Belleau Wood. In July, Allied forces led by Marshal Ferdinand Foch of France, began a counteroffensive designed to defeat Germany once and for all. American reinforcements began flooding the ports of Liverpool in England and Brest and Saint-Nazaire in France. The "doughboys" (a nickname for soldiers dating back to Civil War-era recruits who joined the army for the money) streamed in at a rate of over 250,000 a month. By September, General Pershing had more than a million Americans in his army.

In late September 1918, the AEF took over the southern part of a 200-mile front in the Meuse-Argonne offensive. In seven weeks of fighting, most through terrible mud and rain, U.S. soldiers used more ammunition than the entire Union army had in the four years of the Civil War. The Germans, exhausted and badly outnumbered, began to fall back and look for a cease-fire. On November 11, 1918, the war ended with the signing of an armistice.

The massive influx of American troops and supplies no doubt hastened the end of the war. About two-thirds of the U.S. soldiers saw at least some fighting, but even they managed to avoid the horrors of the sustained trench warfare that had marked the earlier years of the war. For most Americans at the front, the war experience was a mixture of fear, exhaustion, and fatigue. Their time in France would remain a decisive moment in their lives. In all, more than 52,000 Americans died in battle. Another 60,000 died from influenza and pneumonia, half of these while still in training camp. More than 200,000 Americans were wounded in the war. These figures, awful as they were, paled against the estimated casualties (killed and wounded) suffered by the European nations: 9 million for Russia, more than 6 million for Germany, nearly 5 million for France, and over 2 million each for Great Britain and Italy.

OVER HERE

In one sense, World War I can be understood as the ultimate progressive crusade, a reform movement of its own. Nearly all the reform energy of the previous two decades was turned toward the central goal of winning the war. The federal government would play a larger role than ever in managing and regulating the wartime economy. Planning, efficiency, scientific analysis, and cooperation were key principles for government agencies and large volunteer organizations. Although much of the regulatory spirit was temporary, the war experience started some important and lasting organizational trends in American life.

Organizing the Economy

In the summer of 1917 President Wilson established the War Industries Board (WIB) as a clearinghouse for industrial mobilization to support the war effort. Led by the successful Wall Street speculator Bernard M. Baruch, the WIB proved a major innovation in expanding the regulatory power of the federal government. It was given broad authority over the conversion of industrial plants to wartime needs, the manufacture of war materials, and the purchase of supplies for the United States and the Allies. The WIB had to balance price controls against war profits. Only by ensuring a fair rate of return on investment could it encourage stepped-up production.

The WIB eventually handled 3,000 contracts worth $14.5 billion with various businesses. Standardization of goods brought large savings and streamlined production. Baruch continually negotiated with business leaders, describing the system as "voluntary cooperation with the big stick in the cupboard." At first Elbert Gary of U.S. Steel refused to accept the government's price for steel and Henry Ford balked at limiting private car production. But when Baruch warned that he would instruct the military to take over their plants, both industrialists backed down.

In August 1917, Congress passed the Food and Fuel Act, authorizing the president to regulate the production and distribution of the food and fuel necessary for the war effort. To lead the Food Administration (FA), Wilson appointed Herbert Hoover, a millionaire engineer who had already won fame for directing a program of war relief for Belgium. He became one of the best-known figures of the war administration. Hoover imposed price controls on certain agricultural commodities, such as sugar, pork, and wheat. These were purchased by the government and then sold to the public through licensed dealers. The FA also raised the purchase price of grain so that farmers would increase production. But Hoover stopped short of imposing mandatory food rationing, preferring to rely on persuasion, high prices, and voluntary controls.

Hoover's success, like George Creel's at the CPI, depended on motivating hundreds of thousands of volunteers in thousands of American communities. The FA coordinated the work of local committees that distributed posters and leaflets urging people to save food, recycle scraps, and substitute for scarce produce. The FA directed patriotic appeals for "Wheatless Mondays, Meatless Tuesdays, and Porkless Thursdays." Hoover exhorted Americans to "go back to simple food, simple clothes, simple pleasures." He urged them to grow their own vegetables. These efforts resulted in a sharp cutback in the consumption of sugar and wheat as well as a boost in the supply of livestock. The resultant increase in food exports helped sustain the Allied war effort.

The enormous cost of fighting the war, about $33 billion, required unprecedentedly large expenditures for the federal government. The tax structure shifted dramatically as a result. Taxes on incomes and profits replaced excise and customs levies as the major source of revenue. The minimum income subject to the graduated federal income tax, in effect only since 1913, was lowered to $1,000 from $3,000, increasing the number of Americans who paid income tax from 437,000 in 1916 to 4,425,000 in 1918. Tax rates were as steep as 70 percent in the highest brackets.

The bulk of war financing came from government borrowing, especially in the form of the popular Liberty Bonds sold to the American public. Bond drives became highly organized patriotic campaigns that ultimately raised a total of $23 billion for the war effort. The administration also used the new Federal Reserve Banks to expand the money supply, making borrowing easier. The federal debt jumped from $1 billion in 1915 to $20 billion in 1920.

The Business of War

Overall, the war meant expansion and high profits for American business. Between 1916 and 1918, Ford Motor Company increased its workforce from 32,000 to 48,000, General Motors from 10,000 to 50,000. Total capital expenditure in U.S. manufacturing jumped from $600 million in 1915 to $2.5 billion in 1918. Corporate profits as a whole nearly tripled between 1914 and 1919, and many large businesses did much better than that. Annual prewar profits for United States Steel had averaged $76 million; in 1917 they were $478 million. The Bethlehem Shipbuilding Company increased its annual profits from $6 million in peacetime to $49 million in wartime. Du Pont quadrupled its assets. The demand for foodstuffs led to a boom in agriculture as well. The total value of farm produce rose from $9.8 billion in 1914 to $21.3 billion by 1918. Expanded farm acreage and increased investment in farm machinery led to a jump of 20–30 percent in overall farm production.

The most important and long-lasting economic legacy of the war was the organizational shift toward corporatism in American business. The wartime need for efficient management, manufacturing, and distribution could be met only by a greater reliance on the productive and marketing power of large corporations. Never before had business and the federal government cooperated so closely. Under war administrators like Baruch and Hoover, entire industries (such as radio manufacturing) and economic sectors (such as agriculture and energy) were organized, regulated, and subsidized. War agencies used both public and private power—legal authority and voluntarism—to hammer out and enforce agreements. Here was the genesis of the modern bureaucratic state.

Some Americans worried about the wartime trend toward a greater federal presence in their lives. As the *Saturday Evening Post* noted, "All this government activity will be called to account and re-examined in due time." Although many aspects of the government–business partnership proved temporary, some institutions and practices grew stronger in the postwar years. Among these were the Federal Reserve Board, the income tax system, the Chamber of Commerce, the Farm Bureau, and the growing horde of lobbying groups that pressed Washington for special interest legislation.

One key example of the long-range impact of the government–business partnership was the infant radio industry. Wireless communication technology found many uses among naval and ground forces in wartime. As in most industries, the Justice Department guaranteed radio manufacturers protection against patent infringement and antitrust suits. These guarantees helped stimulate research and the mass production of radios for airplanes, ships, and infantry. In 1919 the government helped create the Radio Corporation of America (RCA), which bought out a British company that had dominated America's wireless system. As part of the deal, the U.S. military was allowed a permanent representative on the RCA board of directors. The creation of RCA, jointly owned by General Electric, American Telephone and Telegraph, and Westinghouse, assured the United States a powerful position in the new age of global communications. It also set the stage for the new radio broadcasting industry of the 1920s.

Labor and the War

Organized labor's power and prestige, though by no means equal to those of business or government, clearly grew during the war. The expansion of the economy, combined with army mobilization and a decline in immigration from Europe, caused a growing wartime labor shortage. As the demand for workers intensified, the federal government was forced to recognize that labor, like any other resource or commodity, would have to be more carefully tended to than in peacetime. For the war's duration, working people generally enjoyed higher wages and a better standard of living. Trade unions, especially those affiliated with the American Federation of Labor (AFL), experienced a sharp rise in membership. In effect, the government took in labor as a junior partner in the mobilization of the economy.

Samuel Gompers, president of the AFL, emerged as the leading spokesman for the nation's trade union movement. An English immigrant and cigar maker by trade, Gompers had rejected the socialism of his youth for a philosophy of "business unionism." By stressing the concrete gains that workers could win through collective bargaining with employers, the AFL had reached a total membership of about 2 million in 1914. Virtually all its members were skilled white males, organized in highly selective crafts in the building trades, railroads, and coal mines.

Gompers pledged the AFL's patriotic support for the war effort, and in April 1918 President Wilson appointed him to the National War Labor Board (NWLB). During 1917 the nation had seen thousands of strikes involving more than a million workers. Wages were usually at issue, reflecting workers' concerns with spiraling inflation and higher prices. The NWLB, co-chaired by labor attorney Frank Walsh and former president William H. Taft, acted as a kind of supreme court for labor, arbitrating disputes and working to prevent disruptions in production. The great majority of these interventions resulted in improved wages and reduced hours of work.

Most important, the NWLB supported the right of workers to organize unions and furthered the acceptance of the eight-hour day for war workers—central aims of the labor movement. It also backed time-and-a-half pay for overtime, as well as the principle of equal pay for women workers. AFL unions gained more than a million new members during the war, and overall union membership rose from 2.7 million in 1914 to more than 5 million by 1920. The NWLB established important precedents for government intervention on behalf of labor.

Wartime conditions often meant severe disruptions and discomfort for America's workers. Overcrowding, rapid workforce turnover, and high inflation rates were typical in war-boom communities. In Bridgeport, Connecticut, a center for small-arms manufacturing, the population grew by 50,000 in less than a year. In 1917 the number of families grew by 12,000, but available housing stock increased by only 6,000 units. Chronic congestion became common in many cities; Philadelphia reported the worst housing shortage in its history.

In the Southwest, the demand for wartime labor temporarily eased restrictions against the movement of Mexicans into the United States. The Immigration Act of 1917, requiring a literacy test and an $8 head tax, had cut Mexican immigration nearly in half, down to about 25,000 per year. But employers complained of severe shortages of workers. Farmers in Arizona's Salt River Valley and southern California needed hands to harvest grain, alfalfa, cotton, and fruit. El Paso's mining and smelting industries, Texas's border ranches, and southern Arizona's railroads and copper mines insisted they depended on unskilled Mexican labor as well.

Responding to these protests, in June 1917 the Department of Labor suspended the immigration law for the duration of the war and negotiated an agreement with the Mexican government permitting some 35,000 Mexican contract laborers to enter the United States. Mexicans let in through this program had to demonstrate they had a job waiting before they could cross the border. They received identification cards and transportation to their place of work from American labor contractors. Pressure from southwestern employers kept the exemptions in force until 1921, well after the end of the war, demonstrating the growing importance of cheap Mexican labor to the region's economy.

If the war boosted the fortunes of the AFL, it also spelled the end for more radical elements of the U.S. labor movement. The Industrial Workers of the World (IWW) had followed a different path from the "pure and simple" trade unionism of Gompers. Unlike the AFL, the IWW concentrated on organizing unskilled workers into all-inclusive industrial unions. The Wobblies denounced capitalism as an unreformable system based on exploitation and they opposed U.S. entry into the war. IWW leaders advised their members to refuse induction for "the capitalists' war."

With vigorous organizing, especially in the West, the IWW had grown in 1916 and 1917. It gained strength among workers in several areas crucial to the war effort: copper mining, lumbering, and wheat harvesting. In September 1917, just after the vigilante attack in Bisbee and the IWW's efforts to expose it, the Wilson administration responded to appeals from western business leaders for a crackdown on the Wobblies. Justice Department agents, acting under the broad authority of the recently passed Espionage Act, swooped down on IWW offices in more than sixty towns and cities, arresting more than 300 people and confiscating files. The mass trials and convictions that followed broke the back of America's radical labor movement and marked the beginning of a powerful wave of political repression.

For Every Fighter a Woman Worker, 1917, *by Ernest Hamlin Baker. This poster, part of the United War Work Campaign of the Young Women's Christian Association, depicted America's women as a civilian army, ready and able to take the place of male workers gone off to fight.*

Women at Work

For many of the 8 million women already in the labor force, the war meant a chance to switch from low-paying jobs, such as domestic service, to higher-paying industrial fields. About a million women workers joined the labor force for the first time. Of the estimated 9.4 million workers directly engaged in war work, some 2.25 million were women. Of these, 1.25 million worked in manufacturing. Female munitions plant workers, train engineers, drill press operators, streetcar conductors, and mail carriers became a common sight around the country.

In response to the widened range of female employment, the Labor Department created the Women in Industry Service (WIS). Directed by Mary Van Kleeck, the service advised employers on using female labor and formulated general standards for the treatment of women workers. The WIS represented the first attempt by the federal government to take a practical stand on improving working conditions for women. Its standards included the eight-hour day, equal pay for equal work, a minimum wage, the prohibition of night work, and the provision of rest periods, meal breaks, and restroom facilities. These standards had no legal force, however, and WIS inspectors found that employers often flouted them. They were accepted nonetheless as goals by nearly every group concerned with improving the conditions of working women.

Many women resented the restrictiveness of the WIS guidelines. Myrtle Altenburg, a Wisconsin widow, complained of being prevented from working on a local railroad. "It is my belief," she wrote the state railway commission, "that a woman can do everything that a man can do that is within her strength. Hundreds and hundreds of women might work and release men for war or war work, could they, the women, be employed on the railroads." Even when hired, women suffered discrimination over pay. Government surveys found that women's average earnings were roughly half of men's in the same industries.

At war's end, women lost nearly all their defense-related jobs. Wartime women railroad workers, for example, were replaced by returning servicemen through the application of laws meant to protect women from hazardous conditions. But the war accelerated female employment in fields already dominated by women. By 1920, more women who worked outside the home did so in white-collar occupations—as telephone operators, secretaries, and clerks, for example—than in manufacturing or domestic service. The new awareness of women's work led Congress to create the Women's Bureau in the Labor Department, which continued the WIS wartime program of education and investigation through the postwar years.

Woman Suffrage

The presence of so many new women wageworkers, combined with the highly visible volunteer work of millions of middle-class women, helped finally to secure the vote for women. Volunteer war work—selling bonds, saving food, organizing benefits—was very popular among housewives and clubwomen. These women played a key role in the success of the Food Administration, and the Women's Committee of the Council of National Defense included a variety of women's organizations.

Until World War I, the fight for woman suffrage had been waged largely within individual states. Western states and territories had led the way. Various forms of woman suffrage had become law in Wyoming in 1869, followed by Utah (1870), Colorado (1893), Idaho (1896), Washington (1910), California (1911), Arizona and Oregon (1912), and Montana and Nevada (1914). The reasons for this regional pattern had less to do with dramatically different notions of gender roles in the West than with the distinctiveness of western politics and society. Rocky Mountain and Pacific coast states did not have the sharp ethnocultural divisions between Catholics and Protestants that hindered suffrage efforts in the East. The close identification in the East between the suffrage and prohibition movements led many Catholic immigrants and German Lutherans to oppose the vote for women because they feared it would lead to prohibition. Mormons in Utah supported woman suffrage as a way to preserve polygamy and defend their distinctive social order from attack.

The U.S. entry into the war provided a unique opportunity for suffrage groups to shift their strategy to a national campaign for a constitutional amendment granting the vote to women. The most important of these groups was the National American Woman Suffrage Association. Before 1917, most American suffragists had opposed the war. Under the leadership of Carrie Chapman Catt, NAWSA threw its support behind the war effort and doubled its membership to 2 million. Catt gambled that a strong show of patriotism would help clinch the century-old fight to win the vote for women. NAWSA pursued a moderate policy of lobbying Congress for a constitutional amendment and calling for state referendums on woman suffrage.

At the same time, more militant suffragists led by a young Quaker activist, Alice Paul, injected new energy and more radical tactics into the movement. Paul had spent several years in England working with militant suffragists there, and in 1913 she returned to the United States to form the Congressional Union within the NAWSA to lobby for a federal amendment. Dissatisfied with the NAWSA's conservative strategy of quiet lobbying and orderly demonstrations, Paul left the organization in 1916. She joined forces with western women voters to form the National Woman's Party. Borrowing from English suffragists, this party pursued a more aggressive and dramatic strategy of agitation. Paul and her supporters picketed the White House, publicly burned President Wilson's speeches, and condemned the president and the Democrats for failing to produce an amendment. In one demonstration they chained themselves to the White House fence and after their

Members of the National Woman's Party picketed President Wilson at the White House in 1917. Their militant action in the midst of the war crisis aroused both anger and sympathy. The NWP campaign helped push the president and the Congress to accept woman suffrage as a "war measure."

arrest went on a hunger strike in jail. The militants generated a great deal of publicity and sympathy.

Although some in the NAWSA objected to these tactics, Paul's radical approach helped make the NAWSA position more acceptable to Wilson. Carrie Chapman Catt used the president's war rhetoric as an argument for granting the vote to women. The fight for democracy, she argued, must begin at home, and she urged passage of the woman suffrage amendment as a "war measure." She won Wilson's support, and in 1917 the president urged Congress to pass a woman suffrage amendment as "vital to the winning of the war." The House did so in January 1918 and a more reluctant Senate approved it in June 1919. Another year of hard work was spent convincing the state legislatures. In August 1920, Tennessee gave the final vote needed to ratify the Nineteenth Amendment to the Constitution, finally making woman's vote legal nationwide.

Prohibition

Significantly, another reform effort closely associated with women's groups triumphed at the same time. The movement to eliminate alcohol from American life had attracted many Americans, especially women, since before the Civil War. Temperance advocates saw drinking as the source of many of the worst problems faced by the working class, including family violence, unemployment, and poverty. By the early twentieth century the Woman's Christian Temperance Union, with a quarter-million members, had become the single largest women's organization in American history.

The moral fervor that accompanied America's entry into the war provided a crucial boost to the cause. With so many breweries bearing German names, the movement benefited as well from the strong anti-German feeling of the war years. Outlawing beer and whiskey would also help to conserve precious grain, prohibitionists argued.

In 1917, a coalition of progressives and rural fundamentalists in Congress pushed through a constitutional amendment providing for a national ban on alcoholic drinks. The Eighteenth Amendment was ratified by the states in January 1919 and became the law of the land one year later. Although Prohibition would create a host of problems in the postwar years, especially as a stimulus for the growth of organized crime, many Americans, particularly native Protestants, considered it a worthy moral reform.

Public Health

Wartime mobilization brought deeper government involvement with public health issues, especially in the realm of sex hygiene, child welfare, and disease prevention. The rate of venereal disease among draftees was as high as 6 percent in some states, presenting a potential manpower problem for the army. In April 1917 the War Department mounted a vigorous campaign against venereal disease, which attracted the energies of progressive era sex reformers—social hygienists and antivice crusaders. Under the direction of Raymond Fosdick and the Commission on Training Camp Activities, the military educated troops on the dangers of contracting syphilis and gonorrhea and distributed condoms to soldiers. "A Soldier who gets a dose," warned a typical poster, "is a Traitor." More than a hundred red-light districts near military bases were closed down, and the army established five-mile "pure zones" to keep prostitutes away from the camps. Yet the sexual double standard still operated. Female activists angrily protested when military authorities, while refusing to arrest soldiers for patronizing prostitutes, arrested women en masse and held them in detention centers.

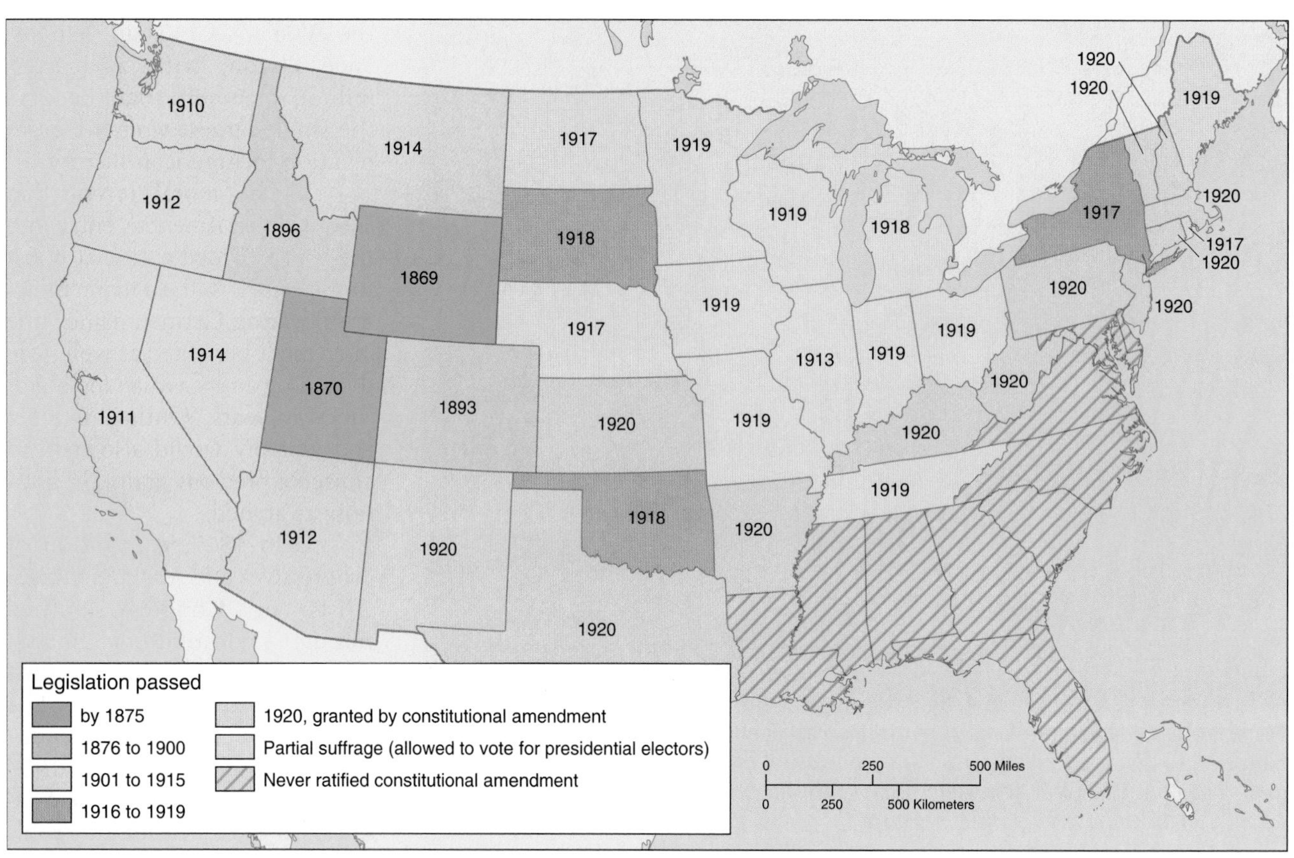

Woman Suffrage by State, 1869–1919 *Dates for the enactment of woman suffrage in the individual states. Years before ratification of the Nineteenth Amendment in 1920, a number of western states had legislated full or partial voting rights for women. In 1917 Montana suffragist Jeannette Rankin became the first woman elected to Congress.*

Source: Barbara G. Shortridge, *Atlas of American Women* (New York: Macmillan, 1987).

The scientific discussions of sex to which recruits were subjected in lectures, pamphlets, and films were surely a first for the vast majority of them. Venereal disease rates for soldiers declined by more than 300 percent during the war. The Division of Venereal Diseases, created in the summer of 1918 as a branch of the U.S. Public Health Service, established clinics offering free medical treatment to infected persons. It also coordinated an aggressive educational campaign through state departments of health.

The wartime boost to government health work continued into the postwar years. The Children's Bureau, created in 1912 as a part of the Labor Department, undertook a series of reports on special problems growing out of the war: the increase in employment of married women, finding day care for children of working mothers, and the growth of both child labor and delinquency. In 1918 Julia C. Lathrop, chief of the bureau, organized a "Children's Year" campaign designed to promote public protection of expectant mothers and infants and to enforce child labor laws. Millions of health education pamphlets were distributed nationwide, and mothers were encouraged to have their infants and children weighed and measured. Thousands of community-based committees enrolled some 11 million women in the drive.

In 1917, Lathrop, who had come to the Children's Bureau from the settlement house movement, proposed a plan to institutionalize federal aid to the states for protection of mothers and children. Congress finally passed the Maternity and Infancy Act in 1921, appropriating over $1 million a year to be administered to the states by the Children's Bureau. In the postwar years, clinics for prenatal and obstetrical care grew out of these efforts and greatly reduced the rate of infant and maternal mortality and disease.

The disastrous influenza epidemic of 1918–19 offered the most serious challenge to national public health during the war years. Part of a worldwide pandemic that claimed as many as 20 million lives, few Americans paid attention to the disease until it swept through military camps and eastern cities in September 1918. A lethal combination of the "flu" and respiratory complications (mainly pneumonia) killed roughly

550,000 Americans in ten months. Most victims were young adults between ages twenty and forty. Professional groups such as the American Medical Association called for massive government appropriations to search for a cure. Congress did appropriate a million dollars to the Public Health Service to combat and suppress the epidemic, but it offered no money for research.

The Public Health Service found itself overwhelmed by calls for doctors, nurses, and treatment facilities. Much of the care for the sick and dying came from Red Cross nurses and volunteers working in local communities across the nation. With a war on, and the nation focused on reports from the battlefront, even a public health crisis of this magnitude went relatively unnoticed. Although funding for the Public Health Service continued to grow in the 1920s, public and private expenditures on medical research were barely one-fiftieth of what they would become after World War II.

REPRESSION AND REACTION

World War I exposed and intensified many of the deepest social tensions in American life. On the local level, as exemplified by the Bisbee deportations, vigilantes increasingly took the law into their own hands to punish those suspected of disloyalty. The push for national unity led the federal government to crack down on a wide spectrum of dissenters from its war policies. The war inflamed racial hatred, and the worst race riots in the nation's history exploded in several cities. At war's end, a newly militant labor movement briefly asserted itself in mass strikes around the nation. Over all these developments loomed the 1917 Bolshevik Revolution in Russia. Radicals around the world had drawn inspiration from what looked like the first successful revolution against a capitalist state. Many conservatives worried that similar revolutions were imminent. From 1918 through 1920 the federal government directed a repressive antiradical campaign that had crucial implications for the nation's future.

Muzzling Dissent: The Espionage and Sedition Acts

The Espionage Act of June 1917 became the government's key tool for the suppression of antiwar sentiment. It set severe penalties (up to twenty years' imprisonment and a $10,000 fine) for anyone found guilty of aiding the enemy, obstructing recruitment, or causing insubordination in the armed forces. The act also empowered the postmaster general to exclude from the mails any newspapers or magazines he thought treasonous. Within a year the mailing rights of forty-five newspapers had been revoked. These included several anti-British and pro-Irish publications, as well as such leading journals of American socialism as the Kansas-based *Appeal to Reason*, which had enjoyed a prewar circulation of half a million, and *The Masses*.

To enforce the Espionage Act, the government had to increase its overall police and surveillance machinery. Civilian intelligence was coordinated by the newly created Bureau of Investigation in the Justice Department. This agency was reorganized after the war as the Federal Bureau of Investigation (FBI). In May 1918 the Sedition Act, an amendment to the Espionage Act, outlawed "any disloyal, profane, scurrilous, or abusive language intended to cause contempt, scorn, contumely, or disrepute" to the government, Constitution, or flag.

In all, more than 2,100 cases were brought to trial under these acts. They became a convenient vehicle for striking out at socialists, pacifists, radical labor activists, and others who resisted the patriotic tide. The most celebrated prosecution came in June 1918 when federal agents arrested Eugene Debs in Canton, Ohio, after he gave a speech defending antiwar protesters. Sentenced to ten years in prison, Debs defiantly told the court: "I have been accused of having obstructed the war. I admit it. Gentlemen, I abhor war. I would oppose the war if I stood alone." Debs served thirty-two months in federal prison before being pardoned by President Warren G. Harding on Christmas Day 1921.

The Supreme Court upheld the constitutionality of the acts in several 1919 decisions. In *Schenck v. United States* the Court unanimously agreed with Justice Oliver Wendell Holmes's claim that Congress could restrict speech if the words "are used in such circumstances and are of such a nature as to create a clear and present danger." The decision upheld the conviction of Charles Schenck for having mailed pamphlets urging potential army inductees to resist conscription. In *Debs v. United States*, the Court affirmed the guilt of Eugene Debs for his antiwar speech in Canton, even though he had not explicitly urged violation of the draft laws. Finally, in *Abrams v. United States*, the Court upheld Sedition Act convictions of four Russian immigrants who had printed pamphlets denouncing American military intervention in the Russian Revolution. The nation's highest court thus endorsed the severe wartime restrictions on free speech.

The deportation of striking miners in Bisbee offered an extreme case of vigilante activity. Thousands of other instances took place as government repression and local vigilantes reinforced each other. The American Protective League, founded with the blessing of the Justice Department, mobilized 250,000 self-appointed "operatives" in more than 600 towns and cities. Members of the league, mostly businessmen, bankers, and former policemen, spied on their neighbors and staged a series of well-publicized "slacker" raids on antiwar protesters and draft evaders. Many communities, inspired by Committee on Public Information campaigns, sought to

THE GREAT MIGRATION: BLACK POPULATION GROWTH IN SELECTED NORTHERN CITIES, 1910–1920

City	1910 No.	1910 Percent	1920 No.	1920 Percent	Percent Increase
New York	91,709	1.9%	152,467	2.7%	66.3%
Chicago	44,103	2.0	109,458	4.1	148.2
Philadelphia	84,459	5.5	134,229	7.4	58.9
Detroit	5,741	1.2	40,838	4.1	611.3
St. Louis	43,960	6.4	69,854	9.0	58.9
Cleveland	8,448	1.5	34,451	4.3	307.8
Pittsburgh	25,623	4.8	37,725	6.4	47.2
Cincinnati	19,739	5.4	30,079	7.5	53.2
Indianapolis	21,816	9.3	34,678	11.0	59.0
Newark	9,475	2.7	16,977	4.1	79.2
Kansas City	23,566	9.5	30,719	9.5	30.4
Columbus	12,739	7.0	22,181	9.4	74.1
Gary	383	2.3	5,299	9.6	1,283.6
Youngstown	1,936	2.4	6,662	5.0	244.1
Buffalo	1,773	0.4	4,511	0.9	154.4
Toledo	1,877	1.1	5,691	2.3	203.2
Akron	657	1.0	5,580	2.7	749.3

Source: U.S. Department of Commerce.

ban the teaching of the German language in their schools or the performance of German music in concert halls.

The Great Migration and Racial Tensions

Economic opportunity brought on by war prosperity triggered a massive migration of rural black Southerners to northern cities. From 1914 to 1920, somewhere between 300,000 and 500,000 African Americans left the rural South for the North. Chicago's black population increased by 65,000, or 150 percent; Detroit's by 35,000, or 600 percent. Acute labor shortages led northern factory managers to recruit black migrants to the expanding industrial centers. The Pennsylvania Railroad alone drew 10,000 black workers from Florida and south Georgia. Black workers eagerly left low-paying jobs as field hands and domestic servants for the chance at relatively high-paying work in meat-packing plants, shipyards, and steel mills.

Kinship and community networks were crucial in shaping what came to be called the Great Migration. They spread news about job openings, urban residential districts, and boardinghouses in northern cities. Black clubs, churches, and fraternal lodges in southern communities frequently sponsored the migration of their members, as well as return trips to the South. Single African American women often made the trip first because they could more easily obtain steady work as maids, cooks, and laundresses. One recalled that "if [white employers] liked the way the women would work in their homes or did ironing, they might throw some work to your husband or son." Relatively few African American men actually secured high-paying skilled jobs in industry or manufacturing. Most had to settle for work as construction laborers, teamsters, janitors, porters, or other low-paid jobs.

The persistence of lynching and other racial violence in the South no doubt contributed to the Great Migration. But racial violence was not limited to the South. Two of the worst race riots in American history occurred as a result of tensions brought on by wartime migration. On July 2, 1917, in East St. Louis, Illinois, a ferocious mob of whites attacked African Americans, killing at least 200. Before this riot, some of the city's manufacturers had been steadily recruiting black labor as a way to keep local union demands down. Unions had refused to allow black workers as members, and politicians had cynically exploited white racism in appealing for votes. In Chicago, on July 27,

1919, antiblack rioting broke out on a Lake Michigan beach. For two weeks white gangs hunted African Americans in the streets and burned hundreds out of their homes. Twenty-three African Americans and 15 whites died, and more than 500 were injured.

In both East St. Louis and Chicago, local authorities held African Americans responsible for the violence. President Wilson refused requests for federal intervention or investigation. A young black veteran who had been chased by a mob in the Chicago riot asked: "Had the ten months I spent in France been all in vain? Were all those white crosses over dead bodies of those dark skinned boys lying in Flanders field for naught? Was democracy a hollow sentiment?"

In terms of service in the armed forces, compliance with the draft, and involvement in volunteer work, African Americans had supported the war effort as faithfully as any group. In 1917, despite a segregated army and discrimination in defense industries, most African Americans thought the war might improve their lot. "If we again demonstrate our loyalty and devotion to our country," advised the *Chicago Defender,* "those injustices will disappear and the grounds for complaint will no longer exist." By the fall of 1919, writing in the *Crisis,* the journal of the National Association for the Advancement of Colored People (NAACP), black author James Weldon Johnson gloomily concluded that "an increased hatred of race was an integral part of wartime intolerance."

This southern African American family is shown arriving in Chicago around 1915. Black migrants to northern cities often faced overcrowding, inferior housing, and a high death rate from disease. But the chance to earn daily wages of $6 to $8 (the equivalent of a week's wages in much of the South), as well as the desire to escape persistent racial violence, kept the migrants coming.

Black disillusionment about the war grew quickly. So did a newly militant spirit. A heightened sense of race consciousness and activism was evident among black veterans and the growing black communities of northern cities. Taking the lead in the fight against bigotry and injustice, the NAACP held a national conference in 1919 on lynching. It pledged to defend persecuted African Americans, publicize the horrors of lynch law, and seek federal legislation against "Judge Lynch." By 1919 membership in the NAACP had reached 60,000 and the circulation of its journal exceeded half a million.

Labor Strife

The relative labor peace of 1917 and 1918 dissolved after the armistice. More than 4 million American workers were involved in some 3,600 strikes in 1919 alone. This unprecedented strike wave had several causes. Most of the modest wartime wage gains were wiped out by spiraling inflation and high prices for food, fuel, and housing. With the end of government controls on industry, many employers withdrew their recognition of unions. Difficult working conditions, such as the twelve-hour day in steel mills, were still routine in some industries. The quick return of demobilized servicemen to the labor force meant layoffs and new concerns about job security.

Several of the postwar strikes received widespread national attention. They seemed to be more than simple economic conflicts, and they provoked deep fears about the larger social order. In February 1919 a strike in the shipyards of Seattle, Washington, over wages escalated into a general citywide strike involving 60,000 workers. A strike committee coordinated the city's essential services for a week in a disciplined, nonviolent fashion. But the local press and Mayor Ole Hanson denounced the strikers as revolutionaries. Hanson effectively ended the strike by requesting federal troops to occupy the city.

In September, Boston policemen went out on strike when the police commissioner rejected a citizens' commission study that recommended a pay raise. Massachusetts governor Calvin Coolidge called in the National Guard to restore order and won a national reputation by crushing the strike. The entire police force was fired. Coolidge declared, "There is no right to strike against the public safety by anybody, anywhere, any time."

The biggest strike took place in the steel industry, involving some 350,000 steelworkers. Centered in several midwestern cities, this epic struggle lasted from September 1919 to January 1920. The AFL had hoped to build on wartime gains in an industry that had successfully resisted unionization before the war. The major demands were union recognition, the eight-hour day, and wage increases. The steel companies used black strike-

The General Strike Committee of Seattle distributed groceries to union families in February 1919. The Seattle general strike had been triggered when shipyard workers walked off the job after failing to gain wage hikes to offset spiraling postwar inflation. The conservative Los Angeles Times *saw the strike as evidence that Bolshevism was a right here and now American menace.*

breakers and armed guards to keep the mills running. Elbert Gary, president of U.S. Steel, directed a sophisticated propaganda campaign that branded the strikers as revolutionaries. Public opinion turned against the strike and condoned the use of state and federal troops to break it. A riot in Gary, Indiana, left eighteen strikers dead. The failed steel strike proved to be the era's most bitter and devastating defeat for organized labor.

AN UNEASY PEACE

The armistice of November 1918 ended the fighting on the battlefield, but the war continued at the peace conference. In the old royal palace of Versailles near Paris, delegates from twenty-seven countries spent five months hammering out a settlement. Yet neither Germany nor Russia was represented. The proceedings were dominated by leaders of the "Big Four": David Lloyd George (Great Britain), Georges Clemenceau (France), Vittorio Orlando (Italy), and Woodrow Wilson (United States). President Wilson saw the peace conference as a historic opportunity to project his domestic liberalism onto the world stage. But the stubborn realities of power politics would frustrate Wilson at Versailles and lead to his most crushing defeat at home.

The Fourteen Points

Wilson arrived in Paris with the United States delegation in January 1919. He brought with him a plan for peace that he had outlined a year earlier in a speech to Congress on U.S. war aims. The Fourteen Points, as they were called, had originally served wartime purposes: to appeal to war opponents in Austria-Hungary and Germany, to convince Russia to stay in the war, and to help sustain Allied morale. As a blueprint for peace, they contained three main elements. First, Wilson offered a series of specific proposals for setting postwar boundaries in Europe and creating new countries out of the collapsed Austro-Hungarian and Ottoman empires. The key idea here was the right of all peoples to "national self-determination." Second, Wilson listed general principles for governing international conduct, including freedom of the seas, free trade, open covenants instead of secret treaties, reduced armaments, and mediation for competing colonial claims. Third, and most important, Wilson called for a League of Nations to help implement these principles and resolve future disputes.

The Fourteen Points offered a plan for world order deeply rooted in the liberal progressivism long associated with Wilson. The plan reflected a faith in efficient government and the rule of law as means for solving international problems. It looked to free trade and commercial development as the key to spreading prosperity. It advocated a dynamic democratic capitalism as a middle ground between Old World autocracy and revolutionary socialism. Wilson's vision was a profoundly moral one, and he was certain it was the only road to a lasting and humane peace.

The most controversial element, both at home and abroad, would prove to be the league. The heart of the league covenant, Article X, called for collective security as the ultimate method of keeping the peace: "The members of the League undertake to respect and preserve as against external aggression the territorial integrity and existing political independence of all Members." In the United States, Wilson's critics would focus on this provision as an unacceptable surrender of the nation's sovereignty and independence in foreign affairs. They also raised constitutional objections, arguing that the American system vested the power to declare war with the Congress. Would membership in the league violate this basic principle of the Constitution?

Wilson in Paris

The president was pleased when the conference at first accepted his plan as the basis for discussions. He also enjoyed wildly enthusiastic receptions from the public in Paris and several other European capitals he visited. France's Clemenceau was less enamored. He sarcastically observed, "God gave us the Ten Commandments, and we broke them. Wilson gave us the Fourteen Points. We shall see." Wilson's plan could not survive the hostile atmosphere at Versailles.

Much of the negotiating at Versailles was in fact done in secret among the Big Four. The ideal of self-determination found limited expression. The independent states of Austria, Hungary, Poland, Yugoslavia, and Czechoslovakia were carved out of the homelands of the beaten Central Powers. But the Allies resisted Wilson's call for independence for the colonies of the defeated nations. A compromise mandate system of protectorates gave the French and British control of parts of the old German and Turkish empires in Africa and West Asia. Japan won control of former German colonies in China. Among those trying, but failing, to influence the treaty negotiations were the sixty-odd delegates to the first Pan African Congress, held in Paris at the same time as the peace talks. The group included Americans W.E.B. Du Bois and William Monroe Trotter as well as representatives from Africa and the West Indies. All were disappointed with the failure of the peace conference to grant self-determination to thousands of Africans living in former German colonies.

Another disappointment for Wilson came with the issue of war guilt. He had strongly opposed the extraction of harsh economic reparations from the Central Powers. But the French and British, with their awful war losses fresh in mind, insisted on making Germany pay. The final treaty contained a clause attributing the war to "the aggression of Germany," and a commission later set German war reparations at $33 billion. Bitter resentment in Germany over the punitive treaty helped sow the seeds for the Nazi rise to power in the 1930s.

The final treaty was signed on June 28, 1919, in the Hall of Mirrors at the Versailles palace. The Germans had no choice but to accept its harsh terms. President Wilson had been disappointed by the secret deals and the endless compromising of his ideals, no doubt underestimating the stubborn reality of power politics in the wake of Europe's most devastating war. He had nonetheless won a commitment to the League of Nations, the centerpiece of his plan, and he was confident that the American people would accept the treaty. The tougher fight would be with the Senate, where a two-thirds vote was needed for ratification.

The Treaty Fight

Preoccupied with peace conference politics in Paris, Wilson had neglected politics at home. His troubles had actually started earlier. Republicans had captured both the House and the Senate in the 1918 elections.

John Christen Johansen, *Signing of the Treaty of Versailles*, 1919, National Portrait Gallery, Smithsonian Institution, Washington, D.C./Art Resource, New York.

Woodrow Wilson, Georges Clemenceau, and David Lloyd George are among the central figures depicted in John Christen Johansen's Signing of the Treaty of Versailles. *But all the gathered statesmen appear dwarfed by their surroundings.*

Wilson had then made a tactical error by including no prominent Republicans in the U.S. peace delegation. He therefore faced a variety of tough opponents to the treaty he brought home.

Wilson's most extreme enemies in the Senate were a group of about sixteen "irreconcilables," opposed to a treaty in any form. Some were isolationist progressives, such as Republicans Robert M. La Follette of Wisconsin and William Borah of Idaho, who opposed the League of Nations as steadfastly as they opposed American entry into the war. Others were racist xenophobes like Democrat James Reed of Missouri. He objected, he said, to submitting questions to a tribunal "on which a nigger from Liberia, a nigger from Honduras, a nigger from India, and an unlettered gentleman from Siam, each have votes equal to the great United States of America."

The less dogmatic but more influential opponents were led by Republican Henry Cabot Lodge of Massachusetts, powerful majority leader of the Senate. They had strong reservations about the League of Nations, especially the provisions for collective security in the event of a member nation's being attacked. Lodge argued that this provision impinged on congressional authority to declare war and placed unacceptable restraints on the nation's ability to pursue an independent foreign policy. Lodge proposed a series of amendments that would have weakened the league. But Wilson refused to compromise, motivated in part by the long-standing hatred he and Lodge felt toward each other. The president decided instead to take his case directly to the American people.

In September, Wilson set out on a speaking tour across the country to drum up support for the league and the treaty. His train traveled 8,000 miles—through the Midwest, to the Pacific, and then back East. The crowds were large and responsive, but they did not change any votes in the Senate. The strain took its toll. On September 25, after speaking in Pueblo, Colorado, the sixty-three-year-old Wilson collapsed from exhaustion. His doctor canceled the rest of the trip. A week later, back in Washington, the president suffered a stroke that left him partially paralyzed. In November, Lodge brought the treaty out of committee for a vote, having appended to it fourteen reservations—that is, recommended changes. A bedridden Wilson stubbornly refused to compromise and instructed Democrats to vote against the Lodge version of the treaty. On November 19, Democrats joined with the "irreconcilables" to defeat the amended treaty, 39 to 55.

Wilson refused to budge. In January, he urged Democrats to either stand by the original treaty or vote it down. The 1920 election, he warned, would be "a great and solemn referendum" on the whole issue. In the final vote, on March 19, 1920, twenty-one Democrats broke with the president and voted for the Lodge version, giving it a majority of 49 to 35. But this was seven votes short of the two-thirds needed for ratification. As a result, the United States never signed the Versailles Treaty, nor did it join the League of Nations. The absence of the United States weakened the League and made it more difficult for the organization to realize Wilson's dream of a peaceful community of nations.

The Russian Revolution and America's Response

Since early 1917, the turmoil of the Russian Revolution had changed the climate of both foreign affairs and domestic politics. The repressive and corrupt regime of Czar Nicholas II had been overthrown in March 1917 by a coalition of forces demanding change. The new provisional government, headed by Alexander Kerensky, vowed to keep Russia in the fight against Germany. But the war had taken a terrible toll on Russian soldiers and civilians, and had become very unpopular. The radical Bolsheviks, led by V. I. Lenin, gained a large following by promising "peace, land, and bread," and they began plotting to seize power. The Bolsheviks followed the teachings of German revolutionary Karl Marx, emphasizing the inevitability of class struggle and the replacement of capitalism by communism.

In November 1917 the Bolsheviks took control of the Russian government. In March 1918, to the dismay of the Allies, the new Bolshevik government negotiated a separate peace with Germany, the Treaty of Brest-Litovsk. Russia was now lost as a military ally, and her defection made possible a massive shift of German troops to the Western Front. As civil war raged within Russia, British and French leaders wanted to help counterrevolutionary forces overthrow the new Bolshevik regime, as well as reclaim military supplies originally sent for use against the Germans.

Although sympathetic to the March revolution overthrowing the czar, President Wilson refused to recognize the authority of the Bolshevik regime. Bolshevism represented a threat to the liberal-capitalist values that Wilson believed to be the foundation of America's moral and material power and that provided the basis for the Fourteen Points. At the same time, however, Wilson at first resisted British and French pressure to intervene in Russia, citing his commitment to national self-determination and noninterference in other countries' internal affairs. "I believe in letting them work out their own salvation, even though they wallow in anarchy for a while," he wrote to one Allied diplomat.

By August 1918, as the Russian political and military situation became increasingly chaotic, Wilson agreed to British and French plans for sending troops to Siberia and northern Russia. Meanwhile, Japan poured troops into Siberia and northern Manchuria in a bid to control the commercially important Chinese Eastern and Trans-Siberian Railways. After the Wilson administration negotiated an agreement that placed these strategic railways under international control, the restoration and protection of the railways became the primary concern of American military forces in Russia. Wilson justified the intervention on trade and commercial grounds, telling Congress, "It is essential that we maintain the policy of the Open Door." But however reluctantly, the United States had in fact become an active, anti-Bolshevik participant in the Russian civil war.

Wilson's idealistic support for self-determination had succumbed to the demands of international power politics. Eventually, some 15,000 American troops served in northern and eastern Russia, with some remaining until 1920. They stayed for two reasons: to counter Japanese influence, and because Wilson did not want to risk alienating the British and French, who opposed withdrawal. The Allied armed intervention widened the gulf between Russia and the West. In March 1919, Russian Communists established the Third International, or Comintern. Their call for a worldwide revolution deepened Allied mistrust, and the Paris Peace Conference essentially ignored the new political reality posed by the Russian Revolution.

The Red Scare

In the United States, strikes, antiwar agitation, even racial disturbances were increasingly blamed on foreign radicals and alien ideologies. Pro-German sentiment, socialism, the IWW, and trade unionism in general, all were conveniently lumped together. The accusation of Bolshevism became a powerful weapon for turning public opinion against strikers and political dissenters of all kinds. In the 1919 Seattle general strike, for example, Mayor Ole Hanson claimed against all evidence that the strikers "want to take possession of our American Government and try to duplicate the anarchy of Russia." Months later the Seattle *Post-Intelligencer,* referring to the IWW, said: "We must smash every un-American and anti-American organization in the land. We must put to death the leaders of this gigantic conspiracy of murder, pillage, and revolution."

In truth, by 1919 the American radicals were already weakened and badly split. The Socialist Party had around 40,000 members. Two small Communist Parties, made up largely of immigrants, had a total of perhaps 70,000. In the spring of 1919, a few extremists mailed bombs to prominent business and political leaders. That June, simultaneous bombings in eight cities killed two people and damaged the residence of Attorney General A. Mitchell Palmer. With public alarm growing, state and federal officials began a coordinated campaign to root out subversives and their alleged Russian connections.

Palmer used the broad authority of the 1918 Alien Act, which enabled the government to deport any immigrant found to be a member of a revolutionary organization prior to or after coming to the United States. In a series of raids in late 1919, Justice Department agents in eleven cities arrested and roughed up several hundred members of the IWW and the Union of Russian Workers. Little evidence of revolutionary intent was found, but 249 people were deported, including prominent anarchists Emma Goldman and Alexander Berkman. In early 1920 some 6,000 people in thirty-three cities, including many U.S. citizens and noncommunists, were arrested and herded into prisons and bullpens. Again, no evidence of a grand plot was found, but another 600 aliens were deported. The Palmer raids had a ripple effect around the nation, encouraging other repressive measures against radicals. In New York, the state assembly refused to seat five duly elected Socialist Party members.

A report prepared by a group of distinguished lawyers questioned the legality of the attorney general's tactics. Palmer's popularity had waned by the spring of 1920, when it became clear that his predictions of revolutionary uprisings were wildly exaggerated. But the Red Scare left an ugly legacy: wholesale violations of constitutional rights, deportations of hundreds of innocent people, fuel for the fires of nativism and intolerance. Business groups, such as the National Association of Manufacturers, found "Red-baiting" to be an effective tool in postwar efforts to keep unions out of their factories. Indeed, the government-sanctioned Red Scare reemerged later in the century as a powerful political force.

The Red Scare took its toll on the women's movement as well. Before the war, many suffragists and feminists had maintained ties and shared platforms with socialist and labor groups. The suffrage movement in particular had brought together women from very different class backgrounds and political perspectives. But the calls for "100 percent Americanism" during and after the war destroyed the fragile alliances that had made a group such as the National American Woman Suffrage Association so powerful. After the war, many women's organizations that had been divided over American involvement in the war reunited under the umbrella of the National Council for Prevention of War. But when military spokesmen in the early 1920s attacked the group for advocating communism, two of its largest affiliates—the General Federation of Women's Clubs and the Parent-Teacher Association—withdrew in fear. Hostility to radicalism marked the political climate of the 1920s, and this atmosphere narrowed the political spectrum for women activists.

The Election of 1920

The presidential contest of 1920 suggested that Americans wanted to retreat from the internationalism, reform fervor, and social tensions associated with the war. Woodrow Wilson had wanted the 1920 election to be a "solemn referendum" on the League of Nations and his conduct of the war. Ill and exhausted, Wilson did not run for reelection. A badly divided Democratic Party compromised on Governor James M. Cox of Ohio as its candidate. A proven vote-getter, Cox distanced himself from Wilson's policies, which had come under withering attack from many quarters.

The Republicans nominated Senator Warren G. Harding of Ohio. A political hack, the handsome and genial Harding had virtually no qualifications to be president, except that he looked like one. Harding's campaign was vague and ambiguous about the Versailles Treaty and almost everything else. He struck a chord with the electorate in calling for a retreat from Wilsonian idealism. "America's present need," he said, "is not heroics but healing; not nostrums but normalcy; not revolution but restoration."

The notion of a "return to normalcy" proved very attractive to voters exhausted by the war, inflation, big government, and social dislocation. Harding won the greatest landslide in history to that date, carrying every state outside the South and taking the popular vote by 16 million to 9 million. Republicans retained their majorities in the House and Senate as well. Socialist Eugene

Debs, still a powerful symbol of the dream of radical social change, managed to poll 900,000 votes from jail. But the overall vote repudiated Wilson and the progressive movement. Americans seemed eager to pull back from moralism in public and international controversies. Yet many of the economic, social, and cultural changes wrought by the war would accelerate during the 1920s. In truth, there could never be a "return to normalcy."

CHRONOLOGY

1903 U.S. obtains Panama canal rights

1904 Roosevelt Corollary justifies U.S. intervention in the Americas

1905 President Theodore Roosevelt mediates peace treaty between Japan and Russia at Portsmouth Conference

1908 Root-Takahira Agreement with Japan affirms status quo in Asia and Open Door policy in China

1911 Mexican Revolution begins

1914 U.S. forces invade Mexico

Panama Canal opens

First World War begins in Europe

President Woodrow Wilson issues proclamation of neutrality

1915 Germany declares war zone around Great Britain

German U-boat sinks *Lusitania*

1916 Pancho Villa raids New Mexico, is pursued by General Pershing

Wilson is reelected

National Defense Act establishes preparedness program

1917 February: Germany resumes unrestricted submarine warfare

March: Zimmermann note, suggesting a German-Mexican alliance, shocks Americans

April: U.S. declares war on the Central Powers

Committee on Public Information is established

May: Selective Service Act is passed

June: Espionage Act is passed

July: Race riot occurs in East St. Louis

War Industries Board is established

August: Food Administration and Fuel Administration are established

November: Bolshevik Revolution begins in Russia

1918 January: Wilson unveils Fourteen Points

April: National War Labor Board is established

May: Sedition Act is passed

June: Eugene Debs is arrested for defending antiwar protesters

U.S. troops begin to see action in France

U.S. troops serve in Russia

November: Armistice ends war

1919 January: Eighteenth Amendment (Prohibition) is ratified

Wilson serves as Chief U.S.negotiator at Paris Peace Conference

June: Versailles Treaty is signed in Paris

July: Race riot breaks out in Chicago

Steel strike begins in several midwestern cities

September: Wilson suffers stroke while touring country in support of Versailles Treaty

November: Henry Cabot Lodge's version of the Versailles Treaty is rejected by the Senate

Palmer raids begin

1920 March: Senate finally votes down Versailles Treaty and League of Nations

August: Nineteenth Amendment (woman suffrage) is ratified

November: Warren G. Harding is elected president

CONCLUSION

Compared to the casualties and social upheavals endured by the European powers, the Great War's impact on American life might appear slight. Yet the war created economic, social, and political dislocations that helped reshape American life long after Armistice Day. Republican administrations invoked the wartime partnership between government and industry to justify an aggressive peacetime policy fostering cooperation between the state and business. Wartime production needs contributed to what economists later called "the second industrial revolution." Patriotic fervor and the exaggerated specter of Bolshevism were used to repress radicalism, organized labor, feminism, and the entire legacy of progressive reform.

The wartime measure of national prohibition evolved into perhaps the most contentious social issue of peacetime. Sophisticated use of sales techniques, psychology, and propaganda during the war helped define the newly powerful advertising and public relations industries of the 1920s. The growing visibility of immigrants and African Americans, especially in the nation's cities, provoked a xenophobic and racist backlash in the politics of the 1920s. More than anything else, the desire for "normalcy" reflected the deep anxieties evoked by America's wartime experience.

REVIEW QUESTIONS

1. What central issues drew the United States deeper into international politics in the early years of the century? How did American presidents justify a more expansive role? What diplomatic and military policies did they exploit for these ends?
2. Compare the arguments for and against American participation in the Great War. Which Americans were most likely to support entry? Which were more likely to oppose it?
3. How did mobilizing for war change the economy and its relationship to government? Which of these changes, if any, spilled over to the postwar years?
4. How did the war affect political life in the United States? What techniques were used to stifle dissent? What was the war's political legacy?
5. To what extent was the war an extension of progressivism?
6. Analyze the impact of the war on American workers. How did the conflict affect the lives of African Americans and women?
7. What principles guided Woodrow Wilson's Fourteen Points? How would you explain the United States' failure to ratify the Treaty of Versailles?

RECOMMENDED READING

Robert H. Ferrell, *Woodrow Wilson and World War I* (1985). A close analysis of Wilson's handling of wartime diplomacy and domestic politics.

Martin Gilbert, *The First World War: A Complete History* (1994). An ambitious overview of the Great War from a global perspective.

Maureen Greenwald, *Women, War, and Work* (1980). The best account of the impact of the war on working women.

David M. Kennedy, *Over Here* (1980). The best, most comprehensive one-volume history of the political and economic impact of the war on the domestic front.

Thomas J. Knock, *To End All Wars: Woodrow Wilson and the Quest for a New World Order* (1992). A fine analysis of Wilson's internationalism, its links to his domestic policies, and his design for the League of Nations.

Walter LaFeber, *The American Age* (1989). A fine survey of the history of U.S. foreign policy that includes an analysis of the pre–World War I era.

Paul L. Murphy, *World War I and the Origin of Civil Liberties* (1979). A good overview of the various civil liberties issues raised by the war and government efforts to suppress dissent.

Ronald Schaffer, *America in the Great War: The Rise of the War Welfare State* (1991). Excellent material on how the war transformed the relationship between business and government and spurred improved conditions for industrial workers.

Joe William Trotter Jr., ed., *The Great Migration in Historical Perspective* (1991). An excellent collection of essays examining the Great Migration, with special attention to issues of class and gender within the African American community.

Neil A. Wynn, *From Progressivism to Prosperity: World War I and American Society* (1986). An illuminating account of the social impact of the war on American life. Effectively connects the war experience with both progressive era trends and postwar developments in the 1920s.

ADDITIONAL BIBLIOGRAPHY

Becoming a World Power

Richard H. Collin, *Theodore Roosevelt's Caribbean* (1990)
John Dobson, *America's Ascent: The United States Becomes a Great Power, 1880–1914* (1978)
Akira Iriye, *Pacific Estrangement* (1972)
Friedrich Katz, *The Secret War in Mexico* (1981)
Burton I. Kaufman, *Efficiency and Expansion* (1974)
Walter LaFeber, *The Panama Canal* (1978)
Lester E. Langley, *The Banana Wars: An Inner History of American Empire, 1900–1934* (1983)
Emily S. Rosenberg, *Spreading the American Dream* (1982)

The Great War

Lloyd E. Ambrosius, *Woodrow Wilson and the American Diplomatic Tradition* (1987)
Paul Fussell, *The Great War and Modern Memory* (1973)
James Joll, *The Origins of the First World War* (1984)
C. Roland Marchand, *The American Peace Movement and Social Reform, 1898–1918* (1973)

American Mobilization

A. E. Barbeau and Florette Henri, *The Unknown Soldiers: Black American Troops in World War I* (1974)
John W. Chambers, *To Raise an Army: The Draft in Modern America* (1987)
J. Garry Clifford, *Citizen Soldiers* (1972)
Edward M. Coffman, *The War to End All Wars* (1968)
Charles Gilbert, *American Financing of World War I* (1970)
Stephen Vaughn, *Holding Fast the Inner Lines: Democracy, Nationalism, and the Committee on Public Information* (1980)
Russell Weigley, *The American Way of War* (1973)

Over Here

Daniel R. Beaver, *Newton D. Baker and the American War Effort, 1917–1919* (1966)
Allen J. Brandt, *No Magic Bullet: A Social History of Venereal Disease in the United States since 1880* (1985)
Valerie J. Conner, *The National War Labor Board* (1983)
Frank L. Grubbs Jr., *Samuel Gompers and the Great War* (1982)
Ellis W. Hawley, *The Great War and the Search for Modern Order*, 2d ed. (1992)
Jeffrey Haydu, *Making American Industries Safe for Democracy* (1997)
John F. McClymer, *War and Welfare: Social Engineering in America, 1890–1925* (1980)
David Montgomery, *The Fall of the House of Labor* (1987)
Barbara Steinson, *American Women's Activism in World War I* (1982)

Repression and Reaction

David Brody, *Labor in Crisis: The Steel Strike of 1919* (1965)
James P. Grossman, *Land of Hope: Chicago, Black Southerners, and the Great Migration* (1989)
Florette Henri, *Black Migration: Movement Northward, 1900–1920* (1975)
Frederick C. Luebke, *Bonds of Loyalty: German Americans and World War I* (1974)
Harold C. Peterson and Gilbert Fite, *Opponents of War, 1917–1918* (1968)
William Preston Jr., *Aliens and Dissenters: Federal Suppression of Radicals, 1903–1933* (1966)
William M. Tuttle Jr., *Race Riot: Chicago in the Red Summer of 1919* (1970)

An Uneasy Peace

Dana Frank, *Purchasing Power: Consumer Organizing, Gender, and the Seattle Labor Movement, 1919–1929* (1994)
Lloyd Gardner, *Safe for Democracy: The Anglo-American Response to Revolution, 1913–1923* (1984)
Robert D. Johnson, *The Peace Progressives and American Foreign Relations* (1995)
N. Gordon Levin Jr., *Woodrow Wilson and World Politics* (1968)
Robert K. Murray, *Red Scare: A Study in National Hysteria, 1919–1920* (1955)
Richard Polenberg, *Fighting Faiths: The Abrams Case, the Supreme Court, and Free Speech* (1987)
Stuart Rochester, *American Liberal Disillusionment in the Wake of World War I* (1977)
Ralph Stone, *The Irreconcilables: The Fight against the League of Nations* (1970)

Biography

Bruce Clayton, *Forgotten Prophet: The Life of Randolph Bourne* (1984)
Kendrick Clements, *Woodrow Wilson: World Statesman* (1987)
Stanley Coben, *A. Mitchell Palmer* (1963)
Arthur S. Link, *Woodrow Wilson: War, Revolution, and Peace* (1979)
Jordan Schwarz, *The Speculator: Bernard M. Baruch in Washington, 1917–1965* (1981)
Frank E. Vandiver, *Black Jack: The Life and Times of John J. Pershing* (1977)
Jacqueline van Voris, *Carrie Chapman Catt* (1987)

CHAPTER TWENTY-THREE

THE TWENTIES

1920–1929

Thomas Hart Benton, *City Activities with Dance Hall* from America Today, 1930. Distemper and egg tempera with oil glaze on gessoed linen, 92 x 134 ½ in. Collection, The Equitable Life Assurance Society of the United States. Photo 1988 by Dorothy Zeidman.

CHAPTER OUTLINE

AMERICAN COMMUNITIES

The Movie Audience and Hollywood: Mass Culture Creates a New National Community

Inside midtown Manhattan's magnificent new Roxy Theater, a sellout crowd eagerly settled in for opening night. Outside, thousands of fans cheered wildly at the arrival of movie stars such as Charlie Chaplin, Gloria Swanson, and Harold Lloyd. A squadron of smartly uniformed ushers guided patrons under a five-story-tall rotunda to some 6,200 velvet-covered seats. The audience marveled at the huge gold and rose-colored murals, classical statuary, plush carpeting, and Gothic-style windows. It was easy to believe newspaper reports that the theater had cost $10 million to build. Suddenly, light flooded the orchestra pit and 110 musicians began playing "The Star Spangled Banner." A troupe of 100 performers took the stage, dancing ballet numbers and singing old southern melodies such as "My Old Kentucky Home" and "Swanee River." Congratulatory telegrams from President Calvin Coolidge and other dignitaries flashed on the screen. Finally, the evening's feature presentation, *The Love of Sunya*, starring Gloria Swanson, began. Samuel L. "Roxy" Rothapfel, the theater's designer, had realized his grand dream—to build "the cathedral of the motion picture."

When Roxy's opened in March 1927, nearly 60 million Americans "worshiped" each week at movie theaters across the nation. The "movie palaces" of the 1920s were designed to transport patrons to exotic places and different times. As film pioneer Marcus Loew put it, "We sell tickets to theaters, not movies." Every large community boasted at least one opulent movie theater. Houston's Majestic was built to represent an ancient Italian garden; it had a ceiling made to look like an open sky, complete with stars and cloud formations. The Tivoli in Chicago featured opulent French Renaissance decor; Grauman's Egyptian in Los Angeles re-created the look of a pharaoh's tomb; and Albuquerque's Kimo drew inspiration from Navajo art and religion.

The remarkable popularity of motion pictures, and later radio, forged a new kind of community. A huge national audience regularly went to the movies, and the same entertainment could be enjoyed virtually anywhere in the country by just about everyone. Movies emerged as the most popular form in the new mass culture, with an appeal that extended far beyond the films themselves, or even the theaters. Americans embraced the cult of celebrity, voraciously consuming fan magazines, gossip columns, and news of the stars. By the 1920s, the production center for this dream world was Hollywood, California, a suburb of Los Angeles that had barely existed in 1890.

Motion picture companies found Hollywood an alluring alternative to the east coast cities where they had been born. Its reliably sunny and dry climate was ideal for year-round filming. Its unique surroundings offered a perfect variety of scenic locations—mountains, desert, ocean—and downtown Los Angeles was only an hour away. Land was cheap and plentiful. And because Los Angeles was the leading nonunion, open-shop city in the country, so was labor. By the early 1920s Hollywood produced more than 80 percent of the nation's motion pictures and was assuming mythical status. The isolation of the town, its great distance from the eastern cities, its lack of traditional sources of culture and learning—all contributed to movie folk looking at life in a self-consciously "Hollywood" way.

With its feel of a modern frontier boomtown, Hollywood was a new kind of American community. It lured the young and cosmopolitan with the promise of upward mobility and a new way of life. Most of the top studio executives were Jewish immigrants from eastern and central Europe. In contrast to most Americans, who hailed from rural areas or small towns, more than half of Hollywood's writers, directors, editors, and actors were born in cities of over 100,000. Two-thirds of its performers were under thirty-five, and three-fourths of its actresses were under twenty-five. More than 90 percent of its writers (women made up one-third to one-half of this key group) had attended college or worked in journalism. The movies this untypical community created evoked the pleasures of leisure, consumption, and personal freedom, redefining the nation's cultural values in the 1920s.

Movie stars dominated Hollywood. Charlie Chaplin, Mary Pickford, Rudolph Valentino, Gloria Swanson, and Douglas Fairbanks became popular idols as much for their highly publicized private lives as for their roles on screen. Many accumulated great wealth, becoming the nation's experts on how to live well. Movie folk built luxurious mansions in a variety of architectural styles and outfitted them with swimming pools, tennis courts, golf courses, and lavish gardens.

Visitors often noted that Hollywood had no museums, art galleries, live theater, or other traditional institutions of high culture. How would the town's wealthy movie elite spend their time and money? By 1916 Charlie Chaplin, a working-class immigrant from the London slums, was earning $10,000 a week for the comedies that made his the most famous face in the world. He recalled trying to figure out what to do with his new wealth. "The money I earned was legendary, a symbol in figures, for I had never actually seen it. I therefore had to do something to prove I had it. So I procured a secretary, a valet, a car, a chauffeur."

Ordinary Americans found it easy to identify with movie stars despite their wealth and status. Unlike industrialists or politicians, stars had no social authority over large groups of employees or voters. They, too, had to answer to a boss, and most had risen from humble beginnings. But above all, Hollywood, like the movies it churned out, represented for millions of Americans new possibilities: freedom, material success, upward mobility, and the chance to remake one's very identity. By the end of the decade the Hollywood "dream factory" had helped forge a national community whose collective aspirations and desires were increasingly defined by those possibilities, even if relatively few Americans realized them during the 1920s.

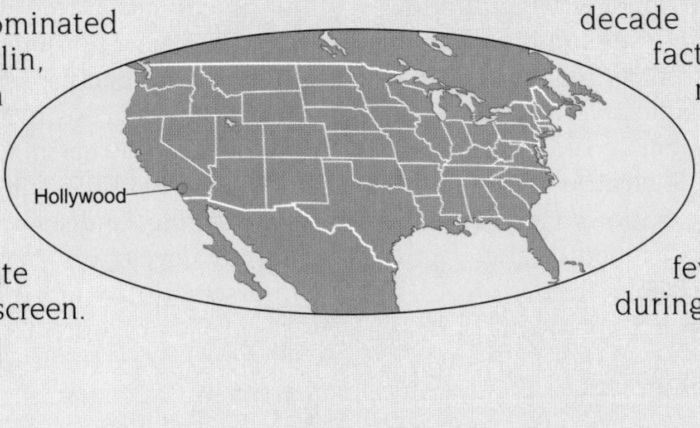

KEY TOPICS

- A second industrial revolution that transforms the economy
- The promise and limits of prosperity in the 1920s
- New mass media and the culture of consumption
- Republican Party dominance
- Political and cultural opposition to modern trends

POSTWAR PROSPERITY AND ITS PRICE

Republican Warren G. Harding won the presidency in 1920, largely thanks to his nostalgic call for a "return to normalcy." But in the decade following the end of World War I, the American economy underwent profound structural changes that guaranteed life would never be "normal" again. The 1920s saw an enormous increase in the efficiency of production, a steady climb in real wages, a decline in the length of the average employee's work week, and a boom in consumer goods industries. Americans shared unevenly in the postwar prosperity, and by the end of the decade certain basic weaknesses in the economy helped to bring on the worst depression in American history. Yet overall, the nation experienced crucial transformations in how it organized its business, earned its living, and enjoyed its leisure time.

The Second Industrial Revolution

The prosperity of the 1920s rested on what historians have called the "second industrial revolution" in American manufacturing, in which technological innovations made it possible to increase industrial output without expanding the labor force. Electricity replaced steam as the main power source for industry in these years, making possible the replacement of older machinery with more efficient and flexible electric machinery. In 1914 only 30 percent of the nation's factories were electrified; by 1929, 70 percent relied on the electric motor rather than the steam engine.

Much of the newer, automatic machinery could be operated by unskilled and semiskilled workers, and it boosted the overall efficiency of American industry. Thus in 1929 the average worker in manufacturing produced roughly three-quarters more per hour than he or she had in 1919. The machine industry itself, particularly the manufacture of electrical machinery, led in productivity gains, enjoying one of the fastest rates of expansion. It employed more workers than any other manufacturing sector—some 1.1 million in 1929—supplying not only a growing home market but 35 percent of the world market as well.

During the late nineteenth century heavy industries such as machine tools, railroads, iron, and steel had pioneered mass-production techniques. These industries manufactured what economists call producer-durable goods. In the 1920s, modern mass-production techniques were increasingly applied as well to newer consumer-durable goods—automobiles, radios, washing machines, and telephones—permitting firms to make large profits while keeping prices affordable. Other consumer-based industries, such as canning, chemicals, synthetics, and plastics, began to change the everyday lives of millions of Americans. With more efficient management, greater mechanization, intensive product research, and ingenious sales and advertising methods, the consumer-based industries helped to nearly double industrial production in the 1920s.

America experienced a building boom during the 1920s, and its construction industry played a large role in the new prosperity. Expenditures for residential housing, nonresidential building, and public construction projects all showed steady growth after 1921. The demand for new housing was unprecedented, particularly with the backlog created during World War I, when little new construction took place. The growth in automobile ownership, as well as improvements in public mass transit, made suburban living more attractive to families and suburban construction more profitable for developers. Commercial banks, savings and loan associations, and insurance companies provided greatly expanded credit for home buying. America's residential mortgage debt jumped from about $8 billion in 1919 to $27 billion in 1929.

The Modern Corporation

The organization and techniques of American business underwent crucial changes during the postwar decade. In the late nineteenth century, individual entrepreneurs such as John D. Rockefeller in oil and Andrew Carnegie in steel had provided a model for

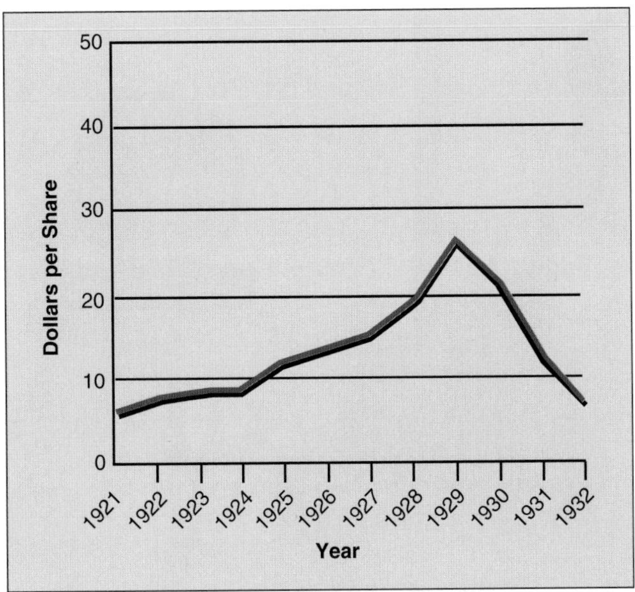

Stock Market Prices, 1921–1932 *Common stock prices rose steeply during the 1920s. Although only about 4 million Americans owned stocks during the period, "stock watching" became something of a national sport.*

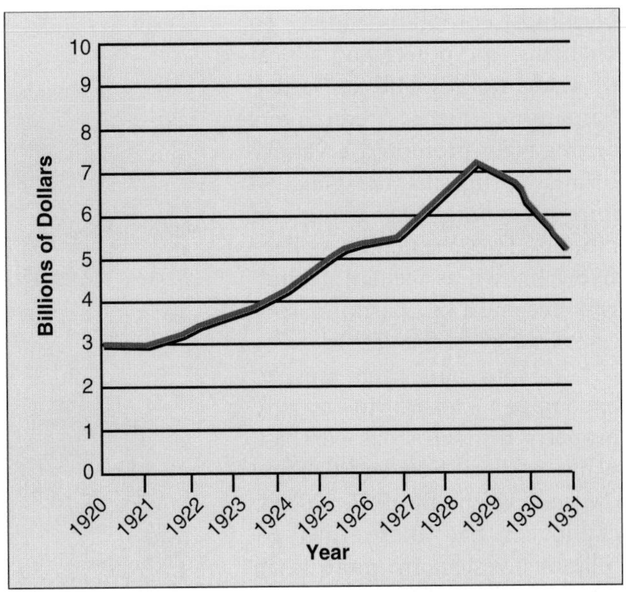

Consumer Debt, 1920–1931 *The expansion of consumer borrowing was a key component of the era's prosperity. These figures do not include mortgages or money borrowed to purchase stocks. They reveal the great increase in "installment buying" for such consumer durable goods as automobiles and household appliances.*

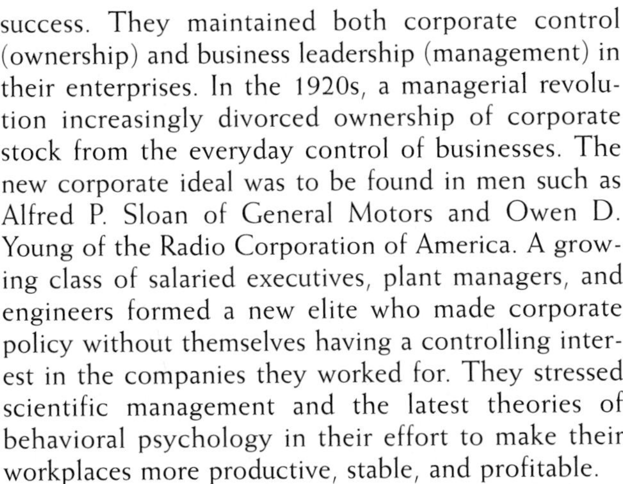

success. They maintained both corporate control (ownership) and business leadership (management) in their enterprises. In the 1920s, a managerial revolution increasingly divorced ownership of corporate stock from the everyday control of businesses. The new corporate ideal was to be found in men such as Alfred P. Sloan of General Motors and Owen D. Young of the Radio Corporation of America. A growing class of salaried executives, plant managers, and engineers formed a new elite who made corporate policy without themselves having a controlling interest in the companies they worked for. They stressed scientific management and the latest theories of behavioral psychology in their effort to make their workplaces more productive, stable, and profitable.

During the 1920s, the most successful corporations were those that led in three key areas: the integration of production and distribution; product diversification; and the expansion of industrial research. Until the end of World War I, for example, the chemical manufacturer Du Pont had specialized in explosives such as gunpowder. After the war Du Pont moved aggressively into the consumer market with a diverse array of products. The company created separate but integrated divisions that produced and distributed new fabrics (such as rayon), paints, dyes, and celluloid products (such as artificial sponges). The great electrical manufacturers—General Electric and Westinghouse—similarly transformed themselves after the war. Previously concentrating on lighting and power equipment, they now diversified into household appliances like radios, washing machines, and refrigerators. The chemical and electrical industries also led the way in industrial research, hiring personnel to develop new products and test their commercial viability.

By 1929 the 200 largest corporations owned nearly half the nation's corporate wealth—that is, physical plant, stock, and property. Half the total industrial income—revenue from sales of goods—was concentrated in 100 corporations. Oligopoly—the control of a market by a few large producers—became the norm. Four companies packed almost three-quarters of all American meat. Another four rolled nine out of every ten cigarettes. National chain grocery stores, clothing shops, and pharmacies began squeezing out local neighborhood businesses. One grocery chain alone, the Great Atlantic and Pacific Tea Company (A&P), accounted for 10 percent of all retail food sales in America. Its 15,000 stores sold a greater volume of goods than Ford Motor Company at its peak. These changes meant that Americans were increasingly members of national consumer communities, buying the same brands all over the country, as opposed to locally produced goods.

Welfare Capitalism

The wartime gains made by organized labor and the active sympathy shown to trade unions by government agencies such as the National War Labor Board troubled most corporate leaders. To challenge the power and appeal of trade unions and collective bargaining, large employers aggressively promoted a variety of new programs designed to improve worker well-being and morale. These schemes, collectively known as welfare capitalism, became a key part of corporate strategy in the 1920s.

One approach was to encourage workers to acquire property through stock-purchase plans or, less frequently, home ownership plans. By 1927, 800,000 employees had more than $1 billion invested in more than 300 companies. Other programs offered workers insurance policies covering accidents, illness, old age, and death. By 1928 some 6 million workers had group insurance coverage valued at $7.5 billion. Many plant managers and personnel departments consciously worked to improve safety conditions, provide medical services, and establish sports and recreation programs for workers. Employers hoped such measures would encourage workers to identify personally with the company and discourage complaints on the job. To some extent they succeeded. But welfare capitalism could not solve the most chronic problems faced by industrial workers: seasonal unemployment, low wages, long hours, and unhealthy factory conditions.

The A&P *grocery chain expanded from* 400 *stores in* 1912 *to more than* 15,000 *by the end of the* 1920s, *making it a familiar sight in communities across* America. A&P *advertisements, like this one from* 1927, *emphasized cleanliness, order, and the availability of name brand goods at discount prices.*

Large corporations also mounted an effective anti-union campaign in the early 1920s called "the American plan," a name meant to associate unionism with foreign and un-American ideas. Backed by powerful business lobbies such as the National Association of Manufacturers and the Chamber of Commerce, campaign leaders called for the open shop, in which no employee would be compelled to join a union. If a union existed, nonmembers would still get whatever wages and rights the union had won—a policy that put organizers at a disadvantage in signing up new members.

The open shop undercut the gains won in a union shop, where new employees had to join an existing union, or a closed shop, where employers agreed to hire only union members. As alternatives, large employers such as U.S. Steel and International Harvester began setting up company unions. Their intent was to substitute largely symbolic employee representation in management conferences for the more confrontational process of collective bargaining. Company unions were often established simultaneously with anti-union campaigns in specific industries or communities.

These management strategies contributed to a sharp decline in the ranks of organized labor. Total union membership dropped from about 5 million in 1920 to 3.5 million in 1926. A large proportion of the remaining union members were concentrated in the skilled crafts of the building and printing trades. A conservative and timid union leadership was also responsible for the trend. William Green, who became president of the American Federation of Labor after the death of Samuel Gompers in 1924, showed no real interest in getting unorganized workers like those in the growing mass-production industries of automobiles, steel, and electrical goods into unions. The federal government, which had provided limited wartime support for unions, now reverted to a more probusiness posture. The Supreme Court in particular was unsympathetic toward unions, consistently upholding the use of injunctions to prevent strikes, picketing, and other union activities.

The Auto Age

In their classic community study *Middletown* (1929), sociologists Robert and Helen Lynd noted the dramatic impact of the car on the social life of Muncie, Indiana. "Why on earth do you need to study what's changing this country?" asked one lifelong Muncie resident in 1924. "I can tell you what's happening in just four letters: A-U-T-O!" This remark hardly seems much of an exaggeration today. No other single development could match the impact of the postwar automobile explosion on the way Americans worked, lived, and played. The auto industry offered the clearest example of the rise to prominence of consumer durables. During the 1920s, America made approximately 85 percent of all the world's passenger cars. By 1929 the motor vehicle industry was the most productive in the United States in terms of value. In that year the industry added 4.8 million new cars to the more than 26 million—roughly one for every five people—already on American roads.

This extraordinary new industry had mushroomed in less than a generation. Its great pioneer, Henry Ford, had shown how the use of a continuous assembly line could drastically reduce the number of worker hours required to produce a single vehicle. Ford revolutionized the factory shop floor with new, custom-built machinery, such as the engine-boring drill press and the pneumatic wrench, and a more efficient layout. "Every piece of work in the shop moves," Ford boasted. "It may move on hooks or overhead chains, going to assembly in the exact order in which the parts are required; it may travel on a moving platform, or it may go by gravity, but the point is that there is no lifting or trucking of anything other than materials." In 1913 it took thirteen hours to produce one automobile. In 1914, at his sprawling new Highland Park assembly plant just outside Detroit, Ford's system finished one car every ninety minutes. By 1925, cars were rolling off his assembly line at the rate of one every ten seconds.

In 1914 Ford startled American industry by inaugurating a new wage scale: $5 for an eight-hour day. This was roughly double the going pay rate for industrial labor, and a shorter workday as well. But in defying the conventional economic wisdom of the day, Ford acted less out of benevolence than out of shrewdness. He understood that workers were consumers as well as producers, and the new wage scale helped boost sales of Ford cars. It also reduced the high turnover rate in his labor force and increased worker efficiency. Roughly two-thirds of the labor force at Ford consisted of immigrants from southern and eastern Europe. By the early 1920s Ford also employed about 5,000 African Americans, more than any other large American corporation. Ford's mass-production system and economies of scale permitted him to progressively reduce the price of his cars, bringing them within the reach of millions of Americans. The famous Model T, thoroughly standardized and available only in black, cost just under $300 in 1924—about three months' wages for the best-paid factory workers.

Finished automobiles roll off the moving assembly line at the Ford Motor Company, Highland Park, Michigan, ca.1920. During the 1920s Henry Ford achieved the status of folk hero, as his name became synonymous with the techniques of mass production. Ford cultivated a public image of himself as the heroic genius of the auto industry, greatly exaggerating his personal achievements.

By 1927 Ford had produced 15 million Model Ts. But by then the company faced stiff competition from General Motors, which had developed an effective new marketing strategy. Under the guidance of Alfred P. Sloan, GM organized into separate divisions, each of which appealed to a different market segment. Cadillac, for example, produced GM's most expensive car, which was targeted at the wealthy buyer; Chevrolet produced its least expensive model, which was targeted at working-class and lower-middle-class buyers. The GM business structure, along with its attempts to match production with demand through sophisticated market research and sales forecasting, became a widely copied model for other large American corporations.

The auto industry provided a large market for makers of steel, rubber, glass, and petroleum products. It stimulated public spending for good roads and extended the housing boom to new suburbs. Showrooms, repair shops, and gas stations appeared in thousands of communities. New small enterprises, from motels to billboard advertising to roadside diners, sprang up as motorists took to the highway. The rapid development of Florida and California, in particular, was partly a response to the growing influence of the automobile and the new possibilities it presented for seeing far-off places.

Automobiles widened the experience of millions of Americans. They made the exploration of the world outside the local community easier and more attractive. For some the car merely reinforced old social patterns, making it easier for them to get to church on Sunday, for example, or visit neighbors. Others used their cars to go to new places, shop in nearby cities, or take vacations. The automobile made leisure, in the sense of getting away from the routines of work and school, a more regular part of everyday life. It undoubtedly also changed the courtship practices of America's youth. Young people took advantage of the car to gain privacy and distance from their parents. "What on earth do you want me to do?" complained one Middletown high school girl to her anxious father. "Just sit around home all evening?" Many had their first sexual experiences in a car.

Until 1924 Henry Ford had disdained national advertising for his cars. But as General Motors gained a competitive edge by making yearly changes in style and technology, Ford was forced to pay more attention to advertising. This ad was directed at "Mrs. Consumer," combining appeals to both female independence and motherly duties.

Cities and Suburbs

Cars also promoted urban and suburban growth. The federal census for 1920 was the first in American history in which the proportion of the population that lived in urban places (those with 2,500 or more people) exceeded the proportion of the population living in rural areas. More revealing of urban growth was the steady increase in the number of big cities. In 1910 there were sixty cities with more than 100,000 inhabitants; in 1920 there were sixty-eight; and by 1930 there were ninety-two. During the 1920s New York grew by 20 percent to nearly 7 million, whereas Detroit, home of the auto industry, doubled its population, to nearly 2 million.

Cities promised business opportunity, good jobs, cultural richness, and personal freedom. They attracted millions of Americans, white and black, from small towns and farms, as well as immigrants from abroad. Immigrants were drawn to cities by the presence there of family and people of like background in already established ethnic communities. In a continuation of the Great Migration that began during World War I, roughly 1.5 million African Americans from the rural south migrated to cities in search of economic opportunities during the 1920s, doubling the black populations of New York, Chicago, Detroit, and Houston.

Cities grew both vertically and horizontally in these years. Skylines around the country were remade as architects took advantage of steel-skeleton construction technology to build skyscrapers. By 1930, American cities boasted nearly 400 buildings more than 20 stories tall. New York's Empire State Building, completed in 1931, was the tallest building in the world, rising 1,250 feet into the sky. It had room for 25,000 commercial and residential tenants in its 102 stories.

Houston offers a good example of how the automobile shaped an urban community. In 1910 it was a sleepy railroad town with a population of about 75,000 that served the Texas Gulf coast and interior. The enormous demand for gasoline and other petroleum products helped transform the city into a busy center for oil refining. Its population soared to 300,000 by the end of the 1920s. Abundant cheap land and the absence of zoning ordinances, combined with the availability of the automobile, pushed Houston to expand horizontally rather than vertically. It became the archetypal decentralized, low-density city, sprawling miles in each direction from downtown, and thoroughly dependent upon automobiles and roads for its sense of community. Other

Sunbelt cities, such as Los Angeles, Miami, and San Diego, experienced similar land use patterns and sharp population growth during the decade.

Suburban communities grew at twice the rate of their core cities, also thanks largely to the automobile boom. Undeveloped land on the fringes of cities became valuable real estate. Grosse Pointe, near Detroit, and Elmwood Park, near Chicago, grew more than 700 percent in ten years. Long Island's Nassau County, just east of New York City, tripled in population. All the new "automobile suburbs" differed in important ways from earlier suburbs built along mass transit lines. The car allowed for a larger average lot size, and in turn lower residential density. It also became essential for commuting to work and encouraged the movement of workplaces out of the central city. The suburbs would increasingly become not only places to live but centers for working and shopping as well.

Exceptions: Agriculture, Ailing Industries

Amid prosperity and progress, there were large pockets of the country that lagged behind. Advances in real income and improvements in the standard of living for workers and farmers were uneven at best. During the 1920s one-quarter of all American workers were employed in agriculture, yet the farm sector failed to share in the general prosperity. The years 1914–19 had been a kind of golden age for the nation's farmers. Increased wartime demand, along with the devastation of much of European agriculture, had led to record-high prices for many crops. In addition, the wartime Food Administration had encouraged a great increase in agricultural production. But with the war's end, American farmers began to suffer from a chronic worldwide surplus of such farm staples as cotton, hogs, and corn.

Prices began to drop sharply in 1920. Cotton, which sold at thirty-seven cents a pound in mid-1920, fell to fourteen cents by year's end. Hog and cattle prices declined nearly 50 percent. By 1921 net farm income was down more than half from the year before. Land values also dropped, wiping out billions in capital investment. Behind these aggregate statistics were hundreds of thousands of individual human tragedies on the nation's 6 million farms. A 1928 song, "Eleven Cent Cotton," expressed the farmer's lament:

'Leven cent cotton, forty cent meat,
How in the world can a poor man eat?
Pray for the sunshine, 'cause it will rain,
Things gettin' worse, drivin' us insane.

During the war many farmers had gone heavily into debt to buy land and expand operations with new machinery. Farm mortgages doubled between 1910 and 1920, from $3.3 billion to $6.7 billion, and another $2.7 billion was added to the total by 1925. These debts saddled farmers with fixed expenses that grew crushingly burdensome as prices spiraled downward. American farm products, moreover, faced stiffer competition abroad from reviving European agriculture and the expanding output from Canada, Argentina, and Australia. Efforts to ease the farmer's plight through governmental reform were largely unsuccessful. Individual farmers, traditionally independent, could not influence the price of commodities they sold or bought. It was extremely difficult for farmers to act collectively.

To be sure, some farmers thrived. Wheat production jumped more than 300 percent during the 1920s. Across the plains of Kansas, Nebraska, Colorado, Oklahoma, and Texas, wheat farmers brought the methods of industrial capitalism to the land. They hitched disc plows and combined harvester-threshers to gasoline-powered tractors, tearing up millions of acres of grassland to create a vast wheat factory. With prices averaging above $1 per bushel over the decade, mechanized farming created a new class of large-scale wheat entrepreneurs on the plains. Ida Watkins, "the Wheat Queen" of Haskell County, Kansas, made a profit of $75,000 from her 2,000 acres in 1926. Hickman Price needed twenty-five combines to harvest the wheat on his Plainview, Texas, farm—34,500 acres stretching over fifty-four square miles. When the disastrous dust storms of the 1930s rolled across the grassless plains, the long-range ecological impact of destroying so much native vegetation became evident.

Improved transportation and chain supermarkets allowed for a wider and more regular distribution of such foods as oranges, lemons, and fresh green vegetables. Citrus, dairy, and truck farmers in particular profited from the growing importance of national markets. But per capita farm income remained well below what it had been in 1919, and the gap between farm and nonfarm income widened. By 1929 the average income per person on farms was $223, compared with $870 for nonfarm workers. By the end of the decade, hundreds of thousands had quit farming altogether for jobs in mills and factories. And fewer farmers owned their land. In 1930, 42 percent of all farmers were tenants, compared with 37 percent in 1919.

The most important initiatives for federal farm relief were the McNary-Haugen bills, a series of complicated measures designed to prop up and stabilize farm prices. The basic idea, borrowed from the old populist proposals of the 1890s, was for the government to purchase farm surpluses and either store them until prices rose or sell them on the world market. The result was supposed to be higher domestic prices for farm products. But President Calvin Coolidge viewed these measures as unwarranted federal interference in the economy and vetoed the McNary-Haugen Farm Relief bill of 1927 when it finally passed Congress. Hard-pressed farmers would not benefit from government relief until the New Deal programs implemented in response to the Great Depression in the 1930s.

Other large sectors of American industry also failed to share in the decade's general prosperity. As oil and natural gas gained in importance, America's coal mines became a less important source of energy. A combination of shrinking demand, new mining technology, and a series of losing strikes reduced the coal labor force by one-quarter. The United Mine Workers, perhaps the strongest AFL union in 1920 with 500,000 members, had shrunk to 75,000 by 1928. Economic hardship was widespread in many mining communities dependent on coal, particularly in Appalachia and the southern Midwest. And those miners who did work earned lower hourly wages.

The number of miles of railroad track actually decreased after 1920 as automobiles and trucks began to displace trains. In textiles, shrinking demand and overcapacity (too many factories) were chronic problems. The women's fashions of the 1920s generally required less material than had earlier fashions, and competition from synthetic fibers such as rayon depressed demand for cotton textiles. To improve profit margins, textile manufacturers in New England and other parts of the Northeast began a long-range shift of operations to the South, where nonunion shops and substandard wages became the rule. Between 1923 and 1933, 40 percent of New England's textile factories closed and nearly 100,000 of the 190,000 workers employed there lost their jobs. Older New England manufacturing centers such as Lawrence, Lowell, Nashua, Manchester, and Fall River were hard hit by this shift.

The center of the American textile industry shifted permanently to the Piedmont region of North and South Carolina. Southern mills increased their work force from 220,000 to 257,000 between 1923 and 1933. By 1933 they employed nearly 70 percent of the workers in the industry. One of the biggest new textile communities was Gastonia, North Carolina, which proudly called itself "the South's City of Spindles." As the dominant employers and overall economic powers in southern textile communities, manufacturers aggressively tried to improve productivity and cut costs. Southern mills generally operated night and day, used the newest labor-saving machinery, and cut back on the wage gains of the World War I years. Southern mill hands paid the price for what they called "stretch-out"—a catchall term describing the changes that had them tending more and more machines, receiving lower wages, working nights, and losing nearly all control over the pace and method of production.

THE NEW MASS CULTURE

New communications media reshaped American culture in the 1920s. The nickname "Roaring Twenties" captures the explosion of image- and sound-making machinery that came to dominate so much of American life. Movies, radio, new kinds of journalism, the recording industry, and a more sophisticated advertising industry were deeply connected with the new culture of consumption. They also encouraged the parallel emergence of celebrity as a defining element in modern life. As technologies of mass impression, the media established national standards and norms for much of our culture—habit, dress, language, sounds, social behavior. For millions of Americans, the new media radically altered the rhythms of everyday life and redefined what it meant to be "normal." To be sure, most working-class families had only limited access to the world of mass consumption—and many had only limited interest in it. But the new mass culture helped redefine the ideal of "the good life" and made the images, if not the substance, of it available to a national community.

Movie-Made America

The early movie industry, centered in New York and a few other big cities, had made moviegoing a regular habit for millions of Americans, especially immigrants and the working class. They flocked to cheap, storefront theaters, called nickelodeons, to watch short Westerns, slapstick comedies, melodramas, and travelogues. By 1914 there were about 18,000 "movie houses" showing motion pictures, more than 7 million daily admissions, and $300 million in annual receipts. With the shift of the industry westward to Hollywood, movies entered a new phase of business expansion.

Large studios such as Paramount, Fox, Metro-Goldwyn-Mayer (M-G-M), Universal, and Warner Brothers dominated the business with longer and more expensively produced movies—feature films. These companies were founded and controlled by immigrants from Europe, all of whom had a talent for discovering and exploiting changes in popular tastes. Adolph Zukor, the Hungarian-born head of Paramount, had been a furrier in New York City. Warsaw-born Samuel Goldwyn, a founder of M-G-M, had been a glove salesman. William Fox, of Fox Pictures, began as a garment cutter in Brooklyn. Most of the immigrant moguls had started in the business by

Mary Pickford, one of the most popular movie stars of the 1910s and 1920s, shown here reading a feminist newspaper in a publicity photo ca.1917. Pickford frequently portrayed young women struggling for economic freedom from men. She wrote weekly columns for women in which she backed suffrage and urged her female readers to be more self-sufficient. Pickford embodied the new, mass media-based "celebrity" of the 1920s.

buying or managing small movie theaters before beginning to produce films.

The studio system, which came to dominate moviemaking, was based on industrial principles. Each studio combined the three functions of production, distribution, and exhibition, and each controlled hundreds of movie theaters around the country. The era of silent films ended when Warner Brothers scored a huge hit in 1927 with *The Jazz Singer*, starring Al Jolson, which successfully introduced sound. New genres—musicals, gangster films, and screwball comedies—soon became popular. The higher costs associated with "talkies" also increased the studios' reliance on Wall Street investors and banks for working capital.

At the heart of Hollywood's success was the star system and the accompanying cult of celebrity. Stars became vital to the fantasy lives of millions of fans. For many in the audience, there was only a vague line separating the on-screen and off-screen adventures of the stars. Studio publicity, fan magazines, and gossip columns reinforced this ambiguity. Film idols, with their mansions, cars, parties, and private escapades, became the national experts on leisure and consumption. Their movies generally emphasized sexual themes and celebrated youth, athleticism, and the liberating power of consumer goods. Young Americans in particular looked to movies to learn how to dress, wear their hair, talk, or kiss. One researcher looking into the impact of moviegoing on young people asked several to keep "motion picture diaries." "Upon going to my first dance I asked the hairdresser to fix my hair like Greta Garbo's," wrote one eighteen-year-old college student. "In speaking on graduation day I did my best to finish with the swaying-like curtsy which Pola Negri taught me from the screen."

Moviemakers attracted new fans by producing more spectacular movies and by building elegant "movie palaces," like the Roxy Theater described in the opening of this chapter, in which to watch them. But many Americans, particularly in rural areas and small towns, worried about Hollywood's impact on traditional sexual morality. They attacked the permissiveness associated with Hollywood life, and many states created censorship boards to screen movies before allowing them to be shown in theaters. In 1921, the popular comedian Roscoe "Fatty" Arbuckle became embroiled in a highly publicized sex scandal when he was accused of raping and murdering actress Virginia Rappe. Although Arbuckle was acquitted, the sensational atmosphere surrounding the case badly frightened studio heads. They resolved to improve their public image.

To counter growing calls for government censorship, Hollywood's studios came up with a plan to censor themselves. In 1922 they hired Will Hays to head the Motion Picture Producers and Distributors of America. Hays was just what the immigrant moguls needed. An Indiana Republican, elder in the Presbyterian Church, and former postmaster general under President Harding, he personified midwestern Protestant respectability. As the movie industry's czar, Hays lobbied against censorship laws, wrote pamphlets defending the movie business, and began setting guidelines for what could and could not be depicted on the screen. He insisted that movies be treated like any other industrial enterprise, for he understood the relationship between Hollywood's success and the growth of the nation's consumer culture. "More and more," Hays argued in 1926, "is the motion picture being recognized as a stimulant to trade. No longer does the girl in Sullivan, Indiana, guess what the styles are going to be in three months. She knows because she sees them on the screen."

Radio Broadcasting

In the fall of 1920, Westinghouse executive Harry P. Davis noticed that amateur broadcasts from the garage of an employee had attracted attention in the local Pittsburgh press. A department store advertised radio sets capable of picking up these "wireless concerts." Davis converted this amateur station to a stronger one at the Westinghouse main plant. Beginning with the presidential election returns that November, station KDKA offered regular nightly broadcasts that were probably heard by only a few hundred people. Radio broadcasting, begun as a service for selling cheap radio sets left over from World War I, would soon sweep the nation.

Before KDKA, wireless technology had been of interest only to the military, the telephone industry, and a few thousand "ham" (amateur) operators who enjoyed communicating with each other. The "radio mania" of the early 1920s was a response to the new possibilities offered by broadcasting. By 1923 nearly 600 stations had been licensed by the Department of Commerce, and about 600,000 Americans had bought radios. Early programs included live popular music, the playing of phonograph records, talks by college professors, church services, and news and weather reports. For millions of Americans, especially in rural areas and small towns, radio provided a new and exciting link to the larger national community of consumption.

Who would pay for radio programs? In the early 1920s, owners and operators of radio stations included radio equipment manufacturers, newspapers, department stores, state universities, cities, ethnic societies, labor unions, and churches. But by the end of the decade commercial (or "toll") broadcasting emerged as the answer. The dominant corporations in the industry—General Electric, Westinghouse, Radio Corporation of America (RCA), and American Telephone and Telegraph (AT&T)—settled on the idea that advertisers would foot the bill for radio. Millions of listeners might be the consumers of radio shows, but sponsors were to be the customers. Only the sponsors and their advertising agencies enjoyed a direct relationship with broadcasters. Sponsors advertised directly or indirectly to the mass audience through such shows as the *Eveready Hour,* the *Ipana Troubadors,* and the *Taystee Loafers*. AT&T leased its nationwide system of telephone wires to allow the linking of many stations into powerful radio networks, such as the National Broadcasting Company (1926) and the Columbia Broadcasting System (1928).

Radio broadcasting created a national community of listeners, just as motion pictures created one of viewers. NBC and CBS led the way in creating popular radio programs that relied heavily on older cultural forms. The variety show, hosted by vaudeville comedians, became network radio's first important format. Radio's first truly national hit, *The Amos 'n' Andy Show* (1928), was a direct descendant of nineteenth-century "blackface" minstrel entertainment. Radio did more than any previous medium to publicize and commercialize previously isolated forms of American music such as country-and-western, blues, and jazz. Broadcasts of baseball and college football games proved especially popular. In 1930, some 600 stations were broadcasting to more than 12 million homes with radios, or roughly 40 percent of American families. By that time all the elements that characterize the present American system of broadcasting—regular daily programming paid for and produced by commercial advertisers, national networks carrying shows across the nation, and mass ownership of receiver sets in American homes—were in place.

New Forms of Journalism

A new kind of newspaper, the tabloid, became popular in the postwar years. The *New York Daily News,* founded in 1919 by Joseph M. Patterson, was the first to develop the tabloid style. Its folded-in-half page size made it convenient to read on buses or subways. The *Daily News* devoted much of its space to photographs and other illustrations. With a terse, lively reporting style that emphasized sex, scandal, and sports, *Daily News* circulation reached 400,000 in 1922 and 1.3 million by 1929.

This success spawned a host of imitators in New York and elsewhere. New papers like the *Chicago Times* and the *Los Angeles Daily News* brought the tabloid style to cities across America, while some older papers, such as the *Denver Rocky Mountain News*, adopted the new format. The circulation of existing dailies was little affected. Tabloids had instead discovered an audience of millions who had never read newspapers before. Most of these new readers were poorly educated working-class city dwellers, many of whom were immigrants or children of immigrants.

The tabloid's most popular new feature was the gossip column, invented by Walter Winchell, an obscure former vaudevillian who began writing his column "Your Broadway and Mine" for the *New York Daily Graphic* in 1924. Winchell described the secret lives of public figures with a distinctive, rapid-fire, slangy style that made the reader feel like an insider. He chronicled the connections among high society, show business stars, powerful politicians, and the underworld. By the end of the decade, scores of newspapers "syndicated" Winchell's column, making him the most widely read—and imitated—journalist in America.

Many critics dismissed the tabloids for being, as one put it, "synonomous with bad taste, vulgarity, and a degenerate sensationalism." But the popularity of the tabloids forced advertising agencies to expand their definition of the consumer market to include working-class and immigrant readers. And advertisers borrowed freely from tabloid techniques—"true confession" stories, racy headlines, shocking photos, sexually charged images—to reach that market.

Journalism followed the larger economic trend toward consolidation and merger. Newspaper chains like Hearst, Gannett, and Scripps-Howard flourished during the 1920s. There was a sizable increase in the number of these chains and in the percentage of total daily circulation that was chain-owned. By the early 1930s, the Hearst organization alone controlled twenty-six dailies in eighteen cities, accounting for 14 percent of the nation's newspaper circulation. One of every four Sunday papers sold in America was owned by the Hearst group. One journalist lamented this standardization in 1930: "When one travels through the country on a Sunday on a fast train and buys Sunday papers, one finds the same 'comics,' the same Sunday magazines, the same special 'features' in almost all of them and, of course, in most of them precisely the same Associated Press news." New forms of journalism, like radio and the movies, contributed to the growth of a national consumer community.

Advertising Modernity

A thriving advertising industry both reflected and encouraged the growing importance of consumer goods in American life. Previously, advertising had been confined mostly to staid newspapers and magazines and offered little more than basic product information. The most creative advertising was usually for dubious products, such as patent medicines. The successful efforts of the government's Committee on Public Information, set up to "sell" World War I to Americans, suggested that new techniques using modern communication media could convince people to buy a wide range of goods and services. As a profession, advertising reached a higher level of respectability, sophistication, and economic power in American life during the 1920s. Total advertising volume in all media—newspapers, magazines, radio, billboards—jumped from $1.4 billion in 1919 to $3 billion in 1929.

The larger ad agencies moved toward a more scientific approach by sponsoring market research and welcoming the language of psychology to their profession. Advertisers began focusing on the needs, desires, and anxieties of the consumer rather than on the qualities of the product. "There are certain things that most people believe," noted one ad agency executive in 1927. "The moment your copy is linked to one of those beliefs, more than half your battle is won." Ad agencies and their clients invested extraordinary amounts of time, energy, and money trying to discover and, to some extent, shape those beliefs. Leading agencies such as Lord and Thomas in Chicago and J. Walter Thompson in New York combined knowledge gained from market research and consumer surveys with carefully prepared ad copy and graphics to sell their clients' wares.

High-powered ad campaigns made new products like Fleischmann's Yeast and Kleenex household words across the country. One of the more spectacular examples of advertising effectiveness involved an old product, Listerine, which had been marketed as a general antiseptic for years by Lambert Pharmaceutical Company. A new ad campaign touting Listerine as a cure for halitosis—a scientific-sounding term for bad breath—boosted Lambert's profits from $100,000 in 1922 to more than $4 million in 1927.

Above all, advertising celebrated consumption itself as a positive good. In this sense the new advertising ethic was a therapeutic one, promising that products would contribute to the buyer's physical, psychic, or emotional well-being. Certain strategies, such as appeals to nature, medical authority, or personal freedom, were used with great success. Many of these themes and techniques are still famil-

Cigarette smoking increased enormously in the 1920s among both men and women, and tobacco companies were among the largest national advertisers. This ad linked smoking to male sexual prowess.

iar today. Well-financed ad campaigns were especially crucial for marketing newer consumer goods such as cars, electrical appliances, and personal hygiene products.

The Phonograph and the Recording Industry

Like radio and movies, the phonograph came into its own in the 1920s as a popular entertainment medium. Originally marketed in the 1890s, early phonographs used wax cylinders that could both record and replay. But the sound quality was poor, and the cylinders were difficult to handle. The convenient permanently grooved disc recordings introduced around World War I were eagerly snapped up by the public, even though discs could not be used to make recordings at home. The success of records transformed the popular music business, displacing both cylinders and sheet music as the major source of music in the home.

Dance crazes such as the fox trot, tango, and grizzly bear, done to complex ragtime and Latin rhythms, boosted the record business tremendously. Dixieland jazz, which recorded well, also captured the public's fancy in the early 1920s, and records provided the music for new popular dances like the Charleston and the black bottom. In 1921 more than 200 companies produced some 2 million records and annual record sales exceeded 100 million.

Record sales declined toward the end of the decade due to competition from radio. But in a broader cultural sense, records continued to transform American popular culture. Record companies discovered lucrative regional and ethnic markets for country music, which appealed primarily to white Southerners, and blues and jazz, which appealed primarily to African Americans. Country musicians like the Carter Family and Jimmie Rodgers and blues singers like Blind Lemon Jefferson and Ma Rainey had their performances put on records for the first time. Their records sold mainly in specialized "hillbilly" and "race" markets. Yet they were also played over the radio, and millions of Americans began to hear musical styles and performers who had previously been isolated. Blues great Bessie Smith sold hundreds of thousands of records and single-handedly kept the fledgling Columbia Record Company profitable. The combination of records and radio started an extraordinary cross-fertilization of American musical styles that continues to this day.

Sports and Celebrity

During the 1920s, spectator sports enjoyed an unprecedented growth in popularity and profitability. As radio, newspapers, magazines, and newsreels exhaustively documented their exploits, athletes took their place alongside movie stars in defining a new culture of celebrity. Big-time sports, like the movies, entered a new corporate phase. Yet it was the athletes themselves, performing extraordinary feats on the field and transcending their often humble origins, who attracted millions of new fans. The image of the modern athlete—rich, famous, glamorous, and often a rebel against social convention—came into its own during the decade.

Major league baseball had more fans than any other sport, and its greatest star, George Herman "Babe" Ruth, embodied the new celebrity athlete. In 1920 the game had suffered a serious public relations disaster with the unfolding of the "Black Sox" scandal. The previous year, eight members of the poorly paid Chicago White Sox had become involved in a scheme to "throw" the World Series in exchange for large sums of money from gamblers. Although they were acquitted in the courts, baseball commissioner Judge Kenesaw Mountain Landis, looking to remove any taint of gambling from the sport, banned the accused players for life. Landis's actions won universal acclaim, but doubts about the integrity of "the national pastime" lingered.

Ruth did more than anyone to repair the damage and make baseball more popular than ever. Born in 1895, he was a product of Baltimore's rough waterfront district. After spending most of his youth in an orphanage for delinquent boys, he broke into baseball as a pitcher for the Boston Red Sox. Traded to the New York Yankees in 1920, he switched to the outfield and began attracting enormous attention with the length and frequency of his home runs. He hit fifty-four in his first year in New York, eclipsing the old record by twenty-nine. The next year he hit fifty-nine. "The Sultan of Swat," as one sportswriter dubbed him, transformed the game. Before Ruth, the "homer" was an infrequent event in a game built around pitching, defense, and speed. Fans now flocked to games in record numbers to see the new, more offensive-oriented baseball.

Ruth was a larger-than-life character off the field as well as on. In New York, media capital of the nation, newspapers and magazines chronicled his enormous appetites—for food, whiskey, expensive cars, and big-city nightlife. He hobnobbed with politicians, movie stars, and gangsters, and he regularly visited sick children in hospitals. Ruth became the first athlete avidly sought after by manufacturers for celebrity endorsement of their products. As one of the most photographed individuals of the era, Ruth's round, beaming face became a familiar image around the world. In 1930, at the onset of the Great Depression, when a reporter told him that his $80,000 salary was more than President Herbert Hoover's, the Babe replied good naturedly, "Well, I had a better year than he did."

Baseball attendance exploded during the twenties, reaching a one-year total of 10 million in 1929. The attendance boom prompted urban newspapers to increase their baseball coverage, and the larger dailies featured separate sports sections. The best sportswriters, such as Grantland Rice, Heywood Broun, and Ring Lardner, brought a poetic sensibility to descriptions of the games and their stars. William K. Wrigley, owner of the Chicago Cubs, discovered that by letting local radio stations broadcast his team's games, the club could win new fans, especially among housewives.

Baseball owners solidified their monopolistic control of the game in 1922 when the Supreme Court, ruling in an antitrust suit, declared that baseball, while obviously a business, was not "trade or commerce in the commonly accepted use of those words." By exempting baseball from antitrust prosecution, the Court gave the game a uniquely favored legal status and also ensured the absolute control of owners over their players. Among those excluded from major league baseball were African Americans, who had been banned from the game by an 1890s' "gentleman's agreement" among owners.

During the 1920s black baseball players and entrepreneurs developed a world of their own, with several professional and semiprofessional leagues catering to expanding African American communities in cities. The largest of these was the Negro National League, organized in 1920 by Andrew "Rube" Foster. Black ball clubs also played exhibitions against, and frequently defeated, teams of white major leaguers. African Americans had their own baseball heroes, such as Josh Gibson and Satchel Paige, who no doubt would have been stars in the major leagues if not for racial exclusion.

The new media configuration of the 1920s created heroes in other sports as well. Radio broadcasts and increased journalistic coverage made college football a big-time sport, as millions followed the exploits of star players such as Illinois's Harold E. "Red" Grange and Stanford's Ernie Nevers. Teams like Notre Dame, located in sleepy South Bend, Indiana, but coached by the colorful Knute Rockne, could gain a wide national following. Sportswriter Grantland Rice contributed to the school's mystique when he dubbed its backfield "the Four Horsemen of Notre Dame." The earnings potential of big-time athletics was not lost on college administrators, and it blurred the old lines separating amateur and professional sports. The center of college football shifted from the old elite schools of the Ivy League to the big universities of the Midwest and Pacific coast, where most of the players were now second-generation Irish, Italians, and Slavs. Athletes like boxers Jack Dempsey and Gene Tunney, tennis players Bill Tilden and Helen Wills, and swimmers Gertrude Ederle and Johnny Weissmuller became household names who brought legions of new fans to their sports.

A New Morality?

Movie stars, radio personalities, sports heroes, and popular musicians became the elite figures in a new culture of celebrity defined by the mass media. They were the model for achievement in the new age. Great events and abstract issues were made real through movie close-ups, radio interviews, and tabloid photos. The new media relentlessly created and disseminated images that are still familiar today: Babe Ruth trotting around the bases after hitting a home run; the wild celebrations that greeted Charles Lindbergh after he completed the first solo transatlantic airplane flight in 1927; the smiling gangster Al Capone, bantering with reporters who transformed his criminal exploits into important news events.

But images do not tell the whole story. Consider one of the most enduring images of "the Roaring Twenties," the flapper. She was usually portrayed on screen, in novels, and in the press as a young, sexually aggressive woman with bobbed hair, rouged cheeks, and short skirt. She loved to dance to jazz music, enjoyed smoking cigarettes, and drank bootleg liquor in cabarets and dance halls. She could also be competitive, assertive, and a good pal. As writer Zelda Fitzgerald put it in 1924: "I think a woman gets more happiness out of being gay, light hearted, unconventional, mistress of her own fate. . . . I want [my daughter] to be a flapper, because flappers are brave and gay and beautiful."

Was the flapper a genuine representative of the 1920s? Did she embody the "new morality" that was so widely discussed and chronicled in the media of the day? The flapper certainly did exist, but she was neither as new nor as widespread a phenomenon as the image would suggest. The delight in sensuality, personal pleasure, and rhythmically complex dance and music had long been key elements of subcultures on the fringes of middle-class society: bohemian enclaves, communities of political radicals, African American ghettos, working-class dance halls. In the 1920s, these activities became normative for a growing number of white middle-class Americans, including women. Jazz, sexual experimentation, heavy makeup, and cigarette smoking spread to college campuses.

Several sources, most of them rooted in earlier years, can be found for the increased sexual openness of the 1920s. Troops in the armed forces during World War I had been exposed to government-sponsored sex education. New psychological and social theories like those of Havelock Ellis, Ellen

Key, and Sigmund Freud stressed the central role of sexuality in human experience, maintaining that sex is a positive, healthy impulse that, if repressed, could damage mental and emotional health. The pioneering efforts of Margaret Sanger in educating women about birth control had begun before World War I (see Chapter 21). In the 1920s, Sanger campaigned vigorously—through her journal *Birth Control Review*, in books, on speaking tours—to make contraception freely available to all women.

Advertisers routinely used sex appeal to sell products. Tabloid newspapers exploited sex with "cheesecake" photos, but they also provided features giving advice on sex hygiene and venereal disease. And movies, of course, featured powerful sex symbols such as Rudolph Valentino, Gloria Swanson, John Gilbert, and Clara Bow. Movies also taught young people an etiquette of sex. One typical eighteen-year-old college student wrote in the motion picture diary she kept for a sociological study: "These passionate pictures stir such longings, desires, and urges as I never expected any person to possess. Just the way the passionate lover held his sweetheart suggests so many beautiful and intimate relations, which even my reenacting a scene does not satisfy any more."

Sociological surveys also suggested that genuine changes in sexual behavior began in the prewar years among both married and single women. Katherine Bement Davis's pioneering study of 2,200 middle-class women, carried out in 1918 and published in 1929, revealed that most used contraceptives and described sexual relations in positive terms. A 1938 survey of 777 middle-class females found that among those born between 1890 and 1900, 74 percent were virgins before marriage; for those born after 1910 the figure dropped to 32 percent. Women born after the turn of the century were twice as likely to have had premarital sex as those born before 1900. The critical change took place in the generation that came of age in the late teens and early twenties. By the 1920s, male and female "morals" were becoming more alike.

This 1925 Judge *cartoon,* Sheik with Sheba, *drawn by John Held, Jr., offered one view of contemporary culture. The flashy new automobile, the hip flask with illegal liquor, the cigarettes, and the stylish "new woman" were all part of the "Roaring Twenties" image.*

THE STATE, THE ECONOMY, AND BUSINESS

Throughout the 1920s, a confident Republican Party dominated national politics, certain that it had ushered in a "new era" in American life. A new and closer relationship between the federal government and American business became the hallmark of Republican policy in both domestic and foreign affairs during the administrations of three successive Republican presidents: Warren Harding (1921–1923), Calvin Coolidge (1923–1929), and Herbert Hoover (1929–1933). And Republicans never tired of claiming that the business-government partnership their policies promoted was responsible for the nation's economic prosperity.

Harding and Coolidge

Handsome, genial, and well-spoken, Warren Harding may have looked the part of a president—but acting like one was another matter. Harding was a product of small-town Marion, Ohio, and the machine politics in his native state. Republican Party officials had made a point of keeping Senator Harding, a compromise choice, as removed from the public eye as possible in the 1920 election. They correctly saw that active campaigning could only hurt their candidate by exposing his shallowness and intellectual weakness. Harding understood his own limitations. He sadly told one visitor to the White House shortly after taking office, "I knew that this job would be too much for me."

Harding surrounded himself with a close circle of friends, "the Ohio gang," delegating to them a great deal of administrative power. The president often conducted business as if he were in the relaxed, convivial, and masculine confines of a small-town saloon. Alice Roosevelt Longworth, Theodore Roosevelt's daughter, described the scene she encountered in Harding's crony-filled study when she tagged along with her husband, Congressman Nicholas Longworth, to a card game: "The air heavy with tobacco smoke, trays with bottles containing every imaginable brand of whiskey [standing] about, cards and poker chips ready at hand—a general atmosphere of waistcoat unbuttoned, feet on the desk, and spitoons alongside." In the summer of 1923 Harding began to get wind of the scandals for which his administration is best remembered. He wearily told his friend Kansas journalist William Allen White: "This is a hell of a job! I have no trouble with my enemies. . . . But my damned friends, . . . White, they're the ones that keep me walking the floor nights."

A series of congressional investigations soon revealed a deep pattern of corruption. Attorney General Harry M. Daugherty had received bribes from violators of the Prohibition statutes. He had also failed to investigate graft in the Veterans Bureau, where Charles R. Forbes had pocketed a large chunk of the $250 million spent on hospitals and supplies. The worst affair was the Teapot Dome scandal involving Interior Secretary Albert Fall. Fall received hundreds of thousands of dollars in payoffs when he secretly leased navy oil reserves in Teapot Dome, Wyoming, and Elk Hills, California, to two private oil developers. He eventually became the first cabinet officer ever to go to jail.

But the Harding administration's legacy was not all scandal. Andrew Mellon, an influential Pittsburgh banker, served as secretary of the treasury under all three Republican presidents of the 1920s. One of the richest men in America, and a leading investor in the Aluminum Corporation of America and Gulf Oil, Mellon believed government ought to be run on the same conservative principles as a corporation. He was a leading voice for trimming the federal budget and cutting taxes on incomes, corporate profits, and inheritances. These cuts, he argued, would free up capital for new investment and thus promote general economic growth. Mellon's program sharply cut taxes for both higher-income brackets and for businesses. By 1926, a person with an income of a million a year paid less than a third of the income tax he or she paid in 1921. Overall, Mellon's policies succeeded in rolling back much of the progressive taxation associated with Woodrow Wilson.

When Harding died in office of a heart attack in August 1923, Calvin Coolidge succeeded to the presidency. Coolidge seemed to most people the temperamental opposite of Harding. Born and raised in rural Vermont, elected governor of Massachusetts, and coming to national prominence only through the 1919 Boston police strike (see Chapter 22), "Silent Cal" was the quintessential New England Yankee. Taciturn, genteel, and completely honest, Coolidge believed in the least amount of government possible. He spent only four hours a day at the office. His famous aphorism, "The business of America is business," perfectly captured the core philosophy of the Republican new era. He was in awe of wealthy

Calvin Coolidge combined a spare, laconic political style with a flair for publicity. He frequently posed in the dress of a cowboy, farmer, or Indian chief.

men such as Andrew Mellon, and he thought them best suited to make society's key decisions.

Coolidge easily won election on his own in 1924. He benefited from the general prosperity and the contrast he provided with the disgraced Harding. Coolidge defeated little-known Democrat John W. Davis, the compromise choice of a party badly divided between its rural and urban wings. Also running was Progressive Party candidate Robert M. La Follette of Wisconsin, who mounted a reform campaign that attacked economic monopolies and called for government ownership of utilities.

In his full term, Coolidge showed most interest in reducing federal spending, lowering taxes, and blocking congressional initiatives. He saw his primary function as clearing the way for American businessmen. They, after all, were the agents of the era's unprecedented prosperity.

Herbert Hoover and the "Associative State"

The most influential figure of the Republican new era was Herbert Hoover, who as secretary of commerce dominated the cabinets of Harding and Coolidge before becoming president himself in 1929. A successful engineer, administrator, and politician, Hoover effectively embodied the belief that enlightened business, encouraged and informed by the government, would act in the public interest. In the modern industrial age, Hoover believed, the government needed only to advise private citizens' groups about what national or international polices to pursue. "Reactionaries and radicals," he wrote in *American Individualism* (1922), "would assume that all reform and human advance must come through government. They have forgotten that progress must come from the steady lift of the individual and that the measure of national idealism and progress is the quality of idealism in the individual."

Hoover thus fused a faith in old-fashioned individualism with a strong commitment to the progressive possibilities offered by efficiency and rationality. Unlike an earlier generation of Republicans, Hoover wanted not just to create a favorable climate for business but to actively assist the business community. He spoke of creating an "associative state," in which the government would encourage voluntary cooperation among corporations, consumers, workers, farmers, and small businessmen. This became the central occupation of the Department of Commerce under Hoover's leadership. Under Hoover, the Bureau of Standards became one of the nation's leading research centers, setting engineering standards for key American industries such as machine tools and automobiles. The bureau also helped standardize the styles, sizes, and designs of many consumer products such as canned goods and refrigerators.

Hoover actively encouraged the creation and expansion of national trade associations. By 1929 there were about 2,000 of them. At industrial conferences called by the Commerce Department, government officials explained the advantages of mutual cooperation in figuring prices and costs and then publishing the information. The idea was to improve efficiency by reducing competition. To some this practice violated the spirit of antitrust laws, but in the 1920s the Justice Department's Antitrust Division took a very lax view of its responsibility. In addition, the Supreme Court consistently upheld the legality of trade associations. Hoover also had a strong influence on presidential appointments to regulatory commissions; most of these went to men who had worked for the very firms the commissions had been designed to supervise. Regulatory commissions thus benefited from the technical expertise brought by industry leaders, but they in turn tended to remain uncritical of the industries they oversaw.

The government thus provided an ideal climate for the concentration of corporate wealth and power. The trend toward large corporate trusts and holding companies had been well under way since the late nineteenth century, but it accelerated in the 1920s. By 1929, the 200 largest American corporations owned almost half the total corporate wealth and about a fifth of the total national wealth. Concentration was particularly strong in manufacturing, retailing, mining, banking, and utilities. The number of vertical combinations—large, integrated firms that controlled the raw materials, manufacturing processes, and distribution networks for their products—also increased. Vertical inegration became common not only in older industries but in the automobile, electrical, radio, motion picture, and other new industries as well.

War Debts, Reparations, Keeping the Peace

The United States emerged from World War I the strongest economic power in the world. The war transformed it from the world's leading debtor nation to its most important creditor. European governments owed the U.S. government about $10 billion in 1919. In the private sector, the war ushered in an era of expanding American investment abroad. As late as 1914 foreign investments in the United States were about $3 billion more than the total of American capital invested abroad. By 1919 that situation was reversed: America had $3 billion more invested abroad than foreigners had invested in the United States. By 1929 the surplus was $8 billion. New York replaced London as the center of international finance and capital markets.

During the 1920s, war debts and reparations were the single most divisive issue in international economics. In France and Great Britain, which both owed the United States large amounts in war loans, many concluded that the Uncle Sam who had offered assistance during wartime was really a loan shark in disguise. In turn, many Americans viewed Europeans as ungrateful debtors. As President Coolidge acidly remarked, "They hired the money, didn't they?" In 1922 the U.S. Foreign Debt Commission negotiated an agreement with the debtor nations that called for them to repay $11.5 billion over a sixty-two-year period. But by the late 1920s, the European financial situation had become so desperate that the United States agreed to cancel a large part of these debts. Continued insistence by the United States that the Europeans pay at least a portion of the debt fed anti-American feeling in Europe and isolationism at home.

The Germans believed that war reparations, set at $33 billion by the Treaty of Versailles, not only unfairly punished the losers of the conflict but, by saddling their civilian economies with such massive debt, also deprived them of the very means to repay. In 1924 Herbert Hoover and Chicago banker Charles Dawes worked out a plan to aid the recovery of the German economy. The Dawes Plan reduced Germany's debt, stretched out the repayment period, and arranged for American bankers to lend funds to Germany. These measures helped stabilize Germany's currency and allowed it to make reparations payments to France and Great Britain. The Allies, in turn, were better able to pay their war debts to the United States.

The horrors of the Great War led millions of citizens, as well as government officials, to advocate curbs on the world's armed forces. In 1921 Secretary of State Charles Evans Hughes took the initiative on arms limitations by inviting representatives from Great Britain, Japan, Italy, France, and China to meet in Washington to discuss reductions in military budgets. Hughes offered to scrap thirty major American ships and asked for comparable actions by the British and Japanese. He asked for a ten-year moratorium on the construction of new battleships and cruisers and proposed limiting naval tonnage. The following year the Five-Power Treaty agreed to this scaling down of navies and also pledged to respect the territorial integrity of China. But the Italians and Japanese soon complained about the treaty's restraints, and ultimately the limits placed on navy construction were abandoned.

The United States never joined the League of Nations, but it maintained an active, if selective, involvement in world affairs. In addition to the Dawes Plan and the American role in naval disarmament, the United States joined the league-sponsored World Court in 1926 and was represented at numerous league conferences. In 1928, with great fanfare, the United States and sixty-two other nations signed the Pact of Paris (better known as the Kellogg-Briand Pact for the U.S. secretary of state Frank B. Kellogg and French foreign minister Aristide Briand who initiated it), which grandly and naively renounced war in principle. Peace groups, such as the Woman's Peace Party and the Quaker-based Fellowship of Reconciliation, hailed the pact for formally outlawing war. But critics charged that the Kellogg-Briand Pact was essentially meaningless since it lacked powers of enforcement and relied solely on the moral force of world opinion. Within weeks of its ratification, the U.S. Congress had appropriated $250 million for new battleships.

Commerce and Foreign Policy

Secretary of State Charles Evans Hughes, a former governor of New York and the Republican candidate for president in 1916, played a leading role in shaping America's postwar foreign policy. Hughes argued that the United States must seek "to establish a *Pax Americana* maintained not by arms but by mutual respect and good will and the tranquilizing processes of reason." Hughes's push for the arms reduction agreements of 1921 went hand in hand with his deep belief that America's economic wealth—not military or political power—could help create a new and prosperous international system free of the rivalries that had led to the disastrous Great War.

Throughout the 1920s, Hughes and other Republican leaders pursued policies designed to expand American economic activity abroad. They understood that capitalist economies must be dynamic; they must expand their markets if they were to thrive. The focus must be on friendly nations and investments that would help foreign citizens to buy American goods. Toward this end, Republican leaders urged close cooperation between bankers and the government as a strategy for expanding American investment and economic influence abroad. They insisted that investment capital not be spent on U.S. enemies, such as the new Soviet Union, or on nonproductive enterprises such as munitions and weapons. Throughout the 1920s, investment bankers routinely submitted loan projects to Hughes and Secretary of Commerce Hoover for informal approval, thus reinforcing the close ties between business investment and foreign policy.

Foreign policy makers were not shy about brandishing America's postwar economic power to gain advantage. In 1926, the British tried to drive up the world price of rubber, a crucial product for the burgeoning automobile industry. Hoover retaliated by threatening a less friendly U.S. attitude toward British loans and war debts and by encouraging American investors to enlarge their rubber plantations in Southeast Asia and Liberia. Within three months, Hoover had succeeded in driving down the price of rubber from $1.21 a pound to 40 cents. For Hoover and other policy makers, American business abroad was simply rugged individualism at work around the globe.

American oil, autos, farm machinery, and electrical equipment supplied a growing world market. Much of this expansion took place through the establishment of branch plants overseas by American companies. America's overall direct investment abroad increased from $3.8 billion in 1919 to $7.5 billion in 1929. Leading the American domination of the world market were General Electric, Ford, and Monsanto Chemical. American oil companies, with the support of the State Department, also challenged Great Britain's dominance in the oil fields of the Middle East and Latin America, forming powerful cartels with English firms.

The strategy of maximum freedom for private enterprise, backed by limited government advice and assistance, significantly boosted the power and profits of American overseas investors. But in Central and Latin America, in particular, aggressive U.S. investment also fostered chronically underdeveloped economies, dependent on a few staple crops (sugar, coffee, cocoa, bananas) grown for export. American investments in Latin America more than doubled between 1924 and 1929, from $1.5 billion to over $3.5 billion. A large part of this money went to taking over vital mineral resources, such as Chile's copper and Venezuela's oil. The growing wealth and power of U.S. companies made it more difficult for these nations to grow their own food or diversify their economies. U.S. economic dominance in the hemisphere also hampered the growth of democratic politics by favoring autocratic, military regimes that could be counted on to protect U.S. investments.

During the 1920s, U.S. negotiators peacefully resolved long-simmering disputes with Mexico over oil and mineral holdings of American companies. The United States withdrew its marines from the Dominican Republic in 1924, after many years of direct military intervention. But in Nicaragua, American troops continued to prop up the conservative government of Adolfo Díaz, who had worked closely with the State Department since the first U.S. intervention in 1911. When a popular revolt led by General Augustino Sandino broke out in 1927, American marines landed and wound up supervising Nicaraguan elections over the next five years. They were not finally withdrawn until 1933, leaving a bitter legacy that would lead to crisis once again in the 1980s.

RESISTANCE TO MODERNITY

One measure of the profound cultural changes of the 1920s was the hostility and opposition expressed toward them by large sectors of the American public. Deep and persistent tensions, with ethnic, racial, and geographical overtones, characterized much of the decade's politics. The postwar Red Scare had given strength to the forces of antiradicalism in politics and traditionalism in culture. Resentments over the growing power of urban culture were very strong in rural and small-town America. The big city, in this view, stood for all that was alien, corrupt, and immoral in the country's life. Several trends and mass movements reflected this anger and the longing for a less complicated past.

Prohibition

The Eighteenth Amendment, banning the manufacture, sale, and transportation of alcoholic beverages, took effect in January 1920. Prohibition was the culmination of a long campaign that associated drinking with the degradation of working-class family life and the worst evils of urban politics. Supporters, a coalition of women's temperance groups, middle-class progressives, and rural Protestants, hailed the new law as "a noble experiment." But it became clear rather quickly that enforcing the new law would be extremely difficult. The Volstead Act of 1919 established a federal Prohibition Bureau to enforce the Eighteenth Amendment. Yet the bureau was severely understaffed, with only about 1,500 agents to police the entire country.

The public demand for alcohol, especially in the big cities, led to widespread lawbreaking. Drinking was such a routine part of life for so many Americans that bootlegging quickly became a big business. Illegal stills and breweries, as well as liquor smuggled in from Canada, supplied the needs of those Americans who continued to drink. Nearly every town and city had at least one "speakeasy," where people could drink and enjoy music and other entertainment. Local law enforcement personnel, especially in the cities, were easily bribed to overlook these illegal establishments. By the early 1920s many eastern states no longer made even a token effort at enforcing the law.

But because liquor continued to be illegal, prohibition gave an enormous boost to violent organized crime. The profits to be made in the illegal liquor trade dwarfed the traditional sources of criminal income—gambling, prostitution, and robbery. The pattern of organized crime in the 1920s closely resembled the larger trends in American business: smaller operations gave way to larger and more complex combinations. Successful organized crime figures, like Chicago's Al "Scarface" Capone, became celebrities in their own right and received heavy coverage in the mass media. Capone himself shrewdly used the rhetoric of the Republican new era to defend himself: "Everybody calls me a racketeer. I call myself a businessman. When I sell liquor it's bootlegging. When my patrons serve it on a silver tray on Lake Shore Drive, it's hospitality."

Organized crime, based on its huge profits from liquor, also made significant inroads into legitimate businesses, labor unions, and city government. By the time Congress and the states ratified the Twenty-first Amendment in 1933, repealing Prohibition, organized crime was a permanent feature of American life. Politically, Prohibition continued to be a controversial issue in national politics, as "wets" and "drys" debated the merits of the law. Prohibition did, in fact, significantly reduce per capita consumption of alcohol. In 1910, annual per capita consumption stood at 2.6 gallons; in 1934 the figure was less than a gallon. Many drinkers—especially wage earners—probably consumed less because of the higher price of bootleg beer and spirits. Yet among young people, especially college students, the excitement associated with speakeasies and lawbreaking contributed to increased drinking during Prohibition.

Immigration Restriction

Sentiment for restricting immigration, growing since the late nineteenth century, reached its peak immediately after World War I. Anti-immigrant feeling reflected the growing preponderance after 1890 of "new immigrants"—those from southern and eastern Europe—over the immigrants from northern and western Europe who had predominated before 1890. Between 1891 and 1920, roughly 10.5 million immigrants arrived from southern and eastern Europe. This was nearly twice as many as arrived in the same years from northern and western Europe.

The "new immigrants" were mostly Catholic and Jewish, and they were darker-skinned than the "old immigrants." To many Americans they seemed more exotic, more foreign, and less willing and able to assimilate the nation's political and cultural values. They were also relatively poorer, more physically isolated in the nation's cities, and less politically strong than earlier immigrants. In the 1890s, the anti-Catholic American Protective Association called for a curb on immigration, and by exploiting the economic depression of that decade it reached a membership of 2.5 million. In 1894 a group of prominent Harvard graduates, including Henry Cabot Lodge and John Fiske, founded the Immigration Restriction League, providing an influential forum for the fears of the nation's elite. The league used newer scientific arguments, based on a flawed application of Darwinian evolutionary theory and genetics, to support its call for immigration restriction.

Theories of scientific racism, which had become more popular in the early 1900s, reinforced anti-immigrant bias. The most influential statement of racial hierarchy was Madison Grant's *The Passing of the Great Race* (1916), which distorted genetic theory to argue that America was committing "race suicide." According to Grant, inferior Alpine, Mediterranean, and Jewish stock threatened to extinguish the superior Nordic race that had made America great. Eugenicists, who enjoyed considerable vogue in these years, held that heredity determined almost all of a person's capacities and that genetic inferiority predisposed people to crime and poverty. Such pseudoscientific thinking sought to explain historical and social development solely as a function of "racial" differences.

Against this background, the war and its aftermath provided the final push for immigration restriction. The "100 percent American" fervor of the

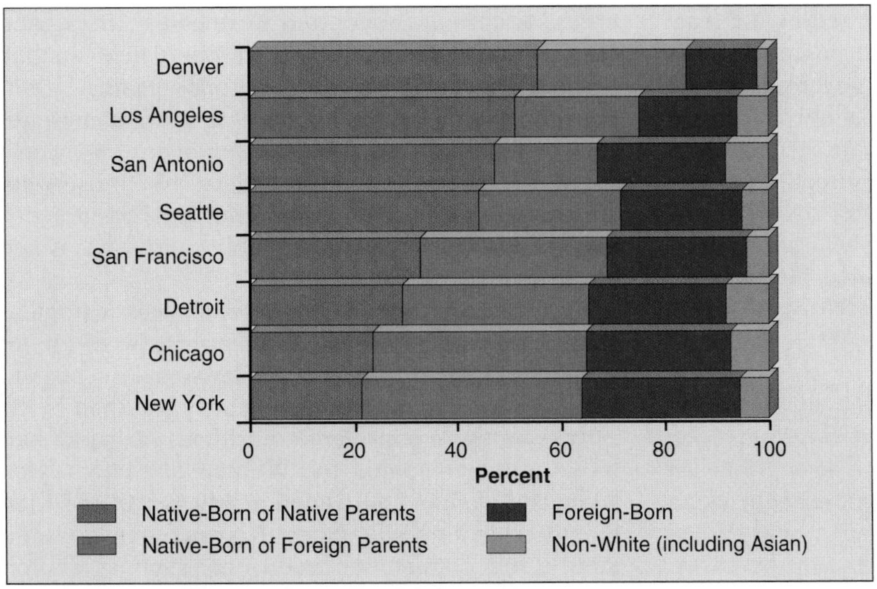

Population Composition of Selected Cities, 1920 *By 1920 the demographic impact of several decades of heavy immigration was especially evident in the nation's cities. The combined population of the foreign-born and those born of foreign parents frequently surpassed that of the native-born of native parents.*

war years fueled nativist passions. So did the Red Scare of 1919–20, which linked foreigners with Bolshevism and radicalism of all kinds in the popular mind. The postwar depression coincided with the resumption of massive immigration, bringing much hostile comment on the relationship between rising unemployment and the new influx of foreigners. The American Federation of Labor proposed stopping all immigration for two years. Sensational press coverage of organized crime figures, many of them Italian or Jewish, also played a part.

In 1921 Congress passed the Immigration Act, setting a maximum of 357,000 new immigrants each year. Quotas limited annual immigration from any European country to 3 percent of the number of its natives counted in the 1910 U.S. census. But restrictionists complained that the new law still allowed too many southern and eastern Europeans in, especially since the northern and western Europeans did not fill their quotas. The Johnson-Reed Immigration Act of 1924 revised the quotas to 2 percent of the number of foreign-born counted for each nationality in the census for 1890, when far fewer southern or eastern Europeans were present in the United States. The maximum total allowed each year was also cut, to 164,000. The quota laws did not apply to Canada, Mexico, or any other nation in the western hemisphere.

The immigration restriction laws reversed earlier practices and became a permanent feature of national policy. Republican congressman Albert Johnson of Washington, co-author of the 1924 act, defended it by claiming that "our capacity to maintain our cherished institutions stands diluted by a stream of alien blood, with all its inherited misconceptions respecting the relationships of the governing power to the governed. . . . The day of unalloyed welcome to all peoples, the day of indiscriminate acceptance of all races, has definitely ended." In effect, Congress had accepted the racial assumptions of such popular, pseudoscientific writers as Madison Grant, basing immigration restriction on a presumed hierarchy of superior and inferior "races."

The Ku Klux Klan

If immigration restriction was resurgent nativism's most significant legislative expression, a revived Ku Klux Klan was its most effective mass movement. The original Klan had been formed in the Reconstruction South as an instrument of white racial terror against newly freed slaves (see Chapter 17). It had died out in the 1870s. The new Klan, born in Stone Mountain, Georgia, in 1915, was inspired by D. W. Griffith's racist spectacle *The Birth of a Nation*, a film released in that year depicting the original KKK as a heroic organization. The new Klan patterned itself on the secret rituals and antiblack hostility of its predecessor, and until 1920 it was limited to a few local chapters in Georgia and Alabama.

When Hiram W. Evans, a dentist from Dallas, became imperial wizard of the Klan in 1922, he transformed the organization. Evans hired professional fund-raisers and publicists and directed an effective recruiting scheme that paid a commission to sponsors of new members. The Klan advocated "100 per cent Americanism" and "the faithful maintenance of White Supremacy." The Klan also staunchly supported the enforcement of Prohibition, and it attacked birth control and Darwinism. The new Klan made a special target of the Roman Catholic Church, labeling it a hostile and dangerous alien power. In a 1926 magazine piece titled "The Klan's Fight for Americanism," Evans alleged that the Church's "theocratic autocracy and its claim to full authority in temporal as well as spiritual matters, all make it impossible for it as a church, or for its members if they obey it, to cooperate in a free democracy in which Church and State have been separated."

The new Klan presented itself as the righteous defender of the embattled traditional values of small-town Protestant America. But ironically, to build its membership rolls, it relied heavily on the publicity, public relations, and business techniques associated with modern urban culture. By 1924 the new Klan counted more than 3 million members across the country. President Harding had joined in a special White House ceremony. Its slogan, "Native, White, Protestant Supremacy," proved especially attractive in the Midwest and South, including many cities. Klansmen boycotted businesses, threatened families, and sometimes resorted to violence—public whippings, arson, and lynching—against their chosen enemies. The Klan's targets sometimes included white Protestants accused of sexual promiscuity, blasphemy, or drunkenness, but most were African Americans, Catholics, and Jews. Support for Prohibition enforcement probably united Klansmen more than any single issue.

On another level, the Klan was a popular social movement. Many members were more attracted by the Klan's spectacular social events and its efforts to reinvigorate community life than by its attacks on those considered outsiders. Perhaps a half million women joined the Women of the Ku Klux Klan, and women constituted nearly half of the Klan membership in some states. Klanswomen drew on family and community traditions, such as church suppers, kin reunions, and gossip campaigns, to defend themselves and their families against what they saw as corruption and immorality. One northern Indiana Klanswoman recalled, "Store owners,

Women members of the Ku Klux Klan in New Castle, Indiana, August 1, 1923. The revived Klan was a powerful presence in scores of American communities during the early 1920s, especially among native-born white Protestants who feared cultural and political change. In addition to preaching "100 percent Americanism," local Klan chapters also served a social function for members and their families.

teachers, farmers . . . the good people, all belonged to the Klan. They were going to clean up the government, and they were going to improve the school books that were loaded with Catholicism." The Klan's power was strong in many communities precisely because it fit so comfortably into the everyday life of white Protestants.

Studies of Klan units suggest that the appeal and activities of the organization varied greatly from community to community. Local conditions and circumstances often attracted followers more than the extremist and nativist appeals of the national office. In Anaheim, California, for example, most Klansmen were migrants from midwestern states who attended mainstream Protestant churches. They focused their anger on the local economic elite, whom they held responsible for failure to enforce Prohibition, a rising crime rate, and runaway economic growth. In Colorado, Prohibition and vice law violations appeared to be the main concern. Vigilante attacks on Catholic priests and Jewish synagogues were more prevalent in cities like Denver and Pueblo, which had small but visible nonwhite Protestant communities.

At its height, the Klan also became a powerful force in Democratic Party politics in Texas, Oklahoma, Indiana, Colorado, Oregon, and other states. It had a strong presence among delegates to the 1924 Democratic National Convention. The Klan began to fade in 1925 when its Indiana leader, Grand Dragon David C. Stephenson, became involved in a sordid personal affair. Stephenson had picked up a young secretary at a party, got her drunk on bootleg liquor, and then assaulted her on a train. After the woman took poison and died, Stephenson was convicted of manslaughter. With one of its most famous leaders disgraced and in jail, the new Klan began to lose members and influence. The success of immigration restriction, the receding concern over Bolshevism, wrangling among Klan leaders, and the general economic prosperity also contributed to the movement's rapid decline by the late 1920s.

Religious Fundamentalism

Paralleling political nativism in the 1920s was the growth of religious fundamentalism. In large numbers of Protestant churches, congregations focused less on religious practice and worship than on social and reform activities in the larger community. By the early 1920s, a fundamentalist revival had developed in reaction to these tendencies. The fundamentalists

Clarence Darrow (left) and William Jennings Bryan at the Scopes Trial in Dayton, Tennessee, in 1925. Their courtroom battle embodied the larger cultural conflict between religious fundamentalism and secular values. In the trial's most dramatic moment, Darrow called Bryan to the witness stand to testify as an expert on the Bible.

emphasized a literal reading of the Bible, and they rejected the tenets of modern science as inconsistent with the revealed word of God. Fundamentalist publications and Bible colleges flourished, particularly among Southern Baptists.

One special target of the fundamentalists was the theory of evolution, first set forth by Charles Darwin in his landmark work *The Origin of Species* (1859). Using fossil evidence, evolutionary theory suggested that over time many species had become extinct and that new ones had emerged through the process of natural selection. These ideas directly contradicted the account of one, fixed creation in the Book of Genesis. Although most Protestant clergymen had long since found ways of blending the scientific theory with their theology, fundamentalists launched an attack on the teaching of Darwinism in schools and universities. By 1925 five southern state legislatures had passed laws restricting the teaching of evolution.

A young biology teacher, John T. Scopes, deliberately broke the Tennessee law in 1925 in order to challenge it in court. The resulting trial that summer in Dayton, a small town near Chattanooga, drew international attention to the controversy. Scopes's defense team included attorneys from the American Civil Liberties Union and Clarence Darrow, the most famous trial lawyer in America. The prosecution was led by William Jennings Bryan, the old Democratic standard-bearer who had thrown himself into the fundamentalist and anti-evolutionist cause. Held in a circus atmosphere in sweltering heat, the trial attracted thousands of reporters and partisans to Dayton and was broadcast across the nation by the radio.

The Scopes "monkey trial"—so called because fundamentalists trivialized Darwin's theory into a claim that humans were descended from monkeys—became one of the most publicized and definitive moments of the decade. The real drama was the confrontation between Darrow and Bryan. Darrow, denied the right to call scientists to testify for the defense, put "the Great Commoner," Bryan, himself on the stand as an expert witness on the Bible. Bryan delighted his supporters with a staunch defense of biblical literalism. But he also drew scorn from many of the assembled journalists, including cosmopolitan types such as H. L. Mencken of the Baltimore Sun, who ridiculed Bryan's simplistic faith. Scopes's guilt was never in question. The jury convicted him quickly, although the verdict was later thrown out on a technicality. Bryan died a week after the trial; his epitaph read simply, "He kept the Faith." The struggle over the teaching of evolution continued in an uneasy stalemate; state statutes were not repealed, but prosecutions for teaching evolution ceased. Fundamentalism, a religious creed and a cultural defense against the uncertainties of modern life, continued to have a strong appeal for millions of Americans.

PROMISES POSTPONED

The prosperity of the twenties was unevenly distributed and enjoyed across America. Older, progressive reform movements that had pointed out inequities faltered in the conservative political climate. But the Republican new era did inspire a range of critics deeply troubled by unfulfilled promises in American life. Feminists sought to redefine their movement in the wake of the suffrage victory. Mexican immigration to the United States shot up, and in the burgeoning Mexican American communities of the Southwest and Midwest, economic and social conditions were very difficult. African Americans, bitterly disappointed by their treatment during and after the war, turned to new political and cultural strategies. Many American intellectuals found themselves deeply alienated from the temper and direction of modern American society.

Feminism in Transition

The achievement of the suffrage removed the central issue that had given cohesion to the disparate forces of female reform activism. In addition, female activists of all persuasions found themselves swimming against a national tide of hostility to political idealism. During the 1920s, the women's movement split into two main wings over a fundamental disagreement about female identity. Should activists stress women's differences from men—their vulnerability and the double burden of work and family—and continue to press for protective legislation, such as laws that limited the length of the work week for women? Or should they emphasize the ways that women were like men—sharing similar aspirations—and push for full legal and civil equality?

In 1920, the National American Woman Suffrage Association reorganized itself as the League of Women Voters. The league represented the historical mainstream of the suffrage movement, those who believed that the vote for women would bring a nurturing sensibility and a reform vision to American politics. This view was rooted in politicized domesticity, the notion that women had a special role to play in bettering society: improving conditions for working women, abolishing child labor, humanizing prisons and mental hospitals, and serving the urban poor. Most league members continued working in a variety of reform organizations, and the league itself concentrated on educating the new female electorate, encouraging women to run for office, and supporting laws for the protection of women and children.

A newer, smaller, and more militant group was the National Woman's Party (NWP), founded in 1916 by militant suffragist Alice Paul. The NWP downplayed the significance of suffrage and argued that women were still subordinate to men in every facet of life. The NWP opposed protective legislation for women, claiming that such laws reinforced sex stereotyping and prevented women from competing with men in many fields. Largely representing the interests of professional and business women, the NWP focused on passage of a brief Equal Rights Amendment (ERA) to the Constitution, introduced in Congress in 1923: "Men and women shall have equal rights throughout the United States and every place subject to its jurisdiction."

Since the ERA would wipe out sex as a legal category, its opponents worried about the loss of hard-won protective legislation that benefited poor and working-class women. Many of the older generation of women reformers opposed the ERA as elitist, arguing that far more women benefited from protective laws than were injured by them. "So long as men cannot be mothers," Florence Kelley declared, "so long legislation adequate for them can never be adequate for wage-earning women; and the cry Equality, Equality, where nature has created inequality, is as stupid and as deadly as the cry of Peace, Peace, where there is no Peace." Mary Anderson, director of the Women's Bureau in the Department of Labor, argued that "women who are wage earners, with one job in the factory and another in the home, have little time and energy left to carry on the fight to better their economic status. They need the help of other women and they need labor laws."

ERA supporters countered that maximum hours laws or laws prohibiting women from night work prevented women from getting many lucrative jobs. According to Harriot Stanton Blatch, daughter of feminist pioneer Elizabeth Cady Stanton, "In many highly paid trades women have been pushed into the lower grades of work, limited in earning capacity, if not shut out of the trade entirely by these so-called protective laws." M. Carey Thomas, president of Bryn Mawr College, defended the ERA with language reminiscent of laissez faire: "How much better by one blow to do away with discriminating against women in work, salaries, promotion and opportunities to compete with men in a fair field with no favour on either side!"

But most women's groups did not think there was a "fair field." Positions solidified. The League of Women Voters, the National Consumers' League, and the Women's Trade Union League opposed the ERA. ERA supporters generally stressed individualism, competition, and the abstract language of "equality" and "rights." ERA opponents emphasized the grim reality of industrial exploitation and the concentration of women workers in low-paying jobs in which they did not compete directly with men. ERA advocates dreamed of a labor market that might be, one in which women might have the widest opportunity. Anti-ERA forces looked at the labor market as it was, insisting it was more important to protect women from existing exploitation. The NWP campaign failed to get the ERA passed by Congress, but the debates it sparked would be echoed during the feminist movement of the 1970s, when the ERA became a central political goal of a resurgent feminism.

A small number of professional women made real gains in the fields of real estate, banking, and journalism. The press regularly announced new "firsts" for women, such as Amelia Earhart's 1928 airplane flight across the Atlantic. Anne O'Hare McCormick won recognition as the "first lady of American journalism" for her reporting and editorial columns in the *New York Times*. As business expanded, a greater percentage of working women were employed in white-collar positions, as opposed to manufacturing and domestic service. In 1900 less than 18 percent of employed women worked in clerical, managerial, sales, and professional areas. By 1930 the number was 44 percent. But studies showed that most of these women were clustered in the low-paying areas of typing, stenography, bookkeeping, cashiering, and sales clerking. Men still dominated in the higher-paid and managerial white-collar occupations.

The most significant, if limited, victory for feminist reformers was the 1921 Sheppard-Towner Act, which established the first federally funded health care program, providing matching funds for states to set up prenatal and child health care centers. These centers also provided public health nurses for house calls. Although hailed as a genuine reform breakthrough, especially for women in rural and isolated communities, the act aroused much opposition. The NWP disliked it for its assumption that all women were mothers. Birth control advocates such as Margaret Sanger complained that contraception was not part of the program. The American Medical Association (AMA) objected to government-sponsored health care and to nurses who functioned outside the supervision of physicians. By 1929, largely as a result of intense AMA lobbying, Congress cut off funds for the program.

Mexican Immigration

While immigration restriction sharply cut the flow of new arrivals from Europe, the 1920s also brought a dramatic influx of Mexicans to the United States. Mexican immigration, which was not included in the immigration laws of 1921 and 1924, had picked up substantially after the outbreak of the Mexican Revolution in 1911, when political instability and economic hardships provided incentives to cross the border to *El Norte*. According to the U.S. Immigration Service, an estimated 459,000 Mexicans entered the United States between 1921 and 1930, more than double the number for the previous decade. The official count no doubt underrepresented the true numbers of immigrants from Mexico. Many Mexicans shunned the main border crossings at El Paso, Texas; Nogales, Arizona; and Calexico, California, and thus avoided paying the $8 head tax and $10 visa fee.

The primary pull was the tremendous agricultural expansion occurring in the American Southwest. Irrigation and large-scale agribusiness had begun transforming California's Imperial and San Joaquin Valleys from arid desert into lucrative fruit and vegetable fields. Cotton pickers were needed in the vast plantations of Lower Rio Grande Valley in Texas and the Salt River Valley in Arizona. The sugar beet fields of Michigan, Minnesota, and Colorado also attracted many Mexican farm workers. American industry had also begun recruiting Mexican workers, first to fill wartime needs and later to fill the gap left by the decline in European immigration.

The new Mexican immigration appeared more permanent than previous waves—that is, more and more newcomers stayed—and, like other immigrants, settled in cities. By 1930 San Antonio's Mexican community accounted for roughly 70,000 people out of a total population of a quarter million. Around 100,000 Mexicans lived in Los Angeles, including 55,000 who attended city schools. Substantial Mexican communities also flourished in midwestern cities such as Chicago, Detroit, Kansas City, and Gary. Many of the immigrants alternated between agricultural and factory jobs, depending on seasonal availability of work. Mexican women often worked in the fields alongside their husbands. They also had jobs as

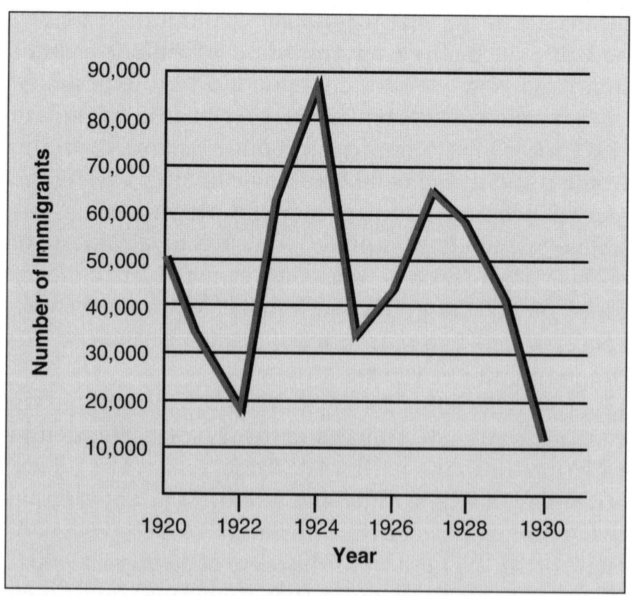

Mexican Immigration to the United States in the 1920s *Many Mexican migrants avoided official border crossing stations so they would not have to pay visa fees. Thus these official figures probably underestimated the true size of the decade's Mexican migration. As the economy contracted with the onset of the Great Depression, immigration from Mexico dropped off sharply.*

Mexican American farm workers are shown pitting apricots near Canoga Park, Los Angeles County, 1924. Most of the more than half million Mexicans who migrated to the United States during the 1920s worked as farm laborers. Migrant families usually traveled and worked together, following the crop harvests.

domestics and seamstresses or took in laundry and boarders.

Racism and local patterns of residential segregation confined most Mexicans to barrios. Housing conditions were generally poor, particularly for recent arrivals, who were forced to live in rude shacks without running water or electricity. Disease and infant mortality rates were much higher than average, and most Mexicans worked at low-paying, unskilled jobs and received inadequate health care. Legal restrictions passed by states and cities made it difficult for Mexicans to enter teaching, legal, and other professions. Mexicans were routinely banned from local public works projects as well. Many felt a deep ambivalence about applying for American citizenship. Loyalty to the Old Country was strong, and many cherished dreams of returning to live out their days in Mexico.

Ugly racist campaigns against Mexicans were common in the 1920s, especially when "cheap Mexican labor" was blamed for local unemployment or hard times. Stereotypes of Mexicans as "greasers" or "wetbacks" were prevalent in newspapers and movies of the day. Nativist efforts to limit Mexican immigration were thwarted by the lobbying of powerful agribusiness interests. The Los Angeles Chamber of Commerce typically employed racist stereotyping in arguing to keep the borders open. Mexicans, it claimed, were naturally suited for agriculture, "due to their crouching and bending habits . . . , while the white is physically unable to adapt himself to them."

Mutual aid societies—*mutualistas*—became key social and political institutions in the Mexican communities of the Southwest and Midwest. They provided death benefits and widows' pensions for members and also served as centers of resistance to

Black Population, 1920 *Although the Great Migration had drawn hundreds of thousands of African Americans to the urban north, the southern states of the former Confederacy still remained the center of the African American population in 1920.*

civil rights violations and discrimination. In 1928, the Federation of Mexican Workers Unions formed in response to a large farm labor strike in the Imperial Valley of California. A group of middle-class Mexican professionals in Texas organized the League of United Latin American Citizens (LULAC) in 1929. The founding of these organizations marked only the beginnings of a long struggle to bring economic, social, and racial equality to Mexican Americans.

The "New Negro"

The Great Migration spurred by World War I showed no signs of letting up during the 1920s, and African American communities in northern cities grew rapidly. By far the largest and most influential of these communities was New York City's Harlem, the demographic and cultural capital of black America. Previously a residential suburb, Harlem began attracting middle-class African Americans in the prewar years. After the war, heavy black migration from the South and the Caribbean encouraged real estate speculators and landlords to remake Harlem as an exclusively black neighborhood. Between 1920 and 1930 nearly 90,000 new arrivals settled in Harlem, giving it a black population of nearly 200,000.

The demand for housing in this restricted geographical area led to skyrocketing rents, but most Harlemites held low-wage jobs. This combination produced extremely overcrowded apartments, unsanitary conditions, and the rapid deterioration of housing stock. Disease and death rates were abnormally high. Harlem was well on its way to becoming a slum. Yet Harlem also boasted a large middle-class population and supported a wide array of churches, theaters, newspapers and journals, and black-owned businesses. It became a magnet for African American intellectuals, artists, musicians, and writers from all over the world. Poet Langston Hughes expressed the excitement of arriving in the community in 1921: "I can never put on paper the thrill of the underground ride to Harlem. I went up the steps and out into the bright September sunlight. Harlem! I stood there, dropped my bags, took a deep breath and felt happy again."

Harlem became the political and intellectual center for what writer Alain Locke called the "New Negro." Locke was referring to a new spirit in the work of black writers and intellectuals, an optimistic faith that encouraged African Americans to develop and celebrate their distinctive culture, firmly rooted in the history, folk culture, and experiences of African American people. This faith was the common denominator uniting the disparate figures associated with the Harlem Renaissance. The assertion of cultural independence resonated in the poetry of Langston Hughes and Claude McKay, the novels of Zora Neale Hurston and Jessie Fauset, the essays of Countee Cullen and James Weldon Johnson, the acting of Paul Robeson, and the blues singing of Bessie Smith. Most would agree with Johnson when he wrote in 1927 that "nothing can go farther to destroy race prejudice than the recognition of the Negro as a creator and contributor to American civilization."

There was a political side to the "New Negro" as well. The newly militant spirit that black veterans had brought home from World War I matured and found a variety of expressions in the Harlem of the 1920s. New leaders and movements began to appear alongside established organizations like the National Association for the Advancement of Colored People. A. Philip Randolph began a long career as a labor leader, socialist, and civil rights activist in these years, editing the *Messenger* and organizing the Brotherhood of Sleeping Car Porters. Harlem was also headquarters to Marcus Garvey's Universal Negro Improvement Association. An ambitious Jamaican immigrant who had moved to Harlem in 1916, Garvey created a mass movement that stressed black economic self-determination and unity among the black communities of the United States, the Caribbean, and Africa. His newspaper, *Negro World,* spoke to black communities around the world, urging black businesses to trade among themselves. With colorful parades and rallies and a central message affirming pride in black identity, Garvey attracted as many as a million members worldwide.

Garvey's best-publicized project was the Black Star Line, a black-owned and -operated fleet of ships that would link people of African descent around the world. But insufficient capital and serious financial mismanagement resulted in the spectacular failure of the enterprise. In 1923, Garvey was found guilty of mail fraud in his fund-raising efforts; he later went to jail and was subsequently deported to England. Despite the disgrace, Harlem's largest newspaper, the *Amsterdam News,* explained Garvey's continuing appeal to African Americans: "In a world where black is despised, he taught them that black is beautiful. He taught them to admire and praise black things and black people."

Harlem in the 1920s also became a popular tourist attraction for "slumming" whites. Nightclubs like the Cotton Club were often controlled by white

A 1925 *pensive portrait of Langston Hughes, one of the leading literary voices of the Harlem Renaissance. Winold Reiss's work suggested Hughes's determination to create poetry out of the everyday life experiences of Harlem's burgeoning African American population.*

organized crime figures. They featured bootleg liquor, floor shows, and the best jazz bands of the day, led by Duke Ellington, Fletcher Henderson, Cab Calloway, and Louis Armstrong. Yet these clubs were rigidly segregated. Black dancers, singers, and musicians provided the entertainment, but no African Americans were allowed in the audience. Chronicled in novels and newspapers, Harlem became a potent symbol to white America of the ultimate good time. Yet the average Harlemite never saw the inside of a nightclub. For the vast majority of Harlem residents, working menial jobs for low wages and forced to pay high rents, the day-to-day reality was depressingly different.

Intellectuals and Alienation

War, Prohibition, growing corporate power, and the deep currents of cultural intolerance troubled many intellectuals in the 1920s. Some felt so alienated from the United States that they left to live abroad. In the early 1920s Gertrude Stein, an American expatriate writer living in Paris, told the young novelist Ernest Hemingway: "All of you young people who served in the war, you are a lost generation." The phrase "a lost generation" was widely adopted as a label for American writers, artists, and intellectuals of the postwar era. Yet it is difficult to generalize about so diverse a community. For one thing, living abroad attracted only a handful of American writers. Alienation and disillusion with American life were prominent subjects in the literature and thought of the 1920s, but artists and thinkers developed these themes in very different ways.

Clifford K. Berryman's 1928 *political cartoon interpreted that year's presidential contest along sectional lines. It depicted the two major presidential contenders as each setting off to campaign in the regions where their support was weakest. For Democrat* Al Smith, *that meant the* West, *and for* Republican Herbert Hoover, *the* East.

The mass slaughter of World War I provoked revulsion and a deep cynicism about the heroic and moralistic portrayal of war so popular in the nineteenth century. Novelists Hemingway and John Dos Passos, who both served at the front as ambulance drivers, depicted the war and its aftermath in world-weary and unsentimental tones. The search for personal moral codes that would allow one to endure life with dignity and authenticity was at the center of Hemingway's fiction. In the taut, spare language of *The Sun Also Rises* (1926) and *A Farewell to Arms* (1929), he questioned idealism, abstractions, and large meanings. As Jake Barnes, the wounded war hero of *The Sun Also Rises* explained, "I did not care what it was all about. All I wanted to know was how to live it."

Hemingway and F. Scott Fitzgerald were the most influential novelists of the era. Fitzgerald joined the army during World War I but did not serve overseas. His work celebrated the youthful vitality of "the Jazz Age" (a phrase he coined) but was also deeply distrustful of the promises of American prosperity and politics. His first novel, *This Side of Paradise* (1920), won a wide readership around the country with its exuberant portrait of "a new generation," "dedicated more than the last to the fear of poverty and the worship of success; grown up to find all Gods dead, all wars fought, all faiths in man shaken." Fitzgerald's finest work, *The Great Gatsby* (1925), written in the south of France, depicted the glamorous parties of the wealthy while evoking the tragic limits of material success.

At home, many American writers engaged in sharp attacks on small-town America and what they viewed as its provincial values. Essayist H. L. Mencken, caustic editor of the *American Mercury*, heaped scorn on fundamentalists, Prohibition, and nativists, while ridiculing what he called the "American booboisie." Mencken understood the power of the small town and despaired of reforming politics. "Our laws," he wrote, "are invented, in the main, by frauds and fanatics, and put upon the statute books by poltroons and scoundrels." Fiction writers also skewered small-town America, achieving commercial and critical success in the process. Sherwood Anderson's *Winesburg, Ohio* (1919) offered a spare, laconic, pessimistic yet compassionate view of middle America. He had a lasting influence on younger novelists of the 1920s.

The most popular and acclaimed writer of the time was novelist Sinclair Lewis. In a series of novels satirizing small-town life, such as *Main Street* (1920) and especially *Babbitt* (1922), Lewis affectionately mocked his characters. His treatment of the central character in *Babbitt*—George Babbitt of Zenith—also had a strong element of self-mockery, for Lewis could offer no alternative set of values to Babbitt's crass self-promotion, hunger for success, and craving for social acceptance.

In 1930 Lewis became the first American author to win the Nobel Prize for literature.

The playwright Eugene O'Neill revolutionized the American stage with his naturalistic and brooding dramas. O'Neill's depictions of the darker side of family life and his exploration of race relations helped push American theater past the melodramatic conventions of the late nineteenth century. Among his influential early plays were *Beyond the Horizon* (1920), *The Emperor Jones* (1921), and *The Great God Brown* (1926). Two expatriate poets, T. S. Eliot and Ezra Pound, were breaking Victorian conventions by pushing American verse in revolutionary new directions. Eliot's *The Waste Land* (1922), perhaps the most influential poem of the century, used the metaphor of impotence to comment on the postwar world.

Another side of intellectual alienation was expressed by writers critical of industrial progress and the new mass culture. The most important of these were a group of poets and scholars centered in Vanderbilt University in Nashville, Tennessee, collectively known as the Fugitives. They included Allen Tate, John Crowe Ransom, Donald Davidson, and Robert Penn Warren, all of whom invoked traditional authority, respect for the past, and older agrarian ways as ideals to live by. The Fugitives attacked industrialism and materialism as modern-day ills. Self-conscious Southerners, they looked to the antebellum plantation-based society as a model for a community based on benevolence toward dependents (such as black people and women) and respect for the land. Their book of essays, *I'll Take My Stand* (1930), was a collective manifesto of their ideas.

Not all intellectuals, of course, were critics of modern trends. Some, like the philosopher John Dewey, retained much of the prewar optimism and belief in progress. But many others, such as Walter Lippmann and Joseph Wood Krutch, articulated a profound uneasiness with the limits of material growth. In his 1929 book *A Preface to Morals*, the urbane and sophisticated Lippmann expressed doubts about the moral health of the nation. Modern science and technological advances could not address more cosmic questions of belief. The erosion of old religious faiths and moral standards, along with the triumph of the new mass culture, had left many people with nothing to believe in. Lippmann called for a new "religion of the spirit" to offer a guide for living an ethical life. He was unclear as to just what the "religion of the spirit" might be. But he was certain that the moralist would have to persuade rather than command people to live the good life. His job would be "not to exhort men to be good but to elucidate what the good is."

The Election of 1928

The presidential election of 1928 served as a kind of national referendum on the Republican new era. It also revealed just how important ethnic and cultural differences had become in defining American politics. The contest reflected many of the deepest tensions and conflicts in American society in the 1920s: native-born versus immigrant; Protestant versus Catholic; Prohibition versus legal drinking; small-town life versus the cosmopolitan city; fundamentalism versus modernism; traditional sources of culture versus the new mass media.

The 1928 campaign featured two politicians who represented profoundly different sides of American life. Al Smith, the Democratic nominee for president, was a pure product of New York City's Lower East Side. Smith came from a background that included Irish, German, and Italian ancestry, and he was raised as a Roman Catholic. After attending parochial school and working in the Fulton Fish Market, he rose through the political ranks of New York's Tammany Hall machine. A personable man with a deep sympathy for poor and working-class people, Smith won a reputation as an effective state legislator in Albany. He served four terms as governor of New York, pushing through an array of laws reforming factory conditions, housing, and welfare programs. Two of his closest advisers were the progressives Frances Perkins and Belle Moskowitz. Smith thus fused older-style machine politics with the newer reform emphasis on state intervention to solve social problems.

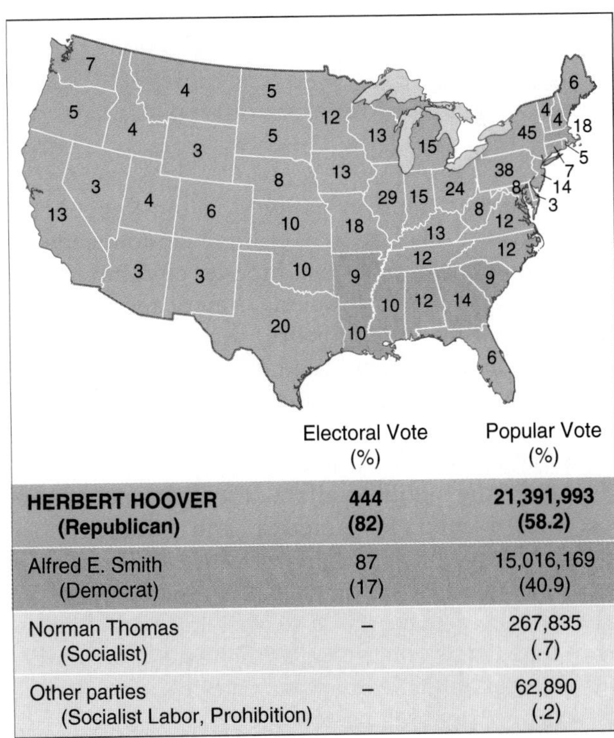

	Electoral Vote (%)	Popular Vote (%)
HERBERT HOOVER (Republican)	**444 (82)**	**21,391,993 (58.2)**
Alfred E. Smith (Democrat)	87 (17)	15,016,169 (40.9)
Norman Thomas (Socialist)	–	267,835 (.7)
Other parties (Socialist Labor, Prohibition)	–	62,890 (.2)

The Election of 1928 *Although Al Smith managed to carry the nation's twelve largest cities, Herbert Hoover's victory in 1928 was one of the largest popular and electoral landslides in the nation's history.*

CHRONOLOGY

1920	Prohibition takes effect Warren G. Harding is elected president Station KDKA in Pittsburgh goes on the air Census reports that urban population is greater than rural population for the first time
1921	First immigration quotas are established by Congress Sheppard-Towner Act establishes first federally funded health care program
1922	Washington conference produces Five-Power Treaty scaling down navies
1923	Equal Rights Amendment is first introduced in Congress Harding dies in office; Calvin Coolidge becomes president
1924	Ku Klux Klan is at height of its influence Dawes Plan for war reparations stabilizes European economies Johnson-Reed Immigration Act tightens quotas established in 1921
1925	Scopes trial pits religious fundamentalism against modernity F. Scott Fitzgerald publishes *The Great Gatsby*
1926	National Broadcasting Company establishes first national radio network
1927	McNary-Haugen Farm Relief bill finally passed by Congress but is vetoed by President Coolidge as unwarranted federal interference in the economy Warner Brothers produces *The Jazz Singer,* the first feature-length motion picture with sound Charles Lindbergh makes first solo flight across the Atlantic Ocean
1928	Kellogg-Briand Pact renounces war Herbert Hoover defeats Al Smith for the presidency
1929	Robert and Helen Lynd publish their classic community study, *Middletown*

Herbert Hoover easily won the Republican nomination after Calvin Coolidge announced he would not run for reelection. Hoover epitomized the successful and forward-looking American. An engineer and self-made millionaire, he offered a unique combination of experience in humanitarian war relief, administrative efficiency, and probusiness policies. Above all, Hoover stood for a commitment to voluntarism and individualism as the best method for advancing the public welfare. He was one of the best-known men in America and promised to continue the Republican control of national politics.

Smith himself quickly became the central issue of the campaign. His sharp New York accent, jarring to many Americans who heard it over the radio, marked him clearly as a man of the city. So did his brown derby and fashionable suits, as well as his promise to work for the repeal of Prohibition. As the first Roman Catholic nominee of a major party, Smith also drew a torrent of anti-Catholic bigotry, especially in the South and Midwest. Nativists and Ku Klux Klanners shamelessly exploited old anti-Catholic prejudices and intimidated participants in Democratic election rallies. But Smith was also attacked from more respectable quarters. Bishop James Cannon, head of the Southern Methodist Episcopal Church, insisted that "no subject of the Pope" should be permitted to occupy the White House. William Allen White, the old and influential progressive editor from Kansas, denounced Smith as the candidate of gambling, prostitution, and liquor interests.

For his part, Smith ran a largely conservative race. He appointed John Raskob, a Republican vice president of General Motors, to manage his campaign, and tried to outdo Hoover in his praise for business. He avoided economic issues such as the unevenness of the prosperity, the plight of farmers, or the growing unemployment. Democrats remained regionally divided over Prohibition, Smith's religion, and the widening split between rural and urban values. Hoover did not have to do much, other than take credit for the continued prosperity.

In retrospect, probably no Democrat could have won in 1928. The incumbent majority party would not lose during prosperous times. Hoover polled 21 million votes to Smith's 15 million, and swept the electoral college 444 to 87, including New York State. Even the Solid South, reliably Democratic since the Civil War, gave five states to Hoover—a clear reflection of the ethnocultural split in the party. Yet the election offered important clues to the future of the Democrats. Smith ran better in the big cities of the North and East than any Democrat in modern times. He outpolled Hoover in the aggregate vote of the nation's twelve largest cities and carried six of them, thus pointing the way to the Democrats' future control of the urban vote.

CONCLUSION

America's big cities, if not dominant politically, now defined the nation's cultural and economic life as never before. The mass media of motion pictures, broadcasting, and chain newspapers brought cosmopolitan entertainments and values to the remotest small communities. The culture of celebrity knew no geographic boundaries. New consumer durable goods associated with mass-production techniques—automobiles, radios, telephones, household appliances—were manufactured largely in cities. The advertising and public relations companies that sang their praises were also distinctly urban enterprises. Even with the curtailing of European immigration, big cities attracted a kaleidoscopic variety of migrants: white people from small towns and farms, African Americans from the rural South, Mexicans from across the border, intellectuals and professionals looking to make their mark.

Many Americans, of course, remained deeply suspicious of postwar cultural and economic trends. Yet the partisans of Prohibition, members of the Ku Klux Klan, and religious fundamentalists usually found themselves on the defensive against what they viewed as alien cultural and economic forces centered in the metropolis. Large sectors of the population did not share in the era's prosperity. But the large numbers who did—or at least had a taste of good times—ensured Republican political dominance throughout the decade. Thus America in the 1920s balanced dizzying change in the cultural and economic realms with conservative politics. The reform crusades that attracted millions during the progressive era were a distant memory. Political activism was no match for the new pleasures promised by technology and prosperity.

REVIEW QUESTIONS

1. Describe the impact of the "second industrial revolution" on American business, workers, and consumers. Which technological and economic changes had the biggest impact on American society?
2. Analyze the uneven distribution of the decade's economic prosperity. Which Americans gained the most, and which were largely left out?
3. How did an expanding mass culture change the contours of everyday life in the decade following World War I? What role did new technologies of mass communication play in shaping these changes? What connections can you draw between the "culture of consumption," then and today?
4. What were the key policies and goals articulated by Republican political leaders of the 1920s? How did they apply these to both domestic and foreign affairs?
5. How did some Americans resist the rapid changes taking place in the post–World War I world? What cultural and political strategies did they employ?
6. Discuss the 1928 election as a mirror of the divisions in American society.

RECOMMENDED READING

John Braemer et al., eds., *Change and Continuity in Twentieth Century America: The 1920s* (1968). A wide-ranging collection of essays on the period, with especially good studies of the resistance to modernity.

Nancy F. Cott, *The Grounding of American Feminism* (1987). Includes a sophisticated analysis of the debates among and between feminists during the 1920s.

Lynn Dumenil, *The Modern Temper: America in the 1920s* (1995). An excellent synthesis of recent scholarship which emphasizes the ambivalence that many Americans felt toward the emergence of modern society.

James J. Flink, *The Car Culture* (1975). The best single volume on the history of the automobile and how it changed American life.

Ellis W. Hawley, *The Great War and the Search for Modern Order* (1979). An influential study of the relations between the state and business and the growth of mass consumer society.

Nancy Maclean, *Behind the Mask of Chivalry: The Making of the Second Ku Klux Klan* (1994). A fine case study of the KKK in Athens, Georgia, with important insights on the Klan's relationship to issues involving gender and class difference.

Roland Marchand, *Advertising the American Dream: Making Way for Modernity, 1920–1940* (1985). A superb, beautifully illustrated account of the rise of the modern advertising industry.

Geoffrey Perrett, *America in the Twenties* (1982). A useful overview of the decade, with very good anecdotal material.

Emily S. Rosenberg, *Spreading the American Dream* (1982). A fine study of American economic and cultural expansion around the world from 1890 to 1945.

Susan Smulyan, *Selling Radio: The Commercialization of American Broadcasting, 1920–1934* (1994). The best analysis of the rise of commercial radio broadcasting in the 1920s.

ADDITIONAL BIBLIOGRAPHY

Postwar Prosperity and Its Price

Irving Bernstein, *The Lean Years: A History of the American Worker, 1919–1933* (1960)
David Brody, *Workers in Industrial America* (1980)
Gilbert C. Fite, *American Farmers: The New Minority* (1981)
Kenneth T. Jackson, *Crabgrass Frontier* (1985)
William Leuchtenberg, *The Perils of Prosperity, 1914–1932* (1958)
Clay McShane, *Down the Asphalt Path* (1994)
Gwendolyn Wright, *Building the American Dream* (1981)
Gerald Zahavi, *Workers, Managers, and Welfare Capitalism* (1988)

The New Mass Culture

Beth A. Bailey, *From Front Porch to Back Seat: Courtship in Twentieth Century America* (1988)
Daniel J. Czitrom, *Media and the American Mind* (1982)
John D'Emilio and Estelle B. Freedman, *Intimate Matters: A History of Sexuality in America* (1988)
Stewart Ewen, *Captains of Consciousness* (1976)
Roland Gelatt, *The Fabulous Phonograph*, rev. ed. (1977)
Jackson Lears, *Fables of Abundance: A Cultural History of Advertising in America* (1994)
Robert Lynd and Helen Lynd, *Middletown* (1929)
Lary May, *Screening Out the Past: The Birth of Mass Culture and the Motion Picture Industry* (1980)
Robert Sklar, *Movie Made America*, rev. ed. (1995)

The State, the Economy, and Business

Guy Alchon, *The Invisible Hand of Planning* (1985)
Warren I. Cohen, *Empire without Tears* (1987)
Louis Galambos and Joseph Pratt, *The Rise of the Corporate Commonwealth* (1988)
Ellis W. Hawley, ed., *Herbert Hoover as Secretary of Commerce* (1974)
John D. Hicks, *Republican Ascendancy, 1921–1933* (1960)
Charles L. Mee, *The Ohio Gang: The World of Warren G. Harding* (1981)
Robert K. Murray, *The Politics of Normalcy* (1973)
Mira Wilkins, *The Maturing of Multinational Enterprise* (1974)
Joan Hoff Wilson, *American Business and Foreign Policy* (1971)

Resistance to Modernity

Katherine M. Blee, *Women and the Klan: Racism and Gender in the 1920s* (1991)
Norman H. Clark, *Deliver Us from Evil: An Interpretation of American Prohibition* (1976)
Lyle W. Dorsett, *Billy Sunday and the Redemption of Urban America* (1991)
John Higham, *Strangers in the Land: Patterns of American Nativism, 1860–1925* (1955)
Henry B. Leonard, *The Open Gates: The Protest against the Movement to Restrict Immigration, 1896–1924* (1980)
George M. Marsden, *Fundamentalism and American Culture* (1980)

Promises Postponed

Stanley Coben, *Rebellion against Victorianism* (1991)
Ruth Schwartz Cowan, *More Work for Mother* (1982)
Ann Douglas, *Terrible Honesty: Mongrel Manhattan in the 1920s* (1995)
Sara M. Evans, *Born for Liberty: A History of Women in America* (1989)
Nathan I. Huggins, *Harlem Renaissance* (1971)
Allan J. Lichtman, *Prejudice and the Old Politics: The Presidential Election of 1928* (1979)
Cary D. Mintz, *Black Culture and the Harlem Renaissance* (1988)
Kathy H. Ogren, *The Jazz Revolution: Twenties America and the Meaning of Jazz* (1989)
Gilbert Osofsky, *Harlem: The Making of a Ghetto* (1965)
Mark Reisler, *By the Sweat of Their Brow: Mexican Immigrant Labor in the United States, 1900–1940* (1976)
George J. Sanchez, *Becoming Mexican American* (1993)
Judith Stein, *The World of Marcus Garvey* (1985)

Biography

Edith L. Blumhofer, *Aimee Semple McPherson* (1993)
David Burner, *Herbert Hoover: The Public Life* (1979)
Robert Creamer, *Babe: The Legend Comes to Life* (1975)
Paula Elder, *Governor Alfred E. Smith: The Politician as Reformer* (1983)
Neal Gabler, *Winchell: Gossip, Power, and the Culture of Celebrity* (1994)
Fred Hobson, *Mencken: A Life* (1994)
Arnold Rampersad, *The Life of Langston Hughes*, 2 vols. (1986–88)
Randy Roberts, *Jack Dempsey* (1979)
David Robinson, *Chaplin* (1985)
Joan Hoff Wilson, *Herbert Hoover: Forgotten Progressive* (1975)

IMMIGRATION & COMMUNITY

The Changing Face of Ethnicity in America

1860–1930

Annual immigration to the United States, which had declined during the late 1850s from a peak of more than 400,000 in 1854, dropped sharply at the onset of the Civil War. But even before the war ended, the pace of immigration revived. From the late nineteenth century until World War I, as America's unprecedented industrial expansion created an unprecedented demand for labor, the rate of immigration increased dramatically, surpassing 1,000,000 in 1905. At the same time, the ethnic background of the immigrants changed, creating a corresponding change in the nation's ethnic landscape.

Before the Civil War most immigrants came from Ireland and Germany. After the war immigrants from Germany and northwestern Europe continued at first to predominate, but by 1896 they had been overtaken by the so-called "New Immigrants" from the countries of southern and eastern Europe. Immigration from Latin America and many Asian countries, although far lower than that from Europe, also increased. Immigration from China, however, slowed considerably after the passage of the Chinese Exclusion Act of 1882.

Overall, between 1860 and 1920 about 28.2 million people immigrated to the United States, and by 1920 these immigrants and their children represented more than one-third of the nation's population. The vast majority of New Immigrants sought better lives for themselves and their families. Driven by economic dislocation, political turmoil, and overpopulation at home, millions of people left their villages for opportunity in distant lands, including Canada, Argentina, Brazil, Australia, and New Zealand as well as the United States. Italians were the largest group among the New Immigrants: between 1880 and 1930 nearly five million came to the United States. Of them, 80 percent were peasants from southern Italy left landless by an agricultural depression.

Religious and ethnic persecution combined with economic hardship to drive the Jews of Russia, Poland, and other eastern European countries to emigrate. Laws in Russia dictated where Jews could live and restricted their opportunities for employment and education. Beginning in 1881, the Russian government encouraged violent attacks known as *pogroms* on Jewish communities. These hardships made the United States appear a beacon of salvation. As a result, the Jewish population of the United States grew from 250,000 in 1877 to more than 4 million in 1927.

Most New Immigrants settled in the nation's urban manufacturing centers, not on farms. Generally poorly educated and lacking industrial skills, they entered the bottom ranks in factories, mines, mills, slaughterhouses, and garment shops. Employers benefited from their numbers to reorganize the workplace and reduce their reliance on highly paid skilled workers. Jews, however, were an exception to this pattern. Many had come from cities and were skilled in craft work and business. Nearly 77 percent of immigrant Jewish men qualified for skilled work in such specialized trades as cigar manufacturing, printing, carpentry, and garment manufacturing. Japanese immigrants—more than 111,000 by 1920—likewise fared well. They had a literacy rate of 99 percent and were able to translate the agricultural experience they brought from Japan to establish themselves as successful farmers of market garden crops in California, where the majority settled.

Most New Immigrants were unmarried young men, and many did not intend to settle permanently in the United States. They hoped instead to earn enough money to return home and buy land or set up a small business. Italian immigrants, nearly 80 percent of them male, and Greek immigrants, more than 90 percent male, had the highest rate of remigration—almost 50 percent. Jews, facing persecution at home, were the least likely to return home. Only 5 percent remigrated. Instead, they saved their wages to bring other family members to the United States. As a result, Jews were the most evenly distributed by sex of the New Immigrants. Only among the Irish did women form the majority of newcomers.

Whether they planned to remigrate or stay, the New Immigrants quickly established distinctive communities, mainly in the nation's large cities or along the West Coast. In 1920 three-quarters of the foreign-born lived in cities. The vast majority of Italians, for example, entered through the port of New York, and nearly one-quarter of them settled nearby. By 1920, 400,000 Italian immigrants were living in sizable communities in Manhattan, Brooklyn, the Bronx, Queens, and Staten Island. In Chicago, one-third of all Italians lived in a single neighborhood on the city's West Side. Across the continent in California, where Italians represented the single largest immigrant group, they gave North Beach in San Francisco a special ethnic flavor.

In many cities the New Immigrants became the numerical majority and dominated political and

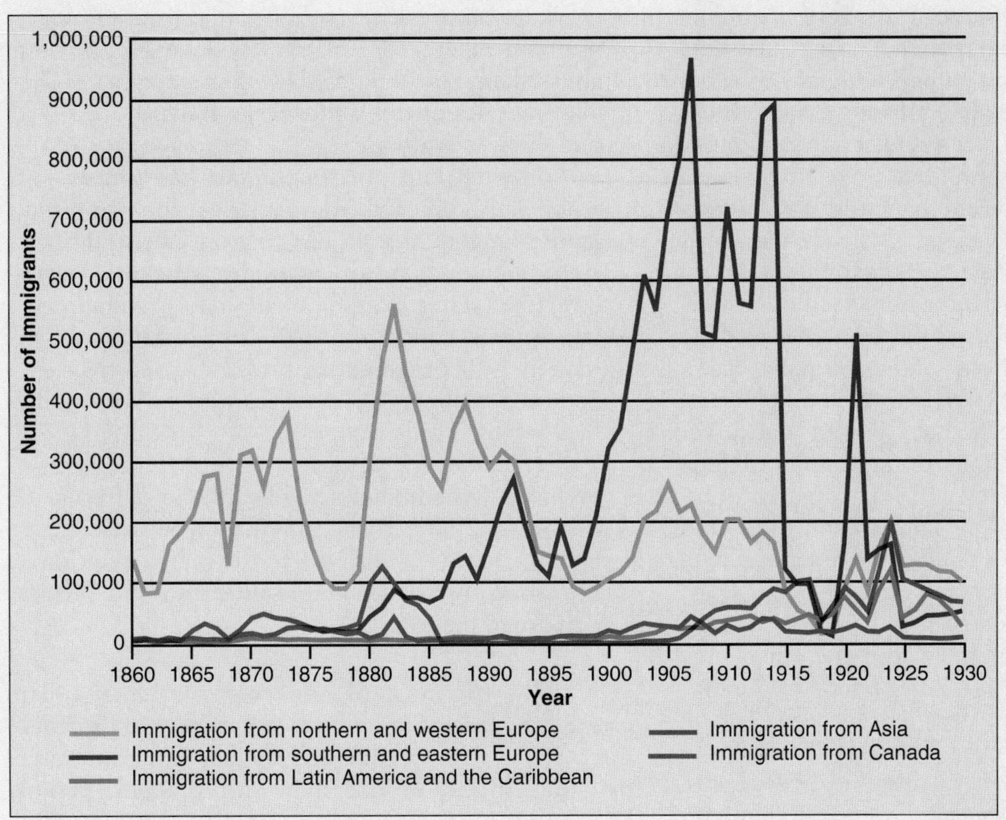

Annual Immigration to the United States, 1860–1930

social institutions. By 1910 in Passaic, New Jersey, for example, 52 percent of the population was foreign-born, most from Russia, Austria-Hungary, or Italy; 32 percent was second-generation (the children of foreign-born); and only 14 percent native-born whites. The immigrant population reshaped Passaic's political landscape, eventually forcing a sweeping reorganization of city government.

Although all New Immigrants tended to concentrate in neighborhoods near the factories or the steel mills where they worked, Italians were the most likely to cluster in so-called ethnic ghettos. Here, in "Little Italy," they spoke their native language, ate familiar foods, and helped their compatriots find jobs and housing. As immigrant communities grew, they sought to recreate Old World cultural patterns through schools, businesses, mutual-aid societies, and fraternal orders. Religious institutions—church and temple—provided the most important link to cultural traditions. Foreign-language newspapers—Germans and Jews produced the largest number—likewise helped forge community solidarity.

Although most old-stock Americans welcomed immigrant labor, many feared the "alien" cultural values and mores of the immigrants themselves. Before the Civil War, nativist, or anti-immigrant, sentiment was directed primarily against Catholics; shortly after the war, its focus was the Chinese. As the new immigration gathered steam in the 1880s, nativist sentiment increasingly turned against *all* immigrants. The nativist reaction to the new immigration found justification in certain intellectual currents of the late nineteenth century. So-called "scientific racism" purported to demonstrate that some racial groups were inherently superior to others, with western Europeans, especially Anglo-Saxons, inevitably ranked at the top, Africans at the bottom, and southern and eastern Europeans not much above them. Social Darwinism similarly claimed to justify social ranking with evolutionary theory.

Until the late nineteenth century, the federal government did little to regulate immigration and instead allowed state governments to set their own policies. But a turning point was reached with the Immigration Act of 1882, which gave the federal government the right to regulate immigration in cooperation with the states. The act laid the foundation for the kind of selective immigration based on race or ethnicity that the Chinese Exclusion Act, also passed in 1882, put into practice. The Immigration Act of 1891 gave the federal government the exclusive power to regulate immigration. The following year, in 1892, the newly centralized immigration reception center opened on Ellis Island.

In 1896, in the midst of a severe economic depression, a bipartisan majority in Congress passed a law requiring all immigrants to pass a literacy test, but it was vetoed by President McKinley. Subsequent efforts to enact such a law met a similar fate until 1917, when fear that the nation would face a wave of immigrants fleeing Europe at the end of World War I generated enough support for Congress to override President Wilson's veto and enact the Immigration Act of 1917. This landmark legislation implemented a literacy test and created an "Asiatic Barred Zone" to deny admission to people from India, Burma, Siam, Afghanistan, Arabia, the Malay Islands, and Polynesia. Foreshadowing the Red Scare that followed World War I, it also tightened restrictions on radicals to exclude members of anarchist and revolutionary organizations.

The era of open-door immigration came to a decisive end in the 1920s. Bills were introduced in Congress to suspend immigration altogether, but legislators compromised on a quota plan based on national origins, which was incorporated into the emergency restriction law passed in 1921. After a series of modifications and heated debates, Congress enacted a law on May 26, 1924, limiting immigration of specific groups to 2 percent of the number recorded by the 1890 census. The consequences were dramatic. European immigration dropped from more than 800,000 in 1921 to less than 150,000 by 1929. In that year, Congress passed the National Origins Act that put the quota system in place on a permanent basis, which, along with the Great Depression, reduced immigration to the United States in the 1930s to the lowest level since 1820.

IN THEIR OWN WORDS

Most immigrants came to the United States hoping to provide a better life for themselves and their families. Walter Lindstrom, who emigrated from Sweden in 1914, began to prepare for this journey when he was only fourteen. After he settled in Chicago, he worked for a time as a hospital orderly, then as a fireman for the railroad, and finally as a cement contractor. At age eighty-three Lindstrom recalled his expectations of a new beginning in America during his childhood on a farm in Sweden.

> My family [in Sweden] had about fifteen acres of poor soil, which did not yield much in the way of crops....I was the oldest child in the family, and also a boy, so I had many chores to do. I had to chop wood, split kindling, carry hay, carry water, and take care of the farm animals....Then in the summer the fields had to be plowed, potatoes planted, harvest to be gathered in the fall, barley to be threshed....Work, work, all the time. No end. No compensation. Only an existence.
>
> I kept on pressing my father that I wanted to go. Somewhere, someplace. Anyplace. Maybe on a ship. Maybe to America. I always remembered the alluring tales of the Wild West—Indians, buffaloes, everything.
>
> And what tales the immigrants had to tell when they returned from America, the promised land! Nuggets of gold hanging on Christmas trees, diamonds on the waysides, sparkling pearls in crystal water begging to be held in human hands. And how good those homecomers looked—fur coats, cuffs on well-creased trousers, and money! Sure, big American bills. Not small like Swedish bills....
>
> I remember the day I left home. Mother had prepared some home-baked beans and salt pork. She was very quiet when I left. Maybe she cried later. Father went with me to the railroad station. He looked pretty sad and I saw tears in his eyes as he wished me well.[1]

By the turn of the century, Italians had created the largest immigrant community in Philadelphia. Many came to the city as laborers contracted by the highly successful entrepreneur, Frank DiBaradino. An immigrant himself from the rural region of Abruzzo, DiBaradino advertised for workers throughout Italy, and, as the proprietor of a steamship ticket agency, he offered them interest-free loans to pay for the Atlantic crossing. By 1940 approximately 37,000 immigrants had taken advantage of his services, which often extended to matchmaking. He not only found jobs on the railroads and in the mines but often personally introduced these men to the women who would become their wives. DiBaradino eventually became the largest labor contractor in Philadelphia. His son later described his father's effective recruiting techniques:

> Agents travelled through the countryside of Abruzzo encouraging and channelizing emigration to Philadelphia with promises of immediate employment. They came as couriers of good fortune. Villagers and country dwellers alike passed on the good tidings that in Philadelphia, some place in America, there were "paesans" who not only had good jobs to give, but who also lent emigrants assistance in obtaining passage across the ocean and in becoming settled among other "paesans" and friends in a strange country. The branch office of the Philadelphia contractors, located in strategic places throughout Abruzzo, became the direct link between the hintermost hamlet in Abruzzo and adjacent regions and the Italian colony in Philadelphia.[2]

Italian immigrants, ca. 1900, on Ellis Island, the main receiving station for nearly three-fourths of all the immigrants from its opening in 1892 until its closing in 1954. Italians were the largest group among the new immigrants.

In 1910 the U.S. Immigration Commission opened the Angel Island detention center, off the coast of San Francisco, for the few Chinese who were allowed to enter the United States following a loosening of the Exclusion Act of 1882. Modeled after Ellis island, the point of entry for most European immigrants, Angel Island housed new arrivals until U.S. immigration inspectors determined whether they were eligible to settle in the United States. The experience made a lasting, often unpleasant impression on the nearly 175,000 Chinese who were detained there before 1940, when the center shut down. In the following passage, a woman immigrant recalls her detention at Angel Island in 1913 when she was nineteen years old.

> There was not much for us to do on the island. In the morning we got up and washed our faces. Afterwards, we had breakfast. After we ate, we napped or washed our own clothes. At lunch time we had congee in a large serving bowl with some cookies. Then at night we had rice with a main dish. You picked at some of it...and that was that. We ate in a huge dining hall....They allowed us to go outside to the yard or even out to the dock, where there were grass and trees, tall and fan-like. The women were allowed to wander around, jump around, and stick our hands or feet into the water to fish out seaweed. Otherwise, the day would have been hard to pass....
>
> I was interrogated one day for several hours. They asked me so much, I broke out in a sweat. Sometimes they would try to trip you: "Your husband said such-and-such and now you say this?" But the answer was out already and it was too late to take it back, so I couldn't do anything about it. If they said you were wrong, then it was up to them whether to land you or not. Later, upon landing, I noticed a white man kept coming around to my husband's laundry and looking at me through the glass window. That was how they checked you out to make sure you didn't go elsewhere.[3]

It was common for men from Eastern Europe to precede other family members. As soon as they earned enough money to pay for the trip and found housing, they usually sent for their wives and children. Such was the case for Abraham Blum, who was born in Romania in 1855 and moved several times in his homeland before deciding to immigrate to the United States. He settled in Philadelphia among his "landsmen," other Jewish immigrants from Romania, and sent for his family. His son, Samuel, later recounted the family's journey to Philadelphia and described the city's checkerboard of ethnic enclaves.

> My father was the first to leave Romania....As far as could be verified, he travelled overland, boarded ship at Antwerp and landed in Philadelphia on March 23, 1900....The second contingent was made up of [his children] Ben, Rose, Gitel and Gitel's fiancé, Moyshe. They traveled a similar route and landed, also in Philadelphia, several months later.
>
> They apparently lost little time in setting up living quarters. Gitel did the house-keeping and the others found work; Rose and Ben in the needle industry and Moyshe at tailoring. My father, I believe, found work as a shoe cutter....
>
> My mother was in charge of bringing the rest of her brood; Kate, myself and Ester, aged ten, six and three respectively. Across Europe to Antwerp and across four thousand miles of ocean, fourteen days of ocean travel, to our destination in Philadelphia. As I finish the foregoing sentence I hesitate, to

marvel at the fortitude and daring of the undertaking, and I well up anew with admiration.

The area in which we settled was at the time a sort of concentrated repository for Jewish immigrants from Russia, Poland and Romania.... From Catherine Street south, the Italian element predominated but they were left behind in a sort of "Little Italy" as the Jewish community by-passed them and began again at about Federal Street, continuing to spread further south. From Second Street east, the Slavic and Polish immigrants were apparently more comfortable, and north of Lombard and west of Sixth was the domain of the earlier arrivals already established and "Americanized"; there were few, if any, black people living in the area at that time.

I recollect that in our immediate area there were Romanian restaurants, Romanian "Chainas" (Tea Houses), their signs showing a large teapot with a smaller teapot superimposed on the same, and there was the "Romanish shiel" (Romanian synagogue), still there on Lombard Street.[4]

Rose Schneiderman (1882–1972), who became a prominent trade union organizer, emigrated from Russia with her family. In this account, published in a popular magazine, *The Independent,* in 1905, she recounts with pride the ups and downs of her family's fortunes and her response to the burdens that fell upon her.

My name is Rose Schneiderman, and I was born in some small city of Russian Poland. I don't know the name of the city, and have no memory of that part of my childhood. When I was about five years of age my parents brought me to this country and we settled in New York.

So my earliest recollections are of living in a crowded street among the East Side Jews, for we also are Jews.

My father got work as a tailor, and we lived in two rooms on Eldridge Street, and did very well, though not so well as in Russia, because mother and father both earned money, and here father alone earned the money, while mother attended to the house. There were then two other children besides me, a boy of three and one of five.

I went to school until I was nine years old, enjoying it thoroughly and making great progress, but then my father died of brain fever and mother was left with three children and another one coming. So I had to stay at home to help her and she went out to look for work....

I was the house worker, preparing the meals and looking after the other children—the baby, a little girl of six years, and a boy of nine. I managed very well, tho the meals were not very elaborate. I could cook simple things like porridge, coffee and eggs, and mother used to prepare the meat before she went away in the morning, so that all I had to do was to put it in the pan at night....

I was finally released by my little sister being taken by an aunt, and the two boys going to the Hebrew Orphan Asylum, which is a splendid institution, and turns out good men. One of these brothers is now a student in the City College, and the other is a page in the Stock Exchange.

When the other children were sent away mother was able to send me back to school, and I stayed in this school (Houston Street Grammar) till I had reached the Sixth Grammar Grade.

Then I had to leave in order to help support the family. I got a place in Hearn's as a cash girl, and after working there three weeks changed to Ridley's, where I remained for two and a half years. I finally left because the pay was so very poor and there did not seem to be any chance of advancement, and a friend told me that I could do better making caps.[5]

After Texas gained its independence from Mexico in 1836 and became a state in 1845, conflict between Anglo Texans and Mexicans persisted, becoming especially acute in the late nineteenth century when political turmoil and economic decline in their homeland prompted many Mexicans to travel northward in search of jobs or education. José Vasconcelos (1882–1959), who became a prominent educator and politician in Mexico, experienced a clash of cultures firsthand after his parents crossed the border to secure better schooling for their children. In his autobiography, *Ulises criollo,* published in 1945, Vasconcelos recalls the ethnic and national rivalries that surfaced in the classroom and on the playground. In the passage below he alludes to the divergent views of Mexicans and Anglos over the legacy of the Battle of the Alamo, a key event in the revolt against Mexico that secured Texas independence.

Piedras Negras [Mexico, opposite Eagle Pass, Texas] was a prosperous town, but it lacked a good school. On the other side of the border, the Yankees matched their concern with material progress with careful attention to education. Because of that my family moved to Eagle Pass when I was about ten years old....

We discussed issues in a democratic manner; the teacher confined herself to directing the debates. Texas independence and the war of 1847 divided the class into rival camps. We constantly talked about the Alamo, the cruel executions carried on

New York City's Lower East Side, photographed by Jacob Riis (1849–1914), ca. 1900. A large number of immigrants established small businesses and lived and worked in this district.

by Santa Anna, and the [treatment of] prisoners of war. There were only a few Mexicans in the class, but we were determined [to defend Mexico]. When I refer to Mexicans I include many who, despite their residence in Texas and their parents' U.S. citizenship, sided with me because of ethnic affinity. Had they done otherwise, they would have still been considered Mexicans because Anglos labeled them as such. Full-fledged Mexicans rarely went to the school. For years I was the only one.

I never felt obligated to make excuses [about Mexican history or Mexican society]. But when it was affirmed in class that one hundred Yankees could chase off one thousand Mexicans, I would rise and say, "That isn't true." I would get even more angry when someone would assert, "Mexicans are a semicivilized people." At home I always heard the opposite, that it was the Yankees who were the newcomers to culture. I would intervene, remarking [to the other students], "But look at Joe [José Vasconcelos]. He is a Mexican. Isn't he civilized? Isn't he a gentleman?" For the moment, that just observation would reestablish cordiality. But that would last only until the next lesson, until we would again read in our textbook phrases and judgments that drove me to ask for permission to refute them. Passions would rise anew. We would make challenging signs to each other. At first I would only have to remain alert in class and be ready to launch my verbal defenses. The other Mexicans would support me and take care of my rivals; during school holidays they would fight them.[6]

Questions

1. Identify the major groups known as the "New Immigrants."
2. Why did the New Immigrants leave their homelands, and why did they choose to settle in particular regions of the United States?
3. What were the major changes in immigration law during 1860–1930 period?
4. How did old-stock Americans greet the New Immigrants?

Sources

1. Joan Morrison and Charlotte Fox Zabusky, *American Mosaic: The Immigrant Experience in the Words of Those Who Lived It* (Pittsburgh: University of Pittsburgh Press, 1993)
2. Jerre Mangione and Ben Morreale, *La Storia: Five Centuries of the Italian American Experience* (New York: HarperCollins, 1992), 50
3. Him Mark Lai, Genny Lim, and Judy Yung, eds., *Island: Poetry and History of Chinese Immigrants on Angel Island, 1910–1940* (Seattle: University of Washington Press, 1980), 72, 117
4. Samuel Blum, unpublished memoir. Copyright Selma Chodoff, 1977.
5. Rose Schneiderman, "A Cap Maker's Story," *The Independent,* 58 (April 27, 1905), pp. 935–936
6. José Vasconcelos, *Ulises criolo,* 2 vols. (Mexico City: Ediciones Botas, 1945), 1:22, 24–27, 29–33, trans. Oscar J. Martinez; reprinted in Oscar J. Martinez, ed., *U.S.–Mexico Borderlands: Historical and Contemporary Perspectives* (Wilmington, Del.: Scholarly Resources, Inc, 1996), 103–106

CHAPTER TWENTY-FOUR

THE GREAT DEPRESSION AND THE NEW DEAL

1929–1940

Domenica del Corriere, Demonstration in New York. Unemployed, depression.

CHAPTER OUTLINE

AMERICAN COMMUNITIES
Sit-Down Strike at Flint: Automobile Workers Organize a New Union

In the gloomy evening of February 11, 1937, 400 tired, unshaven, but very happy strikers marched out of the sprawling automobile factory known as Fisher Body Number 1. Most carried American flags and small bundles of clothing. A makeshift banner on top of the plant announced "Victory Is Ours." A wildly cheering parade line of a thousand supporters greeted the strikers at the gates. Shouting with joy, honking horns, and singing songs, the celebrants marched to two other factories to greet other emerging strikers. After forty-four days, the great Flint sit-down strike was over.

Flint, Michigan, was the heart of production for General Motors, the largest corporation in the world. In 1936 GM's net profits had reached $285 million, and its total assets were $1.5 billion. Originally a center for lumbering and then carriage making, Flint had boomed with the auto industry during the 1920s. Thousands of migrants streamed into the city, attracted by assembly line jobs averaging about $30 a week. By 1930 Flint's population had grown to about 150,000 people, 80 percent of whom depended on work at General Motors. A severe housing shortage made living conditions difficult. Tar-paper shacks, tents, even railroad cars were the only shelter available for many. Parts of the city resembled a mining camp.

The Great Depression hit Flint very hard. Employment at GM fell from a 1929 high of 56,000 to fewer than 17,000 in 1932. As late as 1938 close to half the city's families were receiving some kind of emergency relief. By that time, as in thousands of other American communities, Flint's private and county relief agencies had been overwhelmed by the needs of the unemployed and their families. Two new national agencies based in Washington, D.C., the Federal Emergency Relief Administration and the Works Progress Administration, had replaced local sources of aid during the economic crisis.

The United Automobile Workers (UAW) came to Flint in 1936 seeking to organize GM workers into one industrial union. The previous year, Congress had passed the National Labor Relations Act (also known as the Wagner Act), which made union organizing easier by guaranteeing the right of workers to join unions and bargain collectively. The act established the National Labor Relations Board to oversee union elections and prohibit illegal anti-union activities by employers. But the obstacles to labor organizing were still enormous. Unemployment was high, and GM had maintained a vigorous anti-union policy for years. By the fall of 1936, the UAW had signed up only a thousand members. The key moment came with the seizure of two Flint GM plants by a few hundred auto workers on December 30, 1936. The idea was to stay in the factories until strikers could achieve a collective bargaining agreement with General Motors. "We don't aim to keep the plants or try to run them," explained one sit-downer to a reporter, "but we want to see that nobody takes our jobs. We don't think we're breaking the law, or at least we don't think we're doing anything really bad."

The sit-down strike was a new and daring tactic that gained popularity among American industrial workers during the 1930s. In 1936 there were 48 sit-downs involving nearly 90,000 workers, and in 1937 some 400,000 workers participated in 477 sit-down strikes. Sit-downs expressed the militant exuberance of the rank and file. As one union song of the day put it:

When they tie the can to a union man,
Sit down! Sit down!
When they give him the sack they'll take him back,
Sit down! Sit down!
When the speed up comes, just twiddle your thumbs,
Sit down! Sit down!
When the boss won't talk don't take a walk,
Sit down! Sit down!

The Flint strikers carefully organized themselves into what one historian called "the sit down community." Each plant elected a strike committee and appointed its own police chief and sanitary engineer. Strikers were divided into "families" of fifteen, each with a captain. No alcohol was allowed, and strikers were careful not to destroy company property. Committees were organized for every conceivable purpose: food, recreation, sanitation, education, and contact with the outside. Sit-downers formed glee clubs and small orchestras to entertain themselves. Using loudspeakers, they broadcast concerts and speeches to their supporters outside the gates. A Women's Emergency Brigade—the strikers' wives, mothers, and daughters—provided crucial support preparing food and maintaining militant picket lines.

As the sit-down strike continued through January, support in Flint and around the nation grew. Overall production in the GM empire dropped from 53,000 vehicles per week to 1,500. Reporters and union supporters flocked to the plants. On January 11, in the so-called Battle of Running Bulls, strikers and their supporters clashed violently with Flint police and private GM guards. Michigan governor Frank Murphy, sympathetic to the strikers, brought in the National Guard to protect them. He refused to enforce an injunction obtained by GM to evict the strikers.

In the face of determined unity by the sit-downers, GM gave in and recognized the UAW as the exclusive bargaining agent in all sixty of its factories. The strike was perhaps the most important in American labor history, sparking a huge growth in union membership in the automobile and other mass-production industries. Rose Pesotta, a textile union organizer, described the wild victory celebration in Flint's overflowing Pengelly Building: "People sang and joked and laughed and cried, deliriously joyful. Victory meant a freedom they had never known before. No longer would they be afraid to join unions."

Out of the tight-knit, temporary community of the sit-down strike emerged a looser yet more permanent kind of community: a powerful, nationwide trade union of automobile workers. The UAW struggled successfully to win recognition and collective bargaining rights from other carmakers, such as Chrysler and Ford. The national UAW, like other new unions in the mass-production industries, was composed of locals around the country. The permanent community of unionized auto workers won significant improvements in wages, working conditions, and benefits. Locals also became influential in the political and social lives of their larger communities—industrial cities such as Flint, Detroit, and Toledo. Nationally, organized labor became a crucial component of the New Deal political coalition and a key power broker in the Democratic Party. The new reality of a national community of organized labor would alter the national political and economic landscape for decades to come.

KEY TOPICS

- Causes and consequences of the Great Depression
- The politics of hard times
- Franklin D. Roosevelt and the two New Deals
- The expanding federal sphere in the West
- American cultural life during the 1930s
- Legacies and limits of New Deal reform

HARD TIMES

No event of the twentieth century had a more profound impact on American life than the Great Depression of the 1930s. Statistics can document a slumping economy, mass unemployment, and swelling relief rolls—but these numbers tell only part of the story. The emotional and psychological toll of these years, what one writer called "the invisible scar," must also be considered in understanding the worst economic crisis in American history. Even today, depression-era experiences retain a central, even mythical, place in the lives and memories of millions of American families.

The Bull Market

Stock trading in the late 1920s captured the imagination of the broad American public. The stock market resembled a sporting arena, millions following stock prices as they did the exploits of Babe Ruth or Jack Dempsey. Many business leaders and economists as much as told Americans that it was their duty to buy stocks. John J. Raskob, chairman of the board of General Motors, wrote an article for the *Ladies' Home Journal* titled "Everybody Ought to Be Rich." A person who saved $15 each month and invested it in good common stocks would, he claimed, have $80,000 within twenty years. The *Saturday Evening Post* printed a poem that captured the fever:

> *Oh, hush thee, my babe, granny's bought some more shares*
> *Daddy's gone out to play with the bulls and the bears,*
> *Mother's buying on tips and she simply can't lose,*
> *And baby shall have some expensive new shoes!*

During the bull market of the 1920s, stock prices increased at roughly twice the rate of industrial production. Paper value far outran real value. By the end of the decade, stocks that had been bought mainly on the basis of their earning power, which was passed on to stockholders in the form of dividends, now came to be purchased only for the resale value after their prices rose. Anyone reading the financial pages of a newspaper would be amazed at the upward climb. In 1928 alone, for example, the price of Radio Corporation of America stock shot up from 85 points to 420; Chrysler stock more than doubled, from 63 to 132.

Yet only about 4 million Americans owned any stocks at all, out of a total population of 120 million. Many of these stock buyers had been lured into the market through easy-credit, margin accounts. Margin accounts allowed investors to purchase stocks by making a small down payment (as low as 10 percent), borrowing the rest from a broker, and using the shares as collateral, or security, on the loan. Just as installment plans had stimulated the automobile and other industries, "buying on the margin" brought new customers to the stock market. Investment trusts, similar to today's mutual funds, attracted many new investors with promises of high returns based on their managers' expert knowledge of the market. Corporations with excess capital found that lending money to stockbrokers was more profitable than plowing it back into their own plants to develop new technologies. All these new approaches to buying stock contributed to an expansive and optimistic atmosphere on Wall Street.

The Crash

Although often portrayed as a one- or two-day catastrophe, the Wall Street crash of 1929 was in reality a steep downward slide. The bull market peaked in early September, and prices drifted downward. On October 23 the Dow Jones industrials lost 21 points in one hour, and many large investors concluded the boom was over. The boom itself rested on expectations of continually rising prices; once those expectations began to melt, the market had to decline. On Monday, October 28, the Dow lost 38 points, or 13 percent of its value. On October 29, "Black Tuesday," the bottom seemed to fall out. Over 16 million shares, more than double the previous record, were traded as panic selling took hold. For many, stocks no buyers were available at any price.

The situation worsened. The market's fragile foundation of credit, based on the margin debt, quickly crumbled. Many investors with margin accounts had no choice but to sell when stock values fell. Since the shares themselves represented the security for their

Stockbrokers, their customers, and employees of the New York Stock Exchange gather nervously on Wall Street during the stock market crash of 1929. October 29 was the worst single day in the 112-year history of the exchange, as panic selling caused many stocks to lose half their value.

loans, more money had to be put up to cover the loans when prices declined. By mid-November about $30 billion in the market price of stocks had been wiped out. Half the value of the stocks listed in the *New York Times* index was lost in ten weeks.

The nation's political and economic leaders downplayed the impact of Wall Street's woes. "The fundamental business of the country," President Herbert Hoover told Americans in late October, "is on a sound and prosperous basis." Secretary of the Treasury Andrew Mellon spoke for many in the financial world when he described the benefits of the slump: "It will purge the rottenness out of the system. High costs of living and high living will come down. People will work harder, live a more moral life. Values will be adjusted, and enterprising people will pick up the wrecks from less competent people." At the end of 1929 hardly anyone was predicting that a depression would follow the stock market crash.

Underlying Weaknesses

It would be oversimple to say that the stock market crash "caused" the Great Depression. But like a person who catches a chill, the economy after the crash became less resistant to existing sources of infection. The resulting sickness revealed underlying economic weaknesses left over from the previous decade. First, workers and consumers by and large received too small a share of the enormous increases in labor productivity. Better machinery and more efficient industrial organization had increased labor productivity enormously. But wages and salaries had not risen nearly as much.

In effect, the automobile of American capitalism had one foot pressed to the accelerator of produc-

DISTRIBUTION OF TOTAL FAMILY INCOME AMONG VARIOUS SEGMENTS OF THE POPULATION, 1929–1944 (IN PERCENTAGES)

Year	Poorest Fifth	Second Poorest Fifth	Middle Fifth	Second Wealthiest Fifth	Wealthiest Fifth	Wealthiest 5 Percent
1929	12.5		13.8	19.3	54.4	30.0
1935–1936	4.1	9.2	14.1	20.9	51.7	26.5
1941	4.1	9.5	15.3	22.3	48.8	24.0
1944	4.9	10.9	16.2	22.2	45.8	20.7

Source: Adapted from U.S. Bureau of the Census, *Historical Statistics of the United States, Colonial Times to 1970*, Bicentennial Edition (Washington, D.C.: U.S. Government Printing Office, 1975), p. 301.

tion and another on the brake of consumption. Between 1923 and 1929 manufacturing output per worker-hour increased by 32 percent. But wages during the same period rose only 8 percent, or one-quarter the rise in productivity. Moreover, the rise in productivity itself had encouraged overproduction in many industries. The farm sector had never been able to regain its prosperity of the World War I years. Farmers suffered under a triple burden of declining prices for their crops, a drop in exports, and large debts incurred by wartime expansion (see Chapter 23).

The most important weakness in the economy was the extremely unequal distribution of income and wealth. In 1929, the top 0.1 percent of American families (24,000 families) had an aggregate income equal to that of the bottom 42 percent (11.5 million families). The top 5 percent of American families received 30 percent of the nation's income; the bottom 60 percent got only 26 percent. About 71 percent of American families had annual incomes below $2,500. Nearly 80 percent of the nation's families (21.5 million households) had no savings; the top 0.1 percent held 34 percent of all savings. The top 0.5 percent of Americans owned 32.4 percent of the net wealth of the entire population—the greatest such concentration of wealth in the nation's history.

The stock market crash undermined the confidence, investment, and spending of businesses and the well-to-do. Manufacturers decreased their production and began laying off workers, and layoffs brought further declines in consumer spending and another round of production cutbacks. A spurt of consumer spending might have checked this downward spiral, but consumers had less to spend as industries laid off workers and reduced work hours. With a shrinking market for products, businesses were hesitant to expand. A large proportion of the nation's banking funds were tied to the speculative bubble of Wall Street stock buying. Many banks began to fail as anxious depositors withdrew their funds, which were uninsured. Thousands of families lost their savings to these failures. An 86 percent plunge in agricultural prices between 1929 and 1933, compared to a decline in agricultural production of only 6 percent, brought suffering to America's farmers.

Mass Unemployment

At a time when unemployment insurance did not exist and public relief was completely inadequate, the loss of a job could mean economic catastrophe for workers

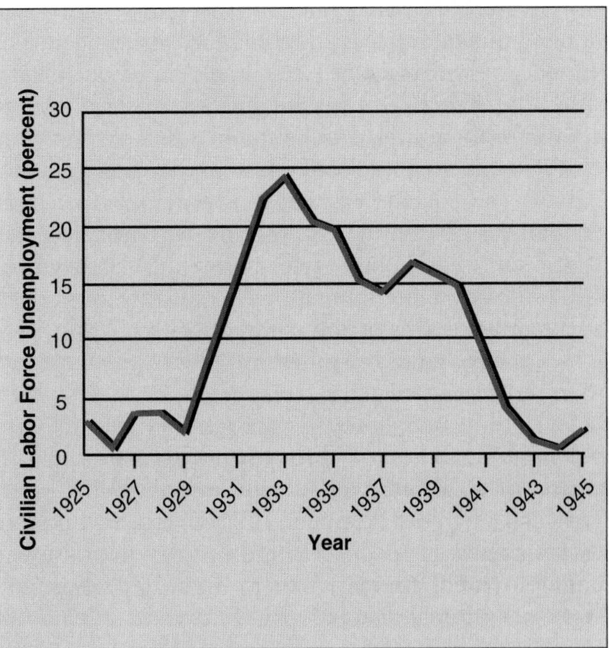

Unemployment, 1929–1945 *In 1939, despite six years of New Deal programs, unemployment still hovered around 18 percent of the workforce. Only the onset of World War II ended the unemployment crisis.*

Source: U.S. Bureau of the Census, *Historical Statistics of the United States, Colonial Times to 1970*, Bicentennial Edition (Washington, D.C.: U.S. Government Printing Office, 1975), p. 135.

and their families. Massive unemployment across America became the most powerful sign of a deepening depression. In 1930 the Department of Labor estimated that 4.2 million workers, or roughly 9 percent of the labor force, were out of work. These figures nearly doubled in 1931, and by 1933, 12.6 million workers—over one-quarter of the labor force—were without jobs. Other sources put the figure that year above 16 million, or nearly one out of every three workers. None of these statistics tells us how long people were unemployed or how many Americans found only part-time work.

What did it mean to be unemployed and without hope in the early 1930s? Figures give us only an outline of the grim reality. Many Americans, raised believing that they were responsible for their own fate, blamed themselves for their failure to find work. Contemporary journalists and social workers noted the common feelings of shame and guilt expressed by the unemployed. Even those who did not blame themselves struggled with feelings of inadequacy, uselessness, and despair. One unemployed Houston woman told a relief caseworker, "I'm just no good, I guess. I've given up ever amounting to anything. It's no use." "Drives a man crazy, or drives him to drink, hangin' around," said an out-of-work Connecticut knife maker. For many, nighttime was the worst. "What is going to become of us?" wondered an Arizona man. "I've lost twelve and a half pounds this month, just thinking. You can't sleep, you know. You wake up about 2 A.M., and you lie and think." A West Virginia man wrote his senator to complain, "My children have not got no shoes and clothing to go to school with, and we haven't got enough bed clothes to keep us warm." For the most desperate, contemplating suicide was not unusual. "Can you be so kind as to advise me as to which would be the most human way to dispose of my self and family, as this is about the only thing that I see left to do," one despondent Pennsylvania man inquired of a state relief agency.

Joblessness proved especially difficult for men between the ages of thirty-five and fifty-five, the period in their lives when family responsibilities were heaviest. Nathan Ackerman, a psychiatrist who went to Pennsylvania to observe the impact of prolonged unemployment on coal miners, found an enormous sense of "internal distress":

> They hung around street corners and in groups. They gave each other solace. They were loath to go home because they were indicted, as if it were their fault for being unemployed. A jobless man was a lazy good-for-nothing. The women punished the men for not bringing home the bacon, by withholding themselves sexually. . . . These men suffered from depression. They felt despised, they were ashamed of themselves. They cringed, they comforted one another. They avoided home.

Dorothea Lange captured the lonely despair of unemployment in White Angel Bread Line, San Francisco, 1933. *During the 1920s Lange had specialized in taking portraits of wealthy families, but by 1932 she could no longer stand the contradiction between her portrait business and "what was going on in the street." She said of this photograph: "There are moments such as these when time stands still and all you can do is hold your breath and hope it will wait for you."*

Unemployment upset the psychological balance in many families by undermining the traditional authority of the male breadwinner. Women, because their labor was cheaper than men's, found it easier to hold onto jobs. Female clerks, secretaries, maids, and waitresses earned much less than male factory workers, but their jobs were more likely to survive hard times. Men responded in a variety of ways to unemployment. Some withdrew emotionally; others became angry or took to drinking. A few committed suicide. One Chicago social worker, writing about unemployment in 1934, summed up the strains she found in families: "Fathers feel they have lost their prestige in the home; there is much nagging, mothers nag at the fathers, parents nag at the children. Children of working age who earn meager salaries find it hard to turn over all their earnings and deny themselves even the greatest necessities and as a result leave home."

Isaac Soyer's Employment Agency, *a 1937 oil painting, offered one of the decade's most sensitive efforts at depicting the anxiety and sense of isolation felt by millions of depression-era job hunters.*

Isaac Soyer, *Employment Agency*, 1937. Oil on canvas 34¼ x 45 inches, (87 x 114.3). Whitney Museum of Art, New York.

Pressures on those lucky enough to have a job increased as well. Anna Novak, a Chicago meat packer, recalled the degrading harassment at the hands of foremen: "You could get along swell if you let the boss slap you on the behind and feel you up. God, I hate that stuff, you don't know!" Fear of unemployment and a deep desire for security marked the depression generation. "I mean there's a conditioning here by the Depression," a sanitation worker told an interviewer many years later. "I'm what I call a security cat. I don't dare switch [jobs]. `Cause I got too much whiskers on it, seniority."

Hoover's Failure

The enormity of the Great Depression overwhelmed traditional—and meager—sources of relief. In most communities across America these sources were a patchwork of private agencies and local government units, such as towns, cities, or counties. They simply lacked the money, resources, and staff to deal with the worsening situation. In large urban centers like Detroit and Chicago, unemployment approached 50 percent by 1932. Smaller communities could not cope either. One West Virginia coal-mining county with 1,500 unemployed miners had only $9,000 to meet relief needs for that year. Unemployed transients, attracted by warm weather, posed a special problem for communities in California and Florida. By the end of 1931 Los Angeles had 70,000 nonresident jobless and homeless men; new arrivals numbered about 1,200 a day.

There was great irony, even tragedy, in President Hoover's failure to respond to human suffering. He had administered large-scale humanitarian efforts during World War I with great efficiency. Yet he seemed to most people a man with little personal warmth. Hoover made his reputation as an engineer and as one who believed in the importance of objective studies of social and economic problems, yet he failed to face the facts of the depression. He ignored all the mounting evidence to the contrary when he claimed in his 1931 State of the Union Address, "Our people are providing against distress from unemployment in true American fashion by magnificent response to public appeal and by action of the local governments."

Hoover resisted the growing calls from Congress and local communities for a greater federal role in relief efforts or public works projects. He worried, as he told Congress after vetoing one measure, about injuring "the initiative and enterprise of the American people." The President's Emergency Committee for Unemployment, established in 1930, and its successor, the President's Organization for Unemployment Relief (POUR), created in 1931, did little more than encourage local groups to raise money to help the unemployed. Walter S. Gifford, chairman of POUR and president of AT&T, insisted that local relief groups could handle the needs of Americans in distress. "My sober and considered judgement," he told Congress in early 1932, "is that at this stage Federal aid would be a disservice to the unemployed."

Hoover's plan for recovery centered on restoring business confidence. His administration's most important institutional response to the depression was the Reconstruction Finance Corporation (RFC), established in early 1932 and based on the War Finance Corporation of the World War I years. The RFC was designed to make government credit available to ailing banks, railroads, insurance companies, and other businesses, thereby stimulating economic activity. The key assumption here was that the credit problem was one of supply (for businesses) rather than demand (from consumers). But given the public's low purchasing power, most businesses were not interested in obtaining loans for expansion.

The RFC managed to save numerous banks and other businesses from going under, but its approach did not hasten recovery. And Hoover was loath to use the RFC to make direct grants to states, cities, or individuals. In July 1932, congressional Democrats pushed through the Emergency Relief Act, which authorized the RFC to lend $300 million to states that had exhausted their own relief funds. Hoover grudgingly signed the bill, but less than $30 million had actually been given out by the end of 1933. Although Congress authorized the RFC to spend money on public works, only a small fraction of its $2 billion budget went to such programs.

Protest and the Election of 1932

By 1932, the desperate mood of many Americans was finding expression in direct, sometimes violent protests that were widely covered in the press. On March 7, communist organizers led a march of several thousand Detroit auto workers and unemployed to the Ford River Rouge factory in nearby Dearborn. When the demonstrators refused orders to turn back, Ford-controlled police fired tear gas and bullets, killing four and seriously wounding fifty others. Some 40,000 people attended a tense funeral service a few days later. Desperate farmers in Iowa organized the Farmers' Holiday Association, aimed at raising prices by refusing to sell produce. In August, some 1,500 farmers turned back cargo trucks outside Sioux City, Iowa, and made a point by dumping milk and other perishables into ditches.

The spring of 1932 also saw the "Bonus Army" begin descending on Washington, D.C. This protest took its name from a 1924 act of Congress that had promised a $1,000 bonus—in the form of a bond that would not mature until 1945—to every veteran of World War I. The veterans who were gathering in Washington demanded immediate payment of the bonus in cash. By summer they and their families numbered around 20,000 and were camped out all over the capital city. Their lobbying convinced the House to pass a bill for immediate payment, but the Senate rejected the bill and most of the veterans left. At the end of July U.S. Army troops led by Chief of Staff General Douglas MacArthur forcibly evicted the remaining 2,000 veterans from their encampment. MacArthur exaggerated the menace of the peaceful demonstrators, insisting they were driven by "the essence of revolution." The spectacle of these unarmed and unemployed men, the heroes of 1918, driven off by bayonets and bullets provided the most disturbing evidence yet of the failure of Hoover's administration.

The congressional elections of 1930 had already revealed a growing dissatisfaction with Hoover's approach. Democrats had won control of the House of Representatives for the first time since 1916 and gained eight seats in the Senate. In 1932, Democrats nominated Franklin D. Roosevelt, governor of New York, as their candidate. Roosevelt's acceptance speech stressed the need for reconstructing the nation's economy. "I pledge you, I pledge myself," he said, "to a new deal for the American people."

Roosevelt's plans for recovery were vague at best. He frequently attacked Hoover for reckless and extravagant spending and accused him of trying to center too much power in Washington. He also spoke of the need for government to meet "the problem of underconsumption" and to help in "distributing wealth and products more equitably." Hoover bitterly condemned Roosevelt's ideas as a "radical departure" from the American way of life. But with the depression growing worse every day, probably any Democrat would have defeated Hoover. The Democratic victory was overwhelming. Roosevelt carried forty-two states, taking the electoral college 472 to 59 and the popular vote by about 23 million to 16 million. Democrats won big majorities in both the House and the Senate. The stage was set for FDR's "new deal."

FDR AND THE FIRST NEW DEAL

No president of this century had a greater impact on American life and politics than Franklin Delano Roosevelt. To a large degree, the New Deal was a product of his astute political skills and the sheer force of his personality. The only president ever elected to four terms, FDR would loom as the dominant personality in American political life through depression and war. Roosevelt's leadership also inaugurated a forty-year-long period during which the Democrats would be the nation's majority party.

FDR the Man

Franklin Delano Roosevelt was born in 1882 in Dutchess County, New York, where he grew up an only child, secure and confident, on his family's vast estate. Franklin's father, James, had made a fortune through railroad investments, but he was already in his fifties when Franklin was born, and it was his mother, Sara Delano, who was the dominant figure in his childhood. Roosevelt's education at Groton, Harvard, and Columbia Law School reinforced the aristocratic values of his family: a strong sense of civic duty, the impor-

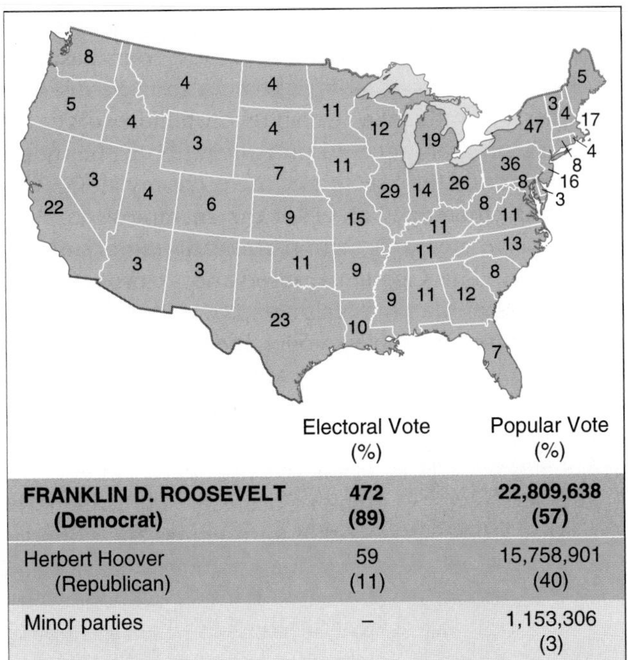

	Electoral Vote (%)	Popular Vote (%)
FRANKLIN D. ROOSEVELT (Democrat)	**472 (89)**	**22,809,638 (57)**
Herbert Hoover (Republican)	59 (11)	15,758,901 (40)
Minor parties	–	1,153,306 (3)

The Election of 1932 *Democrats owed their overwhelming victory in 1932 to the popular identification of the depression with the Hoover administration. Roosevelt's popular vote was about the same as Hoover's in 1928, and FDR's electoral college margin was even greater.*

tance of competitive athletics, and a commitment to public service.

In 1905 Franklin married his distant cousin, Anna Eleanor Roosevelt, niece of President Theodore Roosevelt. Eleanor would later emerge as an influential adviser and political force on her own. Franklin turned to politics as a career early on. He was elected as a Democrat to the New York State Senate in 1910, served as assistant navy secretary from 1913 to 1920, and was nominated for vice president by the Democrats in the losing 1920 campaign.

In the summer of 1921 Roosevelt was stricken with polio at his summer home. He was never to walk again without support. The disease strengthened his relationship with Eleanor, who encouraged him not only to fight his handicap but to continue his political career. The disease and FDR's response to it proved a turning point. His patience and determination in fighting the illness transformed him. The wealthy aristocrat, for whom everything had come relatively easy, now personally understood the meaning of struggle and hardship. "Once I spent two years lying in bed trying to move my big toe," he recalled. "After that anything else seems easy."

Elected governor of New York in 1928, Roosevelt served two terms and won a national reputation for reform. As governor, his achievements included instituting unemployment insurance, strengthening child labor laws, providing tax relief for farmers, and providing pensions for the old. As the depression hit the state, he slowly increased public works and set up a Temporary Emergency Relief Administration. With his eye on the White House, he began assembling a group of key advisers, the "brains trust," who would follow him to Washington. The central figures were Columbia Law School professor and progressive Raymond Moley; two economists, Rexford G. Tugwell and Adolf A. Berle; and attorneys Samuel Rosenman, Basil O'Connor, and Felix Frankfurter. The "brain trusters" shared a faith in the power of experts to set the economy right and a basic belief in government-business cooperation. They rejected the old progressive dream of re-creating an ideal society of small producers. Structural economic reform, they argued, must accept the modern reality of large corporate enterprise based on mass-production and distribution.

Restoring Confidence

In the first days of his administration Roosevelt conveyed a sense of optimism and activism that helped restore the badly shaken confidence of the nation. "First of all," he told Americans in his Inaugural Address on March 4, 1933, "let me assert my firm belief that the only thing we have to fear is fear itself." The very next day he issued an executive order calling for a four-day "bank holiday" to shore up the country's ailing financial system. More than 1,300 banks failed in 1930, more than 2,000 in 1931. Contemporary investigations had revealed a disquieting pattern of stock manipulation, illegal loans to bank officials, and tax evasion that helped erode public confidence in the banking system. Between election day and the inauguration, the banking system had come alarmingly close to shutting down altogether due to widespread bank failures and the hoarding of currency.

Roosevelt therefore called for a special session of Congress to deal with the banking crisis as well as with unemployment aid and farm relief. On March 12 he broadcast his first "fireside chat" to explain the steps he had taken to meet the financial emergency. These radio broadcasts became a standard part of Roosevelt's political technique, and they proved enormously successful. They gave courage to ordinary Americans and communicated a genuine sense of compassion from the White House.

Congress immediately passed the Emergency Banking Act, which gave the president broad discretionary powers over all banking transactions and foreign exchange. It authorized healthy banks to reopen only under licenses from the Treasury Department and provided for greater federal authority in managing the affairs of failed banks. By the middle of March about half the country's banks, holding about

90 percent of the nation's deposits, were open for business again. Banks began to attract new deposits from people who had been holding back their money. The bank crisis had passed.

The Hundred Days

From March to June of 1933—"the Hundred Days"—FDR pushed through Congress an extraordinary number of acts designed to combat various aspects of the depression. What came to be called the New Deal was no unified program to end the depression but rather an improvised series of reform and relief measures, some of which seemed to contradict each other. Roosevelt responded to pressures from Congress, from business, and from organized labor, but he also used his own considerable influence over public opinion to get his way. His program focused on reviving both the industrial and agricultural sectors of the economy along with providing emergency relief for the unemployed.

Five measures were particularly important and innovative. The Civilian Conservation Corps (CCC), established in March as an unemployment relief effort, provided work for jobless young men in protecting and conserving the nation's natural resources. Road construction, reforestation, flood control, and national park improvements were some of the major projects performed in work camps across the country. CCC workers received room and board and $30 each month, up to $25 of which had to be sent home to dependents. By the time the program was phased out in 1942, more than 2.5 million youths had worked in some 1,500 CCC camps.

This 1933 Vanity Fair *cartoon depicting the inauguration of* Franklin D. Roosevelt *captures the contrasting moods of the ebullient, victorious* FDR *and the glum, defeated* Herbert Hoover.

In May, Congress authorized $500 million for the Federal Emergency Relief Administration (FERA). Half the money went as direct relief to the states; the rest was distributed on the basis of a dollar of federal aid for every three dollars of state and local funds spent for relief. This system of outright federal grants differed significantly from Hoover's approach, which provided only for loans. Establishment of work relief projects, however, was left to state and local governments. To direct the FERA Roosevelt turned to Harry Hopkins, an experienced reformer from the world of New York social work. A brilliant administrator with a special commitment to ending racial discrimination in relief work, Hopkins became the New Deal's most influential figure in relief policies and one of Roosevelt's most trusted advisers.

The Agricultural Adjustment Administration (AAA) was set up to provide immediate

OVERVIEW

KEY LEGISLATION OF THE FIRST NEW DEAL ("HUNDRED DAYS," MARCH 9–JUNE 16, 1933)

Legislation	Purpose
Emergency Banking Relief Act	Enlarged federal authority over private banks Government loans to private banks
Civilian Conservation Corps	Unemployment relief Conservation of natural resources
Federal Emergency Relief Administration	Direct federal money for relief, funneled through state and local governments
Agricultural Adjustment Administration	Federal farm aid based on parity pricing and subsidy
Tennessee Valley Authority	Economic development and cheap electricity for Tennessee Valley
National Industrial Recovery Act	Self-regulating industrial codes to revive economic activity
Public Works Administration	Federal public works projects to increase employment and consumer spending

relief to the nation's farmers. The AAA established a new federal role in agricultural planning and price setting. It established parity prices for basic farm commodities, including corn, wheat, hogs, cotton, rice, and dairy products. The concept of parity pricing was based on the purchasing power that farmers had enjoyed during the prosperous years of 1909 to 1914. That period now became the benchmark for setting the prices of farm commodities. The AAA also incorporated the principle of subsidy, whereby farmers received benefit payments in return for reducing acreage or otherwise cutting production where surpluses existed. The funds for these payments were to be raised from new taxes on food processing.

The AAA raised total farm income and was especially successful in pushing up the prices of wheat, cotton, and corn. But it had some troubling side effects as well. Landlords often failed to share their AAA payments with tenant farmers, and they frequently used benefits to buy tractors and other equipment that displaced sharecroppers. Many Americans were disturbed, too, by the sight of surplus crops, livestock, and milk being destroyed while millions went hungry. The Southern Tenant Farmers Union (STFU), founded in 1934, emerged as an important voice of protest against AAA policies. Active in six states and composed of about thirty thousand tenant farmers (over half of whom were black), the STFU protested evictions, called strikes to raise farm labor wages, and challenged landlords to give tenants their fair share of subsidy payments. The STFU succeeded in drawing national attention to the plight of sharecroppers and tenant farmers, but it failed to influence national farm policy. The 1937 Bankhead-Jones Tenancy Act offered a very limited program of loans to tenant farmers, and the AAA remained a boon to large landlords.

The Tennessee Valley Authority (TVA) proved to be one of the most unique and controversial projects of the New Deal era. It had its origins in the federal government's effort during World War I to build a large hydroelectric power complex and munitions plant on the Tennessee River at Muscle Shoals, Alabama. During the 1920s, Republican senator George W. Norris of Nebraska had led an unsuccessful fight to provide for permanent government operation of the Muscle Shoals facilities on behalf of the area's population. The TVA, an independent public corporation, built dams and power plants, produced cheap fertilizer for farmers, and, most significantly, brought cheap electricity for the first time to thousands of people in six southern states. Denounced by some as a dangerous step toward socialism, the TVA stood for decades as a model of how careful government planning could dramatically improve the social and economic welfare of an underdeveloped region.

On the very last of the Hundred Days, Congress passed the National Industrial Recovery Act, the closest attempt yet at a systematic plan for economic recovery. It had two main parts. The National Recovery Administration (NRA) sought to stimulate production and competition in business by means of industrial codes regulating prices, output, and trade practices. In theory, each industry would be self-governed by a code hammered out by representatives of business, labor, and the consuming public. Once approved by the NRA in Washington, led by General Hugh Johnson and symbolized by the distinctive Blue Eagle stamp, the codes would have the force of law. In practice, almost all the NRA codes were written by the largest firms in any given industry; labor and consumers got short shrift. The sheer administrative complexities involved with code writing and compliance made a great many people unhappy with the NRA's operation. Overall, the NRA looked to business and industry leaders to find a way to recovery.

The second component, the Public Works Administration (PWA), led by Secretary of the Interior Harold Ickes, authorized $3.3 billion for the construction of roads, public buildings, and other projects. The idea was to provide jobs and thus stimulate the economy through increased consumer spending. A favorite image for this kind of spending was "priming the pump." Just as a farmer had to prime a pump with water before it could draw more water from the well, the government had to prime the economy with jobs for the unemployed. Eventually the PWA spent over $4.2 billion building roads, schools, post offices, bridges, courthouses, and other public buildings around the country. In thousands of communities today, these structures remain the most tangible reminders of the New Deal era.

LEFT TURN AND THE SECOND NEW DEAL

The Hundred Days legislative package tried to offer something for everybody. Certainly the active, can-do spirit in Washington brought reassurance that the nation was back on track. Yet the depression remained a stark reality for many millions. From the beginning, the New Deal had loud and powerful critics who complained bitterly that FDR had overstepped the traditional boundaries of government action. Others were angry that Roosevelt had not done nearly enough. These varied voices of protest helped shape the political debates of FDR's first term. Ultimately, they would push the New Deal in more radical directions.

Roosevelt's Critics

Criticism of the New Deal came from the right and the left. On the right, pro-Republican newspapers and the American Liberty League, a group of conservative businessmen organized in 1934, denounced Roosevelt and his advisers. They held the administration responsible for what they considered an attack on property rights, the growing welfare state, and the decline of personal liberty. Dominated by wealthy executives of Du Pont and General Motors, the league attracted support from a group of conservative Democrats, including Al Smith, the former presidential candidate, who declared the New Deal's laws "socialistic." The league supported anti-New Dealers for Congress, but in the 1934 election Democrats built up their majorities from 310 to 319 in the House and from 60 to 69 in the Senate—an unusually strong showing for the incumbent party in a midterm election.

Some of Roosevelt's staunchest early supporters turned critical. Father Charles E. Coughlin, a Catholic priest in suburban Detroit, attracted a huge national radio audience of 40 million listeners with passionate sermons attacking Wall Street, international bankers, and "plutocratic capitalism." Coughlin at first supported Roosevelt and the New Deal, and he tried to build a close personal relationship with the president. But by 1934 the ambitious Coughlin, frustrated by his limited influence on the administration, began attacking FDR. Roosevelt was a tool of special interests, he charged, who wanted dictatorial powers. New Deal policies were part of a communist conspiracy, threatening community autonomy with centralized federal power. Coughlin finally broke with FDR and founded the National Union for Social Justice. In 1936 the Coughlin-dominated Union Party nominated William Lemke, an obscure North Dakota congressman, to run for president. Lemke polled only 900,000 votes, but Coughlin continued his biting attacks on Roosevelt through 1940.

More troublesome for Roosevelt and his allies were the vocal and popular movements on the left. These found the New Deal too timid in its measures. In California, well-known novelist and socialist Upton Sinclair entered the 1934 Democratic primary for governor by running on a program he called EPIC, for End Poverty in California. He proposed a $50 a month pension for all poor people over age sixty. His campaign also emphasized a government-run system of "production for use" (rather than profit) workshops for the unemployed. Sinclair shocked local and national Democrats by winning the primary easily. He lost a close general election only because the Republican candidate received heavy financial and tactical support from wealthy Hollywood studio executives and frightened regular Democrats.

Another Californian, Francis E. Townsend, a retired doctor, created a large following among senior citizens with his Old Age Revolving Pension plan. He called for payments of $200 per month to all people over sixty, provided the money was spent within thirty days. The pensions would be financed by a national 2 percent tax on all commercial transactions. This plan managed to attract a nationwide following of more than 3 million by 1936. But Townsend's plan was essentially regressive, since it proposed to tax all Americans equally, regardless of their income.

Huey Long, Louisiana's flamboyant backcountry orator, posed the greatest potential threat to Roosevelt's leadership. Long had captured Louisiana's governorship in 1928 by attacking the state's entrenched oil industry and calling for a radical redistribution of wealth. In office, he significantly improved public education, roads, medical care, and other public services, winning the loyalty of the state's poor farmers and industrial workers. Elected to the U.S. Senate in 1930, Long came to Washington with national ambitions. He at first supported Roosevelt, but in 1934 his own presidential ambitions and his impatience with the pace of New Deal measures led to a break with Roosevelt.

Long organized the Share Our Wealth Society. Its purpose, he thundered, "was to break up the swollen fortunes of America and to spread the wealth among all our people." Limiting the size of large fortunes, Long promised, would mean a homestead worth $5,000 and a $2,500 annual income for everyone. Although Long's economics were fuzzy at best, he undoubtedly touched a deep nerve with his "Every Man a King" slogan. The Democratic National Committee was shocked when a secret poll in the summer of 1935 revealed that Long might attract 3 or 4 million votes. Only his assassination that September by a disgruntled political enemy prevented Long's third-party candidacy, which might have proved disastrous for FDR.

In the nation's workplaces and streets, a rejuvenated and newly militant labor movement also loomed as a force to be reckoned with. In many industrial cities Unemployed Councils, organized largely by the Communist Party, held marches and rallies demanding public works projects and relief payments. Section 7a of the National Industrial Recovery Act required that workers be allowed to bargain collectively with employers, through representatives of their own choosing. Though this provision of the NIRA was not enforced, it did help raise expectations and spark union organizing. Almost 1.5 million workers took part in some 1,800 strikes in 1934. But employers resisted unionization nearly everywhere, often with violence and the help of local and state police.

In Minneapolis, a local of the International Brotherhood of Teamsters won a bloody strike against the combined opposition of the union's own national officials, vehemently anti-union employers, and a brutal city police force. Violence against strikers helped unite the city's working classes. The Minneapolis Central Labor Union was prepared to support a general strike, and the funeral of a striker shot by police drew 100,000 people. In San Francisco in 1934, a general strike in support of striking members of the International Longshoremen's Association (ILA) effectively shut down the city. Employer use of strikebreakers and violent intimidation prompted an outpouring of support for the ILA from the city's working class, as well as from many shopkeepers and middle-class professionals. When the ILA accepted government arbitration, it won on its main issue—control over the hiring halls on the waterfront. In both Minneapolis and San Francisco, workers had demonstrated the power of labor solidarity and mass protest.

The Second Hundred Days

The popularity of leaders like Sinclair, Townsend, and Long suggested Roosevelt might be losing electoral support among workers, farmers, the aged, and the unemployed. In early 1935 Roosevelt and his closest advisers responded by turning left and concentrating on a new program of social reform. They had three major goals: strengthening the national commitment to creating jobs; providing security against old age, unemployment, and illness; and improving housing conditions and cleaning slums. What came to be called "the Second Hundred Days" marked the high point of progressive lawmaking in the New Deal.

In April the administration pushed through the Emergency Relief Appropriation Act, which allocated $5 billion for large-scale public works programs for the jobless. New Deal economists, following the theories of Britain's John Maynard Keynes, argued that each government dollar spent had a multiplier effect, pumping two or three dollars into the depressed gross national product. The major responsible agency here was the Works Progress Administration (WPA), led by Harry Hopkins. Born and raised in Iowa, Hopkins had pursued a social work career in New York City. Streetwise, driven by a deep moral passion to help the less fortunate, and impatient with bureaucracy, Hopkins emerged as the key figure in New Deal relief programs. People often referred to him as the "assistant president." Over the next seven years Hopkins oversaw the employment of more than 8 million Americans on a vast array of construction projects: roads, bridges, dams, airports, and sewers. Among the most innovative WPA programs were community service projects that employed thousands of jobless artists, musicians, actors, and writers.

The landmark Social Security Act of 1935 provided for old-age pensions and unemployment insur-

OVERVIEW

KEY LEGISLATION OF THE SECOND NEW DEAL (1935–1938)

Legislation	Purpose
Emergency Relief Appropriations Act (1935) (includes Works Progress Administration)	Large-scale public works program for the jobless
Social Security Act (1935)	Federal old-age pensions and unemployment insurance
National Labor Relations Act (1935)	Federal guarantee of right to organize trade unions and collective bargaining
Resettlement Administration (1935)	Relocation of poor rural families Reforestation and soil erosion projects
National Housing Act (1937)	Federal funding for public housing and slum clearance
Fair Labor Standards Act (1938)	Federal minimum wage and maximum hours

ance. A payroll tax on workers and their employers created a fund from which retirees received monthly pensions after age sixty-five. Payment size depended upon how much employees and their employers had contributed over the years. The unemployment compensation plan established a minimum weekly payment and a minimum number of weeks during which those who lost jobs could collect. The Social Security Board administered this complex system of federal-state cooperation. The original law failed to cover domestics and farm workers, many of whom were Latinos and African Americans. It also made no provisions for casual laborers or public employees. The old-age pensions were quite small at first, as little as $10 a month. And to collect unemployment, one had to have first lost a job. But the law, which has since been amended many times, established the crucial principle of federal responsibility for America's most vulnerable citizens.

Roosevelt and congressional New Dealers called for new legislation to strengthen labor's right to organize after the Supreme Court, in May 1935, ruled the NIRA unconstitutional, including its provisions protecting union organizing. In July 1935, Congress passed the National Labor Relations Act, often called the Wagner Act for its chief sponsor, Democratic senator Robert F. Wagner of New York. The new law had far-reaching implications for American politics and the economy. For the first time, the federal government guaranteed the right of American workers to join or form independent labor unions and bargain collectively for improved wages, benefits, and working conditions. The National Labor Relations Board would conduct secret-ballot elections in shops and factories to determine which union, if any, workers desired as their sole bargaining agent. The law also defined and prohibited unfair labor practices by employers, including firing workers for union activity. The Wagner Act, described as "the Magna Carta for labor," quickly proved a boon to union growth, especially in previously unorganized industries such as automobiles, steel, and textiles. It set the stage for the sit-down strike in Flint and for General Motors' eventual acceptance of union labor in its factories.

Finally, the Resettlement Administration (RA) produced one of the most utopian New Deal programs, one designed to create new kinds of model communities. Established by executive order and led by key brain truster Rexford G. Tugwell, the RA helped destitute farm families relocate to more productive areas. It granted loans for purchasing land and equipment, and it directed reforestation and soil erosion projects, particularly in the hard-hit Southwest. Due to lack of funds and poor administration, however, only about 1 percent of the projected 500,000 families were actually moved.

Tugwell, one of the New Deal's most ardent believers in planning, was more successful in his efforts at creating model greenbelt communities combining the best of urban and rural environments. "My idea," he wrote, "is to go just outside centers of population, pick up cheap land, build a whole community and entice people into it." Though his vision was only partially fulfilled, several of these communities, such as Greenhills, near Cincinnati, and Greendale, near Milwaukee, still thrive.

Labor's Upsurge: Rise of the CIO

In 1932 the American labor movement was nearly dead. Only 2.8 million workers were union members, a half-million fewer than in 1929 and more than 2 million fewer than in 1920. Yet by 1942, unions claimed more than 10.5 million members, nearly a third of the total nonagricultural work force. This remarkable turnaround was one of the key events of the depression era. The growth in the size and power of the labor movement permanently changed the work lives and economic status of millions, as well as the national and local political landscapes.

At the core of this growth was a series of dramatic successes in the organization of workers in large-scale, mass-production industries such as automobiles, steel, rubber, electrical goods, and textiles. Workers in these fields had largely been ignored by the conservative, craft-conscious unions that dominated the American Federation of Labor. At the 1935 AFL convention, a group of more militant union officials led by John L. Lewis (of the United Mine Workers) and Sidney Hillman (of the Amalgamated Clothing Workers) formed the Committee for Industrial Organization (CIO). Their goal was to organize mass-production workers by industry rather than by craft. They emphasized the need for opening the new unions to all, regardless of a worker's level of skill. And they differed from nearly all old-line AFL unions by calling for the inclusion of black and women workers.

Lewis was the key figure in the CIO. The gruff son of a Welsh miner, Lewis was articulate, ruthless, and very ambitious. He saw the new legal protection given by the Wagner Act as a historic opportunity. But despite the Act—whose constitutionality was unclear until 1937—Lewis knew that establishing permanent unions in the mass-production industries would be a bruising battle. He committed the substantial resources of the United Mine Workers to a series of organizing drives, focusing first on the steel and auto industries. Many CIO organizers were communists or radicals of other persuasions, and their dedication, commitment, and willingness to work within disciplined organizations proved invaluable in the often dangerous task of creating industrial unions. Of the roughly 200 full-time organizers on the payroll of the Steel Workers Organizing Committee in 1937, almost a third were members of the Communist Party.

Militant rank-and-file unionists were often ahead of Lewis and other CIO leaders. The sit-down strike—refusing to work but staying in the factory to prevent "scab" workers from taking over—emerged as a popular tactic among rubber and auto workers. After the dramatic breakthrough in the Flint sit-down strike at General Motors, membership in CIO unions grew rapidly. In eight months, membership in the United Automobile Workers alone soared from 88,000 to 400,000. CIO victories in the steel, rubber, and electrical industries followed, but often at a very high cost. One bloody example of the perils of union organizing was the 1937 Memorial Day Massacre in Chicago. In a field near the struck Republic Steel Mill in South Chicago, police fired into a crowd of union supporters, killing ten workers and wounding scores more.

Overall, the success of the CIO's organizing drives was remarkable. In 1938 CIO unions, now boasting nearly 4 million members, withdrew from the AFL and reorganized themselves as the Congress of Industrial Organizations. Ahead lay many hard battles organizing workers in such nonunion bastions as the Ford Motor Company and the textile plants of the South. But for the first time ever, the labor movement had gained a permanent place in the nation's mass-production industries. Organized labor took its place as a key power broker in Roosevelt's New Deal and the national Democratic Party. Frances Perkins, FDR's secretary of labor and the nation's first woman cabinet member, captured the close relationship between the new unionism and the New Deal: "Programs long thought of as merely labor welfare, such as shorter hours, higher wages, and a voice in the terms of conditions of work, are really essential economic factors for recovery."

The New Deal Coalition at High Tide

Did the American public support Roosevelt and his New Deal policies? Both major political parties looked forward to the 1936 elections as a national referendum, and the campaign itself was an exciting and hard-fought contest. Very few political observers predicted its lopsided result.

Republicans nominated Governor Alfred M. Landon of Kansas, who had gained attention by surviving the Democratic landslide of 1934. Landon, an easygoing, colorless man with little personal magnetism, emphasized a nostalgic appeal to traditional American values. His campaign served as a lightning rod for all those, including many conservative Democrats, who were dissatisfied with Roosevelt and the direction he had taken. Al Smith, the Democratic nominee in 1928, categorically denounced the New Deal as "socialistic" and supported Landon. Kansas Republican William Allen White, editor of the *Emporia Gazette*, attacked the New Deal for building up the federal government and creating "a great political machine centered in Washington."

American Tragedy, 1937, oil on canvas, 29½ x 39½ inches. Private Collection, Terry Dintenfass Gallery. Photo by Philip Evergood.

Philip Evergood, American Tragedy (1937). *A classic example of the social realism characteristic of much depression-era art, this painting depicts the police violence against strikers at the Republic Steel Mill. Evergood was one of many artists who found work in the* Federal Art Project *painting murals in public buildings.*

Roosevelt attacked the "economic royalists" who denied that government "could do anything to protect the citizen in his right to work and his right to live." At the same time, FDR was careful to distance himself from radicalism. "It was this administration," he declared, "which saved the system of private profit and free enterprise after it had been dragged to the brink of ruin." As Roosevelt's campaign crossed the country, his advisers were heartened by huge and enthusiastic crowds, especially in large cities like Chicago and Pittsburgh. Still, the vast majority of the nation's newspapers endorsed Landon. And a widely touted "scientific" poll by the *Literary Digest* forecast a Republican victory in November.

Election day erased all doubts. Roosevelt carried every state but Maine and Vermont, polling 61 percent of the popular vote. Democrats increased their substantial majorities in the House and Senate as well. The *Literary Digest,* it turned out, had drawn the sample for its poll from people whose addresses were listed in telephone directories and car registration records, thus omitting the poorer Americans who had no telephones or cars—and who supported Roosevelt. In 1936 the Democrats drew millions of new voters into the political process and at the same time forged a new coalition of voters that would dominate national politics for two generations.

This "New Deal coalition," as it came to be known, included traditional-minded white southern Democrats, big-city political machines, industrial workers of all races, trade unionists, and many depression-hit farmers. The Democrats' strong showing in the ethnic wards of America's large urban centers amplified a trend that had begun with Al Smith's 1928 campaign. Roosevelt was especially popular among first- and second-generation immigrants of Catholic and Jewish descent. Organized labor put an unprecedented amount of money and people power into Roosevelt's reelection. Black voters in the North and West, long affiliated with the Republicans as the party of Abraham Lincoln, went Democratic in record numbers. The Great Depression was by no means over. But the New Deal's active response to the nation's misery, particularly the bold initiatives taken in 1935, had obviously struck a powerful chord with the American electorate.

THE NEW DEAL AND THE WEST

The New Deal had a more profound impact on the West than on any other region in the nation. Western citizens received more from the federal government in per capita payments for welfare, work relief, and loans than the people of any other section. But perhaps more important, New Deal programs, based on a philosophy of rational planning of resource use, transformed western agriculture, water and energy sources, and Indian policy. From Great Plains farming communities in Kansas and Oklahoma to Pacific coast cities such as Los Angeles and Seattle, federal subsidy and management became an integral part of western life. In the process, the New Deal helped propel the West into the modern era. The region's economic development and politics would now be dominated by a combination of Washington-based bureaucracies, large-scale agriculture, and new industrial enterprises.

The Dust Bowl

An ecological and economic disaster of unprecedented proportions struck the southern Great Plains in the mid-1930s. The region had suffered several drought years in the early 1930s. Such dry spells occurred regularly in roughly twenty-year cycles. But this time the parched earth became swept up in violent dust storms the likes of which had never been seen before. The dust storms were largely the consequence of years of stripping the landscape of its natural vegetation. During World War I, wheat fetched record-high prices on the world market, and for the next twenty years Great Plains farmers turned the region into a vast wheat factory.

The wide flatlands of the Great Plains were especially suited to mechanized farming, and gasoline-powered tractors, disc plows, and harvester-thresher combines increased productivity enormously. Back in 1830 it had taken some fifty-eight hours of labor to bring an acre of wheat to the granary; in much of the Great Plains a hundred years later it required less than three hours. As wheat prices fell in the 1920s, farmers broke still more land to make up the difference with increased production. Great Plains farmers had created an ecological time bomb that exploded when drought returned in the early 1930s. With native grasses destroyed for the sake of wheat growing, there was nothing left to prevent soil erosion. Dust storms blew away tens of millions of acres of rich topsoil, and thousands of farm families left the region. Those who stayed suffered deep economic and psychological losses from the calamity. The hardest-hit regions were western Kansas, eastern Colorado, western Oklahoma, the Texas Panhandle, and eastern New Mexico. It was the calamity in this southern part of the Plains that prompted a Denver journalist to coin the phrase "Dust Bowl."

Black blizzards of dust a mile and a half high rolled across the landscape, darkening the sky and whipping the earth into great drifts that settled over hundreds of miles. Dust storms made it difficult for humans and livestock to breathe and destroyed crops and trees over vast areas. Dust storms turned day into night, terrifying those caught in them. "Dust pneumonia" and other respiratory infections afflicted thousands, and many travelers found themselves stranded in automobiles and trains unable to move. The worst storms occurred in the early spring of 1935. A Garden City, Kansas, woman gave an account of her experience for the *Kansas City Times*:

> All we could do about it was just sit in our dusty chairs, gaze at each other through the fog that filled the room and watch that fog settle slowly and silently, covering everything—including ourselves—in a thick, brownish gray blanket. When we opened the door swirling whirlwinds of soil beat against us unmercifully. The door and windows were all shut tightly, yet those tiny particles seemed to seep through the very walls. It got into cupboards and clothes closets; our faces were as dirty as if we had rolled in the dirt; our hair was gray and stiff and we ground dirt between our teeth.

Several federal agencies intervened directly to relieve the distress. Many thousands of Great Plains farm families were given direct emergency relief by the Resettlement Administration. Other federal assistance included crop and seed loans, moratoriums on loan payments, and temporary jobs with the Works Progress Administration. In most Great Plains counties, from one-fifth to one-third of the families applied for relief; in the hardest-hit communities, as many as 90 percent of the families received direct government aid. The Agricultural Adjustment Administration paid wheat farmers millions of dollars not to grow what they could not sell and encouraged the diversion of acreage from soil-depleting crops like wheat to soil-enriching crops such as sorghum.

To reduce the pressure from grazing cattle on the remaining grasslands, the Drought Relief Service of the Department of Agriculture purchased more than 8 million head of cattle in 1934 and 1935. For a brief time, the federal government was the largest cattle owner in the world. This agency also lent ranchers money to feed their remaining cattle. The Taylor Grazing Act of 1934 brought stock grazing on 8 million acres of public domain lands under federal management.

The federal government also pursued longer-range policies designed to alter land-use patterns, reverse soil erosion, and nourish the return of grass-

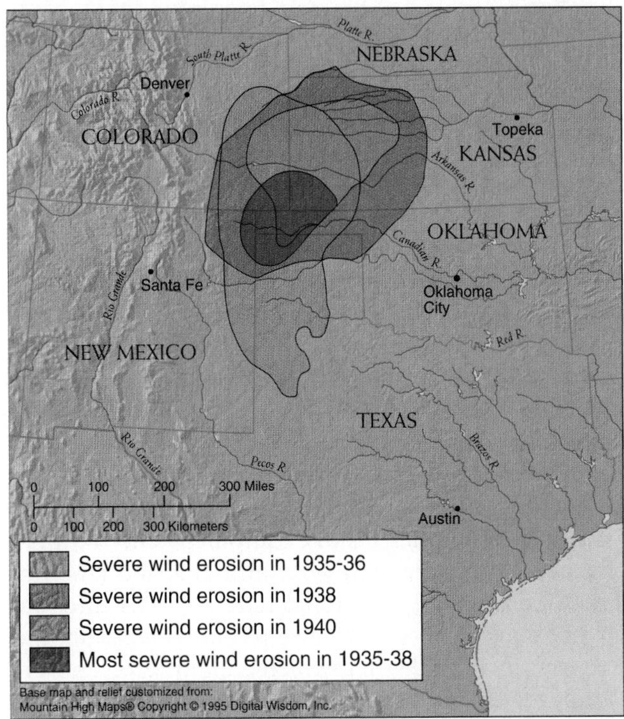

The Dust Bowl, 1935–1940 *This map shows the extent of the Dust Bowl in the southern Great Plains. Federal programs designed to improve soil conservation, water management, and farming practices could not prevent a mass exodus of hundreds of thousands out of the Great Plains.*

Years of Dust. *This 1936 poster by the artist and photographer Ben Shahn served to publicize the work of the Resettlement Administration, which offered aid to destitute farm families hit hard by the Dust Bowl. Shahn's stark imagery here was typical of the documentary aesthetic associated with Depression-era art and photography.*

lands. The Department of Agriculture, under Secretary Henry A. Wallace, sought to change farming practices. The spearhead for this effort was the Soil Conservation Service (SCS), which conducted research into controlling wind and water erosion, set up demonstration projects, and offered technical assistance, supplies, and equipment to farmers engaged in conservation work on farms and ranches. The SCS pumped additional federal funds into the Great Plains and created a new rural organization, the soil conservation district, which administered conservation regulations locally.

By 1940 the acreage subject to blowing in the Dust Bowl area of the southern plains had been reduced from roughly 50 million acres to less than 4 million acres. In the face of the Dust Bowl disaster, New Deal farm policies had restricted market forces in agriculture. But the return of regular rainfall and the outbreak of World War II led many farmers to abandon the techniques that the SCS had taught them to accept. Wheat farming expanded and farms grew as farmers once again pursued commercial agriculture with little concern for its long-term effects on the land.

While large landowners and ranchers reaped sizable benefits from AAA subsidies and other New Deal programs in the southern plains, tenant farmers and sharecroppers received very little. In the cotton lands of Texas, Oklahoma, Missouri, and Arkansas, thousands of tenant and sharecropper families were forced off the land. They became part of a stream of roughly 300,000 people, disparagingly called "Okies," who migrated to California in the 1930s. California migrants included victims of the Dust Bowl, but the majority were blue-collar workers and small businessmen looking to improve their economic lot. California suffered from the depression along with the rest of the nation, but it still offered more jobs, higher wages, and higher relief payments than the states of the southern plains. Most Okies could find work only as poorly paid agricultural laborers in the fertile San Joaquin and Imperial Valley districts. There they faced discrimination and scorn as "poor white trash" while they struggled to create communities amid the squalor of migrant labor camps. Only with the outbreak of World War II and the pressing demand for labor were migrants able to significantly improve their situation.

Mexican farm laborers faced stiff competition from Dust Bowl refugees. By the mid-1930s they no longer dominated California's agricultural workforce. In 1936 an estimated 85 to 90 percent of the state's migratory workers were white Americans, as compared to less than 20 percent before the depression. Mexican farm worker families who managed to stay employed in California, Texas, and Colorado saw their wages plummet.

Southwestern communities, responding to racial hostility from unemployed whites and looking for ways to reduce their welfare burden, campaigned to deport Mexicans and Mexican Americans. Employers, private charities, and the Immigration and Naturalization Service joined in this effort. Authorities made little effort to distinguish citizens from aliens; most of the children they deported had been born in the United States and were citizens. Los Angeles County had the most aggressive campaign, using boxcars to ship out more than 13,000 Mexicans between 1931 and 1934. The hostile climate convinced thousands more to leave voluntarily. Approximately one-third of Los Angeles's 150,000 Mexican and Mexican American residents left the city in the early 1930s. Overall, nearly one-half million left the United States during the decade. Some

Mexican deportees crossed the border with a melancholy song on their lips:

> *And so I take my leave,*
> *may you be happy.*
> *Here the song ends,*
> *but the depression goes on forever.*

Water Policy

The New Deal ushered in the era of large-scale water projects designed to provide irrigation and cheap power and to prevent floods. The long-range impact of these undertakings on western life was enormous. The key government agency in this realm was the Bureau of Reclamation of the Department of the Interior, established under the National Reclamation Act of 1902. The bureau's original responsibility had been to construct dams and irrigation works and thereby encourage the growth of small farms throughout the arid regions of the West. Until the late 1920s the bureau's efforts had been of little consequence, providing irrigation for only a very small portion of land. But its fortunes changed when its focus shifted to building huge multipurpose dams designed to control entire river systems.

The first of these projects was the Boulder Dam (later renamed the Hoover Dam). The dam, actually begun during the Hoover administration, was designed to harness the Colorado River, wildest and most isolated of the major western rivers. Its planned benefits included flood prevention, the irrigation of California's Imperial Valley, the supplying of domestic water for southern California, and the generation of cheap electricity for Los Angeles and southern Arizona. Hoover, however, had opposed the public power aspect of the project, arguing that the government ought not to compete with private utility companies. This position was contrary to that of most Westerners, who believed cheap public power was critical for development. Roosevelt's support for government-sponsored power projects was a significant factor in his winning the political backing of the West in 1932 and subsequent election years.

Boulder Dam was completed in 1935 with the help of funds from the Public Works Administration. Its total cost was $114 million, which was to be offset by the sale of the hydroelectric power it generated. Los Angeles and neighboring cities built a 259-mile aqueduct, costing $220 million, to channel water to their growing populations. Lake Mead, created by construction of the dam, became the world's largest artificial lake, extending 115 miles up the canyon and providing a popular new recreation area. The dam's irrigation water helped make the Imperial Valley, covering over 500,000 acres, one of the most productive agricultural districts in the world.

The success of Boulder Dam transformed the Bureau of Reclamation into a major federal agency with huge resources at its disposal. In 1938 it completed the All-American Canal—an 80-mile channel connecting the Colorado River to the Imperial Valley, with a 130-mile branch to the Coachella Valley. The canal cost $24 million to build and carried a flow of water equal to that of the Potomac River. More than a million acres of desert land were opened up to the cultivation of citrus fruits, melons, vegetables, and cotton. Irrigation districts receiving water promised to repay, without interest, the cost of the canal over a forty-year period. This interest-free loan was in effect a huge government subsidy to the private growers who benefited from the canal.

In 1935 the bureau began the giant Central Valley Project (CVP). The Central Valley, stretching through the California interior, is a 500-mile oblong watershed with an average width of 125 miles. The idea was to bring water from the Sacramento River in the North down to the arid lands of the larger San Joaquin Valley in the South. Completed in 1947, the project eventually cost $2.3 billion. The CVP stored water and transferred it to the drier southern regions of the state. It also provided electricity, flood control, and municipal water. The federal government, local municipalities, and buyers of electric power paid most of the cost, and the project proved a boon to large-scale farmers in the Sacramento and San Joaquin River Valleys.

The largest power and irrigation project of all was the Grand Coulee Dam, northwest of Spokane, Washington. Completed in 1941, it was designed to convert the power of the Columbia River into cheap electricity and to irrigate previously uncultivated land, thereby stimulating the economic development of the Pacific Northwest. The construction of Grand Coulee employed tens of thousands of workers and pumped millions of dollars into the region's badly depressed economy. Between 1933 and 1940 Washington State ranked first in per capita federal expenditures. In the longer run, Grand Coulee provided the cheapest electricity in the United States and helped attract new manufacturing to a region previously dependent on the export of raw materials, such as lumber and metals.

These technological marvels and the new economic development they stimulated were not without an environmental and human cost. The Grand Coulee and smaller dams nearby reduced the Columbia River, long a potent symbol of the western wilderness, to a string of lakes. Spawning salmon could no longer run the river above the dam. In California, the federal guarantee of river water made a relative handful of large farmers fabulously wealthy. But tens of thousands of farm workers, mostly of Mexican descent, labored in the newly fertile fields for very low wages, and their health suffered from contact with pesticides.

The New Deal and Water *This map illustrates U. S. drainage areas and the major large-scale water projects begun or completed by federal agencies in them during the New Deal. By providing irrigation, cheap power, flood control, and recreation areas, these public works had a historically unprecedented impact on America's western communities.*

The Colorado River, no longer emptying into the Pacific, began to build up salt deposits, making its water increasingly unfit for drinking or irrigation. Water pollution in the form of high salinity continues to plague the 2,000 mile river to this day.

A New Deal for Indians

The New Deal brought important changes and some limited improvements to the lives of Indians. In 1933 some 320,000 Indian people, belonging to about 200 tribes, lived on reservations. Most were in Oklahoma, Arizona, New Mexico, and South Dakota. Indian people suffered from the worst poverty of any group in the nation and an infant mortality rate twice that of the white population. The incidence of alcoholism and other diseases such as tuberculosis and measles was much higher on the reservation than off. Half of all those on reservations were landless, forced to rent or live with relatives. The Bureau of Indian Affairs (BIA), oldest of the federal bureaucracies in the West, had a long history of corruption and mismanagement. The BIA had for years tried to assimilate Indians through education and had routinely interfered with Indian religious affairs and tribal customs. In 1928 the Merriam Report, prepared by the Institute for Government Research, had offered a scathing and widely publicized critique of BIA mismanagement. But the Hoover administration made no effort to reform the agency.

In 1933 President Roosevelt appointed John Collier to bring change to the BIA. Collier had deep roots in progressive-era social work and community organizing in eastern big-city slums. During the 1920s he had become passionately interested in Indian affairs after spending time in Taos, New Mexico. He became involved with the struggle of the Pueblo Indians to hold onto their tribal lands, and he had served as executive secretary of the American Indian Defense Association. As the new BIA head, Collier pledged to "stop wronging the Indians and to rewrite the cruel and stupid laws that rob them and crush their family lives." Collier brought a reformer's zeal to his new job, and he quickly demonstrated his bureaucratic skills. He halted the sale of Indian lands, obtained emergency conservation work for 77,000 Indians under the CCC program, and secured millions of dollars in PWA funds to finance Indian day schools on the reservations. He also fired incompetent and corrupt BIA officials and insisted that those who remained respect tribal customs.

Most important, Collier became the driving force behind the Indian Reorganization Act (IRA) of 1934. The IRA reversed the allotment provisions of the Dawes Severalty Act of 1887, which had weakened tribal sovereignty by shifting the distribution of land from tribes to individuals (see Ch.18). The new legislation permitted the restoration of surplus reservation lands to tribal ownership and allocated funds for the purchase of additional lands and for economic development. At its heart, the IRA sought to restore tribal structures by making the tribes instruments of the federal government. Any tribe that ratified the IRA could then elect a tribal council that would enjoy federal recognition as the legal tribal government. In this way, Collier argued, tribes would be "surrounded by the protective guardianship of the federal government and clothed with the authority of the federal government." He fought first to get the legislation through a reluctant Congress, which, uneasy with reversing the long-standing policy of Indian assimilation, insisted on many changes to Collier's original plan.

The more difficult battle involved winning approval by Indian peoples. Collier's efforts to win acceptance of the IRA met with mixed results on the reservations. Linguistic barriers made it nearly impossible for some tribes to fully assess the plan. The Papagos of southern Arizona, for example, had no words for "budget" and "representative." Their language made no distinction among the terms "law," "rule," "charter," and "constitution," and they used the same word for "president," "reservation agent," "king," and "Indian commissioner." In all, 181 tribes organized governments under the IRA, while 77 tribes rejected it.

The Navajos, the nation's largest tribe with over 40,000 members, rejected the IRA, illustrating some of the contradictions embedded in federal policy. The Navajo refusal came as a protest against the BIA's forced reduction of their livestock, part of a soil conservation program. The government blamed Navajo sheep for the gullying and erosion that threatened to fill in Lake Mead and make Boulder Dam inoperable. But the hundreds of thousands of sheep in the Navajos' herds were central to their economy and society. They used sheep for barter, to pay religious leaders, and as their primary source of meat.

The Navajos believed the erosion stemmed not from overgrazing but from lack of sufficient water and inadequate acreage on the reservation. Howard Gorman, a Navajo political leader, angrily responded to Collier's last-minute personal appearance before the tribal council: "This thing, the thing you said that will make us strong, what do you mean by it? We have been told that not once but many times this same thing, and all it is is a bunch of lies. . . . You're wasting your time coming here and talking to us." Facing loss of half their sheep, Navajos took their anger out on Collier, rejecting the reorganization plan.

Under Collier's tenure, the BIA became much more sensitive to Indian cultural and religious freedom. The number of Indian people employed by the BIA itself increased from a few hundred in 1933 to more than 4,600 in 1940. Collier trumpeted the principle of Indian political autonomy, a radical idea for the day. But in practice, both the BIA and Congress regularly interfered with reservation governments, especially in money matters. Collier often dictated economic programs for tribes, which Congress usually underfunded. For the long run, Collier's most important legacy was the reassertion of the status of Indian tribes as semisovereign nations. In 1934 a Department of the Interior lawyer, Nathan Margold, wrote a legal opinion that tribal governments retained all their original powers—their "internal sovereignty"—except when these were specifically limited by acts of Congress. In later years U.S. courts would uphold the Margold Opinion, leading to a significant restoration of tribal rights and land to Indian peoples of the West.

DEPRESSION-ERA CULTURE

American culture in the 1930s, like all other aspects of national life, was profoundly shaped by the Great Depression. The themes and images in various cultural forms frequently reflected depression-related problems. Yet contradictory messages coexisted, sometimes within the same novel or movie. With American capitalism facing its worst crisis, radical expressions of protest and revolution were more common than ever. But there were also strong celebrations of individualism, nostalgia for a simpler, rural past, and searches for core American virtues. The 1930s also saw important shifts in the organization and production of culture. For a brief but significant moment, the federal government offered substantial and unprecedented support to artists and writers. In the realm of popular culture, Hollywood movies, network radio broadcasting, and big-band jazz achieved a central place in the everyday lives of Americans.

A New Deal for the Arts

The depression hit America's writers, artists, and teachers just as hard as blue-collar workers. In 1935, the WPA allocated $300 million for the unemployed in these fields. Over the next four years, Federal Project No. 1, an umbrella agency covering writing, theater, music, and the visual arts, proved to be one of the most

A Works Progress Administration (WPA) poster from 1938. The primary goal of federal relief projects, WPA officials stressed, was to rebuild the individual worker's confidence and self-respect. Typically, this poster uses only male laborers in its illustrations, reflecting a gender bias common in New Deal relief efforts.

innovative and successful New Deal programs. "Federal One," as it was called, offered work to desperate artists and intellectuals, enriched the cultural lives of millions, and left a substantial legacy of artistic and cultural production. Nearly all these works were informed by the spirit of the documentary impulse, a deep desire to record and communicate the experiences of ordinary Americans. Photographer Lewis Hine defined the documentary attitude simply and clearly: "I wanted to show the things that had to be corrected. I wanted to show the things that had to be appreciated."

At its height, the Federal Writers Project employed 5,000 writers on a variety of programs. Most notably, it produced a popular series of state and city guidebooks, each combining history, folklore, and tourism. The 150-volume "Life in America" series included valuable oral histories of former slaves, studies of ethnic and Indian cultures, and pioneering collections of American songs and folk tales. Work on the Writers Project helped many American writers to survive, hone their craft, and go on to great achievement and prominence. These included Ralph Ellison, Richard Wright, Margaret Walker, John Cheever, Saul Bellow, and Zora Neale Hurston. Novelist Anzia Yezierska recalled a strong spirit of camaraderie among the writers: "Each morning I walked to the Project as light hearted as if I were going to a party." For poet Muriel Rukeyser, the FWP embodied an essential part of the era: "The key to the 30s was the joy to awake and see life entire and tell the stories of real people."

The Federal Theater Project (FTP), under the direction of the dynamic Hallie Flanagan of Vassar College, reached as many as 30 million Americans with its productions. The FTP sought to expand the audience for theater beyond the regular patrons of the commercial stage. Tickets for its productions were cheap, and it made variety of dramatic forms available. Among its most successful productions were the "Living Newspaper" plays based on contemporary controversies and current events. *Power* concerned the public ownership of utilities; *Triple A Plowed Under* dealt with farm problems; *Injunction Granted* documented unionizing struggles. Other FTP productions brought classics as well as new plays to communities. Among the most successful productions were T. S. Eliot's *Murder in the Cathedral,* Maxwell Anderson's *Valley Forge,* and Orson Welles's version of *Macbeth,* set in Haiti with an all-black cast.

The FTP often came under attack from congressional critics who found it too radical. But Flanagan defended her vision of a theater that confronted political issues. If the plays were mixed with politics, she wrote, "it was because life in our country was mixed with politics. These Arts projects were coming up, through, and out of the people." The FTP supported scores of community-based theatrical units around the country, giving work and experience to actors, playwrights, directors, and set designers. It brought vital and exciting theater to millions who had never attended before.

Two smaller but similar programs were the Federal Music Project (FMP) and the Federal Art Project (FAP). The FMP, under Nikolai Sokoloff of the Cleveland Symphony Orchestra, employed 15,000 musicians and financed hundreds of thousands of low-priced public concerts by touring orchestras. The Composers' Forum Laboratory supported new works by American composers such as Aaron Copland and William Schuman.

Among the painters who received government assistance through the FAP were Willem de Kooning, Jackson Pollock, and Louise Nevelson. The FAP also employed painters and sculptors to teach studio skills and art history in schools, churches, and settlement houses. The *Index of American Design* was a comprehensive compilation of American folk art from colonial times. The FAP also commissioned artists to paint hundreds of murals on the walls of post offices, meeting halls, courthouses, and other government buildings. Many of these, done in the style of the revolutionary Mexican muralists Diego Rivera and José Clemente Orozco, emphasized political and social themes. All these projects, declared Holger Cahill, director of the FAP, were aimed at "raising a generation sensitive to their visual environment and capable of helping to improve it."

The Documentary Impulse

"You can right a lot of wrongs with 'pitiless publicity,'" Franklin Roosevelt once declared. Social change, he argued, "is a difficult thing in our civilization unless you have sentiment." During the 1930s an enormous number of artists, novelists, journalists, photographers, and filmmakers tried to document the devastation wrought by the depression in American communities. They also depicted people's struggles to cope with and reverse hard times. Some of these efforts were consciously linked to promoting political action, often as part of a radical commitment to overthrowing capitalism. Others were interested less in fomenting social change than in recording vanishing ways of life. Mainstream mass media, such as the photo essays found in *Life* magazine or "March of Time" newsreels, also adapted this stance.

Regardless of political agendas or the medium employed, what one historian calls "the documentary impulse" became a prominent style in 1930s cultural expression. At its core, the documentary impulse directly influenced its audience's intellect and feelings through documentary "evidence" of social problems and human suffering. The most direct and influential expression of the documentary style was the photograph. In 1935 Roy Stryker, chief of the Historical Section of the Resettlement Administration (later part of the Farm Security Administration), gathered a remarkable group of photographers to help document the work of the agency. Stryker encouraged them to photograph whatever caught their interest, even if the pictures had no direct connection with RA projects. These photographers, including Dorothea Lange, Walker Evans, Arthur Rothstein, Russell Lee, Ben Shahn, and Marion Post Wolcott, left us the single most significant visual record of the Great Depression.

The photographers traveled through rural areas, small towns, and migrant labor camps, often not stopping even long enough to learn the names of their subjects. They produced powerful images of despair and resignation as well as hope and resilience. These photographs were reproduced in newspapers and magazines across America. Individual images could be interpreted in different ways, depending on context and captions. Stryker believed that the faces of the subjects were most memorable. "You could look at the people," he wrote, "and see fear and sadness and desperation. But you saw something else, too. A determination that not even the depression could kill. The photographers saw it—documented it."

That double vision, combining a frank portrayal of pain and suffering with a faith in the possibility of overcoming disaster, could be found in many other cultural works of the period. John Steinbeck's *Grapes of Wrath* (1939) sympathetically portrayed the hardships of Oklahoma Dust Bowl migrants on their way to California. "We ain't gonna die out," Ma Joad asserts near the end of the book. "People is goin' on—changing' a little, maybe, but goin' right on." A similar, if more personal, ending could be found in Margaret Mitchell's 1936 best-seller *Gone with the Wind*. Although this romantic novel was set in the Civil War–era South, many Americans identified with Scarlett O'Hara's determination to overcome the disaster of war and the loss of Rhett Butler. "With the spirit of her people who would not know defeat, even when it stared them in the face, she raised her chin. She could get Rhett back. She knew she could."

Many writers interrupted their work to travel around the country and discover the thoughts and feelings of ordinary people. "With real events looming larger than any imagined happenings," novelist Elizabeth Noble wrote, "documentary films and still photographs, reportage and the like have taken the place once held by the grand invention." Writers increasingly used documentary techniques to communicate the sense of upheaval around the nation. In *Puzzled America* (1935), Sherwood Anderson wrote of the psychological toll taken by unemployment. American men, especially, he wrote, were losing "that sense of being some part of the moving world of activity, so essential to an American man's sense of his manhood—the loss of this essential something in the joblessness can never be measured in dollars." Yet writers also found a remarkable absence of bitterness and a great deal of faith. James Rorty, in *Where Life Is Better* (1936), was actually encouraged by his cross-country trip. "I had rediscovered for myself a most beautiful land, and a most vital, creative, and spiritually unsubdued people."

Waiting for Lefty

For some, the capitalist system itself, with its enormous disparities of private wealth amid desperate poverty, was the culprit responsible for the Great Depression. Relatively few Americans became communists or socialists in the 1930s (at its height, the Communist

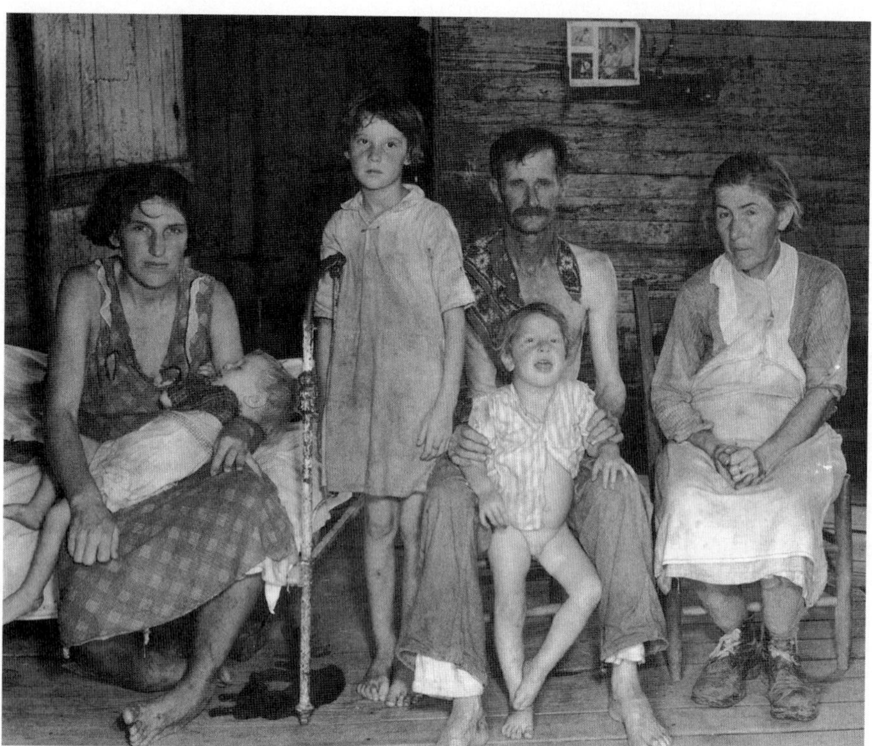

Sharecropper Family, *by Walker Evans, 1939. This photograph of the Bud and Ivy Woods family was first published in the 1941 book* Let Us Now Praise Famous Men, *with text by James Agee. Unlike some documentary photographers of the era, Evans's spare, direct pictures revealed his subjects to be not merely victims but strong and complex individuals as well. Largely ignored in the 1930s, Evans's work enjoyed a critical revival during the 1960s.*

Party of the United States had perhaps 100,000 members), and many of these remained active for only a brief time. Yet Marxist analysis, with its emphasis on class conflict and the failures of capitalism, had a wide influence on the era's thought and writing.

Some writers joined the Communist Party believing it to be the best hope for political revolution. They saw in the Soviet Union an alternative to an American system that appeared mired in exploitation, racial inequality, and human misery. Communist writers, like the novelist Michael Gold and the poet Meridel LeSueur, sought to radicalize art and literature, and they celebrated collective struggle over individual achievement. Gold's *Jews without Money* (1930) was one of the more successful attempts at a proletarian novel. It dramatized the sense of being locked into a system that could deliver only despair rather than prosperity. Granville Hicks, an editor of the communist magazine the *New Masses,* flatly declared: "If there is any other working interpretation of the apparent chaos than that which presents itself in terms of the class struggle, it has not been revealed."

A more common pattern for intellectuals, especially when they were young, was brief flirtation with communism. Many African American writers, attracted by the Communist Party's militant opposition to lynching, job discrimination, and segregation, briefly joined the party or found their first supportive audiences there. These included Richard Wright, Ralph Ellison, and Langston Hughes. Many playwrights and actors associated with New York's influential Group Theater were part of the Communist Party orbit in those years. One production of the group, Clifford Odets's *Waiting for Lefty* (1935), depicted a union organizing drive among taxi drivers. At the play's climax, the audience was invited to join the actors in shouting "Strike!" A commercial and political success, it offered perhaps the most celebrated example of radical, politically engaged art.

Left-wing influence reached its height after 1935 during the "Popular Front" period. Alarmed by the rise of fascism in Europe, communists around the world followed the Soviet line of uniting with liberals and all other antifascists. The American Communist Party adopted the slogan "Communism is Twentieth-Century Americanism." Communists became strong supporters of Roosevelt's New Deal, and their influence was especially strong within the various WPA arts projects. Some 3,200 Americans volunteered for the Communist Party–organized Abraham Lincoln Brigade, which fought in the Spanish civil war on the republican side against the fascists led by Francisco Franco. The Lincolns' sense of commitment and sacrifice appealed to millions of Americans sympathetic to the republican cause. Communists and other radicals, known for their dedication and effectiveness, also played a leading role in the difficult CIO unionizing drives in the auto, steel, and electrical industries. The successful sit-down strike at General Motors in Flint benefited from the organizing efforts of Communist Party activists who lent their expertise and helped keep the strikers and their families focused and supplied with food.

Hollywood in the 1930s

Commercial popular culture also boomed in the depression years. The coming of "talking pictures" toward the end of the 1920s helped make movies the most popular entertainment form of the day. More than 60 percent of Americans attended one of the nation's 20,000 movie houses each week. Through fan maga-

Reginald Marsh, Twenty Cent Movie, 1936. Egg tempera on composition board. 40 x 40 in. Whitney Museum of American Art, New York.

Reginald Marsh, Twenty Cent Movie, 1936. *Marsh documented the urban landscape of the 1930s with great empathy, capturing the city's contradictory mix of commercialism, optimism, energy, and degradation. The popularity of Hollywood films and their stars reached new heights during the Great Depression.*

zines and gossip columns they followed the lives and careers of movie stars more avidly than ever. With so many movies being churned out by Hollywood studios for so many fans, it is difficult to generalize about the cultural impact of individual films. Moviegoing itself, usually enjoyed with friends, family, or a date, was perhaps the most significant development of all.

It is too easy to dismiss movies as mere escapism. The more interesting question is, What were people escaping to? Several film genres proved enormously popular during the 1930s. Gangster films did very well in the early depression years. *Little Caesar* (1930), starring Edward G. Robinson, and *Public Enemy* (1931), with James Cagney, set the standard. They all depicted violent criminals brought to justice by society—but along the way they gave audiences a vicarious exposure to the pleasures of wealth, power, and lawbreaking. Social disorder could also be treated comically, as in such Marx Brothers films as *Duck Soup* (1933) and *A Night at the Opera* (1935). Mae West's popular comedies, such as *She Done Him Wrong* (1933) and *I'm No Angel* (1933), made people laugh by subverting expectations about sex roles. West was an independent woman, not afraid of pleasure. When Cary Grant asked her, "Haven't you ever met a man who could make you happy?" she replied, "Sure, lots of times."

Movie musicals offered audiences extravagant song-and-dance spectacles, as in Busby Berkeley's *Gold Diggers of 1933* and *42nd Street* (1933). "Screwball comedies" featured sophisticated, fast-paced humor and usually paired popular male and female stars: Clark Gable and Claudette Colbert in *It Happened One Night* (1934), Katharine Hepburn and Cary Grant in *Bringing Up Baby* (1938). A few movies, notably from the Warner Brothers studio, tried to offer a more "socially conscious" view of depression-era life. These included *I Am a Fugitive from a Chain Gang* (1932), *Wild Boys of the Road* (1933), and *Black Legion* (1936). By and large, however, Hollywood avoided confronting controversial social or political issues.

Some 1930s filmmakers expressed highly personal visions of core American values. Two who succeeded in capturing both popular and critical acclaim were Walt Disney and Frank Capra. By the mid-1930s, Disney's animated cartoons had become moral tales that stressed keeping order and following the rules. The Mickey Mouse cartoons and the full-length features, such as *Snow White and the Seven Dwarfs* (1937), pulled back from the fantastic stretching of time and space in earlier cartoons. Capra's comedies, such as *Mr. Deeds Goes to Town* (1936) and *You Can't Take It with You* (1938), idealized a small-town America with close families and comfortable homes. Although Capra's films dealt with contemporary problems more than most—unemployment, government corruption, economic monopoly—he made no critique of the social and economic system. Rather, he seemed to suggest that most of the country's ills could be solved if only its leaders learned the old-fashioned values of "common people"—kindness, loyalty, charity.

The Golden Age of Radio

Radio broadcasting emerged as the most powerful medium of communication in the home, profoundly changing the rhythms and routines of everyday life. In 1930 roughly 12 million American homes, 40 percent of the total, had a radio set. By the end of the decade radios could be found in 90 percent of the nation's homes. Advertisers dominated the structure and content of American radio, forming a powerful alliance with the two large networks, the National Broadcasting Company (NBC) and the Columbia Broadcasting System (CBS). The Federal Communications Commission, established in 1934, continued long-standing policies that favored commercial broadcasting over other arrangements, such as municipal or university programming. By 1937 NBC and CBS controlled about 90 percent of the wattage in the American broadcasting industry. Nearly all network shows were produced by advertising agencies.

The depression actually helped radio expand. An influx of talent arrived from the weakened worlds of vaudeville, ethnic theater, and the recording industry. The well-financed networks offered an attractive outlet to advertisers seeking a national audience. Radio programming achieved a regularity and professionalism absent in the 1920s, making it much easier for a listener to identify a show with its sponsor. Companies with national distribution paid thousands of dollars an hour to networks; by 1939 annual radio advertising revenues totaled $171 million.

Much of network radio was based on older cultural forms. The variety show, hosted by comedians and singers and based on the old vaudeville format, was the first important style. It featured stars like Eddie Cantor, Ed Wynn, Kate Smith, and Al Jolson, who constantly plugged the sponsor's product. The use of a studio audience re-created the human interaction so necessary in vaudeville. The popular comedy show *Amos 'n' Andy* adapted the minstrel "blackface" tradition to the new medium. White comedians Freeman Gosden and Charles Correll used only their two voices to invent a world of stereotyped African Americans for their millions of listeners.

The spectacular growth of the daytime serial, or soap opera, dominated radio drama. Aimed mainly at women working in the home, these serials alone constituted 60 percent of all daytime shows by 1940. Soaps such as *Ma Perkins, Helen Trent,* and *Clara Lou and Em* revolved around strong, warm female characters who provided advice and strength to weak, indecisive friends and relatives. Action counted very little; the development of character and relationships was all-important. Contemporary studies found that the average soap opera fan regularly tuned in to six or more different series. Evening radio dramas included thrillers such as *Inner Sanctum* and *The Shadow,* which emphasized crime and suspense. These shows made great use of music and sound effects to sharpen their impact.

In the later 1930s serious drama bloomed briefly, independent of commercial sponsorship, over CBS's Columbia Workshop. Archibald MacLeish's *Fall of the City,* a parable about fascism, and Orson Welles's *War of the Worlds,* a superrealistic adaptation of the H. G. Wells classic, proved the persuasive power of radio. Welles's show convinced many who tuned in that a Martian invasion was actually underway. Radio became a key factor in politics as well, as President Roosevelt showed early on with his popular fireside chats.

Finally, radio news arrived in the 1930s, showing the medium's potential for direct and immediate coverage of events. Network news and commentary shows multiplied rapidly over the decade. Complex political and economic issues and the impending European crisis fueled a news hunger among Americans. A 1939 survey found that 70 percent of Americans relied on the radio as their prime source of news. Yet commercial broadcasting, dominated by big sponsors and large radio manufacturers, failed to cover politically controversial events, such as labor struggles. The most powerful station in the country, WLW in Cincinnati, refused to even mention strikes on the air. NBC routinely canceled programs it feared might undermine "public confidence and faith."

The Swing Era

One measure of radio's cultural impact was its role in popularizing jazz. Before the 1930s, jazz was heard largely among African Americans and a small coterie of white fans and musicians. Regular broadcasts of live performances began to expose a broader public to the music. So did radio disc jockeys who played jazz records on their shows. Bands led by black artists such as Duke Ellington, Count Basie, and Benny Moten began to enjoy reputations outside of traditional jazz centers like Chicago, Kansas City, and New York.

Benny Goodman became the key figure in the "swing era," largely through radio exposure. Goodman, a white, classically trained clarinetist, had been inspired by African American bandleaders Fletcher Henderson and Don Redman. These men created arrangements for big bands that combined harmonic call-and-response patterns with breaks for improvised solos. Goodman purchased a series of arrangements from Henderson, smoothing out the sound but keeping the strong dance beat. His band's late-Saturday-night broadcasts began to attract attention.

The Benny Goodman band at the Meadowbrook Lounge, Cedar Grove, New Jersey, 1941. After his breakthrough into national prominence in 1935, Goodman became one of the first white bandleaders to hire and feature African American musicians. Although most in the audience were undoubtedly dancing to "the King of Swing," note the crowd of serious listeners gathered around the bandstand.

In 1935, at the Palomar Ballroom in Los Angeles, Goodman made the breakthrough that established his enormous popularity. When the band started playing the Henderson arrangements, the young crowd, primed by the radio broadcasts, roared its approval and began to dance wildly. Goodman's music was perfect for doing the jitterbug or lindy hop, dances borrowed from African American culture. As "the King of Swing," Goodman helped make big-band jazz a hit with millions of teenagers and young adults from all backgrounds. In the late 1930s, big-band music by the likes of Goodman, Basie, Jimmie Lunceford, and Artie Shaw accounted for the majority of million-selling records.

Despite the depression, the mass culture industry expanded enormously during the 1930s. Millions of Americans no doubt used mass culture as a temporary escape from their problems, but the various meanings they drew from movies, radio, and popular music were by no means monolithic. In most communities, Americans, especially young people, identified more closely than ever with the national communities forged by modern media. If mass culture offered little in the way of direct responses to the economic and social problems of the day, it nonetheless played a more integral role than ever in shaping the rhythms and desires of the nation's everyday life.

THE LIMITS OF REFORM

In his second Inaugural Address Roosevelt emphasized that much remained to be done to remedy the effects of the depression. Tens of millions of Americans were still denied the necessities for a decent life. "I see one third of a nation ill-housed, ill-clad, ill-nourished," the president said. With his stunning electoral victory, the future for further social reform seemed bright. Yet by 1937 the New Deal was in retreat. A rapid political turnaround over the next two years put continuing social reform efforts on the defensive.

Court Packing

FDR and his advisers were frustrated by several Supreme Court rulings declaring important New Deal legislation unconstitutional. In May 1935, in *Schecter v. United States,* the Court found the National Recovery Administration unconstitutional in its entirety. The grounds included excessive delegation of legislative power to the executive and the regulation of business that was intrastate, as opposed to national, in character. In early 1936, ruling in *Butler v. United States,* the Court invalidated the Agricultural Adjustment Administration, declaring it an unconstitutional attempt at regulating agriculture. The Court was composed mostly of Republican appointees, six of whom were over seventy. Roosevelt looked for a way to get more friendly judges on the high court.

In February 1937 FDR asked Congress for legislation that would expand the Supreme Court from nine to a maximum of fifteen justices. The president would be empowered to make a new appointment whenever an incumbent judge failed to retire upon reaching age seventy. Roosevelt argued that age prevented justices from keeping up with their workload, but few people believed this logic. Newspapers almost unanimously denounced FDR's "court-packing bill."

Even more damaging was the determined opposition from a coalition of conservatives and outraged New Dealers in the Congress, such as Democratic senator Burton K. Wheeler of Montana. The president gamely fought on, maintaining that his purpose was simply to restore the balance of power among the three branches of the federal government. As the battle dragged on through the spring and summer, FDR's claims weakened. Conservative justice Willis Van Devanter announced plans to retire, giving Roosevelt the chance to make his first Court appointment.

More important, the Court upheld the constitutionality of some key laws from the second New Deal, including the Social Security Act and the National Labor Relations Act. At the end of August, FDR backed off from his plan and accepted a compromise bill that reformed lower court procedures but left the Supreme Court untouched. FDR lost the battle for his judiciary proposal, but he may have won the war for a more responsive Court. Still, the political price was very high. The Court fight badly weakened Roosevelt's relations with Congress. Many more conservative Democrats now felt free to oppose further New Deal measures.

The Women's Network

The Great Depression and the New Deal brought some significant changes for women in American economics and politics. Most women continued to perform unpaid domestic labor within their homes, work that was not covered by the Social Security Act. A growing minority, however, also worked for wages and salaries outside the home. Women represented 24.3 percent of all workers in 1930; by 1940, 25.1 percent of the workforce was female. There was also an increase in married working women as a result of hard times. Between 1930 and 1940 the proportion of married women among the female workforce jumped from 28.8 percent to 35 percent. Jobs in which men predominated, such as construction and heavy industry, were hardest hit by the depression. In contrast, secretarial, sales, and other areas long associated with women's labor were less affected. But sexual stereotyping still routinely forced women into low-paying and low-status jobs.

The New Deal brought a measurable, if temporary, increase in women's political influence. For those women associated with social reform, the New Deal opened up possibilities to effect change. A "women's network," linked by personal friendships and professional connections, made its presence felt in national politics and government. Most of the women in this network had long been active in movements promoting suffrage, labor law reform, and welfare programs.

Eleanor Roosevelt became a powerful political figure in her own right, actively using her prominence as First Lady to fight for the liberal causes she believed in. She revolutionized the role of the political wife by taking a position involving no institutional duties and turning it into a base for independent action. Privately, she enjoyed great influence with her husband, and her support for a cause could give it instant credibility. She worked behind the scenes with a wide network of women professionals and reformers whom she had come to know in the 1920s. She was a strong supporter of protective labor legislation for women, and her overall outlook owed much to the social reform tradition of the women's movement. "When all is said and done," she wrote in *It's Up to the Women* (1933), "women are different from men. They are equal in many ways, but they cannot refuse to acknowledge their differences. . . . Their physical functions in life are different and perhaps in the same way the contributions which they are to bring to the spiritual side of life are different."

One of Eleanor Roosevelt's first public acts as First Lady was to convene a White House Conference on the Emergency Needs of Women, in November 1933. She helped Ellen Woodward, head of women's projects in the Federal Emergency Relief Administration, find jobs for 100,000 women, ranging from nursery school teaching to sewing. Roosevelt worked vigorously for antilynching legislation, compulsory health insurance, and child labor reform and fought racial discrimination in New Deal relief programs. She saw herself as the guardian of "human values" within the administration, a buffer between depression victims and government bureaucracy. She frequently testified before legislative committees, lobbied her husband privately and the Congress publicly, and wrote a widely syndicated newspaper column.

Eleanor Roosevelt's closest political ally was Molly Dewson. A long-time social worker and suffragist, Dewson wielded a good deal of political clout as director of the Women's Division of the national Democratic Party. Under her leadership women for the first time played a central role in shaping the party platform and running election campaigns. Dewson proved a tireless organizer, traveling to cities and towns around the country and educating women about Democratic policies and candidates. Her success impressed the president, and he relied on her judgment in recommending political appointments. Dewson placed more than a hundred women in New Deal positions.

Perhaps Dewson's most important success came in persuading FDR to appoint Frances Perkins secretary of labor—the first woman cabinet member in U.S. history. A graduate of Mount Holyoke College and a veteran activist for social welfare and reform, Perkins had served as FDR's industrial commissioner in New York before coming to Washington. As labor secretary, Perkins embodied the gains made by women in appointive offices. Her department was responsible for creating the Social Security Act and the Fair Labor Standards Act of 1938, both of which incorporated protective measures long advocated by women reformers. Perkins defined feminism as "the movement of women to participate in service to society." Yet despite the best efforts of the "women's network," women never constituted more than 19 percent of those employed by work relief programs, even though they made up 37 percent of the unemployed.

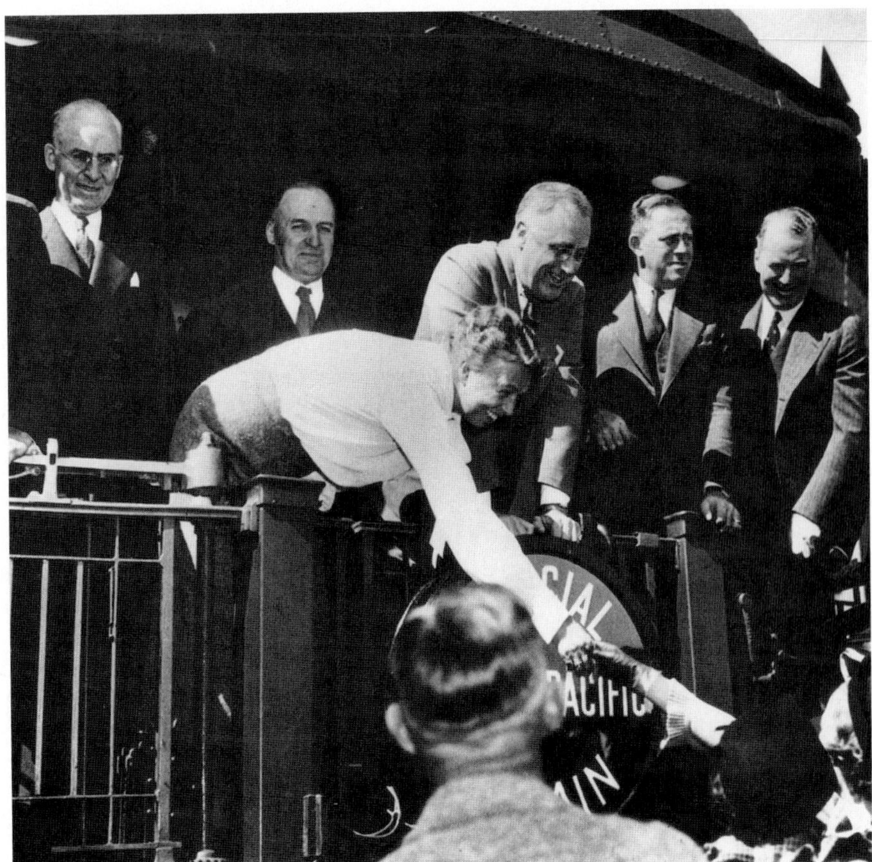

Eleanor Roosevelt on a campaign tour with her husband in Nebraska, 1935. *Long active in women's organizations and Democratic Party circles, she used political activity both to maintain her independence and make herself a valuable ally to* FDR. *"The attitude of women toward change in society," she argued, "is going to determine to a great extent our future in this country."*

New Deal agencies opened up spaces for scores of women in the federal bureaucracy. These women were concentrated in Perkins's Labor Department, the FERA and WPA, and the Social Security Board. In addition, the social work profession, which remained roughly two-thirds female in the 1930s, grew enormously in response to the massive relief and welfare programs. In sum, although the 1930s saw no radical challenges to existing male and female roles, working-class women and professional women held their own and managed to make some gains.

A New Deal for Minorities?

"The Negro was born in Depression," recalled Clifford Burke. "It only became official when it hit the white man." Long near the bottom of the American economic ladder, African Americans suffered disproportionately through the difficult days of the 1930s . The old saying among black workers that they were "last hired, first fired" was never more true than during times of high unemployment. With jobs made scarce by the depression, even traditional "Negro occupations"—domestic service, cooking, janitorial work, elevator operating—were coveted. One white clerk in Florida expressed a widely held view among white Southerners when he defended a lynch mob attack on a store with black employees: "A nigger hasn't got no right to have a job when there are white men who can do the work and are out of work."

Overall, the Roosevelt administration made little overt effort to combat the racism and segregation entrenched in American life. FDR was especially worried about offending the powerful southern Democratic congressmen who were a key element in his political coalition. And local administration of many federal programs meant that most early New Deal programs routinely accepted discrimination. The CCC established separate camps for African Americans. The NRA labor codes tolerated lower wages for black workers doing the same jobs as white workers. African Americans could not get jobs with the TVA. In Atlanta, relief payments for black clients averaged $19.29 per month, compared with $32.66 for white clients. When local AAA committees in the South reduced acreage and production to boost prices, thousands of black sharecroppers and farm laborers were forced off the land. Racism was also embedded in the entitlement provisions of the Social Security Act. The act excluded domestics and casual laborers—workers whose ranks were disproportionately African Americans—from old-age insurance.

Yet some limited gains were made. President Roosevelt issued an executive order in 1935 banning discrimination in WPA projects. In the cities the WPA, paying minimum wages of $12 a week, enabled thousands of African Americans to survive. Between 15 and 20 percent of all WPA employees were black people, although African Americans made up less than 10 percent of the nation's population. The Public Works Administration, under Harold Ickes, constructed a number of integrated housing complexes and employed more than its fair share of black workers in construction.

FDR appointed several African Americans to second-level positions in his administration. This group became known as "the Black Cabinet." Mary McLeod Bethune, an educator who rose from a sharecropping background to found Bethune-Cookman College, proved a superb leader of the Office of Minority Affairs in the National Youth Administration. Her most successful programs substantially reduced black illiteracy. Harvard-trained Robert Weaver advised the president on economic affairs and in 1966 became the first black cabinet member when he was appointed secretary of housing and urban development. Yet Roosevelt himself was diffident about advancing civil rights. Typically, he spoke out against lynching in the South, but unlike his wife, he refused to support legislation making it a federal crime. Nor would he risk alienating white Southerners by working for long-denied voting rights for African Americans in the South.

Hard times were especially trying for Mexican Americans as well. As the Great Depression drastically reduced the demand for their labor, they faced massive layoffs, deepening poverty, even starvation. In Houston, a settlement association survey made in 1935 reported that "no group are greater sufferers from the present economic situation than members of the Mexican colony." As with African Americans, New Deal programs did little to help Mexicans and Mexican Americans. The AAA benefited large growers, not stoop laborers. Neither the National Labor Relations Act nor the Social Security Act made any provisions for farm laborers. The Federal Emergency Relief Administration and the Works Progress Administration did, at first, provide relief and jobs to the needy irrespective of citizenship status. But after 1937 the WPA eliminated aliens from eligibility, causing great hardship for thousands of Mexican families. In San Antonio, for example, the WPA allocated 1,800 jobs for needy pecan shellers, but only 700 Mexicans could qualify due to citizenship requirements.

The New Deal record for minorities was mixed at best. African Americans, especially in the cities, benefited from New Deal relief and work programs, though this assistance was not color-blind. Black industrial workers made inroads into labor unions affiliated with the CIO. The New Deal made no explicit attempt to attack the deeply rooted patterns of racism and discrimination in American life. The deteriorating economic and political conditions faced by Mexicans and Mexican Americans resulted in a mass reverse exodus. Yet by 1936, for the first time ever, a majority of black voters had switched their political allegiance to the Democrats—concrete evidence that they supported the directions taken by FDR's New Deal.

The Roosevelt Recession

The nation's economy had improved significantly by 1937. Unemployment had declined to "only" 14 percent (9 million people), farm prices had improved to 1930 levels, and industrial production was slightly higher than the 1929 mark. Economic traditionalists, led by Secretary of the Treasury Henry Morgenthau, called for reducing the federal deficit, which had grown to more than $4 billion in fiscal year 1936. Roosevelt, always uneasy about the growing national debt, called for large reductions in federal spending, particularly in WPA and farm programs. Federal Reserve System officials, worried about inflation, tightened credit policies.

Rather than stimulating business, the retrenchment brought about a steep recession. The stock market collapsed in August 1937, and industrial output and farm prices plummeted. Most alarming was the big increase in unemployment. By March 1938 the jobless rate hovered around 20 percent, with more than 13 million people looking for work. As conditions worsened, Roosevelt began to blame the "new depression" on a "strike of capital," claiming businessmen had refused to invest because they wanted to hurt his prestige. In truth, the administration's own severe spending cutbacks were more responsible for the decline.

The blunt reality was that even after five years the New Deal had not brought about economic recovery. Throughout 1937 and 1938 the administration drifted. Roosevelt received conflicting advice on the economy. Some advisers, suspicious of the reluctance of business to make new investments, urged a massive antitrust campaign against monopolies. Others urged a return to the Keynesian strategy of "priming the economic pump" with more federal spending. Emergency spending bills in the spring of 1938 pumped new life into the WPA and the PWA. But Republican gains in the 1938 congressional elections (eighty seats in the House, seven in the Senate) made it harder than ever to get new reform measures through.

There were a couple of important exceptions. The 1938 Fair Labor Standards Act established the first federal minimum wage (twenty-five cents an hour) and set a maximum work week of forty-four hours for all employees engaged in interstate commerce. The National Housing Act of 1937, also known as the Wagner-Steagall Act, funded public housing construction and slum clearance and provided rent subsidies for low-income families. But by and large, by 1938 the reform whirlwind of the New Deal was over.

CONCLUSION

Although American capitalism and democracy survived the cataclysm of the Great Depression, the New Deal failed in its central mission. It was never able to bring full economic recovery or end the scourge of mass unemployment. Only the economic boom that accompanied World War II would do that. Far from being the radical program its conservative critics charged, the New Deal did little to alter fundamental property relations or the distribution of wealth. Indeed, most of its programs largely failed to help the most powerless groups in America—migrant workers, tenant farmers and sharecroppers, African Americans, and other minorities.

But the New Deal profoundly changed many areas of American life. Overall, it radically increased the role of the federal government in American lives and communities. Western and southern communities in particular were transformed through federal intervention in water, power, and agricultural policies. Relief programs and the Social Security system established at least the framework for a welfare state. For the first time in American history, the national government took responsibility for assisting its needy citizens. And also for the first time, the federal government guaranteed the rights of workers to join trade unions, and it set standards for minimum wages and maximum hours. In politics, the New Deal established the Democrats as the majority party. Some version of the Roosevelt New Deal coalition would dominate the nation's political life for another three decades.

The New Deal's efforts to end racial and gender discrimination were modest at best. Some of the more ambitious programs, such as subsidizing the arts or building model communities, enjoyed only brief success. Other reform proposals, such as national

CHRONOLOGY

1929	Stock market crash
1930	Democrats regain control of the House of Representatives
1932	Reconstruction Finance Corporation established to make government credit available
	Bonus Army marches on Washington
	Franklin D. Roosevelt elected president
1933	Roughly 13 million workers unemployed
	The "hundred days" legislation of the First New Deal
	Twenty-first Amendment repeals Prohibition (Eighteenth Amendment)
1934	Indian Reorganization Act repeals Dawes Severalty Act and reasserts the status of Indian tribes as semisovereign nations
	Growing popularity of Father Charles E. Coughlin and Huey Long, critics of Roosevelt
1935	Second New Deal
	Committee for Industrial Organization (CIO) established
	Dust storms turn the southern Great Plains into the Dust Bowl
	Boulder Dam completed
1936	Roosevelt defeats Alfred M. Landon in reelection landslide
	Sit-down strike begins at General Motors plants in Flint, Michigan
1937	General Motors recognizes United Automobile Workers
	Roosevelt's "Court-packing" plan causes controversy
	Memorial Day Massacre in Chicago demonstrates the perils of union organizing
	"Roosevelt recession" begins
1938	CIO unions withdraw from the American Federation of Labor to form the Congress of Industrial Organizations
	Fair Labor Standards Act establishes the first federal minimum wage

health insurance, never got off the ground. Conservative counterpressures, especially after 1937, limited what could be changed.

Still, the New Deal did more than strengthen the presence of the national government in people's lives. It also fed expectations that the federal presence would intensify. Washington became a much greater center of economic regulation and political power, and the federal bureaucracy grew in size and influence. With the coming of World War II, the direct role of national government in shaping American communities would expand beyond the dreams of even the most ardent New Dealer.

REVIEW QUESTIONS

1. What were the underlying causes of the Great Depression? What consequences did it have for ordinary Americans, and how did the Hoover administration attempt to deal with the crisis?
2. Analyze the key elements of Franklin D. Roosevelt's first New Deal program. To what degree did these succeed in getting the economy back on track and in providing relief to suffering Americans?
3. How did the so-called Second New Deal differ from the first? What political pressures did Roosevelt face that contributed to the new policies?
4. How did the New Deal reshape western communities and politics? What specific programs had the greatest impact in the region? How are these changes still visible today?
5. Evaluate the impact of the labor movement and radicalism on the 1930s. How did they influence American political and cultural life?
6. To what extent were the grim realities of depression reflected in popular culture? To what degree were they absent?
7. Discuss the long- and short-range effects of the New Deal on American political and economic life. What were its key successes and failures? What legacies of New Deal-era policies and political struggles can you find in contemporary America?

RECOMMENDED READING

Anthony J. Badger, *The New Deal: The Depression Years, 1933–1940* (1989). Recent and very useful overview that emphasizes the limited nature of New Deal reforms.

John Braeman et al., eds., *The New Deal: The State and Local Levels* (1975). Good collection of essays analyzing the workings of the New Deal in local communities throughout the nation.

Alan Brinkley, *The End of Reform: New Deal Liberalism in Recession and War* (1995). A sophisticated analysis of the political and economic limits faced by New Deal reformers from 1937 through World War II.

Lizabeth Cohen, *Making a New Deal: Industrial Workers in Chicago, 1919–1939* (1990). A brilliant study that demonstrates the transformation of immigrant and African American workers into key actors in the creation of the CIO and in New Deal politics and illuminates the complex relationship between ethnic cultures and mass culture.

Michael Demming, *The Cultural Front: The Laboring of American Culture in the Twentieth Century* (1997). A provocative reinterpretation of 1930s culture, emphasizing the impact of the Popular Front and its lasting influence on American modernism and mass culture.

Richard Lowitt, *The New Deal and the West* (1984). A comprehensive study of the New Deal's impact in the West, with special attention to water policy and agriculture.

Robert S. McElvaine, *The Great Depression: America, 1929–1941* (1984). The best one-volume overview of the Great Depression. It is especially strong on the origins and early years of the worst economic calamity in American history.

Lois Scharf, *To Work and to Wed* (1980). Examines female employment and feminism during the Great Depression.

Harvard Sitkoff, *A New Deal for Blacks* (1978). Focuses on the narrow gains made by African Americans from New Deal measures, as well as the racism that pervaded most government programs.

William Stott, *Documentary Expression and Thirties America* (1973). A very thoughtful account of the documentary impulse and its relationship to the political and social upheavals of the era.

Studs Terkel, *Hard Times* (1970). The best oral history of the Great Depression. It includes a very wide range of voices recalling life in the depression era.

ADDITIONAL BIBLIOGRAPHY

Hard Times

Michael A. Bernstein, *The Great Depression* (1987)
David Burner, *Herbert Hoover* (1978)
Roger Daniels, *The Bonus March* (1971)
John A. Garraty, *The Great Depression* (1986)
Susan E. Kennedy, *The Banking Crisis of 1933* (1973)
Robert S. McElvaine, ed., *Down and Out in the Great Depression* (1983)
Janet Poppendieck, *Breadlines Knee-Deep in Wheat* (1986)
Elmos Wicker, *The Banking Panics of the Great Depression* (1996)

FDR and the First New Deal

Paul K. Conkin, *The New Deal*, 2d ed. (1975)
Steve Fraser and Gary Gerstle, eds., *The Rise and Fall of the New Deal Order* (1988)
Ellis Hawley, *The New Deal and the Problem of Monopoly* (1966)
William Leuchtenberg, *The FDR Years* (1995)
Percy M. Merill, *Roosevelt's Forest Army* (1981)
James S. Olson, *Saving Capitalism* (1988)
Albert U. Romasco, *The Politics of Recovery: Roosevelt's New Deal* (1983)
Theodore M. Saloutos, *The American Farmer and the New Deal* (1982)

Left Turn and the Second New Deal

Kristi Andersen, *The Creation of a Democratic Majority, 1928–1936* (1979)
Irving Bernstein, *The Turbulent Years: A History of the American Worker, 1933–1941* (1970)
Alan Brinkley, *Voices of Protest: Huey Long, Father Coughlin, and the New Deal* (1982)
Peter Friedlander, *The Emergence of a UAW Local* (1975)
Gary Gerstle, *Working Class Americanism* (1989)
Robin D. G. Kelley, *Hammer and Hoe: Alabama Communists during the Great Depression* (1990)
Joseph P. Lash, *Dealers and Dreamers* (1988)
Roy Lubove, *The Struggle for Social Security* (1968)
Robert H. Zieger, *The CIO, 1935–1955* (1995)

The New Deal and the West

James M. Gregory, *American Exodus: The Dust Bowl Migration and Okie Culture in California* (1989)
Norris Hundley Jr., *The Great Thirst: California and Water, 1770s–1990s* (1992)
Laurence Kelly, *The Assault on Assimilation: John Collier and the Origins of Indian Policy Reform, 1920–1954* (1983)
Vicki Ruiz, *Cannery Women/Cannery Lives: Mexican Women, Unionization, and the California Food Processing Industry, 1930–1950* (1987)
Charles J. Shindo, *Dust Bowl Migrants in the American Imagination* (1997)
Graham D. Taylor, *The New Deal and American Indian Tribalism* (1980)
Donald Worster, *Dust Bowl* (1979)

Depression-Era Culture

Vivian Gornick, *The Romance of American Communism* (1976)
Harvey Kleher, *The Heyday of American Communism* (1984)
J. Fred MacDonald, *Don't Touch That Dial* (1979)
Richard McKinzie, *The New Deal for Artists* (1973)
Barbara Melosh, *Engendering Culture: Manhood and Womanhood in New Deal Public Art and Theater* (1991)
David P. Peeler, *Hope among Us Yet* (1987)
Richard H. Pells, *Radical Visions and American Dreams: Culture and Social Thought in the Depression* Years (1973)
Thomas Schatz, *The Genius of the System: Hollywood Filmmaking in the Studio Era* (1988)
Richard Schickel, *The Disney Version* (1968)
Martin Williams, *Jazz in Its Own Time* (1989)

The Limits of Reform

Francisco E. Balderrama, *Decade of Betrayal: Mexican Repatriation in the 1930's* (1995)
Mark Naison, *Communists in Harlem during the Depression* (1983)
James T. Patterson, *Congressional Conservatism and the New Deal* (1967)
Winifred Wandersee, *Women's Work and Family Values: 1920–1940* (1981)
Susan Ware, *Beyond Suffrage: Women in the New Deal* (1981)
______, *Partner and I: Molly Dewson, Feminism, and New Deal Politics* (1987)
Nancy J. Weiss, *Farewell to the Party of Lincoln: Black Politics in the Age of FDR* (1983)
Robert L. Zangrando, *The NAACP Crusade against Lynching* (1980)

Biography

Blanche W. Cook, *Eleanor Roosevelt*, vol. 1 (1992)
Kenneth S. Davis, *FDR*, 4 vols. (1972, 1975, 1986, 1992)
Steven Fraser, *Labor Will Rule: Sidney Hillman and the Rise of American Labor* (1991)
Dorothy Healey and Maurice Isserman, *California Red: A Life in the American Communist Party* (1990)
J. Joseph Huthmacher, *Robert F. Wagner and the Rise of Urban Liberalism* (1968)
Nelson Lichtenstein, *The Most Dangerous Man in Detroit: Walter Reutter and the Fate of American Labor* (1995)
George Martin, *Madame Secretary: Frances Perkins* (1976)
George McJimsey, *Harry Hopkins* (1987)
Karen Becker Ohrn, *Dorothea Lange and the Documentary Tradition* (1980)
Lois Scharf, *Eleanor Roosevelt* (1987)
Robert Zieger, *John L. Lewis* (1988)

CHAPTER TWENTY-FIVE

WORLD WAR II

1941–1945

Back Him Up, Christie's Images.

AMERICAN COMMUNITIES
Los Alamos, New Mexico

Chapter Outline

On Monday, July 16, 1945, at 5:29:45 A.M., Mountain War Time, the first atomic bomb exploded in a brilliant flash visible in three states. Within just seven minutes, a huge, multicolored, bell-shaped cloud soared 38,000 feet into the atmosphere and threw back a blanket of smoke and soot to the earth below. The heat generated by the blast was four times the temperature at the center of the sun, and the light produced rivaled that of nearly twenty suns. Even ten miles away people felt a strong surge of heat. The giant fireball ripped a crater a half-mile wide in the ground, fusing the desert sand into glass. The shock wave blew out windows in houses more than 200 miles away. The blast killed every living creature—squirrels, rabbits, snakes, plants, and insects—within a mile and the smells of death lingered for nearly a month.

Very early that morning, Ruby Wilkening had driven to a nearby mountain ridge, where she joined several other women waiting for the blast. Wilkening worried about her husband, a physicist, who was already at the test site. No one knew exactly what to expect, not even the scientists who developed the bomb.

The Wilkenings were part of a unique community of scientists who had been marshaled for war. President Franklin D. Roosevelt, convinced by Albert Einstein and other physicists that the Nazis might successfully develop an atomic bomb, had inaugurated a small nuclear research program in 1939. Soon after the United States entered World War II, Roosevelt, convinced by scientists that they could produce an atomic weapon in time to affect the outcome of the war, increased the resources available to what was now known as the Manhattan Project and placed it under the direction of the Army Corps of Engineers. By December 1942 a team headed by Italian-born Nobel Prize-winner Enrico Fermi had produced the first chain reaction in uranium under the University of Chicago's football stadium. Now the mission was to build a new, formidable weapon of war, the atomic bomb.

The government moved the key researchers and their families to Los Alamos in the remote and sparsely populated Sangre de Cristo Mountains of New Mexico, a region of soaring peaks, ancient Indian ruins, modern Pueblos, and villages occupied by the descendents of the earliest Spanish settlers. The scientists and their families arrived in March 1943. They occupied a former boys' preparatory school until new houses could be built. Some families doubled up in rugged log cabins or nearby ranches. Telephone service to the outside world was poor, and the mountain roads were so rough that changing flat tires became a tiresome but familiar routine. Construction of new quarters proceeded slowly, causing nasty disputes between the "long-hairs" (scientists) and the "plumbers" (army engineers) in charge of the grounds. Despite the chaos, outstanding American and European scientists eagerly signed up. Most were young, with an average age of twenty-seven, and quite a few were recently married. Many couples began their families at Los Alamos, producing a total of nearly a thousand babies between 1943 and 1949.

The scientists and their families formed an exceptionally close-knit community, united by the need for secrecy and their shared antagonism toward their army guardians. The military atmosphere was oppressive. Homes and laboratories were cordoned off by barbed wire and guarded by military police. Everything, from linens to food packages, was stamped "Government Issue." Security personnel followed the scientists whenever they left Los Alamos. The scientists' homes were wired for sound, and several scientists were reprimanded for discussing their work with their wives. All outgoing mail was censored. Well-known scientists commonly worked under aliases—Fermi became "Eugene Farmer"—and code names were used for such terms as atom, bomb, and uranium fission. The birth certificates of babies born at Los Alamos listed their place of birth simply as rural Sandoval County, and children registered without surnames at nearby public schools. Even automobile accidents went unreported, and newspapers carried no wedding announcements or obituaries. Only a group thoroughly committed to the war effort could accept such restrictions on personal liberty.

A profound urgency motivated the research team, which included refugees from Nazi Germany and Fascist Italy and a large proportion of Jews. The director of the project, California physicist J. Robert Oppenheimer, promoted a scientific élan that offset the military style of commanding general Leslie Groves. Just thirty-eight, slightly built, and deeply emotional, "Oppie" personified the idealism that helped the community of scientists overcome whatever moral reservations they held about placing such a potentially ominous weapon in the hands of the government.

In the Technical Area of Los Alamos, Oppenheimer directed research from an office with a desk, long tables, and blackboard along the walls in a typical two-story army building. At seven o'clock each workday morning, the siren dubbed "Oppie's Whistle" called the other scientists to their laboratories to wrestle with the theoretical and practical problems of building an atomic device. Once a week Oppenheimer called together the heads of the various technical divisions to discuss their work in round-table conferences. From May to November 1944, after the bomb had been designed, the key issue was testing it. Many scientists feared a test might fail, scattering the precious plutonium at the bomb's core and discrediting the entire project. Finally, with plutonium production increasing, the Los Alamos team agreed to test "the gadget" at a site 160 miles away.

The unprecedented scientific mobilization at Los Alamos mirrored changes occurring throughout American society as the nation rallied behind the war effort. Sixteen million men and women left home for military service and nearly as many moved to take advantage of wartime jobs. Several states in the South and Southwest experienced huge surges in population. California alone grew by 2 million people, a large proportion from Mexico. Many broad social changes with roots in earlier times—the economic expansion of the West, the erosion of farm tenancy among black people in the South and white people in Appalachia, and the increasing employment of married women—accelerated during the war. The United States, initially reluctant to enter the war, emerged from it the world's leading superpower and free from the weight of the Great Depression. The events of the war eroded old communities, created new ones like Los Alamos, and transformed nearly all aspects of American society.

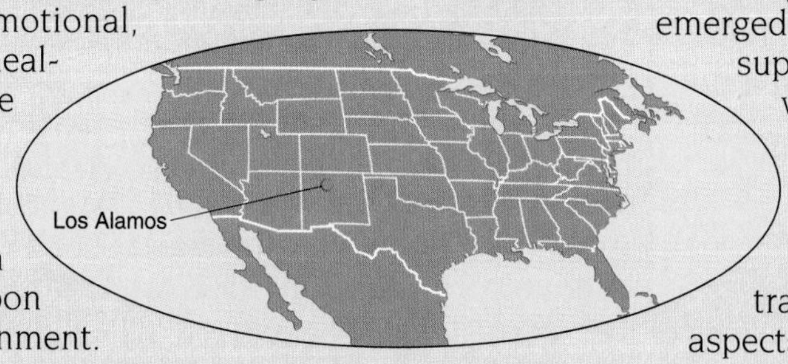

KEY TOPICS

- The events leading to Pearl Harbor and declaration of war
- The marshaling of national resources for war
- American society during wartime
- The mobilization of Americans into the armed forces
- The war in Europe and Asia
- Diplomacy and the atomic bomb

THE COMING OF WORLD WAR II

The Great Depression was not confined to the United States. It was a worldwide economic decline that further undermined a political order that had been shaky since World War I. Production declined by nearly 40 percent, international trade dropped by as much as two-thirds, and unemployment rose. While rivalries for markets and access to raw materials intensified, political unrest spread across Europe and Asia. Demagogues played upon nationalist hatreds, fueled by old resentments and current despair, and offered solutions in the form of territorial expansion by military conquest.

Preoccupied with restoring the domestic economy, President Franklin D. Roosevelt had no specific plan to deal with growing conflict elsewhere in the world. Moreover, the majority of Americans strongly opposed foreign entanglements. But as debate over diplomatic policy heated up, terrifying events overseas pulled the nation steadily toward war.

The Shadows of War

War spread first across Asia. Militarist-imperialist leaders in Japan, which suffered economically from loss of trade during the 1930s, determined to make their nation the richest in the world. The Japanese army seized control of Manchuria in 1931 and in 1932 installed a puppet government there. When reprimanded by the League of Nations, Japan simply withdrew from the organization. In 1937 Japan provoked full-scale war with an invasion of northern China. When it seized control of the capital city of Nanking, Japan's army murdered as many as 300,000 Chinese men, women, and children and destroyed much of the city. Within the year Japan controlled all but China's western interior and threatened all Asia and the Pacific.

Meanwhile, the rise of authoritarian nationalism in Italy and Germany cast a dark shadow over Europe. The economic hardships brought on by the Great Depression—and in Germany resentment over the harsh terms of the Versailles Treaty that ended World War I—fueled the rise of demagogic mass movements. Glorifying war as a test of national virility, the Italian Fascist dictator Benito Mussolini, who had seized power in 1922, declared, "We have buried the putrid corpse of liberty." In Germany, the National Socialists (Nazis), led by Adolf Hitler, combined militaristic rhetoric with a racialist doctrine of Aryan (Nordic) supremacy that claimed biological superiority for the blond-haired and blue-eyed peoples of northern Europe and classified nonwhites, including Jews, as "degenerate races."

Hitler, who had the backing of major industrialists such as the weapons manufacturer Krupp and the support of about a third of the German electorate, was appointed Chancellor of Germany in 1933. With his brown-shirted storm troopers ruling the streets, he quickly seized absolute authority, destroying opposition parties and effectively making himself dictator of the strongest nation in central Europe. Renouncing the disarmament provisions of the Versailles treaty, he began, with no effective protest from France and Britain, to rebuild Germany's armed forces. Intending to make Germany the center of a new civilization, the Nazi leader built up a vast industrial infrastructure for an army of a half-million men poised to conquer Europe. In 1936 Italy allied with Germany to form the Rome-Berlin Axis. In November 1937 Hitler announced plans to obtain *Lebensraum*—living space and farmland for Germany's growing population—through territorial expansion. The prospect of war grew as both Mussolini and Hitler began to act on their imperial visions. In 1935 Italy sent troops to Ethiopia and formally claimed the impoverished African kingdom as a colony. Both Germany and Italy supported the fascist insurrection of General Francisco Franco in the Spanish Civil War that broke out in 1936. In 1936 also, Hitler sent troops to occupy the Rhineland, a region demilitarized by the Versailles Treaty, and prepared to advance on central Europe. In 1938 he sent troops into his native Austria, annexing it to Germany.

Hitler next turned his attention to Czechoslovakia, a country which both Britain and France were pledged by treaty to assist. War seemed imminent. But Britain and France surprised Hitler by agreeing, at a conference in Munich the last week of September 1938, to allow Germany to annex the Sudetenland, a part of Czechoslovakia bordering Germany. In return, Hitler pledged to stop his territorial advance. Less than six months later, in March 1939, Hitler seized the rest of Czechoslovakia.

By the fall of 1938, the world was becoming increasingly aware of the shocking character of Hitler's regime, especially its virulent racial doctrines. After 1935, when Hitler published the notorious Nuremberg Laws denying civil rights to Jews, the campaign against them became steadily more vicious. On the night of November 9, 1938, Nazi storm troopers rounded up Jews, beating them mercilessly and murdering an untold number. They smashed windows in Jewish shops, hospitals, and orphanages and burned synagogues to the ground. This attack came to be known as *Kristallnacht*, "the Night of Broken Glass." The Nazi government soon expropriated Jewish property and excluded Jews from all but the most menial forms of employment. Pressured by Hitler, Hungary and Italy also enacted laws against Jews.

Isolationism

Americans responded cautiously to these events. World War I had left a legacy of strong isolationist sentiment. Popular films such as *All Quiet on the Western Front* (1930) vividly depicted the horrors of war, including atrocities against civilians. Senseless slaughter might be a centuries-old way of life in Europe, many reasoned, but not for the United States, which should stay clear of foreign wars. As late as 1937, nearly 70 percent of Americans responding to a Gallup poll stated that U.S. involvement in World War I had been a mistake.

This sentiment won strong support in Congress. In 1934, a special committee headed by Republican senator Gerald P. Nye of North Dakota had charged weapons manufacturers with driving the United States into World War I in the hopes of windfall profits, which, in fact, many realized. To deter future entanglements, Congress passed three Neutrality Acts in 1935, 1936, and 1937 authorizing the president to deny American firms the right to sell or ship munitions to belligerent nations.

College students, seeing themselves as future cannon fodder, strongly opposed foreign entanglements. In 1933, 39 percent of those polled stated that they would refuse to fight in any war; 33 percent would fight only if the United States were attacked. Three years later, 500,000 boycotted classes in a nationwide "student strike" to demonstrate their opposition to any preparation for war.

Isolationism spanned the political spectrum. In 1938 socialist Norman Thomas gathered leading liberals and trade unionists into the Keep America Out of War Congress; the communist-influenced American League against War and Fascism claimed more than 1 million members. Meanwhile, Republican senator Robert A. Taft of Ohio, son of former president William Howard Taft, argued that a new war would harm American democracy by enlarging the federal government and tightening its grip on the citizenry.

In 1940 the arch-conservative America First Committee was formed to oppose U.S. intervention. The group was particularly strong in the Midwest. Some America Firsters championed the Nazis while others simply advocated American neutrality. Chaired by top Sears executive Robert E. Wood, the America First Committee quickly gained attention because its members included such well-known personalities as movie stars Robert Young and Lillian Gish, automobile manufacturer Henry Ford, and Charles A. Lindbergh, famous for his 1927 solo flight across the Atlantic. Within a year, America First had launched more than 450 chapters.

Roosevelt Readies for War

While Americans looked on anxiously, the twists and turns of world events prompted President Franklin D. Roosevelt to ready the nation for war. In October 1937 he had called for international cooperation to "quarantine the aggressors." "Let no one imagine that America will escape, that America may expect mercy, that this Western Hemisphere will not be attacked." But a poll of Congress revealed that a two-thirds majority opposed economic sanctions, calling any such plan a "back door to war." Forced to draw back, Roosevelt nevertheless won from Congress $1 billion in appropriations to enlarge the navy. But as late as January 1939, in his annual address to Congress, Roosevelt insisted that the United States must use all means "short of war" to deter aggression.

Everything changed on September 1, 1939, when Hitler invaded Poland. Committed by treaty to defend Poland against unprovoked attack, Great Britain and France issued a joint declaration of war against Germany two days later. After the fall of Warsaw at the end of the month, the fighting slowed to a near halt. Even along their border, French and German troops did not exchange fire. From the east, however, the invasion continued. Just two weeks before Hitler overran Poland, the Soviet Union had stunned the world by signing a nonaggression pact with its former enemy. The Red Army now entered Poland, and the two great powers proceeded to split the hapless nation between them. Soviet forces then headed north, invading Finland on November 30. The European war had begun.

Calculating that the United States would stay out of the war, Hitler began a crushing offensive against western Europe in April 1940. Using the technique of *Blitzkrieg* (lightning war)—massed, fast-moving columns of tanks supported by air power—that had overwhelmed Poland, Nazi troops moved first against

OCTOBER 2, 1938
EUROPEAN WAR

If England and France go to war against Germany do you think the United States can stay out?

Yes	57%
No	43

By Region

	Yes	*No*
New England	46%	54%
Middle Atlantic	61	39
East Central	60	40
West Central	57	43
South	60	40
West	51	49

Interviewing Date 9/15–20/1938, Survey #132, Question #4

FEBRUARY 21, 1940
EUROPEAN WAR

If it appears that Germany is defeating England and France, should the United States declare war on Germany and send our army and navy to Europe to fight?

Yes	23%
No	77

7 percent expressed no opinion.

Interviewing Date 2/2–7/1940, Survey #183-K, Question #6

DECEMBER 16, 1940
EUROPEAN WAR

Do you think it was a mistake for the United States to enter the last World War?

Yes	39%
No	42
No opinion	19

By Political Affiliation
Democrats

Yes	33%
No	46
No opinion	21

Republicans

Yes	46%
No	38
No opinion	16

Interviewing Date 11/21–30/1940, Survey #244-K, Question #6

Gallup Polls: European War and World War I, 1938–1940 *These three polls conducted by the American Institute of Public Opinion indicate the persistence of isolationist sentiment and popular criticism of U.S. involvement in World War I. Many respondents believed the United States, despite its commitments to European allies, should stay out of war. After 1940, in the aftermath of Nazi military victories in Europe, many Americans reconsidered their opposition, fearing a threat to democracy in their own nation.*

Germany's northern neighbors. After taking Denmark and Norway, the Nazi armored divisions swept over Holland, Belgium, and Luxembourg and sent more than 338,000 British troops into retreat across the English Channel from Dunkirk. Hitler's army, joined by the Italians, easily conquered France in June 1940. Hitler now turned toward England. In the battle of Britain, Nazi bombers pounded population and industrial centers while U-boats cut off incoming supplies.

Even with Great Britain under attack, opinion polls indicated Americans' determination to stay out of the war. But most Americans, like Roosevelt himself, believed that the security of the United States depended on both a strong defense and the defeat of Germany. Invoking the Neutrality Act of 1939, which permitted the sale of arms to Britain, France, and China, the president clarified his position: "all aid to the Allies short of war." In May 1940 he began to transfer surplus U.S. planes and equipment to the Allies. In September the president secured the first peacetime military draft in American history, the Selective Service Act of 1940, which sent 1.4 million men to army training camps by July 1941. Yet even when he secured huge congressional appropriations for the production of airplanes and battleships, Roosevelt did so in the name of "hemispheric defense," not intervention.

President Roosevelt could not yet admit the inevitability of U.S. involvement—especially during an election year. His popularity had dropped with the "Roosevelt recession" that began in 1937, raising doubts that he could win what would be an unprecedented third term. Waiting until July 1940, the eve of the Democratic Party convention, Roosevelt announced that world events compelled him to accept a party "draft" for renomination. In his campaign he promised voters not to "send your boys to any foreign wars." Roosevelt and his vice-presidential candidate Henry Wallace won by a margin of 5 million popular votes over the Republican dark-horse candidate, Wendell L. Willkie of Indiana.

Roosevelt now moved more aggressively to aid the Allies in their struggle with the Axis powers. In his annual message to Congress, he proposed a bill that would allow the president to sell, exchange, or lease arms to any country whose defense appeared vital to

Japanese attack planes devastated the U.S. fleet stationed on the Hawaiian island of Oahu. Before December 7, 1941, few Americans had heard of Pearl Harbor, but the "sneak" attack became a symbol of Japanese treachery and the necessity for revenge.

U.S. security. Passed by Congress in March, 1941, the Lend-Lease Act made Great Britain the first beneficiary of massive aid. Roosevelt also extended the U.S. "security zone" nearly halfway across the Atlantic Ocean and ordered the Coast Guard to seize any German-controlled or German ships that entered an American port. He directed Germany and Italy to close their U.S. consulates and ordered U.S. ships to shoot any Nazi vessel in U.S. "defensive waters" on sight. After Congress authorized the merchant marine to sail fully armed while conveying lend-lease supplies directly to Britain, a formal declaration of war was only a matter of time.

In August 1941 Roosevelt met secretly at sea off Newfoundland with British prime minister Winston Churchill to map military strategy and declare "common principles." Known as the Atlantic Charter, their proclamation specified the right of all peoples to live in freedom from fear, want, and tyranny. The Atlantic Charter also called for free trade among all nations, an end to territorial seizures, and disarmament. Eventually endorsed by the Soviet Union and fourteen other nations, the Atlantic Charter pledged to all nations—vanquished as well as victors—the right to self-determination.

By this time the European war had moved to a new stage. Hitler had conquered the Balkans and then set aside the expedient Nazi-Soviet Pact to resume his quest for the entire European continent. In June 1941

Hitler launched an invasion of the Soviet Union, promising its rich agricultural land to German farmers. Observing this dramatic escalation, the United States moved closer to intervention.

Pearl Harbor

Throughout 1940 and much of 1941 the United States focused on events in Europe, but the war in Asia went on. Roosevelt, anticipating danger to American interests in the Pacific, had directed the transfer of the Pacific Fleet from bases in California to Pearl Harbor, on the island of Oahu, Hawai'i, in May 1940. On September 27 Japan formally joined Germany and Italy as the Asian partner of the Axis alliance. Under the terms of the expanded alliance, Germany would support Japan's seizure of Dutch, British, and French colonial possessions as part of its attempt to create a regional bloc under its rule.

The United States and Japan each played for time. Roosevelt wanted to save his resources to fight against Germany, while Japan's leaders gambled that America's preoccupation with Europe might allow them to conquer all of Southeast Asia, including the French colonies in Indochina (Vietnam, Cambodia, and Laos) and the British possessions of Burma and India. When Japan occupied Indochina in July, 1941, however, Roosevelt responded by freezing Japanese assets in the United States and cutting off its oil supplies.

Confrontation with Japan now looked likely. U.S. intelligence had broken the Japanese diplomatic code, and the president knew that Japan was preparing for war against the western powers. Roosevelt's advisers expected an attack in the southern Pacific or British Malaya sometime after November. General Douglas MacArthur alerted his command in the Philippines.

Japan, however, intended to knock the United States out of the Pacific in a single blow. Early Sunday morning, December 7, 1941, Japanese carriers launched an attack on Pearl Harbor that caught American forces completely off guard. Sailors on the decks of American ships looked up to see Japanese dive-bombers in the sky above them. Loudspeakers warned: "Japs are coming! Japs attacking us! Go to your battle stations!" Within two hours, Japanese pilots had destroyed nearly 200 American planes and badly damaged the fleet; more than 2,400 Americans were killed and nearly 1,200 wounded. On the same day, Japan struck U.S. bases on the Philippines, Guam, and Wake Island.

On December 8, declaring the attack on Pearl Harbor a date that "will live in infamy," Roosevelt asked Congress for a declaration of war against Japan. With only one dissenting vote—by pacifist Jeannette Rankin of Montana, who had voted against U.S. entry into World War I in 1917—Congress acceded. The United States had not yet declared war on Japan's European allies, but Hitler made that unnecessary when he asked the Reichstag on December 11 to support war against the "half Judaized and the other half Negrified" American nation. Mussolini joined him in the declaration, and the United States on the same day recognized that a state of war existed with Germany and Italy. World War II now began for Americans.

President Franklin D. Roosevelt signs the declaration of war against Japan, December 8, 1941, a day after the attack on Pearl Harbor. Congressional leaders, many of whom had earlier hoped to keep the United States out of war, here unite around the president and his policies.

ARSENAL OF DEMOCRACY

Late in 1940 President Roosevelt called upon all Americans to make the nation "an arsenal of democracy." During the next three years, the economic machinery that had failed during the 1930s was swiftly retooled for military purposes, with dramatic results. The Great Depression suddenly ended. Never before had the federal government poured so much energy and money into production or assigned such a great army of experts to manage it. This marshaling of resources involved a concentration of power in the federal government that exceeded anything planned by the New Deal.

Mobilizing for War

A few days after the United States declared war on Germany, Congress passed the War Powers Act, which established a precedent for executive authority that would endure long after the war's end. The president gained the power to reorganize the federal government and create new agencies; to establish programs censoring all news and information and abridging civil liberties; to seize property owned by foreigners; and even to award government contracts without competitive bidding.

Roosevelt promptly created special wartime agencies. At the top of his agenda was a massive reorientation and management of the economy, and an alphabet soup of new agencies arose to fill any gaps in production. The Supply Priorities and Allocation Board (SPAB) oversaw the use of scarce materials and resources vital to the war, adjusting domestic consumption (even ending it for some products such as automobiles) to military needs. The Office of Price Administration (OPA) checked the threat of inflation from the government's sudden massive spending by imposing price controls. The National War Labor Board (NWLB) mediated disputes between labor and management, halting strikes and also controlling inflation by limiting wage increases. The War Manpower Commission (WMC) directed the mobilization of military and civilian services. And the Office of War Mobilization (OWM), headed by James F. Byrnes, coordinated operations among all these agencies.

Several new agencies focused on domestic propaganda. The attack on Pearl Harbor evoked an outpouring of rage against Japan and effectively quashed much opposition to U.S. intervention. Still, for most Americans, World War II would remain a foreign war, and the government stepped in to fan the fires of patriotism and to shape public opinion. In June 1942 the president created the Office of War Information (OWI) to coordinate information from the multiplying federal agencies and to engage the press, radio, and film industry in an informational campaign—in short, to sell the war to the American people.

The OWI gathered data and controlled the release of news, emphasizing the need to make reports on the war both dramatic and encouraging. Like the Committee on Public Information during World War I, during the first twenty-one months of the war the new agency banned the publication of advertisements, photographs, and newsreels showing American dead, fearing that such images would demoralize the public. In 1943, worrying that Americans had become overconfident, officials changed their policy. A May issue of Newsweek featured graphic photographs of Americans wounded in battle, explaining that "to harden home-front morale, the military services have adopted a new policy of letting civilians see photographically what warfare does to men who fight." To spare families unnecessary grief, throughout the war the OWI prohibited the publication of any photograph revealing the identity of the American dead. The OWI also published leaflets and booklets for the armed services and flooded enemy ranks with subversive propaganda.

Propaganda also fueled the selling of war bonds. Secretary of the Treasury Henry Morgenthau Jr. not only encouraged Americans to buy government bonds to finance the war but planned a campaign "to use bonds to sell the war, rather than vice versa." Bonds, the ads for them claimed, were a good investment that gave everyone an opportunity "to have a financial stake in American democracy." Buying them would "mean bullets in the bellies of Hitler's hordes!" Discovering through research that Americans felt more antagonism to Japan than Germany, Morgenthau directed his staff to use more negative stereotypes of the Japanese in their advertising copy. Polls showed, however, that most depression-stung Americans bought war bonds mainly to invest safely, to counter inflation, and to save for postwar purchases.

The federal government also sponsored various measures to prevent subversion of the war effort. Concerned about enemy propaganda, the Office of Facts and Figures hired political scientist Harold Lasswell of Yale University to devise a means to measure the patriotic content of magazines and newspapers. The Federal Bureau of Investigation (FBI) was kept busy, its appropriation rising from $6 million to $16 million in just two years. The attorney general authorized wiretapping in cases of espionage or sabotage, but the FBI used it extensively—and illegally—in domestic surveillance. The Joint Chiefs of Staff created the Office of Strategic Services (OSS) to assess the enemy's military strength, to gather intelligence information, and to oversee espionage activities. Its head, Colonel William Donovan, envisioned the OSS as an "adjunct to military strategy" and engaged leading social scientists to plot psychological warfare against the enemy.

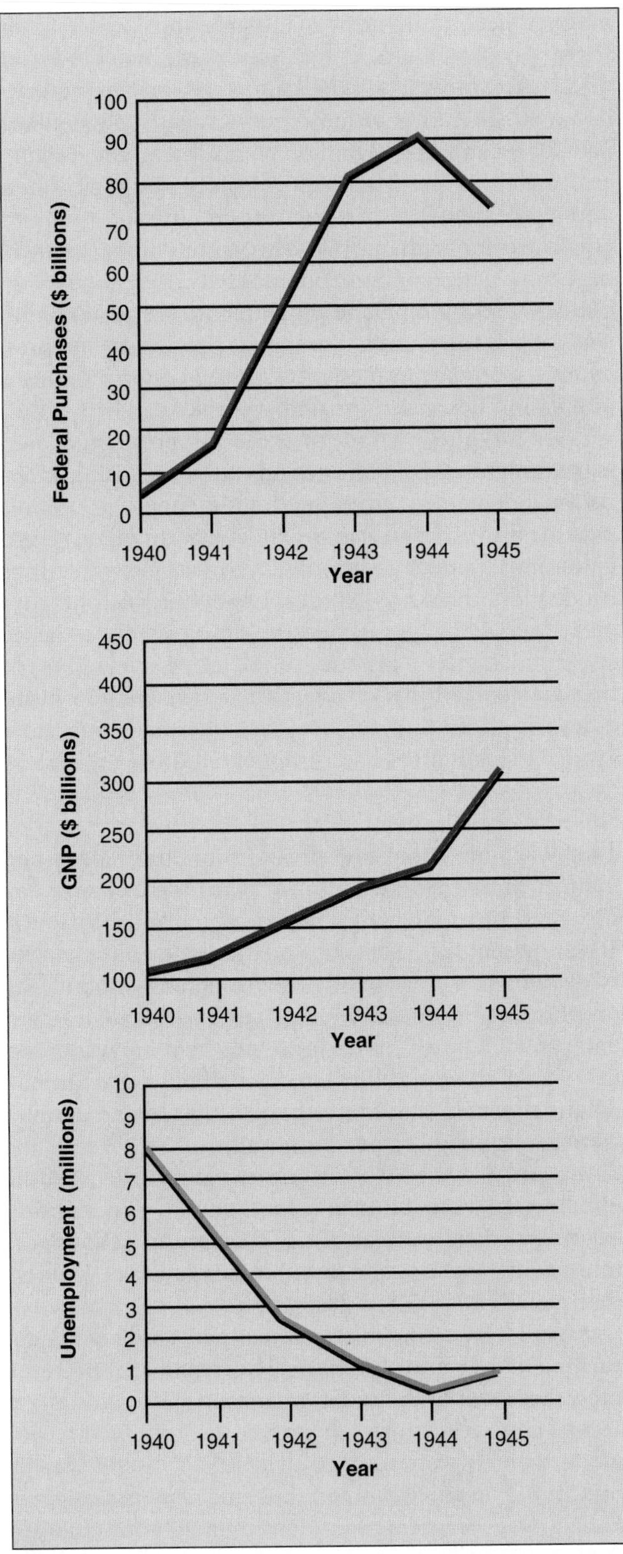

Effects of War Spending, 1940–1945 *Wartime spending had a multiplier effect on the U.S. economy. Government contracts with industry rapidly increased the gross national product, and the sharp upswing in production utilized all available workers and sharply reduced unemployment.*

Source: Robert L. Heilbroner, *The Economic Transformation of America* (New York: Harcourt, Brace, 1977), p. 205.

One important outcome of these activities was to increase the size of the government many times over its New Deal level, which conservatives already considered far too large. It cost about $250 million a day to fight the war. As a result, the federal government spent twice as much during the war as it had during the nation's entire history up to then. The federal budget grew to ten times its peacetime amount during the New Deal. Defense spending rose from $9 million to $98 million, and the number of federal employees nearly quadrupled, from a little over 1 million in 1940 to nearly 4 million by the war's end.

Despite this pattern of expansion, however, the New Deal itself fell victim to the war. As President Roosevelt announced in 1942, "Dr. New Deal" had been replaced by "Dr. Win the War." No longer carrying the heavy responsibility of bringing the nation out of the Great Depression, his administration directed all its resources toward securing the planes, ships, guns, and food required for victory. Moreover, the 1942 elections weakened the New Deal coalition by unseating many liberal Democrats. The Republicans gained forty-six new members in the House of Representatives, nine in the Senate. Republicans now had greater opportunity to quash proposals to extend the social programs instituted during the 1930s.

One by one, New Deal agencies vanished. One of the most popular programs, the Civilian Conservation Corps, secured funds from Congress, but only to cover its liquidation. In December 1942 the Works Progress Administration, which handled various forms of work relief, was given, in Roosevelt's words, a "wartime furlough"; a few months later Congress granted the agency an "honorable discharge." Major New Deal agencies, including the National Youth Administration and the Federal Writers Project, were dismantled by 1943.

Economic Conversion

The decisive factor for victory, even more than military prowess and superior strategy, would be, many observers agreed, the ability of the United States to outproduce its enemies. The country enjoyed many advantages to meet this challenge: a large industrial base, abundant natural resources (largely free from interference by the war), and a civilian population large enough to permit it to increase both its labor force and its armed forces. The war would lift the United States out of the Great Depression and create the biggest economic boom in the history of any nation. But first the entire civilian economy had to be both expanded and transformed for the production of arms and other military supplies.

Economic conversion resulted from a combination of government spending and foreign orders for military supplies. The American public firmly opposed rearmament until 1938, when expenditures for military purposes amounted to only 1.5 percent of the federal budget. The revision of neutrality legislation in 1939 eased previous restrictions on the sale of war materials to France and Great Britain, creating a huge market and boosting production significantly. By the summer of 1941 the federal government was pouring vast amounts into defense production. Six months after the attack on Pearl Harbor its allocations topped $100 billion for equipment and supplies that exceeded what American firms had produced in any previous war. Facing war orders too large to fill, American industries were now primed for all-out production.

Before the Japanese attack on Pearl Harbor, President Roosevelt counted on American businesses to manage their own war-related industries. After announcing a goal of 60,000 planes, 45,000 tanks, and 8 million tons of ships for 1942, Roosevelt formed the War Production Board in January of that year. He directed the new agency to "exercise general responsibility" for the economy. By June, nearly half of everything produced in the United States was war material.

Every economic indicator pointed upward. The gross national product (accounting for inflation) rose from $88.6 billion in 1939 to $198.7 billion in five years. Investment in new plants and equipment, including the manufacture of newly discovered synthetic rubber and fabrics, made possible an increase of 50 percent in the nation's productive capacity and the creation of 17 million jobs. Factories operated around-the-clock, seven days a week. With better equipment and more motivation, American workers proved twice as productive as the Germans, five times as productive as the Japanese. No wonder the actual volume of industrial output expanded at the fastest rate in American history. Military production alone grew from 2 percent of the 1939 total gross national product to 40 percent of the 1943 total. "Something is happening," announced Time magazine, "that Adolf Hitler does not understand . . . it is the miracle of production."

Businesses scored huge profits from military contracts. The government provided low-interest loans and even direct subsidies for the expansion of construction of facilities, with generous tax write-offs for retooling. The 100 largest corporations, which manufactured 30 percent of all goods in 1940, garnered 70 percent of all war and civilian contracts and the bulk of the war profits. On the other hand, many small businesses closed, a half-million between 1941 and 1943 alone.

Defense production transformed entire regions. The impact was strongest in the West—the major staging area for the war in the Pacific—where the federal government spent nearly $40 billion for military and industrial expansion. California secured 10 percent of all federal funds, and by 1944 Los Angeles had become the nation's second largest manufacturing center, only slightly behind Detroit. The South also benefited from 60 of the army's 100 new camps. Its textile factories hummed: the army alone required nearly 520 million pairs of socks and 230 million pairs of pants. The southern branch of the Manhattan Project, the Oak Ridge, Tennessee, facility for the production of uranium, employed more than 80,000 workers during 1945, its peak year. The economic boom lifted entire populations out of sharecropping and tenancy into well-paid industrial jobs in the cities and pumped unprecedented profits into southern business. Across the country the rural population decreased by almost 20 percent.

Despite a "Food for Freedom" program, American farmers could not keep up with the rising international demand or even the domestic market for milk, potatoes, fruits, and sugar. The Department of Agriculture reached its goals only in areas such as livestock production, thanks to skyrocketing wholesale prices for meat. The war also speeded the development of large-scale, mechanized production of crops, including the first widespread use of chemical fertilizers and pesticides. By 1945 farm income had doubled, but thousands of small farms had disappeared, never to return.

New Workers

The wartime economy brought an unprecedented number of new workers into the labor force. The *bracero* program, negotiated by United States and Mexico in 1942, opened to Mexicans short-term employment in trades previously closed to them, such as shipbuilding on the Pacific coast. More than 200,000 Mexicans entered the United States legally to help harvest crops. In 1944 a survey published by the Bureau of Indian Affairs reported that more than 46,000 Indian peoples were working in either agriculture or industry. The Sioux and Navajos, for example, were hired in large numbers to help build military depots and military training centers. African Americans found new opportunities in industry, and the number of black workers rose from 2,900,000 to 3,800,000.

The war most dramatically altered the wage-earning patterns of women. The female labor force grew by over 50 percent, reaching 19.5 million in 1945. The rate of growth proved especially high for white women over the age of thirty-five, and for the first time married women became the majority of female wage earners. The employment rate changed comparatively little for African American women; fully 90 percent had been in the labor force in 1940. However, many black women left domestic service for higher-paying jobs in manufacturing.

Despite this jump in employment rates, neither government nor industry rushed to recruit women. Well into the summer of 1942 the Department of War advised

Facing a shortage of workers and increased production demands, the War Manpower Commission and the Office of War Information conducted a campaign to recruit women into the labor force. Women were encouraged to "take a job for your husband/son/brother" and to "keep the world safe for your children." Higher wages also enticed many women to take jobs in factories producing aircraft, ships, and ordnance. This photograph shows women working on the assembly line at Douglas Aircraft's plant in Long Beach, California, in 1944.

businesses to hold back from hiring women "until all available male labor in the area had first been employed." Likewise, neither government nor industry expected women to stay in their jobs when the war ended. Recruitment campaigns targeted "Mrs. Stay-at-Home" yet underscored the temporary aspect of her wartime service. "Rosie the Riveter" appeared in posters and advertisements as the model female citizen, but only "for the duration." In Washington, D.C., women bus drivers were given badges to wear on their uniforms that read: "I am taking the place of a man who went to war."

For the most part, advertisers used conventional gender stereotypes to make wartime jobs appealing to women. Recruitment posters and informational films depicted women's new industrial jobs as simple variations of domestic tasks. Where once housewives sewed curtains for their kitchens, they now produced silk parachutes. Their skill with a vacuum cleaner easily translated into riveting on huge ships. "Instead of cutting a cake," one newsreel explained, "this woman [factory worker] cuts the pattern of aircraft parts. Instead of baking a cake, this woman is cooking gears to reduce the tension in the gears after use."

In practice, however, many stereotypes broke down. Women mined coal, repaired aircraft engines, cut and welded sheet metal, and operated forklifts and drill presses. On the Pacific coast, more than one-third of all workers in aircraft and shipbuilding were women. One female African American ship welder recalled: "There is nothing in the training to prepare you for the excruciating noise you get down in the ship. Any who were not heart-and-soul determined to stick it out would fade out right away. . . . And it isn't only your muscles that must harden. It's your nerve, too."

Compared to the Great Depression, when married women were barred from many jobs, World War II opened up new fields. The number of women automobile workers, for example, jumped from 29,000 to 200,000, that of women electrical workers from 100,000 to 374,000. Polled near the end of the war, the overwhelming majority—75 percent—of women workers expressed a desire to keep working, preferably at the same jobs. One woman spoke for many in describing her wartime work as "thrilling" and "exciting," adding that it was also "something women have never been allowed to do before." Many also candidly admitted that they most of all liked earning good money. One woman reported that her assembly-line job in the aircraft industry paid $1.15 per hour, a huge increase over the hourly wage she formerly earned as a waitress: 20 cents, with no tips allowed.

Although wartime employment changed the lives and raised the expectations of many new workers, the major advances proved short-lived. As early as 1943 some industries began planning to lay off women as war production wound down. With jobs reserved for returning veterans, women in industry saw their numbers diminish rapidly; as many as 4 million lost their jobs between 1944 and 1946. Although skyrocketing inflation propelled many married women back into the labor force by the end of the decade, they did not pick up lucrative jobs in heavy industry.

Wartime Strikes

Although 17 million new jobs were created during the war, the economic gains were unevenly distributed. Wages increased by as much as 50 percent but never as fast as profits or prices. This widely reported dispar-

Strikes and Lockouts in the United States, 1940–1945

Year	Number of Strikes	Number of Workers Involved	Number of Man-Days Idle	Percent of Total Employed
1940	2,508	576,988	6,700,872	2.3
1941	4,288	2,362,620	23,047,556	8.4
1942	2,968	839,961	4,182,557	2.8
1943	3,752	1,981,279	13,500,529	6.9
1944	4,956	2,115,637	8,721,079	7.0
1945	4,750	3,467,000	38,025,000	12.2

Despite "no-strike" pledges, workers staged wildcat strikes in the war years. Union leaders negotiated shorter hours, higher wages, and seniority rules and helped to build union membership to a new height. When the war ended, nearly 30 percent of all nonagricultural workers were union members.

Source: "Work Stoppages Caused by Labor-Management Disputes in 1945," *Monthly Labor Review*, May 1946, p. 720; and Martin Glaberman, *War Time Strikes* (Detroit: Bewick, 1980), p. 36.

ity produced one of the most turbulent periods in American labor history.

Labor strife began even before U.S. involvement in World War II. Only two weeks after the 1940 election, workers struck at the Vultee aircraft plant in Los Angeles. After the attorney general denounced the strikers as unpatriotic and the FBI began to harass participants, workers throughout the city walked off their jobs in sympathy with the aircraft workers. In April 1941 the president himself intervened in a large strike at Allis Chalmers near Milwaukee, threatening seizure of the plant and forcing a settlement after 75 days of work stoppage. Later that year Roosevelt ordered troops to break the North American Aviation strike at Inglewood, California.

More workers went on strike in 1941, before the United States entered the war, than in any previous year except 1919. Rising production orders and tightening labor markets made strikes feasible: jobs were plentiful, and business leaders, anticipating hefty profits, had reason to settle quickly. This climate prompted a militant union drive at Ford Motor Company's enormous River Rouge plant, and the United Auto Workers (UAW) emerged as one of the most powerful labor organizations in the world.

Once the United States entered the war, the major unions agreed to no-strike pledges for its duration. The National War Labor Board, with representatives from business and labor, encouraged employers to allow unions in their plants, and unions secured contracts that included automatic dues checkoff, high wages, and new fringe benefits such as pension plans. Total union membership increased from 10.5 million to 14.7 million, with women's share alone rising from 11 to 23 percent.

Unions also enrolled 1,250,000 African Americans, twice the prewar number. But many white workers resisted this change. "Hate strikes" broke out in plants across the country when African Americans were hired or promoted to jobs customarily held by white workers. For example, at a U.S. Rubber Company factory in Detroit, more than half the workers walked out in 1943 when African American women began to operate the machinery. Such strikes usually ended quickly because black workers refused to back down.

Rank-and-file union members staged other illegal "wildcat" strikes. The most dramatic, a walkout of more than a half-million coal miners in 1943 led by the rambunctious John L. Lewis, withstood the attacks of the government and the press. Roosevelt repeatedly ordered the mines seized, only to find, as Lewis retorted, that coal could not be mined with bayonets. The Democratic majority in Congress passed the first federal antistrike bill, giving the president power to penalize strikers, even to draft them. And yet the strikes grew in size and number, reaching a level greater than in any other four-year period in American history.

THE HOME FRONT

Most Americans thoroughly appreciated the burst of prosperity brought on by wartime production. But they also experienced dramatic and unanticipated changes in the ways they worked and lived. Food rationing, long workdays, and separation from loved ones were just a few of the new conditions of daily life. Americans in communities across the country endured four intense years of adjustment.

Most Americans were happy and proud to make whatever sacrifices they could to help bring about the Allied victory. But alongside national unity ran deep conflicts on the home front. Racial and ethnic hostilities flared repeatedly and on several occasions erupted in violence.

Families in Wartime

Despite the uncertainties of wartime, or perhaps because of them, men and women rushed into marriage. The surge in personal income caused by the wartime economic boom meant that many young couples could afford to set up their own households—something their counterparts in the 1930s had not been able to do. As one social scientist remarked at the time, "Economic conditions were ripe for a rush to the altar." For other couples, the prospect of separation provided the incentive. The U.S. Census Bureau estimated that between 1940 and 1943 at least a million more people married than would have been expected had there been no war. The marriage rate skyrocketed, peaking in 1946. The median age for first marriage for women dropped to an unprecedented low of 20.3 years. But by 1946 the number of divorces also set records.

Housing shortages were acute, and rents were high. So scarce were apartments that taxi drivers became, for an extra fee, up-to-the-minute guides to vacancies. Able to set their own terms, landlords frequently discriminated against families with children and even more so against racial minorities. To ease these pressures, the National Housing Agency kicked off the "Share Your Home" campaign, which ultimately encouraged 1.5 million families to open their homes to friends, relatives, or strangers. The federal government also financed the construction of low-cost housing projects, which furnished approximately 2 million new residential units.

Supplying a household was scarcely less difficult. Although retailers extended their store hours into the evenings and weekends, shopping had to be squeezed in between long hours on the job. Extra planning was necessary for purchasing government-rationed staples such as meat, cheese, sugar, milk, coffee, gasoline, and even shoes. Many women found it nearly impossible to manage both a demanding job and a household; this dual responsibility contributed to high turnover and absentee rates in factories. A 1943 survey reported that 40 percent of all women who left war plants did so for marital or household reasons rather than because of unsatisfactory wages or working conditions.

The care of small children became a major problem. Wartime employment or military service often separated husbands and wives, leaving children

Students at Officers' Training School at Northwestern University, who were not allowed to marry until they were commissioned as ensigns, apply for marriage licenses in Chicago, August 20, 1943, shortly before graduation. These young couples helped the marriage rate skyrocket during World War II.

in the hands of only one parent. But even when families stayed together, both adults often worked long hours, sometimes on different shifts. Although the War Manpower Commission estimated that as many as 2 million children needed some form of child care, federally funded day-care centers served less than 10 percent of defense workers' children. Polls indicated that the majority of mothers would in any case refuse to send their youngsters to a public child-care center. In some communities, industries and municipal governments established limited facilities that could not keep up with the rapid increase in the number of "latchkey" children.

Juvenile delinquency rose during the war. With employers often relaxing minimum age requirements for employment, many teenagers quit school for the high wages of factory jobs. Between 1941 and 1944 high school enrollments decreased by 1.2 million. Runaways drifted from city to city, finding temporary work at wartime plants or at military installations. Gangs formed in major urban areas, leading to brawling, prostitution, or automobile thefts for joy rides. Overall, however, with so many young men either employed or serving in the armed forces, crime by juvenile as well as adult males declined. In contrast, complaints against girls, mainly for sexual offenses or for running away from home, increased significantly. In response, local officials created various youth agencies and charged them with developing more recreational and welfare programs.

In 1944 the U.S. Office of Education and the Children's Bureau inaugurated a back-to-school campaign. Local school boards appealed to employers to hire only older workers, and toward the end of the war the student dropout rate began to decline. The public schools, meanwhile, expanded their curriculums to include nutrition, hygiene, first aid, and the political context of the war itself. Although many teachers had quit to take better-paying jobs in industry, those who remained often organized scrap and salvage missions, war bond drives, Victory gardens, and letter-writing campaigns. In many localities, the school stood at the center of community war efforts.

Public health improved greatly during the war. Forced to cut back on expenditures for medical care during the Great Depression, many Americans now spent large portions of their wartime paychecks on doctors, dentists, and prescription drugs. But even more important were the benefits provided to the more than 16 million men inducted into the armed forces and their dependents. The majority of young, well-trained physicians and dentists worked in uniform, providing their services at government expense. The number of doctors and dentists also increased dramatically: the graduating classes of 1944 were twice as large as those of any prewar year. Nationally, incidences of such communicable diseases as typhoid fever, tuberculosis, and diphtheria dropped considerably, the infant death rate fell by more than a third, and life expectancy increased by three years. The death rate in 1942, excluding battle deaths, was the lowest in the nation's history. In the South and Southwest, however, racism and widespread poverty combined to halt or even reverse these trends. These regions continued to have the highest infant and maternal mortality rates in the nation.

The Internment of Japanese Americans

After the attack on Pearl Harbor, many Americans feared an invasion of the mainland and suspected Japanese Americans of secret loyalty to an enemy government. On December 8, 1941, the federal government froze the financial assets of those born in Japan, known as Issei, who had been barred from U.S. citizenship. Politicians, patriotic organizations, and military officials, meanwhile, called for the removal of all Americans of Japanese descent from Pacific coastal areas. Although a State Department intelligence report certified their loyalty, Japanese Americans—two-thirds of whom were American-born citizens—became the only ethnic group singled out for legal sanctions.

Charges of sedition masked long-standing racial prejudices. The press began to use the word "Jap" in headlines, while political cartoonists employed blatant racial stereotypes. Popular songs appeared with titles like "You're a Sap, Mister Jap, to Make a Yankee Cranky." The head of the Western Defense Command, General John L. DeWitt, called the Japanese "an enemy race," bound by "racial affinities" to their homeland no matter how many generations removed. "The very fact that no sabotage has taken place to date," an army report suggested, with twisted logic, "is a disturbing and confirming indication that action will be taken."

On February 19, 1942, President Roosevelt signed Executive Order 9066, suspending the civil rights of Japanese Americans and authorizing the exclusion of approximately 110,000 men, women, and children from (mainly) California, Oregon, Washington, and southern Arizona. While the government confiscated most of their personal property, the army began to round up and remove them from the communities where they lived and worked.

During the spring of 1942, Japanese American families received one week's notice to close up their businesses and homes before being transported to one of the ten internment camps managed by the War Relocation Authority. The guarded camps were located as far away as Arkansas, although the majority had been set up in isolated districts of Utah, Colorado, Idaho, Arizona, Wyoming, and California. Karl G. Yoneda described his quarters at Manzanar, California:

> There were no lights, stoves, or window panes. My two cousins and I, together with seven others, were crowded into a 25 x 30 foot room. We slept on army cots with our clothes on. The next morning we discovered that there were no toilets or washrooms. . . . We saw GIs manning machine guns in the watchtowers. The barbed wire fence which surrounded the camp was visible against the background of the snow-covered Sierra mountain range. "So this is the American-style concentration camp," someone remarked.

By August, virtually every West Coast resident who had at least one Japanese grandparent had been interned.

The Japanese American Citizens League charged that "racial animosity" rather than military necessity had dictated the internment policy. Despite the protest of the American Civil Liberties Union and several church groups against the abridgment of the civil rights of Japanese Americans, the Supreme Court in *Korematsu v. U.S.* (1944) upheld the constitutionality of relocation on grounds of national security. By this time a program of gradual release was in place, although the last center, at Tule Lake, California, did not close until March 1946. In protest, nearly 6,000 Japanese Americans renounced their U.S. citizenship. Japanese Americans had lost homes and businesses valued at $500 million in what many historians judge the worst violation of American civil liberties during the war. Not until 1988 did the U.S. Congress vote reparations of $20,000 and a public apology to each of the 60,000 surviving victims.

Civil Rights and Race Riots

Throughout the war, African American activists conducted a "Double V" campaign, mobilizing not only for Allied victory but for their own rights as citizens. "The army is about to take me to fight for democracy," one Detroit resident said, "but I would as leave fight for democracy right here." Black militants demanded, at a minimum, fair housing and equal employment opportunities. President Roosevelt responded in a lukewarm fashion, supporting advances in civil rights that would not, in his opinion, disrupt the war effort.

Before the United States entered the war, A. Philip Randolph, president of both the Brotherhood of Sleeping Car Porters and the National Negro Congress, had organized the March on Washington Movement. At a planning meeting in Chicago a black woman had proposed sending African Americans to Washington, D.C., "from all over the country, in jalopies, in trains, and any way they can get there until we get some action from the White House." Local rallies were held across the country in preparation for the "great rally" of no less than 100,000 people at the Lincoln Memorial on the Fourth of July.

Eager to stop the movement, President Roosevelt met with Randolph, who proposed an executive order "making it mandatory that Negroes be permitted to work." Randolph reviewed several drafts before approving the text that became, on June 25, 1941, Executive Order 8802 banning discrimination in defense industries and government. The president later appointed a Fair Employment Practices Committee to hear complaints and to take "appropriate steps to redress grievances." Randolph called off the march but did not disband his all-black March on Washington organization. He remained determined to "shake up white America."

Byron Takashi Tsuzuki, *Forced Removal, Act II*, 1944. Japanese American National Museum, Collection of August and Kitty Nakagawa.

Byron Takashi Tsuzuki, Forced Removal, Act II, 1944. *This Japanese American artist illustrates the forced relocation of Japanese Americans from their homes to one of ten inland camps in 1942. About 110,000 Japanese Americans were interned during World War II, some for up to four years. Beginning in January 1945, they were allowed to return to the Pacific coast.*

Other civil rights organizations formed during wartime to fight both discrimination and Jim Crow practices, including segregation in the U.S. armed forces. The interracial Congress of Racial Equality (CORE), formed by pacifists in 1942, staged sit-ins at Chicago, Detroit, and Denver restaurants that refused to serve African Americans. In several cities, CORE used nonviolent means to challenge racial segregation in public facilities. Meanwhile, membership in the National Association for the Advancement of Colored People (NAACP), which took a strong stand against discrimination in the military, grew from 50,000 in 1940 to 450,000 in 1946.

The struggle for equality took shape within local communities. Approximately 1.2 million African Americans left the rural South to take jobs in wartime industries. They faced not only serious housing shortages but whites who were determined to keep them out of the best jobs and neighborhoods. In February 1942, when twenty black families attempted to move into new federally funded apartments adjacent to a Polish American community in Detroit, a mob of 700 white protesters halted the moving vans and burned a cross on the project's grounds. The police overlooked the white rioters but arrested black youths. Finally, two months later, 1,000 state troopers supervised the move of these families into the Sojourner Truth Homes, named after the famous abolitionist and former slave.

Racial violence reached its wartime peak during the summer of 1943, when 274 conflicts broke out in nearly fifty cities. In Detroit, twenty-five blacks and nine whites were killed and more than 700 were injured. After the riot, one writer reported: "I thought that I had witnessed an experience peculiar to the Deep South. On the streets of Detroit I saw again the same horrible exhibition of uninhibited hate as they fought and killed one another—white against black—in a frenzy of homicidal mania, without rhyme or reason." The poet Langston Hughes, who supported U.S. involvement in the war, wrote:

Looky here, America
What you done done—
Let things drift
Until the riots come

Yet you say we're fighting
For democracy.
Then why don't democracy
Include me?

I ask you this question
Cause I want to know
How long I got to fight
BOTH HITLER—AND JIM CROW.

The poet and educator Pauli Murray summed up the situation in a letter sent to President Roosevelt: "It is my conviction . . . that the problem of race, intensified by economic conflict and war nerves . . . will eventually . . . occupy a dominant position as a national domestic problem." Her words proved prescient.

Horace Pippin (1888–1946). Mr. *Prejudice*, 1943. Oil on canvas, 18 x 14 inches. Philadelphia Museum of Art, Gift of Dr. and Mrs. Matthew T. Moore. Photo by Graydon Wood.

This painting is by Horace Pippin, a self-taught African American artist who began painting as therapy for an injury suffered while serving with the U.S. Army's 369th Colored Infantry Regiment during World War I. It is one of a series drawn during World War II illustrating the contradiction between the principles of libery and justice, for which Americans were fighting abroad, and the reality of race prejudice at home.

Zoot-suit Riots

On the night of June 4, 1943, sailors poured into nearly 200 cars and taxis to drive through the streets of East Los Angeles in search of Mexican Americans dressed in zoot suits. The sailors assaulted their victims at random, even chasing one youth into a movie theater and stripping him of his clothes while the audience cheered. Riots broke out and continued for five days.

Two communities had collided, with tragic results. The sailors had only recently been uprooted from their hometowns and regrouped under the strict discipline of boot camp. Now stationed in southern California while awaiting departure overseas, they came face-to-face with

Mexican American teenagers wearing long-draped coats, pegged pants, pocket watches with oversized chains, and big floppy hats. To the sailors, the zoot suit was not just a flamboyant fashion. Unlike the uniform the young sailors wore, the zoot suit signaled a lack of patriotism.

The zoot-suiters, however, represented less than 10 percent of their community's youth. More than 300,000 Mexican Americans were serving in the armed forces, in numbers greater than their proportion of the draft-age population and in the most hazardous branches, the paratrooper and marine corps. Many others were employed in war industries in Los Angeles, which had become home to the largest community of Mexican Americans in the nation. For the first time Mexican Americans were finding well-paying jobs, and, like African Americans, they expected their government to protect them from discrimination.

There were several advances during the war. The Fair Employment Practices Committee fostered a limited expansion of civil rights. The Spanish-Speaking People's Division in the Office of Inter-American Affairs established centers in Denver, Salt Lake City, and Los Angeles to bring together community, business, and educational leaders in programs on Latin American culture. The office also developed programs to instill cultural pride and self-esteem among Mexican American children. School districts in California and throughout the Southwest introduced lessons on the Mexican heritage and encouraged bilingual education. Many schools also added vocational training classes to channel graduates into wartime industry.

But these new programs did little to ease the bitter racial and cultural conflict that on occasion became vicious. In Los Angeles, military and civilian authorities eventually contained the zoot-suit riots by ruling several sections of the city off limits to military personnel. The Los Angeles City Council passed legislation making the wearing of a zoot suit in public a criminal offense. Later, the Joint Finding Committee on Un-American Activities in California conducted hearings to determine whether foreign enemy agents had plotted the unrest. Nevertheless, many Mexican Americans expressed concern about their personal safety; some feared that, after the government rounded up the Japanese, they would be the next group sent to internment camps.

Popular Culture and "The Good War"

Global events shaped the lives of American civilians but appeared to touch them only indirectly in their everyday activities. Food shortages, long hours in the factories, and even fears for loved ones abroad did not take away all the pleasures of full employment and prosperity. With money in their pockets, Americans spent freely at vacation resorts, country clubs, race-tracks, nightclubs, dance halls, and movie theaters. Sales of books skyrocketed, and spectator sports attracted huge audiences.

This Mexican American zoot-suiter wears the typical thigh-length, broad-lapel jacket with padded shoulders, baggy trousers pegged at the cuff, and a broad-brimmed felt hat. A dramatic contrast to the military uniforms of the day, the zoot suit symbolized cultural rebellion.

Popular culture, especially music, seemed to bridge the growing racial divisions of the neighborhood and the workplace. Transplanted southern musicians, black and white, brought their regional styles to northern cities and adapted them quickly to the electric amplification of nightclubs and recording studios. "They'd made them steel guitars cry and whine," Ray Charles later remembered. Played on jukeboxes in bars, bus stations, and cafes, "country" and "rhythm & blues" not only won over new audiences but also inspired musicians themselves to crisscross old boundaries. The International Sweethearts of Rhythm, a group of black and white women singers, started in the Mississippi Delta but soon pleased audiences throughout the United States.

Many songs featured war themes. Personal sentiment meshed with government directive to depict a "good war," justifying massive sacrifice and dedicated to a worthy and even noble cause. The plaintive "A Rainbow at Midnight" by country singer Ernest Tubb expressed the hope of a common "dogface" soldier looking beyond the misery and horror to the promise of a brighter tomorrow. "Till Then," recorded by the harmonious black quartet, the Mills Brothers, offered the prospect of a romantic reunion when "the world will be free." The era's best-known tune, Irving Berlin's "White Christmas," evoked a lyrical nostalgia of past celebrations with family and friends close by. On the lighter side, novelty artist Spike Jones made his name with the "razz" or "Bronx cheer," in "We're Going to Ffft in the Fuehrer's Face."

Hollywood artists meanwhile threw themselves into a perpetual round of fund-raising and morale-boosting public events. Movie stars called on fans to buy war bonds and to support the troops. Combat films such as *Action in the North Atlantic* made heroes of ordinary Americans under fire, depicting GIs of different races and ethnicities discovering their common humanity. Movies with antifascist themes, such as *Tender Comrade,* promoted friendship among Russians and Americans, while films like *Since You Went Away* portrayed the loyalty and resilience of families with servicemen stationed overseas.

The wartime spirit also infected the juvenile world of comics. The climbing sales of nickel "books" spawned a proliferation of patriotic superheroes such as Flash, Hawkman, the Green Lantern, Captain Marvel, and the more comical Plastic Man. Captain America, created by the famed comic artist Jack Kirby, was a frail soldier who, when injected with a wonder drug, began delivering punches at Adolf Hitler even before the United States entered the war. Kirby went on to create "boy Commandos," intensifying juvenile identification with battlefield action. Even Bugs Bunny put on a uniform and fought sinister-looking enemies.

Fashion designers did their part. Padded shoulders and straight lines became popular for both men and women; BVD, a leading manufacturer of underwear, designed civilian clothing to resemble military attire. Patriotic Americans, such as civil defense volunteers and Red Cross workers, fancied uniforms, and women employed in defense plants wore pants, often for the first time. Restrictions on materials also influenced fashion. Production of nylon stockings was halted because the material was needed for parachutes. To save material, women's skirts were shortened, while the War Production Board encouraged cuffless "Victory Suits" for men. Executive Order M-217 restricted the colors of shoes manufactured during the war to "black, white, navy blue, and three shades of brown."

Never to see a single battle, safeguarded by two oceans, many Americans nevertheless experienced the war years as the most intense of their entire lives. Popular music, Hollywood movies, radio programs, and advertisements—all screened by the Office of War Information—encouraged a sense of personal involvement in a collective effort to preserve democracy at home and to save the world from fascism. No one was excluded, no action considered insignificant. Even casual conversation came under the purview of the government, which warned that "Loose Lips Sink Ships."

MEN AND WOMEN IN UNIFORM

During World War I, American soldiers served for a relatively brief period and in small numbers. A quarter-century later, World War II mobilized 16.4 million Americans into the armed forces. Although only 34 percent of men who served in the army saw combat—the majority during the final year of the war—the experience had a powerful impact on nearly everyone. Whether working in the steno pool at Great Lakes Naval Training Center in northern Illinois or slogging through mud with rifle in hand in the Philippines, many men and women saw their lives reshaped in unpredictable ways. Uprooted from their communities, they suddenly found themselves among strangers, in an unfamiliar geographical setting, and under a severe military regimen.

Creating the Armed Forces

Before the European war broke out in 1939, the majority of the 200,000 men in the U.S. armed forces were employed as military police, engaging in such tasks as patrolling the Mexican border or occupying colonial possessions, such as the Philippines. Neither the army nor the navy was prepared for the scale of combat World War II entailed. Only the Marine Corps, which had been planning since the 1920s to wrest control of the western Pacific from Japan, was poised to fight. Once mobilized for war, however, the United States became a first-rank military power.

On October 16, 1940, National Registration Day, all men between the ages of twenty-one and thirty-six were legally obligated to register for military service. Just two weeks later more than 5,000 local draft boards began to draw the first numbers to send men off to camps for one year of training. After the United States entered the war, the draft age was lowered to eighteen, and local boards were instructed to choose first from the youngest.

One-third of the men examined by the Selective Service were rejected. Surprising numbers were refused induction because they were physically unfit for military service, and nearly 1 million were rejected because of "neuropsychiatric disorders or emotional problems." At a time when only one American in four graduated from high school, induction centers turned away many conscripts because they were functionally illiterate.

But those who passed the screening tests joined the best-educated army in history: nearly half of white draftees had graduated from high school and 10 percent had attended college. Once inducted, soldiers spent the first month learning basic military skills such as shooting a rifle, pitching a tent, digging a foxhole, and saluting an officer.

The officer corps, whose top-ranking members were from the Command and General Staff School at Fort Leavenworth, tended to be highly professional, politically conservative, and personally autocratic. General Douglas MacArthur, supreme commander in the Pacific theater, was said to admire the discipline of the German army and to disparage political democracy. General Dwight D. Eisenhower, however, supreme commander of the Allied forces in Europe, projected a new and contrasting spirit. Distrusted by MacArthur and many of the older brass, Eisenhower appeared to his troops a model of fair play, encouraging young men to follow him into the officer corps for idealistic rather than career reasons.

The democratic rhetoric of the war and the sudden massive expansion of the armed forces contributed to this transformation of the officer corps. A shortage of officers during World War I had prompted a huge expansion of the Reserve Officer Training Corps, but its drilling and discipline alone

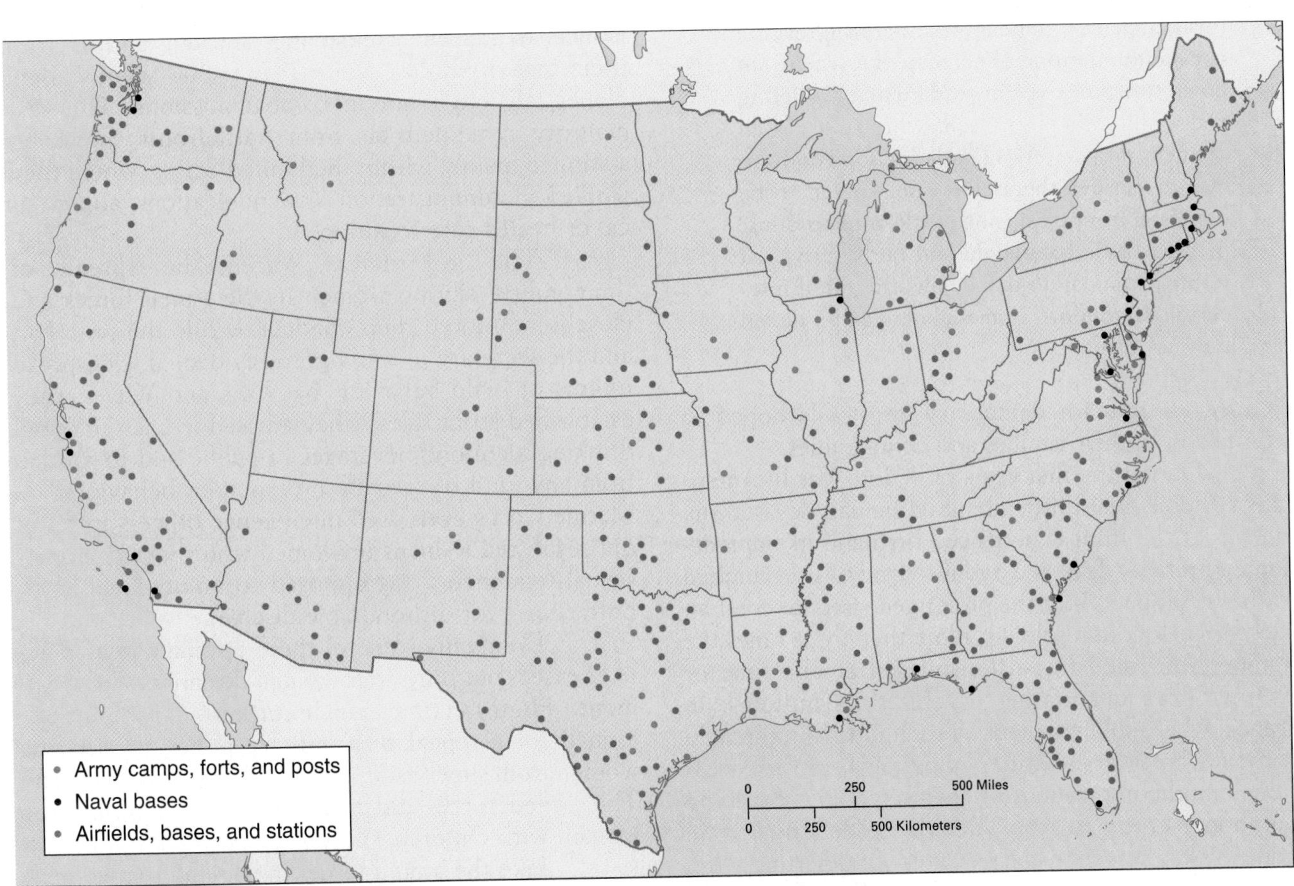

Wartime Army Camps, Naval Bases, and Airfields *Their locations chosen for political as well as defense reasons, military facilities were rapidly constructed in every state. The many facilities located in the South and West helped open these areas to economic development and an influx of new migrants.*

Source: Clifford L. Lord and Elizabeth H. Lord, *Lord & Lord Historical Atlas of the United States*, rev. ed. (New York: Holt, 1953), p. 309.

could not create good officers, and it was still insufficient to meet the demand for trained officers. Racing to make up for the deficiency, Army Chief of Staff George Marshall opened schools for officer candidates. In 1942, in seventeen-week training periods, these schools produced more than 54,000 platoon leaders. Closer in sensibility to the civilian population, these new officers were the kinds of leaders Eisenhower sought.

Most GIs (short for "government issue"), who were the vast majority of draftees, had limited contact with officers at the higher levels and instead forged bonds with their company commanders and men within their own combat units. "Everyone wants someone to look up to when he's scared," one GI explained. Most of all, soldiers depended on the solidarity of the group and the loyalty of their buddies to pull through the war.

The majority of GIs endured military discipline "to get the task done," as revealed in numerous polls. They longed foremost for peace. "In the magazines," wrote the popular war correspondent Ernie Pyle,

> war seemed romantic and exciting, full of heroics and vitality. . . . Certainly there were great tragedies, unbelievable heroism, even a constant undertone of comedy. But when I sat down to write, I saw instead men . . . suffering and wishing they were somewhere else . . . all of them desperately hungry for somebody to talk to besides themselves, no women to be heroes in front of, damned little wine to drink, precious little song, cold and fairly dirty, just toiling from day to day in a world full of insecurity, discomfort, homesickness and a dulled sense of danger.

Pledged to fight for democracy, most GIs hoped to return soon to their families and communities.

During the first years of World War II, Americans at home heard little about its human devastation, but GIs at the front experienced firsthand its unprecedented brutality, fear, and agony. Many GIs succumbed to "battle fatigue" from the prolonged stress of combat. More than 1 million soldiers, more than three times the number who died in battle, suffered at one time or another from debilitating psychiatric symptoms. In France, where soldiers spent up to 200 days in the field without a break from fighting, thousands cracked, occasionally inflicting wounds on themselves in order to be sent home. One who simply fled the battlefront, Private Eddie Slovik, was tried and executed for desertion—the first such execution since the Civil War. Slovik had been singled out as an example. Most deserters were sentenced to hard labor in military stockades. Only in 1944 did the army devise a rotation system to relieve exhausted soldiers.

Women Enter the Military

Before World War II women served in the armed forces mainly as nurses and clerical workers. The Army Nurse Corps, created in 1901, and the Navy Nurse Corps, formed in 1908, were scarcely military organizations. Recruits earned neither military pay nor rank and received scant public recognition for their services.

With the approach of World War II, Massachusetts Republican congresswoman Edith Nourse Rogers proposed legislation for the formation of a women's corps. The army instead drafted its own bill, which Rogers sponsored, creating in May 1942 the Women's Army Auxiliary Corps (WAAC), later changed to Women's Army Corps (WAC). In 1942–43 other bills established a women's division of the navy (WAVES), the Women's Airforce Service Pilots, and the Marine Corps Women's Reserve. Overall, more than 350,000 women served in World War II, two-thirds of them in the WACS and WAVES. As a group, they were better educated and more skilled than the average soldier.

Although barred from combat, women were not necessarily protected from danger. Nurses accompanied the troops into combat in Africa, Italy, and France, treated men under fire, and dug and lived in their own foxholes. More than 1,000 women flew planes, although not in combat missions. The vast majority remained far from battlefronts, however, stationed mainly within the United States, where they worked in administration, communications, and clerical or health-care facilities.

The government feared the spread of "immorality" among women in the armed forces and closely monitored their conduct. While the president and the secretary of war vigorously denied widespread rumors of "wild behavior" by Wacs and Waves, they established strict rules. They advised women to avoid drinking alcoholic beverages in public and to abstain from any kind of sexually promiscuous behavior. The Marine Corps even used intelligence officers to ferret out suspected lesbians or women who showed "homosexual tendencies" (as opposed to homosexual acts), both causes for dishonorable discharge.

Eventually some of these discriminatory practices eased, but only after women demanded fair treatment. High-ranking female officers, for example, argued for a repeal of a military policy prohibiting women from supervising male workers, even in offices. The armed forces did not, however, lift its ban on women with children.

Like the armed forces in general, the women's services were marked by racial segregation, despite government declarations of egalitarianism. Black women and white women ate in separate mess halls and slept in separate barracks. At the beginning of the war, black nurses were admitted to serve only black

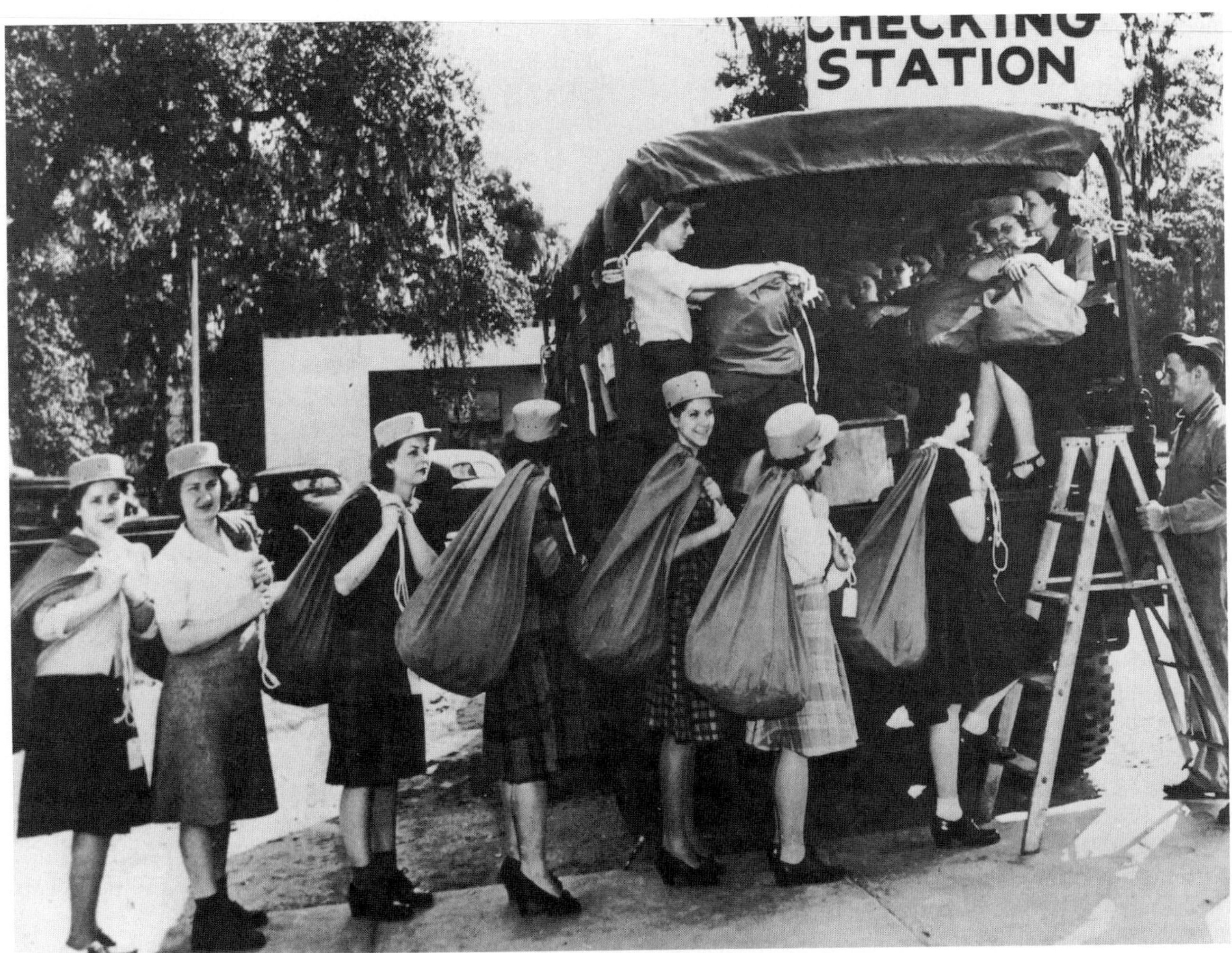

New recruits to the Women's Army Corps (WAC) *pick up their clothing "issue" (allotment). These volunteers served in many capacities, from nursing men in combat to performing clerical and communications duties "stateside" (within the* United States). *Approximately* 140,000 *women served in the* WACS *during* World War II.

soldiers, and the WAVES refused all black women on the ground that the navy had no black airmen to attend. Only in 1944 did Roosevelt order the navy to incorporate black Waves, and fewer than 100 served.

Old Practices and New Horizons

The draft brought hundreds of thousands of young African American men into the army, where they would join all-black regiments commanded by white officers. Secretary of War Henry Stimson refused to challenge this policy, saying that the army could not operate effectively as "a sociological laboratory." African Americans nevertheless enlisted at a rate 60 percent above their proportion of the general population.

By 1944 black soldiers represented 10 percent of the army's troops, and overall approximately 1 million African Americans served in the armed forces during World War II. The majority served in the Signal, Engineer, and Quartermaster Corps, mainly in construction or stevedore work. Only a small minority were permitted to rise to fighting status and lower officer ranks, and only toward the end of the war when the shortage of infantry neared a crisis. An all-black tank squadron earned distinction in Germany. And despite the very small number of African Americans admitted to the Air Force, the 99th Pursuit Squadron gained high marks in action against the feared German air force, the Luftwaffe. Even the Marine Corps and the Coast Guard agreed to end their historic exclusion of African Americans, although they recruited and promoted only a small number.

The ordinary black soldier, sailor, or marine, saw no benefit from the late-in-the-war gains of a few. Throughout 1941 race riots initiated by whites against blacks broke out at training bases, especially in the South. Serving in segregated, low-prestige units, African Americans encountered discrimination everywhere, from the army canteen to the religious chapels. Even the blood banks kept blood segregated by race (although a black physician, Dr. Charles Drew, had invented the process for storing plasma). Toward the end of the war, segregation began to break down, if only in post stores and recreational facilities.

The army also grouped Japanese Americans into segregated units, sending most to fight far from the Pacific theater. Better educated than the average soldier, many Nisei soldiers who knew Japanese served state-side as interpreters and translators. When the army decided to create a Nisei regiment, more than 10,000 volunteers stepped forward, only one in five of whom was accepted. The Nisei 442d fought heroically in Italy and France and became the most decorated regiment in the war.

Despite segregation, the armed forces ultimately pulled Americans of all varieties out of their communities. Many Jews and other second-generation European immigrants, for example, described their stint in the military as an "Americanizing" experience. Many Indian peoples left reservations for the first time, approximately 25,000 serving in the armed forces. For many African Americans, military service provided a bridge to postwar civil rights agitation. Amzie Moore, who later helped to organize the Mississippi Freedom Democratic Party, traced his understanding that "people are just people" to his experiences in the armed forces during World War II.

Many homosexuals also discovered a wider world. Despite a policy barring them from military service, most slipped through mass screening at induction centers. Moreover, the emotional pressures of wartime, especially the fear of death, encouraged close friendships, and homosexuals in the military often found more room than in civilian life to express their sexual orientation openly. In army canteens, for example, men often danced with one another, whereas in civilian settings they would have been subject to ridicule or even arrest for such activity. "The war is a tragedy to my mind and soul," one gay soldier confided, "but to my physical being, it's a memorable experience." Lesbian Wacs and Waves had similar tales.

Most soldiers looked back at the war, with all its dangers and discomforts, as the greatest experience they would ever know. As the *New Republic* predicted in 1943, they met fellow Americans from every part of the country and recognized for the first time in their lives "the bigness and wholeness of the United States." "Hughie was a Georgia cracker, so he knew something about moonshine," remembered one soldier. Another fondly recalled "this fellow from Wisconsin we called 'Moose.' " The army itself promoted these expectations of new experience. *Twenty-Seven Soldiers* (1944), a government-produced film for the troops, showed Allied soldiers of several nationalities all working together in harmony.

Overseas Occupation

As a liberating or occupying force, Americans stationed overseas had a mixed record. Children especially welcomed the GIs, who brought candy and chewing gum. But civilians in areas not controlled by Axis powers often resented the presence of American troops, whose demands for entertainment could turn their communities into red-light zones for drinking and prostitution.

Few Britishers welcomed the nearly 3 million GIs who were stationed in their country between 1942 and 1945. "It is difficult to go anywhere in London without having the feeling that Britain is now Occupied Territory," complained novelist George Orwell in 1943. The privileges of American troops also irked the British. American soldiers enjoyed a standard of living that surpassed that of both the military and civilian populations of Europe. A GI earned three times as much pay as his British counterpart, and consumed an average of four pounds of rations daily. Even their uniforms outshone those of the British, who mocked: "They're overfed, overpaid, overdressed, oversexed—and over here."

The relationship between GIs and civilians was worse on the Continent. At first, the French welcomed the American troops as soldiers of liberation. But the Americans arrived in 1944, when several million Europeans were without homes and nearly everyone was living on the brink of starvation. The GIs themselves were war-weary or war-crazed, and not a few committed petty robberies or rapes in towns and villages en route to Paris. "Intoxication," one study found, "was the largest contributing factor to crime in the European Theater of Operations."

In Belgium and southern Holland, however, where Nazi rule had been harsh, American soldiers were greeted as heroes. City restaurants were renamed "Cafe Texas" or "Cafe Alaska." Civilians cheered the Americans and eagerly shared—or traded sexual favors for—their supply of chewing gum, cash, and cigarettes. Despite government-sponsored precautions, the rate of venereal disease ran at 42 per 1,000 soldiers.

Prisoners of War

Approximately 120,000 Americans became prisoners of war (POWs). Those captured by the Germans were taken back to camps—*Olfags* for officers or *Stalags* for enlisted men—where they sat out the remainder of the war, mainly fighting boredom. Registered by the Swiss Red Cross, they could receive packages of supplies and occasionally join work brigades. By contrast, Russian POWs were starved and occasionally murdered in German camps.

Conditions for POWs in the Pacific were, however, worse than abysmal. Of the 20,000 Americans captured in the Philippines early in the war, only 40 percent survived to return home in 1945. At least 6,000 American and Filipino prisoners, beaten and denied food and water, died on the notorious eighty-

Sidney Simon, *P.O.W.s at Bilibid Prison*, 1945. Oil on canvas, 25 x 30 inches. Center of Military History, U.S. Army.

A painting by Sidney Simon of American POWs freed from Japanese captors at Bilibid prison, in Manila, 1945, after the U.S. reconquest of the Philippines. The battle of the Philippine Sea and the battle of Leyte Gulf during the previous year had nearly broken Japanese resistance in the area, but the cleanup process revealed the awful price that Americans and their Filipino allies had paid. As prisoners of war, they had suffered terribly from malnutrition and improperly attended wounds and from an unsparing and inhumane Japanese military code of behavior.

mile "Death March" through the jungles on the Bataan Peninsula in 1942. After the survivors reached the former U.S. air base Camp O'Donnell, hundreds died weekly in a cesspool of disease and squalor.

The Japanese army felt only contempt for POWs; its own soldiers evaded capture by killing themselves. The Imperial Army assigned its most brutal troops to guard prisoners and imposed strict and brutal discipline in the camps. In a postwar survey, 90 percent of former POWs from the Pacific reported that they had been beaten. A desire for retribution, as well as racist attitudes, prompted GIs to treat Japanese prisoners far more brutally than enemy soldiers captured in Europe or Africa.

THE WORLD AT WAR

During the first year of declared war, the Allies remained on the defensive. Hitler's forces held the European Continent and pounded England with aerial bombardments while driving deep into Russia and across northern Africa to take the Suez Canal. The situation in the Pacific was scarcely better. Just two hours after the attack on Pearl Harbor, Japanese planes struck the main U.S. base in the Philippines and demolished half the air force commanded by General Douglas MacArthur. Within a short time, MacArthur was forced to withdraw his troops to the Bataan Peninsula, admitting that Japan had practically seized the Pacific.

The War in Europe

Roosevelt called the news "all bad," and his military advisers predicted a long fight to victory.

But the Allies enjoyed several important advantages: vast natural resources and a skilled workforce with sufficient reserves to accelerate the production of weapons and ammunitions; the determination of millions of antifascists throughout Europe and Asia; and the capacity of the Soviet Union to endure immense losses. Slowly at first, but then with quickening speed, these advantages made themselves felt.

Soviets Halt Nazi Drive

The weapons and tactics of World War II were radically different from those of World War I. Unlike World War I, which was fought by immobile armies kept behind trenches by bursts of machine-gun fire, World War II

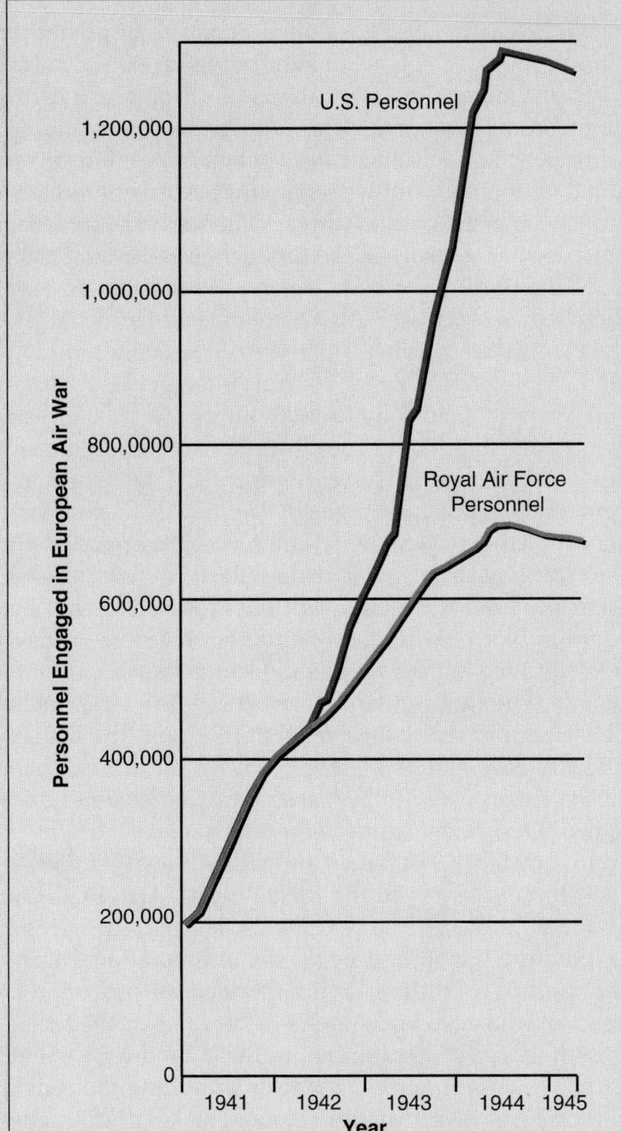

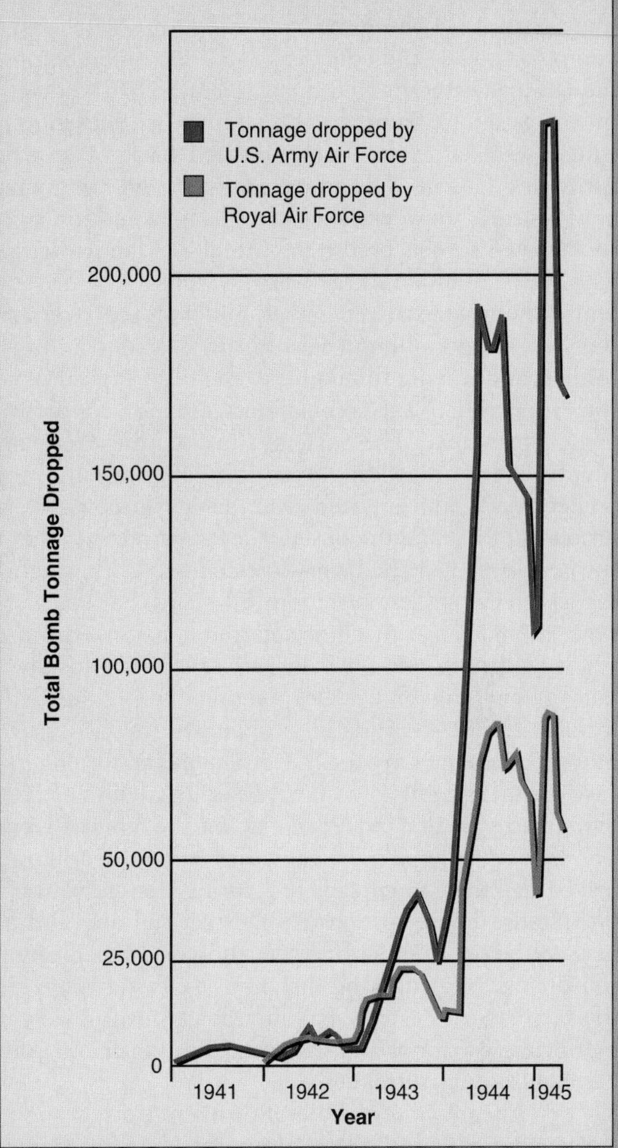

World War II: Personnel and Bombs

The offensive phase of the Allied campaign against the Axis unfolded late in the war. Major defeats in the Soviet Union and Africa deprived Germany of the resources needed to expand the war. The British and Americans, with an almost endless supply of materials and personnel, proceeded to overpower Germany and its European allies. Germans had ruled the skies early in the war. By 1943, Allied planes destroyed the German and Italian systems of transportation and supply, making cities almost unlivable. As British and Americans troops continued to pour into Europe, Allied victory became inevitable.

was a war of offensive maneuvers punctuated by surprise attacks. Its chief weapons were tanks and airplanes, combining mobility and concentrated firepower. Also of major importance were artillery and explosives, which according to some estimates accounted for over 30 percent of the casualties. Major improvements in communication systems, mainly two-way radio transmission and radiotelephony permitting commanders to stay in contact with division leaders, also played a decisive role from the beginning of the war.

Early on, Hitler had used these methods to seize the advantage, purposefully creating terror among the stricken populations of western Europe as he routed their armies. The Royal Air Force, however, fought the Luftwaffe to a standstill in the Battle of Britain, frustrating Hitler's hopes of invading England. In the summer of 1941, he turned his attention to the east, hoping to invade and conquer the Soviet Union before the United States entered the war. But he had to delay the invasion to come to the support of Mussolini, whose weak army had been pushed back in North Africa and Greece. The attack on Russia did not come until June 22, six weeks later than planned and too late to achieve its goals before the brutal Russian winter.

The burden of the war now fell on the Soviet Union. From June to September, Hitler's forces overran the Red Army, killing or capturing nearly 3 million soldiers and leaving thousands to die from exposure or starvation. But Nazi commanders did not count on civilian resistance. The Soviets rallied, cutting German supply lines and sending every available resource to Soviet troops concentrated just outside Moscow. After furious fighting and the onset of severe winter weather, the Red Army launched a massive counterattack, catching the freezing German troops off guard. For the first time, the Nazi war machine suffered a major setback.

Turning strategically away from Moscow, during the summer of 1942 German troops headed toward Crimea and the rich oil fields of the Caucasus. Still set on conquering the Soviet Union and turning its vast resources to his own use, Hitler decided to attack Stalingrad, a major industrial city on the Volga River. The Soviets suffered more casualties during the following battles than Americans did during the entire war. But intense house-to-house and street fighting and a massive Soviet counteroffensive took an even greater toll on the Nazi fighting machine. By February 1943 the German Sixth Army had met defeat, overpowered by Soviet war troops and weapons. More than 100,000 German soldiers surrendered.

Already in retreat but plotting one last desperate attempt to halt the Red Army, the Germans threw most of their remaining armored vehicles into action at Kursk, in the Ukraine, in July 1943. The clash quickly developed into the greatest land battle in history. More than 2 million troops and 6,000 tanks went into action. After another stunning defeat, the Germans had decisively lost the initiative. Their only option was to delay the advance of the Red Army against their homeland.

Meanwhile, the Soviet Union had begun to recover from its early losses, even as tens of millions of its own people remained homeless and near starvation. Assisted by the U.S. Lend-Lease program, by 1942 the Soviets were outproducing Germany in many types of weapons and other supplies. Nazi officers and German civilians alike began to doubt that Hitler could win the war. The Soviet victories had turned the tide of the war.

The Allied Offensive

In the spring of 1942, Germany, Italy, and Japan commanded a territory extending from France to the Pacific Ocean. They controlled central Europe and a large section of the Soviet Union as well as considerable parts of China and the southwestern Pacific. But their momentum was flagging. American shipbuilding outpaced the punishment Nazi submarines inflicted on allied shipping, and sub-sinking destroyers greatly reduced the submarines' threat. The United States far outstripped Germany in the production of landing craft and amphibious vehicles, two of the most important innovations of the war. Also outnumbered by the Allies, the German air force was limited to defensive action. On land, the United States and Great Britain had the trucks and jeeps to field fully mobile armies, while German troops marched in and out of Russia with packhorses.

Still, German forces represented a mighty opponent on the European Continent. Fighting the Nazis there almost by themselves, the Soviets repeatedly appealed for the creation of a Second Front, an Allied offensive against Germany from the West. The Allies focused instead on securing North Africa and then on an invasion of Italy, hoping to move from there into Central Europe.

On the night of October 23–24, 1942, near El Alamein in the deserts of western Egypt, the British Eighth Army halted a major offensive by the German Afrika Korps, headed by General Edwin Rommel, the famed "Desert Fox." Although suffering heavy losses—approximately 13,000 men and more than 500 tanks—their forces destroyed the Italian North African Army and much of Germany's Afrika Korps. Americans entered the war in Europe as part of Operation Torch, the landing of British and American troops on the coast of Morocco and Algeria in November 1942 that was the largest amphibious military landing to that date. The Allies then fought their way along the coast, entering Tunis in triumph six months later. With the surrender of a quarter-million Germans and Italians in Tunisia in May 1943, the Allies controlled North Africa and had a secure position in the Mediterranean.

During the North African campaign, the Allies announced that they would accept nothing less than the unconditional surrender of their enemies. In January 1943, Roosevelt and Churchill had met in Casablanca in Morocco and ruled out any possibility of negotiation with the Axis powers. Roosevelt's supporters hailed the policy as a clear statement of goals, a promise to the world that the scourge of fascism would be completely banished. Stalin, who did not attend the meeting, criticized the policy, fearing that it would only increase the enemy's determination to fight to the end. Other critics similarly charged that the demand for total capitulation would serve to prolong the war and lengthen the casualty list.

Allied aerial bombing further increased pressure on Germany. Many U.S. leaders believed that in the B-17 Flying Fortress, the air force possessed the ultimate weapon, "the mightiest bomber ever built."

The U.S. Army Air Corps described this bomber as a "humane" weapon, capable of hitting specific military targets and sparing the lives of civilians. But when weather or darkness required pilots to depend on radar for sightings, they couldn't distinguish clearly between factories and schools or between military barracks and private homes, and bombs might fall within a range of nearly two miles from the intended target. American pilots preferred to bomb during daylight hours, while the British bombed during the night. Bombing missions over the Rhineland and the Ruhr successfully took out many German factories. But the Germans responded by relocating their plants, often dispersing light industry to the countryside.

Determined to break German resistance, the Royal Air Force redirected its main attack away from military sites to cities, including fuel dumps and public transportation. Hamburg was practically leveled. Between 60,000 and 100,000 people were killed, and 300,000 buildings were destroyed. Sixty other cities were hit hard, leaving 20 percent of Germany's total residential area in ruins. The very worst raid of the war—650,000 incendiary bombs dropped on the city of Dresden, destroying 8 square miles and killing 135,000 civilians—had no military value.

The Allied strategic air offensive weakened the German economy and undermined civilian morale. Moreover, in trying to defend German cities and factories, the *Luftwaffe* sacrificed many of its fighter planes. When the Allies finally invaded western Europe in the summer and fall of 1944, they would enjoy superiority in the air.

The Allied Invasion of Europe

During the summer of 1943, the Allies began to advance on southern Italy. On July 10 British and American troops stormed Sicily from two directions and conquered the island in mid-August. King Vittorio Emmanuel dismissed Mussolini, calling him "the most despised man in Italy," and Italians, by now disgusted with the Fascist government, celebrated in the streets. Italy surrendered to the Allies on September 8, and Allied troops landed on the southern Italian peninsula. But Hitler sent new divisions into Italy, occupied the northern peninsula, and effectively stalled the Allied campaign. When the European war ended, the German and Allied armies were still battling on Italy's rugged terrain.

Elsewhere in occupied Europe, armed uprisings against the Nazis spread. The brutalized inhabitants of Warsaw's Jewish ghetto repeatedly rose up against their tormentors during the winter and spring of 1943. Realizing that they could not hope to defeat superior forces, they finally sealed off their quarter, executed collaborators, and fought invaders, street by street and house by house. Scattered revolts followed in the Nazi labor camps, where military prisoners of war and civilians were being worked to death on starvation rations.

Partisans were active in many sections of Europe, from Norway to Greece and from Poland to France. Untrained and unarmed by any military standard, organized groups of men, women, and children risked their lives to distribute antifascist propaganda, taking action against rich and powerful Nazi collaborators. They smuggled food and weapons to clandestine resistance groups and prepared the way for Allied offensives. As Axis forces grew weaker and partially withdrew, the partisans worked more and more openly, arming citizens to fight for their own freedom.

Meanwhile, Stalin continued to push for a second front. Stalled in Italy, the Allies prepared in early 1944 for Operation Overlord, a campaign to retake the continent with a decisive counterattack through France. American and British forces began by filling the southern half of England with military camps. All leaves were canceled. New weapons, such as amphibious armored vehicles, were carefully camouflaged. Fortunately, Hitler had few planes or ships left, so the Germans could defend the coast only with fixed bunkers whose location the Allies ascertained. Operation Overlord began with a preinvasion air assault that dropped 76,000 tons of bombs on Nazi targets.

The Allied invasion finally began on "D-Day," June 6, 1944. Under steady German fire the Allied fleet brought to the shores of Normandy more than 175,000 troops and more than 20,000 vehicles—an accomplishment unimaginable in any previous war. Although the Germans had responded slowly, anticipating an Allied strike at Calais instead, at Omaha Beach they had prepared their defense almost perfectly. Wave after wave of Allied landings met machine gun and mortar fire, and the tides filled with corpses and those pretending to be dead. Some 2,500 troops died, many before they could fire a shot. In the next six weeks, nearly 1 million more Allied soldiers came ashore, broke out of Normandy, and prepared to march inland.

As the fighting continued, all eyes turned to Paris, the premier city of Europe. Allied bombers pounded factories producing German munitions on the outskirts of the French capital. As dispirited German soldiers retreated, many now hoping only to survive, the French Resistance unfurled the French flag at impromptu demonstrations on Bastille Day, July 14. On August 10, railway workers staged one of the first successful strikes against Nazi occupiers, and three days later the Paris police defected to the Resistance, which proclaimed in leaflets that "the hour of liberation has come." General Charles de Gaulle, accompanied by

D-Day landing, June 6, 1944, marked the greatest amphibious maneuver in military history. Troop ships ferried Allied soldiers from England to Normandy beaches. Within a month, nearly 1 million men had assembled in France, ready to retake western and central Europe from German forces.

Allied troops, arrived in Paris on August 25 to become president of the reestablished French Republic.

One occupied European nation after another now swiftly fell. But the Allied troops had only reached a resting place between bloody battles.

The High Cost of European Victory

In September 1944 Allied commanders searched for a strategy to end the war quickly. Missing a spectacular chance to move through largely undefended territory and on to Berlin, they turned north instead, intending to open the Netherlands for Allied armies on their way to Germany's industrial heartland. Faulty intelligence reports overlooked a well-armed German division at Arnhem, Holland, waiting to cut Allied paratroopers to pieces. By the end of the battle, the Germans had captured 6,000 Americans.

In a final, desperate effort to reverse the Allied momentum, Hitler directed his last reserves, a quarter-million men, at Allied lines in the Belgian forest of the Ardennes. In what is known as the Battle of the Bulge, the Germans took the Allies by surprise, driving them back 50 miles before they were stopped. This last effort—the bloodiest single campaign Americans had been involved in since the battle of Gettysburg—exhausted the German capacity for counterattack. After Christmas day 1944, the Germans fell back, retreating toward their own territory.

The end was now in sight. In March 1945 the Allies rolled across the Rhine and took the Ruhr valley with its precious industrial resources. The defense of Germany, now hopeless, had fallen into the hands of young teenagers and elderly men. By the time of the German surrender, May 8, Hitler had committed suicide in a Berlin bunker and high Nazi officials were planning their escape routes. The casualties of the Allied European campaign had been enormous, if still small compared to those of the Eastern Front: more than 200,000 killed and almost 800,000 wounded, missing, or dead in nonbattle accidents and unrelated illness.

The War in Asia and the Pacific

The war that had begun with Pearl Harbor rapidly escalated into scattered fighting across a region of the world far larger than all of Europe, stretching from Southeast Asia to the Aleutian Islands. Japan followed up its early advantage by cutting the supply routes between Burma and China, crushing the British navy, and seizing the Philippines, Hong Kong, Wake Island, British Malaya, and Thailand. Although China offically joined the Allies on December 9, 1941, and General Stillwell arrived in March as commander of the China-Burma-India theater, the military mission there remained on the defensive. Meanwhile, after tenacious fighting at the Bataan Peninsula and on the island of Corregidor, the U.S. troops not captured or killed retreated to Australia.

At first, nationalist and anticolonial sentiment played into Japanese hands. Japan succeeded with only 200,000 men because so few inhabitants of the imperial colonies of Britain and France would fight to defend them. Japan installed puppet "independent" governments in Burma and the Philippines. But the new Japanese empire proved terrifyingly cruel. A panicky exodus of refugees precipitated a famine in Bengal, India, which took nearly 3,500,000 lives in 1943. Nationalists from Indochina to the Philippines turned against the Japanese, establishing guerrilla armies that cut Japanese supply lines and prepared the way for Allied victory.

Six months after the disaster at Pearl Harbor, the United States began to regain naval superiority in the central Pacific and halt Japanese expansion. In a carrier duel with spectacular aerial battles at the Battle of the Coral Sea on May 7 and 8, the United States blocked a Japanese threat to Australia. A month later, the Japanese fleet converged on Midway Island, which was strategically vital to American communications and the defense of Hawai'i. American strategists, however, thanks to specialists who had broken Japanese codes, knew when and where the Japanese planned to attack. The two carrier fleets, separated by hundreds of miles, clashed at the Battle of Midway on June 4. American planes sank four of Japan's vital aircraft carriers and destroyed hundreds of planes, ending Japan's offensive threat to Hawai'i and the west coast of the United States.

But the war for the Pacific was far from over. By pulling back their offensive perimeter, the Japanese concentrated their remaining forces. Their commanders calculated that bitter fighting, with high casualties on both sides, would wear down the American troops. The U.S. command, divided between General Douglas MacArthur in the southwest Pacific and Admiral Chester Nimitz in the central Pacific, needed to develop a counterstrategy to strangle the Japanese import-based economy and to retake strategic islands closer to the homeland.

The Allies launched their counteroffensive campaign on the Solomon Islands and Papua, near New Guinea. American and Australian ground forces fought together through the jungles of Papua, while the marines prepared to attack the Japanese stronghold of Guadalcanal. American forces ran low on food and ammunition during the fierce six-month struggle on Guadalcanal, while the Japanese were reduced to eating roots and berries. American logistics were not always well planned: a week before Christmas in the subtropical climate, a shipment of winter coats arrived! But with strong supply lines secured in a series of costly naval battles, the Amer-

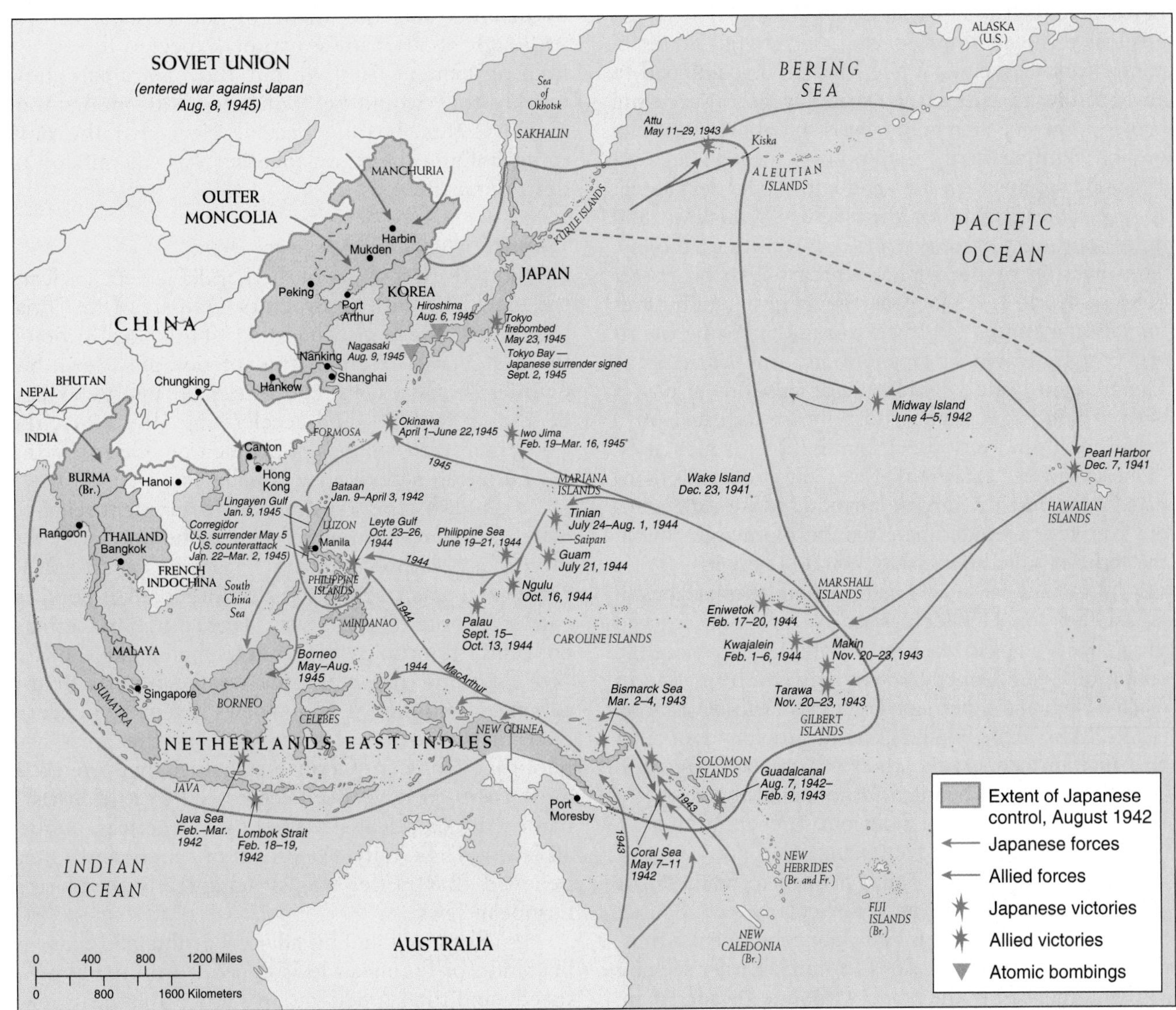

War in the Pacific *Across an ocean battlefield utterly unlike the European theater, Allies battled Japanese troops near their homeland.*

icans were finally victorious in February 1943 when the Japanese abandoned Guadalcanal.

For the next two years, the U.S. navy and marine corps, in a strategy known as "island hopping," pushed to capture a series of important atolls from their well-armed Japanese defenders and open a path to Japan. The first of these assaults, which cost more than 1,000 Marines their lives, was on Tarawa, in November 1943, in the Gilbert Islands. In subsequent battles in 1944, American forces occupied Guam, Saipan, and Tinian in the Marianas Islands, within air range of the Japanese home islands. In another decisive naval engagement, the Battle of the Philippine Sea, fought in June 1944, the Japanese fleet suffered a crippling loss.

In October 1944 General MacArthur led a force of 250,000 to retake the Philippines. In a bid to defend the islands, practically all that remained of the Japanese navy threw itself at American invaders in the Battle of Leyte Gulf, the largest naval battle in history. The Japanese lost eighteen ships, leaving the United States in control of the Pacific. While MacArthur continued to advance toward Luzon, the marines waged a successful battle on the small but important island of Iwo Jima. The ground fighting in the Philippines, meanwhile, cost 100,000 Filipinos their lives and left Manila devastated.

The struggle for the island of Okinawa, 800 miles southwest of Tokyo, proved even more bloody. The invasion of the island, which began on Easter Sunday, April 1, 1945, was the largest amphibious operation mounted by Americans in the Pacific war. It was met by waves of Japanese airborne *kamikaze* (or "divine wind") pilots flying suicide missions in planes with a 500-pound bomb and only enough fuel for a one-way flight. On the ground, U.S. troops used flame-throwers, each with three hundred gallons of napalm, against the dug-in Japanese. More Americans died or were wounded here than at Normandy. In all, the fighting killed more than 200,000 people.

Air and sea attacks on mainland Japan had begun to take their toll. U.S. submarines had drastically reduced the ability of ships to reach Japan with supplies. Since the taking of Guam, American bombers had been able to reach Tokyo and other Japanese cities, with devastating results. Massive fire bombings burned thousands of civilians alive in their mostly wood or bamboo homes and apartments and left hundreds of thousands homeless.

Japan could not hold out forever. Without a navy or air force, the government could not transport the oil, tin, rubber, and grain needed to maintain its soldiers. Great Britain and particularly the United States, however, pressed for quick unconditional surrender. They had special reasons to hurry. Earlier seeking a commitment from the Soviet Union to invade Japan, they now looked beyond the war, determined to prevent the Red Army from taking any territories held by the Japanese. These calculations and the anticipation that an invasion would be extremely bloody set the stage for the use of a secret weapon that American scientists had been preparing: the atomic bomb.

THE LAST STAGES OF WAR

From the attack on Pearl Harbor until mid-1943, President Roosevelt and his advisers focused on military strategy rather than on plans for peace. But once the defeat of Nazi Germany appeared in sight, high government officials began to reconsider their diplomatic objectives. Roosevelt wanted both to crush the Axis powers and to establish a system of collective security to prevent another world war. He knew he could not succeed without the cooperation of the other key leaders, Stalin and Churchill.

During 1944 and 1945, the "Big Three" met to hammer out the shape of the postwar world. Although none of these nations expected to reach a final agreement, neither did they anticipate how quickly they would be confronted with momentous global events. It soon became clear that the only thing holding the Allies together was the mission of destroying the Axis.

The Holocaust

Not until the last stages of the war did Americans learn the extent of Hitler's atrocities. As part of his "final solution to the Jewish question," Hitler had ordered the systematic extermination of not only Jews but Gypsies, homosexuals, and others of "inferior" races. Beginning in 1933, and accelerating after 1941, the Nazis murdered millions of people from Germany and the European nations they conquered.

During the war the U.S. government released little information on what came to be known as the Holocaust. Although liberal magazines such as the *Nation* and small committees of intellectuals tried to call attention to what was happening in German concentration camps, major news media like the *New York Times* and *Time* magazine treated reports of the camps and killings as minor news items. The experience of World War I, during which the press had published stories of German atrocities that proved in most cases to have been fabricated by the British, had bred a skeptical attitude in the American public. As late as 1943, only 43 percent of Americans polled believed that Hitler was systematically murdering European Jews.

Roosevelt and his advisers maintained that the liberation of European Jews depended primarily on a speedy and total Allied victory. When American Jews pleaded for a military strike against the rail lines leading to the notorious extermination camp in Auschwitz,

Leslie Cole, *Belsen Camp. The Compound for Women.* Imperial War Museum, London.

Belsen Camp: The Compound for Women, *painted by American artist Leslie Cole, depicts Belsen as the Allied troops found it when they invaded Germany in 1945.*

Poland, the War Department replied that Allied armed forces would not be employed "for the purpose of rescuing victims of enemy oppression unless such rescues are the direct result of military operations conducted with the objective of defeating the armed forces of the enemy." In short, the government viewed civilian rescue as a diversion of precious resources.

Allied troops discovered the death camps when they invaded Germany and liberated Poland. When Eisenhower and General George S. Patton visited the Ohrdruf concentration camp in April 1945, they found barracks crowded with corpses and crematories still reeking of burned flesh. "I want every American unit not actually in the front lines to see this place," Eisenhower declared. "We are told that the American soldier does not know what he is fighting for. Now, at least, he will know what he is fighting against." At Buchenwald in the first three months of 1944, more than 14,000 prisoners were murdered. In all, the Holocaust claimed the lives of as many as 6 million Jews, 250,000 Gypsies, and 60,000 homosexuals, among others.

The Yalta Conference

In preparing for the end of the war, Allied leaders began to reassess their goals. The Atlantic Charter, drawn up before the United States had entered the war, stated noble objectives for the world after the defeat of fascism: national self-determination, no territorial aggrandizement, equal access of all peoples to raw materials and collaboration for the improvement of economic opportunities, freedom of the seas, disarmament, and "freedom from fear and want." Now, four years later, Roosevelt—ill and exhausted—realized that neither Great Britain nor the Soviet Union intended to abide by any code of conduct that compromised its national security or conflicted with its economic interests in other nations or in colonial territories. Stalin and Churchill soon reached a new agreement, one that projected their respective "spheres of influence" over the future of central Europe.

In February 1945 Roosevelt held his last meeting with Churchill and Stalin at Yalta, a Crimean resort on the Black Sea. Seeking their cooperation, the president recognized that prospects for postwar peace also depended on compromise. Although diplomats avoided the touchy phrase "spheres of influence"—the principle according to which the great powers of the nineteenth century had described their claims to dominance over other nations—it was clear that this principle guided all negotiations. Neither the United States nor Great Britain did more than object to the Soviet Union's plan to retain the Baltic states and part of Poland as a buffer zone to protect it against any future German aggression. In return, Britain planned to reclaim its empire in Asia, and the United States hoped to hold several Pacific islands in order to monitor any military resurgence in Japan. Stalin also affirmed his pledge to enter the war against Japan and approved plans for a future world organization, which Roosevelt championed.

Roosevelt announced to Congress that the Yalta meeting had been a "great success," proof that the wartime alliance remained intact. Privately, however, the president concluded that the outcome of the conference revealed that the Atlantic Charter had been nothing more than "a beautiful idea."

The death of Franklin Roosevelt of a stroke on April 12, 1945 cast a dark shadow over all hopes for long-term, peaceful solutions to global problems. Stung by a Republican congressional comeback in 1942, Roosevelt had rebounded in 1944 to win an unprecedented fourth term as president. In an overwhelming electoral college victory (432 to 99), he had defeated Republican New York governor Thomas E. Dewey. Loyal Democrats continued to link their

On August 6, 1945, a U.S. B-29 bomber dropped "Little Boy," an atomic bomb, on Hiroshima, killing nearly 80,000 Japanese civilians and injuring another 70,000. Three days later, "Fat Man" destroyed Nagasaki, killing 40,000 and injuring 60,000 more. On August 14, the government of Japan surrendered, bringing an end to the war.

hopes for peace to Roosevelt's leadership, but the president did not live to witness the surrender of Germany on May 8, 1945. And now, as new and still greater challenges were appearing, the nation's great pragmatic idealist was gone.

The Atomic Bomb

Roosevelt's death made cooperation among the Allied nations much more difficult. His successor, Harry S. Truman, who had been a Kansas City machine politician, a Missouri judge, and a U.S. senator, lacked diplomatic experience as well as Roosevelt's personal finesse. The new president had no intention of making concessions to the war-devastated Soviets. Shortly after taking office, Truman announced to his secretary of state, "We must stand up to the Russians at this point and not be easy with them."

As a result, negotiations at the Potsdam Conference, held just outside Berlin from July 17 to August 2, 1945, lacked the spirited cooperation characteristic of the wartime meetings of Allied leaders that Roosevelt had attended. The American, British, and Soviet delegations had a huge agenda, including reparations, the future of Germany, and the status of other Axis powers such as Italy. They agreed to demand Japan's unconditional surrender and to try Nazi leaders as war criminals. But they were sharply divided over most other issues.

It was during the Potsdam meetings that Truman first learned about the successful testing of an atomic bomb in New Mexico. Until this time, the United States had been pushing the Soviet Union to enter the Pacific war as a means to avoid a costly U.S. land invasion. But after Secretary of State Stimson received a cable reading "Babies satisfactorily born," U.S. diplomats concluded that they no longer needed assistance from the Soviet Union to bring the war to an end.

American diplomats knew that the emperor of Japan was prepared to end the fighting if the Allies would set aside the stipulation of unconditional surrender. At first, Truman considered accepting a slight modification, such as allowing the emperor to continue to head the Japanese nation. But the president also went forward with the plan to deploy the atomic bomb. As Truman later stated, he had no moral reservations about making this decision. He understood that the three bombs on hand had been developed specifically for this purpose. He therefore endorsed the principal outcome of the Potsdam Conference, a warning to Japan to surrender immediately or face "complete and utter destruction."

On August 3, 1945, Japan wired its refusal to surrender. Three days later, the Army Air Force B-29 bomber Enola Gay dropped the bomb that destroyed the Japanese city of Hiroshima. Approximately 80,000 people died on August 6; in the following weeks thousands more died from radiation poisoning or burns; by 1950 the death toll reached 200,000. "I was greatly moved," Truman reported when he heard the news.

An editorialist wrote in the Japanese *Nippon Times*, "This is not war, this is not even murder; this is pure nihilism . . . a crime against God which strikes at the very basis of moral existence." In the United States, several leading religious publications echoed this view. The *Christian Century* interpreted the use of the bomb as a "moral earthquake" that made the long-denounced use of poison gas by Germany in World War I utterly insignificant by comparison.

CHRONOLOGY

1931	September: Japan occupies Manchuria
1933	March: Adolf Hitler seizes power
	May: Japan quits League of Nations
1935	October: Italy invades Ethiopia
1935–1937	Neutrality Acts authorize the president to block the sale of munitions to belligerent nations
1937	August: Japan invades China
	October: Franklin D. Roosevelt calls for international cooperation against aggression
1938	March: Germany annexes Austria
	September: Munich Agreement lets Germany annex Sudeten Czechoslovakia
	November: Kristallnacht, Nazis attack Jews and destroy Jewish property
1939	March: Germany annexes remainder of Czechoslovakia
	August: Germany and the Soviet Union sign nonaggression pact
	September: Germany invades Poland; World War II begins
	November: Soviet Union invades Finland
1940	April–June: Germany's *Bliztkrieg* sweeps over Western Europe
	September: Germany, Italy, and Japan—the Axis powers—conclude a military alliance
	First peacetime military draft in American history
	November: Roosevelt is elected to an unprecedented third term
1941	March: Lend-Lease Act extends aid to Great Britain
	May: German troops secure the Balkans
	A. Philip Randolph plans March on Washington movement for July
	June: Germany invades Soviet Union
	Fair Employment Practices Committee formed
	August: The United States and Great Britain agree to the Atlantic Charter
	December: Japanese attack Pearl Harbor; United States enters the war
1942	January: War mobilization begins
	February: Executive order mandates internment of Japanese Americans
	May–June: Battles of Coral Sea and Midway give the United States naval superiority in the Pacific
	August: Manhattan Project begins
	November: United States stages amphibious landing in North Africa; Operation Torch begins
1943	January: Casablanca conference announces unconditional surrender policy
	February: Soviet victory over Germans at Stalingrad
	April–May: Coal miners strike
	May: German Afrika Korps troops surrender in Tunis
	July: Allied invasion of Italy
	Summer: Race riots break out in nearly fifty cities
1944	June–August: Operation Overlord and liberation of Paris
	November: Roosevelt elected to fourth term
1945	February: Yalta Conference renews American-Soviet alliance
	February–June: United States captures Iwo Jima and Okinawa in Pacific
	April: Roosevelt dies in office; Harry Truman becomes president
	May: Germany surrenders
	July–August: Potsdam Conference
	August: United States drops atomic bombs on Hiroshima and Nagasaki; Japan surrenders

Most Americans learned about the atomic bomb for the first time on August 7, when the news media reported the destruction and death it had wrought in Hiroshima. But concerns about the implications of this new weapon were soon overwhelmed by an outpouring of relief when Japan surrendered on August 14 after a second bomb destroyed Nagasaki. In Los Alamos, New Mexico, horns and sirens blared in exultation. Proud of his scientific accomplishment, Oppenheimer nevertheless reported that he was a "little scared of what I have made."

The decision to use the atomic bomb against Japan remains one of the most controversial aspects of the war. Although Truman stated in his memoirs, written much later, that he gave the order with the expectation of saving "a half a million American lives" in ground combat, no such official estimate exists. An intelligence document of April 30, 1946, states, "The dropping of the bomb was the pretext seized upon by all leaders as the reason for ending the war, but . . . [even if the bomb had not been used] the Japanese would have capitulated upon the entry of Russia into the war." There is no question, however, that the use of nuclear force did strengthen the U.S. diplomatic mission. It certainly intimidated the Soviet Union, which would soon regain its status as a major enemy of the United States. Truman and his advisers in the State Department knew that their atomic monopoly could not last, but they hoped that in the meantime the United States could play the leading role in building the new world order.

CONCLUSION

The new tactics and weapons of the Second World War, such as massive air raids and the atomic bomb, made warfare incomparably more deadly than before to both military and civilian populations. Between 40 and 50 million people died in World War II—four times the number in World War I—and half the casualties were women and children. More than 405,000 Americans died and more than 670,000 were wounded. Although slight compared to the casualties suffered by other Allied nations—more than 20 million Soviets died during the war—the human cost of World War II for Americans was second only to that of the Civil War.

Coming at the end of two decades of resolutions to avoid military entanglements, the war pushed the nation's leaders to the center of global politics and into risky military and political alliances that would not outlive the war. The United States emerged the strongest nation in the world, but in a world where the prospects for lasting peace appeared increasingly remote.

If World War II raised the nation's international commitments to a new height, its impact on ordinary Americans was not so easy to gauge. Many new communities formed as Americans migrated in mass numbers to new regions that were booming as a result of the wartime economy. Enjoying a rare moment of full employment, many workers new to well-paying industrial jobs anticipated further advances against discrimination. Exuberant at the Allies' victory over fascism and the return of the troops, the majority were optimistic as they looked ahead.

REVIEW QUESTIONS

1. Describe the response of Americans to the rise of nationalism in Japan, Italy, and Germany during the 1930s. How did President Franklin D. Roosevelt ready the nation for war?
2. What role did the federal government play in gearing up the economy for wartime production?
3. How did the war affect the lives of American women?
4. Discuss the causes and consequences of the Japanese American internment program.
5. Describe the role of popular culture in promoting the war effort at home.
6. How did military service affect the lives of those who served in World War II?
7. What were the main points of Allied military strategy in both Europe and Asia?
8. How successful were diplomatic efforts in ending the war and in establishing the terms of peace?

RECOMMENDED READING

Stephen E. Ambrose, *D-Day, June 6, 1944: The Climactic Battle of World War II* (1994). A vivid and extremely readable, moment-by-moment reconstruction of the preparation and battle, relying heavily upon the oral histories of American veterans.

Allan Berube, *Coming Out under Fire: The History of Gay Men and Women in World War Two* (1991). A study of government policy toward homosexuals during the war and the formation of a gay community. Berube offers many insights into the new opportunities offered homosexuals through travel and varied companionship and of the effects of sanctions against them.

John Morton Blum, *V Was for Victory: Politics and American Culture during World War II* (1976). A colorful narration of American society and culture during wartime. Blum seeks to recreate the patriotic spirit that quelled potential conflict among diverse groups during wartime.

Paul Boyer, *By the Bomb's Early Light: American Thought and Culture at the Dawn of the Atomic Age* (1985). An analysis of the intellectual and cultural assumptions in relation to atomic weaponry. Boyer examines the development of a political logic, on the part of President Harry Truman and others, that made use of atomic weapons against the Japanese inevitable.

Wayne S. Cole, *Roosevelt and the Isolationists, 1932–45* (1983). Shows the president and his critics sparring over foreign policy issues. Cole analyzes the complexities of liberal-conservative divisions over war and offers insights into the logic of conservatives who feared the growth of a permanent bureaucratic, militarized state.

Richard M. Dalfiume, *Desegregation of the U.S. Armed Forces: Fighting on Two Fronts, 1939–1953* (1969). Analyzes wartime race relations in the military. By examining the official mechanisms to end discrimination and the remaining patterns of racism in the armed forces, Dalfiume reveals how changing attitudes from the top ran up against old assumptions among enlisted men and women.

Roger Daniels, *Concentration Camps USA: Japanese Americans and World War II* (1981). Perhaps the best account of Japanese American internment. Daniels details the government programs, the experiences of detention and camp life, and the many long-term consequences of lost liberty.

Sherna Berger Gluck, *Rosie the Riveter Revisited: Women, the War, and Social Change* (1987). An oral history-based study of women workers during World War II. Gluck's interviewees reveal the diversity of experiences and attitudes of women workers as well as their common feelings of accomplishment.

Gerald F. Linderman, *The World within War: America's Combat Experience in World War II* (1997). Emphasizes the less glamorous aspects of war, mainly the strains placed on the combat soldiers on the front lines. Linderman examines in especially close detail the grim experiences of Army infantrymen and the Marine riflemen who fought in the Pacific campaign.

Katrina R. Mason, *Children of Los Alamos: An Oral History of the Town Where the Atomic Age Began* (1995). Recollections of those who spent their childhood in Los Alamos. They describe their affection for the geographical setting as well as sense of safety growing up in a community so well protected. They also comment on the ethnic diversity of those who populated the town and on the pride they took in their parents' contribution to building the bomb and ending the war.

Neil R. McMillan, ed., *Remaking Dixie: The Impact of World War II on the American South* (1997). A collection of essays on the impact of World War II on the South that pay special attention to the experiences of African Americans and women. Several authors question the degree to which southern society was transformed by wartime mobilization.

Robert J. Moskin, *Mr. Truman's War: The Final Victories of World War II and the Birth of the Postwar World* (1996). A lively history of the final stages of World War II, including the surrender of Germany and the emergence of postwar foreign policy. Moskin provides an assessment of the impact of the war on social and economic conditions in the United States.

William M. Tuttle Jr., *"Daddy's Gone to War": The Second World War in the Lives of America's Children* (1993). Draws from 2,500 letters that the author solicited from men and women in their fifties and sixties about their wartime childhood memories.

David S. Wyman, *The Abandonment of the Jews: America and the Holocaust, 1941–1945* (1984). A detailed examination of U.S. immigration policy and response to Hitler's program of genocide. Wyman shows both the indifference of the Roosevelt administration to appeals for Allied protection of Jews and the inclinations of leading American Jewish organizations to stress the formation of a future Jewish state above the protection of European Jewry.

ADDITIONAL BIBLIOGRAPHY

Coming of World War II

Cynthia Ellet, *Conscientious Objectors and the Second World War* (1991)

Sheldon H. Harris, *Factories of Death: Japanese Biological Warfare, 1932–1945, and the American Cover Up* (1994)

Akira Iriye, *The Origins of the Second World War in Asia and the Pacific* (1988)

Deborah Lipstadt, *Beyond Belief: The American Press and the Coming of the Holocaust, 1933–1945* (1992)

Ernest Mandel, *The Meaning of the Second World War* (1986)
Frank P. Mintz, *Revisionism and the Origins of Pearl Harbor* (1985)
Geoffrey S. Smith, *To Save a Nation* (1992)

Arsenal of Democracy and the Home Front

Karen Anderson, *Wartime Women* (1981)
Beth Bailey and David Farber, *The First Strange Place: The Alchemy of Race and Sex in World War II Hawaii* (1993)
Alison R. Bernstein, *American Indians and World War II* (1991)
Dominic J. Capeci and Martha Wilkerson, *Layered Violence: The Detroit Rioters of 1943* (1991)
Paul D. Casdorph, *Let the Good Times Roll: Life at Home in America during World War II* (1989)
Thomas Doherty, *Hollywood, American Culture and World War II* (1993)
Lewis A. Erenberg and Susan E. Hirsch, eds., *The War in American Culture: Society and Consciousness during World War II* (1996)
George Q. Flynn, *The Mess in Washington: Manpower Mobilization in World War II* (1979)
Evelyn Nakano Glenn, *Issei, Nisei, War Bride* (1986)
Maurice Isserman, *Which Side Were You On? The American Communist Party during World War II* (1982)
John W. Jeffries, *Wartime America* (1996)
Amy Kesselman, *Fleeting Opportunities: Women Shipyard Workers in Portland and Vancouver during World War II* (1990)
Nelson Lichtenstein, *Labor's War at Home: The CIO in World War II* (1982)
Gary Y. Okihiro, *Whispered Silences: Japanese Americans and World War II* (1996)
Richard Polenberg, *War and Society: The United States, 1941–1945* (1972).
George H. Roeder, *The Censored War: American Visual Experience during World War II* (1993)
Ronald Schaffer, *America in the Great War: The Rise of the War Welfare State* (1991)
Bartholomew H. Sparrow, *From the Outside In: World War II and the American State* (1996)
Harold Vatter, *The U.S. Economy in World War II* (1985)

World at War

Russell A. Buchanan, *Black Americans in World War II* (1977)
Jean H. Cole, *Women Pilots of World War II* (1992)
Conrad C. Crane, *Bombs, Cities, and Civilians* (1993)
John W. Dower, *War without Mercy* (1986)
Paul Fussell, *Wartime: Understanding Behavior in the Second World War* (1989)
Akira Iriye, *Power and Culture: The Japanese-American War, 1941–1945* (1981)
Peter Maslowski, *Armed with Cameras: The American Military Photographers of World War II*(1996)
Nathan Miller, *War at Sea: A Naval History of World War II* (1995)
Brenda L. Moore, *To Serve My Country: The Story of the Only African American WACS Stationed Overseas During World War II* (1996)
David Reynolds, *Rich Relations: The American Occupation of Britain, 1942–1945* (1995)
Ronald H. Spector, *Eagle against the Sun: The American War with Japan* (1985)
Mark A. Stoler, *The Politics of the Second Front* (1977)
Russell P. Weigley, *Eisenhower's Lieutenants: The Campaign for France and Germany, 1944–1945* (1981)

Last Stages of War

Lloyd C. Gardner, *Architects of Illusion* (1970).
____, *Spheres of Influence: The Great Powers Partition Europe, from Munich to Yalta* (1993)
Gabriel Kolko, *Politics of War* (1968, 1990)
Charles E. Neu, *The Troubled Encounter: The United States and Japan* (1975, 1979)
Keith Sainsbury, *The Turning Point: Roosevelt, Stalin, Churchill, and Chiang-Kai-Shek, 1943* (1985)
Kenneth E. Shewmaker, *Americans and Chinese Communists, 1927–1945* (1971)
Paul Varg, *The Closing of the Door: Sino-American Relations, 1936–1946* (1973)

Atomic Bomb

Gar Alperovitz, *The Decision to Use the Atomic Bomb and the Architecture of an American Myth* (1995)
Barton J. Bernstein, ed., *The Atomic Bomb* (1976)
Michael S. Sherry, *The Rise of American Air Power* (1987)
Martin J. Sherwin, *A World Destroyed: The Atomic Bomb and the Grand Alliance* (1975)
Michael B. Stoff and Jonathan F. Fanton, eds., *The Manhattan Project* (1991)

Biography

Stephen E. Ambrose, *Supreme Commander: War Years of General Dwight D. Eisenhower* (1970)
Robert Dallek, *Franklin D. Roosevelt and American Foreign Policy* (1979)
Carlo D'Este, *Patton: A Genius for War* (1995)
Thomas Hughes, *Over Lord: General Pete Quesada and the Triumph of Tactical Air Power in World War II* (1995)
Steve Neal, *Dark Horse: A Biography of Wendell Willkie* (1984)
Paula F. Pfeffer, *A. Philip Randolph* (1990)
John Hubbard Preston, *Apocalypse Undone: My Survival of Japanese Imprisonment during World War II* (1990)

CHAPTER TWENTY-SIX

THE COLD WAR

1945–1952

Poster from 1947: Is This Tomorrow—*America under Communism!* Michael Barson/Archive Photos.

Chapter Outline

AMERICAN COMMUNITIES

University of Washington, Seattle: Students and Faculty Face the Cold War

In May 1948, a philosophy professor at the University of Washington in Seattle answered a knock on his office door. Two state legislators, members of the state's Committee on Un-American Activities, entered. "Our information," they charged, "puts you in the center of a communist conspiracy."

The accused professor, Melvin Rader, had never been a communist. A self-described liberal, Rader drew fire because he had joined several organizations supported by communists. During the 1930s, in response to the rise of Nazism and fascism, Rader had become a prominent political activist in his community. At one point he served as president of the University of Washington Teacher's Union, which had formed during the upsurge of labor organizing during the New Deal. When invited to join the Communist Party, Rader bluntly refused. "The experience of teaching social philosophy had clarified my concepts of freedom and democracy," he later explained. "I was an American in search of a way—but it was not the communist way."

Despite this disavowal, Rader was caught up in a Red Scare that curtailed free speech and political activity on campuses throughout the United States. At some universities, such as Yale, the Federal Bureau of Investigation (FBI) set up camp with the consent of the college administration, spying on students and faculty, screening the credentials of job or scholarship applicants, and seeking to entice students to report on their friends or roommates. The University of Washington administration turned down the recommendation of the Physics Department to hire J. Robert Oppenheimer because the famed atomic scientist had become a vocal opponent of the arms race and the proliferation of nuclear weapons.

Although one state legislator claimed that "not less than 150 members" of the University of Washington faculty were subversives, the state's Committee on Un-American Activities turned up just six members of the Communist Party. These six were brought up before the university's Faculty Committee on Tenure and Academic Freedom, charged with violations ranging from neglect of duty to failing to inform the university administration of their party membership. Three were ultimately dismissed, while the other three were placed on probation.

What had provoked this paranoia? Instead of peace in the wake of World War II, a pattern of cold war—icy relations—prevailed between the United States and the Soviet Union. Uneasy allies during World War II, the two superpowers now viewed each other as archenemies, and nearly all other nations lined up with one or the other of them. Within the United States, the cold war demanded pledges of absolute loyalty from citizens in every institution, from the university to trade unions and from the mass media to government itself.

If not for the outbreak of the cold war, this era would have marked one of the most fruitful in the history of higher education. The Servicemen's Readjustment Act, popularly known as the GI Bill of Rights, passed by Congress in 1944, offered stipends covering tuition and living expenses to veterans attending vocational schools or college. By the 1947–48 academic year, the federal government was subsidizing nearly half of all male college students. Between 1945 and 1950, 2.3 million students benefited from the GI Bill, at a cost of more than $10 billion.

At the University of Washington the student population in 1946 had grown by 50 percent over its prewar peak of 10,000, and veterans represented fully two-thirds of the student body. A quickly expanded faculty taught into the evening to use classroom space efficiently. Meanwhile, the state legislature pumped in funds for the construction of new buildings, including dormitories and prefabricated units for married students.

According to many observers, a feeling of community flourished among these war-weary undergraduates. Often the first in their families to attend college, they joined fellow students in campaigns to improve the campus. Married, often fathers of young children, they expected university administrators to treat them as adults. They wanted less supervision of undergraduate social life, more affordable housing, and better cultural opportunities than had previously been the case. On some campuses, film societies and student-run cooperatives vied with fraternities and sororities as centers of undergraduate social activity.

The cold war put a damper on these community-building efforts. FBI director J. Edgar Hoover testified that the college campuses were centers of "red propaganda," full of teachers "tearing down respect for agencies of government, belittling tradition and moral custom and . . . creating doubts in the validity of the American way of life." Due to communistic teachers and "communist-line textbooks," a senator lamented, thousands of parents sent "their sons and daughters to college as good Americans," only to see them return home "four years later as wild-eyed radicals."

These extravagant charges were never substantiated, but conservatives who had long regarded campuses as centers of homosexuality and atheism leaped at the opportunity presented by the cold war to take revenge on them. Several states, including Washington, enacted or revived "loyalty acts," obligating all state employees to swear in writing their loyalty to the United States and to disclaim membership in any subversive organization. Nationwide, approximately 200 faculty members were dismissed outright and many others were denied tenure. Thousands of students simply left school, dropped out of organizations, or changed friends after "visits" from FBI agents or interviews with administrators. The main effect on campus was the restraint of free speech generally and fear of criticizing U.S. racial, military, or diplomatic policies in particular.

This gloomy mood reversed the wave of optimism that had swept through America only a few years earlier. V-J Day, marking Victory over Japan, had erupted into a two-day national holiday of wild celebrations, complete with ticker-tape parades, spontaneous dancing, and kisses for returned GIs. Americans, living in the richest and most powerful nation in the world, finally seemed to have gained the peace they had fought and sacrificed to win. But peace proved fragile and elusive.

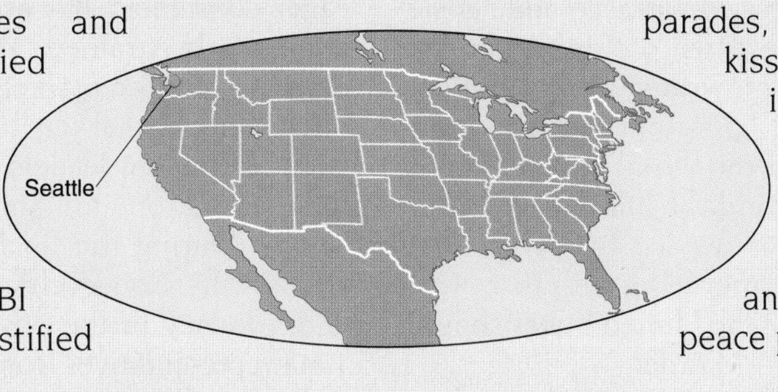

Seattle

KEY TOPICS

- **Prospects for world peace at end of World War II**
- **Diplomatic policy during the cold war**
- **The Truman presidency**
- **Anticommunism and McCarthyism**
- **Cold war culture and society**
- **The Korean War**

GLOBAL INSECURITIES AT WAR'S END

The war that had engulfed the world from 1939 to 1945 created an international interdependence that no country could ignore. The legendary African American folk singer Leadbelly (Huddie Ledbetter) added a fresh lyric to an old spiritual melody: "We're in the same boat, brother. . . . And if you shake one end you're going to rock the other." Never before, not even at the end of World War I, had hopes been so strong for a genuine "community of nations." But most Americans also recognized, a 1945 opinion poll revealed, that prospects for a durable peace rested on harmony among the Allies, especially between the Soviet Union and the United States.

Diplomatic conflict between these two competitors for world leadership had been the rule since the Russian Revolution of 1917. The threat of fascism had merely placed this rivalry on hold. Following World War II, opposing national interests and combative leaders made a continued U.S.-Soviet alliance impossible. Only the prospect of mutual destruction prevented the United States and the Soviet Union, the world's two most powerful nations, from precipitating another world war.

"The American Century"

In 1941 Henry Luce, publisher of *Time, Life,* and *Fortune* magazines, had forecast the dawn of "the American Century." Americans must, he wrote, "accept wholeheartedly our duty and our opportunity as the most powerful and vital nation in the world and in consequence to assert upon the world the full impact of our influence, for such means as we see fit." This bold pronouncement reflected the prevailing faith that, with the rest of the world in ruins, the United States should establish the principles of world order.

Americans had good reason to be confident about their prospects for setting the terms of peace. Compared with Great Britain and France, reduced to second-rate powers too weak to hold their once vast empires, the United States had not only escaped the ravages of the war but had actually prospered from it. Between 1940 and 1944 industrial production rose by 90 percent, agricultural output by 20 percent. By June 1945 the capital assets of manufacturing had increased 65 percent over prewar levels, largely because of government subsidies, and were equal in value to approximately half the entire world's goods and services.

And yet the foundation of this vigorous economy appeared fragile. Above all, Americans feared the return of widespread unemployment. Memories of the Great Depression were still fresh, and many older Americans could recall the steep economic downturn that had followed World War I. Economists understood that it was the massive government spending associated with wartime industry, rather than New Deal programs, that had ended the nightmare of the 1930s. A great question loomed: What would happen when wartime production slowed and millions of troops returned home?

"We need markets—big markets—in which to buy and sell," answered Assistant Secretary of State for Economic Affairs Will Clayton. Just to maintain the current level of growth, the United States needed an estimated $14 billion in exports—an unprecedented amount. Many business leaders looked to the Soviet Union as a potential trading partner. The president of the U.S. Chamber of Commerce testified that the Soviet Union, desperate to rebuild its war-torn society, could become, "if not our biggest, at least our most eager consumer." But as diplomatic relations became increasingly strained, this prospect vanished. With eastern European markets threatened and large chunks of former colonial territories closed off, U.S. business and government leaders became yet more determined to secure Europe for American trade and investment.

During the final stages of the war, President Franklin D. Roosevelt's advisers laid plans to secure U.S. primacy in the postwar global economy. In July 1944 representatives from forty-four Allied nations met at Bretton Woods, New Hampshire, and established the International Bank for Reconstruction and Development (World Bank) and the International Monetary Fund (IMF) to help rebuild war-torn Europe and to assist the nations of Asia, Latin America, and Africa. By stabilizing exchange rates to permit the expansion of international trade, the IMF would deter currency conflicts and trade wars—two maladies of the 1930s that were largely responsible for the political instability and national rivalries leading to World War II. The IMF was also seen as a means for blocking any rivals to U.S. economic leadership.

As the principal supplier of funds for the IMF and the World Bank—more than $7 billion to each—the United States could unilaterally shape the world economy by determining the allocation of loans. Its representatives could withhold funds from those nations that threatened to nationalize industry, for instance, while generously rewarding those that opened themselves to American investments. Foreign currencies were pegged to the U.S. dollar, a monetary policy that further enhanced the power of American bankers.

The Soviet Union interpreted "the American Century," and especially its aggressive economic programs, as a return to the policy that had guided international affairs since the Russian Revolution: a strategy to destroy communism. For this reason, the Soviet Union simply refused to join either the World Bank or the IMF, regarding them as part of a concerted endeavor by the United States to remake the world in its own capitalist image. By spurning these financial institutions, the Soviet Union cut off the possibility of aid to its own people as well as to its eastern European client states. Equally important, the Soviet Union isolated itself economically.

The United Nations and Hopes for Collective Security

A thin hope remained amid the gloom of disunity between the two superpowers. A month after the conference at Bretton Woods, Allied leaders met to lay plans for a system of collective security, the United Nations (UN). The dream of international cooperation had been seeded earlier by President Roosevelt. Had Americans agreed to join the League of Nations—as President Woodrow Wilson had pleaded in 1919—then perhaps, Roosevelt suggested, the second world war might have been averted. In late summer and fall 1944 at the Dumbarton Oaks estate in Washington, D.C., and again in April 1945 in San Francisco, the Allies worked to shape the United Nations as an international agency that would arbitrate disputes among members as well as impede aggressors, by military force if necessary. Opinion polls showed that nearly 80 percent of Americans favored U.S. membership in the UN.

Appointed to the UN delegation by President Harry Truman in 1946, Eleanor Roosevelt (1884–1962) pressured the organization to adopt the Declaration of Human Rights in 1948. In this photograph, taken in 1946, the former First Lady is exchanging ideas with Warren Austin, also a delegate to the United Nations.

From its inception the UN had only limited ability to carry out its mission. The organization represented all member nations through its General Assembly, which met for the purpose of debate but not for adjudication. The "primary responsibility for the maintenance of international peace and security" lay exclusively with the Security Council, which had five permanent members (the United States, Great Britain, the Soviet Union, France, and Nationalist China) and six temporary members elected for two-year terms. Because each permanent member enjoyed absolute veto power, the Security Council could censure an act of aggression by any of its members only if that nation abstained from the vote. Without this provision, the United States would not have joined the United Nations, but because of it, the UN could not assume the role of world peacekeeper that its architects had envisioned.

During its first decade, the UN operated strictly along lines dictated by the cold war. The Western nations held the balance of power and rigorously maintained their position by controlling the admission of new member nations. They successfully excluded Communist China, for example, thus ensuring that the UN would bolster their own political interests. The polarization between East and West made negotiated settlements virtually impossible.

The UN achieved its greatest success with its humanitarian programs for the victims of world war. Its relief agency provided the war-torn countries of Europe and Asia with billions of dollars for medical supplies, food, and clothing. The UN also dedicated itself to protecting human rights; its high standards for human dignity were due significantly to the lobbying of Eleanor Roosevelt, the president's widow and one of the first U.S. delegates to the world organization. In December 1948 the UN adopted the Universal Doctrine of Human Rights that affirmed the inalienable rights of all people to religious and civil liberty.

The trial of top Nazi officials by the International Court of Justice in 1945 and 1946 proved to be a high point of post-war international cooperation. At these proceedings, known as the Nuremberg trials, twenty-one of the twenty-four defendants were found guilty of "war crimes and atrocities." The testimony revealed the ghastly details of the organized cruelty of the Nazi regime, including the attempt to exterminate Jews, Gypsies, homosexuals, and others in the "final solution." Responding to the attempt by the accused to defend themselves with the claim that they had only followed orders, the panel of judges propounded the Nuremberg Principle: No soldier or civilian could be required, or should obey, an order—whatever its source—that conflicted with basic humanitarian tenets. Put forward by Robert Jackson, associate justice of the U.S. Supreme Court and chief U.S. prosecutor at the trials, this ruling was later affirmed by the United Nations. In the long run, however, the UN lacked the power and authority to enforce these principles any more than the ideals of human rights.

The Division of Europe

The Atlantic Charter of 1941 committed the Allies to recognize the right of all nations to self-determination and renounce all claims to new territories as the spoils of war. Following a limited period of occupation, the Allies pledged to hold free, democratic elections in those areas taken from the Axis powers and then to relinquish control to the new governments. As polls revealed, however, most Americans were skeptical of this plan. The Allied leaders themselves, moreover, violated the charter's main points before the war had ended, dividing occupied Europe into spheres of influence (see Chapter 25).

So long as Franklin Roosevelt remained alive, this strategy had seemed reconcilable with world peace. Convinced of his ability to maneuver Josef Stalin and the Soviets person to person and situation by situation, the president had balanced his own international idealism with his belief that the United States was entitled to extraordinary influence in Latin America and the Philippines and that other great powers might have similar privileges or responsibilities elsewhere. "We shall have to take the responsibility for world collaboration," he said in an address to Congress, "or we shall have to bear the responsibility for another world conflict."

Roosevelt also recognized the diplomatic consequences of the brutal European ground war that had been fought largely on Soviet territory: the Soviet Union's unnegotiable demand for territorial security along its European border. The nation lay in ruins, with 20 million dead, more than 70,000 villages destroyed, and nearly 25 million people homeless; its steel and agricultural production was down to half of prewar levels. Roosevelt believed that by offering economic assistance he might ease Stalin's fears and loosen the Soviet grip on conquered nations. But by the time of the Potsdam Conference in July 1945, the Soviet Union had already consolidated its influence over most of eastern Europe and the little Baltic states. Only the Yugoslavians and Albanians, who had turned back fascist forces without the Red Army's assistance, could claim nominal independence.

Hopes for cooperation between the Soviet Union and the United States further unraveled in central Europe. France, Great Britain, the Soviet Union, and the United States had divided Germany temporarily into four occupation zones, each governed by one of them. But the Allies could not agree on long-term plans. Having borne the brunt of German aggression, France and the Soviet Union both opposed reunification of Germany. The Soviet Union also demanded heavy reparations along with a limit on postwar reindustrialization. Roosevelt appeared to agree with the Soviets. "We have got to be tough with Germany, and I mean the German people not just the Nazis," he concluded. "We . . . have got to treat them in such a manner so they can't just go on reproducing people who want to continue the way they have in the past." But American business leaders, envisioning a new center for U.S. commerce, shared Winston Churchill's hope of rebuilding Germany into a powerful counterforce against the Soviet Union and a strong market for U.S. and British goods.

The division of Germany forecast the shape of the new world order. West Germany became more and more "American" as the United States directed the reconstruction of its capitalist economy and canceled voters' mandates for government ownership of coal mines and major industries. While guiding liberal politicians into top government positions, U.S. advisers began a program of amnesty for a former Nazi elite, which controlled large sectors of business and the civil service, in order to stabilize the government against a resurgence of a once-strong German socialist movement. Meanwhile, the Soviets dragged industrial equipment out of impoverished East Germany for their own domestic needs and imposed a harsh discipline on the inhabitants. Despite promising to deliver the economy over to German workers, the Soviets took no steps toward democracy in East Germany.

"The main prize of the victory" over the Axis powers was, a State Department document had noted in November 1945, a "limited and temporary power to establish the kind of world we want to live in." But this prediction failed to account for the dissolution of the alliance between the western powers and the Soviet Union. Winston Churchill, swearing to preserve the British colonial empire, had himself parleyed with Stalin to establish spheres of influence. Yet he refused to accept Soviet demands for control over eastern Europe as a buffer against future invasions from the West. The more forcefully Stalin resisted plans for Western-style governments and Western influence right up to the Soviet borders, the more Western leaders cried foul. In a speech delivered in Fulton, Missouri, in March 1946, Churchill declared that "an iron curtain has descended across the [European] Continent." The dream of a community of nations had dissolved, but perhaps it had never been more than a fantasy contrived to maintain a fragile alliance amid the urgency of World War II.

THE POLICY OF CONTAINMENT

Many Americans believed that Franklin D. Roosevelt, had he lived, would have been able to stem the tide of tensions between the Soviet Union and the United States. Harry S. Truman, who became president when FDR died in April 1945, sorely lacked FDR's talent for diplomacy. More comfortable with southern or conservative Democrats than with polished New Dealers, the new president liked to talk tough and act defiantly. He did not hesitate to flaunt the U.S. monopoly of the atomic bomb. Just ten days after he took office, Truman complained that U.S.-Soviet negotiations had been a "one-way street." He vowed to "baby" the Soviets no longer, adding that if they did not like it they could "go to hell."

Truman replaced Roosevelt's diplomatic advisers with a hard-line team of new advisers. Drawing on their advice, he aimed to establish U.S. leadership in the world through a race for power that would exhaust communist resources. In the short run, Truman determined to maintain U.S. military superiority and prevent communism from spreading outside the Soviet Union. Containment, a doctrine uniting military, economic, and diplomatic strategies to turn back communism and to secure for the United States the leading role in world affairs, now became the linchpin of U.S. foreign policy.

The Truman Doctrine

Truman showed his cards early in 1947 when a crisis erupted in the Mediterranean, a region considered a British sphere. When civil war broke out in Greece and Great Britain announced its plan to withdraw all economic and military aid, U.S. diplomatic leaders began to fear a move into this territory by the Soviet Union. They knew that Stalin was not directly involved in the crisis, but they also recognized that the Soviet Union would derive enormous benefits from a communist victory in nearby Greece. To forestall this possibility, Truman decided to take over Britain's historic role as the dominant power in this area. The president made his case by insisting that without U.S. intervention all of the oil-rich Middle East would fall under Soviet control.

Such a commitment demanded something many Americans feared: an expenditure of hundreds of millions of dollars and the responsibility for controlling a region far outside the Western Hemisphere and the Pacific. If he hoped to sway public opinion as well as the fiscally conservative Republican Congress, advised Republican senator Arthur H. Vandenberg of Michigan, chair of the Foreign Relations Committee, the president would have to "scare hell out of the country."

In early March 1947 Truman swung into action. Speaking at Baylor University, he linked the survival of the American system of free enterprise to Western victory in Greece. A week later, on March 12, appearing before Congress, the president argued: "At the present moment in world history, nearly every nation must choose between alternative ways of life. . . . One way of life is based upon the will of the majority, and is distinguished by free institutions . . . and freedom from political oppression. The second way of life is based upon the will of a minority forcibly imposed on the majority . . . and the suppression of personal freedoms." Never mentioning the Soviet Union by name, the president appealed for all-out resistance to a "certain ideology," wherever it appeared in the world. The preservation of peace and the freedom of all Americans depended, Truman insisted, on containing communism.

Truman won the day. Congress approved his request to appropriate $400 million in aid for Greece and Turkey, and this assistance helped the Greek monarchy crush the rebel movement. Truman's victory took the sting out of Republican criticisms and buoyed his popularity for the upcoming 1948 election. It also helped to turn Americans against their former ally and to generate popular support for a campaign against communism, both at home and abroad. Moreover, by exaggerating the immediacy of the Soviet threat, Truman was able to wield his executive power to control the legislative agenda, much as a president would do in time of war.

The significance of what became known as the Truman Doctrine far outlasted the events in the Mediterranean: the United States had declared its right to intervene to save other nations from communist subversion. As early as February 1946, foreign-policy adviser George Kennan had sent an 8,000-word "long telegram" to the State Department insisting that Soviet fanaticism could be quelled only by ongoing military and diplomatic pressure. In July 1947 he reaffirmed his belief. Writing under the pseudonym "X" in *Foreign Affairs*, Kennan explained that the future of democracy depended on two possibilities: "either the break-up [of communism] or the gradual mellowing of Soviet power." Despite complaints from critics such as Walter Lippmann, who described this position as a "strategic monstrosity," requiring an

VERVIEW

Major Cold War Policies

Policy	Date	Provisions
Truman Doctrine	1947	Pledged the United States to the containment of communism in Europe and elsewhere. The doctrine was the foundation of Truman's foreign policy. It impelled the United States to support any nation whose stability was threatened by communism or the Soviet Union.
Federal Employees Loyalty and Security Program	1947	Established by Executive Order 9835, this program barred communists and fascists from federal employment and outlined procedures for investigating current and prospective federal employees.
Marshall Plan	1947	U.S. program to aid war-torn Europe, also known as the European Recovery Program. The Marshall Plan was a cornerstone in the U.S. use of economic policy to contain communism.
National Security Act	1947	Established Department of Defense (to coordinate the three armed services), the National Security Council (to advise the president on security issues), and the Central Intelligence Agency (to gather and evaluate intelligence data).
North Atlantic Treaty Organization (NATO)	1948	A military alliance of twelve nations formed to deter possible aggression of the Soviet Union against Western Europe.
NSC-68	1950	National Security Council Paper calling for an expanded and aggressive U.S. defense policy, including greater military spending and higher taxes.
Internal Security Act (also known as the McCarran Act and the Subversive Activities Control Act)	1950	Legislation providing for the registration of all communist and totalitarian groups and authorizing the arrest of suspect persons during a national emergency.
Immigration and Nationality Act (also known as McCarran-Walter Immigration Act)	1952	Reaffirmed the national origins quota system but tightened immigration controls, barring homosexuals and people considered subversive from entering the United States.

endless diffusion of American resources for military operations around the world, containment served as the cornerstone of U.S. foreign policy for the next several decades.

The Marshall Plan

The Truman Doctrine directly inspired the European Recovery Program, commonly known as the Marshall Plan. Introduced in a commencement speech at

Harvard University on June 5, 1947, by secretary of state and former army chief of staff George C. Marshall, the plan aimed to reduce "hunger, poverty, desperation, and chaos" and to restore "the confidence of the European people in the economic future of their own countries and of Europe as a whole." In this region, the Truman administration did not fear a Soviet invasion as much as the political consequences of total disintegration of the region's economy. Indirectly, the Marshall Plan aimed to turn back both socialist and communist bids for power in northern and western Europe.

The Marshall Plan in effect brought recipients of aid into a bilateral agreement with the United States. The western European nations, seventeen in all, received nearly $13 billion between 1948 and 1951; more than half went to West Germany, France, and Great Britain. The seventeen nations also ratified the General Agreement on Tariffs and Trade (GATT), which reduced commercial barriers among member nations and opened all to U.S. trade.

Located deep within communist East Germany, West Berlin was suddenly cut off from the West when Josef Stalin blockaded all surface traffic in an attempt to take over the war-torn city. Between June 1948 and May 1949, British and U.S. pilots made 272,000 flights, dropping food and fuel to civilians. The Berlin Airlift successfully foiled the blockade, and the Soviet Union reopened access on May 12.

Considered by many historians the most successful postwar U.S. diplomatic venture, the Marshall Plan created the climate for a viable capitalist economy in western Europe. Industrial production in that region rose by 200 percent between 1947 and 1952. Deflationary programs cut wages and increased unemployment, but profits soared and the standard of living improved. Under U.S. leadership, the nations of western Europe rallied to become a major center of American trade and investment.

The Marshall Plan drove a further wedge between the United States and the Soviet Union. Stalin denounced the plan as an American scheme to rebuild Germany and to incorporate it into an anti-Soviet bloc. The architects of the Marshall Plan, however, had never expected the Soviet Union to participate. As one planner noted, if the recovery program included funds to help the communist nations, "the whole project would probably be unworkable." As the president readily acknowledged, the Truman Doctrine and the Marshall Plan were "two halves of the same walnut."

The Berlin Crisis and the Formation of NATO

Once the Marshall Plan was in place, the strategy of containment began to take clear shape in Germany. In June 1948 the Western allies decided to incorporate the American, French, and British occupation zones into a single nation, the Federal Republic of West Germany. Already alarmed by their plan to rebuild German industry, Stalin perceived this new move as yet another threat to Soviet security. On June 24, 1948, he responded by stopping all traffic to West Berlin, formally controlled by the Western allies but located hundreds of miles within Soviet-occupied East Germany.

Divided Europe *During the cold war, Europe was divided into opposing military alliances, the North American Treaty Organization (NATO) and the Warsaw Pact (communist bloc).*

The Soviet retaliation created for Truman both a crisis and an opportunity for confrontation. The president believed that Stalin intended to take over Berlin, thus putting not only the future of Germany but the governing role of the Western powers in jeopardy. Although his advisers were reluctant to risk war by challenging Stalin militarily, the president refused to show any sign of weakness. He threatened to use atomic weapons against the Soviets, and he even sent two squadrons of B-29s to the U.S. military base in Great Britain. But this plan was quickly abandoned, and the United States began, with help from the Royal Air Force, an airlift of historic proportions—Operation Vittles, which delivered nearly 2 million tons of supplies to West Berliners. Finally, in May 1949, the Soviet Union conceded defeat and lifted the blockade. Within a few weeks, East Germany and West Germany were established as separate states.

The Berlin crisis made a U.S.-led military alliance against the Soviets attractive to western European nations. In April 1949 ten European nations, Canada, and the United States formed the North Atlantic Treaty Organization (NATO), a mutual defense pact in which "an armed attack against one or more of them . . . shall be considered an attack against them all." NATO complemented the Marshall Plan, strengthening economic ties among the member nations by, according to one analyst, keeping "the Russians out, the Americans in, and the Germans down." It also deepened divisions between eastern and western Europe, making a permanent military mobilization on both sides almost inevitable.

By mid-1949 Truman and his advisers were basking in the glow of their victories. The U.S. Senate had ratified the first formal military treaty with a European nation since the Revolutionary War era—a giant step away from isolationism. Congress also approved $1.3 billion in military aid, which involved the creation of U.S. Army bases and the deployment of American troops abroad. Critics such as isolationist senator Robert A. Taft warned that the United States could not afford to police all of Europe without sidetracking domestic policies and undercutting the UN. But opinion polls revealed strong support for Truman's tough line against the Soviets.

Between 1947 and 1949, the Truman administration had defined the policies that would shape the cold war for decades to come. The Truman Doctrine explained the ideological basis of containment; the Marshall Plan put into place its economic underpinnings in western Europe; and NATO created the mechanisms for military enforcement. When NATO extended membership to a rearmed West Germany in May 1955, the Soviet Union responded by creating a counterpart, the Warsaw Pact, including East Germany. The division of East and West was complete.

The Cold War in Asia

Triumphant in western Europe, Truman managed only a mixed record in Asia. In some areas, he proved that the United States could contain communism without massive displays of military strength. Elsewhere, the Truman Doctrine did not work, and the results were disastrous for the president.

The United States achieved its greatest success in occupied Japan. General Douglas MacArthur directed an interim government in a modest reconstruction program that included land reform, the creation of independent trade unions, abolition of contract marriages and granting of woman suffrage, sweeping demilitarization, and, eventually, a constitutional democracy that barred communists from all posts. Increasingly more wary of the Soviet Union than of a resurgent Japan, American leaders planned to rebuild the Japanese economy and integrate Japan, like West Germany, into an anti-Soviet bloc. In return for its sovereignty, granted in 1952, Japan agreed to house huge U.S. military bases, thus placing U.S. troops and weapons strategically close to the Soviet Union's Asian rim. U.S. advisers, meanwhile, prepared a new group of business leaders who were eager to build a capitalist economy in Japan and willing to quash anti-American dissent with a powerful national police. Economically, the United States took control, forbidding Japan to trade with the Soviet Union and, later, the People's Republic of China.

Truman scored smaller but significant victories in both Indonesia and the Philippines. When a nationalist revolution in the Dutch East Indies began to threaten U.S. interests, the State Department forced Holland to grant independence to its colony, and the sovereign state of Indonesia was created in 1949. The United States had granted formal independence to the Philippines in 1946 but retained major naval bases there as well as influence over Filipino foreign and domestic affairs. In response to a major uprising of peasants hungry for land, the United States directed massive amounts of aid to nationalist leader Ramón Magsaysay, who crushed the rebellion. General MacArthur adamantly defended the role of the United States, describing the Philippines to Congress in 1950 as a "mighty bulwark of Christianity in the Far East."

The situation in China could not be handled so easily. Unwilling to take strong diplomatic or economic measures against the escalating Japanese invasion during the 1930s, American officials nevertheless felt compelled to prop up the corrupt and sagging Jiang Jieshi (Chiang Kai-shek) regime after China officially joined the Allies in 1941. Under General Joseph Stilwell, however, the U.S. military mission of the China-Burma-India theater remained largely defensive. The Communist Red Army, led by Mao Zedong, assumed more and more of the fighting as the war drew to a close.

American diplomats on the scene, observing the shift of forces closely, warned Jiang that without major reforms—especially the breaking up of large landholdings and the feeding of starving people—his forces were bound to lose the loyalty of ordinary Chinese. Increasingly desperate for a solution, the Americans tried to convince Jiang to turn over the reins of government to a less corrupt group of moderates. Some urged reconciliation of the U.S. government with the rising military and political hero, Mao, either alone or in coalition with Jiang.

All these plans failed when Jiang insisted on fighting the communists after Japan had been defeated. Sorely misjudging his resources and launching an all-out offensive against his communist adversaries, Jiang precipitated the collapse of his government. When the victory of Mao's forces became inevitable, U.S. diplomats broke off relations with Jiang, and Secretary of State Dean Acheson issued a 1,054-page "White Paper" explaining that the situation was "beyond the control of the government of the United States." By mid-1949, the majority of Jiang's troops surrendered, and his Nationalist government retreated to the island of Formosa (Taiwan). Enjoying wide support among the rural 85 percent of China's population, Mao took control of the mainland.

The news of China's "fall" to communism created an uproar in the United States. The Asia First wing of the Republican Party, which envisioned the Far East rather than Europe as the prime site of future U.S. overseas economic expansion, blamed the Truman administration for "losing" China. Although China was never America's possession to lose, the bipartisan anti-communist sentiment fueled by Truman's actions placed him in the delicate position of holding the "Iron Curtain" in place across the world. Republicans described Truman's explanation for communist victory as a "white-wash of a wishful, do-nothing policy," and the Democrats as a "party of treason" to national security.

The president had repeatedly insisted that communism was a "conspiracy" of depraved power-mongers with no basis of popular support. The "China Lobby," which represented economic interests but also had roots in Christian missionary ties to Asia, continued to use Truman's own rhetoric against him. *Time* magazine, the voice of publisher and China Lobby enthusiast Henry Luce, was especially vitriolic. Boxed in, Truman seemed once more as he had to many during his early months in office, a small-time politician powerless and incompetent to shape American affairs.

After Stalin signed a formal alliance with Mao in February 1950, the rhetoric of the cold war became yet more pronounced. The perceived threat of "international communism" came to dominate American foreign policy for the next twenty years.

Atomic Diplomacy

The policy of containment depended on the ability of the United States to back up its commitments through military means, and Truman relied on the U.S. monopoly of atomic weapons to pressure the Soviets to cooperate. On August 9, 1945, the day U.S. planes bombed Nagasaki, the president told Americans, "We must constitute ourselves trustees of this new force—to prevent its misuse, and to turn it into the channels of service to mankind." In a survey conducted one month later, 85 percent of the respondents wanted the United States to retain sole possession of the bomb for as long as possible. Many scientists nevertheless warned that once the bomb had been exploded, the "secret" could no longer be guarded.

After the war, many Americans favored control of atomic power by the United Nations. But a plan drafted by American financier Bernard M. Baruch failed to win approval by the Soviet Union. When negotiations stalled, the United States quickly put aside all plans for international cooperation. In 1946 Congress passed the Atomic Energy Act, which granted the newly established Atomic Energy Commission control of all research and development under the strictest standards of national security.

The United States began to stockpile atomic weapons and conduct additional tests on the Bikini Islands in the Pacific. By 1949, the number of bombs had grown from thirteen to fifty. By 1950, as a scientific adviser subsequently observed, the United States "had a stockpile capable of somewhat more than reproducing World War II in a single day."

Despite warnings to the contrary by leading scientists, U.S. military analysts continued to downplay Soviet nuclear capability. The Military Intelligence Division of the War Department estimated it would take the Soviet Union three to ten years to produce an atomic bomb. In August 1949, the Soviet Union proved them wrong by testing its own atomic bomb. "There is only one thing worse than one nation having the atomic bomb," Nobel Prize-winning scientist Harold C. Urey said, "that's two nations having it."

Within a few years, both the United States and the Soviet Union had tested hydrogen bombs a thousand times more powerful than the primitive weapons dropped on Hiroshima and Nagasaki in 1945. Both proceeded to stockpile bombs and to put nuclear warheads on missiles, inaugurating the fateful nuclear arms race that scientists had feared since 1945. The two superpowers were now firmly locked into the cold war. The nuclear arms race imperiled their futures, diverted their economies, and fostered fears of impending doom. When he heard of the Soviet detonation of the bomb, Senator Vandenberg remarked presciently, "This is now a different world." Prospects for global peace had faded, and despite the Allied victory in World War II, the world had again divided into hostile camps.

THE TRUMAN PRESIDENCY

Truman's aggressive, gutsy personality suited the confrontational mood of the cold war. He linked the Soviet threat in Europe to the need for a strong presidency. Meanwhile, he reached out to voters alarmed at Republican intent on dismantling the New Deal. Pressed to establish his own political identity, "Give 'em Hell" Harry successfully portrayed himself as a fierce fighter against all challengers, yet loyal to Roosevelt's legacy.

"To Err Is Truman"

In marked contrast with his illustrious predecessor, Harry Truman was a virtual unknown to most Americans. Within a year of assuming office, he rated lower in public approval than any twentieth-century president except Roosevelt's own predecessor, Herbert Hoover, who had been blamed for the Great Depression. The twin responsibilities of reestablishing peacetime conditions—demobilizing the troops and reconverting the economy—seemed to overwhelm the new president's administration. Repeatedly lashing out at his detractors and withdrawing unpopular proposals after public outcries, he also had trouble convincing Americans of his sincerity. "To err is Truman," critics jeered.

As commander in chief, Truman angered servicemen and -women eager to return home. Quite a few combat veterans were surprised to find themselves shipped off to the Philippines to put down labor and agrarian unrest. Members of Congress received bundles of protest letters, "Bring Daddy Home" clubs formed throughout the country, and in January 1946 demonstrations broke out in Manila. Spreading across the Pacific, the "Bring the Boys Home" movement so alarmed Truman that he reversed course and, in a dramatic radio address, promised a rapid demobilization. Under his orders the War Department gave in, but the president had already damaged his record.

At home, Truman did no better. In handling the enormous task of reconverting the economy to peacetime production, he appeared both inept and mean-spirited. The president faced millions of restless would-be consumers tired of rationing and eager to spend their wartime savings. The demand for consumer items rapidly outran supply, fueling inflation and creating a huge black market; business profits skyrocketed along with retail prices. When Congress proposed to extend wartime controls over prices, Truman vetoed the bill.

In 1945 and 1946, the country appeared ready to explode. While homemakers protested rising prices by boycotting neighborhood stores, industrial workers struck in unprecedented numbers. Employers, fearing a rapid decline to depression-level profits, determined to slash wages or at least hold them steady; workers wanted a bigger cut of the huge war profits they had heard about. As police and strikers clashed, citywide general strikes spread from transit workers to other laborers. In Oakland, Pittsburgh, and Rochester, the strikes halted all commerce for days. Alarmed by the spectacle of nearly 4.6 million workers on picket lines, the new president proposed to seize the mines and to induct striking railroad workers into the army. The Senate, however, killed this plan by a 70 to 13 vote.

Congress defeated most of Truman's proposals for reconversion. One week after Japan's surrender, the president introduced a twenty-one-point program that included greater unemployment compensation, higher minimum wages, and housing assistance. Later he added proposals for national health insurance and atomic energy legislation. Congress turned back the bulk of these bills, passing the Employment Act of 1946 only after substantial modification. The act created a new executive body, the Council of Economic Advisers, which would confer with the president and formulate policies for maintaining employment, production, and purchasing power. But the measure failed to grant the fiscal means to guarantee full employment, thus undermining Truman's chief effort to advance beyond the New Deal.

By 1946 Truman's popularity had dipped to 32 percent. One joke began with a reflection on what

Police and strikers confront each other in Los Angeles during one of many postwar strikes in 1946. *Employers wanted to cut wages, and workers refused to give up the higher living standard achieved during the war.*

Roosevelt would do if still alive, only to end by asking "What would Truman do if he were alive?" Republicans, sensing victory in the upcoming off-year elections, asked the voters, "Had enough?" Apparently the voters had. They censored Truman and the Democrats, giving Republicans majorities in both houses of Congress and in the state capitols. In office, the Republicans set out to turn back the New Deal. And in a symbolic repudiation of Roosevelt they passed an amendment establishing a two-term limit for the presidency.

The Republicans, dominant in Congress for the first time since 1931, prepared a full counteroffensive against the constituency most hated by business: organized labor. Unions had by this time reached a peak in size and power, with membership topping 15 million and encompassing nearly 40 percent of all wage earners. To halt this movement, the Republican-dominated Eightieth Congress passed the Taft-Hartley Act in 1947.

The Labor-Management Relations Act, as Taft-Hartley was officially known, outlawed many practices approved by the Wagner Act of 1935 (see Chapter 24), such as the closed shop, the secondary boycott, and the use of union dues for political activities. It also mandated an eighty-day cooling-off period in the case of strikes affecting national safety or health. Called the "slave labor bill" by union activists, Taft-Hartley furthermore required all union officials to swear under oath that they were not communists—a cold war mandate that abridged freedoms ordinarily guaranteed by the First Amendment. Those unions that refused to cooperate were denied the services of the National Labor Relations Board, which arbitrated strikes and issued credentials to unions. In short, the Taft-Hartley Act made it more difficult for workers to establish unions in their industry or trade.

Truman regained some support from organized labor when he vetoed the Taft-Hartley Act, saying it would "conflict with important principles of our democratic society." Congress, however, overrode his veto, and Truman himself went on to invoke the act against strikers. Members of the president's own party now proposed that he resign or sought to persuade General Dwight Eisenhower to accept the Democratic nomination for president in the upcoming national election.

The 1948 Election

Although lacking a strong candidate, Democrats gingerly approached the 1948 election—the first presidential contest since the inauguration of the cold war—as an opportunity to campaign for their own post-New Deal agenda. In preparation, a group headed by Eleanor Roosevelt, labor leaders Philip Murray and Walter Reuther, and theologian Reinhold Niebuhr, among others, met in January 1947 to form Americans for Democratic Action (ADA). This body became the most important liberal lobby of the postwar era. Determined to defeat the Republicans, ADA moved to reorient the Democratic Party itself, which appeared to be breaking up on the shoals of cold war politics.

"As long as Franklin Roosevelt was President," wrote a journalist in the British *New Statesman* in 1948, "life was politically simple. . . . There was a place for [liberals] on the New Deal bandwagon, and until the driver died, some of them were permitted to sit on the front seat." The new president, however, had already divided the liberal community. Truman frankly considered some of Roosevelt's closest advisers to be "crackpots and the lunatic fringe." By late 1946 he had forced out the remaining social planners who had staffed the Washington bureaus for over a decade, including one of the best-loved New Dealers, Secretary of the Interior Harold Ickes.

Truman had also fired his secretary of commerce, Henry A. Wallace, for advocating a more conciliatory policy toward the Soviet Union. Wallace, however, would not retreat and made plans to run for president as candidate of the newly formed Progressive Party. Having served as Roosevelt's vice president and secretary of agriculture, Wallace was well known as a long-time champion of New Deal liberalism. He vowed to expand New Deal programs, to move swiftly and boldly toward full employment, racial equality, and stronger trade unions, and to work in harmony with the Soviet Union. As the election neared, Wallace remarked after a speech before 32,000 enthusiastic supporters, "We're on the march. We're really rolling now."

The deepening cold war soon quashed Wallace's chances. Rallying around the president, ADA denounced the Progressive Party for lining up "with the force of Soviet totalitarianism." Truman himself, as well as many conservatives, accused Wallace of being a tool of communists. These timely Red-baiting attacks took a toll on the poorly organized and underfunded Wallace campaign, driving many liberals from its ranks, including future Democratic presidential candidate George McGovern. Moreover, Wallace, who never subscribed to communism, refused to fend off these charges, considering them a dangerous by-product of anticommunist hysteria.

Meanwhile, Truman, in an unusually shrewd strategic move, repositioned himself to discredit congressional Republicans. He proposed programs calling for federal funds for education and new housing and a national program of medical insurance that he knew the Republicans would kill, and he called Congress back for a fruitless special session in 1948. He then hammered away at the Republican controlled "do-nothing Congress" to good effect in his reelection campaign, warning voters that if Republicans won the White House, the United States would become "an economic colony of Wall Street."

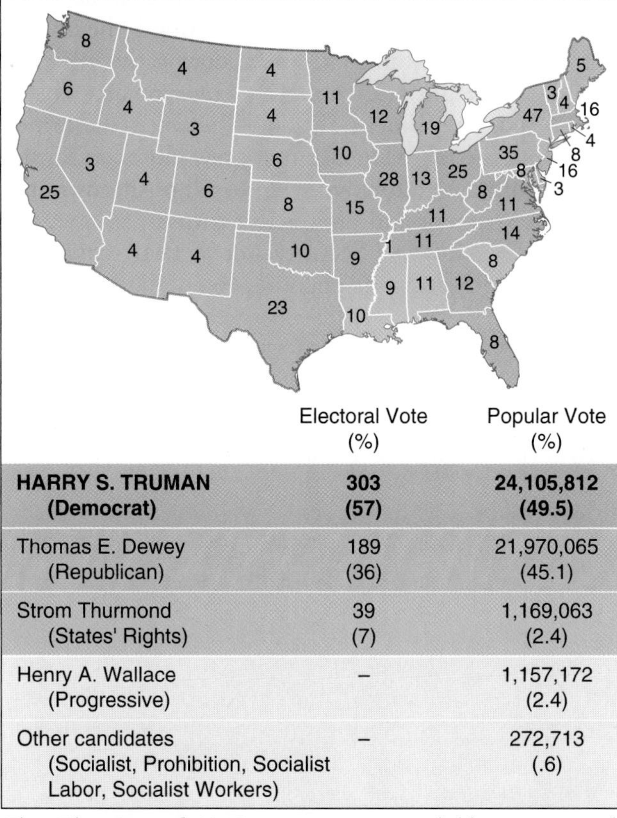

	Electoral Vote (%)	Popular Vote (%)
HARRY S. TRUMAN (Democrat)	**303 (57)**	**24,105,812 (49.5)**
Thomas E. Dewey (Republican)	189 (36)	21,970,065 (45.1)
Strom Thurmond (States' Rights)	39 (7)	1,169,063 (2.4)
Henry A. Wallace (Progressive)	–	1,157,172 (2.4)
Other candidates (Socialist, Prohibition, Socialist Labor, Socialist Workers)	–	272,713 (.6)

The Election of 1948 *Harry Truman holds up a copy of the* Chicago Tribune *with headlines confidently and mistakenly predicting the victory of his opponent, Thomas E. Dewey. An initially unpopular candidate, Truman made a whistle-stop tour of the country by train to win 49.5 percent of the popular vote to Dewey's 45.1 percent.*

A second tactic seemed to backfire. Pressed by ADA leaders to cut Wallace's lead on civil rights, Truman issued executive orders in July 1948 desegregating the armed forces and banning discrimination in the federal civil service. He also endorsed a plank on racial equality that he personally considered too strongly worded. In response, some 300 southern delegates bolted from the Democratic National Convention and formed a States' Rights ("Dixiecrat") ticket headed by Governor J. Strom Thurmond of South Carolina, known for his segregationist views. With the South as good as lost, and popular New York governor Thomas E. Dewey heading the Republican ticket, Truman appeared hopelessly far from victory.

Yet as the election neared, Truman managed to restore essential components of the New Deal coalition. Fear of the Republicans won back the bulk of organized labor, while the recognition of the new State of Israel in May 1948 helped prevent the defection of many liberal Jewish voters from Democratic ranks. The success of the Berlin airlift also buoyed Truman's popularity. By election time, Truman had deprived Henry Wallace of nearly all his liberal support. Meanwhile, Dewey, who had run a hard-hitting campaign against Roosevelt in 1944, expected to coast to victory. By campaigning vigorously, Truman won back Democrats except in the South, where Thurmond took four states. The president carried most of the states and trounced Dewey 303 to 189 in the electoral college. Congressional Democrats again had majorities in both houses. Truman's campaign had retained the loyalty of those Americans who feared a reversal of the New Deal. "Harry Truman won the election," concluded the *New Republic,* "because Franklin Roosevelt had worked so well."

The Fair Deal

President Truman laid out his domestic agenda in January 1949. "Every segment of our population and every individual has a right to expect from our Government a fair deal," he affirmed. The return of Democratic majorities in the House and Senate, he hoped, would enable him to translate campaign promises into concrete legislative achievements. But a powerful bloc of conservative southern Democrats and midwestern Republicans defeated most of the president's plans.

Truman could claim only a few victories. Congress passed a National Housing Act in 1949, promoting federally funded construction of low-income housing. It also raised the minimum wage from forty to seventy-five cents per hour and expanded the Social Security program to cover an additional 10 million people. Otherwise, Truman made little headway. He and congressional liberals introduced a variety of bills to weaken southern segregationism: making lynching a federal crime; outlawing the poll tax; prohibiting discrimination in interstate transportation. These measures were all defeated by southern-led filibusters. Proposals to create a national health insurance plan, provide federal aid for education, and repeal or modify Taft-Hartley remained bottled up in committees. Truman himself appeared to lose interest in the liberal agenda as his cold war foreign policy increasingly took priority over domestic issues.

Truman managed best to lay out the basic principles of cold war liberalism. Toning down the rhetoric of economic equality espoused by the visionary wing of the Roosevelt coalition, his Fair Deal exalted economic growth—not the reapportionment of wealth or political power—as the proper mechanism for ensuring social harmony and national welfare. His administration insisted, therefore, on an ambitious program of expanded foreign trade while relying on the federal government to encourage high levels of productivity at home. Although dropping at the end of World War II, federal expenditures remained at least seven times greater than during their New Deal peak in the 1930s.

The Truman administration effectively used the threat of military confrontation with the Soviet Union to increase the size of the defense budget. By the end of Truman's second term, defense allocations accounted for 10 percent of the gross national product, directly or indirectly employed hundreds of thousands of well-paid workers, and subsidized some of the nation's most profitable corporations. This vast financial outlay, guided through Congress by legislators seeking economic benefits for their constituents, created the rationale for permanent, large-scale military spending as a basic stimulus to economic growth. A vigorous anticommunist crusade at home strengthened the underpinnings of this ambitious cold war program.

THE COLD WAR AT HOME

In June 1946, Attorney General Tom C. Clark announced that the United States had become the target of "a sinister and deep-seated plot on the part of Communists, ideologists, and small groups of radicals" to capture unions, cause strikes, and prevent lawful authorities from maintaining order. FBI director J. Edgar Hoover estimated that there were at least 100,000 communists in the nation. Four years later, Republican senator Joseph R. McCarthy announced that he held lists of communists serving secretly in government agencies. This information, he declared, showed that the United States had already fallen prey to subversive influences. The specter of a prolonged cold war with the Soviet Union had encouraged many Americans, including the nation's leaders, to become obsessed with problems of national security, real or imagined, and to resort to extreme measures to solve them.

The National Security State

The cold war served as the rationale for a massive reordering of governmental power. Only a powerful leader in charge of a vast bureaucracy, it was argued, could hope to curtail the international communist conspiracy. Invoking national security, the president now claimed executive authority normally reserved for wartime. Within a decade after the end of World War II, a huge federal bureaucracy, dependent on military spending and increasingly devoted to surveillance at home and abroad, had greatly changed the relationship of the federal government to everyday affairs.

National defense took up increasingly large portions of the nation's resources. Shortly before the war, the federal workforce totaled about 900,000 civilians, with about 10 percent engaged in security work; by war's end, the government employed nearly 4 million people, of whom 75 percent worked in national security agencies. The Pentagon, which had opened in 1943 as the largest office building in the world, housed the Joint Chiefs of Staff and 35,000 military personnel. Similarly, when the State Department consolidated its various divisions in 1961, it abandoned the nearly thirty separate buildings acquired during the 1950s to take over an eight-story structure covering an area the size of four city blocks. The ties between the armed forces and the State Department grew closer, as former military officers routinely began to fill positions in the State Department and diplomatic corps.

The National Security Act of 1947, passed by Congress with Truman's encouragement, laid the foun-

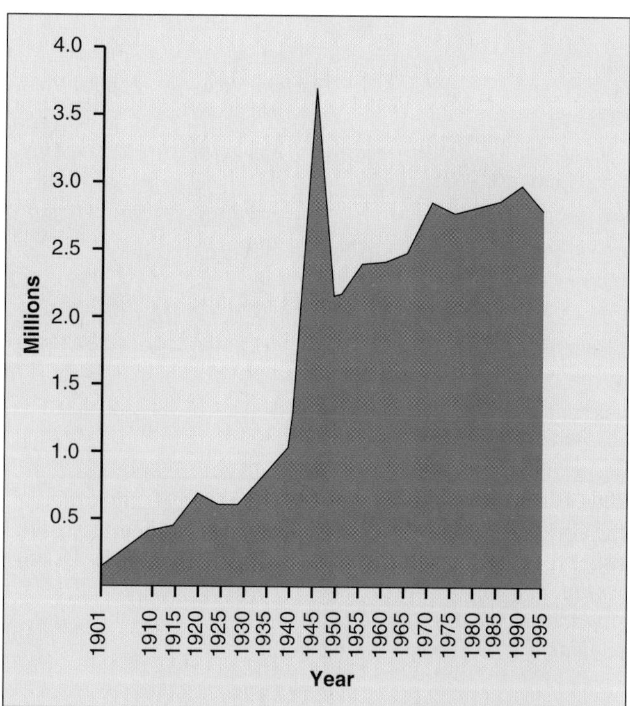

Number of Employees in the Executive Branch, 1901–1995 *The federal bureaucracy, which reached a peak of nearly four million people during World War II, remained at unprecedentedly high levels during the cold war.*

Source: U.S. Bureau of the Census, *Historical Statistics of the United States, Colonial Times through 1970*; *Statistical Abstract of the United States, 1997* dation for this expansion. The act established the Department of Defense and the National Security Council (NSC) to administer and coordinate defense policies and to advise the president. The Central Intelligence Agency (CIA), with roots in the wartime Office of Strategic Services, was established to obtain political, military, and economic information from around the world. Although information about the CIA was classified—that is, secret from both Congress and the public—historians have estimated that the agency soon dwarfed the State Department in number of employees and size of budget. By late 1947, as Harrison Baldwin of the *New York Times* noted, there was an ominous trend toward "militarization of [the] government and of the American state of mind."

In March 1947, Truman signed Executive Order 9835, establishing the Federal Employees Loyalty and Security Program. The program barred members of the Communist Party—as well as fascists and anyone guilty of "sympathetic association" with either—from federal employment. It also outlined procedures for investigating current and prospective federal employees. An employee could be dismissed merely on "reasonable grounds for belief that the person is disloyal." Later amendments added "homosexuals" as potential security risks on the grounds that they might succumb to blackmail by enemy agents.

Many state and municipal governments enacted loyalty programs and required public employees, including teachers at all levels, to sign loyalty oaths. In Detroit, the loyalty review board included city officials, FBI agents, and executives from the auto industry. Positions involving security clearances were closed off to many scientists and engineers, including several who had worked on the Manhattan Project. In all, some 6.6 million people underwent loyalty and security checks. Although no spies or saboteurs turned up, nearly 500 government workers were fired and nearly 6,000 more chose to resign.

Attorney General Clark aided this effort by publishing a list of hundreds of potentially subversive organizations selected by criteria so vague that any views "hostile or inimical to the American form of government" (as Clark's assistants noted in a memo) could make an organization liable for investigation and prosecution. There was, moreover, no right of appeal.

Although designed primarily to screen federal employees, the attorney general's list effectively outlawed many political and social organizations, indirectly stigmatizing hundreds of thousands of individuals who had done nothing illegal. Church associations, civil rights organizations, musical groups, and even summer camps appeared on the list. Some, like the Civil Rights Congress, played important roles in defending imprisoned African Americans. Others, like the Jewish Music Alliance and Camp Kinderland, mainly served the cultural interests of Jewish Americans.

Membership in a listed group provided the rationale for dismissal at nearly every level of government. Fraternal and social institutions, especially popular among aging European immigrants of various nationalities, were among the largest organizations destroyed. The state of New York, for example, legally dismantled the International Workers' Order, which had provided insurance to nearly 200,000 immigrants and their families. Only a handful of organizations had the funds to challenge the listing legally; most simply closed their doors. Even past membership in a listed group—during the desperate 1930s many liberals had been briefly active in communist or communist-related movements—quickly became grounds for suspicion and likely dismissal. As a result, millions faced investigation and potential ruin.

In 1950 Congress overrode the president's veto to pass a bill that Truman called "the greatest danger to freedom of press, speech, and assembly since the Sedition Act of 1798." The Internal Security (McCarran) Act required communist organizations to register with the Subversive Activities Control Board and authorized the arrest of suspect persons during a national emergency. The Immigration and Nationality Act, sponsored by Republican senator Pat McCarran of Nevada and adopted in 1952, again over Truman's veto, barred people deemed "subversive" or "homosexual" from becoming citizens or even from visiting the United States. It also empowered the attorney general to deport immigrants who were members of communist organizations, even if they had become citizens. Challenged repeatedly on constitutional grounds, the Subversive Activities Control Board remained in place until 1973, when it was terminated.

The Red Scare in Hollywood

Anticommunist Democratic representative Martin Dies of Texas, who had chaired a congressional committee on "un-American activities" since 1938, told reporters at a press conference in Hollywood in 1944:

> Hollywood is the greatest source of revenue in this nation for the Communists and other subversive groups. . . . Two elements stand out in . . . the making of pictures which extoll foreign ideology—propaganda for a cause which seeks to spread its ideas to our people[,] and the "leftist" or radical screenwriters. . . . In my opinion, [motion picture executives] will do well to halt the propaganda pictures and eliminate every writer who has un-American ideas.

A few years later, Dies's successor, J. Parnell Thomas of New Jersey (later convicted and imprisoned for bribery), directed the committee to investigate supposed communist infiltration of the movie industry.

Renamed and made a permanent standing committee in 1945, the House Un-American Activities Committee (HUAC) conducted an investigation of the entertainment industry that was one of the most spectacular and troubling domestic antisubversive campaigns of the cold war. HUAC had the power to subpoena witnesses and to compel them to answer all questions or face contempt of Congress charges. The results were sometimes absurd. In well-publicized hearings held in Hollywood in October 1947, HUAC heard the mother of actress Ginger Rogers explain that her daughter, duped into appearing in the pro-Soviet wartime film *Tender Comrade (1943)*, "had been forced" to read the subversive line "Share and share alike, that's democracy." Conservative novelist Ayn Rand added that *The Song of Russia* (1944) had intentionally deceived the American public by showing Russians smiling! The committee found ample evidence of leftist sympathies but none of the subversive activity it alleged. Meanwhile, the studios announced that no writer, technician, or actor who refused to denounce communism would be employed again.

HUAC encouraged testimony by "friendly witnesses" such as Ronald Reagan and Gary Cooper. Barbara Stanwyck testified that her husband, Robert Taylor, another friendly witness, could not have been influenced by communist ideas because he never read books; he even prepared gourmet meals solely "from the pictures" in cookbooks. The committee intimidated many witnesses into naming suspect friends and coworkers in order to be cleared for future work in Hollywood. Only a few former communists, such as television superstar Lucille Ball, were too popular to be damaged by the bad publicity.

A small but prominent minority refused to cooperate with HUAC. By claiming the freedoms of speech and association guaranteed by the First and Sixth Amendments to the Constitution, they became known as "unfriendly witnesses." Many had worked in Hollywood films celebrating America's working people, a popular depression-era theme but now considered indicative of subversive intentions. During World War II, many of these same screenwriters and actors had teamed up on films attacking fascism. Among the most prominent "unfriendly witnesses" were actors Orson Welles, Zero Mostel, and Charlie Chaplin, and Oscar-winning screenwriter Ring Lardner Jr. Humphrey Bogart led a stars' delegation to "Defend the First Amendment" before Congress, but generated only headlines. A handful of dissenters served prison sentences for contempt of Congress. Meanwhile, the privately published *Red Channels: The Report of Communist Influence in Radio and Television* (1950) persuaded advertisers to cancel their accounts with many programs considered friendly to the Soviet Union, the United Nations, or liberal causes. Hollywood studios refused to employ any writer, director, or actor who refused to cooperate with HUAC. The resulting blacklist, which remained in effect until the 1960s, limited the production of films dealing directly with social or political issues.

Hollywood studios themselves played into the mounting fears, releasing by 1954 more than forty films with titles such as *I Married a Communist* (1950) and *The Red Menace* (1949) that sensationalized the communist threat. The television industry sponsored the dramatic series *The Hunter,* featuring the adventures of an American businessman fighting communist agents throughout the Free World. Few of these films or programs were popular, however.

Spy Cases

In August 1948, HUAC opened public hearings with a star witness: Whittaker Chambers, *Time* magazine editor and former communist, who confessed to spying for the Soviet Union during the 1930s. Chambers named as a fellow communist Alger Hiss, a veteran of Roosevelt's State Department, Roosevelt's adviser at Yalta, and at the time of the hearings president of the prestigious Carnegie Endowment for International Peace. After Hiss denied any affiliation with the Communist Party and proceeded to sue his accuser for slander, Chambers revealed a cache of microfilms of secret documents—hidden in a pumpkin patch on his farm in Maryland—he claimed Hiss had passed to him.

Republican representative Richard Nixon of California described this evidence as proof of "the most serious series of treasonable activities . . . in the history of America" but refused to allow anyone to examine the mysterious documents. (Many years later, the notorious "Pumpkin Papers" were revealed to be Bureau of Standards data, available in most public libraries.) Because a statute of limitations for espionage precluded a charge of treason, a federal grand jury in January 1950 convicted Hiss of perjury only (for denying he knew Chambers), and he received a five-year prison term.

Many Democrats, including Truman himself, at first dismissed the allegations against Hiss—conveniently publicized at the start of the 1948 election campaign—as a red herring, a Republican maneuver to convince the public that Democrats had allowed communists to infiltrate the federal government. Indeed, Nixon himself circulated a pamphlet entitled *The Hiss Case* to promote his candidacy for vice president. Two years later, Hiss was released from prison, still claiming his innocence.

The most dramatic spy case of the era involved Julius Rosenberg, former government engineer, and his wife, Ethel, who were accused of stealing and plotting

I Married a Communist, *movie poster,* 1950. *In this Hollywood movie, an evil subversive blackmails a shipping executive with a shady past, while fellow communists fool longshoremen into striking. This sensationalistic treatment of the "communist threat" merges the familiar image of the gangster with the malevolent Soviet Union. Like most anticommunist films,* I Married a Communist *was commercially unsuccessful.*

to convey atomic secrets to Soviet agents during World War II. The government's case against the Rosenbergs rested on the testimony of their supposed accomplices, some of them secretly coached by the FBI. In March 1951 a jury found them guilty of conspiring to commit espionage. The American press showed them no sympathy, but around the world the Rosenbergs were defended by citizens' committees and their convictions protested in large-scale demonstrations. Scientist Albert Einstein, the pope, and the president of France, among many prominent figures, all pleaded for clemency. The Rosenbergs maintained their innocence to the end, insisting they were being persecuted as Jews and for holding leftist political beliefs. They died in the electric chair on June 19, 1953.

McCarthyism

In a sensational Lincoln Day speech to the Republican Women's Club of Wheeling, West Virginia, on February 9, 1950, Republican senator Joseph R. McCarthy of Wisconsin announced that the United States had been sold out by the "traitorous actions of those who have been treated so well by the nation." These "bright young men who have been born with silver spoons in their mouths"—such as Secretary of State Dean Acheson, whom McCarthy called a "pompous diplomat in striped pants, with a phony English accent"—were part of a conspiracy, he charged, of more than 200 communists working in the State Department.

A few days later, after a drinking bout, McCarthy, pressed by reporters to name some of these alleged communists, said "I'm not going to tell you anything. I just want you to know I've got a pailful [of dirt] . . . and I'm going to use it where it does the most good." Actually, he had no names, and later investigations uncovered not a single communist in the State Department. But for several years, McCarthy issued wild accusations and led a flamboyant offensive against not only New Deal Democrats but the entire Truman administration for failing to defend the nation's security. Democrats were "soft on communism," he charged; they had "lost" China. His name has provided the label for the entire campaign to silence critics of the cold war: McCarthyism.

Behind the blitz of publicity—McCarthy's staff assistant, lawyer Roy Cohn, called it "showbiz"—the previously obscure junior senator from Wisconsin had struck a chord. Communism seemed to many Americans to be much more than a military threat—indeed, nothing less than a demonic force capable of undermining basic values. It compelled patriots to proclaim themselves ready for atomic warfare: "Better Dead Than Red." McCarthy also had help from the American Legion and the Chamber of Commerce, prominent religious leaders such as the Catholic Francis Cardinal Spellman, and union leaders wishing to consolidate their power by eliminating dissenters. Many of his fellow campaigners shared his deep resentment toward the east coast diplomatic elite who had come to power with the New Deal. McCarthyism, as a historian wrote at the time, was at least partly "the revenge of the noses that for 20 years of fancy parties were pressed against the outside window pane."

Ironically, however, the targets of McCarthyism were not members of the elite but groups with little political clout, such as African Americans, Jews, the foreign-born, and homosexuals. They were carefully chosen not so much for their political sympathies but because they would be too weak or fearful to strike back at their accusers. Civil rights organizations faced the severest persecution since the 1920s. The Civil Rights Congress and the Negro Youth Council, for instance, were destroyed after frequent charges of communist influence. W. E. B. Du Bois, the renowned African American historian, and famed concert singer (and former All-American football hero) Paul Robeson had public appearances canceled and their right to travel abroad abridged.

In attacks on women's organizations and homosexual groups, meanwhile, anticommunist rhetoric cloaked deep fears about changing sexual mores. HUAC published a pamphlet quoting a Columbia professor as saying that "girls' schools and women's colleges contain some of the most loyal disciples of Russia . . . often frustrated females." Republican Party chair Guy Gabrielson warned that "sexual perverts" who were possibly "as dangerous as actual Communists" had infiltrated the government. Aided by FBI reports, the federal government fired up to sixty homosexuals per month in the early 1950s. Dishonorable discharges from the U.S. armed forces for homosexuality, an administrative procedure without appeal, also increased dramatically, to 2,000 per year. Noted historian Arthur Schlesinger Jr., bitterly opposed to the former vice president Henry Wallace's crusade against the cold war, accused Wallace's supporters of wanting "something secret, sweaty and furtive," acting like "homosexuals in a boys' school." Critics of cold war policies, Schlesinger Jr. suggested, were not "real" men or, perhaps, "real" women either.

Hank Walker, *Life–Time Magazine*

The tables turned on Senator Joseph McCarthy (1908–57) after he instigated an investigation of the U.S. Army for harboring communists. A congressional committee then investigated McCarthy for attempting to make the Army grant special privileges to his staff aide, Private David Schine. During the televised hearings, Senator McCarthy—shown here with his staff assistant Roy Cohn—discredited himself. In December 1954, the Senate voted to censure him.

But much of this rhetoric was merely divisive opportunism, a ruthless attempt to gain power and fame by exploiting cold war fears. Although McCarthy's own chief aide, Roy Cohn, was himself a secret homosexual, and FBI director J. Edgar Hoover a secret transvestite, both used their influence to heighten anxieties about such "abnormal" or "perverted" orientations.

McCarthy succeeded in his campaign of intimidation partly because he brilliantly used the media to his own advantage. He also perfected the inquisitorial technique, asking directly, "Are you now, or have you ever been, a Communist?" By showing the press a blatantly doctored photo of Democratic senator Millard E. Tydings of Maryland talking with Soviet leaders, he helped defeat Tydings for reelection in 1950. When the distinguished liberal Republican Margaret Chase Smith of Maine appealed to fellow senators for support in a "Declaration of Conscience" against McCarthy's smear tactics, she secured only nine votes.

McCarthyism took hold so effectively because the way had been paved for it by the inflammatory rhetoric of the Truman Doctrine. Conservatives and liberals alike routinely compared communists to Satan or invasive bacteria, thereby promoting not only paranoia but hysteria. Attorney General J. Howard McGrath sounded a typical alarm in 1949: "Communists . . . are everywhere—in factories, offices, butcher shops, on street corners, in private businesses. . . . At this very moment [they are] busy at work—undermining your government, plotting to destroy the liberties of every citizen, and feverishly trying in whatever way they can, to aid the Soviet Union."

Joseph McCarthy and his fellow Red-hunters eventually burned themselves out. During televised congressional hearings in 1954, not only did McCarthy fail to prove wild charges of communist infiltration of the army but in the glare of the television cameras he appeared deranged. Cowed for years, the Senate finally condemned him for "conduct unbecoming a member." Although its energy was spent, McCarthyism left great damage in its wake. Many repressive state and federal laws remained in effect and basic freedoms of speech and assembly had been eroded. Dissent had become dangerous.

AGE OF ANXIETY

At the end of World War II, while much of the world lay in rubble, the United States began the longest, steadiest period of economic growth and prosperity in its history. "We have about 50 percent of the world's wealth," George Kennan noted in 1948, "but only 3.6 percent of its population." Very large pockets of poverty remained, and not all Americans benefited from the postwar abundance. Nonetheless, millions of Americans achieved middle-class status, often through programs subsidized by the federal government.

Prosperity did not dispel an anxious mood, fueled in part by the reality and the rhetoric of the cold war and nuclear proliferation. Many Americans also feared an economic backslide. If war production had ended the hardships of the Great Depression, how would the economy fare in peacetime? No one could say. Above all, peace itself seemed precarious. President Truman himself suggested that World War III appeared inevitable, and his secretary of state, Dean Acheson, warned the nation to keep "on permanent alert." McCarthyism raised the spectre of internal as well as distant enemies. To ease their apprehensions, many Americans turned their attention inward, focusing on a personal life they could understand and influence instead of the uncertainties of foreign affairs.

Even the ultimate symbol of postwar prosperity, the new home in the suburbs, reflected more than simple self-confidence. In 1950 the *New York Times* ran advertisements that captured a chilling quality of the boom in real estate: country properties for the Atomic Age located at least fifty miles outside major cities—the most likely targets, it was believed, of a Soviet nuclear attack. To protect their families in light of this possibility, not a few suburbanites built bomb shelters adjoining their homes. These underground structures reinforced with concrete and steel and outfitted with sufficient provisions to maintain a family for several weeks after an atomic explosion signaled a widespread anxiety about life in postwar American communities.

The Two-Income Family

The postwar prosperity propelling the suburban boom helped to strengthen the domestic ideal of the nuclear family. But many Americans also interpreted their rush toward marriage and parenthood, as one writer put it, as

DISTRIBUTION OF TOTAL PERSONAL INCOME AMONG VARIOUS SEGMENTS OF THE POPULATION, 1947–1970 (IN PERCENTAGES)*

Year	Poorest Fifth	Second Poorest Fifth	Middle Fifth	Second Wealthiest Fifth	Wealthiest Fifth	Wealthiest 5 Percent
1947	3.5	10.6	16.7	23.6	45.6	18.7
1950	3.1	10.5	17.3	24.1	45.0	18.2
1960	3.2	10.6	17.6	24.7	44.0	17.0
1970	3.6	10.3	17.2	24.7	44.1	16.9

Despite the general prosperity of the postwar era, the distribution of income remained essentially unchanged.

*Monetary income only.

Source: Adapted from U.S. Bureau of the Census, Historical Statistics of the United States, Colonial Times to 1970, Bicentennial ed. (Washington, D.C.: U.S. Government Printing Office, 1975), p. 292.

a "defense—an impregnable bulwark" against the anxieties of the era. Financial well-being could not in itself offset the insecurities provoked by the cold war.

Young couples were marrying younger and producing more children than at any time in the past century. The national fertility rate had reached an all-time low during the Great Depression, bottoming out in 1933 at 75 per 1,000 women. A decade later, after wartime production had revived the economy, the birth rate climbed to nearly 109 per 1,000 women. The U.S. Census Bureau predicted that this spurt would be temporary. To everyone's surprise, the birth rate continued to grow at a record pace, peaking at over 118 per 1,000 women in 1957. The "baby boom" lasted well into the 1960s.

This model is displaying the ideal kitchen of the 1950s. The "American way of life," defined as a high standard of living, was one of the tangible fruits of U.S. victory in World War II.

Postwar prosperity also sparked a spending spree of trailblazing proportions. "The year 1946," *Life* magazine proclaimed, "finds the U.S. on the threshold of marvels, ranging from runless stockings and shineless serge suits to jet-propelled airplanes that will flash across the country in just a little less than the speed of sound." The conversion from wartime to peacetime production took longer than many eager shoppers had hoped, but by 1950 the majority of Americans could own consumer durables, such as automatic washers, and small appliances, from do-it-yourself power tools to cameras. By the time Harry Truman left office two-thirds of all American households claimed at least one television set.

These two trends—the baby boom and high rates of consumer spending—encouraged a major change in the middle-class family. Having worked during World War II, often in occupations traditionally closed to them, many women wished to continue in full-time employment. Reconversion to peacetime production forced the majority from their factory positions, but most women quickly returned, taking jobs at a faster rate than men and providing half the total growth of the labor force. By 1952, 2 million more wives worked than during the war. Gone, however, were the high-paying unionized jobs in manufacturing. Instead, most women found minimum-wage jobs in the expanding service sector: clerical work, health care and education, and restaurant, hotel, and retail services. Mothers of young children were the most likely to be employed. "If it weren't for the children," one wife explained,

> I'd be tempted to try to get along on one salary, even if it meant skimping. But we need two incomes to enable us to have a house with a yard that the children can play in; to live in a neighborhood where I don't have to worry about their playmates; to provide a guitar for the musical one and dancing lessons for the one who needs to improve her muscular co-ordination—not to mention teeth-straightening and medical insurance and the bonds we are stowing away for their education.

Older women whose children were grown might work because they had come to value a job for its own sake. Younger women often worked for reasons of "economic necessity"—that is, to maintain a middle-class standard of living that now required more than one income.

Even though most women sought employment primarily to support their families, they ran up against popular opinion and expert advice urging them to return to their homes. Public opinion registered resounding disapproval—by 86 percent of those surveyed—of a married woman's working if jobs were scarce and her husband could support her. Commentators even appealed for a return to an imaginary "traditional" family, where men alone were breadwinners and women stayed happily at home, as a bulwark against communism. Noting that most Soviet women worked in industry, nervous writers insisted that American men and women must stop the spread of communism by playing complementary but utterly different roles. Just as the Truman Doctrine and the Marshall Plan responded to pitfalls abroad, the American family might limit, or "contain," dangers at home—if "restored" to its "traditional" form and function in the democratic nation.

This campaign began on a shrill note. Ferdinand Lundberg and Marynia Farnham, in their best-selling *Modern Woman: The Lost Sex* (1947), attributed the "super-jittery age in which we live" to women's abandonment of the home to pursue careers. To counter this trend, they proposed federally funded psychotherapy to readjust women to their housewifely roles and cash subsidies to encourage them to bear more children.

Articles in popular magazines, television shows, and high-profile experts chimed in with similar messages. Talcott Parsons, the distinguished Harvard sociologist, delineated the parameters of the "democratic" family: husbands served as breadwinners while wives—"the emotional hub of the family"—stayed home to care for their families. In the first edition of *Baby and Child Care* (1946), the child-rearing advice manual that soon outsold the Bible, Benjamin Spock similarly advised women to devote themselves full time, if financially possible, to their maternal responsibilities. "Women have many careers," another expert explained, "but only one vocation—motherhood."

Patterns of women's higher education reflected this conservative trend. Having made slight gains during World War II when college-age men were serving in the armed forces or working in war industries, women lost ground after the GI Bill created a huge upsurge in male enrollment. Women represented 40 percent of all college graduates in 1940 but only 25 percent a decade later. College administrators, disturbed by the trend toward women's employment, called for a new curriculum that would prepare women instead for marriage and motherhood. James Madison Wood, president of Stephens College in Columbia, Missouri, prescribed home economics as the foundation of women's higher education, with such curriculum highlights as child care and interior decoration. "The college years," he argued, "must be rehearsal periods for the major performance"—that is, for their roles as wives and mothers—of women's lives.

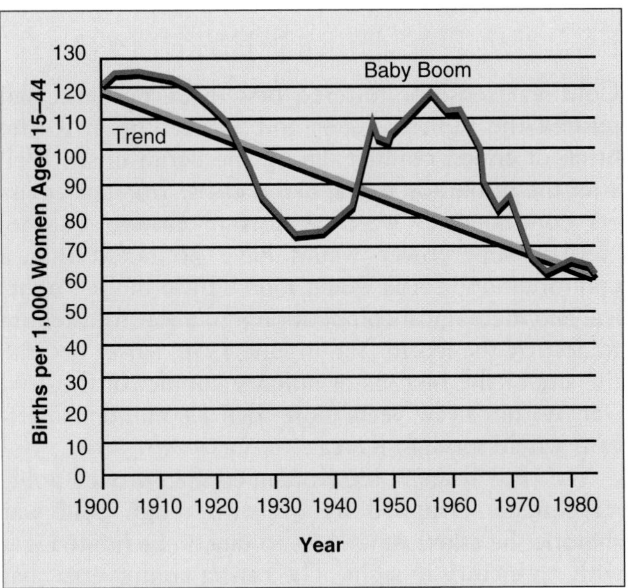

U.S. Birth Rate, 1930–1980 *The bulge of the "baby boom," a leading demographic factor in the postwar economy, stands out for this fifty-year period.*

These policies and prescriptions ran counter to the trend that was bringing ever more middle-class women into the workforce to help support their families. As early as 1947 *Life* magazine reflected an awareness of this conflict in a thirteen-page feature, "American Woman's Dilemma." How could women comfortably take part in a world beyond the home, the article asked, and at the same time heed the advice of FBI director J. Edgar Hoover, who exhorted the nation's women to fight "the twin enemies of freedom—crime and communism" by fulfilling their singular role as "homemakers and mothers"?

Religion and Education

Cold war fears helped to make Baptist Billy Graham one of the most popular evangelical ministers of the era and star of the first major televised "crusades" for religious revival. Born in Charlotte, North Carolina, in 1918, Graham had grown up believing that all doubts about the literal truth of the Bible were traps set by Satan. He gave a spiritual twist to cold war anxieties, warning against the decline of "God-centered homes" and the increased number of wives who tried to "wear the trousers" of the family. Moral contagion, juvenile delinquency, and communism could be halted only by what Graham called an "immediate decision for Christ." Politically, Graham aligned himself with the Republican Party and supported a large military budget to protect the United States, which he saw as the last hope of Christianity.

The message of anticommunism also permeated public education. In an era of higher education reshaped by the GI Bill, and of primary education expanding to meet the postwar baby boom, the nation invested more than funds in its school system. According to guidelines set down by the Truman administration, teachers were to "strengthen national security through education," specifically redesigning their lesson plans to illustrate the superiority of the American democratic system over

Soviet communism. In 1947 the federal Office of Education launched the "Zeal for Democracy" program for implementation by school boards nationwide. Meanwhile, schoolchildren were also taught to prepare themselves for a surprise Soviet attack by ducking under their desks and closing their eyes against the blinding light of a nuclear bomb.

Leading historians, such as Samuel Eliot Morison, insisted that fellow scholars shape their interpretations of the nation's past to highlight traditional values, especially the sanctity of private property. Richard Hofstadter's prize-winning *American Political Tradition* (1948) described in detail the uniquely American faith in "the economic virtues of capitalist culture as necessary qualities of man." Historians like Hofstadter portrayed earlier critics of this consensus, such as the populists, as mentally unbalanced and dangerous to American democracy.

Many teachers and students spurned these new educational programs and interpretations of American history. A fearless minority of scholars protested infringements on their academic freedom by refusing to sign loyalty oaths and by writing books pointing out the potential dangers of U.S. foreign and domestic policies of the cold war. But the chilling atmosphere, such as the political climate pervading the campus of the University of Washington, made many individuals more reluctant to express contrary opinions or ideas.

The Cultural Noir

Anxieties intensified by the cold war surfaced as major themes in popular culture. One of the most acclaimed Hollywood films of the era, the winner of nine Academy Awards, *The Best Years of Our Lives* (1946), followed the stories of three returning veterans as they tried to readjust to civilian life. The former soldiers found that the dreams of reunion with family and loved ones that had sustained them through years of fighting now seemed hollow. In some cases, their wives and children had become so self-reliant that the men had no clear function to perform in the household; in other cases, the prospect for employment appeared dim. The feeling of community shared with wartime buddies dissipated, leaving only a profound sense of loneliness.

The genre of film *noir* (French for "black") deepened this mood into an aesthetic. Movies like *Out of the Past, Detour,* and *They Live by Night* featured stories of ruthless fate and betrayal. Their protagonists were usually strangers or loners falsely accused of crimes or trapped into committing them. The high-contrast lighting of these black and white films accentuated the difficulty of distinguishing friend from foe. Feelings of frustration and loss of control came alive in tough, cynical characters played by actors such as Robert Mitchum and Robert Ryan. The Hollywood blacklist, however, soon barred many of the most talented directors and writers of *noir* films from further production.

Plays and novels also described alienation and anxiety in vivid terms. Playwright Arthur Miller, in *Death of a Salesman* (1949), sketched an exacting portrait of self-destructive individualism. Willy Loman, the play's hero, is obsessively devoted to his career in sales but nevertheless a miserable failure. Worse, he has trained his sons to excel in personal presentation and style—the very methods prescribed by standard American success manuals—making them both shallow and materialistic. J. D. Salinger's widely praised novel *Catcher in the Rye* (1951) explored the mental anguish of a teenage boy estranged from the crass materialism of his parents.

Cold war anxiety manifested itself in a flurry of unidentified flying object (UFO) sightings. Thousands of Americans imagined that a communistlike invasion from outer space was already under way, or they hoped that superior creatures might arrive to show the way to world peace. The U.S. Air Force discounted the sightings of flying saucers, but dozens of private researchers and faddists claimed to have been contacted by aliens. Hollywood films fed these beliefs. The popular movie *The Day the Earth Stood Still* (1951) delivered a message of world peace in which a godlike being implores earthlings to abandon their weaponry before they destroy the planet. Other popular science fiction films carried a different message. In *The Invasion of the Body Snatchers* (1956), for example, a small town is captured by aliens who take over the minds of its inhabitants when they fall asleep, a subtle warning against apathy toward the threat of communist "subversion."

END OF THE DEMOCRATIC ERA

Cold war tensions festered first in Europe and had pushed the United States and Soviet Union to the brink of armed conflict during the Berlin crisis. Well after the resolution of the Berlin crisis, Truman's advisers continued to watch events in eastern Europe. Neither superpower would have predicted that a confrontation in Asia would soon transform their political and ideological competition into a war threatening to destroy the world. Yet, in June 1950, Korea became the site of the first major military conflict of the cold war. Within a few years more than 1.8 million Americans would serve in Korea.

For Truman, the Korean conflict proved political suicide. Trapped by his own tough cold war rhetoric, he asked Americans to sanction a limited war with no victory in sight. The raging controversy that followed Truman's actions in Korea ended the twenty-year Democratic lock on the presidency and the greatest era of reform in U.S. history.

American soldiers fought in Korea under the command of General Douglas MacArthur until President Truman named General Matthew Ridgway as his replacement in April 1951. Nearly 1.8 million Americans served in Korea.

The Korean War

On June 25, 1950, President Truman was called back to Washington, D.C., from his home in Independence, Missouri. The State Department had just received a cablegram reporting a military attack on South Korea by communist-controlled North Korea. Secretary of State Acheson immediately set up an emergency meeting of the UN Security Council to request action. Determined to carve a niche in history by "being tough" on communists, Truman now had to live up to his promise.

Korea, a colony of Japan since 1910, had been divided along its 38th parallel between U.S. and Soviet forces following the Axis defeat in 1945, making its two halves into zones of occupation cold war-style. By mid-1949, the two superpowers had withdrawn from the small peninsula, leaving their respective dependent governments in charge. In the South (the Republic of Korea) the United States backed the unpopular dictatorship of Syngman Rhee, while the Soviet Union sponsored a communist government in North Korea (the Democratic People's Republic of Korea) under Kim Il Sung.

Some experienced diplomats such as George Kennan regarded the conflict between the two Koreas as a civil war. Truman, however, treated the invasion as a major Soviet test of the U.S. policy of containment, an act of aggression that had to be met with force. "Korea is the Greece of the Far East," the president announced. "If we are tough enough now, if we stand up to them like we did in Greece three years ago, they won't take any next steps," he explained. The Soviets, on the other hand, regarded the invasion as the consequence of former anti-Japanese military leader Kim Il Sung's plan to overthrow a government of past collaborators with the Japanese and unite the two Koreas. While supplying military equipment, Moscow insisted that it had neither ordered nor directed the attack. Having recently been accused of "selling out" eastern Europe and "losing" China, Truman felt compelled to act.

Three days after the invasion, the president sought approval from the UN Security Council to send in troops. Due to a boycott of the Council by the Soviet delegate, who could have vetoed the decision, the Security Council agreed. Two-thirds of Americans polled approved the president's decision to send troops under the command of General Douglas MacArthur.

Military events seemed at first to justify the president's decision. Seoul, the capital of South Korea, had fallen to North Korean troops within weeks of the invasion, and communist forces continued to push south until they had taken most of the peninsula. The situation appeared grim until Truman authorized MacArthur to carry out an amphibious landing at Inchon, which he did on September 15, 1950. With tactical brilliance and good fortune, the general orchestrated a military campaign that halted the communist drive. By October, UN troops had retaken South Korea.

Basking in victory, the Truman administration could not resist the temptation to expand its war aims. Hoping to prove that Democrats were not soft on communism, the president and his advisers decided to roll back the communists beyond the 38th parallel to

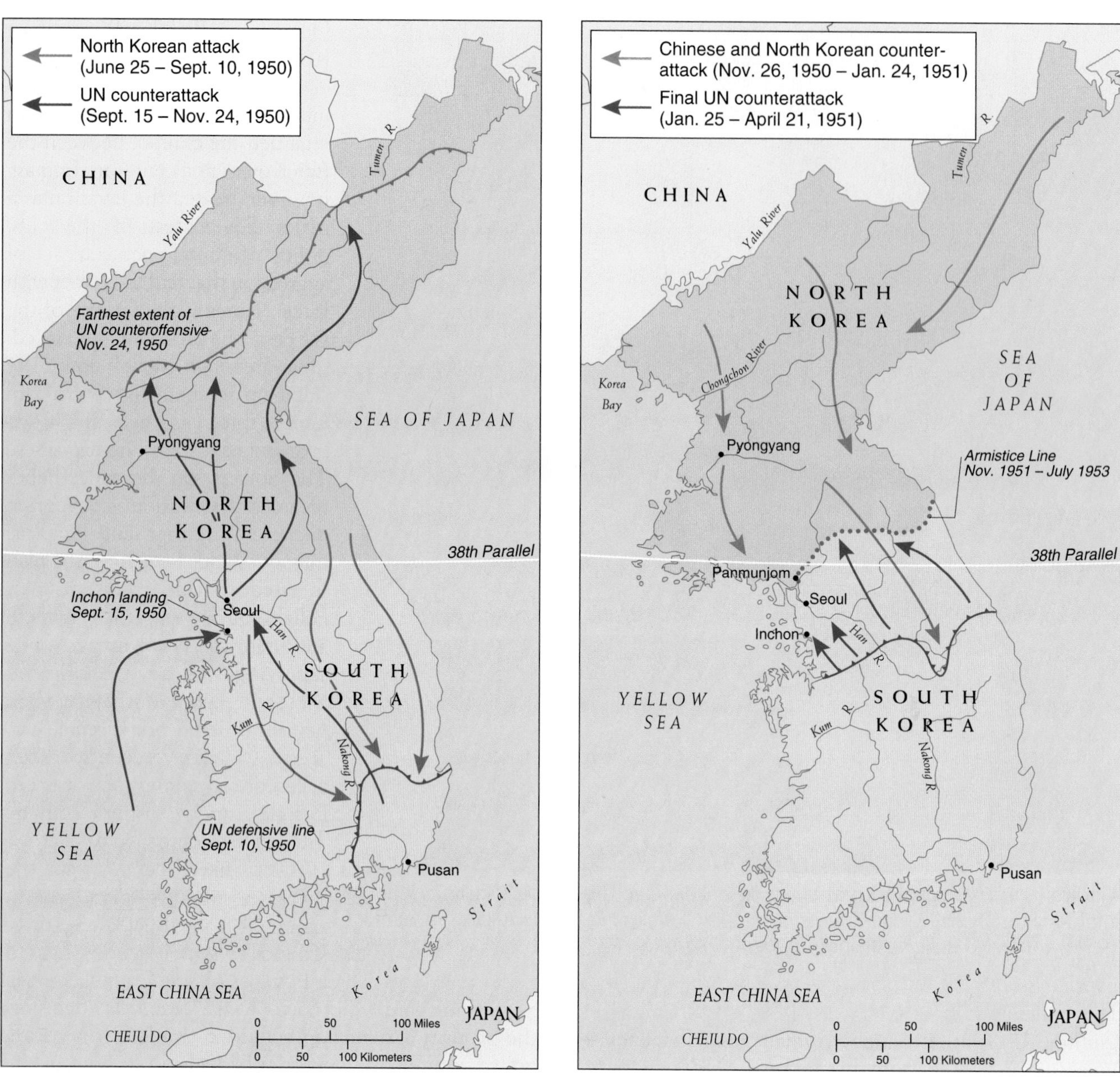

The Korean War *The intensity of battles underscored the strategic importance of Korea in the cold war.*

the Chinese border and thereby reunite Korea as a showcase for democracy. Until this point, China had not been actively involved in the war. But it now warned that any attempt to cross the dividing line would be interpreted as a threat to its national security. Truman flew to Wake Island in the Pacific on October 15 for a conference with MacArthur, who assured the president of a speedy victory, promising to have the UN troops "home by Christmas."

Overconfident, MacArthur had sorely miscalculated. Chinese premier Zhou Enlai ordered Chinese troops to mass at the Yalu River. Suddenly, and without any air support, the Chinese attacked on November 26. MacArthur's force was all but crushed. European allies warned against escalation, and White House officials debated using the atomic bomb. The Chinese drove the UN troops back into South Korea, where they regrouped and in March began pushing back to the 38th parallel. By summer 1951, a stalemate had been reached very near the old border. Negotiations for a settlement went on for the next eighteen months amid heavy fighting.

"There is no substitute for victory," MacArthur insisted as he tried without success to convince Truman to prepare for a new invasion of communist territory. Encouraged by strong support at home, he continued to provoke the president by speaking out against official policy, calling for bombing of supply lines in China and a naval blockade of the Chinese coast—actions certain to lead to a Chinese-American war. Finally, on April 10, 1951, Truman dismissed MacArthur for insubordination and other unauthorized activities. As General Omar N. Bradley later remarked, MacArthur had proposed "the wrong war, at the wrong place and at the wrong time, and with the wrong enemy." He had also placed himself above the civilian commander in chief of the armed forces.

The Legacy of "The Sour Little War"

The Korean War had profound implications for the use of executive power. By instituting a peacetime draft in 1948 and then ordering American troops into Korea, Truman had bypassed congressional authority. Senator Robert Taft called the president's actions "a complete usurpation" of democratic checks and balances. Truman sidestepped such criticisms and their constitutional implications by carefully referring to the military deployment not as a U.S. war but as a UN-sanctioned "police action."

The president derived his authority from NSC-68, a paper adopted by the National Security Council in April 1950 that reinterpreted the basic policy of containment as well as decision making at the highest levels of government. Describing communism as "a new fanatic faith" that "seeks to impose its absolute authority over the rest of the world," NSC-68 pledged the United States not only to drive back communist influence wherever it appeared but also to "foster the seeds of destruction within the Soviet Union." As Dean Acheson observed later, NSC-68 was the new "fundamental" paper of U.S. foreign policy. Its use demonstrated, one historian observed, a "centralization of power" in which the entire government "had literally been compressed or consolidated into the President and his like-minded appointees."

The Korean War, which permitted Truman to activate NSC-68, also provided the president the public rationale for a rapid and permanent military buildup, including the allocation of at least 20 percent of the gross national product to national defense. Between 1950 and 1953, when the conflict subsided, military spending rose from $13 billion to more than $50 billion annually. By 1952 the U.S. Army had grown to 3.6 million, or six times its size at the beginning of the conflict. At the same time, the federal government accelerated the development of nuclear bombs and weapons, including the first hydrogen, or H, bomb, which was tested in November 1952. By the time it ended, the war had cost the United States approximately $100 billion.

The outcome of the Korean War did nothing to improve Truman's case for rolling back communism. Negotiations and fighting proceeded in tandem until the summer of 1953, when a settlement was reached in which both North Korea and South Korea occupied almost the same territory as when the war began. Approximately 54,000 Americans died in Korea; the North Koreans and Chinese lost well over 2 million people. The UN troops had employed both "carpet bombing" (intense, destructive attack on a given area) and napalm (jellied gasoline bombs), destroying most of the housing and food supplies in both Koreas. True to the pattern of modern warfare, which emerged during World War II, the majority of civilians killed were women and children. Nearly 1 million Koreans were left homeless.

For the United States, the Korean War extended the principle of containment far beyond Europe and enlarged the geographical range of the cold war to include East Asia. The war also lined up the People's Republic of China and the United States as unwavering enemies for the next twenty years and heightened the U.S. commitment to Southeast Asia. Now, as one historian commented, the "frontiers on every continent were going to remain frontiers in the traditional American meaning of a frontier—a region to penetrate and control and police and civilize."

The Korean War, moreover, did much to establish an ominous tradition of "unwinnable" conflicts that left many Americans skeptical of official policy. Truman had initially rallied popular support for U.S. intervention by contrasting the communist North with the "democratic" South, thus casting the conflict in the ideological terms of the cold war. MacArthur's early victories had promised the liberation of North Korea and even the eventual disintegration of the Soviet and Chinese regimes. But with the tactical stalemate came mass disillusionment.

In retrospect many Americans recognized that Truman, in fighting communism in Korea, had pledged the United States to defend a corrupt government and a brutal dictator. Decades later the Korean War inspired the dark comedy *M*A*S*H*, adapted for television from the film written by Hollywood screenwriter Ring Lardner Jr., an "unfriendly witness" before HUAC who was jailed during the Korean War for contempt of Congress. As late as 1990, members of Congress were still debating the terms of a Korean War memorial. "It ended on a sad note for Americans," one historian has concluded, "and the war and its memories drifted off into a void."

Truman's Downfall

There was only one burning issue during the election campaign of 1952: the Korean War. Opinion polls indicated widespread frustration with Truman's conduct of the war. Although respondents did not know what they wanted instead—an invasion of China, as MacArthur had planned, or an immediate withdrawal of U.S.

troops—they were clearly angry at the leader who had created the bloody deadlock.

Truman's popularity had wavered continually since he took office in 1945, but it sank to an all-time low in the early 1950s shortly after he dismissed MacArthur as commander of the UN troops in Korea. The White House received thousands of letters and telegrams calling for Truman's impeachment. If Congress did not get rid of the Truman-Acheson team, McCarthy roared, "Asia, the Pacific and Europe may be lost to Communism" and "Red waters may lap at all of our shores." MacArthur, meanwhile, returned home a hero, welcomed by more than 7 million fans in New York City alone.

Richard Nixon used the new medium of television to convince American voters that he had not established an illegal slush fund in his campaign for the vice presidency in 1952. Viewers responded enthusiastically to his melodramatic delivery and swamped the Republican campaign headquarters with telegrams endorsing his candidacy.

A furious but short-lived MacArthur-for-president campaign began. On April 19, 1951, MacArthur gave an impassioned address to a joint session of the Congress. Legislators, many with tears in their eyes, gave him a standing ovation. But over the next two months, as the Senate Armed Services and Foreign Relations Committees conducted joint hearings about MacArthur's dismissal, the general's popularity rapidly fell. George Marshall, Omar Bradley, and the Joint Chiefs all testified that they had never subscribed to MacArthur's strategy for the war. Moreover, in light of General MacArthur's challenge to presidential authority, they believed that there had been "no other course but to relieve him" of his duties in Korea.

While discrediting MacArthur, the hearings also revealed the extent of popular dissatisfaction with Truman. Newspapers reported that officials in his administration had been dealing in kickbacks for government contracts, just the kind of corruption that critics had predicted when Truman replaced veteran New Dealers with his political cronies. Business and organized labor complained about the price and wage freezes imposed during the Korean War. A late-1951 Gallup poll showed the president's approval rating at 23 percent. In early 1952, Truman announced he would not run for reelection, a decision rare for a president eligible for another term.

Truman left the Democratic Party in disarray. The Democrats' best hope for victory now lay in convincing Dwight Eisenhower to run on the Democratic ticket, although his reputation as a moderate conservative suggested no continuity with party traditions. When Eisenhower politely refused their offers, Democratic leaders turned to the popular but uncharismatic governor of Illinois, Adlai E. Stevenson Jr.

Admired for his honesty and intelligence, Stevenson offered no solutions to the conflict in Korea, the accelerating arms race, or the cold war generally. Accepting the Democratic nomination, Stevenson candidly admitted that "the ordeal of the twentieth century is far from over," a prospect displeasing to voters aching for peace.

The Republicans made the most of the Democrats' dilemma. Without proposing any sweeping answers of their own, they pointed to all the obvious shortcomings of their opponents. The Korean stasis dovetailed with the "K_1C_2"—Korea, communism, and corruption—line of attack on the Democratic administration. Traditional Republican conservatives wanted to nominate Robert Taft, shrewd critic of Truman's "imperial" presidency and author of the antilabor Taft-Hartley Act. But when opinion polls showed that Dwight Eisenhower possessed an "unprecedented" 64 percent approval rating, and when "Ike" allowed himself to be "drafted" for the Republican nomination, his candidacy was certain.

Eisenhower styled himself the moderate. He wisely avoided the negative impressions made by the unsuccessful 1948 Republican candidate, Thomas

CHRONOLOGY

1941	Henry Luce forecasts the dawn of "the American Century"
1944	GI Bill of Rights benefits World War II veterans
	International Monetary Fund and World Bank founded
1945	Franklin D. Roosevelt dies in office; Harry S. Truman becomes president
	United Nations charter signed
	World War II ends
	Strike wave begins
	Truman proposes program of economic reforms
1946	Employment Act creates Council of Economic Advisers
	Churchill's Iron Curtain speech
	Atomic Energy Act establishes Atomic Energy Commission
	Republicans win control of Congress
	Benjamin Spock publishes *Baby and Child Care*
1947	Americans for Democratic Action founded
	Truman Doctrine announced; Congress appropriates $400 million in aid for Greece and Turkey
	Federal Employees Loyalty and Security Program established and attorney general's list of subersive organizations authorized
	Marshall Plan announced
	Taft-Hartley Act restricts union activities
	National Security Act establishes Department of Defense, the National Security Council, and the Central Intelligence Agency
	House Un-American Activities Committee hearings in Hollywood
1948	Ferdinand Lundberg and Marynia Farnham publish *Modern Woman: The Lost Sex*
	State of Israel founded
	Berlin blockade begins
	Henry Wallace nominated for president on Progressive Party ticket
	Truman announces peacetime draft and desegregates U.S. armed forces and civil service
	Truman wins election; Democrats sweep both houses of Congress
1949	Truman announces Fair Deal
	North Atlantic Treaty Organization (NATO) created
	Communists led by Mao Zedong take power in China
	Berlin blockade ends
	Soviet Union explodes atomic bomb
1950	Alger Hiss convicted of perjury
	Senator Joseph McCarthy begins anticommunist crusade
	Soviet Union and the People's Republic of China sign an alliance
	Adoption of NSC-68 consolidates presidential war powers
	Korean War begins
	Internal Security (McCarran) Act requires registration of communist organizations and arrest of communists during national emergencies
1951	Truman dismisses General Douglas MacArthur
	Armistice talks begin in Korea
1952	Immigration and Nationality Act retains quota system, lifts ban on immigration of Asian and Pacific peoples, but bans "subversives" and homosexuals
	United States explodes first hydrogen bomb
	Dwight D. Eisenhower wins presidency; Richard Nixon becomes vice president
1953	Julius and Ethel Rosenberg executed for atomic espionage
	Armistice ends fighting in Korea
1954	Army-McCarthy hearings end
1955	Warsaw Pact created

Dewey, who had seemed as aggressive as Truman on foreign policy and simultaneously eager to overturn the New Deal domestic legislation. Eisenhower knew better: voters wanted peace and government-assisted prosperity. He neither threatened to widen the war nor supported the stalemate created by Truman. Eisenhower promised instead "an early and honorable" peace and avoided questions of finance or the economy. His advisers warned him: "The chief reason that people want to vote for you is because they think you have more ability to keep us out of another war."

Meanwhile, Eisenhower's vice-presidential candidate, Richard Nixon, waged a relentless and defamatory attack on Stevenson, calling him "Adlai the Appeaser" and the "Ph.D. graduate of Dean Acheson's cowardly College of Communist Containment." Senator Joseph McCarthy chimed in, proclaiming that with club in hand he might be able to make "a good American" of Stevenson. A month before the election, McCarthy went on network television with his requisite "exhibits" and "documents," this time purportedly showing that the Democratic presidential candidate had promoted communism at home and abroad. These outrageous charges kept the Stevenson campaign off balance.

The Republican campaign was itself not entirely free of scandal: the vice-presidential candidate had been caught accepting personal gifts from wealthy benefactors. Nixon chose to plead his case on national television. Describing his wife Pat's "good Republican cloth coat" and their modest style of living, he contritely admitted that he had indeed accepted one gift, a puppy named Checkers that his daughters loved and that he refused to give back. "The Poor Richard Show," as critics called the event, defused the scandal without answering the most important charges.

Eisenhower, meanwhile, continued to enchant the voters as a peace candidate. Ten days before the election he dramatically announced, "I shall go to Korea" to settle the war. Eisenhower received 55 percent of the vote and carried thirty-nine states, in part because he brought out an unusually large number of voters in normally Democratic areas. He won the popular vote in much of the South and in the northern cities of New York, Chicago, Boston, and Cleveland. The New Deal coalition of ethnic and black voters, labor, northern liberals, and southern conservatives no longer commanded a majority. But the victory was most clearly a sign of Eisenhower's own popularity. Riding his coattails, the Republicans regained control of Congress, but their margin in the Senate was only one seat.

CONCLUSION

Dwight Eisenhower's election diminished the intensity of the cold war mood without actually halting the conflict. "The Eisenhower Movement," wrote Walter Lippmann, was a "mission in American politics" to restore a sense of community among the American people. In a larger sense, many of the issues of the immediate post–World War II years seemed to have been settled, or put off for a distant future. The international boundaries of communism were frozen with the Chinese Revolution, the Berlin blockade, and now the Korean War. Meanwhile, at home cold war defense spending had become a permanent part of the national budget, an undeniable drain on tax revenues but an important element in the government contribution to economic prosperity. If the nuclear arms race remained a cause for anxiety, joined by more personal worries about the changing patterns of family life, a sense of relative security nevertheless spread. Prospects for world peace had dimmed, but the worst nightmares of the 1940s had eased as well.

REVIEW QUESTIONS

1. Discuss the origins of the cold war and the sources of growing tensions between the United States and the Soviet Union at the close of World War II.
2. Describe the basic elements of President Harry Truman's policy of containment. How did the threat of atomic warfare affect this policy?
3. Compare the presidencies of Franklin D. Roosevelt and Harry S. Truman, both Democrats.
4. Describe the impact of McCarthyism on American political life. How did the anticommunist campaigns affect the media? What were the sources of Senator Joseph McCarthy's popularity? What brought about his downfall?
5. How did the cold war affect American culture?
6. Discuss the role of the United States in Korea in the decade after World War II. How did the Korean War affect the 1952 presidential election?
7. Why did Dwight D. Eisenhower win the 1952 presidential election?

RECOMMENDED READING

Warren I. Cohen, *America in the Age of Soviet Power, 1945–1991* (1993). A volume in the "Cambridge History of American Foreign Relations" series, this study examines the origins of the cold war in policies ending World War II, including the breakup of the colonial empires, and concludes with the collapse of communism in the Soviet Union.

Martin Bauml Duberman, *Paul Robeson* (1988). A biography of the renowned African American singer and actor who was driven from the stage for political reasons. Duberman shows Robeson as a great artist but also a self-conscious representative of black rights who felt compelled to oppose U.S. foreign policy and suddenly lost his public career as a result.

Townsend Hoopes and Douglas Brinkley, *FDR and the Creation of the U.N.* (1997). A concise account of the founding the United Nations, from Franklin D. Roosevelt—whose "initiative and determination" laid the groundwork for the world organization—to Harry Truman.

Joyce Kolko and Gabriel Kolko, *The Limits of Power: The World and United States Foreign Policy, 1945–1954* (1972). A detailed commentary arguing that U.S. efforts to control the post-war world were thwarted by the complexities of international politics, especially the efforts of colonized nations to gain independence.

George Lipsitz, *A Rainbow at Midnight: Labor and Culture in the 1940s* (1994). A vivid account of economic and cultural hopes, uneasiness, and disappointments after World War II. Lipsitz shows how struggles for economic democracy were defeated and how popular culture—for example, country-and-western music and rock 'n' roll, as well as stock car racing and roller derby—arose in blue-collar communities.

Elaine Tyler May, *Homeward Bound: American Families in the Cold War Era* (1988). A lively account of the effects on family life and women's roles of the national mood of "containment." May argues that government policy became part of a popular culture that solidified the cold war era's "feminine mystique."

David G. McCullough, *Truman* (1992). An uncritical rendition of Truman's personal life and political career. Through personal correspondence and other documents, McCullough details Truman's view of himself and the generally favorable view of him held by supporters of cold war liberalism.

Patrick McGilligan and Paul Buhle, *Tender Comrades: A Backstory of the Hollywood Blacklist* (1997). A collection of interviews with thirty-five victims of the Hollywood Blacklist, including some of the most important writers, directors, and film stars. The collection is especially valuable for its detailing of film production during the years of World War II and afterward, including the creation of *film noir*.

Joanne Meyerowitz, ed., *Not June Cleaver: Women and Gender in Postwar America, 1945–1960* (1994). A collection of essays that refute the common stereotype of women as homebound during the postwar era.

Victor S. Navasky, *Naming Names* (1980). A fascinating account of government informants, McCarthyism, and the blacklist. Navasky presents especially interesting treatments of academic life, where blacklisting had only a slight impact, and Hollywood, where McCarthyism changed American popular culture.

David M. Oshinsky, *A Conspiracy So Immense: The World of Joe McCarthy* (1983). A study of McCarthyism that presents a keen view of McCarthy as a product of his background and the political conditions of the time, as well as a clever politician who found widespread support in the Republican Party.

Daniel Yergin, *Shattered Peace: The Origins of the Cold War and the National Security State* (1977). A lucid analysis of the motives of the Americans and the Soviets that led to a full-scale arms race. Yergin argues that each side misinterpreted the motives of the other and thereby lost the opportunity to attain world peace.

ADDITIONAL BIBLIOGRAPHY

Global Insecurities and the Policy of Containment

H. W. Brands Jr., *The Devil We Knew: Americans and the Cold War* (1993)

Robert Frazier, *Anglo-American Relations with Greece: The Coming of the Cold War, 1942–47* (1991)

James L. Gormly, *The Collapse of the Grand Alliance, 1945–1948* (1987)

Burton Hersh, *The Old Boys: The American Elite and the Origins of the CIA* (1992)

Michael J. Hogan, *The Marshall Plan* (1987)

Timothy P. Ireland, *Creating the Entangling Alliance: The Origins of NATO* (1981)

Bruce R. Kuniholm, *The Origins of the Cold War in the Near East* (1980)

Walter LeFeber, *America, Russia, and the Cold War, 1945–1980*, 7th ed. (1993)
Robert L. Messer, *The End of an Alliance: James F. Byrnes, Roosevelt, Truman, and the Origins of the Cold War* (1982)
Thomas G. Paterson, *Meeting the Communist Threat* (1988)
Michael Schaller, *American Occupation of Japan: The Origins of the Cold War in Asia* (1985)
Telford Taylor, *The Anatomy of the Nuremberg Trials: A Personal Memoir* (1992)
Imanuel Wexler, *The Marshall Plan Revisited* (1983)

The Truman Presidency

Jack Ballard, *Shock of Peace* (1983)
Andrew J. Dunar, *The Truman Scandals and the Politics of Morality* (1984)
Melvyn P. Leffler, *A Preponderance of Power: National Security, the Truman Administration, and the Cold War* (1992)
Donald McCoy, *The Presidency of Harry S. Truman* (1984)
Gary W. Reichard, *Politics as Usual* (1988)

The Cold War at Home

Michael R. Belknap, *Cold War Political Justice: The Smith Act, the Communist Party, and American Civil Liberties* (1977)
David Callahan, *Dangerous Capabilities: Paul Nitze and the Cold War* (1990)
Larry Ceplair and Steven Englund, *The Inquisition in Hollywood: Politics in the Film Community, 1930–1960* (1980)
Sigmund Diamond, *Compromised Campus: The Collaboration of Universities with the Intelligence Communities, 1945–1995* (1992)
Richard M. Freeland, *The Truman Doctrine and the Origins of McCarthyism* (1972, 1985)
Richard M. Fried, *Nighmare in Red* (1990)
Robert Griffith, *The Politics of Fear: Joseph R. McCarthy and the Senate*, 2d ed. (1987)
Mike Nielson and Gene Mailes, *Hollywood's Other Blacklist: Union Struggles in the Studio System* (1996)
Kenneth O'Reilly, *Hoover and the Un-Americans: The FBI, HUAC, and the Red Menace* (1983)
Ellen W. Schrecker, *No Ivory Tower: McCarthyism in the Universities* (1988)

Age of Anxiety

Michael Barson, *"Better Dead Than Red!" A Nostalgic Look at the Golden Years of Russiaphobia, Red-Baiting, and Other Commie Madness* (1992)
Paul Boyer, *By the Bomb's Early Light: American Thought and Culture at the Dawn of the Atomic Age* (1985)
Ann Fagan Ginger and David Christian, eds., *The Cold War against Labor: An Anthology* (1987)
Fred Inglis, *The Cruel Peace: Everyday Life in the Cold War* (1991)
Stuart W. Leslie, *The Cold War and American Science* (1993)
J. Fred MacDonald, *Television and the Red Menace* (1985)
Lary May, ed., *Recasting America: Culture and Politics in the Age of the Cold War* (1989)
Richard G. Powers, *G-Men: Hoover's FBI in American Popular Culture* (1983)
Andrews Ross, *No Respect: Intellectuals and Popular Culture* (1989)
Leila Rupp and Verta Taylor, *Survival in the Doldrums: The American Women's Rights Movement, 1945 to the 1960s* (1987)
Nora Sayre, *Running Time: Films of the Cold War* (1982)
Arlene Skolnick, *Embattled Paradise: The American Family in an Age of Uncertainty* (1991)

Korean War

Albert Cowdrey, *The Medics' War* (1987)
Bruce Cumings, *The Origins of the Korean War* (1981)
Rosemary Foot, *The Wrong War* (1985)
Jon Halliday and Bruce Cumings, *Korea* (1988)
D. Clayton James, *Refighting the Last War: Command and Crisis in Korea, 1950–1953* (1992)
John Toland, *In Mortal Combat: Korea, 1950–1953* (1992)

Biography

Curt Gentry, *J. Edgar Hoover: The Man and the Secrets* (1991)
Wilson D. Miscamble, *George F. Kennan and the Making of American Foreign Policy, 1947–1950* (1992)
Robert P. Newman, *Owen Lattimore and the "Loss" of China* (1992)
Michael Schaller, *Douglas MacArthur* (1989)
Athan G. Theoharis and John Stuart Cox, *The Boss: J. Edgar Hoover and the Great American Inquisition* (1988)

CHAPTER TWENTY-SEVEN

AMERICA AT MIDCENTURY

1952–1963

Andy Warhol, *Campbell's Soup Can*. Saatchi Collection, London/A.K.G., Berlin/Superstock.

CHAPTER OUTLINE

AMERICAN COMMUNITIES
Popular Music in Memphis

The nineteen-year-old singer was peering nervously out over the large crowd. He knew that people had come to Overton Park's outdoor amphitheater that hot, sticky July day in 1954 to hear the headliner, country music star Slim Whitman. Sun Records, a local Memphis label, had just released the teenager's first record, and it had begun to receive some airplay on local radio. But the singer and his two bandmates had never played in a setting even remotely as large as this one. And their music defied categories: it wasn't black and it wasn't white; it wasn't pop and it wasn't country. But when the singer launched into his version of a black blues song called "That's All Right," the crowd went wild. "I came offstage," the singer later recalled, "and my manager told me that they was hollering because I was wiggling my legs. I went back out for an encore, and I did a little more, and the more I did, the wilder they went." Elvis Presley had arrived.

Elvis combined a hard-driving, rhythmic approach to blues and country music with a riveting performance style, inventing the new music known as rock 'n' roll. An unprecedented cultural phenomenon, rock 'n' roll was a music made largely for and by teenagers. In communities all over America, rock 'n' roll brought teens together around jukeboxes, at sock hops, in cars, and at private parties. It demonstrated the enormous consumer power of American teens. Rock 'n' roll also embodied a postwar trend accelerating the integration of white and black music. This cultural integration prefigured the social and political integration won by the civil rights movement.

Located halfway between St. Louis and New Orleans on the Mississippi River, Memphis had become a thriving commercial city by the 1850s, with an economy centered on the lucrative cotton trade of the surrounding delta region. It grew rapidly in the post–Civil War years, attracting a polyglot population of white businessmen and planters, poor rural whites and blacks, and German and Irish immigrants. By the early twentieth century Memphis also boasted a remarkable diversity of popular theater and music, including a large opera house, numerous brass bands, vaudeville and burlesque, minstrel shows, jug bands, and blues clubs.

Like most American cities, Memphis enjoyed healthy growth during World War II, with lumber mills, furniture factories, and chemical manufacturing supplementing the cotton market as sources of jobs and prosperity. And like the rest of the South, Memphis was a legally segregated city; whites and blacks lived, went to school, and worked apart. Class differences among whites were important as well. Like thousands of other poor rural whites in these years, Elvis Presley had moved from Mississippi to Memphis in 1949, where his father found work in a munitions plant. The Presleys were poor enough to qualify for an apartment in Lauderdale Courts, a Memphis public housing project. To James Conaway, who grew up in an all-white, middle-class East Memphis neighborhood, people like the

Presleys were "white trash." Negroes, he recalled, were "not necessarily below the rank of a country boy like Elvis, but of another universe, and yet there was more affection for them than for some whites."

Gloria Wade-Gayles, who lived in the all-black Foote Homes housing project, vividly remembered that her family and neighbors "had no illusion about their lack of power, but they believed in their strength." For them, strength grew from total immersion in a black community that included ministers, teachers, insurance men, morticians, barbers, and entertainers. "Surviving meant being black, and being black meant believing in our humanity, and retaining it, in a world that denied we had it in the first place."

Yet in the cultural realm, class and racial barriers could be challenged. Elvis Presley grew up a dreamy, shy boy, who turned to music for emotional release and spiritual expression. He soaked up the wide range of music styles available in Memphis. The Assembly of God Church his family attended featured a renowned hundred-voice choir. Elvis and his friends went to marathon all-night "gospel singings" at Ellis Auditorium, where they enjoyed the tight harmonies and emotional style of white gospel quartets.

Elvis also drew from the sounds he heard on Beale Street, the main black thoroughfare of Memphis and one of the nation's most influential centers of African American music. In the postwar years, local black rhythm and blues artists like B. B. King, Junior Parker, and Muddy Waters attracted legions of black and white fans with their emotional power and exciting showmanship. At the Handy Theater on Beale Street, the teenaged Elvis Presley, like thousands of other white young people, heard black performers at the "Midnight Rambles"—late shows for white people only. Elvis himself performed along with black contestants in amateur shows at Beale Street's Palace Theater. Nat D. Williams, a prominent black Memphis disc jockey and music promoter, recalled how black audiences responded to Elvis's unique style. "He had a way of singing the blues that was distinctive. He could sing 'em not necessarily like a Negro, but he didn't sing 'em altogether like a typical white musician. . . . Always he had that certain humanness about him that Negroes like to put in their songs."

The expansion of the broadcasting and recording industries in the postwar years also contributed to the weakening of racial barriers in the musical realm. Two Memphis radio stations featured the hard-driving rhythm and blues music that was beginning to attract a strong following among young white listeners. These Memphis stations also featured spirituals by African American artists such as Mahalia Jackson and Clara Ward.

Elvis himself understood his debt to black music and black performers. "The colored folks," he told an interviewer in 1956, "been singing and playing it just like I'm doing now, man, for more years than I know. They played it like that in the shanties and in their juke joints and nobody paid it no mind until I goosed it up. I got it from them."

Dissatisfied with the cloying pop music of the day, white teenagers across the nation were increasingly turning to the rhythmic drive and emotional intensity of black rhythm and blues. They quickly adopted rock 'n' roll (the term had long been an African American slang expression for dancing and sexual intercourse) as their music. But it was more than just music: it was also an attitude, a celebration of being young, and a sense of having something that adult authority could not understand or control.

When Sun Records sold Presley's contract to RCA Records in 1956, Elvis became an international star. Records like "Heartbreak Hotel," "Don't Be Cruel," and "Jailhouse Rock" shot to the top of the charts and blurred the old boundaries between pop, country, and rhythm and blues. By helping to accustom white teenagers to the style and sound of black artists, Elvis helped establish rock 'n' roll as an interracial phenomenon. Institutional racism would continue to plague the music business—many black artists were routinely cheated out of royalties and severely underpaid—but the music of postwar Memphis at least pointed the way toward the exciting cultural possibilities that could emerge from breaking down the barriers of race. It also gave postwar American teenagers a newfound sense of community.

Memphis

KEY TOPICS

- Post–World War II prosperity
- Suburban life: ideal and reality
- The emergence of youth culture
- Television, mass culture, and their critics
- Foreign policy in the Eisenhower years
- John F. Kennedy and the promise of a New Frontier

AMERICAN SOCIETY AT MIDCENTURY

With the title of his influential work, *The Affluent Society* (1958), economist John Kenneth Galbraith gave a label to postwar America. Galbraith observed that American capitalism had worked "quite brilliantly" in the years since World War II. But Americans, he argued, needed to spend less on personal consumption and devote more public funds to schools, medical care, cultural activities, and social services. For most Americans, however, strong economic growth was the defining fact of the postwar period. A fierce desire for consumer goods and the "good life" imbued American culture, and the deeply held popular belief in a continuously expanding economy and a steadily increasing standard of living—together with the tensions of the cold war—shaped American social and political life.

The Eisenhower Presidency

Dwight D. Eisenhower's landslide election victory in 1952 set the stage for the first full two-term Republican presidency since that of Ulysses S. Grant. At the core of Eisenhower's political philosophy lay a conservative vision of community. He saw America as a corporate commonwealth, similar to the "associative state" envisioned by Herbert Hoover a generation earlier (see Chapter 23). Eisenhower believed the industrial strife, high inflation, and fierce partisan politics of the Truman years could be corrected only through cooperation, self-restraint, and disinterested public service. As president, Eisenhower emphasized limiting the New Deal trends that had expanded federal power, and he encouraged a voluntary, as opposed to regulatory, relationship between government and business. Social harmony and "the good life" at home were closely linked, in his view, to maintaining a stable and American-led international order abroad.

Eisenhower viewed his leadership style as crucial for achieving the goal of a harmonious, corporate-led society. That style owed something to his roots in turn-of-the-century Kansas and his socialization in the military. In the army he had risen through the command structure by playing it safe, keeping his own counsel, and allowing his subordinates to apprise him of his options. He once described his views on leadership to a critic: "It's persuasion—and conciliation—and patience. It's long, slow, tough work. That's the only kind of leadership I know or believe in—or will practice."

Consciously, Eisenhower adopted an evasive style in public, and he was fond of the phrase "middle of the road." He told a news conference, "I feel pretty good when I'm attacked from both sides. It makes me more certain I'm on the right track." Intellectuals and liberals found it easy to satirize Eisenhower for his blandness, his frequent verbal gaffes, his vagueness, and his often contradictory pronouncements. The majority of the American public, however, evidently agreed with Eisenhower's easygoing approach to his office. He kept the conservative and liberal wings of his party united and appealed to many Democrats and independents.

Eisenhower wanted to run government in a businesslike manner while letting the states and corporate interests guide domestic policy and the economy. He appointed nine businessmen to his first cabinet, including three with ties to General Motors. Former GM chief Charles Wilson served as secretary of defense and epitomized the administration's economic views with his famous aphorism "What's good for General Motors business is good for America." In his appointments to the Federal Trade Commission, the Federal Communications Commission, and the Federal Power Commission, Eisenhower favored men congenial to the corporate interests they were charged with regulating. Eisenhower also secured passage of the Submerged Lands Act in 1953, which transferred $40 billion worth of disputed offshore oil lands from the federal government to the Gulf states. This transfer ensured a greater role for the states and private companies in the oil business—and cost the Treasury billions in lost revenues.

In the long run, the Eisenhower administration's lax approach to government regulation accelerated a trend toward the destruction of the natural environment. Oil exploration in Louisiana's bayous, for example, began the massive degradation of America's largest wetlands. Water diversion policies in Florida seriously damaged the biggest tropical forest in the United States. The increased use of toxic chemicals, begun during World War II and largely unregulated by law, placed warehouses of poisons in hundreds of sites, many abutting military installations. Virtually unregulated use and disposal of the pesticide DDT poisoned birds and other animals and left permanent toxic scars in the environment.

At the same time, Eisenhower accepted the New Deal legacy of greater federal responsibility for social welfare. He rejected calls from conservative Republicans, for example, to dismantle the Social Security system. His administration agreed to a modest expansion of Social Security and unemployment insurance and small increases in the minimum wage. Ike also created the Department of Health, Education and Welfare, appointing Oveta Culp Hobby as its secretary, making her the second woman to hold a cabinet post. In agriculture, Eisenhower continued the policy of parity payments designed to sustain farm prices. Between 1952 and 1960, federal spending on agriculture jumped from about $1 billion to $7 billion.

This photo, which appeared in a 1950 issue of Life Magazine, *posed a family of pioneer suburbanites in front of their* Levittown, New York, *home. The prefabricated house was built in* 1948.

Eisenhower proved hesitant to use fiscal policy to pump up the economy, which went into recession after the Korean War ended in 1953 and again in 1958, when the unemployment rate reached 7.5 percent. The administration refused to cut taxes or increase spending to stimulate growth. Eisenhower feared starting an inflationary spiral more than he worried about unemployment or poverty. By the time he left office, he could proudly point out that real wages for an average family had risen 20 percent during his term. With low inflation and steady, if modest, growth, the Eisenhower years brought greater prosperity to most Americans. Long after he retired from public life, Ike liked to remember his major achievement as having created "an atmosphere of greater serenity and mutual confidence."

Subsidizing Prosperity

During the Eisenhower years the federal government played a crucial role in subsidizing programs that helped millions of Americans achieve middle-class status. Federal aid helped people to buy homes, attend college and technical schools, and live in newly built suburbs. Much of this assistance expanded on programs begun during the New Deal and World War II. The Federal Housing Administration (FHA), established in 1934, extended the government's role in subsidizing the housing industry. The FHA insured long-term mortgage loans made by private lenders for home building. By putting the full faith and credit of the federal government behind residential mortgages, the FHA attracted new private capital into home building and revolutionized the industry. A typical FHA mortgage required less than 10 percent for a down payment and spread low-interest monthly payments over thirty years.

Yet FHA policies also had long-range drawbacks. FHA insurance went overwhelmingly to new residential developments, usually on the fringes of urban areas, hastening the decline of older, inner-city neighborhoods. A bias toward suburban, middle-class communities manifested itself in several ways: it was FHA policy to favor the construction of single-family projects while discouraging multi-unit housing, to refuse loans for the repair of older structures and rental units, and to require for any loan guarantee an "unbiased professional estimate" rating the property, the prospective borrower, and the neighborhood. In practice, these estimates resulted in blatant discrimination against communities that were racially mixed. The FHA's Underwriting Manual bluntly warned: "If a neighborhood is to retain stability, it is necessary that properties shall continue to be occupied by the same social and racial classes." FHA policies in effect inscribed the racial and income segregation of suburbia in public policy.

Wife and children of the typical white, middle-class family greet the breadwinning father arriving home from work. Such images, which appeared frequently in popular magazines, idealized the home as the safe haven from the tensions of the office and enshrined the family as the source of happiness and security.

The majority of suburbs were built as planned communities. One of the first was Levittown, which opened in Hempstead, Long Island, in 1947, on 1,500 acres of former potato fields. Developer William Levitt, who described his firm as "the General Motors of the housing industry," was the first entrepreneur to bring mass-production techniques to home building. All building materials were precut and prefabricated at a central factory, then assembled on-site into houses by largely unskilled, nonunion labor. In this way Levitt put up hundreds of identical houses each week. Eventually, Levittown encompassed more than 17,000 houses and 82,000 people. Yet in 1960 not one of Levittown's residents was African American.

The revolution in American life wrought by the 1944 Servicemen's Readjustment Act, known as the GI Bill of Rights, extended beyond its impact on higher education (see Chapter 26). In addition to educational grants, the act provided returning veterans with low-interest mortgages and business loans, thus subsidizing the growth of the suburbs as well as the postwar expansion of higher education. Through 1956, nearly 10 million veterans received tuition and training benefits under the act. VA-insured loans totaled more than $50 billion by 1962, providing assistance to millions of former GIs who started businesses.

The Federal Highway Act of 1956 gave another key boost to postwar growth, especially in the suburbs. It originally authorized $32 billion for the construction of a national interstate highway system. Financing was to come from new taxes on gasoline, as well as on oil, tires, buses, and trucks. Key to this ambitious program's success was that these revenues were held separately from general taxes in a Highway Trust Fund. By 1972 the program had become the single largest public works program in American history; 41,000 miles of highway were built at a cost of $76 billion. Federal subsidy of the interstate highway system stimulated both the automobile industry and suburb building. But it also accelerated the decline of American mass transit and older cities. By 1970, the nation possessed the world's best roads and one of its worst public transportation systems.

The shadow of the cold war prompted the federal government to take new initiatives in aid for education. After the Soviet Union launched its first Sputnik satellite in the fall of 1957, American officials worried that the country might be lagging behind the

Soviets in training scientists and engineers. The Eisenhower administration, with the bipartisan support of Congress, pledged to strengthen support for educating American students in mathematics, science, and technology. The National Defense Education Act (NDEA) of 1958 allocated $280 million in grants—tied to matching grants from the states—for state universities to upgrade their science facilities. The NDEA also created $300 million in low-interest loans for college students, who had to repay only half the amount if they went on to teach in elementary or secondary school after graduation. In addition, the NDEA provided fellowship support for graduate students planning to go into college and university teaching. The NDEA represented a new consensus on the importance of high-quality education to the national interest.

Suburban Life

The suburban boom strengthened the domestic ideal of the nuclear family as the model for American life. In particular, the picture of the perfect suburban wife—efficient, patient, always charming—became a dominant image in television, movies, and magazines. Suburban domesticity was usually presented as women's only path to happiness and fulfillment. This cultural image often masked a stifling existence defined by housework, child care, and boredom. In the late 1950s Betty Friedan, a wife, mother, and journalist, began a systematic survey of her Smith College classmates. She found "a strange discrepancy between the reality of our lives as women and the image to which we were trying to conform." Friedan expanded her research and in 1963 published *The Feminine Mystique*, a landmark book that articulated the frustrations of suburban women and helped to launch a revived feminist movement.

The postwar rebirth of religious life was strongly associated with suburban living. In 1940 less than half the American population belonged to institutionalized churches; by the mid-1950s nearly three-quarters identified themselves as church members. A church-building boom was centered in the expanding suburbs. Best-selling religious authors such as Norman Vincent Peale and Bishop Fulton J. Sheen offered a shallow blend of reassurance and "the power of positive thinking." They stressed individual solutions to problems, opposing social or political activism. Their emphasis on the importance of belonging, of fitting in, meshed well with suburban social life and the ideal of family-centered domesticity.

California came to embody postwar suburban life. At the center of this lifestyle was the automobile. Cars were a necessity for commuting to work. California also led the nation in the development of drive-in facilities: motels, movies, shopping malls, fast-food restaurants, and banks. More than 500 miles of highways would be constructed around Los Angeles alone. In Orange County, southeast of Los Angeles, the "centerless city" emerged as the dominant form of community. The experience of one woman resident was typical: "I live in Garden Grove, work in Irvine, shop in Santa Ana, go to the dentist in Anaheim, my husband works in Long Beach, and I used to be the president of the League of Women Voters in Fullerton."

Contemporary journalists, novelists, and social scientists contributed to the popular image of suburban life as essentially dull, conformist, and peopled exclusively by the educated middle class. John Cheever, for example, won the National Book Award for *The Wapshot Chronicle* (1957), a novel set in fictional Remsen Park, "a community of four thousand identical homes." Psychiatrist Richard Gordon's *Split Level Trap* (1960) focused on the emotional problems he observed among the suburban families of Bergen County, New Jersey. Yet these writers tended to obscure the real class and ethnic differences found among and between suburban communities. Many new suburbs had a distinctively blue-collar cast. Milpitas, California, for example, grew up around a Ford auto plant about fifty miles outside San Jose. Its residents were blue-collar assembly line workers and their families rather than salaried, college-educated, white-

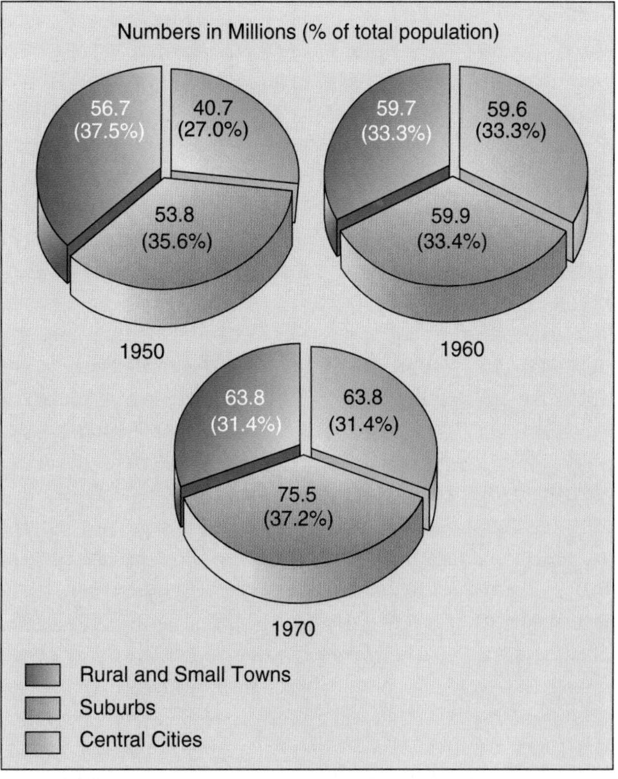

The Growth of the Suburbs, 1950–1970 *Suburban growth, at the expense of older inner cities, was one of the key social trends in the twenty-five years following World War II. By 1970, more Americans lived in suburbs than in either inner cities or rural areas.*

Source: Adapted from U.S. Bureau of the Census, *Current Censuses, 1930–1970* (Washington, D.C.: U.S. Government Printing Office, 1975).

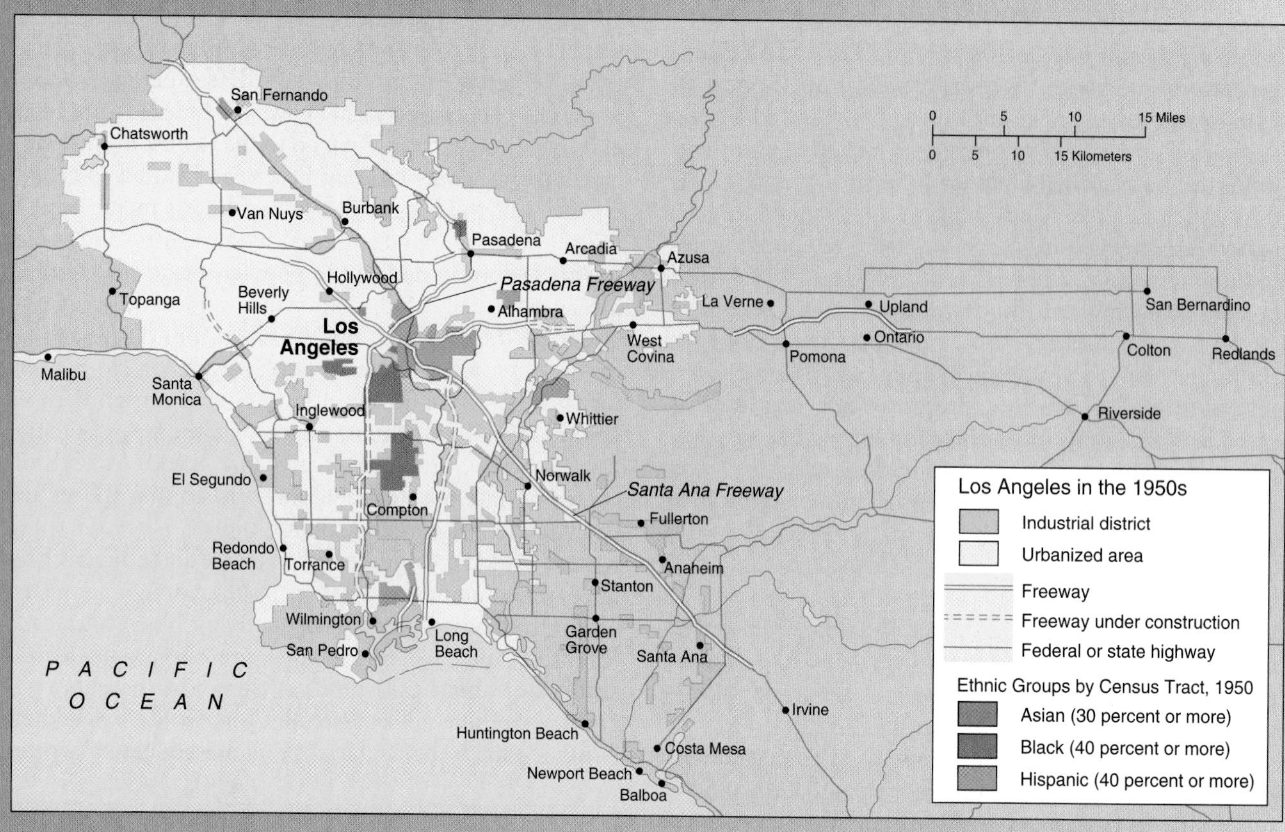

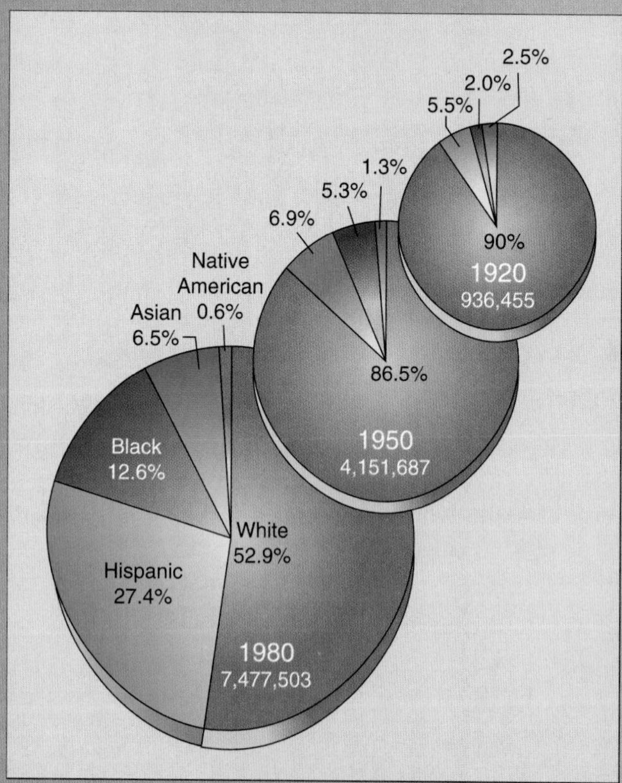

L. A. County Population

The Changing Face of Postwar Los Angeles

Los Angeles epitomized two postwar American trends: the rapid growth of western cities and the rapid expansion of the suburbs. Spurred by government funding, it boasted the highest per capita ownership of both private homes and automobiles of any American city. Federal tax policies subsidized home ownership, and loan guarantees through the Federal Housing Administration and the Veterans Administration made home mortgages available to millions. The state's Collier-Burns Act of 1947 committed gasoline taxes and auto registration fees to building a high-speed freeway system in metropolitan Los Angeles. The Federal Highway Act of 1956 supplemented these funds by incorporating some of the freeways into the national highway system. By 1960 Los Angeles had 250 miles of freeways. By the 1970s, about two-thirds of downtown Los Angeles was devoted to the automobile.

Postwar Los Angeles also evolved into one of the most ethnically diverse cities in the nation. What had been an overwhelmingly white Protestant population began to change during World War II with the influx of African American, Mexican, and Indian factory workers. By the 1970s Korean, Filipino, Vietnamese, and other Asian immigrants, along with newcomers from Mexico and Central America, had radically altered the city's ethnic character. But Los Angeles neighborhoods and suburbs remained largely segregated by race and ethnicity.

collar employees. Self-segregation and zoning ordinances gave some new suburbs as distinctively Italian, Jewish, or Irish ethnic identities as older urban neighborhoods. For millions of new suburbanites, architectural and psychological conformity was an acceptable price to pay for the comforts of home ownership, a small plot of land, and a sense of security and status.

Lonely Crowds and Organization Men

Perhaps the most ambitious and controversial critique of postwar suburban America was sociologist David Riesman's *The Lonely Crowd* (1950). Riesman argued that modern America had given birth to a new kind of character type, the "other-directed" man. Previously the nation had cultivated "inner-directed" people—self-reliant individualists who early on in life had internalized self-discipline and moral standards. By contrast, the "other-directed" person typical of the modern era was peer-oriented. Morality and ideals came from the overarching desire to conform. Americans, Riesman thought, were now less likely to take risks or act independently. Their thinking and habits had come to be determined by cues they received from the mass media.

Similarly, William H. Whyte's *Organization Man* (1956), a study of the Chicago suburb of Park Forest, offered a picture of people obsessed with fitting into their communities and jobs. In place of the old Protestant ethic of hard work, thrift, and competitive struggle, Whyte believed, middle-class suburbanites now strived mainly for a comfortable, secure niche in the system. They held to a new social ethic, he argued: "a belief in the group as the source of creativity; a belief in 'belongingness' as the ultimate need of the individual." Sloan Wilson's *Man in the Grey Flannel Suit,* a 1955 best-seller, featured a hero who rejects the top position at his firm. His boss sympathizes with this reluctance to sacrifice, telling him, "There are plenty of good positions where it's not necessary for a man to put in an unusual amount of work."

The most radical critic of postwar society, and the one with the most enduring influence, was Texas-reared sociologist C. Wright Mills. In *White Collar* (1951), Mills analyzed the job culture that typified life for middle-class salaried employees, office workers, and bureaucrats. "When white collar people get jobs," he wrote, "they sell not only their time and energy, but their personalities as well. They sell by the week or month their smiles and their kindly gestures, and they must practice the prompt repression of resentment and aggression." In *The Power Elite* (1956), Mills argued that a small, interconnected group of corporate executives, military men, and political leaders had come to dominate American society. The arms race in particular, carried out in the name of cold war policies, had given an unprecedented degree of power to the military-industrial complex.

The Expansion of Higher Education

American higher education experienced rapid growth after the war. This expansion both reflected and reinforced other trends in postwar society. The number of students enrolled in colleges and universities climbed from 2.6 million in 1950 to 3.2 million in 1960. It then more than doubled—to 7.5 million—by 1970, as the baby boom generation came of age. Most of these new students attended greatly enlarged state university systems. Main campuses at state universities in Michigan, Wisconsin, California, and other states grew bigger than ever, enrolling as many as 40,000 students. Technical colleges and "normal schools" (designed originally for the training of teachers) were upgraded and expanded into full-fledged universities, as in the branches of the State University of New York, founded in 1948.

Several factors contributed to this explosion. A variety of new federal programs, including the GI Bill and the National Defense Education Act, helped subsidize college education for millions of new students. Government spending on research and development in universities, especially for defense-related projects, pumped further resources into higher education. Much of this money supported programs in graduate work, reflecting an important postwar shift in the priorities of American universities. Graduate education and faculty research now challenged traditional undergraduate teaching as the main locus of university activity and power.

Colleges and universities by and large accepted the values of postwar corporate culture. By the mid-1950s, 20 percent of all college graduates majored in business or other commercial fields. The college degree was a gateway to the middle class. It became a requirement for a whole range of expanding white-collar occupations in banking, insurance, real estate, advertising and marketing, and other corporate enterprises. As much as educating young people, colleges trained them for careers in technical, professional, and management positions. Most administrators accommodated large business interests, which were well represented on university boards of trustees. Universities themselves were increasingly run like businesses, with administrators adopting the language of input-output, cost effectiveness, and quality control.

Researchers found college students in the 1950s generally absorbed the conventions and attitudes associated with working in a corporate environment. A typical Iowa State student told one writer, "You have to be very careful not to associate with the wrong clan of people, an introvert that isn't socially acceptable, guys who dress in the fashion of ten years ago. These people are just not accepted—and, if you associate with them, you're not accepted either."

Health and Medicine

Dramatic improvements in medical care allowed many Americans to enjoy longer and healthier lives. During the war the federal government had poured unprecedented amounts of money into medical research and the diffusion of new techniques. The armed forces had immunized and treated millions of servicemen and women for diseases ranging from syphilis to tuberculosis. New antibiotics such as penicillin were manufactured and distributed on a mass basis, and after the war they became widely available to the general population. Federal support for research continued after the war with the reorganization of the National Institutes of Health in 1948. Federal agencies, led by the National Institute of Mental Health, founded in 1949, also expanded research on and treatment of mental illness.

By 1960 many dreaded epidemic diseases, such as tuberculosis, diphtheria, whooping cough, and measles, had virtually disappeared from American life. Perhaps the most celebrated achievement of postwar medicine was the victory over poliomyelitis. Between 1947 and 1951 this disease, which usually crippled those it did not kill, struck an annual average of 39,000 Americans. In 1952, 58,000 cases, most of them children, were reported. Frightened parents warned children to stay away from crowded swimming pools and other gathering places. In 1955 Jonas Salk pioneered the first effective vaccine against the disease, using a preparation of killed virus. A nationwide program of polio vaccination, later supplemented by the oral Sabin vaccine, virtually eliminated polio by the 1960s.

Yet the benefits of "wonder drugs" and advanced medical techniques were not shared equally by all Americans. More sophisticated treatments and expensive new hospital facilities sharply increased the costs of health care. The very poor and many elderly Americans found themselves unable to afford modern medicine. Thousands of communities, especially in rural areas and small towns, lacked doctors or decent hospital facilities. Critics of the medical establishment charged that the proliferation of medical specialists and large hospital complexes had increased the number of unnecessary surgical operations, especially for women and children. The decline of the general practitioner—the family doctor—meant fewer physicians made house calls; more and more people went to hospital emergency rooms or outpatient clinics for treatment. Unreasonable faith in sophisticated medical technologies also contributed to the proliferation of iatrogenic ailments—sickness brought on by treatment for some other illness.

The American Medical Association (AMA), which certified medical schools, did nothing to increase the flow of new doctors. The number of physicians per 100,000 people actually declined between 1950 and 1960; the shortage was made up by doctors trained in other countries. The AMA also lobbied hard against efforts to expand government responsibility for the public's health. President Harry Truman had advanced a plan for national health insurance, to be run along the lines of Social Security. President Dwight Eisenhower had proposed a program that would offer government assistance to private health insurance companies. The AMA denounced both proposals as "socialized medicine." It helped block direct federal involvement in health care until the creation of Medicare (for the elderly) and Medicaid (for the poor) in 1965.

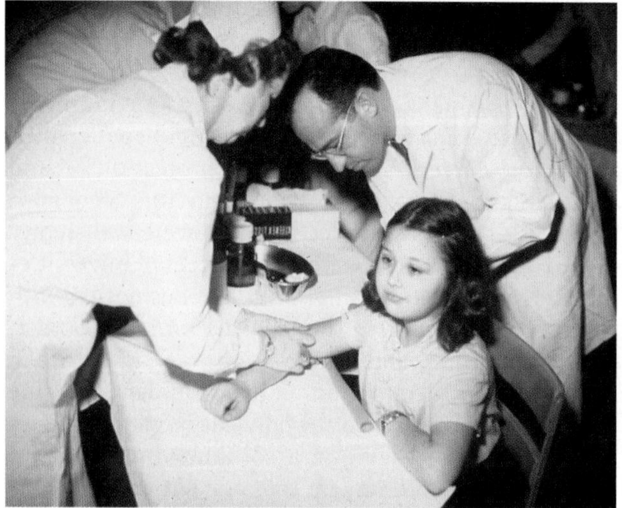

Dr. Jonas E. Salk and nurse administered polio vaccine to Pauline Antloger, a student at Sunnyside School in Pittsburgh, 1955. Dr. Salk's scientific breakthrough of a killed-virus polio vaccine led to an array of viral vaccines to cure other diseases, such as hepatitis.

YOUTH CULTURE

The term "teenager," describing someone between thirteen and nineteen, entered standard usage only at the end of World War II. According to the *Dictionary of American Slang*, the United States is the only country with a word for this age group and the only country to consider it "a separate entity whose influence, fads, and fashions are worthy of discussion apart from the adult world." The fifteen years following World War II saw unprecedented attention to America's adolescents. Deep fears were expressed about everything from teenage sexuality and juvenile delinquency to young people's driving habits, hairstyles, and choice of clothing. At the same time, advertisers and businesses pursued the disposable income of America's affluent youth with a vengeance. Teenagers often found themselves caught between their desire to carve out their own separate sphere and the pressure to become an adult as quickly as possible.

The Youth Market

Birth rates had accelerated gradually during the late 1930s and more rapidly during the war years. The children born in those years had by the late 1950s grown into the original teenagers, the older siblings of the celebrated baby boom of 1946–64. They came of age in a society that, compared with that of their parents and the rest of the world, was uniquely affluent. Together, the demographic growth of teens and the postwar economic expansion created a burgeoning youth market. Manufacturers and advertisers rushed to cash in on the special needs and desires of young consumers: cosmetics, clothing, radios and phonographs, and cars.

Before Elvis Presley became the ultimate teen idol, his life in Memphis mirrored the experiences of millions of American teenagers. In high school he was an average student at best, and he took part-time jobs to help out the family; after graduation he worked as a truck driver and as an electrician's helper. He enjoyed making the rounds of movies, roller rinks, and burger joints with his friends, and he dreamed of owning his own Cadillac. Like many teens, Elvis obsessed over the latest stylish clothing—which he could not afford. He could often be found haunting the shop windows at the Lansky Brothers clothing store on Beale Street in Memphis.

In 1959, *Life* summarized the new power of the youth market. "Counting only what is spent to satisfy their special teenage demands," the magazine reported, "the youngsters and their parents will shell out about $10 billion this year, a billion more than the total sales of GM." In addition, advertisers and market researchers found that teenagers often played a critical, if hard-to-measure, role as "secret persuaders" in a family's large purchases. Specialized market research organizations, such as Eugene Gilbert & Company and Teen-Age Survey Incorporated, sprang up to serve business clients eager to attract teen consumers and instill brand loyalty. Through the 1950s and into the 1960s, teenagers had a major, sometimes dominant, voice in determining America's cultural fads.

To many parents, the emerging youth culture was a dangerous threat to their authority. One mother summarized this fear in a revealing, if slightly hysterical, letter to *Modern Teen*:

> Don't you realize what you are doing? You are encouraging teenagers to write to each other, which keeps them from doing their school work and other chores. You are encouraging them to kiss and have physical contact before they're even engaged, which is morally wrong and you know it. You are encouraging them to have faith in the depraved individuals who make rock and roll records when it's common knowledge that ninety per cent of these rock and roll singers are people with no morals or sense of values.

The increasing uniformity of public school education also contributed to the public recognition of the special status of teenagers. In 1900, about one of every eight teenagers was in school; by the 1950s, the figure was six out of eight. Psychologists wrote guidebooks for parents, two prominent examples being Dorothy Baruch's *How to Live with Your Teenager* (1953) and Paul Landis's *Understanding Teenagers* (1955). Social scientists stressed the importance of peer pressure for understanding teen behavior. "The teenage group," Landis observed in *Understanding Teenagers*, "is self sufficient now as in no previous generation." The larger point here is that traditional sources of adult authority and socialization—the marketplace, schools, child-rearing manuals, the mass media—all reinforced the notion of teenagers as a special community, united by age, rank, and status.

"Hail! Hail! Rock 'n' Roll!"

The demands of the new teen market, combined with structural changes in the postwar American mass media, reshaped the nation's popular music. As television broadcasting rapidly replaced radio as the center of family entertainment, people began using radios in new ways. The production of portable transistor radios and car radios grew rapidly in the 1950s as listeners increasingly tuned them in for diversion from or an accompaniment to other activities. Locally produced radio shows, featuring music, news, and disc jockeys, replaced the old star-studded network programs. By 1956, 2,700 AM radio stations were on the air across the United States, with about 70 percent of their broadcast time given to record shows. Most of these concentrated on popular music for the traditional white adult market: pop ballads, novelty songs, and show tunes.

In the recording industry, meanwhile, a change was in the air. Small independent record labels led the way in aggressively recording African American rhythm and blues artists. Atlantic, in New York, developed the most influential galaxy of artists, including Ray Charles, Ruth Brown, the Drifters, Joe Turner, LaVerne Baker, and the Clovers. Chess, in Chicago, had the blues-based singer-songwriter-guitarists Chuck Berry and Bo Diddley and the "doo-wop" group the Moonglows. In New Orleans, Imperial had the veteran pianist-singer Fats Domino, while Specialty unleashed the outrageous Little Richard on the world. On radio, over jukeboxes, and in record stores, all of these African American artists "crossed over," adding millions of white teenagers to their solid base of black fans.

The older, more established record companies, such as RCA, Decca, M-G-M, and Capitol, had largely ignored black music. Their response to the new trend was to offer slick, toned-down "cover" versions by white pop singers of rhythm and blues originals. Cover versions were invariably pallid imitations, artistically inferior to the originals. One has only to compare, say, Pat Boone's covers of Fats Domino's "Ain't That a Shame" or Little Richard's "Tutti Frutti" to hear how much was lost. While African American artists began to enjoy newfound mass acceptance, there were limits to how closely white kids could identify with black performers. Racism, especially in so sexually charged an arena as musical performance, was still a powerful force in American life. Because of the superior promotional power of the major companies and the institutional racism in the music business, white cover versions almost always outsold the black originals.

This photo of Elvis Presley singing at a 1956 state fair in Memphis captured his dramatic stage presence. Performing with only a trio, his sound was spare but hard driving. Both the music and Presley's stage moves owed a great deal to African American rhythm and blues artists.

Alan Freed, a popular white Cleveland disc jockey, refused to play cover versions on his "Moondog Matinee" program. He played only original rhythm and blues music, and he popularized the term "rock 'n' roll" to describe it. Freed promoted concerts around the Midwest featuring black rhythm and blues artists, and these attracted enthusiastic audiences of both black and white young people. In 1954 the music trade magazine *Billboard* noted this trend among white teenagers: "The present generation has not known the rhythmically exciting dance bands of the swing era. It therefore satisfies its hunger for 'music with a beat' in modern r&b (rhythm and blues) groups." The stage was thus set for the arrival of white rock 'n' roll artists who could exploit the new sounds and styles.

As a rock 'n' roll performer and recording artist, Elvis Presley reinvented American popular music. His success challenged the old lines separating black music from white, and pop from rhythm and blues or country. As a symbol of rebellious youth and as the embodiment of youthful sexuality, Elvis revitalized American popular culture. In his wake came a host of white rock 'n' rollers, many of them white Southerners like Elvis: Jerry Lee Lewis, Buddy Holly, the Everly Brothers, Roy Orbison. But the greatest songwriter and the most influential guitarist to emerge from this first "golden age of rock 'n' roll" was Chuck Berry, an African American from St. Louis who worked part-time as a beautician and house painter. Berry proved especially adept at capturing the teen spirit with humor, irony, and passion. He composed hits around the trials and tribulations of school ("School Days"), young love ("Memphis"), cars ("Maybellene"), and making it as a rock 'n' roller ("Johnny B. Goode"). As much as anyone, Berry created music that defined what it meant to be young in postwar America.

Almost Grown

At least some of the sense of difference, of uniqueness, associated with adolescence came from teens themselves. Teenage consumers remade the landscape of popular music into their own turf. The dollar value of annual record sales nearly tripled between 1954 and 1959, from $213 million to $603 million. New magazines aimed exclusively at teens flourished in the postwar years. *Modern Teen, Teen Digest,* and *Dig* were just a few. Most teen magazines, like rock 'n' roll music, focused on the rituals, pleasures, and sorrows surrounding teenage courtship. Paradoxically, behavior patterns among white middle-class teenagers in the 1950s and early 1960s exhibited a new kind of youth orientation and at the same time a more pronounced identification with adults.

While many parents worried about the separate world inhabited by their teenage children, many teens seemed determined to become adults as quickly as possible. Postwar affluence multiplied the number of two-car families, making it easier for sixteen-year-olds to win driving privileges formerly reserved for eighteen-year-olds. Girls began dating, wearing brassieres and nylon stockings, and using cosmetics at an earlier age than before—twelve or thirteen rather than fifteen or sixteen. Several factors contributed to this trend, including a continuing decline in the age of menarche (first menstruation), the sharp drop in the age of marriage after World War II, and the precocious social climate of junior high schools (institutions that became widespread only after 1945). The practice of going steady, derived from the college custom of fraternity and sorority pinning, became commonplace among high schoolers. By the late 1950s, eighteen had become the most common age at which American females married.

Teenagers often felt torn between their identification with youth culture and pressures to assume adult responsibilities. Many young people juggled part-time jobs with school and very active social lives. Teen-oriented magazines, music, and movies routinely dispensed advice and sympathy regarding this dilemma. Rock 'n' roll songs offered the most sympathetic treatments of the conflicts teens experienced over work ("Summertime Blues"), parental authority ("Yakety Yak"), and the desire to look adult ("Sweet Little Sixteen"). By 1960 sociologist James S. Coleman reflected a growing consensus when he noted that postwar society had given adolescents "many of the instruments which can make them a functioning community: cars, freedom in dating, continual contact with the opposite sex, money, and entertainment, like popular music and movies, designed especially for them."

Deviance and Delinquency

Many adults held rock 'n' roll responsible for the apparent decline in parental control over teens. A psychiatrist writing in the *New York Times* described rock as "a cannibalistic and tribalistic kind of a music" and "a communicable disease." Many clergymen and church leaders declared it "the devil's music." Much of the opposition to rock 'n' roll, particularly in the South, played on long-standing racist fears that white females might be attracted to black music and black performers. The undercurrent beneath all this opposition was a deep anxiety over the more open expression of sexual feelings by both performers and audiences.

Paralleling the rise of rock 'n' roll was a growing concern with an alleged increase in juvenile delinquency. An endless stream of magazine articles, books, and newspaper stories asserted that criminal behavior among the nation's young was chronic. Gang fights, drug and alcohol abuse, car theft, and sexual offenses received the most attention. The U.S. Senate established a special subcommittee on juvenile delinquency. Highly publicized hearings in 1955 and 1956 convinced much of the public that youthful criminals were terrorizing the country. Although crime statistics do suggest an increase in juvenile crime during the 1950s, particularly in the suburbs, the public perception of the severity of the problem was surely exaggerated.

In retrospect, the juvenile delinquency controversy tells us more about anxieties over family life and the erosion of adult authority than about crime patterns. Teenagers seemed more defined by and loyal to their peer culture than to their parents. A great deal of their music, speech, dress, and style was alien and threatening. The growing importance of the mass media in defining youth culture brought efforts to regulate or censor media forms believed to cause juvenile delinquency. For example, psychologist Fredric Wertham led a crusade that forced the comic book industry to adopt a code strictly limiting the portrayal of violence and crime.

As reactions to two of the most influential "problem youth" movies of the postwar era indicate, teens and their parents frequently interpreted depictions of youthful deviance in the mass media in very different ways. In *The Wild One* (1954), Marlon Brando played the crude, moody leader of a vicious motorcycle gang. Most adults thought of the film as a critique of mindless gang violence, but many teenagers identified with the Brando character, who, when asked, "What are you rebelling against?" coolly replied, "Whattaya got?" In *Rebel without a Cause* (1955), James Dean, Natalie Wood, and Sal Mineo played emotionally troubled youths in an affluent California suburb. The movie suggests that parents can cause delinquency when they fail to conform to conventional roles—Dean's father wears an apron and his mother is domineering. But on another level, the film suggests that young people can form their own families, without parents.

Brando and Dean, along with Elvis, were probably the most popular and widely imitated teen idols of the era. For most parents, they were vaguely threatening figures whose sexual energy and lack of discipline placed them outside the bounds of middle-class respectability. For teens, however, they offered an irresistible combination of rough exterior and sensitive core. They embodied, as well, the contradiction of individual rebellion versus the attractions of a community defined by youth.

MASS CULTURE AND ITS DISCONTENTS

No mass medium ever achieved such power and popularity as rapidly as television. The basic technology for broadcasting visual images with sound had been developed by the late 1930s, and television demonstrations were among the most popular exhibits at the 1939 New York World's Fair. But World War II and corporate competition postponed television's introduction to the public until 1946. By 1960, nearly nine in ten American families owned at least one set, which was turned on an average of more than five hours a day. Television reshaped leisure time and political life. It also helped create a new kind of national community defined by the buying and selling of consumer goods.

Important voices challenged the economic trends and cultural conformity of the postwar years. Academics, journalists, novelists, and poets offered a variety of works criticizing the overall direction of American life. These critics of what was dubbed "mass society" were troubled by the premium American culture put on conformity, status, and material consumption. Although a distinct minority, these critics were persistent. Many of their ideas and prescriptions would reverberate through the political and cultural upheavals of the 1960s and 1970s.

Television: Tube of Plenty

Television constituted a radical change from radio, and its development as a mass medium was quicker and less chaotic. The three main television networks—NBC, CBS, ABC—grew directly from radio organizations. A short-lived fourth network, Dumont, grew from a television manufacturing business. The Federal Communications Commission oversaw the licensing of stations and set technical standards. The networks led the industry from the start, rather than following individual stations, as radio had done. Nearly all TV stations were affiliated with one or more of the networks; only a handful of independent stations could be found around the country.

Television not only depended on advertising, it also transformed the advertising industry. The television business, like radio, was based on the selling of time to advertisers who wanted to reach the mass audiences tuning into shows. Radio had offered entire shows produced by and for single sponsors, usually advertisers who wanted a close identification between their product and a star. But the higher costs of television production forced key changes. Sponsors left production of programs to the networks, independent producers, and Hollywood studios.

Sponsors now bought scattered time slots for spot advertisements rather than bankrolling an entire show. Ad agencies switched their creative energy to producing slick thirty-second commercials rather than entertainment programs. A shift from broadcasting live shows to filming them opened up lucrative opportunities for reruns and foreign export. The total net revenue of the TV networks and their affiliated stations in 1947 was about $2 million; by 1957 it was nearly $1 billion. Advertisers spent $58 million on TV shows in 1949; ten years later the figure was almost $1.5 billion.

The staple of network radio, the comedy-variety show, was now produced with pictures. The first great national TV hit, *The Milton Berle Show*, followed this format when it premiered in 1948. Radio stars such as Jack Benny, Edgar Bergen, George Burns and Gracie Allen, and Eddie Cantor switched successfully to television. Boxing, wrestling, the roller derby, and other sporting events were also quite popular. For a brief time, original live drama flourished on writer-oriented shows such as *Goodyear Television Playhouse* and *Studio One*. In addition, early television featured an array of situation comedies with deep roots in radio and vaudeville.

Set largely among urban ethnic families, early shows like *I Remember Mama, The Goldbergs, The Life of Riley, Life with Luigi,* and *The Honeymooners* often featured working-class families struggling with the dilemmas posed by consumer society. Most plots turned around comic tensions created and resolved by consumption: contemplating home ownership,

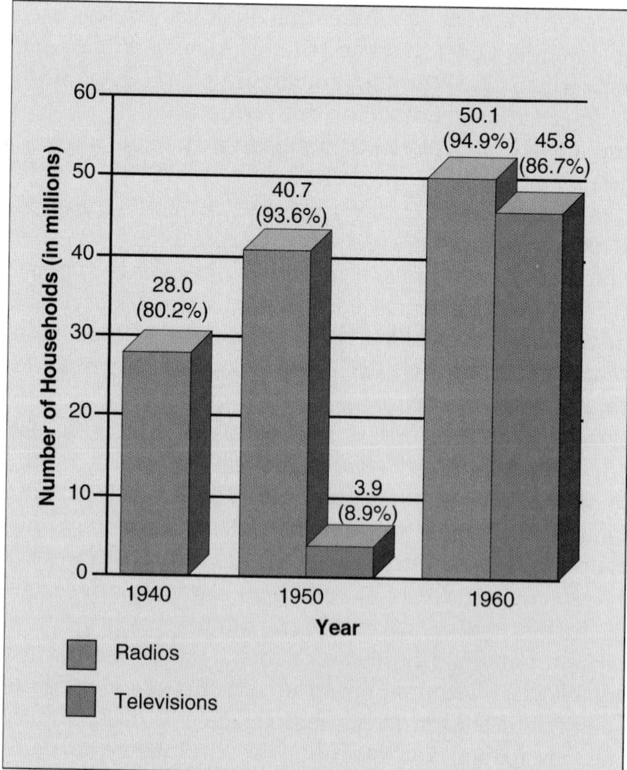

Radio and Television Ownership, 1940–1960

By 1960 nearly 90 percent of American households owned at least one television set, as TV replaced radio as the nation's dominant mass medium of entertainment. Radio ownership rose as well, but Americans increasingly listened to radio as an accompaniment to other activities, such as driving.

A Motorola television advertisement from Woman's Home Companion, 1951. Manufacturers designed TV sets as living room furniture and emphasized their role in fostering family togetherness.

going out on the town, moving to the suburbs, buying on credit, purchasing a new car. Generational discord and the loss of ethnic identity were also common themes. To some degree, these early shows mirrored and spoke to the real dilemmas facing families that had survived the Great Depression and the Second World War and were now finding their place in a prosperous consumer culture.

By the late 1950s all the urban ethnic comedy shows were off the air. A new breed of situation comedies presented non-ethnic white, affluent, and insular suburban middle-class families. Shows like *Father Knows Best, Leave It to Beaver, The Adventures of Ozzie and Harriet,* and *The Donna Reed Show* epitomized the ideal suburban American family of the day. Their plots focused on genial crises, usually brought on by children's mischief and resolved by kindly fathers. In retrospect, what is most striking about these shows is what is absent—politics, social issues, cities, white ethnic groups, African Americans, and Latinos were virtually unrepresented.

Television cut deeply into the filmgoing habits of Americans. The audience for movies began a steep decline from the high point of 1948. Hollywood tried desperately to compete with its new rival by pushing spectacular new techniques such as Cinerama, CinemaScope, and 3-D. By the mid-1950s, studios had begun to sell off their valuable backlog of films to the networks; old movies thus became a staple of television programming. Many TV shows were produced on the same Hollywood back lots that had churned out "B" pictures in the 1930s and 1940s. Two of the most popular genres of television in these years were old movie standbys: Westerns (*Gunsmoke, Cheyenne, The Rifleman*) and crime dramas (*Dragnet, Highway Patrol, The Untouchables*).

Television also demonstrated a unique ability to create overnight fads and crazes across the nation. Elvis Presley's 1956 appearances on several network television variety shows, including those hosted by Milton Berle and Ed Sullivan, catapulted him from regional success to international stardom. Successful television advertising campaigns made household names out of previously obscure products. A memorable example of TV's influence came in 1955 when Walt Disney produced a series of three one-hour shows on the life of frontier legend Davy Crockett. The tremendous success of the series instantly created a $300 million industry of Davy Crockett shirts, dolls, toys, and coonskin caps.

Television and Politics

Prime-time entertainment shows carefully avoided any references to the political issues of the day. Network executives bowed to the conformist climate created by the domestic cold war. Any hint of political controversy could scare off sponsors, who were extremely sensitive to public protest. Anticommunist crusaders set themselves up as private watchdogs, warning of alleged subversive influence in the broadcasting industry. In 1950 one such group published *Red Channels* (see Chapter 26), a book branding 151 of the most well-known writers, directors, and actors in radio and television as communists or communist dupes. Television executives responded by effectively blacklisting many talented individuals.

As in Hollywood, the cold war chill severely restricted the range of political discussion on television. Any honest treatment of the conflicts in American society threatened the consensus mentality at the heart of the television business. Even public affairs and documentary programs were largely devoid of substantial political debate. An important exception was Edward R. Murrow's *See It Now* on CBS—but that show was off the air by 1955. Television news did not come into its own until 1963, with the beginning of half-hour nightly network newscasts. Only then did television's extraordinary power to rivet the nation's attention during a crisis become clear.

Still, some of the ways that TV would alter the nation's political life emerged in the 1950s. Television made Democratic senator Estes Kefauver of Tennessee a national political figure through live coverage of his 1951 Senate investigation into organized crime. It also contributed to the political downfall of Senator Joseph McCarthy in 1954 by showing his cruel bullying tactics during Senate hearings into alleged subversive influence in the army. In 1952, Republican vice-presidential candidate Richard M. Nixon effectively used an emotional, direct television appeal to voters—the "Checkers" speech—to counter charges of corruption (see Chapter 26).

The 1952 election also brought the first use of TV political advertising for presidential candidates. The Republican Party hired a high-powered ad agency, Batten, Barton, Durstine & Osborn, to create a series of short, sophisticated advertisements touting Dwight D. Eisenhower. The Democrats were content to buy a few half-hour blocks of TV time for long speeches by their nominee, Adlai Stevenson. The BBD&O campaign saturated TV with twenty-second Eisenhower spots for two weeks before election day. Ever since then, television image making has been the single most important element in American electoral politics.

Jack Kerouac, founding voice of the Beat literary movement, in front of a neon lit bar, ca. 1950. Kerouac's public readings, often to the accompaniment of live jazz music, created a performance atmosphere underlining the connections between his writing style and the rhythms and sensibility of contemporary jazz musicians.

Culture Critics

From both the left and the right, an assortment of writers expressed anger, fear, and plain disgust with the power of American mass culture. It would, they feared, overwhelm traditional standards of beauty, truth, and quality. Indeed, the urge to denounce the mass media for degrading the quality of American life tended to unite radical and conservative critics. Thus Marxist writer Dwight Macdonald sounded an old conservative warning when he described mass culture as "a parasite, a cancerous growth on High Culture." Society's most urgent problem, Macdonald claimed, was a "a tepid, flaccid Middlebrow Culture that threatens to engulf everything in its spreading ooze."

Critics of mass culture argued that the audiences for the mass media were atomized, anonymous, and detached. The media themselves had become omnipotent, capable of manipulating the attitudes and behavior of the isolated individuals in the mass. These critics undoubtedly overestimated the power of the media. They ignored the preponderance of research suggesting that most people watched and responded to mass media in family, peer group, and other social settings. The critics also missed the genuine vitality and creative brilliance to be found within mass culture: African American music; the films of Nicholas Ray, Elia Kazan, and Howard Hawks; the experimental television of Ernie Kovacs; the satire of *Mad* magazine.

Many of these critics achieved great popularity themselves, suggesting that the public was deeply ambivalent about mass culture. One of the best-selling authors of the day was Vance Packard, whose 1957 exposé *The Hidden Persuaders* showed how advertisers exploited motivational research into the irrational side of human behavior. Paul Goodman won a wide audience for his *Growing Up Absurd* (1960), which charged that America made it very difficult for young people to find meaningful work, sexual fulfillment, or a true sense of community. Goodman was only one of the thinkers at the end of the decade whose work pointed toward the coming youth rebellion in culture and politics.

The Beats

Some of the sharpest dissents from the cultural conformity of the day came from a group of writers known collectively as the Beats. Led by the novelist Jack Kerouac and the poet Allen Ginsberg, the Beats shared a distrust of the American virtues of progress, power, and material gain. Kerouac, born and raised in a working-class French Canadian family in Lowell, Massachusetts, coined the term "beat" in 1948. It meant for him a "weariness with all the forms of the modern industrial state"—conformity, militarism, blind faith in technological progress. The Beat sensibility celebrated spontaneity, friendship, jazz, open sexuality, drug use, and the outcasts of American society. Like Elvis Presley and other white rock 'n' rollers, the Beats also identified with black music and black culture. But for the Beats, it was the music, language, and dress of jazz musicians that caught their attention rather than the rhythm and blues that had attracted so many white teenagers.

Kerouac championed what he called the "spontaneous prose" style of writing—"first thought, best thought"—and he filled scores of notebooks with his observations, poems, and accounts of his friends' lives. These notebooks provided the basis for his published works. His novel *On the Road* became the Beat manifesto. Originally written in 1951, the novel was not published until 1957. It chronicled the tumultuous adventures of Kerouac's circle of friends as they traveled by car back and forth across America. The main character, Dean Moriarty, became a potent symbol of freedom and rebellion, "mad to live, mad to talk, mad to be saved, desirous of everything at the same time." Many readers mistook Dean for Kerouac, a sensitive and complex artist. The instant celebrity brought by the book exacerbated the alcoholism that drove Kerouac to an early death at age forty-seven in 1969.

Allen Ginsberg had grown up in New Jersey in an immigrant Jewish family. His father was a poet and teacher, and his mother had a history of mental problems. After being expelled from Columbia University, Ginsberg grew close to Kerouac and another writer, William Burroughs. At a 1955 poetry reading in San Francisco, Ginsberg introduced his epic poem *Howl* to a wildly enthusiastic audience:

> *I saw the best minds of my generation destroyed*
> *by madness, starving hysterical naked,*
> *dragging themselves through the negro streets at dawn*
> *looking for an angry fix,*
> *angelheaded hipsters burning for the ancient heavenly*
> *connection*
> *to the starry dynamo in the machinery of night.*

Howl was published in 1956 and was quickly confiscated by police as "obscene and indecent." A highly publicized trial led to a landmark legal decision that the poem was literature, not pornography. *Howl* became one of the best-selling poetry books in the history of publishing, and it established Ginsberg as an important new voice in American literature.

Beat writers received a largely antagonistic, even virulent reception from the literary establishment. But millions of young Americans read their work and became intrigued by their alternative visions. The mass media soon managed to trivialize the Beats. A San Francisco journalist coined the term "beatnik," and by the late 1950s it had become associated with affected men and women dressed in black, wearing sunglasses and berets, and acting rebellious and alienated. *Life* did a highly negative photo portrayal of beatniks, hiring models for the spread. On television, *The Many Loves of Dobie Gillis* even featured a comic beatnik character, Maynard G. Krebs. But Beat writers like Kerouac, Ginsberg, Burroughs, Diane DiPrima, Gary Snyder, LeRoi Jones, and others continued to produce serious work that challenged America's official culture. They foreshadowed the mass youth rebellion and counterculture to come in the 1960s.

THE COLD WAR CONTINUED

Eisenhower's experience in foreign affairs had been one of his most attractive assets as a presidential candidate. His success as supreme commander of the Allied forces in World War II owed as much to diplomatic skill as to military prowess. As president, Eisenhower sustained the anticommunist rhetoric of cold war diplomacy, and his administration persuaded Americans to accept the cold war stalemate as a more or less permanent fact. Eisenhower developed new strategies for containment and for the support of United States power abroad, including a greater reliance on nuclear weapons and the aggressive use of the Central Intelligence Agency (CIA) for covert action. Yet Eisenhower also resolved to do everything he could to forestall an all-out nuclear conflict. He recognized the limits of raw military power. He accepted a less than victorious end to the Korean War, and he avoided a full military involvement in Indochina. Ironically, Eisenhower's promotion of high-tech strategic weaponry fostered development of a military-industrial complex. By the time he left office in 1961, he felt compelled to warn the nation of the growing dangers posed by burgeoning military spending.

The "New Look" in Foreign Affairs

Although Eisenhower recognized that the United States was engaged in a long-term struggle with the Soviet Union, he feared that permanent mobilization for the cold war might overburden the American economy and result in a "garrison state." He therefore pursued a high-tech, capital intensive defense policy that emphasized America's qualitative advantage in strategic weaponry. The "new look" in foreign affairs promised to reduce the military budget by exploiting America's atomic and air superiority.

The emphasis on massive retaliation, the administration claimed, would also make possible cuts in the military budget. As Secretary of Defense Charles Wilson said, the goal was to "get more bang for the buck." Eisenhower largely succeeded in stabilizing the defense budget. Between 1954 and 1961 absolute spending rose only $800 million, from $46.6 billion to $47.4 billion. Military spending as an overall percentage of the federal budget fell from 66 percent to 49 percent during his two terms. Much of this saving was gained through the increased reliance on nuclear weapons and long-range delivery systems, which were relatively less expensive than conventional forces.

Secretary of State John Foster Dulles emerged as a key architect of American policy, giving shape to Eisenhower's views. Raised a devout Presbyterian and trained as a lawyer, Dulles had been involved in diplomatic affairs since World War I. He brought a strong sense of righteousness to his job, an almost missionary belief in America's responsibility to preserve the "free world" from godless, immoral communism. Dulles articulated a more assertive policy toward the communist threat by calling not simply for containment but for a "rollback." The key would be greater reliance on America's nuclear superiority. This policy appealed to Republicans, who had been frustrated by the restriction of United Nations forces to conventional arms during the Korean War.

President Dwight D. Eisenhower (left), meeting with John Foster Dulles, who served as secretary of state until his death in 1959.

The "new look" conflicted, however, with Eisenhower's own sense of caution, especially during moments of crisis in eastern Europe and potential military confrontation with the Soviet Union. The limits of a policy based on nuclear strategy became painfully clear when American leaders faced tense situations that offered no clear way to intervene without provoking full-scale war.

When East Berliners rebelled against the Soviets in 1953, cold war hard-liners thought they saw the long awaited opportunity for rollback. But precisely how could the United States respond? Public bitterness over the Korean conflict merged with Eisenhower's sense of restraint and in the end, apart from angry denunciations, the United States did nothing to prevent the Soviets from crushing the rebellion. U.S. leaders faced the same dilemma on a grander scale when Hungarians revolted against their Soviet-dominated communist rulers in 1956, staging a general strike and taking over the streets and factories in Budapest and other cities. The United States opened its gates to thousands of Hungarian refugees, but despite urgent requests, it refused to intervene when Soviet tanks and troops crushed the revolt. Eisenhower recognized that the Soviets would defend their own borders, and all of eastern Europe as well, by all-out military force if necessary.

The death of Josef Stalin in 1953 and the worldwide condemnation of his crimes, revealed by his successor, Nikita Khrushchev, in 1956, gave Eisenhower fresh hope for a new spirit of peaceful coexistence between the two superpowers. Khrushchev, in a gesture of goodwill, withdrew Soviet troops from Austria. The first real rollback had been achieved by negotiations and a spirit of common hope, not threats or force. In 1958 Khrushchev, probing American intentions and hoping to redirect the Soviet economy toward the production of more consumer goods, unilaterally suspended nuclear testing. Tensions rose again that year when the Soviet leader, threatened by a revived West Germany, demanded that the Western Allies leave Berlin within six months. But after Khrushchev made a twelve-day trip to America in 1959, he suspended the deadline and relations warmed. Khrushchev visited an Iowa farm, went sightseeing in Hollywood, and spent time with Eisenhower at Camp David, the presidential retreat in Maryland.

The two leaders achieved nothing concrete, but with summit diplomacy seeming to offer at least a psychological thaw in the cold war, the press began referring to "the spirit of Camp David." In early 1960 Khrushchev called for another summit in Paris, to discuss German reunification and nuclear disarmament. Eisenhower, meanwhile, planned his own friendship tour of the Soviet Union. But in May 1960 the Soviets shot down an American U-2 spy plane gathering intelligence on Soviet military installations. A deeply embarrassed Eisenhower at first denied the existence of U-2 flights, but the Soviets produced the pilot, Francis Gary Powers, who readily confessed. The summit collapsed when Eisenhower refused Khrushchev's demands for an apology and an end to the spy flights.

The U-2 incident demonstrated the limits of personal diplomacy in resolving the deep structural rivalry between the superpowers. Although Eisenhower knew from earlier U-2 flights that the Soviet Union had undertaken no major military buildup, he had agreed with Congress to a hike of $2.5 billion in military spending in 1957. The launching of the first space-orbiting satellite by the Soviets in October of that year provided a new incentive. Sputnik demonstrated Soviet technological prowess and upset Americans' precarious sense of security. Urged to sponsor the building of "fallout shelters" for the entire population in case of nuclear attack, Eisenhower rejected what he called "the negative stuff." He supported instead a program of more federal funds for science education, as provided in the National Defense Education Act of 1958. Yet, in Congress a bipartisan majority voted to increase the military budget by another $8 billion in 1958, thereby accelerating the arms race and expanding the defense sector of the economy.

Covert Action

Eisenhower combined the overt threat of massive retaliation in his "new look" approach to foreign affairs with a heavy reliance on covert interventions by the Central Intelligence Agency (CIA). He had been an enthusiastic supporter of covert operations during World War II, and during his presidency CIA-sponsored covert paramilitary operations became a key facet of American foreign policy. With the American public wary of direct U.S. military interventions, the CIA promised a cheap, quick, and quiet way to depose hostile or unstable regimes. Eisenhower increasingly relied on the CIA to destabilize emerging third world governments deemed too radical or too friendly with the Soviets. Covert actions also proved vital for propping up more conservative regimes under siege by indigenous revolutionaries. These actions were particularly effective in the former colonial areas of Asia, Africa, and the Caribbean.

For CIA director, Eisenhower named Allen Dulles, brother of the secretary of state and a former leader in the CIA's World War II precursor, the Office of Strategic Services. The CIA's mandate was to collect and analyze information, but it did much more under Dulles's command. Thousands of covert agents stationed all over the world carried out a wide range of political activities. Some agents arranged large, secret financial payments to friendly political parties, such as the conservative Christian Democrats in Italy and Latin America or foreign trade unions opposed to socialist policies. Other agents secretly funded and guided intellectuals in, for instance, the Congress of Cultural Freedom, a prestigious group of liberal writers in Europe and the United States.

While the United States moderated its stance toward the Soviet Union and its eastern European satellites, it hardened its policies in the third world. The need for anticommunist tactics short of all-out military conflict pushed the Eisenhower administration to develop new means of fighting the cold war. The premise rested on encouraging confusion or rivalry within the communist sphere and on destabilizing or destroying anticapitalist movements around the world.

The Soviet Union tried to win influence in Africa, Asia, and Latin America by appealing to a shared "anti-imperialism" and by offering modest amounts of foreign aid. In most cases, communists played only small roles in third world independence movements. But the issue of race and the popular desire to recover national resources from foreign investors inflamed already widespread anti-European and anti-American feelings. When new nations or familiar allies threatened to interfere with U.S. regional security arrangements, or to expropriate the property of American businesses, the Eisenhower administration turned to covert action and military intervention.

Intervening around the World

The Central Intelligence Agency produced a swift, major victory in Iran in 1953. The country's popular prime minister, Mohammed Mossadegh, had nationalized Britain's Anglo-Iranian Oil Company, and the State Department worried that this might set a precedent throughout the oil-rich Middle East. Kermit Roosevelt, CIA chief in Iran, organized and financed an opposition to Mossadegh within the Iranian army and on the streets of Teheran. This CIA-led move-

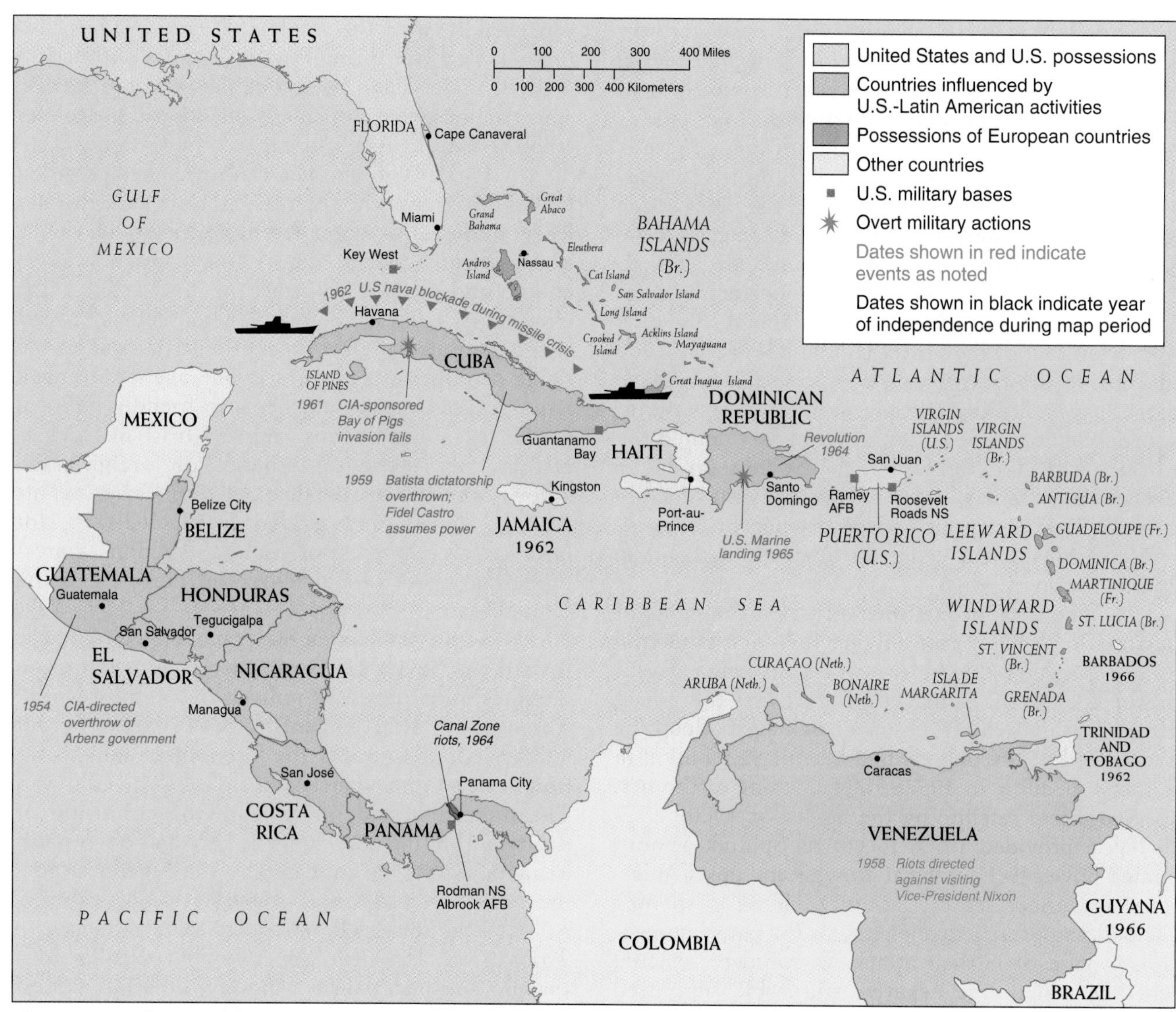

The U.S. in the Caribbean, 1948–1966 *U.S. military intervention and economic presence grew steadily in the Caribbean following World War II. After 1960, opposition to the Cuban Revolution dominated U.S. Caribbean policies.*

ment forced Mossadegh out of office and replaced him with Riza Shah Pahlavi. The shah proved his loyalty to his American sponsors by renegotiating oil contracts so as to assure American companies 40 percent of Iran's oil concessions.

The rivalry between Israel and its Arab neighbors complicated U.S. policy in the rest of the Middle East. The Arab countries launched an all-out attack on Israel in 1948 immediately after the United States and the Soviet Union had recognized its independence. Israel repulsed the attack, drove thousands of Palestinians from their homes, occupied territory that hundreds of thousands of others had fearfully fled, and seized lands far in excess of the terms of a United Nations-sponsored armistice of 1949. The Arab states refused to recognize Israel's right to exist and subjected it to a damaging economic boycott. Meanwhile, hundreds of thousands of Palestinians languished in refugee camps. Eisenhower believed that Truman had perhaps been too hasty in encouraging the Israelis. Yet most Americans supported the new Jewish state as a refuge for a people who had suffered so much persecution.

Israel stood as a reliable U.S. ally in an unstable region. Arab nationalism continued to vex American policy makers, culminating in the Suez crisis of 1956. Egyptian president Gamal Abdel Nasser, a leading voice of Arab nationalism, looked for American and British economic aid. He had long dreamed of building the Aswan High Dam on the Nile to create more arable land and provide cheap electric power. When negotiations broke down, Nasser announced he would nationalize the strategically sensitive Suez Canal, and he turned to the Soviet Union for aid. Eisenhower refused European appeals for U.S. help in seizing the Suez Canal and returning it to the British. When British, French, and Israeli forces attacked Egypt in October 1956, the United States sponsored a UN resolution calling for a cease-fire and a withdrawal of foreign forces. Yielding to this pressure and to Soviet threats of intervention, the British and French withdrew, and eventually so did the Israelis. Eisenhower had won a major diplomatic battle through patience and pressure, but he did not succeed in bringing lasting peace to the troubled region.

The most publicized CIA intervention of the Eisenhower years took place in Guatemala, where a fragile democracy had taken root in 1944. President Jácobo Arbenz Guzmán, elected in 1950, aggressively pursued land reform and encouraged the formation of trade unions. At the time, 2 percent of the Guatemalan population owned 72 percent of all farmland. Arbenz also challenged the long-standing dominance of the American-based United Fruit Company by threatening to expropriate hundreds of thousands of acres that United Fruit was not cultivating. The company had powerful friends in the administration (CIA director Dulles had sat on its board of trustees), and it began intensive lobbying for U.S. intervention. United Fruit linked the land reform program to the evils of international communism, and the CIA spent $7 million training antigovernment dissidents based in Honduras.

The American navy stopped ships bound for Guatemala and seized their cargo, and on June 14, 1954, a U.S.-sponsored military invasion began. Guatemalan citizens resisted by seizing United Fruit buildings, but U.S. Air Force bombing saved the invasion effort. Guatemalans appealed in vain to the United Nations for help. Meanwhile, President Eisenhower publicly denied any knowledge of CIA activities. The newly appointed military leader, Carlos Castillo Armas, flew to the Guatemalan capital in a U.S. embassy plane. Widespread terror followed, unions were outlawed, and thousands arrested. United Fruit circulated photos of Guatemalans murdered by the invaders, labeling them "victims of communism." In 1957 Castillo Armas was assassinated, and a decades-long civil war ensued between military factions and peasant guerrillas.

American intervention in Guatemala increased suspicion of and resentment against American foreign policy throughout Central and Latin America. Vice President Nixon declared that the new Guatemalan government had earned "the overwhelming support of the Guatemalan people." But in 1958, while making a "goodwill" tour of Latin America, Nixon was stoned by angry mobs in Caracas, Venezuela, suggesting that U.S. actions in the region had triggered an anti-American backlash.

In Indochina, the United States provided France with massive military aid and CIA cooperation in its desperate struggle to maintain its colonial empire. From 1950 to 1954 the United States poured $2.6 billion (about three-quarters of the total French costs) into the fight against the nationalist Vietminh movement, led by communist Ho Chi Minh. When Vietminh forces surrounded 25,000 French troops at Dien Bien Phu in March 1954, France pleaded with the United States to intervene directly. Secretary of State Dulles and Vice President Nixon, among others, recommended the use of tactical nuclear weapons and a commitment of ground troops. But Eisenhower, recalling the difficulties of the Korean conflict, rejected this call. "I can conceive of no greater tragedy," he said, "than for the United States to become engaged in all-out war in Indochina."

At the same time, Eisenhower feared that the loss of one country to communism would inevitably lead to the loss of others. As he put it, "You have a row of dominoes set up, and you knock over the first one and what will happen to the last one is the certainty that it will go over quickly." According to this so-called domino theory, the "loss" of Vietnam would threaten other Southeast Asian nations, such as Laos, Thailand, the Philippines, and perhaps even India and Australia. After the French surrender at Dien Ben Phu, a conference in Geneva established a cease-fire and a temporary division of Vietnam along the 17th parallel into northern and southern sectors. The Geneva accord called for reunification and national elections in 1956. But the United States, although it had attended the conference along with the Soviet Union and China, refused to sign the accord. In response to the Vietnam situation the Eisenhower administration created the Southeast Asia Treaty Organization (SEATO) in 1954. This NATO-like security pact included the United States, Great Britain, France, Australia, New Zealand, Thailand, the Philippines, and Pakistan, and was dominated by the United States.

South Vietnamese leader Ngo Dinh Diem, a former Japanese collaborator and a Catholic in a country that was 90 percent Buddhist, quickly alienated many peasants with his corruption and repressive policies. American economic and military aid, along with continuing covert CIA activity, was crucial in keeping the increasingly isolated Diem in power. Both Diem and Eisenhower refused to permit the 1956 elections stipulated in Geneva, because they knew popular hero Ho Chi Minh would easily win. By 1959 Diem's harsh and unpopular government in

Venezuelan soldiers (right) tried to disperse rioters who attacked Vice President Richard M. Nixon's car in Caracas during his 1958 "goodwill tour." Demonstrations such as these revealed a reservoir of resentment in Latin America against the interventionist policies of the United States in the region.

Saigon faced a civil war; thousands of peasants had joined guerrilla forces determined to drive him out. Eisenhower's commitment of military advisers and economic aid to South Vietnam, based on cold war assumptions, laid the foundation for the Vietnam War of the 1960s.

Ike's Warning: The Military-Industrial Complex

Throughout the 1950s small numbers of peace advocates in the United States had pointed to the ultimate illogic of the "new look" in foreign policy. The increasing reliance on nuclear weapons, they argued, did not strengthen national security but rather threatened the entire planet with extinction. They demonstrated at military camps, atomic test sites, and missile-launching ranges, often getting arrested to make their point. Reports of radioactive fallout around the world rallied a larger group of scientists and prominent intellectuals against further nuclear testing. In Europe, a Ban the Bomb movement gained a wide following; an American counterpart, the National Committee for a Sane Nuclear Policy (SANE), claimed 25,000 members by 1958. The Women's International League for Peace and Freedom collected petitions calling for a test ban. The Student Peace Union, founded in 1959, established units on many campuses. Small but well-publicized actions against civil defense drills took place in several big cities: protesters marched on the streets rather than entering bomb shelters.

As he neared retirement, President Eisenhower came to share some of the protesters' anxiety and doubts about the arms race. Ironically, Eisenhower found it difficult to restrain the system he helped create. He chose to devote his Farewell Address, delivered in January 1961, to warning the nation about the dangers of what he termed "the military-industrial complex." Its total influence, he cautioned, "economic, political, even spiritual—is felt in every city, every statehouse, every office of the federal government." The conjunction of a large military establishment and a large arms industry, Eisenhower noted, was new in American history. "The potential for the disastrous rise of misplaced power exists and will persist. We must never let the weight of this combination endanger our liberties or democratic processes."

The old soldier understood perhaps better than most the dangers of raw military force. Eisenhower's public posture of restraint and caution in foreign affairs accompanied an enormous expansion of American economic, diplomatic, and military strength. Yet the Eisenhower years also demonstrated the limits of power and intervention in a world that did not always conform to the simple dualistic assumptions of cold war ideology.

JOHN F. KENNEDY AND THE NEW FRONTIER

No one could have resembled Dwight Eisenhower less in personality, temperament, and public image than John Fitzgerald Kennedy. The handsome son of a prominent, wealthy Irish American diplomat, husband of a fashionable, trend-setting heiress, forty-two-year-old JFK embodied youth, excitement, and sophistication. As only the second Catholic candidate for president—the first was Al Smith in 1928—Kennedy ran under the banner of the New Frontier. His liberalism inspired idealism and hope in millions of young people at home and abroad. In foreign affairs, Kennedy generally followed, and in some respects deepened, the cold war precepts that dominated postwar policy making. But by the time of his assassination in 1963, he may have been veering away from the hard-line anticommunist ideology he had earlier embraced. What a second term might have brought remains debatable, but his death ended a unique moment in American public life.

The Election of 1960

John F. Kennedy's political career began in Massachusetts, which elected him to the House in 1946 and then the Senate in 1952. Kennedy won the Democratic nomination after a bruising series of primaries in which he defeated party stalwarts Hubert Humphrey of Minnesota and Lyndon B. Johnson of Texas. Unlike Humphrey and Johnson, Kennedy had not been part of the powerful group of insiders who dominated the Senate. But he drew strength and financial support from a loyal coterie of friends and family, including his father, Joseph P. Kennedy, and his younger brother Robert. Vice President Richard M. Nixon, the Republican nominee, had faithfully served the Eisenhower administration for eight years, and was far better known than his younger opponent. The Kennedy campaign stressed its candidate's youth and his image as a war hero. During his World War II tour of duty in the Pacific, Kennedy had bravely rescued one of his crew after their PT boat had been sunk. Kennedy's supporters also pointed to his intellectual ability. JFK had won the Pulitzer Prize in 1957 for his book *Profiles in Courage*, which in fact had been written largely by aides.

The election featured the first televised presidential debates. Political analysts have long argued over the impact of these four encounters, but agree that they moved television to the center of presidential politics, making image and appearance more critical than ever. Nixon appeared nervous and the camera made him look unshaven. Kennedy, in contrast, benefited from a confident manner and telegenic good looks. Both candidates emphasized foreign policy. Nixon defended the Republican record and stressed his own maturity and experience. Kennedy hammered away at the alleged "missile gap" with the Soviet Union and promised more vigorous executive leadership. He also countered the anti-Catholic prejudice of evangelical Protestants with a promise to keep church and state separate.

Kennedy squeaked to victory in the closest election since 1884. He won by a little more than 100,000 votes out of nearly 69 million cast. He ran

Studio television set for one of the four Kennedy-Nixon presidential debates, October 1960. Howard K. Smith of CBS News was the moderator. Eighty-five million viewers watched at least one of the debates, which both reflected and increased the power of television in the electoral process.

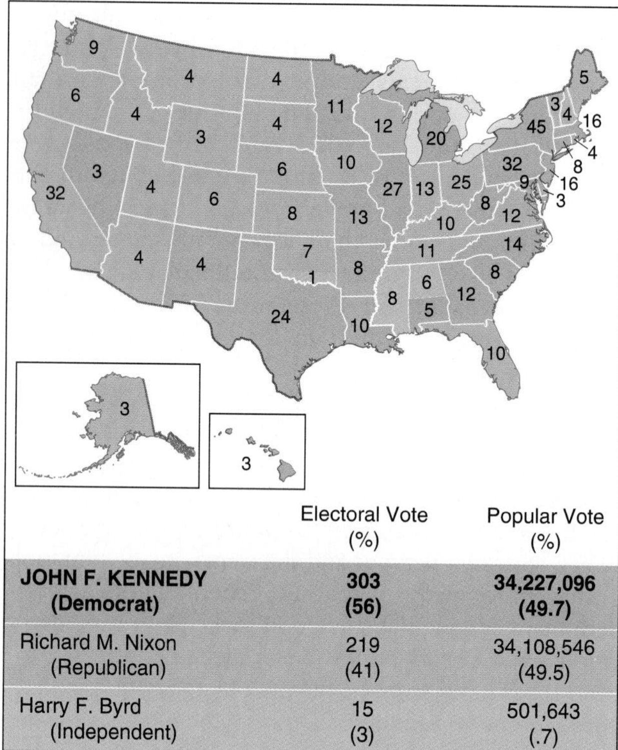

	Electoral Vote (%)	Popular Vote (%)
JOHN F. KENNEDY (Democrat)	**303 (56)**	**34,227,096 (49.7)**
Richard M. Nixon (Republican)	219 (41)	34,108,546 (49.5)
Harry F. Byrd (Independent)	15 (3)	501,643 (.7)

The Election of 1960 *Kennedy's popular vote margin over Nixon was only a little over 100,000, making this one of the closest elections in American history.*

poorly in the South, but won the Catholic vote so overwhelmingly that he carried most of the Northeast and Midwest. Though the margin of victory was tiny, Kennedy was a glorious winner. Surrounding himself with prestigious Ivy League academics, Hollywood movie stars, and talented artists and writers, he imbued the presidency with an aura of celebrity. The inauguration brought out a bevy of poets, musicians, and fashionably dressed politicians from around the world. The new administration promised to be exciting and stylish, a modern-day Camelot peopled by heroic young men and beautiful women. The new president's ringing inaugural address ("Ask not what your country can do for you—ask what you can do for your country") had special resonance for a whole generation of young Americans.

New Frontier Liberalism

Kennedy promised to revive the long-stalled liberal domestic agenda. His New Frontier advocated such liberal programs as a higher minimum wage, greater federal aid for education, increased Social Security benefits, medical care for the elderly, support for public housing, and various antipoverty measures. Yet the thin margin of his victory and the stubborn opposition of conservative southern Democrats in Congress made it difficult to achieve these goals. Congress refused, for example, to enact the administration's attempt to extend Social Security and unemployment benefits to millions of uncovered workers. Congress also failed to enact administration proposals for aid to public schools, mass-transit subsidies, and medical insurance for retired workers over sixty-five.

There were a few New Frontier victories. Congress did approve a modest increase in the minimum wage (to $1.25 per hour), agreed to a less ambitious improvement in Social Security, and appropriated $5 billion for public housing. It also passed the Manpower Retraining Act, appropriating $435 million to train the unemployed. The Area Redevelopment Act provided federal funds for rural, depressed Appalachia. The Higher Education Act of 1963 offered aid to colleges for constructing buildings and upgrading libraries. One of the best-publicized New Frontier programs was the Peace Corps, in which thousands of mostly young men and women traveled overseas for two-year stints in underdeveloped countries. There they provided technical and educational assistance in setting up health care programs and improving agricultural efficiency. As a force for change, the Peace Corps produced modest results, but it epitomized Kennedy's promise to provide opportunities for service for a new generation of idealistic young people.

Kennedy helped revive the issue of women's rights with his Presidential Commission on the Status of Women, led by Eleanor Roosevelt. The commission's 1963 report was the most comprehensive study of women's lives ever produced by the federal government. It documented the ongoing discrimination faced by American women in the workplace and in the legal system, as well as the inadequacy of social services such as day care. It called for federally supported day-care programs, continuing education programs for women, and an end to sex bias in Social Security and unemployment benefits. The commission also insisted that more women be appointed to policy-making positions in government. One concrete legislative result, the Equal Pay Act of 1963, made it illegal for employers to pay men and women different wages for the same job. The law did not do much to improve women's economic status, since most working women were employed in job categories, such as secretary or clerk, that included no men. But the issue of economic inequality had at least been put on the public agenda. President Kennedy also directed executive agencies to prohibit sex discrimination in hiring and promotion. The work of the commission contributed to a new generation of women's rights activism.

Taking a more aggressive stance on stimulating economic growth and creating new jobs than had Eisenhower, Kennedy relied heavily on Walter Heller, chair of the Council of Economic Advisers (CEA).

Heller emphasized the goal of full employment, which he believed could be attained through deficit spending, encouragement of economic growth, and targeted tax cuts. The administration thus pushed lower business taxes through Congress, even at the cost of a higher federal deficit. The Revenue Act of 1962 encouraged new investment and plant renovation by easing tax depreciation schedules for business. Kennedy also gained approval for lower U.S. tariffs as a way to increase foreign trade. To help keep inflation down, he intervened in the steel industry in 1961 and 1962, pressuring labor to keep its wage demands low and management to curb price increases.

Kennedy also increased the federal commitment to a wholly new realm of government spending: the space program. The National Aeronautics and Space Administration (NASA) had been established under Eisenhower in response to the Soviet success with Sputnik. In 1961, driven by the cold war motivation of beating the Soviets to the moon and avoiding "another Sputnik," Kennedy won approval for a greatly expanded space program. He announced the goal of landing an American on the moon by the end of the decade. NASA eventually spent $33 billion before reaching this objective in 1969. This program of manned space flight—the Apollo missions—appealed to the public, acquiring a science fiction aura. In space, if not on earth, the New Frontier might actually be reached.

Overall, Kennedy's most long-lasting achievement as president may have been his strengthening of the executive branch itself. He insisted on direct presidential control of details that Eisenhower had left to advisers and appointees. Moreover, under Kennedy the White House staff assumed many of the decision-making and advisory functions previously held by cabinet members. This arrangement increased Kennedy's authority, since these appointees, unlike cabinet secretaries, escaped congressional oversight and confirmation proceedings. White House aides also lacked an independent constituency; their power and authority derived solely from their ties to the president. Kennedy's aides, "the best and the brightest," as he called them, dominated policy making. With men such as McGeorge Bundy directing foreign affairs and Theodore Sorensen coordinating domestic issues, Kennedy began a pattern whereby American presidents increasingly operated through small groups of fiercely loyal aides, often acting in secret.

Astronaut John H. Glenn as he prepared for the first American manned space orbit of the earth. The space program of the early 1960s emphasized the technical training and courage of astronauts, consciously creating a set of public heroes as a way to ensure popular support and congressional funding.

Kennedy and the Cold War

During Kennedy's three years in office his approach to foreign policy shifted from aggressive containment to efforts at easing U.S.-Soviet tensions. Certainly when he first entered office, Kennedy and his chief aides considered it their main task to confront the communist threat. In his first State of the Union Address, in January 1961, Kennedy told Congress that America must seize the initiative in the cold war. The nation must "move outside the home fortress, and . . . challenge the enemy in fields of our own choosing." To head the State Department Kennedy chose Dean Rusk, a conservative former assistant to Truman's secretary of state, Dean Acheson. Secretary of Defense Robert McNamara, a Republican and Ford Motor Company executive, was determined to streamline military procedures and weapons buying. McNamara typified the technical, cost-efficient, superrational approach to policy making. Allen Dulles, Eisenhower's CIA director, remained at his post. These and other officials believed with Kennedy that Eisenhower had timidly accepted stalemate when the cold war could have been won.

Kennedy built up American nuclear and conventional weapons systems. Between 1960 and 1962 defense appropriations increased by nearly a third, from $43 billion to $56 billion. JFK expanded Eisenhower's policy of covert operations, deploying the Army's elite Special Forces as a supplement to CIA covert operations in counterinsurgency battles against third world guerrillas. These soldiers, fighting under the direct orders of the president, could provide "rapid response" to "brush-fire" conflicts where Soviet influence threatened American interests. The Special Forces, authorized by Kennedy to wear the green berets that gave them their unofficial name, reflected the president's desire as president to acquire greater flexibility, secrecy, and independence in the conduct of foreign policy.

The limits on the ability of covert action and the Green Berets to further American interests became apparent in Southeast Asia. In Laos, where the United States had ignored the 1954 Geneva agreement and installed a friendly military regime, the CIA-backed government could not defeat Soviet-backed Pathet Lao guerrillas. The president had to arrange with the Soviets to neutralize Laos. In neighboring Vietnam, the situation proved more difficult. When Communist Vietcong guerrillas launched a civil war in South Vietnam against the U.S.-supported government in Saigon, Kennedy began sending hundreds of Green Berets and other military advisers to support the rule of Ngo Dinh Diem. In May 1961, in response to North Vietnamese aid to the Vietcong, Kennedy ordered a covert action against Ho Chi Minh's government that included sabotage and intelligence gathering.

Kennedy's approach to Vietnam reflected an analysis of the situation in that country by two aides, General Maxwell Taylor and Walt Rostow, who saw it through purely cold war eyes. "The Communists are pursuing a clear and systematic strategy in Southeast Asia," Taylor and Rostow concluded, ignoring the inefficiency, corruption, and unpopularity of the Diem government. By 1963, with Diem's army unable to contain the Vietcong rebellion, Kennedy had sent nearly 16,000 support and combat troops to South Vietnam. By then, a wide spectrum of South Vietnamese society had joined the revolt against the hated Diem, including highly respected Buddhist monks and their students. Americans watched in horror as television news reports showed footage of Buddhists burning themselves to death on the streets of Saigon—the ultimate protest against Diem's repressive rule. American press and television also reported the mounting casualty lists of U.S. forces in Vietnam. The South Vietnamese army, bloated by U.S. aid and weakened by corruption, continued to disintegrate. In the fall of 1963, American military officers and CIA operatives stood aside with approval as a group of Vietnamese generals removed President Diem, killing him and his top advisers. It was the first of many coups that racked the South Vietnamese government over the next few years.

In Latin America, Kennedy looked for ways to forestall various revolutionary movements that were gaining ground. The erosion of peasant landholdings had accelerated rapidly after 1950. Huge expanses of fertile land long devoted to subsistence farming were converted to business-dominated agriculture that grew staple crops for export (bananas, coffee, sugar). Millions of impoverished peasants were forced to relocate to already overcrowded cities. In 1961 Kennedy unveiled the Alliance for Progress, a ten-year, $100 billion plan to spur economic development in Latin America. The United States committed $20 billion to the project, with the Latin nations responsible for the rest. The main goals included greater industrial growth and agricultural productivity, more equitable distribution of income, and improved health and housing.

Kennedy intended the program as a kind of Marshall Plan that would benefit the poor and middle classes of the continent. The alliance did help raise growth rates in Latin American economies. But the expansion in export crops and in consumption by the tiny upper class did little to aid the poor or encourage democracy. The United States hesitated to challenge the power of dictators and extreme conservatives who were staunch anticommunist allies. Thus the alliance soon degenerated into just another foreign aid program, incapable of generating genuine social change.

The Cuban Revolution and the Bay of Pigs

The direct impetus for the Alliance for Progress was the Cuban Revolution of 1959, which loomed over Latin America. The U.S. economic domination of Cuba that began with the Spanish American War (see Chapter 20) had continued through the 1950s. American-owned business controlled all of Cuba's oil production, 90 percent of its mines, and roughly half of its railroads and sugar and cattle industries. Havana, the island's capital, was an attractive tourist center for Americans, and U.S. crime syndicates shared control of the island's lucrative gambling, prostitution, and drug trade with dictator Fulgencio Batista. In the early 1950s a peasant-based revolutionary movement, led by Fidel Castro, began gaining strength in the rural districts and mountains outside Havana.

On New Year's Day 1959, after years of guerilla war, the rebels entered Havana and seized power amid great public rejoicing. For a brief time, Castro seemed a hero to many North Americans as well. The *New York Times* had conducted sympathetic interviews with Castro in 1958, while he was still fighting in Cuba's mountains. Many young people visited the island and returned with enthusiastic reports. Famous writers such as James Baldwin and Ernest Hemingway embraced Castro. The CIA and President Eisenhower, however, shared none of this exuberance. Castro's land reform program, involving the seizure of acreage from the tiny minority that controlled much of the fertile land, threatened to set an example for other Latin American countries. Although Castro had not joined the Cuban Communist Party, he turned to the Soviet Union after the United States withdrew economic aid. He began to sell sugar to the Soviets and soon nationalized American-owned oil companies and other enterprises. Eisenhower established an economic boycott of Cuba in 1960, then severed diplomatic relations.

Kennedy inherited from Eisenhower plans for a U.S. invasion of Cuba, including the secret arming and training of Cuban exiles. The CIA drafted the invasion plan, which was based on the assumption that a U.S.-led invasion would trigger a popular uprising of the Cuban people and bring down Castro. Kennedy went along with the plan, but at the last moment decided not to supply an Air Force cover for the operation. On April 17, 1961, a ragtag army of 1,400 counterrevolutionaries led by CIA operatives landed at the Bay of Pigs, on Cuba's south coast. Castro's efficient and loyal army easily subdued them. At the United Nations, Ambassador Adlai Stevenson, deceived by presidential aides, flatly denied any U.S. involvement, only to learn the truth later.

The debacle revealed that the CIA, blinded by cold war assumptions, had failed to understand the Cuban Revolution. There was no popular uprising against Castro. Instead, the invasion strengthened Castro's standing among the urban poor and peasants, already attracted by his programs of universal literacy and medical care. As Castro stifled internal opposition, many Cuban intellectuals and professionals fled to the United States. An embarrassed Kennedy reluctantly took the blame for the abortive invasion, and his administration was censured time and again by third world delegates to the United Nations. American liberals criticized Kennedy for plotting Castro's overthrow, while conservatives blamed him for not supporting the invasion. Despite the failure, Kennedy remained committed to getting rid of Castro and keeping up the economic boycott. The CIA continued to support anti-Castro operations and launched at least eight attempts to assassinate the Cuban leader.

The Missile Crisis

The aftermath of the Bay of Pigs led to the most serious confrontation of the cold war: the Cuban missile crisis of October 1962. Frightened by U.S. belligerency, Castro asked Soviet premier Khrushchev for military help. Khrushchev responded in the summer of 1962 by shipping to Cuba a large amount of sophisticated weaponry, including intermediate-range nuclear missiles. In early October U.S. reconnaissance planes found camouflaged missile silos dotting the island. Several Kennedy aides demanded an immediate bombing of Cuban bases, arguing that the missiles had decisively changed the strategic global advantage the United States had previously enjoyed. Other aides rejected this analysis, pointing out that American cities had been vulnerable to Soviet intercontinental ballistic missiles (ICBMs) since 1957.

A tense meeting of President John F. Kennedy (bending over table at right) and his Cabinet, October 29, 1962, in the midst of the Cuban missile crisis. The White House released a carefully selected series of such photos to convey the seriousness of the choices faced by the president and his advisers.

The president and his advisers pondered their options in a series of tense meetings. Secretary of Defense McNamara was probably closest to the truth when he asserted, "I don't believe it's primarily a military problem. It's primarily a domestic political problem." Kennedy's aggressive attempts to exploit Cuba in the 1960 election now came back to haunt him, as he worried that his critics would accuse him of weakness in failing to stand up to the Soviets. The disastrous Bay of Pigs affair still rankled. Even some prominent Democrats, including Senator J. William Fulbright, chair of the Senate Foreign Relations Committee, called for an invasion of Cuba.

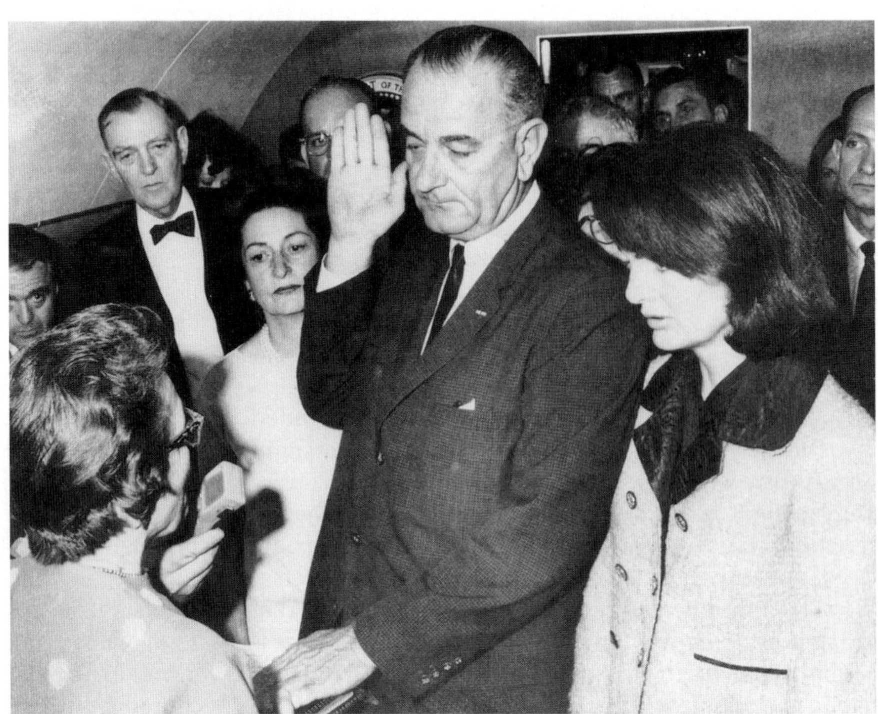

Vice President Lyndon B. Johnson took the oath of office as president aboard Air Force One after the assassination of John F. Kennedy, November 22, 1963. Onlookers included the grief-stricken Jacqueline Kennedy (right) and Lady Bird Johnson (left). This haunting photo captured both the shock of Kennedy's assassination and the orderly succession of power that followed.

Kennedy went on national television on October 22. He announced the discovery of the missile sites, demanded the removal of all missiles, and ordered a strict naval blockade of all offensive military equipment shipped to Cuba. He also requested an emergency meeting of the UN Security Council and promised that any missiles launched from Cuba would bring "a full retaliatory response upon the Soviet Union." For a tense week, the American public wondered if nuclear Armageddon was imminent. Eyeball to eyeball, the two superpowers waited for each other to blink. On October 26 and 27 Khrushchev yielded, ordering twenty-five Soviet ships off their course to Cuba, thus avoiding a challenge to the American blockade.

Khrushchev offered to remove all the missiles in return for a pledge from the United States not to invade Cuba. Khrushchev later added a demand for removal of American weapons from Turkey, as close to the Soviet Union as Cuba is to the United States. Kennedy secretly assured Khrushchev that the United States would dismantle the obsolete Jupiter missiles in Turkey. On November 20, after weeks of delicate negotiations, Kennedy publicly announced the withdrawal of Soviet missiles and bombers from Cuba, pledged to respect Cuban sovereignty, and promised that U.S. forces would not invade the island.

The crisis had passed. The Soviets, determined not to be intimidated again, began the largest weapons buildup in their history. For his part Kennedy, perhaps chastened by this flirtation with nuclear disaster, made important gestures toward peaceful coexistence with the Soviets. In a June 1963 address at American University, Kennedy called for a rethinking of cold war diplomacy. Both sides, he said, had been "caught up in a vicious and dangerous cycle in which suspicion on one side breeds suspicion on the other, and new weapons beget counterweapons." It was important "not to see only a distorted and desperate view of the other side. . . . No government or social system is so evil that its people must be considered as lacking in virtue."

Shortly after, Washington and Moscow set up a "hot line"—a direct phone connection to permit instant communication during times of crisis. More substantial was the Limited Nuclear Test-Ban Treaty, signed in August by the United States, the Soviet Union, and Great Britain. The treaty prohibited aboveground, outer space, and underwater nuclear weapons tests. It eased international anxieties over radioactive fallout. But underground testing continued to accelerate for years. The limited test ban was perhaps more symbolic than substantive, a psychological breakthrough in East-West relations after a particularly tense three years.

The Assassination of President Kennedy

The assassination of John F. Kennedy in Dallas on November 22, 1963, sent the entire nation into shock and mourning. Just forty-six years old and president

CHRONOLOGY

1950	David Riesman publishes *The Lonely Crowd*
1952	Dwight D. Eisenhower is elected president
1953	CIA installs Riza Shah Pahlavi as leader of Iran
1954	Vietminh force French surrender at Dien Bien Phu CIA overthrows government of Jácobo Arbenz Guzmán in Guatemala United States explodes first hydrogen bomb
1955	Jonas Salk pioneers vaccine for polio James Dean stars in the movie *Rebel without a Cause*
1956	Federal Highway Act authorizes Interstate Highway System Elvis Presley signs with RCA Eisenhower is reelected Allen Ginsberg publishes *Howl*
1957	Soviet Union launches Sputnik, first space-orbiting satellite Jack Kerouac publishes *On the Road*
1958	National Defense Education Act authorizes grants and loans to college students
1959	Nikita Khrushchev visits the United States
1960	Soviets shoot down U-2 spy plane John F. Kennedy is elected president Almost 90 percent of American homes have television
1961	President Kennedy creates "Green Berets" Bay of Pigs invasion of Cuba fails
1962	Cuban missile crisis brings the world to the brink of a superpower confrontation
1963	Report by the Presidential Commission on the Status of Women documents ongoing discrimination Limited Nuclear Test-Ban Treaty is signed President Kennedy is assassinated Betty Friedan publishes *The Feminine Mystique*

for only three years, Kennedy quickly ascended to martyrdom in the nation's consciousness. Millions had identified his strengths—intelligence, optimism, wit, charm, coolness under fire—as those of American society. In life, Kennedy had helped place television at the center of American political life. Now in the aftermath of his death, television riveted a badly shocked nation. One day after the assassination, the president's accused killer, an obscure political misfit named Lee Harvey Oswald, was himself gunned down before television cameras covering his arraignment in Dallas. Two days later tens of millions watched the televised spectacle of Kennedy's funeral, trying to make sense of the brutal murder. Although a special commission headed by Chief Justice Earl Warren found the killing to be the work of Oswald acting alone, many Americans doubted this conclusion. Kennedy's death gave rise to a host of conspiracy theories, none of which seems provable. In 1979 a House committee concluded that more than one gunman had fired on the presidential motorcade; but FBI scientists disputed this finding.

As Adlai Stevenson, one of Kennedy's longtime political rivals in the Democratic Party, noted in his eulogy to the president, "No one will ever know what this blazing political talent might have accomplished had he been permitted to live and labor long in the cause of freedom." We will never know, of course, what Kennedy might have achieved in a second term. But in his 1,000 days as president, he demonstrated a capacity to change and grow in office. Having gone to the brink during the missile crisis, he managed to launch new initiatives toward peaceful coexistence. At the time of his death, relations between the United States and the Soviet Union were more amicable than at any time since the end of World War II. Much of the domestic liberal agenda of the New Frontier would be finally implemented by Kennedy's successor, Lyndon B. Johnson, who dreamed of creating a Great Society.

CONCLUSION

America in 1963 still enjoyed the full flush of its postwar economic boom. To be sure, millions of Americans, particularly African Americans and Latinos, did not share in the good times. But millions of others had managed to achieve middle-class status since the early 1950s. An expanding economy, cheap energy, government subsidies, and a dominant position in the world marketplace had made the hallmarks of "the good life" available to more Americans than ever. The postwar "American dream" promised home ownership, college education, secure employment at decent wages, affordable appliances, and the ability to travel—for one's children if not for one's self. The nation's public culture—its schools, mass media, politics, advertising—presented a powerful consensus based on the idea that the American dream was available to all who would work for it.

The presidential transition from the grandfatherly Dwight Eisenhower to the charismatic John F. Kennedy symbolized for many a generational shift as well. By 1963 young people had more influence than ever before in shaping the nation's political life, its media images, and its burgeoning consumer culture. Kennedy himself inspired millions of young Americans to pursue public service and to express their political idealism. But even by the time of Kennedy's death, the postwar consensus and the conditions that nurtured it were beginning to unravel.

REVIEW QUESTIONS

1. How did postwar economic prosperity change the lives of ordinary Americans? Which groups benefited most and which were largely excluded from "the affluent society"?
2. What role did federal programs play in expanding economic opportunities?
3. Analyze the origins of postwar youth culture. How was teenage life different in these years from previous eras? How did popular culture both reflect and distort the lives of American youth?
4. How did mass culture become even more central to American everyday life in the two decades following World War II? What problems did various cultural critics identify with this trend?
5. How did cold war politics and assumptions shape American foreign policy in these years? What were the key interventions the United States made in Europe and the third world?
6. Evaluate the domestic and international policies associated with John F. Kennedy and the New Frontier. What continuities with Eisenhower-era politics do you find in the Kennedy administration? How did JFK break with past practices?

RECOMMENDED READING

Erik Barnouw, *Tube of Plenty* (1982). The best one-volume history of television, with excellent material on the new medium's impact upon cultural and political life.

James B. Gilbert, *A Cycle of Outrage* (1986). An insightful analysis of juvenile delinquency and its treatment by social scientists and the mass media during the 1950s.

Peter Guralnick, *Last Train to Memphis: The Rise of Elvis Presley* (1994). The best biography of Presley and a stunning portrait of the milieu that produced him.

Kenneth T. Jackson, *Crabgrass Frontier* (1985). The most comprehensive overview of the history of American suburbs. Jackson provides a broad historical context for understanding postwar suburbanization, and offers an excellent analysis of the impact of government agencies such as the Federal Housing Administration.

George Lipsitz, *Time Passages* (1990). An illuminating set of essays charting developments in American popular culture, especially strong analysis of music and early television.

Elaine Tyler May, *Homeward Bound: American Families in the Cold War* (1988). A thoughtful social history linking family life of the 1950s with the political shadow of the cold war.

Gerald Nicosia, *Memory Babe: A Critical Biography of Jack Kerouac* (1983). Both the best biography of this key Beat writer and the best analysis of the Beat generation.

Chester Pach Jr. and Elmo Richardson, *The Presidency of Dwight D. Eisenhower*, rev. ed. (1991). A good recent overview of the Eisenhower administration.

Herbert Parmet, *JFK* (1983). A solid, balanced examination of the Kennedy presidency.

James T. Patterson, *Grand Expectations: Postwar America, 1945–1974* (1996). A comprehensive overview of postwar life that centers on the "grand expectations" evoked by unprecedented prosperity.

ADDITIONAL BIBLIOGRAPHY

American Society at Mid-Century

Charles C. Alexander, *Holding the Line: The Eisenhower Era, 1952–1961* (1975)
David Calleo, *The Imperious Economy* (1982)
Barbara B. Clowse, *Brainpower for the Cold War* (1981)
Stephanie Coontz, *The Way We Never Were* (1992)
John P. Diggins, *The Proud Decades: America in War and Peace, 1941–1960* (1988)
Scott Donaldson, *The Suburban Myth* (1969)
Benita Eisler, *Private Lives: Men and Women of the Fifties* (1986)
Herbert Gans, *The Levittowners* (1967)
Delores Hayden, *Redesigning the American Dream* (1984)
Kenneth W. Olson, *The GI Bill, the Veterans, and the Colleges* (1974)

Youth Culture

Wini Breines, *Young, White, and Miserable: Growing Up Female in the Fifties* (1992)
Thomas Doherty, *Teen Pics* (1994)
Nelson George, *The Death of Rhythm and Blues* (1988)
Charlie Gillett, *The Sound of the City*, rev. ed. (1983)
William Graebner, *Coming of Age in Buffalo* (1990)
John A. Jackson, *Big Beat Heat: Alan Freed and the Early Years of Rock 'n' Roll* (1991)
Douglas T. Miller and Marion Novak, *The Fifties: The Way We Really Were* (1977)
David P. Szatmary, *Rockin' in Time: A Social History of Rock and Roll* (1991)
Ed Ward et al., *Rock of Ages* (1987)

Mass Culture and Its Discontents

James L. Baughman, *The Republic of Mass Culture* (1992)
George Lipsitz, *Class and Culture in Cold War America* (1981)
J. Fred MacDonald, *Television and the Red Menace* (1985)
David Marc, *Demographic Vistas: Television and American Culture* (1984)
Karal Ann Merling, *As Seen On TV: The Visual Culture of Everyday Life in the 1950's* (1995)
Richard H. Pells, *The Liberal Mind in a Conservative Age* (1984)
Lynn Spigel, *Make Room for TV* (1992)
Ella Taylor, *Prime Time Families* (1989)
Stephen J. Whitfield, *The Culture of the Cold War* (1991)

The Cold War Continued

Stephen Ambrose, *Ike's Spies* (1981)
David L. Anderson, *Trapped by Success: The Eisenhower Administration and Vietnam, 1953–1961* (1991)
Richard J. Barnet, *Intervention and Revolution* (1972)
Robert Divine, *Eisenhower and the Cold War* (1981)
Richard Immerman, *The CIA in Guatemala* (1982)
Gabriel Kolko, *Confronting the Third World* (1988)
Richard A. Melanson and David A. Mayers, eds., *Reevaluating Eisenhower* (1986)
Peter Wyden, *Bay of Pigs* (1980)

John F. Kennedy and the New Frontier

Michael Beschloss, *The Crisis Years* (1991)
Thomas Brown, *JFK: The History of an Image* (1988)
Noam Chomsky, *Rethinking Camelot* (1993)
James N. Giglio, *The Presidency of John F. Kennedy* (1991)
Trumbull Higgins, *The Perfect Failure: Kennedy, Eisenhower and the CIA at the Bay of Pigs* (1988)
Walter LaFeber, *Inevitable Revolutions* (1983)
Richard Mahoney, *JFK: Ordeal in Africa* (1983)
Thomas G. Paterson, ed., *Kennedy's Quest for Victory* (1989)
Richard E. Welch Jr., *Response to Revolution: The United States and Cuba, 1959–1961* (1985)
Garry Wills, *The Kennedy Imprisonment* (1983)

Biography

Stephen Ambrose, *Eisenhower*, 2 vols. (1983, 1984)
Chuck Berry, *The Autobiography* (1987)
David Burner, *John F. Kennedy and a New Generation* (1988)
Carol George, *God's Salesman: Norman Vincent Peale and the Power of Positive Thinking* (1993)
Townsend Hoopes, *The Devil and John Foster Dulles* (1973)
Daniel Horowitz, *Vance Packard and American Social Criticism* (1994)
Irving L. Horowitz, *C. Wright Mills: American Utopian* (1983)
Barry Miles, *Allen Ginsberg* (1989)
Thomas C. Reeves, *A Question of Character: A Life of John F. Kennedy* (1991)

CHAPTER TWENTY-EIGHT

THE CIVIL RIGHTS MOVEMENT

1945–1966

Romare Bearden, *Watching the Trains Go By*, 1964. Collection of Philip J. and Suzanne Schiller, American Social Commentary Art, 1930–1970. Photo by Sharon Goodman. © Romare Bearden Foundation/Licensed by VAGA, New York, NY.

Chapter Outline

AMERICAN COMMUNITIES

The Montgomery Bus Boycott: An African American Community Challenges Segregation

A steady stream of cars and pedestrians jammed the streets around the Holt Street Baptist Church in Montgomery, Alabama. By early evening a patient, orderly, and determined crowd of more than 5,000 African Americans had packed the church and spilled over onto the sidewalks. Loudspeakers had to be set up for the thousands who could not squeeze inside. After a brief prayer and a reading from Scripture, all attention focused on the twenty-six-year-old minister who was to address the gathering. "We are here this evening," he began slowly, "for serious business. We are here in a general sense because first and foremost we are American citizens, and we are determined to apply our citizenship to the fullness of its means."

Sensing the expectant mood of the crowd, the minister got down to specifics. Rosa Parks, a seamstress and well-known activist in Montgomery's African American community, had been taken from a bus, arrested, and put in jail for refusing to give up her seat to a white passenger on December 1, 1955. Composing roughly half the city's 100,000 people, Montgomery's black community had long endured the humiliation of a strictly segregated bus system. Drivers could order a whole row of black passengers to vacate their seats for one white person. And black people had to pay their fares at the front of the bus and then step back outside and reenter through the rear door. The day of the mass meeting, more than 30,000 African Americans had answered a hastily organized call to boycott the city's buses in protest of Mrs. Parks's arrest. As the minister quickened his cadence and drew shouts of encouragement, he seemed to gather strength and confidence from the crowd. "You know, my friends, there comes a time when people get tired of being trampled over by the iron feet of oppression. There comes a time, my friends, when people get tired of being flung across the abyss of humiliation, when they experience the bleakness of nagging despair."

Even before he concluded his speech, it was clear to all present that the bus boycott would continue for more than just a day. The minister laid out the key principles that would guide the boycott—nonviolence, Christian love, unity. In his brief but stirring address the minister created a powerful sense of communion. "If we are wrong, justice is a lie," he told the clapping and shouting throng. "And we are determined here in Montgomery to work and fight until justice runs down like water and righteousness like a mighty stream." Historians would look back at Montgomery, he noted, and have to say: " 'There lived a race of people, black people, fleecy locks and black complexion, of people who had the moral courage to stand up for their rights.' And thereby they injected a new meaning into the veins of history and of civilization."

The Reverend Dr. Martin Luther King Jr. made his way out of the church amid waves of applause and rows of hands reaching out to touch him. His prophetic speech catapulted him into leadership of the Montgomery bus boycott—but he had not started the movement. When Rosa Parks was arrested, local activists with deep roots in the black protest tradition galvanized the community with the idea of a boycott. Mrs. Parks herself had served for twelve years as secretary of the local NAACP chapter. She was a committed opponent of segregation and was thoroughly respected in the city's African American community. E. D. Nixon, president of the Alabama NAACP and head of the local Brotherhood of Sleeping Car Porters union, saw Mrs. Parks's arrest as the right case on which to make a stand. It was Nixon who brought Montgomery's black ministers together on December 5 to coordinate an extended boycott of city buses. They formed the Montgomery Improvement Association (MIA) and chose Dr. King as their leader.

While Nixon organized black ministers, Jo Ann Robinson, an English teacher at Alabama State College, spread the word to the larger black community. Robinson led the Women's Political Council (WPC), an organization of black professional women founded in 1949. With her WPC allies, Robinson wrote, mimeographed, and distributed 50,000 copies of a leaflet telling the story of Mrs. Parks's arrest and urging all African Americans to stay off city buses on December 5. They did. Now the MIA faced the more difficult task of keeping the boycott going. Success depended on providing alternate transportation for the 30,000 to 40,000 maids, cooks, janitors, and other black working people who needed to get to work.

The MIA coordinated an elaborate system of car pools, using hundreds of private cars and volunteer drivers to provide as many as 20,000 rides each day. Many people walked. Local authorities, although shocked by the discipline and sense of purpose shown by Montgomery's African American community, refused to engage in serious negotiations. With the aid of the NAACP, the MIA brought suit in federal court against bus segregation in Montgomery. Police harassed boycotters with traffic tickets and arrests. White racists exploded bombs in the homes of Dr. King and E. D. Nixon. The days turned into weeks, then months, but still the boycott continued. All along, mass meetings in Montgomery's African American churches helped boost morale with singing, praying, and stories of individual sacrifice. One elderly woman, refusing all suggestions that she drop out of the boycott on account of her age, made a spontaneous remark that became a classic refrain of the movement: "My feets is tired, but my soul is rested."

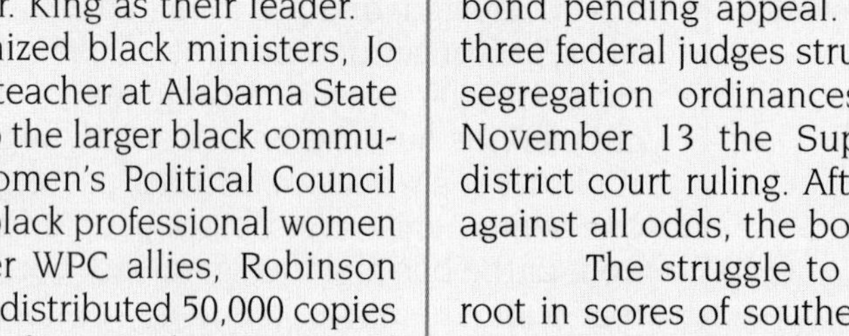

The boycott reduced the bus company's revenues by two-thirds. In February 1956 city officials obtained indictments against King, Nixon, and 113 other boycotters under an old law forbidding hindrance to business without "just cause or legal excuse." A month later King went on trial. A growing contingent of newspaper reporters and TV crews from around the country watched as the judge found King guilty, fined him $1,000, and released him on bond pending appeal. But on June 4, a panel of three federal judges struck down Montgomery's bus segregation ordinances as unconstitutional. On November 13 the Supreme Court affirmed the district court ruling. After eleven hard months and against all odds, the boycotters had won.

The struggle to end legal segregation took root in scores of southern cities and towns. African American communities led these fights, developing a variety of tactics, leaders, and ideologies. With white allies, they engaged in direct-action protests such as boycotts, sit-ins, and mass civil disobedience as well as strategic legal battles in state and federal courts. The movement was not without its inner conflicts. Tensions between local movements and national civil rights organizations flared up regularly. Within African American communities, long-simmering distrust between the working classes and rural folk on the one hand and middle-class ministers, teachers, and business people on the other sometimes threatened to destroy political unity. There were generational conflicts between African American student activists and their elders. But overall, the civil rights movement created new social identities for African Americans and profoundly changed American society.

Montgomery

KEY TOPICS

- Legal and political origins of the African American civil rights struggle
- Martin Luther King's rise to leadership
- Student protesters and direct action in the South
- Civil rights and national politics
- Civil Rights Act of 1964 and Voting Rights Act of 1965
- America's other minorities

ORIGINS OF THE MOVEMENT

The experiences of African Americans during World War II and immediately after laid the foundation for the civil rights struggle of the 1950s and 1960s. Nearly 1 million black men and women had served in the armed forces. The discrepancy between fighting totalitarianism abroad while enduring segregation and other racist practices in the military embittered many combat veterans and their families. Between 1939 and 1945 nearly 2 million African Americans found work in defense plants and another 200,000 entered the federal civil service. Black union membership doubled, reaching more than 1.2 million. But the wartime stress on national unity and consensus largely muted political protests. With the war's end, African Americans and their white allies determined to push ahead for full political and social equality.

Civil Rights after World War II

The boom in wartime production spurred a mass migration of nearly a million black Southerners to northern cities. Forty-three northern and western cities saw their black population double during the 1940s. Although racial discrimination in housing and employment was by no means absent in northern cities, greater economic opportunities and political freedom continued to attract rural African Americans after the war. With the growth of African American communities in northern cities, black people gained significant influence in local political machines in such cities as New York, Chicago, and Detroit. Within industrial unions such as the United Automobile Workers and the United Steel Workers, white and black workers learned the power of biracial unity in fighting for better wages and working conditions. Harlem congressman Adam Clayton Powell Jr. captured the new mood of 1945 when he wrote that black people were eager "to make the dream of America become flesh and blood, bread and butter, freedom and equality."

After the war, civil rights issues returned to the national political stage for the first time since Reconstruction. Black voters had already begun to switch their allegiance from the Republicans to the Democrats during the New Deal. A series of symbolic and substantial acts by the Truman administration solidified that shift. In 1946 Truman created a President's Committee on Civil Rights. Its report, *To Secure These Rights* (1947), set out an ambitious program to end racial inequality. Recommendations included a permanent civil rights division in the Justice Department, voting rights protection, antilynching legislation, and a legal attack on segregated housing. Yet, although he publicly endorsed nearly all the proposals of the new committee, Truman introduced no legislation to make them law.

Truman and his advisers walked a political tightrope on civil rights. They understood that black voters in several key northern states would be pivotal in the 1948 election. At the same time, they worried about the loyalty of white southern Democrats adamantly opposed to changing the racial status quo. In July 1948 the president made his boldest move on behalf of civil rights, issuing an executive order barring segregation in the armed forces. When liberals forced the Democratic National Convention to adopt a strong civil rights plank that summer, a group of outraged Southerners walked out and nominated Governor Strom Thurmond of South Carolina for president on a States' Rights ticket. Thurmond carried four southern states in the election. But with the help of over 70 percent of the northern black vote, Truman barely managed to defeat Republican Thomas E. Dewey in November. The deep split over race issues would continue to rack the national Democratic Party for a generation.

Electoral politics was not the only arena for civil rights work. During the war, membership in the National Association for the Advancement of Colored People had mushroomed from 50,000 to 500,000. Working- and middle-class urban black people provided the backbone of this new membership. The NAACP conducted voter registration drives and lobbied against discrimination in housing and employment. Its Legal Defense and Education Fund, vigorously led by special counsel Thurgood Marshall, mounted several significant legal challenges to segregation laws. In *Morgan v. Virginia* (1946), the Supreme

Court declared that segregation on interstate buses was an undue burden on interstate commerce. Other Supreme Court decisions struck down all-white election primaries, racially restrictive housing covenants, and the exclusion of blacks from law and graduate schools.

The NAACP's legal work demonstrated the potential for using federal courts in attacking segregation. Courts were one place where black people, using the constitutional language of rights, could make forceful arguments that could not be voiced in Congress or at political conventions. But federal enforcement of court decisions was often lacking. In 1947 a group of black and white activists tested compliance with the Morgan decision by traveling on a bus through the Upper South. This "Freedom Ride" was cosponsored by the Christian pacifist Fellowship of Reconciliation (FOR) and its recent offshoot, the Congress of Racial Equality (CORE), which was devoted to interracial, nonviolent direct action. In North Carolina, several riders were arrested and sentenced to thirty days on a chain gang for refusing to leave the bus.

Two symbolic "firsts" raised black expectations and inspired pride. In 1947 Jackie Robinson broke the color barrier in major league baseball, winning rookie-of-the-year honors with the Brooklyn Dodgers. Robinson's courage in the face of racial epithets from fans and players paved the way for the black ballplayers who soon followed him to the big leagues. In 1950 United Nations diplomat Ralph Bunche won the Nobel Peace Prize for arranging the 1948 Arab-Israeli truce. However, Bunche later declined an appointment as undersecretary of state because he did not want to subject his family to the humiliating segregation laws of Washington, D.C.

Cultural change could have political implications as well. In the 1940s, African American musicians created a new form of jazz that revolutionized American music and asserted a militant black consciousness. Although black musicians had pioneered the development of swing and, earlier, jazz, white bandleaders and musicians had reaped most of the recognition and money from the public. Artists such as Charlie Parker, Dizzy Gillespie, Thelonius Monk, Bud Powell, and Miles Davis revolted against the standard big-band format of swing, preferring small groups and competitive jam sessions to express their musical visions. The new music, dubbed "bebop" by critics and fans, demanded a much more sophisticated knowledge of harmony and melody and featured more complex rhythms and extended improvisation than previous jazz styles.

In urban black communities the "boppers" consciously created a music that, unlike swing, white popularizers found difficult to copy or sweeten. These black artists insisted on independence from the white-defined norms of show business. Serious about both their music and the way it was presented, they refused to cater to white expectations of grinning, easygoing black performers. Although most boppers had roots in the South, they preferred the relative freedom they found in northern urban black communities. Many northern black (and white) youths identified with the distinctive music, language, and dress of the boppers. In both their music and their public image, these musicians presented a rebellious alternative to the traditional image of the African American entertainer.

The Segregated South

In the postwar South, still home to over half the nation's 15 million African Americans, the racial situation had changed little since the Supreme Court had sanctioned "separate but equal" segregation in *Plessy v. Ferguson* (discussed in Chapter 20). In practice, segregation meant separate but unequal. A tight web of state and local ordinances enforced strict separation of the races in schools, restaurants, hotels, movie theaters, libraries, restrooms, hospitals, even cemeteries, and the facilities for black people were consistently inferior to those for whites. There were no black policemen in the Deep South and only a handful of black lawyers. "A white man," one scholar observed, "can steal from or maltreat a Negro in almost any way without fear of reprisal, because the Negro cannot claim the protection of the police or courts."

Charlie Parker (alto sax) and Miles Davis (trumpet) with their group in 1947, at the Three Deuces Club in New York City. Parker and Davis were two creative leaders of the "bebop" movement of the 1940s. Working in northern cities, boppers reshaped jazz music and created a distinct language and style that was widely imitated by young people. They challenged older stereotypes of African American musicians by insisting that they be treated as serious artists.

Signs designating "White" and "Colored" rest rooms, waiting rooms, entrances, benches, and even water fountains were a common sight in the segregated South. They were a constant reminder that legal separation of the races in public spaces was the law of the land.

In the late 1940s only about 10 percent of eligible southern black people voted, most of these in urban areas. A combination of legal and extralegal measures kept all but the most determined black people disfranchised. Poll taxes, all-white primaries, and discriminatory registration procedures reinforced the belief that voting was "the white man's business." African Americans who insisted on exercising their right to vote, especially in remote rural areas, faced physical violence—beatings, shootings, lynchings. A former president of the Alabama Bar Association expressed a commonly held view when he declared, "No Negro is good enough and no Negro will ever be good enough to participate in making the law under which the white people of Alabama have to live."

Outsiders often noted that despite Jim Crow laws (see Chapter 20) contact between blacks and whites was ironically close. The mass of black Southerners worked on white-owned plantations and in white households. One black preacher neatly summarized the nation's regional differences this way: "In the South, they don't care how close you get as long as you don't get too big; in the North, they don't care how big you get as long as you don't get too close." The South's racial code forced African Americans to accept, at least outwardly, social conventions that reinforced their low standing with whites. A black person did not shake hands with a white person, or enter a white home through the front door, or address a white person except formally.

In these circumstances, survival and self-respect depended to a great degree on patience and stoicism. Black people learned to endure humiliation by keeping their thoughts and feelings hidden from white people. Paul Laurence Dunbar, an African American poet, captured this bitter truth in his turn-of-the-century poem "We Wear the Mask."

We wear the mask that grins and lies,
It hides our cheeks and shades our eyes,
This debt we pay to human guile;
With torn and bleeding hearts we smile,
And mouth with myriad subtleties.
Why should the world be over-wise,
In counting all our tears and sighs?
Nay, let them only see us, while
We wear the mask.

Brown v. Board of Education

Since the late 1930s, the NAACP had chipped away at the legal foundations of segregation. Rather than making a frontal assault on the *Plessy* separate-but-equal rule, civil rights attorneys launched a series of suits seeking complete equality in segregated facilities. The aim of this strategy was to make segregation so prohibitively expensive that the South would be forced to dismantle it. In the 1939 case *Missouri v. ex.rel. Gaines*, the Supreme Court ruled that the University of Missouri law school must either admit African Americans or build another, fully equal law school for them. NAACP lawyers pushed their arguments further, asserting that equality could not be measured simply by money or physical plant. In *McLaurin v. Oklahoma State Regents* (1950), the Court agreed with Thurgood Marshall's argument that regulations forcing a black law student to sit, eat, and study in areas apart from white students inevitably created a "badge of inferiority."

By 1951, Marshall had begun coordinating the NAACP's legal resources for a direct attack on the separate-but-equal doctrine. The goal was to overturn *Plessy* and the constitutionality of segregation itself. For a test case, Marshall combined five lawsuits challenging segregation in public schools. One of these suits argued the case of Oliver Brown of Topeka, Kansas, who sought to overturn a state law permitting cities to maintain segregated schools. The law forced Brown's eight-year-old daughter Linda to travel by bus to a black school even though she lived only three blocks from an all-white elementary school. The Supreme Court heard initial arguments on the cases, grouped together as *Brown v. Board of Education*, in December 1952.

In his argument before the Court, Thurgood Marshall tried to establish that separate facilities, by definition, denied black people their full rights as American citizens. Marshall used sociological and psychological evidence that went beyond standard legal arguments. For example, he cited the research of African American psychologist Kenneth B. Clark, who had studied the self-esteem of black children in New York City and in segregated schools in the South. Using black and white dolls and asking the children which they preferred, Clark illustrated how black children educated in segregated schools developed a negative self-image. When Chief Justice Fred Vinson died suddenly in 1953, President Dwight Eisenhower appointed California Governor Earl Warren to fill the post. After hearing further arguments, the Court remained divided on the issue of overturning *Plessy*. Warren, eager for a unanimous decision, patiently worked at convincing two holdouts. Using his political skills to persuade and achieve compromise, Warren urged his colleagues to affirm a simple principle as the basis for the decision.

On May 17, 1954, Warren read the Court's unanimous decision aloud. "Does segregation of children in public schools solely on the basis of race . . . deprive the children of the minority group of equal educational opportunities?" The chief justice paused. "We believe that it does." Warren made a point of citing several of the psychological studies of segregation's effects. He ended by directly addressing the constitutional issue. Segregation deprived the plaintiffs of the equal protection of the laws guaranteed by the Fourteenth Amendment. "We conclude that in the field of public education the doctrine of 'separate but equal' has no place. Separate educational facilities are inherently unequal." "Any language in *Plessy v. Ferguson* contrary to this finding is rejected."

African Americans and their liberal allies around the country hailed the decision and the legal genius of Thurgood Marshall. Marshall himself predicted that all segregated schools would be abolished within five years. Black newspapers were full of stories on the imminent dismantling of segregation. The *Chicago Defender* called the decision "a second emancipation proclamation." But the issue of enforcement soon dampened this enthusiasm. To gain a unanimous decision, Warren had had to agree to let the Court delay for one year its ruling on how to implement desegregation. This second *Brown* ruling, handed down in May 1955, assigned responsibility for desegregation plans to local school boards. The Court left it to federal district judges to monitor compliance, requiring only that desegregation proceed "with all deliberate speed." Thus, although the Court had made a momentous and clear constitutional ruling, the need for compromise dictated gradual enforcement by unspecified means.

Crisis in Little Rock

Resistance to *Brown* took many forms. Most affected states passed laws transferring authority for pupil assignment to local school boards. This prevented the NAACP from bringing statewide suits against segregated school systems. Counties and towns created layers of administrative delays designed to stop implementation of *Brown*. Some school boards transferred public school property to new, all-white private "academies." State legislatures in Virginia, Alabama, Mississippi, and Georgia, resurrecting pre–Civil War doctrines, passed resolutions declaring their right to "interpose" themselves between the people and the federal government and to "nullify" federal laws. In 1956, 101 congressmen from the former Confederate states signed the Southern Manifesto, urging their states to refuse compliance with desegregation. President Dwight Eisenhower declined to publicly endorse *Brown*, contributing to the spirit of southern resistance. "I don't believe you can change the hearts of men with laws or decisions," he said. Privately, the pres-

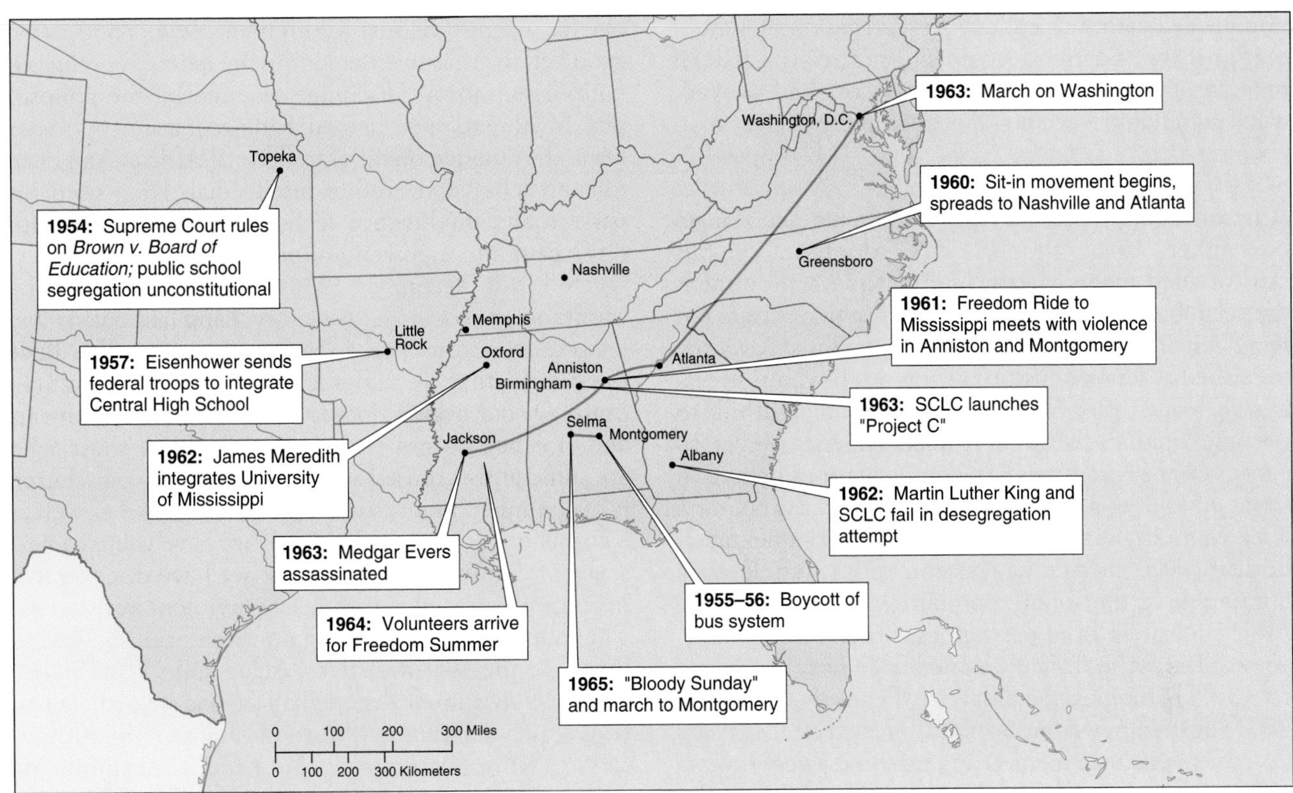

Map of the Civil Rights Movement *Key battlegrounds in the struggle for racial justice in communities across the South.*

ident opposed the *Brown* decision, and he later called his appointment of Earl Warren as chief justice "the biggest damn fool mistake I ever made."

In Little Rock, Arkansas, the tense controversy over school integration became a test case of state versus federal power. A federal court ordered public schools to begin desegregation in September 1957, and the local school board made plans to comply. But Governor Orval Faubus, facing a tough reelection fight, decided to make a campaign issue out of defying the court order. He dispatched Arkansas National Guard troops to Central High School to prevent nine black students from entering. For three weeks, armed troops stood guard at the school. Screaming crowds, encouraged by Faubus, menaced the black students, beat up two black reporters, and chanted "Two, four, six, eight, we ain't going to integrate."

At first, President Eisenhower tried to intervene quietly, gaining Faubus's assurance that he would protect the nine black children. But when Faubus suddenly withdrew his troops, leaving the black students at the mercy of the white mob, Eisenhower had to move. On September 24 he placed the Arkansas National Guard under federal control and ordered a thousand paratroopers of the 101st Airborne Division to Little Rock. The nine black students arrived in a U.S. Army car. With fixed bayonets, the soldiers protected the students as they finally integrated Little Rock High School. Eisenhower, the veteran military commander, justified his actions on the basis of upholding federal authority and enforcing the law. He made no endorsement of desegregation. But as the first president since Reconstruction to use armed federal troops in support of black rights, Eisenhower demonstrated that the federal government could, indeed, protect civil rights. Unfazed, Governor Faubus kept Little Rock high schools closed during the 1958–59 academic year to prevent what he called "violence and disorder."

NO EASY ROAD TO FREEDOM, 1957–62

The legal breakthrough represented by the *Brown* decision heartened opponents of segregation everywhere. Most important, *Brown* demonstrated the potential for using the federal court system as a weapon against discrimination and as a means of protecting the full rights of citizenship. Yet the widespread opposition to *Brown* and its implications showed the limits of a strictly legal strategy. In Little Rock, the ugly face of white racism received wide coverage in the mass media and quickly sobered the more optimistic champions of integration. However welcome Eisenhower's intervention, his reluctance to endorse desegregation suggested that civil rights activists could still not rely on federal help. As the Montgomery bus boycott had proved, black communities would have to help themselves first.

Martin Luther King and the SCLC

When it ended with the Supreme Court decision in November 1956, the 381-day Montgomery bus boycott had made Martin Luther King a prominent national figure. In January 1957 *Time* magazine put King on its cover. The *New York Times Magazine* published a detailed history of the bus boycott, focusing on King's role. NBC's *Meet the Press* invited him to become only the second African American ever to appear on that program. Speaking invitations poured in from universities and organizations around the country. King himself was an extraordinary and complex man. Born in 1929 in Atlanta, he enjoyed a middle-class upbringing as the son of a prominent Baptist minister. After graduating from prestigious Morehouse College, an all-black school, King earned a divinity degree at Crozer Theological Seminary in Pennsylvania and a Ph.D. in theology from Boston University.

In graduate school King explored a very diverse range of philosophers and political thinkers—the ancient Greeks, French Enlightenment thinkers, the German idealists, and Karl Marx. He was drawn to the social Christianity of American theologian Walter Rauschenbusch, who insisted on connecting religious faith with struggles for social justice. Above all King admired Mohandas Gandhi, a lawyer turned ascetic who had led a successful nonviolent resistance movement against British colonial rule in India. Gandhi taught his followers to confront authorities with a readiness to suffer, in order to expose injustice and force those in power to end it. This tactic of nonviolent civil disobedience required discipline and sacrifice from its followers, who were sometimes called upon to lay their lives on the line against armed police and military forces.

Like Gandhi and many of the Christian saints he had studied, King grappled with inner doubts about his faith and true mission. Since childhood he had suffered from extreme mood swings. He was charming and popular, but also self-restrained and dignified. Even after becoming pastor of Montgomery's Dexter Avenue Baptist Church in 1954, King often agonized over his inner emotions, including his religious faith. The rigorous discipline required by the philosophy of nonviolence helped King to master his inner turmoil. A unique blend of traditional African American folk preacher and erudite intellectual, King used his passion and intelligence to help transform a community's pain into a powerful moral force for change.

In a December 1956 address celebrating the Montgomery bus boycott victory, King laid out six key lessons from the year-long struggle. "(1) We have discovered that we can stick together for a common cause; (2) our leaders do not have to sell out; (3) threats and violence do not necessarily intimidate those who are sufficiently aroused and non-violent; (4) our church is becoming militant, stressing a social gospel as well as a gospel of personal salvation; (5) we have gained a new sense of dignity and destiny; (6) we have discovered a new and powerful weapon—non-violent resistance." The influence of two visiting northern pacifists, Bayard Rustin of the War Resisters' League and Glenn Smiley of the Fellowship of Reconciliation, had helped deepen King's own commitment to the Gandhian philosophy.

King recognized the need to exploit the momentum of the Montgomery movement. In early 1957, with the help of Rustin and other aides, he brought together nearly 100 black ministers to found the Southern Christian Leadership Conference (SCLC). The clergymen elected King president and his close friend, the Reverend Ralph Abernathy, trea-

After eleven months of nonviolent struggle, the Reverend Dr. Martin Luther King, Jr., leader of the Montgomery Bus Boycott, and the Reverend Glenn Smiley, of the Fellowship of Reconciliation, were among the group enjoying the first integrated bus ride in Montgomery. They were pictured here sitting at the front of the bus.

The second day of the sit-in at the Greensboro, North Carolina, Woolworth's lunch counter, February 2, 1960. From left: Joseph McNeil, Franklin McCain, Billy Smith, and Clarence Henderson. The Greensboro protest sparked a wave of sit-ins across the South, mostly by college students, demanding an end to segregation in restaurants and other public places.

surer. The SCLC called upon black people "to understand that nonviolence is not a symbol of weakness or cowardice, but as Jesus demonstrated, nonviolent resistance transforms weakness into strength and breeds courage in the face of danger."

Previously, the struggle for racial equality had been dominated by a northern elite focusing on legal action. The SCLC now envisioned the southern black church, preaching massive nonviolent protest, as leading the fight. The SCLC gained support among black ministers, and King vigorously spread his message in speeches and writings. But the organization failed to spark the kind of mass, direct-action movement that had made history in Montgomery. Instead, the next great spark to light the fire of protest came from what seemed at the time a most unlikely source: black college students.

Sit-Ins: Greensboro, Nashville, Atlanta

On Monday, February 1, 1960, four black freshmen from North Carolina Agricultural and Technical College in Greensboro sat down at the whites-only lunch counter in Woolworth's. They politely ordered coffee and doughnuts. As the students had anticipated while planning the action in their dorm rooms, they were refused service. Although they could buy pencils or toothpaste, black people were not allowed to eat in Woolworth's. But the four students stayed at the counter until closing time. Word of their actions spread quickly, and the next day they returned with over two dozen supporters. On the third day, students occupied sixty-three of the sixty-six lunch counter seats. By Thursday they had been joined by three white students from the Women's College of the University of North Carolina in Greensboro. Scores of sympathizers overflowed Woolworth's and started a sit-in down the street in S. H. Kress. On Friday hundreds of black students and a few whites jammed the lunch counters.

The week's events made Greensboro national news. City officials, looking to end the protest, offered to negotiate in exchange for an end to demonstrations. But white business leaders and politicians proved unwilling to change the racial status quo, and the sit-ins resumed on April 1. In response to the April 21 arrest of forty-five students for trespassing, an outraged African American community organized an economic boycott of targeted stores. With the boycott cutting deeply into merchants' profits, Greensboro's leaders reluctantly gave in. On July 25, 1960, the first African American ate a meal at Woolworth's.

The Greensboro sit-in sent a shock wave throughout the South. During the next eighteen months 70,000 people—most of them black students, a few of them white allies—participated in sit-ins against segregation in dozens of communities. More than 3,000 were arrested. African Americans had discovered a new form of direct-action protest, dignified and powerful, which white people could not ignore. The sit-in movement also transformed participants' self-image, empowering them psychologically and emotionally. Franklin McCain, one of the original four Greensboro students, later recalled a great feeling of soul cleansing: "I probably felt better on that day than I've ever felt in my life. Seems like a lot of feelings of guilt or what-have-you suddenly left me, and I felt as though I had gained my manhood, so to speak, and not only gained it, but had developed quite a lot of respect for it."

In Nashville, Reverend James Lawson, a northern-born black minister, had led workshops in nonviolent resistance since 1958. Lawson had served a jail term as a conscientious objector during the Korean War and had become active in the Fellowship of Reconciliation. He had also spent three years as a missionary in India, where he learned close-up the Gandhian methods of promoting social change. Lawson gathered around him a group of deeply committed black students from Fisk, Vanderbilt, and other Nashville colleges. Young activists there talked not only of ending segregation but also of creating a "Beloved Community" based on Christian idealism and Gandhian principles.

In the spring of 1960 more than 150 Nashville students were arrested in disciplined sit-ins aimed at desegregating downtown lunch counters. Lawson, who preached the need for sacrifice in the cause of justice, found himself expelled from the divinity school at Vanderbilt. Lawson and other veterans of the Nashville sit-ins, such as John Lewis, Diane Nash, and Marion Barry, would go on to play influential roles in the national civil rights movement. The Nashville group developed rules of conduct that became a model for protesters elsewhere: "Don't strike back or curse if abused. . . . Show yourself courteous and friendly at all times. . . . Report all serious incidents to your leader in a polite manner. Remember love and nonviolence."

The most ambitious sit-in campaign developed in Atlanta, the South's largest and richest city, home to the region's most powerful and prestigious black community. Students from Morehouse, Spelman, and the other all-black schools that made up Atlanta University took the lead. On March 15, 1960, 200 young black people staged a well-coordinated sit-in at restaurants in City Hall, the State Capitol, and other government offices. Police arrested and jailed seventy-six demonstrators that day, but the experience only strengthened the activists' resolve. Led by Julian Bond and Lonnie King, two Morehouse undergraduates, the students formed the Committee on an Appeal for Human Rights. In full-page advertisements in Atlanta newspapers the students demanded an end to segregation and also demanded jobs, equal housing and education, and better health services for the city's black people. We will "use every legal and non-violent means at our disposal to secure full citizenship rights as members of this great democracy of ours," the students promised. Over the summer they planned a fall campaign of large-scale sit-ins at major Atlanta department stores and a boycott of downtown merchants. Their slogan became "Close out your charge account with segregation, open up your account with freedom." In October 1960 Martin Luther King and thirty-six students were arrested when they sat down in the all-white Magnolia Room restaurant in Rich's Department Store. As in Greensboro and Montgomery, the larger African American community in Atlanta supported the continuing sit-ins, picketing, and boycotts. The campaign stretched on for months, and hundreds of protesters went to jail. The city's business leaders finally relented in September 1961, and desegregation came to Atlanta.

SNCC and the "Beloved Community"

The sit-in movement pumped new energy into the civil rights cause, creating a new generation of activists and leaders. Mass arrests, beatings, and vilification in the southern white press only strengthened the resolve of those in the movement. Students also had to deal with the fears of their families, many of whom had made great sacrifices to send them off to college. John Lewis, a seminary student in Nashville, remembered his mother in rural Alabama pleading with him to "get out of that mess, before you get hurt." Lewis wrote to his parents that he acted out of his Christian conscience: "My soul will not be satisfied until freedom, justice, and fair play become a reality for all people."

The new student militancy also caused discord within black communities. The authority of local African American elites had traditionally depended on their influence and cooperation with the white establishment. Black lawyers, schoolteachers, principals, and businessmen had to maintain regular and cordial relations with white judges, school boards, and politicians. Student calls for freedom disturbed many community leaders worried about upsetting traditional patronage networks. Some black college presidents, pressured by trustees and state legislators, sought to moderate or stop the movement altogether. The president of Southern University in Baton Rouge, the largest black college in the nation, suspended eighteen sit-in leaders in 1960 and forced the entire student body of 5,000 to reapply to the college so that agitators could be screened out.

An April 1960 conference of 120 black student activists in Raleigh, North Carolina, underlined the generational and radical aspects of the new movement. The meeting had been called by Ella Baker, executive director of the SCLC, to help the students assess their experiences and plan future actions. Fifty-five at the time, Baker had for years played an important behind-the-scenes role in the civil rights cause, serving as a community organizer and field secretary for the NAACP before heading the staff of the SCLC. She understood the psychological importance of the students' remaining independent of adult control. She counseled them to resist affiliating with any of the national civil rights organizations. Baker also encouraged the trend toward group-centered leadership among the students. She later commented that social movements needed "the development of people who are interested not in being leaders as much as in developing leadership among other people."

With Baker's encouragement, the conference voted to establish a new group, the Student Nonviolent Coordinating Committee (SNCC). The strong influence of the Nashville students, led by James Lawson, could be found in the SNCC statement of purpose:

> We affirm the philosophical or religious ideal of nonviolence as the foundation of our purpose, the presupposition of our faith, and the manner of our action. Nonviolence as it grows from Judaic-Christian tradition seeks a social order of justice permeated by love. Integration of human endeavor represents the crucial first step towards such a society.
>
> By appealing to conscience and standing on the moral nature of human existence, nonviolence nurtures the atmosphere in which reconciliation and justice become actual possibilities.

In the fall of 1960 SNCC established an organizational structure, a set of principles, and a new style of civil rights protest. The emphasis was on fighting segregation through direct confrontation, mass action, and civil disobedience. SNCC fieldworkers initiated and supported local, community-based activity. Three-quarters of the first fieldworkers were less than twenty-two years old. Leadership was vested in a nonhierarchical Coordinating Committee, but local groups were free to determine their own direction. SNCC people distrusted bureaucracy and structure; they stressed spontaneity and improvisation. Bob Moses, a former Harvard graduate student and New York City schoolteacher, best expressed the freewheeling SNCC attitude: "Go where the spirit say go and do what the spirit say do." Over the next few years SNCC was at the forefront of nearly every major civil rights battle.

The Election of 1960 and Civil Rights

The issue of race relations was kept from center stage during the very close presidential campaign of 1960. As vice president, Richard Nixon had been a leading Republican voice for stronger civil rights legislation. In contrast, Democratic nominee Senator John F. Kennedy had played virtually no role in the congressional battles over civil rights during the 1950s. But during the campaign, their roles reversed. Kennedy praised the sit-in movement as part of a revival of national reform spirit. He declared, "It is in the American tradition to stand up for one's rights—even if the new way is to sit down." While the Republican platform contained a strong civil rights plank, Nixon, eager to court white southern voters, minimized his own identification with the movement. In October, when Martin Luther King was jailed after leading a demonstration in Atlanta, Kennedy telephoned Coretta Scott King to reassure her and express his personal support. Kennedy's brother Robert telephoned the judge in the case and angrily warned him that he had violated King's civil rights and endangered the national Democratic ticket. The judge released King soon afterward.

News of this intervention did not gain wide attention in the white South, much to the relief of the Kennedys. The race was tight, and they knew they could not afford to alienate traditional white southern Democrats. But the campaign effectively played up the story among black voters all over the country. Kennedy won 70 percent of the black vote, which helped put him over the top in such critical states as Illinois, Texas, Michigan, and Pennsylvania and secure his narrow victory over Nixon. Many civil rights activists optimistically looked forward to a new president who would have to acknowledge his political debt to the black vote.

But the very closeness of his victory constrained Kennedy on the race question. Democrats had lost ground in the House and Senate, and Kennedy had to worry about alienating conservative southern Democrats who chaired key congressional committees. Passage of major civil rights legislation would be virtually impossible. The new president told leaders such as Roy Wilkins of the NAACP that a strategy of "minimum legislation, maximum executive action" offered the best road to change. The president did appoint some forty African Americans to high federal positions, including Thurgood Marshall to the federal appellate court. He established a Committee on Equal Employment Opportunity, chaired by Vice President Lyndon B. Johnson, to fight discrimination in the federal civil service and in corporations that received government contracts.

Most significantly, the Kennedy administration sought to invigorate the Civil Rights Division of the Justice Department. That division had been created by the Civil Rights Act of 1957, which authorized the attorney general to seek court injunctions to protect people denied their right to vote. But the Eisenhower administration had made little use of this new power. Robert Kennedy, the new attorney general, began assembling a staff of brilliant and committed attorneys, headed by Washington lawyer Burke Marshall. Kennedy encouraged them to get out of Washington and get into the field wherever racial troubles arose. In early 1961, when Louisiana school officials balked at a school desegregation order, Robert Kennedy warned them that he would ask the federal court to hold them in contempt. When Burke Marshall started court proceedings, the state officials gave in. But the new, more aggressive mood at Justice could not solve the central political dilemma: how to move forward on civil rights without alienating southern Democrats. Pressure from the newly energized southern civil rights movement soon revealed the true difficulty of that problem. The movement would also provoke murderous outrage from white extremists determined to maintain the racial status quo.

A Freedom Riders' bus burns after being firebombed in Anniston, Alabama, May 14, 1961. After setting the bus afire, whites attacked the passengers fleeing the smoke and flames. Violent scenes like this one received extensive publicity in the mass media and helped compel the Justice Department to enforce court rulings banning segregation on interstate bus lines.

Freedom Rides

In the spring of 1961 James Farmer, national director of CORE, announced plans for an interracial Freedom Ride through the South. The goal was to test compliance with court orders banning segregation in interstate travel and terminal accommodations. CORE had just recently made Farmer its leader in an effort to revitalize the organization. One of the founders of CORE in 1942, Farmer had worked for various pacifist and socialist groups and served as program director for the NAACP. He designed the Freedom Ride to induce a crisis, in the spirit of the sit-ins. "Our intention," Farmer declared, "was to provoke the southern authorities into arresting us and thereby prod the Justice Department into enforcing the law of the land." CORE received financial and tactical support from the SCLC and several NAACP branches. It also informed the Justice Department and the Federal Bureau of Investigation of its plans, but received no reply.

On May 4 seven blacks and six whites split into two interracial groups and left Washington on public buses bound for Alabama and Mississippi. At first the two buses encountered only isolated harassment and violence as they headed south. But when one bus entered Anniston, Alabama, on May 14 an angry mob surrounded it, smashing windows and slashing tires. Six miles out of town, the tires went flat. A firebomb tossed through a window forced the passengers out. The mob then beat the Freedom Riders with blackjacks, iron bars, and clubs, and the bus burst into flames. A caravan of cars organized by the Birmingham office of the SCLC rescued the wounded. Another mob attacked the second bus in Anniston, leaving one Freedom Rider close to death and permanently brain-damaged.

The violence escalated. In Birmingham, a mob of forty whites waited on the loading platform and attacked the bus that managed to get out of Anniston. Although police had been warned to expect trouble, they did nothing to stop the mob from beating the Freedom Riders with pipes and fists, nor did they make any arrests. FBI agents observed and took notes but did nothing. The remaining Freedom Riders decided to travel as a single group on the next lap, from Birmingham to Montgomery, but no bus would take them. Stranded and frightened, they reluctantly boarded a special flight to New Orleans arranged by the Justice Department. On May 17 the CORE-sponsored Freedom Ride disbanded.

But that was not the end of the Freedom Rides. SNCC leaders in Atlanta and Nashville assembled a fresh group of volunteers to continue the trip. On May 20 twenty-one Freedom Riders left Birmingham for Montgomery. The bus station in the Alabama capital was eerily quiet and deserted as they pulled in. But when the passengers left the bus a mob of several hundred whites rushed them, yelling "Get those niggers!" and clubbing people to the ground. James Zwerg, a white Freedom Rider from the University of Wisconsin, had his spinal cord severed. John Lewis, veteran of the Nashville sit-in movement, suffered a brain concussion. As he lay in a pool of blood, a policeman handed him a state court injunction forbidding interracial travel in Alabama. The mob indiscriminately beat journalists and clubbed John Siegenthaler, a Justice Department attorney sent to observe the scene. It took police more than an hour to halt the rioting. Montgomery's police commissioner later said, "We have no intention of standing guard for a bunch of troublemakers coming into our city."

The mob violence and the indifference of Alabama officials made the Freedom Ride page-one news around the country and throughout the world. Newspapers in Europe, Africa, and Asia denounced the hypocrisy of the federal government. The Kennedy administration, preparing for the president's first summit meeting with Soviet premier Nikita Khrushchev, saw the situation as a threat to its international prestige. On May 21, an angry mob threatened to invade a support rally at Montgomery's First Baptist Church. A hastily assembled group of 400 U.S. marshals, sent by Robert Kennedy, barely managed to keep the peace. The attorney general called for a cooling-off period, but Martin Luther King, James Farmer, and the SNCC leaders announced that the Freedom Ride would continue. When Robert Kennedy warned that the racial turmoil would embarrass the president in his meeting with Khrushchev, Ralph Abernathy of the SCLC replied, "Doesn't the Attorney General know that we've been embarrassed all our lives?"

A bandaged but spirited group of twenty-seven Freedom Riders prepared to leave Montgomery for Jackson, Mississippi, on May 24. To avoid further violence Robert Kennedy arranged a compromise through Mississippi senator James Eastland. In exchange for a guarantee of safe passage through Mississippi, the federal government promised not to interfere with the arrest of the Freedom Riders in Jackson. This Freedom Ride and several that followed thus escaped violence. But more than 300 people were arrested that summer in Jackson on charges of traveling "for the avowed purpose of inflaming public opinion." Sticking to a policy of "jail, no bail," Freedom Riders clogged the prison, where they endured beatings and intimidation by prison guards that went largely unreported in the press. Their jail experiences turned most of them into committed core leaders of the student movement.

The Justice Department eventually petitioned the Interstate Commerce Commission to issue clear rules prohibiting segregation on interstate carriers. At the end of 1962 CORE proclaimed victory in the battle against Jim Crow interstate travel. By creating a crisis, the Freedom Rides had forced the Kennedy administration to act. But they also revealed the unwillingness of the federal government to fully enforce the law of the land. The Freedom Rides exposed the ugly face of southern racism to the world. At the same time, they reinforced white resistance to desegregation. The jailings and brutality experienced by Freedom Riders made clear to the civil rights community the limits of moral suasion alone for effecting change.

The Albany Movement: The Limits of Protest

Where the federal government chose not to enforce the constitutional rights of black people, segregationist forces tenaciously held their ground, especially in the more remote areas of the Deep South. In Albany, a small city in southwest Georgia, activists from SNCC, the NAACP, and other local groups formed a coalition known as the Albany movement. Starting in October 1961 and continuing for more than a year, thousands of Albany's black citizens marched, sat in, and boycotted as part of a citywide campaign to integrate public facilities and win voting rights. More than a thousand people spent time in jail. In December, the arrival of Martin Luther King and the SCLC transformed Albany into a national symbol of the struggle.

But the gains at Albany proved minimal. Infighting among the various civil rights organizations hurt the cause. Local SNCC workers opposed the more cautious approach of NAACP officials, even though the more established organization paid many of the campaign's expenses. The arrival of King guaranteed national news coverage, but local activists worried that his presence might undermine the community focus and their own influence. Most important, Albany police chief Laurie Pritchett shrewdly deprived the movement of the kind of national sympathy won by the Freedom Riders. Pritchett filled the jails with black demonstrators, kept their mistreatment to a minimum, and prevented white mobs from running wild. "We met 'nonviolence' with 'nonviolence,' " he boasted.

King himself was twice arrested in the summer of 1962, but Albany officials quickly freed him to avoid negative publicity. The Kennedy administration kept clear of the developments in Albany, hoping to help the gubernatorial campaign of "moderate" Democrat Carl Sanders. By late 1962 the Albany movement had collapsed, and Pritchett proudly declared the city "as segregated as ever." One activist summed up the losing campaign: "We were naive enough to think we could fill up the jails. Pritchett was hep to the fact that we couldn't. We ran out of people before he ran out of jails." Albany showed that mass protest without violent white reaction and direct federal intervention could not end Jim Crow.

The successful battle to integrate the University of Mississippi in 1962 contrasted with the failure at Albany and reinforced the importance of federal intervention for guaranteeing civil rights to African Americans. In the fall of 1962 James Meredith, an Air Force veteran and a student at all-black Jackson State College, tried to register as the first black student at the university. Governor Ross Barnett defied a federal court order and personally blocked Meredith's path at the admissions office. When Barnett refused to assure Robert Kennedy that Meredith would be protected, the attorney general dispatched 500 federal marshals to the campus. Over the radio, Barnett encouraged resistance to the "oppressive power of the United States," and an angry mob of several thousand whites, many of them armed, laid siege to the campus on September 30. A night of violence left 2 people dead and 160 marshals wounded, 28 from gunfire. President Kennedy ordered 5,000 army troops onto the campus to stop the riot. A federal guard remained to protect Meredith, who graduated the following summer.

THE MOVEMENT AT HIGH TIDE, 1963–65

The tumultuous events of 1960–62 convinced civil rights strategists that segregation could not be dismantled merely through orderly protest and moral persuasion. Only comprehensive civil rights legislation, backed by the power of the federal government, could guarantee full citizenship rights for African Americans. To build the national consensus needed for new laws, civil rights activists looked for ways to gain broader support for their cause. By 1963, their sense of urgency had led them to plan dramatic confrontations that would expose the violence and terror routinely faced by southern blacks. With the whole country—indeed, the whole world—watching, the movement reached the peak of its political and moral power.

Birmingham

At the end of 1962, Martin Luther King and his SCLC allies decided to launch a new campaign against segregation in Birmingham, Alabama. After the failure in Albany, King and his aides looked for a way to shore up his leadership and inject new momentum into the freedom struggle. They needed a major victory. Birmingham was the most segregated big city in America, and it had a deep history of racial violence. African Americans endured total segregation in schools, restaurants, city parks, and department store dressing rooms. Although black people constituted more than 40 percent of the city's population, fewer than 10,000 of Birmingham's 80,000 registered voters were black. The city's prosperous steel industry relegated black workers to menial jobs.

Working closely with local civil rights groups led by the longtime Birmingham activist Reverend Fred Shuttlesworth, the SCLC carefully planned its campaign. The strategy was to fill the city jails with protesters, boycott downtown department stores, and enrage Public Safety Commissioner Eugene "Bull" Connor. In April, King arrived with a manifesto demanding an end to racist hiring practices and segregated public accommodations and the creation of a biracial committee to oversee desegregation. "Here in Birmingham," King told reporters, "we have reached the point of no return." Connor's police began jailing hundreds of demonstrators, including King himself, who defied a state court injunction against further protests.

Held in solitary confinement for several days, King managed to write a response to a group of Birmingham clergy who had deplored the protests. King's *Letter from Birmingham Jail* was soon widely reprinted and circulated as a pamphlet. It set out the key moral issues at stake, and scoffed at those who claimed the campaign was illegal and ill timed. King wrote:

> We know through painful experience that freedom is never voluntarily given by the oppressor; it must be demanded by the oppressed. Frankly, I have never yet engaged in a direct action campaign that was "well timed" in the view of those who have not suffered unduly from the disease of segregation. For years now I have heard the word "Wait!" It rings in the ear of every Negro with a piercing familiarity. This "Wait" has almost always meant "Never." We must come to see, with one of our distinguished jurists, that "justice too long delayed is justice denied."

After King's release on bail, the campaign intensified. The SCLC kept up the pressure by recruiting thousands of Birmingham's young students for a "children's crusade." In early May, Bull Connor's forces

Police dogs attacked a seventeen-year-old civil rights demonstrator for defying an anti-parade ordinance in Birmingham, Alabama, May 3, 1963. He was part of the "children's crusade" organized by SCLC in its campaign to fill the city jails with protesters. More than 900 Birmingham schoolchildren went to jail that day.

began using high-powered water cannons, billy clubs, and snarling police dogs to break up demonstrations. Millions of Americans reacted with horror to the violent scenes from Birmingham shown on national television. Many younger black people, especially from the city's poor and working-class districts, began to fight back, hurling bottles and bricks at police. On May 10, mediators from the Justice Department negotiated an uneasy truce. The SCLC agreed to an immediate end to the protests. In exchange, businesses would desegregate and begin hiring African Americans over the next three months, and a biracial city committee would oversee desegregation of public facilities.

King claimed "the most magnificent victory for justice we've ever seen in the Deep South." But whites such as Bull Connor and Governor George Wallace denounced the agreement. A few days after the announcement, more than a thousand robed Ku Klux Klansmen burned a cross in a park on the outskirts of Birmingham. When bombs rocked SCLC headquarters and the home of King's brother, a Birmingham minister, enraged blacks took to the streets and pelted police and fire fighters with stones and bottles. President Kennedy ordered 3,000 army troops into the city and prepared to nationalize the Alabama Guard. The violence receded, and white city business people and politicians began to carry out the agreed-upon pact. But in September a bomb killed four black girls in a Birmingham Baptist church, reminding the city and the world that racial harmony was still a long way off.

The Birmingham campaign and the other protests it sparked over the next seven months engaged more than 100,000 people and led to nearly 15,000 arrests. The civil rights community now drew support from millions of Americans, black and white, who were inspired by the protesters and repelled by the face of southern bigotry. At the same time, Birmingham changed the nature of black protest. The black unemployed and working poor who joined in the struggle brought a different perspective from that of the students, professionals, and members of the religious middle class who had dominated the movement before Birmingham. They cared less about the philosophy of nonviolence and more about immediate gains in employment and housing and an end to police brutality. The urgent cries for "Freedom now!" were more than simply a demand to end legal segregation, and they were a measure as well of how far the movement had traveled in the seven years since the end of the Montgomery bus boycott.

JFK and the March on Washington

The growth of black activism and white support convinced President Kennedy the moment had come to press for sweeping civil rights legislation. Continuing white resistance in the South also made clearer than ever the need for federal action. In June 1963, Alabama governor George Wallace threatened to personally block the admission of two black students to the state university. Only the deployment of National Guard troops, placed under federal control by the president, ensured the students' safety and their peaceful admission into the University of Alabama.

It was a defining moment for Kennedy. On June 11 the president went on national television and offered his personal endorsement of the civil rights activism. Reviewing the racial situation, Kennedy told his audience that America would not be fully free until all its citizens were free. "We face . . . a moral crisis as a country and a people. It cannot be met by repressive police action. It cannot be left to increased demonstrations in the streets. It cannot be quieted by token moves or talk. It is a time to act in the Congress, in your state and local legislative body, and, above all, in all our daily lives." The next week Kennedy asked Congress for a broad law that would ensure voting rights, outlaw segregation in public facilities, and bolster federal authority to deny funds for discriminatory programs. Knowing they would face a stiff fight from congressional conservatives, administration officials began an intense lobbying effort in support of the law. After three years of fence sitting, Kennedy finally committed his office and his political future to the civil rights cause.

Movement leaders lauded the president's initiative. Yet they understood that racial hatred still haunted the nation. Only a few hours after Kennedy's television speech, a gunman murdered Medgar Evers, leader of the Mississippi NAACP, outside his home in Jackson. To pressure Congress and demonstrate the

Reverend Dr. Martin Luther King, Jr., acknowledging the huge throng at the historic March on Washington for "jobs and freedom," August 28, 1963. The size of the crowd, the stirring oratory and song, and the live network television coverage produced one of the most memorable political events in the nation's history.

urgency of their cause, a broad coalition of civil rights groups planned a massive, nonviolent March on Washington. The idea had deep roots in black protest. A. Philip Randolph, head of the Brotherhood of Sleeping Car Porters, had originally proposed such a march in 1941 to protest discrimination against blacks in the wartime defense industries. Now, more than twenty years later, Randolph, along with his aide Bayard Rustin, revived the concept and convinced leaders of the major civil rights groups to support it.

The Kennedy administration originally opposed the march, fearing it would jeopardize support for the president's civil rights bill in Congress. But as plans for the rally solidified, Kennedy reluctantly gave his approval. Leaders from the SCLC, the NAACP, SNCC, the Urban League, and CORE—the leading organizations in the civil rights community—put aside their tactical differences to forge a broad consensus for the event. John Lewis, the young head of SNCC who had endured numerous brutal assaults, planned a speech that denounced the Kennedys as hypocrites. Lewis's speech enraged Walter Reuther, the white liberal leader of the United Auto Workers union, which had helped finance the march. Reuther threatened to turn off the loudspeakers he was paying for, believing Lewis's speech would embarrass the Kennedys. Randolph, the acknowledged elder statesman of the movement, convinced Lewis at the last moment to tone down his remarks. "We've come this far," he implored. "For the sake of unity, change it."

On August 28, 1963, more than a quarter of a million people, including 50,000 whites, gathered at the Lincoln Memorial to rally for "jobs and freedom." Union members, students, teachers, clergy, professionals, musicians, actors—Americans from all walks of life joined the largest political assembly in the nation's history until then. The sight of all those people holding hands and singing "We Shall Overcome," led by the white folk singer Joan Baez, would not be easily forgotten. At the end of a long, exhilarating day of speeches and freedom songs, Martin Luther King provided an emotional climax. Combining the democratic promise of the Declaration of Independence with the religious fervor of his Baptist heritage, King stirred the crowd with his dream for America:

> I have a dream today that one day this nation will rise up and live out the true meaning of its creed: "We hold these truths to be self-evident—that all men are created equal." . . . When we allow freedom to ring, when we let it ring from every village and every hamlet, from every state and every city, we will be able to speed up that day when all of God's children—black men and white men, Jews and Gentiles, Protestants and Catholics—will be able to join hands and sing in the words of the old Negro spiritual, "Free at last! Free at last! Thank God almighty, we are free at last!"

LBJ and the Civil Rights Act of 1964

An extraordinary demonstration of interracial unity, the March on Washington stood as the high-water mark in the struggle for civil rights. It buoyed the spirits of movement leaders as well as the liberals pushing the new civil rights bill through Congress. But the assassination of John F. Kennedy on November 22, 1963, in Dallas threw an ominous cloud over the whole nation and the civil rights movement in particular. In the Deep South, many ardent segregationists welcomed the president's death because of his support for civil rights. Most African Americans probably shared the feelings of Coretta Scott King, who recalled her family's vigil: "We felt that President Kennedy had been a friend of the Cause and that with him as President we could continue to move forward. We watched and prayed for him."

Lyndon Baines Johnson, Kennedy's successor, had never been much of a friend to civil rights. As a senator from Texas (1948–60, including six years as majority leader), Johnson had been one of the shrewdest and most powerful Democrats in Congress. Throughout the 1950s he had worked to obstruct the passage and enforcement of civil rights laws—though as vice president he had ably chaired Kennedy's working group on equal employment. Johnson reassured a grieving nation that "the ideas and the ideals which [Kennedy] so nobly represented must and will be translated into effective action." Even so, civil rights activists looked upon Johnson warily as he took over the Oval Office.

As president, Johnson realized that he faced a new political reality, one created by the civil rights movement. Eager to unite the Democratic Party and prove himself as a national leader, he seized on civil rights as a golden political opportunity. "I knew that if I didn't get out in front on this issue," he later recalled, "they [the liberals] would get me. They'd throw up my background against me, they'd use it to prove that I was incapable of bringing unity to the land I loved so much. . . . I had to produce a civil rights bill that was even stronger than the one they'd have gotten if Kennedy had lived." Throughout the early months of 1964, the new president let it be known publicly and privately that he would brook no compromise on civil rights.

Johnson exploited all his skills as a political insider. He cajoled, flattered, and threatened key members of the House and Senate. Working with the president, the fifteen-year-old Leadership Conference on Civil Rights coordinated a sophisticated lobbying effort in Congress. Groups such as the NAACP, the AFL-CIO, the National Council of Churches, and the American Jewish Congress made the case for a strong civil rights bill. The House passed the bill in February by a 290–130 vote. The more difficult fight would be in the Senate, where a southern filibuster promised to block the bill or weaken it. But by June, Johnson's persistence had paid off and the southern filibuster had collapsed.

On July 2, 1964, Johnson signed the Civil Rights Act of 1964. Every major provision had survived intact. This landmark law represented the most significant civil rights legislation since Reconstruction. It prohibited discrimination in most places of public accommodation; outlawed discrimination in employment on the basis of race, color, religion, sex, or national origin; outlawed bias in federally assisted programs; authorized the Justice Department to institute suits to desegregate public schools and other facilities; created the Equal Employment Opportunity Commission; and provided technical and financial aid to communities desegregating their schools.

OVERVIEW

LANDMARK CIVIL RIGHTS LEGISLATION, SUPREME COURT DECISIONS, AND EXECUTIVE ORDERS

Year	Decision, law, or executive order	Significance
1939	*Missouri v. ex.rel.Gaines*	Required University of Missouri Law School either to admit African Americans or build another, fully equal law school
1941	Executive Order 8802 (by President Roosevelt)	Banned racial discrimination in defense industry and government offices; established Fair Employment Practices Committee to investigate violations
1946	*Morgan v. Virginia*	Ruled that segregation on interstate buses violated federal law and created an "undue burden" on interstate commerce
1948	Executive Order 9981 (by President Truman)	Desegregated the U.S. armed forces
1950	*McLaurin v. Oklahoma State Regents*	Ruled that forcing an African American student to sit, eat, and study in segregated facilities was unconstitutional because it inevitably created a "badge of inferiority"
1950	*Sweatt v. Painter*	Ruled that an inferior law school created by the University of Texas to serve African-Americans violated their right to equal protection and ordered Herman Sweatt to be admitted to University of Texas Law School
1954	*Brown v. Board of Education of Topeka I*	Declared "separate educational facilities are inherently unequal," thus overturning *Plessy v. Ferguson* (1896) and the "separate but equal" doctrine as it applied to public schools
1955	*Brown v. Board of Education of Topeka II*	Ordered school desegregation to begin with "all deliberate speed," but offered no timetable
1957	Civil Rights Act	Created Civil Rights Division within the Justice Department
1964	Civil Rights Act	Prohibited discrimination in employment and most places of public accommodation on basis of race, color, religion, sex, or national origin; outlawed bias in federally assisted programs; created Equal Employment Opportunity Commission
1965	Voting Rights Act	Authorized federal supervision of voter registration in states and counties where fewer than half of voting age residents were registered; outlawed literacy and other discriminatory tests in voter registration

Mississippi Freedom Summer

While President Johnson and his liberal allies won the congressional battle for the new civil rights bill, activists in Mississippi mounted a far more radical and dangerous campaign than any yet attempted in the South. In the spring of 1964 a coalition of workers led by SNCC launched the Freedom Summer project, an ambitious effort to register black voters and directly challenge the iron rule of segregation. Mississippi stood as the toughest test for the civil rights movement, racially and economically. It was the poorest, most backward state in the nation, and had remained largely untouched by the freedom struggle. African Americans constituted 42 percent of the state's population, but fewer than 5 percent could register to vote. Median black family income was under $1,500 a year, roughly one-third that of white families. A small white planter elite controlled most of the state's wealth, and a long tradition of terror against black people had maintained the racial caste system.

After they were barred from the floor of the August 1964 National Democratic convention, members of the Mississippi Freedom Democratic Party were led by Fanny Lou Hamer in a song-filled protest outside the hotel.

Bob Moses of SNCC and Dave Dennis of CORE planned Freedom Summer as a way of opening up this closed society to the glare of national publicity. The project recruited over 900 volunteers, mostly white college students, to aid in voter registration, teach in "freedom schools," and help build a "freedom party" as an alternative to Mississippi's all-white Democratic Party. Organizers expected violence, which was precisely why they wanted white volunteers. Dave Dennis later explained their reasoning: "The death of a white college student would bring on more attention to what was going on than for a black college student getting it. That's cold, but that was also in another sense speaking the language of this country." Mississippi authorities prepared for the civil rights workers as if expecting a foreign army, beefing up state highway patrols and local police forces.

On June 21, while most project volunteers were still undergoing training in Ohio, three activists disappeared in Neshoba County, Mississippi, when they went to investigate the burning of a black church that was supposed to serve as a freedom school. Six weeks later, after a massive search belatedly ordered by President Johnson, FBI agents discovered the bodies of the three—white activists Michael Schwerner and Andrew Goodman, and a local black activist, James Chaney—buried in an earthen dam. Goodman and Schwerner had been shot once; Chaney had been severely beaten before being shot three times. Over the summer, at least three other civil rights workers died violently. Project workers suffered 1,000 arrests, 80 beatings, 35 shooting incidents, and 30 bombings in homes, churches, and schools.

Within the project, simmering problems tested the ideal of the Beloved Community. Black veterans of SNCC resented the affluent white volunteers, many of whom had not come to terms with their own racial prejudices. White volunteers, staying only a short time in the state, often found it difficult to communicate in the southern communities with local African Americans, who were wary of breaking old codes of deference. Sexual tensions between black male and white female volunteers also strained relations. A number of both black and white women, led by Ruby Doris Robinson, Mary King, and Casey Hayden, began to raise the issue of women's equality as a companion goal to racial equality. The day-to-day reality of violent reprisals, police harassment, and constant fear took a hard toll on everyone.

The project did manage to rivet national attention on Mississippi racism, and it won enormous sympathy from northern liberals. Among their concrete accomplishments, the volunteers could point with pride to more than forty freedom schools that brought classes in reading, arithmetic, politics, and African American history to thousands of black children. Some 60,000 black voters signed up to join the Mississippi Freedom Democratic Party (MFDP). In August 1964 the MFDP sent a slate of delegates to the Democratic

National Convention looking to challenge the credentials of the all-white regular state delegation.

In Atlantic City, the idealism of Freedom Summer ran into the more cynical needs of the national Democratic Party. Lyndon Johnson opposed the seating of the MFDP because he wanted to avoid a divisive floor fight. He was already concerned that Republicans might carry a number of southern states in November. But MFDP leaders and sympathizers gave dramatic testimony before the convention, detailing the racism and brutality in Mississippi politics. "Is this America," asked Fannie Lou Hamer, "the land of the free and the home of the brave, where we are threatened daily because we want to live as decent human beings?" Led by vice-presidential nominee Senator Hubert Humphrey, Johnson's forces offered a compromise that would have given the MFDP a token two seats on the floor. Bitter over what they saw as a betrayal, the MFDP delegates turned the offer down. Within SNCC, the defeat of the MFDP intensified African American disillusionment with the Democratic Party and the liberal establishment.

Born Malcolm Little, Malcolm X (1925–65) took the name "X" as a symbol of the stolen identity of African slaves. He emerged in the early 1960s as the foremost advocate of racial unity and black nationalism. The Black Power movement, initiated in 1966 by SNCC members, was strongly influenced by Malcolm X.

Malcolm X and Black Consciousness

Frustrated with the limits of nonviolent protest and electoral politics, younger activists within SNCC found themselves increasingly drawn to the militant rhetoric and vision of Malcolm X, who since 1950 had been the preeminent spokesman for the black nationalist religious sect, the Nation of Islam (NOI). Founded in depression-era Detroit by Elijah Muhammad, the NOI, like the followers of black nationalist leader Marcus Garvey in the 1920s (see Chapter 23) aspired to create a self-reliant, highly disciplined, and proud community—a separate "nation" for black people. Elijah Muhammad preached a message of racial solidarity and self-help, criticized crime and drug use, and castigated whites as "blue-eyed devils" responsible for the world's evil. During the 1950s the NOI (also called Black Muslims) successfully organized in northern black communities, appealing especially to criminals, drug addicts, and others living on the margins of urban life. It operated restaurants, retail stores, and schools as models for black economic self-sufficiency.

The man known as Malcolm X had been born Malcolm Little in 1925 and raised in Lansing, Michigan. His father, a preacher and a follower of Marcus Garvey, was killed in a racist attack by local whites. In his youth, Malcolm led a life of petty crime, eventually serving a seven-year prison term for burglary. While in jail he educated himself and converted to the Nation of Islam. He took the surname "X" to symbolize his original African family name, lost through slavery. Emerging from jail in 1952, he became a dynamic organizer, editor, and speaker for the Nation of Islam. He spoke frequently on college campuses as well on the street corners of black neighborhoods like New York's Harlem. He encouraged his audiences to take pride in their African heritage and to consider armed self-defense rather than relying solely on nonviolence—in short, to break free of white domination "by any means necessary."

Malcolm ridiculed the integrationist goals of the civil rights movement. Black Muslims, he told audiences, do not want "to integrate into this corrupt society, but to separate from it, to a land of our own, where we can reform ourselves, lift up our moral standards, and try to be godly." In his best-selling *Autobiography of Malcolm X* (1965), he admitted that his position was extremist. "The black race here in North America is in extremely bad condition. You show me a black man who isn't an extremist," he argued, "and I'll show you one who needs psychiatric attention."

In 1964, troubled by Elijah Muhammad's personal scandals (he faced paternity suits brought by two young female employees) and eager to find a more politically effective approach to improving conditions for blacks, Malcolm X broke with the Nation of Islam. He made a pilgrimage to Mecca, the Muslim holy city, where he met Islamic peoples of all colors and underwent a "radical alteration in my whole outlook about 'white' men." He returned to the United States as El-Hajj Malik El-Shabazz, abandoned his black separatist views, and founded the Organization of Afro-American Unity. Malcolm now looked for common ground with the civil rights movement, addressing a Mississippi Freedom Democrats rally in Harlem and meeting with SNCC activists. He stressed the international links between the civil rights struggle in America and the problems facing emerging African nations. On February 21, 1965, Malcolm X was assassinated during a speech at Harlem's Audubon Ballroom. His assailants were members of a New Jersey branch of the NOI, possibly infiltrated by the FBI.

"More than any other person," remarked black author Julius Lester, "Malcolm X was responsible for the new militancy that entered The Movement in 1965." SNCC leader John Lewis thought Malcolm had been the most effective voice "to articulate the aspirations, bitterness, and frustrations of the Negro people," forming "a living link between Africa and the civil rights movement in this country." In his death he became a martyr for the idea that soon became known as Black Power. As much as anyone, Malcolm X pointed the way to a new black consciousness that celebrated black history, black culture, the African heritage, and black self-sufficiency.

Selma and the Voting Rights Act of 1965

Lyndon Johnson won reelection in 1964 by a landslide, capturing 61 percent of the popular vote. Of the 6 million black people who voted in the election, 2 million more than in 1960, an overwhelming 94 percent cast their ballots for Johnson. Republican candidate Senator Barry Goldwater managed to carry only his home state of Arizona and five Deep South states, where fewer than 45 percent of eligible black people could vote. With Democrats in firm control of both the Senate and the House, civil rights leaders believed the time was ripe for further legislative gains. Johnson and his staff began drafting a tough voting rights bill in late 1964, partly with an eye toward countering Republican gains in the Deep South with newly registered black and Democratic voters. Martin Luther King and the SCLC shared this goal of passing a strong voting rights law that would provide southern black people with direct federal protection of their right to vote.

Once again, movement leaders plotted to create a crisis that would arouse national indignation, pressure Congress, and force federal action. King and his aides chose Selma, Alabama, as the target of their campaign. Selma, a city of 27,000 some fifty miles west of Montgomery, had a notorious record of preventing black voting. Of the 15,000 eligible black voters in Selma's Dallas County, registered voters numbered only in the hundreds. In 1963, local activists Amelia Boynton and Reverend Fred Reese had invited SNCC workers to aid voter registration efforts in the community. But they had met a violent reception from county sheriff Jim Clark. Sensing that Clark might be another Bull Connor, King arrived in Selma in January 1965, just after accepting the Nobel Peace Prize in Oslo. "We are not asking, we are demanding the ballot," he declared. King, the SCLC staff, and SNCC workers led daily marches on the Dallas County Courthouse, where hundreds of black citizens tried to get their names added to voter lists. By early February, Clark had imprisoned more than 3,000 protesters.

Despite the brutal beating of Reverend James Bevel, a key SCLC strategist, and the killing of Jimmy

Voting rights demonstrators rallied in front of the state capitol in Montgomery, Alabama, March 25, 1965, after a four day, fifty-four mile trek from Selma. The original 3,000 marchers were joined by over 30,000 supporters by the end of their journey.

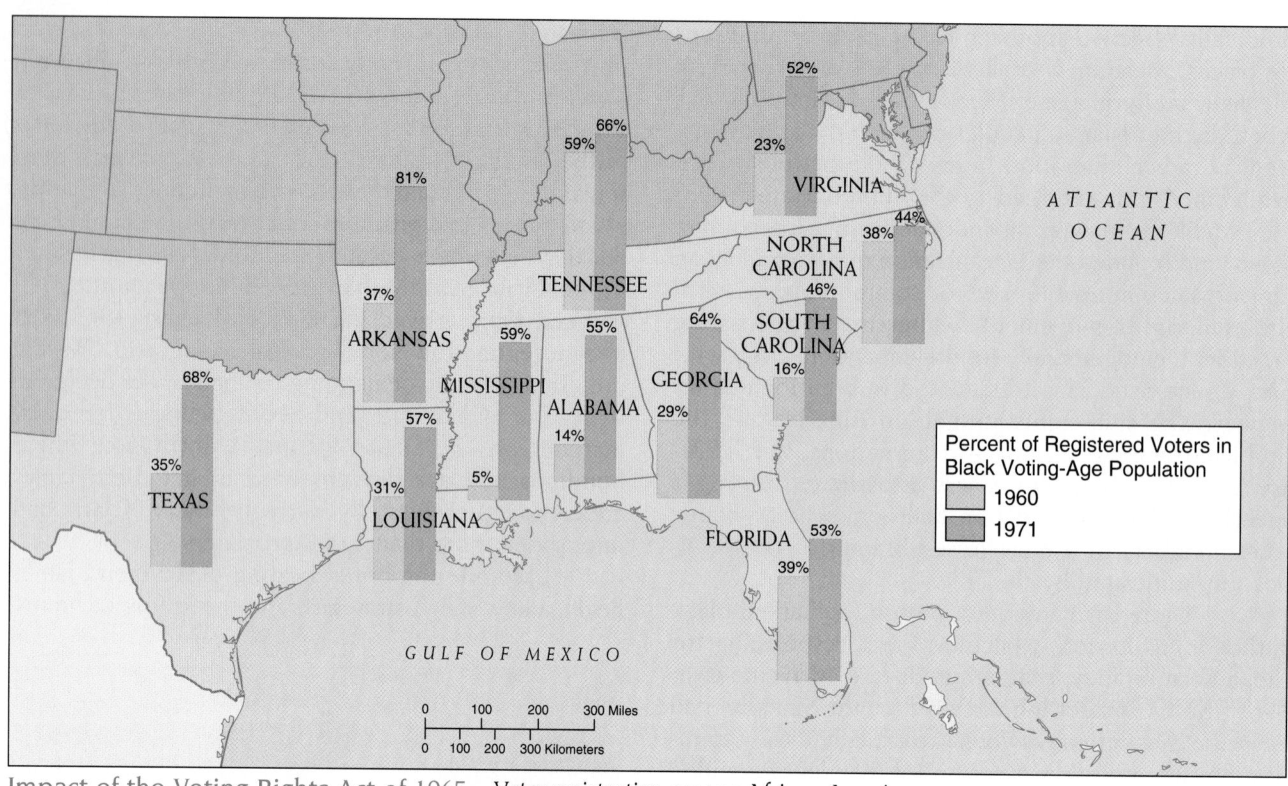

Impact of the Voting Rights Act of 1965 *Voter registration among African Americans in the South increased significantly between* 1960 *and* 1971.

Lee Jackson, a young black demonstrator in nearby Marion, the SCLC failed to arouse the level of national indignation it sought. Consequently, in early March SCLC staffers called on black activists to march from Selma to Montgomery, where they planned to deliver a list of grievances to Governor Wallace. On Sunday, March 7, while King preached to his church in Atlanta, a group of 600 marchers crossed the Pettus Bridge on the Alabama River, on their way to Montgomery. A group of mounted, heavily armed county and state lawmen blocked their path and ordered them to turn back. When the marchers did not move, the lawmen attacked with billy clubs and tear gas, driving the protesters back over the bridge in a bloody rout. More than fifty marchers had to be treated in local hospitals.

The dramatic "Bloody Sunday" attack received extensive coverage on network television, prompting a national uproar. Demands for federal intervention poured into the White House from all over the country. King issued a public call for civil rights supporters to come to Selma for a second march on Montgomery. But a federal court temporarily enjoined the SCLC from proceeding with the march. King found himself trapped. He reluctantly accepted a face-saving compromise: in return for a promise from Alabama authorities not to harm marchers, King would lead his followers across the Pettus Bridge, stop, pray briefly, and then turn back. This plan outraged the more militant SNCC activists and sharpened their distrust of King and the SCLC.

But just when it seemed the Selma movement might die, white racist violence revived it. A gang of white toughs attacked four white Unitarian ministers who had come to Selma to participate in the march. One of them, Reverend James J. Reeb of Boston, died of multiple skull fractures. His death brought new calls for federal action. On March 15, President Johnson delivered a televised address to a joint session of Congress to request passage of a voting rights bill. In a stirring speech, the president fused the political power of his office with the moral power of the movement. "Their cause must be our cause, too. Because it is not just Negroes, but really all of us who must overcome the crippling legacy of bigotry and injustice. And," he concluded firmly, invoking the movement's slogan, "we shall overcome." Johnson also prevailed upon federal judge Frank Johnson to issue a ruling allowing the march to proceed, and he warned Governor Wallace not to interfere.

On March 21 Martin Luther King led a group of more than 3,000 black and white marchers out of Selma on the road to Montgomery, where the bus boycott that marked the beginning of his involvement had occurred nine years before. Four days later they arrived at the Alabama statehouse. Their ranks had been swelled by more than 30,000 supporters, including hundreds of prominent politicians, entertainers, and black leaders. "I know some of you are asking today," King told the crowd, " 'How long will it take?' " He went on in a rousing, rhythmic cadence:

> I come to say to you this afternoon, however difficult the moment, however frustrating the hour, it will not be long because truth pressed to earth will rise again. How long? Not long, because no lie can live forever. How long? Not long, because you will reap what you sow. How long? Not long, because the arc of the moral universe is long but it bends toward justice. How long? Not long, because mine eyes have seen the glory of the coming of the Lord!

In August 1965 President Johnson signed the Voting Rights Act into law. It authorized federal supervision of registration in states and counties where fewer than half of voting-age residents were registered. It also outlawed literacy and other discriminatory tests that had been used to prevent blacks from registering to vote. Between 1964 and 1968, black registrants in Mississippi leaped from 7 percent to 59 percent of the statewide black population; in Alabama, from 24 percent to 57 percent. In those years the number of southern black voters grew from 1 million to 3.1 million. For the first time in their lives, black Southerners in hundreds of small towns and rural communities could enjoy full participation in American politics. Ten years after the Montgomery bus boycott, the civil rights movement had reached a peak of national influence and interracial unity.

FORGOTTEN MINORITIES, 1945–65

The civil rights movement revolved around the aspirations and community strength of African Americans. The historic injustices of slavery, racism, and segregation gave a moral and political urgency to the black struggle for full citizenship rights. Yet other minorities as well had long been denied their civil rights. After World War II, Latinos, Indian peoples, and Asian Americans began making their own halting efforts to improve their political, legal, and economic status. They faced strong opposition from institutional racism and various economic interests that benefited from keeping these groups in a subordinate position. By the late 1960s, the success of the black civil rights movement had inspired these minority groups to adopt more militant strategies of their own.

Mexican Americans

The Mexican American community in the West and Southwest included both longtime U.S. citizens—who found white authorities nonetheless unwilling to recognize their rights—and non-citizen immigrants from Mexico. After World War II, several Mexican American political organizations sought to secure equal rights and equal opportunity for their community by stressing its American identity. The most important of these groups were the League of United Latin American Citizens (LULAC), founded in Texas in 1928, and the GI Forum, founded in Texas in 1948 by Mexican American veterans of World War II. Both emphasized the learning of English, assimilation into American society, improved education, and the promotion of political power through voting. LULAC successfully pursued two important legal cases that anticipated *Brown v. Board of Education*. In *Mendez v. Westminster,* a 1947 California case, and in the 1948 *Delgado* case in Texas, the Supreme Court upheld lower-court rulings that declared segregation of Mexican Americans unconstitutional. Like *Brown*, these two decisions did not immediately end segregation, but they offered pathbreaking legal and psychological victories to Mexican American activists. LULAC won another significant legal battle in the 1954 *Hernandez* decision, in which the Supreme Court ended the exclusion of Mexican Americans from Texas jury lists.

Mexican migration to the United States increased dramatically during and after World War II. The *bracero* program, a cooperative effort between the U.S. and Mexican governments, brought some 300,000 Mexicans to the United States during the war as temporary agricultural and railroad workers. American agribusiness came to depend on Mexicans as a key source of cheap farm labor, and the program continued after the war. Most *braceros* endured harsh work, poor food, and substandard housing in the camps in which they lived. Some migrated into the newly emerging barrio neighborhoods in cities such as San Antonio, Los Angeles, El Paso, and Denver. Many *braceros* and their children became American citizens, but most returned to Mexico. Another group of postwar Mexican immigrants were the *mojados*, or "wetbacks," so called because many swam across the Rio Grande River to enter the United States illegally.

In 1954, in an effort to curb the flow of undocumented immigrants from Mexico, the Eisenhower administration launched the massive "Operation Wetback." Over the next three years Immigration Service agents rounded up some 3.7 million allegedly illegal migrants and sent them back over the border. Immigration agents made little effort to distinguish the so-called illegals from *braceros* and Mexican American citizens. Many families were broken up, and thousands who had lived in the United States for a decade or more found

Delegates to the 1948 National Convention of the League of United Latin American Citizens met in Kingsville, Texas. After World War II, LULAC grew to about 15,000 members active in two hundred local councils, mostly in Texas and California.

themselves deported. Many deportees were denied basic civil liberties, such as due process, and suffered physical abuse and intimidation. Most Mexican Americans had ambivalent feelings about *mojados* and Operation Wetback. The deportations tended to improve job opportunities and wages for those who remained. Yet the so-called illegals were considered members of *la raza*, the larger Mexican American community, and family ties between these groups were common. LULAC and the *Asociación Nacional Mexico-Americana*, founded in 1950, tried in vain to curb abuses against aliens and Mexican Americans. Among Mexican Americans, Operation Wetback left a bitter legacy of deep mistrust and estrangement from Anglo culture and politics.

Puerto Ricans

The United States took possession of the island of Puerto Rico in 1898, during the final stages of the Spanish-American War. The Jones Act of 1917 made the island an unincorporated territory of the United States and granted U.S. citizenship to all Puerto Ricans. Over the next several decades, Puerto Rico's economic base shifted from a diversified, subsistence-oriented agriculture to a single export crop—sugar. U.S. absentee owners dominated the sugar industry, claiming most of the island's arable land, previously tilled by small farmers growing crops for local consumption. Puerto Rico's sugar industry grew enormously profitable, but few island residents benefited from this expansion. By the 1930s, unemployment and poverty were widespread and the island was forced to import its foodstuffs.

Small communities of Puerto Rican migrants had begun to form in New York City during the 1920s. The largest was on the Upper East Side of Manhattan—*el barrio* in East Harlem. During World War II, labor shortages led the federal government to sponsor the recruitment of Puerto Rican workers for industrial jobs in New Jersey, Philadelphia, and Chicago. But the "great migration" took place from 1945 to 1964. During these two decades the number of Puerto Ricans living on the mainland jumped from less than 100,000 to roughly 1 million. Economic opportunity was the chief impetus for this migration, for the island suffered from high unemployment rates and low wages.

The advent of direct air service between Puerto Rico and New York in 1945 made the city easily accessible. The Puerto Rican community in East (or Spanish) Harlem mushroomed, and new communities in the South Bronx and Brooklyn began to emerge. By 1970 there were about 800,000 Puerto Ricans in New York—more than 10 percent of the city's population. New Puerto Rican communities also took root in Connecticut, Massachusetts, New Jersey, and the Midwest. Puerto Ricans frequently circulated between the island and the mainland, often returning home when economic conditions on the mainland were less favorable.

The experience of Puerto Rican migrants both resembled and differed from that of other immigrant groups in significant ways. Like Mexican immigrants, Puerto Ricans were foreign in language, culture, and experience, yet unlike them they entered the United States as citizens. Many Puerto Ricans were also African Americans. Racial and ethnic discrimination came as a double shock, since Puerto Ricans, as citizens, entered the United States with a sense of entitlement. In New York, Puerto Ricans found themselves barred from most craft unions, excluded from certain neighborhoods, and forced to take jobs largely in the low-paying garment industry and service trades. Puerto Rican children were not well served by a public school system insensitive to language differences and too willing to track Spanish-speaking students into obsolete vocational programs.

By the early 1970s, Puerto Rican families were substantially poorer on average than the total population of the country, and they had the lowest median income of any Latino groups. The steep decline in manufacturing jobs and in the garment industry in New York during the 1960s and 1970s hit the Puerto Rican community especially hard. So did the city's fiscal crisis, which brought sharp cuts in funding for schools, health care, libraries, government jobs, and other public services traditionally available to immigrant groups. The structural shift in the U.S. economy away from manufacturing and toward service and high-technology jobs reinforced the Puerto Rican community's goal of improving educational opportunities for its members. The struggle to establish and improve bilingual education in schools became an important part of this effort. Most Puerto Ricans, especially those who had succeeded in school and achieved middle-class status, continued to identify strongly with their Puerto Rican heritage and the Spanish language.

Indian Peoples

The postwar years also brought significant changes in the status and lives of Indian peoples. Congress reversed the policies pursued under the New Deal, which had stressed Indian sovereignty and cultural independence. Responding to a variety of pressure groups, including mining and other economic interests wishing to exploit the resources on Indian reservations, Congress adopted a policy known as "termination," designed to cancel Indian treaties and terminate sovereignty rights. In 1953 it passed House Concurrent Resolution 108, which allowed Congress to terminate a tribe as a political entity by passing legislation specific to that tribe. The leader of the termination forces, Senator Arthur Watkins of Utah, declared the new law meant that "the concept that the Indian people exist within the United States as independent nations has been rejected." Supporters of termination had varied motives, but the policy added up to the return of enforced assimilation for solving the "Indian problem."

George Gillette (left foreground), chairman of the Fort Berthold Indian Council, wept as Secretary of Interior J. A. Krug signed a contract buying 155,000 acres of the tribe's best land in North Dakota for a reservoir project, May 20, 1948. "The members of the tribal council sign this contract with heavy hearts," Gillette said.

Between 1954 and 1962, Congress passed twelve termination bills covering more than sixty tribes, nearly all in the West. Even when tribes consented to their own termination, they discovered that dissolution brought unforeseen problems. For example, members of the Klamaths of Oregon and the Paiutes of Utah received large cash payments from the division of tribal assets. But after these one-time payments were spent, members had to take poorly paid, unskilled jobs to survive. Many Indian peoples became dependent on state social services and slipped into poverty and alcoholism.

Along with termination, the federal government gave greater emphasis to a relocation program aimed at speeding up assimilation. The Bureau of Indian Affairs encouraged reservation Indians to relocate to cities, where they were provided housing and jobs. For some, relocation meant assimilation, intermarriage with whites, and the loss of tribal identity. Others, homesick and unable to adjust to an alien culture and place, either returned to reservations or wound up on the margins of city life. Still others regularly traveled back and forth. In some respects, this urban migration paralleled the larger postwar shift of rural peoples to cities and suburbs.

Indians increasingly came to see termination as a policy geared mainly to exploiting resources on Indian lands. By the early 1960s a new movement was emerging to defend Indian sovereignty. The National Congress of American Indians (NCAI) condemned termination, calling for a review of federal policies and a return to self-determination. The NCAI led a political and educational campaign that challenged the goal of assimilation and created a new awareness among white people that Indians had the right to remain Indians. When the termination policy ended in the early 1960s, it had affected only about 3 percent of federally recognized Indian peoples.

Taking their cue from the civil rights movement, Indian activists used the court system to reassert sovereign rights. Indian and white liberal lawyers, many with experience in civil rights cases, worked through the Native American Rights Fund, which became a powerful force in western politics. A series of Supreme Court decisions, culminating in *U.S. v. Wheeler* (1978), reasserted the principle of "unique and limited" sovereignty. The Court recognized tribal independence except where limited by treaty or Congress.

The Indian population had been growing since the early years of the century, but most reservations had trouble making room for a new generation. Indians suffered increased rates of poverty, chronic unemployment, alcoholism, and poor health. The average Indian family in the early 1960s earned only one-third of the average family income in the United States. Those who remained in the cities usually became "ethnic Indians," identifying themselves more as Indians than as members of specific tribes. By the late 1960s ethnic Indians had begun emphasizing civil rights over tribal rights, making common cause with African Americans and other minorities. The National Indian Youth Council (NIYC), founded in 1960, tried to unite the two causes of equality for individual Indians and special status for tribes. But the organization faced difficult contradictions between a common Indian identity, emphasizing Indians as a single ethnic group, and tribal identity, stressing the citizenship of Indians in separate nations.

Asian Americans

The harsh relocation program of World War II devastated the Japanese American community on the west coast (see Chapter 25). But the war against Nazism also helped weaken older notions of white superiority and racism. During the war the state of California had aggressively enforced an alien land law by confiscating property declared illegally held by Japanese. In November 1946 a proposition supporting the law appeared on the state ballot. But, thanks in part to a campaign by the Japanese American Citizens League (JACL) reminding voters of the wartime contributions of Nisei (second-generation) soldiers, voters overwhelmingly rejected the referendum. One JACL leader hailed the vote as proof that "the people of California will not approve discriminatory and prejudiced treatment of persons of Japanese ancestry." Two years later the Supreme Court declared the law unconstitutional, calling it "nothing more than outright racial discrimination."

The 1952 Immigration and Nationality Act (see Chapter 26) removed the old ban against Japanese immigration, and also made Issei (first-generation Japanese Americans) eligible for naturalized citizenship. Japanese Americans, who lobbied hard for the new law, greeted it with elation. "It gave the Japanese equality with all other immigrants," said JACL leader Harry Takagi, "and that was the principle we had been struggling for from the very beginning." By 1965 some 46,000 immigrant Japanese, most of them elderly Issei, had taken their citizenship oaths. One of these wrote a poem to celebrate the achievement:

> *Going steadily to study English,*
> *Even through the rain at night,*
> *I thus attain,*
> *Late in life,*
> *American citizenship.*

The Immigration and Nationality Act allowed immigration from the "Asian-Pacific Triangle." It was nonetheless racially discriminatory, in that each country in Asia was permitted only 100 immigrants a year. In addition, the act continued the national-origins quotas of 1924 for European countries. The civil rights struggle helped spur a movement to reform immigration policies. "Everywhere else in our national life, we have eliminated discrimination based on national origins," Attorney General Robert Kennedy told Congress in 1964. "Yet, this system is still the foundation of our immigration law."

In 1965 Congress passed a new Immigration and Nationality Act, abolishing the national-origins quotas and providing for the admission each year of 170,000 immigrants from the Eastern Hemisphere and 120,000 from the Western Hemisphere. The new law set a limit of 20,000 per country from the Eastern Hemisphere—these immigrants to be admitted on a first-come, first-served basis—and established preference categories for professional and highly skilled immigrants.

The 1965 act would have a profound effect on Asian American communities, opening the way for a new wave of immigration. In the twenty years following the act the number of Asian Americans soared from 1 million to 5 million. Four times as many Asians settled in the United States in this period as in the entire previous history of the nation. This new wave also brought a strikingly different group of Asian immigrants. In 1960 the Asian American population was 52 percent Japanese, 27 percent Chinese, and 20 percent Filipino. In 1985, the composition was 21 percent Chinese, 21 percent Filipino, 15 percent

CHRONOLOGY

1941 Executive Order 8802 forbids racial discrimination in defense industries and government

1946 In *Morgan v. Virginia,* U.S. Supreme Court rules that segregation on interstate buses is unconstitutional

President Harry Truman creates the Committee on Civil Rights

1947 Jackie Robinson becomes the first African American on a major league baseball team

1948 President Truman issues executive order desegregating the armed forces

1954 In *Brown v. Board of Education,* Supreme Court rules segregated schools inherently unequal

1955 Supreme Court rules that school desegregation must proceed "with all deliberate speed"

Montgomery bus boycott begins

1956 Montgomery bus boycott ends in victory as the Supreme Court affirms a district court ruling that segregation on buses is unconstitutional

1957 Southern Christian Leadership Conference (SCLC) is founded

President Dwight Eisenhower sends in federal troops to protect African American students integrating Little Rock, Arkansas, high school

1960 Sit-in movement begins as four college students sit at a lunch counter in Greensboro, North Carolina, and ask to be served

Student Nonviolent Coordinating Committee (SNCC) founded

1960 Board of Indian Commissioners is created

Buffalo Bill, the King of the Border Men, sets off "Wild West" publishing craze

1961 Freedom Rides begin

1962 James Meredith integrates the University of Mississippi

The Albany movement fails to end segregation in Albany, Georgia

1963 SCLC initiates campaign to desegregate Birmingham, Alabama

Medgar Evers, leader of the Mississippi NAACP, is assassinated

March on Washington; Martin Luther King Jr. delivers his historic "I Have a Dream" speech

1964 Mississippi Freedom Summer project brings students to Mississippi to teach and register voters

President Johnson signs the Civil Rights Act of 1964

Civil rights workers Michael Schwerner, James Chaney, and Andrew Goodman are found buried in Philadelphia, Mississippi

Mississippi Freedom Democratic Party (MFDP) is denied seats at the 1964 Democratic Presidential Convention

1965 SCLC and SNCC begin voter registration campaign in Selma, Alabama

Malcolm X is assassinated

Civil rights marchers walk from Selma to Montgomery

Voting Rights Act of 1965 is signed into law

Japanese, 12 percent Vietnamese, 11 percent Korean, 10 percent Asian Indian, 4 percent Laotian, and 3 percent Cambodian. These newcomers included significant numbers of highly educated professionals and city dwellers, a sharp contrast with the farmers and rural peoples of the past.

CONCLUSION

The mass movement for civil rights was arguably the most important domestic event of the twentieth century. The struggle that began in Montgomery in December 1955 ultimately transformed race relations in thousands of American communities. By the early 1960s this community-based movement had placed civil rights at the very center of national political life. It achieved its greatest successes by invoking the law of the land to destroy legal segregation and win individual freedom for African Americans. The Civil Rights Act of 1964 and the Voting Rights Act of 1965 testified to the power of an African American and white liberal coalition. Yet the persistence of racism, poverty, and ghetto slums challenged a central assumption of liberalism: that equal protection of constitutional rights would give all Americans equal opportunities in life. By the mid-1960s, many black people had begun to question the core values of liberalism, the benefits of alliance with whites, and the philosophy of nonviolence. At the same time, a conservative white backlash against the gains made by African Americans further weakened the liberal political consensus.

In challenging the persistence of widespread poverty and institutional racism, the civil rights movement called for deep structural changes in American life. By 1967, Martin Luther King was articulating a broad and radical vision linking the struggle against racial injustice to other defects in American society. "The black revolution," he argued, "is much more than a struggle for the rights of Negroes. It is forcing America to face all its interrelated flaws—racism, poverty, militarism, and materialism. It is exposing evils that are deeply rooted in the whole structure of our society." Curing these ills would prove far more difficult than ending legal segregation.

REVIEW QUESTIONS

1. What were the key legal and political antecedents to the civil rights struggle in the 1940s and early 1950s? What organizations played the most central role? Which tactics continued to be used, and which were abandoned?
2. How did African American communities challenge legal segregation in the South? Compare the strategies of key organizations, such as the NAACP, SNCC, SCLC, and CORE.
3. Discuss the varieties of white resistance to the civil rights movement. Which were most effective in slowing the drive for equality?
4. Analyze the civil rights movement's complex relationship with the national Democratic Party between 1948 and 1964. How was the party transformed by its association with the movement? What political gains and losses did that association entail?
5. What legal and institutional impact did the movement have on American life? How did it change American culture and politics? Where did it fail?
6. What relationship did the African American struggle for civil rights have with other American minorities? How—if at all—did these minorities benefit? Did they build their own versions of the movement?

RECOMMENDED READING

Taylor Branch, *Parting the Waters: America in the King Years, 1954–1963* (1988); *Pillar of Fire: America in the King Years, 1963–1965* (1998). A deeply researched and monumental narrative history of the southern civil rights movement organized around the life and influence of Reverend Martin Luther King Jr.

Clayborne Carson, *In Struggle: SNCC and the Black Awakening of the 1960s* (1981). The most comprehensive history of the Student Nonviolent Coordinating Committee, arguably the most important civil rights organization. Carson stresses the evolution of SNCC's radicalism during the course of the decade.

William Chafe, *Civilities and Civil Rights: Greensboro, North Carolina, and the Black Struggle for Equality* (1980). Examines the community of Greensboro from 1945 to 1975. Chafe focuses on the "etiquette of civility" and its complex relationship with the promise of racial justice, along with black protest movements and relations between the city's blacks and whites.

David Chappell, *Inside Agitators: White Southerners in the Civil Rights Movement* (1994). The best recent analysis of white involvement in the movement.

Sara Evans, *Personal Politics: The Roots of Women's Liberation in the Civil Rights Movement and the New Left* (1979). A pathbreaking study showing the important connections between the struggle for black rights and the rebirth of feminism.

Aldon D. Morris, *The Origins of the Civil Rights Movement: Black Communities Organizing for Change* (1984). An important study combining history and social theory. Morris emphasizes the key role of ordinary black people, acting through their churches and other community organizations before 1960.

Howell Raines, *My Soul Is Rested: Movement Days in the Deep South Remembered* (1977). The best oral history of the civil rights movement, drawing from a wide range of participants and points of view. It is brilliantly edited by Raines, who covered the events as a journalist.

Jo Ann Gibson Robinson, *The Montgomery Bus Boycott and the Women Who Started It*, ed. David J. Garrow (1987). An important memoir by one of the key behind-the-scenes players in the Montgomery bus boycott. Robinson stresses the role of middle- and working-class black women in the struggle.

Mark Tushnet, *Making Civil Rights Law: Thurgood Marshall and the Supreme Court, 1936–1961* (1994). An in-depth examination of Marshall's critical role in leading the legal fight against segregation.

Robert Weisbrot, *Freedom Bound: A History of America's Civil Rights Movement* (1990). One of the best single-volume syntheses of the movement. Weisbrot is especially strong on the often turbulent relations between black activists and white liberals and the relationship between civil rights and broader currents of American reform.

ADDITIONAL BIBLIOGRAPHY

Origins of the Movements

Michael R. Belknap, *Federal Law and Southern Order* (1987)
William C. Berman, *The Politics of Civil Rights in the Truman Administration* (1970)
A. Russell Buchanan, *Black Americans in World War II* (1977)
Richard M. Dalfiume, *Desegregation of the U.S. Armed Forces* (1969)
Scott DeVeaux, *The Birth of BeBop* (1998)
Elizabeth Huckaby, *Crisis at Central High* (1980)
Martin Luther King Jr., *Stride toward Freedom* (1958)
Richard Kluger, *Simple Justice* (1977)
Bernard Schwartz, *Inside the Warren Court* (1987)
___, *The NAACP's Legal Strategy against Segregated Education* (1987)
Jules Tygiel, *Baseball's Great Experiment: Jackie Robinson and His Legacy* (1983)
Stephen J. Whitfield, *A Death in the Delta: The Story of Emmett Till* (1989)
C. Vann Woodward, *The Strange Career of Jim Crow*, 3d ed. (1974)

No Easy Road to Freedom, 1957–62

Jack Bloom, *Class, Race, and the Civil Rights Movement* (1987)
James Farmer, *Lay Bare the Heart* (1985)
James Forman, *The Making of Black Revolutionaries* (1985)
David J. Garrow, *The FBI and Martin Luther King Jr.* (1983)
Ann Moody, *Coming of Age in Mississippi* (1970)
Cleveland Sellers with Robert Terrell, *The River of No Return* (1973)
Harris Wofford, *Of Kennedys and Kings* (1980)
Miles Wolff, *Lunch at the 5&10* (1990)
Howard Zinn, *SNCC: The New Abolitionists* (1965)

The Movement at High Tide, 1963–65

Seth Cagin and Philip Dray, *We Are Not Afraid* (1988)
David J. Garrow, *Protest at Selma* (1978)
Hugh Davis Graham, *The Civil Rights Era* (1990)
Henry Hampton and Steve Fayer, *Voices of Freedom: An Oral History of the Civil Rights Movement* (1990)
Stephen Lawson, *Black Ballots* (1976)
Doug McAdam, *Freedom Summer* (1988)
Harvard Sitkoff, *The Struggle for Black Equality, 1954–1992* (1993)
Mark Stern, *Calculating Visions: Kennedy, Johnson, and Civil Rights* (1992)
Sheyann Webb and Rachel West Nelson, *Selma, Lord, Selma* (1980)
Charles Whalen and Barbara Whalen, *The Longest Debate: A Legislative History of the 1964 Civil Rights Act* (1985)

Forgotten Minorities, 1945–65

Rodolfo Acuna, *Occupied America*, 3d ed. (1981)
Manuel Alers-Montalvo, *The Puerto Rican Migrants of New York* (1985)
Frank T. Bean and Marta Tienda, *The Hispanic Population of the United States* (1988)
Larry Burt, *Tribalism in Crisis: Federal Indian Policy, 1953–1961* (1982)
Donald Fixico, *Termination and Relocation: Federal Indian Policy, 1945–1960* (1986)
Mario T. Garcia, *Mexican Americans* (1989)
Virginia Sanchez Korrol, *From Colonia to Community* (1983)
Benjamin Marquez, *LULAC* (1993)
Ronald Takaki, *Strangers from a Different Shore: A History of Asian Americans* (1989)

Biography

Paul K. Conkin, *Big Daddy from the Pedernales: Lyndon Baines Johnson* (1986)
David J. Garrow, *Bearing the Cross: Martin Luther King, Jr., and the Southern Christian Leadership Conference* (1986)
David Levering Lewis, *King: A Biography*, 2d ed. (1978)
Malcolm X, with Alex Haley, *The Autobiography of Malcolm X* (1965)
Kay Mills, *This Little Light of Mine: The Life of Fannie Lou Hamer* (1993)
Bruce Perry, *Malcolm: The Life of a Man Who Changed Black America* (1991)
Paula F. Pfeffer, *A. Philip Randolph* (1990)

CHAPTER TWENTY-NINE

WAR ABROAD, WAR AT HOME

1965–1974

Bernard Perlin, *Mayor Richard Daley*, 1968. Collection of Philip J. and Suzanne Schiller, American Social Commentary Art, 1930–70.

AMERICAN COMMUNITIES
Uptown, Chicago, Illinois

CHAPTER OUTLINE

During Freedom Summer of 1964, while teams of northern college students traveled south to join voter registration campaigns among African Americans, a small group moved to Chicago to help the city's poor people take control of their communities and to demand better city services. They targeted a neighborhood known as Uptown, a one-mile-square section five miles north of the Loop, the city center. The residents, many only recently transplanted from the poverty of the Appalachian South, lived in crowded tenements or in once-elegant mansions now subdivided into tiny, run-down apartments. Four thousand people lived on just one street running four blocks, 20 percent of them on welfare. Chicago civic authorities had also selected this neighborhood for improvement. Designating it a Conservation Area under the terms of the Urban Renewal Act, they applied for federal funds in order to upgrade the housing for middle-income families and, in effect, to clear out the current residents. In contrast, the student organizers intended to mobilize the community "so as to demand an end to poverty and the construction of a decent social order."

With the assistance of the Packinghouse Workers union, the students formed Jobs or Income Now (JOIN), opened a storefront office, and invited local residents to work with them to halt the city's plans. They spent hours and hours listening to people, drawing out their ideas and helping them develop scores of additional programs. Confronting the bureaucracy of the welfare and unemployment compensation offices stood high on their list. They also campaigned against Mayor Richard Daley's policy of "police omnipresence" that had a fleet of squad cars and paddy wagons continually patrolling the neighborhood. To curb police harassment, they demanded the creation of civilian review boards. They also helped establish new social clubs, a food-buying cooperative, a community theater, and a health clinic. Within a few years, Uptown street kids had formed the Young Patriots organization, put out a community newspaper, *Rising Up Angry*, and staffed free breakfast programs.

Chicago JOIN was one of ten similar projects sponsored by Students for a Democratic Society (SDS). Impatient with the nation's chronic poverty and cold war politics, twenty-nine students from nine universities had met in June 1960 to form a new kind of campus-based political organization. SDS soon caught the attention of liberal students, encouraging them, as part of the nation's largest college population to date, to make their voices heard. By its peak in 1968, SDS had 350 chapters and between 60,000 and 100,000 members. Its principle of participatory democracy—with its promise to give people control over the decisions affecting their lives—appealed to a wider following of more than a million students.

In June 1962 in Port Huron, Michigan, the founding members of SDS issued a declaration of principles, drafted mainly by graduate student Tom Hayden. "We are people . . . bred in at least modest comfort, housed now in universities," *The Port Huron Statement* opened, "looking uncomfortably to the world we inherit." The dire effects of poverty and social injustice, it continued, were not the only dismaying things about American society. A deeper ailment plagued American politics. Everyone, including middle-class students with few material wants, suffered from a sense of "loneliness, estrangement, and alienation." *The Port Huron Statement* defined SDS as a new kind of political movement that would bring people "out of isolation and into community." Through participatory democracy, not just the poor but all Americans could overcome their feelings of "powerlessness [and hence] resignation before the enormity of events." As one organizer explained, programs like JOIN were attempts to create a poor people's movement as well as a means for students themselves to live an "authentic life" outside the constraints of middle-class society.

SDS began with a campaign to reform the university, especially to disentangle the financial ties between campus-based research programs and the military-industrial complex. Later it expanded to the nation's cities, sending small groups of students to live and organize in the poor communities of Boston, Louisville, Cleveland, and Newark as well as Chicago.

Ultimately, few of these projects succeeded in mobilizing the poor to political action. Protests against local government did little to combat unemployment, and campaigns for better garbage collection or more playgrounds rarely evolved into lasting movements. Nevertheless, organizers did succeed in bringing many neighborhood residents "out of isolation and into community." By late 1967 SDS prepared to leave JOIN in the hands of the people it had organized, which was its goal from the beginning.

Chicago

Initially, even Lyndon Baines Johnson promoted the ideal of civic participation. The Great Society, as the president called his domestic program, promised more than the abolition of poverty and racial inequality. In May 1964 at the University of Michigan the president described his goal as a society "where every child can find knowledge to enrich his mind and to enlarge his talents," where "the city of man serves not only the needs of the body and the demands of commerce but the desire for beauty and the hunger for community."

By 1967 the Vietnam War had upset the domestic agendas of both SDS and the Johnson administration. If SDSers had once believed they could work with liberal Democrats to reduce poverty in the United States, they now interpreted social injustice at home as the inevitable consequence of dangerous and destructive foreign policies pursued by liberals and conservatives alike. SDS threw its energies into the movement against the war in Vietnam. President Johnson, meanwhile, pursued a foreign policy that would swallow up the funding for his own plans for a war on poverty and precipitate a very different war at home, Americans against Americans. As hawks and doves lined up on opposite sides, the Vietnam War created a huge and enduring rift. SDS member Richard Flacks had warned that the nation had to "choose between devoting its resources and energies to maintaining military superiority and international hegemony or rechanneling those resources and energies to meeting the desperate needs of its people." Ultimately, even President Johnson himself understood that the "bitch of a war" in Asia ruined "the woman I really loved—the Great Society." The dream of community did not vanish, but consensus appeared increasingly remote as the United States fought—and eventually lost—the longest war in its history.

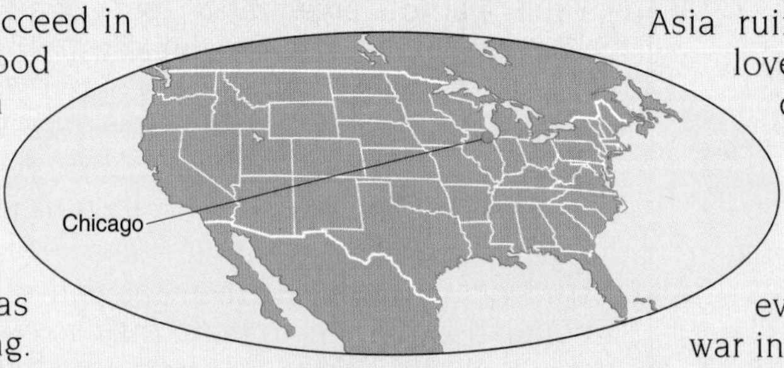

KEY TOPICS

- Widening U.S. involvement in the war in Vietnam
- "The sixties generation" and the antiwar movement
- Poverty and urban crisis
- The election of 1968
- The rise of "liberation" movements
- The Nixon presidency and the Watergate conspiracy

VIETNAM: AMERICA'S LONGEST WAR

The Vietnam War had its roots in the Truman Doctrine and its goal of containing communism (see Chapter 26). After the defeat of the French by the communist forces of Ho Chi Minh in 1954, Vietnam emerged as a major zone of cold war contention. President John Kennedy called it "the cornerstone of the Free World in Southeast Asia, the keystone in the arch, the finger in the dike," a barrier to the spread of communism throughout the region and perhaps the world. President Lyndon Johnson sounded the same note at the beginning of his presidency. He told the public that North Vietnam was intent on conquering South Vietnam, defeating the United States, and extending "the Asiatic dominion of communism." With American security at stake, he concluded, Americans had little choice but to fight for "the principle for which our ancestors fought in the valleys of Pennsylvania."

Vietnam was not Valley Forge, however, and the United States ultimately paid a huge price for its determination to turn back communism in Indochina. More than 50,000 Americans died in an unwinnable overseas war that only deepened divisions at home.

Johnson's War

Although President Kennedy had greatly increased the number of military advisors in South Vietnam (see Chapter 27), it was his successor, Lyndon B. Johnson, who made the decision to engage the United States in a major war there. At first, Johnson simply hoped to stay the course in Vietnam. Facing a presidential election in November 1964, he knew that a major military setback would cripple his election campaign. But he was equally determined to avoid the fate of President Truman, who had bogged down politically after "losing" China to communism and producing a stalemate in Korea. Within days of taking office, the new president said he intended to do his utmost to help South Vietnam win its "contest against the externally directed and supported Communist conspiracy."

Throughout the winter and spring of 1964, as conditions grew steadily worse in South Vietnam, Johnson and his advisors quietly laid the groundwork for a sustained bombing campaign against North Vietnam. In early August, they found a pretext to set this plan in motion. After two U.S. destroyers in the Gulf of Tonkin, off the coast of North Vietnam, reported attacks by North Vietnamese patrol boats, Johnson retaliated by ordering air strikes against bases in North Vietnam.

Johnson now appealed to Congress to pass a resolution giving him the authority "to take all necessary measures" and "all necessary steps" to defend U.S. armed forces and to protect Southeast Asia "against aggression or subversion." This Tonkin Gulf resolution, secretly drafted six weeks before the incident for which it was named, passed the Senate on August 7 with only two dissenting votes and moved unanimously through the House. It served, in Undersecretary of State Nicholas Katzenbach's words, as the "functional equivalent" of a declaration of war.

Ironically, Johnson campaigned for the presidency with a call for restraint in Vietnam. He assured voters that "we are not about to send American boys nine or ten thousand miles away from home to do what Asian boys ought to be doing for themselves." This strategy helped him win a landslide victory over conservative Republican Barry Goldwater of Arizona, who had proposed the deployment of nuclear weapons in Vietnam.

With the election behind him, Johnson now faced a hard decision. The limited bombing raids against North Vietnam had failed to slow the movement of the communist Vietcong forces across the border into the South. Meanwhile, the government in Saigon, the capital city of South Vietnam, appeared near collapse. Faced with the prospect of a communist victory, the president chose to escalate U.S. involvement in Vietnam massively.

Deeper into the Quagmire

In early February 1965, Johnson found a rationale to justify massive bombing of the North. The Vietcong had fired at the barracks of the U.S. Marine base at Pleiku in the central highlands of Vietnam, killing 8 and wounding more than 100 Americans. Waving the list of casualties, the president rushed into an emergency meeting of the National Security Council to announce that the time had passed for keeping "our guns over the mantel and our shells in the cupboard." He ordered immediate reprisal bombing of North Vietnam and one week later, on February 13, authorized Operation Rolling Thunder, a campaign of gradually intensifying air attacks.

Johnson and his advisers hoped that the air strikes against North Vietnam would demonstrate U.S. resolve "both to Hanoi and to the world" and make the deployment of ground forces unnecessary. Intelligence reports, however, suggested that the bombing had little impact and noted, moreover, that North Vietnam was now sending troops into South Vietnam. With retreat his only alternative, Johnson decided to introduce ground troops for offensive operations.

Once Rolling Thunder had begun, President Johnson found it increasingly difficult to speak frankly with the American public about his policies. Initially, he announced that only two battalions of marines were being assigned to Danang to defend the airfields where bombing runs began. But six week later 50,000 U.S. troops were in Vietnam. By November 1965 the total topped 165,000, and more troops were on the way. But even after Johnson authorized a buildup to 431,000 troops in mid-1966, victory was still nowhere in sight.

The strategy pursued by the Johnson administration and implemented by General William Westmoreland—a war of attrition—was based on the premise that continued bombing would eventually exhaust North Vietnam's resources. Meanwhile, U.S. ground forces would defeat the Vietcong in South Vietnam, forcing its soldiers to defect and supporters to scatter, thereby restoring political stability to South Vietnam's pro-western government. As Johnson once boasted, the strongest military power in the world surely could crush a communist rebellion in a "pissant" country of peasants.

In practice, the United States wreaked havoc in South Vietnam, tearing apart its society and bringing ecological devastation to its land. Intending to locate and eradicate the support network of the Vietcong, U.S. ground troops conducted search-and-destroy missions throughout the countryside. They attacked villagers and their homes. Seeking to ferret out Vietcong sympathizers, U.S. troops turned at any one time as many as 4 million people—approximately one quarter of the population of South Vietnam—into refugees. By late 1968, the United States had dropped more than 3 million tons of bombs on Vietnam, and eventually delivered more than three times the tonnage dropped by the Allies on all fronts during World War II. The United States also conducted the most destructive chemical warfare in history. To deprive the Vietcong of camouflage, American troops used herbicides to defoliate forests. During Operation Ranch Hand, which ran between 1965 and 1971, 17.6 million gallons of Agent Orange were sprayed over approximately 3.6 million acres of South Vietnam.

Several advisers urged the president to inform the American people about his decisions on Vietnam, even to declare a state of national emergency. But Johnson feared he would lose momentum on domestic reform, including his antipoverty programs, if he drew attention to foreign policy. Seeking to avoid "undue excitement in the Congress and in domestic public opinion," he held to a course of intentional deceit.

The Credibility Gap

Johnson's popularity had surged at the time of the Tonkin Gulf resolution, skyrocketing in one day from 42 to 72 percent, according to a Louis Harris poll. But afterward it waned rapidly. The war dragged on. Every night network television news publicized the latest American body count. No president had worked so hard to control the news media, but by 1967 Johnson found himself badgered at press conferences by reporters who accused the president of creating a credibility gap.

Scenes of human suffering and devastation recorded by television cameras increasingly undermined the administration's moral justification of the war with claims that it was a necessary defense of freedom and democracy in South Vietnam. During the early 1960s network news had either ignored Vietnam or had been patriotically supportive of U.S. policy. Beginning with a report on a ground operation against the South Vietnamese village of Cam Ne by Morley Safer for CBS News in August 1965, however, the tenor of news reporting changed. Although government officials described the operation as a strategic destruction of "fortified Vietcong bunkers," the CBS *Evening News* showed pictures of Marines setting fire to the thatched homes of civilians. After CBS aired Safer's report, President Johnson complained bitterly to the news director. But more critical commentary soon followed. By 1967, according to a noted media observer, "every subject tended to become Vietnam." Televised news reports now told of new varieties of American cluster bombs, which released up to 180,000 fiberglass shards, and showed the nightmarish effects of the defoliants used on forests in South Vietnam to uncover enemy strongholds.

Coverage of the war in the print media also became more skeptical of Johnson's policies. By 1967 independent news teams were probing the government's official claims. Harrison Salisbury, Pulitzer Prize-winning *New York Times* reporter, questioned the administration's claims that its bombing of the North precisely targeted military objectives, charging that U.S. planes had bombed the population center of Hanoi, capital of North Vietnam, and intentionally ravaged villages in the South. As American military deaths climbed at the rate of more than 800 per month during the first half of 1967, newspaper coverage of the war focused yet more intently on such disturbing events.

The most vocal congressional critic of Johnson's war policy was Democratic senator J. William Fulbright of Arkansas, who chaired the Senate Foreign Relations Committee and who had personally speeded the passage of the Tonkin Gulf resolution. A strong supporter of the cold war, Fulbright had decided that the war in Vietnam was unwinnable and destructive to domestic reform. In *Arrogance of Power,* a book published in 1966 that became a national best-seller, he proposed a negotiated withdrawal from a neutralized Southeast Asia. At first Fulbright stood nearly alone: in October 1966 only 15 percent of Congress favored a negotiated settlement. But he soon persuaded prominent Democrats in Congress, such as Frank Church, Mike Mansfield, and George McGovern, to put aside their personal loyalty to Johnson and oppose his conduct of the war. In 1967 the Congress passed a nonbinding resolution appealing to the United Nations to help negotiate an end to hostilities. Meanwhile, some of the nation's most trusted European allies called for restraint in Vietnam.

Refugees, Binh Dinh Province, 1967. The massive bombing and ground combat broke apart the farming communities of South Vietnam, creating huge numbers of civilian casualties and driving millions into quickly constructed refugee camps or already overcrowded cities. Approximately 25 percent of the South Vietnamese population fled their native villages, many never to return.

The impact of the war, which cost Americans $21 billion per year, was also felt at home. Johnson convinced Congress to levy a 10 percent surcharge on individual and corporate taxes. Later adjustments in the national budget tapped the Social Security fund, heretofore safe from interference. Inflation raced upward, fed by spending on the war. Johnson replaced advisers who questioned his policy, but as casualties multiplied, more and more Americans began to question his handling of the war.

A GENERATION IN CONFLICT

As the war in Vietnam escalated, Americans from all walks of life demanded an end to U.S. involvement. Debates raged everywhere, from families to informal community meetings to the halls of Congress. Eventually the antiwar movement won over a majority. But between 1965 and 1971, its years of peak activity, it had a distinctly generational character. At the forefront were the baby boomers who were just coming of age.

This so-called sixties generation, the largest generation in American history, was also the best educated so far. By the late 1960s, nearly half of all young adults between the ages of 18 and 21 were enrolled in college. In 1965 there were 5 million college students; in 1973 the number had doubled to 10 million. Public universities made the largest gains; by 1970 eight had more than 30,000 students apiece. Many of these young people combined protest against the war in Vietnam with a broader, penetrating critique of American society. Through music, dress, and even hairstyle, many expressed a deep estrangement from the values and aspirations of their parents' generation. As early as 1967, when opposition to the war had begun to swell, "flower children" were putting daisies in the rifle barrels of troops stationed to quash campus protests, providing a seemingly innocent counterpoint to the grim news of slaughter abroad.

These young people believed they heralded a "culture of life" against the "culture of death" symbolized by the war. Campus organizations such as SDS, which had begun in the early 1960s in an attempt to build community, now turned against the government. SDS encouraged many college students to take a militant stand against the war, calling for an immediate and unconditional withdrawal of U.S. troops from Vietnam.

"The Times They Are A-Changin'"

The first sign of a new kind of protest was the free speech movement at the University of California at Berkeley in 1964. That fall, civil rights activists returned to the campus from Freedom Summer in Mississippi. They soon began to picket Bay Area stores that practiced discrimination in hiring and to recruit other students to join them. When the university administration moved to prevent them from setting up information booths on campus, eighteen groups protested, including the arch-conservative Students for Goldwater, claiming that their right to free speech had been abridged. The administration responded by sending police to break up the protest rally and arrest participants. University president Clark Kerr met with students, agreed not to press charges, and seemed set to grant them a small space on campus for political activity. Then, under pressure from conservative regents, Kerr reversed himself and announced in November that the university planned to press new charges against the free speech movement's leaders. On December 2 a crowd of 7,000 gathered to protest this decision. Joining folk singer Joan Baez in singing "We Shall Overcome," a group of students marched toward the university's administration building where they planned to stage a sit-in until Kerr rescinded his order. The police arrested nearly 800 students in the largest mass arrest in California history.

Mario Savio, a Freedom Summer volunteer and philosophy student, explained that the free speech movement wanted more than just the right to conduct political activity on campus. He spoke for many students when he complained that the university had become a faceless bureaucratic machine rather than a community of learning. Regulating the activities of students while preparing them for colorless lives as corporation clerks, the university made them "so sick at heart" that they had decided to put their "bodies upon the gears" to make it stop.

The free speech movement's social critique resonated among college students. Across the country they began to demand a say in the structuring of their education. Brown University students, for example, demanded a revamp of the curriculum that would eliminate all required courses and make grades optional. Students also protested campus rules that treated students as children instead of as adults. After a string of campus protests, most large universities, including the University of California, relinquished *in loco parentis* (in the place of parents) policies and allowed students to live off-campus and to set their own hours.

Across the bay in San Francisco, other young adults staked out a new form of community —a counterculture. In 1967, "the Summer of Love," the population of the Haight-Ashbury district swelled by 75,000 as youthful adventurers gathered for the most celebrated "be-in" of the era. Although the *San Francisco Chronicle* featured a headline reading "Mayor Warns Hippies to Stay Out of Town," masses of long-haired young men and women dressed in bell-bottoms and tie-dyed T-shirts were undeterred. They congregated in "the Haight" to listen to music, take drugs, and "be" with each other. "If you're going to San Francisco," a popular rock group sang, "be sure to wear some flowers in your hair . . . you're going to meet some gentle people there." In the fall, the majority returned to their own communities, often bringing with them a new lifestyle. *Time* magazine announced the appearance of new "hippie enclaves . . . in every major U.S. city from Boston to Seattle, from Detroit to New Orleans."

The generational rebellion took many forms, including a revolution in sexual behavior that triggered countless quarrels between parents and their maturing sons and daughters. During the 1960s more teenagers experienced premarital sex—by the decade's end three-quarters of all college seniors had engaged in sexual intercourse—and far more talked about it openly than in previous eras. With birth control widely available, including the newly developed "pill," many young women, who were no longer deterred from sex by fear of pregnancy, rejected premarital abstinence. "We've

Young women, dressed in hippie garb, flash the peace sign in protest against the war in Vietnam.

discarded the idea that the loss of virginity is related to degeneracy," one college student explained. "Premarital sex doesn't mean the downfall of society, at least not the kind of society that we're going to build." Many heterosexual couples chose to live together outside marriage, a practice few parents condoned. A much smaller but significant number formed communes—approximately 4,000 by 1970—where members could share housekeeping and child care as well as sexual partners.

An antiwar demonstrator places a flower, a symbol of peace, in the rifle barrel of troops during the March on the Pentagon in October 1967. Nearly 100,000 opponents of the Vietnam War gathered in Washington, D.C., and hundreds were arrested as they attempted to storm the entrance to the Pentagon.

Psychedelic and other hallucinogenic drugs played a large part in this counterculture. Harvard professor Timothy Leary urged young people to "turn on, tune in, drop out" and also advocated the mass production and distribution of LSD (lysergic acid diethylamide), which was not criminalized until 1968. Marijuana, illegal yet readily available, was often paired with rock music in a collective ritual of love and laughter. Singer Bob Dylan taunted adults with the lyrics of his hit single, "Everybody must get stoned."

Music played a large part in defining the counterculture. With the emergence of rock 'n' roll in the 1950s, popular music had begun to express a deliberate generational identity (see Chapter 27), a trend that gained momentum with the emergence of the British rock group, the Beatles, in 1964. Folk music, which had gained popularity on campuses in the early 1960s with the successful recordings of Peter, Paul, and Mary, Phil Ochs, Judy Collins, as well as Joan Baez, continued to serve the voice of protest. Shortly after Freedom Summer, folk singer Bob Dylan issued a warning to parents:

> *Your sons and your daughters*
> *are beyond your command*
> *Your old road is*
> *rapidly agin'.*
> *Please get out of the new one*
> *If you can't lend your hand*
> *For the times they are a-changin'.*

By 1965 Dylan himself had turned to the electric guitar and rock, which triumphed as the musical emblem of a generation.

At a farm near Woodstock, New York, more than 400,000 people gathered in August 1969 for a three-day rock concert and to give witness to the ideals of the counterculture. Thousands took drugs while security officials and local police stood by, some stripped off their clothes to dance or swim, and a few even made love in the grass. "We were exhilarated," one reveler recalled. "We felt as though we were in liberated territory."

The Woodstock Nation, as the counterculture was renamed by the media, did not actually represent the sentiments of most young Americans. But its attitudes and styles, especially its efforts to create a new community, did speak for the large minority seeking a peaceful alternative to the intensifying climate of war. "We used to think of ourselves as little clumps of weirdos," rock star Janis Joplin explained. "But now we're a whole new minority group." Another interpreter, Charles Reich, whose *The Greening of America* (1970) became a best-seller, defined the counterculture as a generation's attempt to create "a form of community in which love, respect, and a mutual search for wisdom replace the competition and separation of the past." The slogan "Make Love, Not War" linked generational rebellion and opposition to the U.S. invasion of Vietnam.

From Campus Protest to Mass Mobilization

Three weeks after the announcement of Operation Rolling Thunder in 1965, peace activists called for a day-long boycott of classes so that students and faculty might meet to discuss the war. At the University of

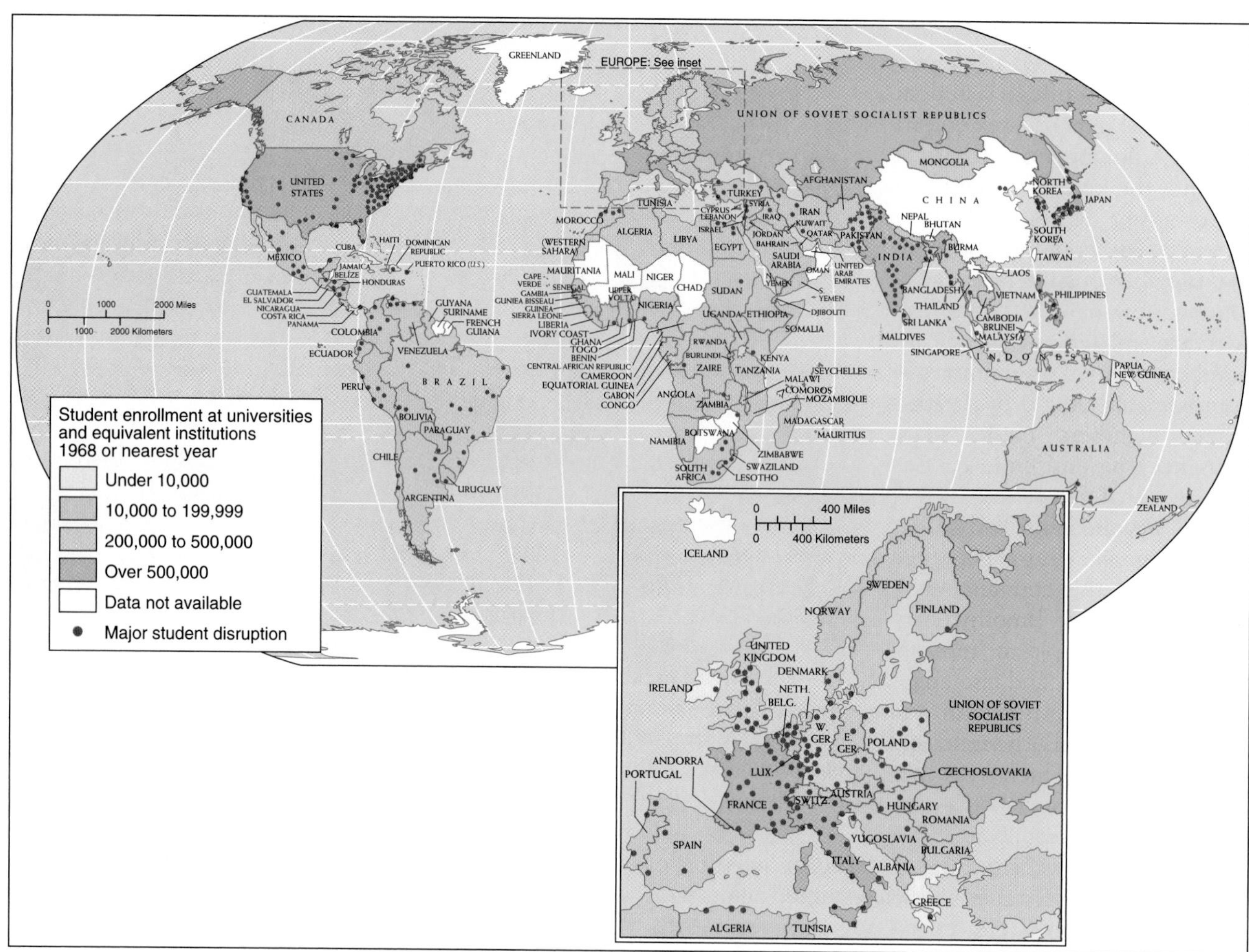

Antiwar Protests on College and University Campuses, 1967–1969 *Campus-based protests against the war in Vietnam, at first centered on the east coast and in California, spread to nearly every region of the country and around the world by the decade's end.*

Michigan in Ann Arbor, more than 3,000 students turned out for sessions held through the night because administrators bowed to pressure of state legislators and refused to cancel classes. During the following weeks, "teach-ins" spread across the United States and as far away as Europe and Japan.

Students also began to protest against war-related research on their campuses. The expansion of higher education in the 1960s had depended largely on federally funded programs, including military research on counterinsurgency tactics and new chemical weapons. Student protesters demanded an end to these programs and, receiving no response from university administrators, turned to civil disobedience. In October 1967, the Dow Chemical Company, manufacturers of napalm, a form of jellied gasoline often used against civilians, sent job recruiters to the University of Wisconsin at Madison despite warnings that a group of students would try to prevent them from conducting interviews. A few hundred students staged a sit-in at the building where the recruitment interviews were scheduled, and 2,000 onlookers gathered outside. Ordered by university administrators to disperse the crowd, the city's police broke glass doors, dragged students through the debris, and clubbed those who refused to move. Suddenly the campus erupted. Students chanted *Sieg Heil* at the police, who attempted to disperse them with tear gas and Mace. Undergraduate students and their teaching assistants boycotted classes for a week. During the next three years, hundreds of similar strikes took place on campuses in every region of the country.

Many student strikes merged opposition to the war with other campus and community issues. At Columbia University, students struck in 1968 against the administration's plans to build a new gymnasium in a city park used by residents of neighboring Harlem. In the Southwest, Mexican American students demonstrated against the use of funds for military projects that might otherwise be allocated to antipoverty and educational programs.

By the late 1960s the peace movement had spread well beyond the campus and commanded a diverse following. While some protesters marched, others held prayer vigils, staged art fairs, distributed leaflets door to door, or simply engaged friends and neighbors in conversation about Vietnam. In April 1967 a day-long antiwar rally at the Sheep Meadow in Manhattan's Central Park drew more than 300,000 people—more than had taken part in the civil rights movement's 1965 March on Washington. Meanwhile, 60,000 protesters turned out in San Francisco. By summer, Vietnam Veterans against the War began to organize returning soldiers and sailors, encouraging them to cast off the medals and ribbons they had won in battle.

The steadily increasing size of antiwar demonstrations provoked conservatives and prowar Democrats to take a stronger stand in support of the war. On the weekend following the huge turn-out in Central Park, the Veterans of Foreign Wars staged a "Loyalty Day" parade in New York City under the banner "One Country, One Flag, Love It or Leave It." Although only 7,500 people participated, the event signaled a hardening of opposition to the peace movement. Several newspaper and magazine editorialists called for the arrest of antiwar leaders on charges of treason. Secretary of State Dean Rusk, appearing on NBC's *Meet the Press,* expressed his concern that "authorities in Hanoi" might conclude, incorrectly, that the majority of Americans did not back their president and that "the net effect of these demonstrations will be to prolong the war, not to shorten it."

Many demonstrators themselves concluded that mass mobilizations alone had little impact on U.S. policy. Some sought to serve as moral witnesses. Despite a congressional act of 1965 providing for a five-year jail term and a $10,000 fine for destroying a draft card, nearly 200 young men destroyed their draft cards at the April Sheep Meadow demonstration and encouraged approximately a half-million more to resist the draft or refuse induction. Two Jesuit priests, Daniel and Philip Berrigan, raided the offices of the draft board in Catonsville, Maryland, in May 1968 and poured homemade napalm over records. A few protesters even doused their clothes with gasoline and set fire to themselves, as Buddhist monks protesting the war had done in Vietnam. Other activists determined to "bring the war home." An estimated 40,000 bombing incidents or bomb threats took place from January 1969 to April 1970; more than $21 million of property was damaged, and forty-three people were killed. Most of the perpetrators were never identified.

Observers at the time noted a similarity between the violence in Vietnam and the violence in the United States. Parallel wars were now being fought, one between two systems of government in Vietnam, another between the American government and masses of its citizens. Those Americans sent to Vietnam were caught in between.

Teenage Soldiers

The Vietnam War era witnessed not only a generation gap but a fissure within the generation of young adults. Whereas the average age of the World War II soldier was twenty-six, the age of those who fought in Vietnam hovered around nineteen. Until late 1969 the Selective Service System—the draft—gave deferments to college students and to workers in selected occupations while recruiting hard in poor communities, advertising the armed forces as a provider of vocational training and social mobility. Working-class young men, disproportionately African American and Latino, signed up in large numbers under these inducements. They also bore the brunt of combat. Whereas college graduates constituted only 12 percent of all soldiers and 9 percent of those who were killed in combat, high school dropouts were the most likely to serve in Vietnam and by far the most likely to die there. This disparity created a rupture that would last well past the end of the war.

Yet the soldiers were not entirely isolated from the changes affecting their generation. GIs in significant numbers smoked marijuana, listed to rock music, and participated in the sexual revolution. In 1968 more than 200 soldiers from Fort Hood, Texas, attended a be-in. But most condemned antiwar protest as the expressions of their privileged peers who did not have to fight.

As the war dragged on, however, some soldiers began to show their frustration. By 1971 many GIs were putting peace symbols on their combat helmets, joining antiwar demonstrations, and staging their own events such as "Armed Farces Day." Sometimes entire companies refused to carry out duty assignments or even to enter battle. A smaller number took revenge by "fragging" their commanding officers with grenades meant for the enemy. Meanwhile African American soldiers closed ranks and often flaunted their racial solidarity by weaving their bootlaces into "slave bracelets" and carrying Black Power canes, which were ebony-colored and topped with a clenched fist. Some openly complained about being asked to fight "a white man's war" and emblazoned their helmets with slogans like "No Gook Ever Called Me Nigger." By 1971, at least fourteen organizations claimed affiliation with RITA, an acronym for "Resistance in the Army." The largest was the American Servicemen's Union, which claimed more than 10,000 members and published its own newspaper, *The Bond*.

The nature of the war fed feelings of disaffection in the armed forces. U.S. troops entering South Vietnam expected a warm welcome from the people whose homeland they had been sent to defend.

Instead, they encountered anti-American demonstrations and placards with slogans like "End Foreign Dominance of Our Country." Hostile Vietnamese civilians viewed the Americans as invaders. The enemy avoided open engagements in which the Americans could benefit from their superior arms and air power. Soldiers found themselves instead stumbling into booby traps as they chased an elusive guerrilla foe through deep, leech-infested swamps and dense jungles swarming with fire ants. They could never be sure who was friend and who was foe. Patently false U.S. government press releases that heralded glorious victories and extolled the gratitude of Vietnamese civilians deepened bitterness on the front lines.

Approximately 8.6 million men and women served in the armed forces, and many returned to civilian life quietly and without fanfare, denied the glory earned by the combat veterans of previous wars. They reentered a society divided over the cause for which they had risked their lives. Tens of thousands suffered debilitating physical injuries. As many as 40 percent of them came back with drug dependencies or symptoms of post-traumatic stress disorder, haunted and depressed by troubling memories of atrocities. Moreover, finding and keeping a job proved to be particularly hard in the shrinking economy of the 1970s. The situation was especially bleak for African American veterans who returned to communities with unemployment rates at least triple the national average. Many veterans felt betrayed either by their own generation or by their government.

President Lyndon B. Johnson talks to James Truesville of Raleigh, North Carolina, at Camp Catoctin, Maryland, where young men from fourteen states were receiving training in basic job skills. One of the most highly touted programs of the War on Poverty, the Job Corps suffered from underfunding and a tendency to teach young trainees obsolete technical skills.

WARS ON POVERTY

During the early 1960s, the civil rights movement spurred a new awareness of and concern with poverty. As poor African Americans from both the rural South and the urban North got involved in political protests, they added the issues of unemployment, low wages, and slum housing to the demands for desegregation and voting rights. The civil rights movement also revealed the close link between racial discrimination and economic inequalities. What good was winning the right to sit at a lunch counter if one could not afford to buy a hamburger?

One of the most influential books of the times, Michael Harrington's *The Other America* (1962), added fuel to this fire. Harrington argued that one-fifth of the nation—as many as 40 to 50 million people—suffered from bad housing, malnutrition, poor medical care, and other deprivations of poverty. He documented the miseries of what he called the "invisible land of the other Americans," the rejects of society who simply did not exist for affluent suburbanites or the mass media. The other America, Harrington wrote, "is populated by failures, by those driven from the land and bewildered by the city, by old people suddenly confronted with the torments of loneliness and poverty, and by minorities facing a wall of prejudice."

These arguments motivated President Johnson to expand the antipoverty program that he had inherited from the Kennedy administration. "That's my kind of program," he told his advisers. "It will help people. I want you to move full speed ahead on it." Ironically, it was another kind of war that ultimately undercut his aspiration to wage "an unconditional war on poverty."

The Great Society

In his State of the Union message in 1964, Johnson announced his plans to build a Great Society. Over the next two years, he used the political momentum of the civil rights movement and the overwhelming Democratic majorities in the House and Senate to push through the most ambitious reform program since the New Deal. In August 1964 the Economic Opportunity Act launched the War on Poverty. It established an Office of Economic Opportunity (OEO), which coordinated a network of federal programs designed to increase opportunities in employment and education.

The programs had mixed results. The Job Corps provided vocational training mostly for urban black youth considered unemployable. Housed in dreary barrackslike camps far from home, trainees often found themselves learning factory skills that were already obsolete. The dropout rate was very high. The Neighborhood Youth Corps managed to provide work for about 2 million young people aged sixteen to twenty-one. But nearly all of these were low-paying, make-work jobs. Educational programs proved more successful. VISTA (Volunteers in Service to America) was a kind of domestic Peace Corps that brought several thousand idealistic teachers into poor school districts.

The most innovative and controversial element of the OEO was the Community Action Program (CAP). The program invited local communities to establish community action agencies (CAAs), to be funded through the OEO. The Economic Opportunity Act included language requiring these agencies to be "developed, conducted, and administered with the maximum feasible participation of residents of the areas and members of the groups served." In theory, as the SDS organizers had also believed, community action would empower the poor by giving them a direct say in mobilizing resources to attack poverty.

By 1966 the OEO was funding more than 1,000 CAAs, mostly in black neighborhoods of big cities. The traditional powers in cities—mayors, business elites, and political machines—generally resisted the CAP's promotion of institutional change. They looked at CAAs as merely another way to dispense services and patronage, with the federal government picking up the tab. A continual tug-of-war over who should control funding and decision making plagued the CAP in most cities, sparking intense power struggles that helped to cripple the antipoverty effort. Such was the case in Chicago, where Mayor Richard Daley demanded absolute control over the allocation of federal funds. After being challenged by OEO activists, Daley denounced the program for "fostering class struggle."

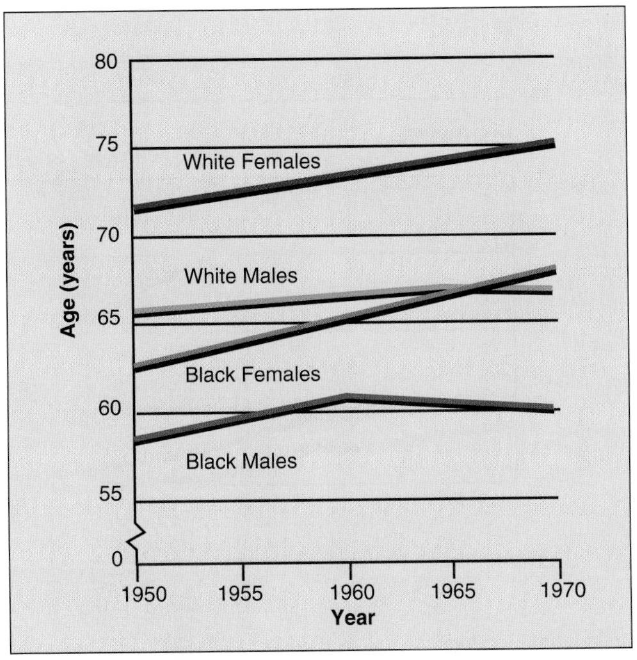

Comparative Figures on Life Expectancy at Birth by Race and Sex, 1950–1970 *Shifting mortality statistics suggested that the increased longevity of females increasingly cut across race lines, but did not diminish the difference between white people and black people as a whole.*

The most successful and popular offshoots of the CAP were the so-called national-emphasis programs, designed in Washington and administered according to federal guidelines. The Legal Services Program, staffed by attorneys, helped millions of poor people in legal battles with housing authorities, welfare departments, police, and slumlords. Head Start and Follow Through reached more than 2 million poor children and significantly improved the long-range educational achievement of participants. Comprehensive Community Health Centers—one-stop clinics—provided basic medical services to poor patients who could not afford to see doctors. Upward Bound helped low-income teenagers develop the skills and confidence needed for college. Birth control programs dispensed contraceptive supplies and information to hundreds of thousands of poor women.

But the root cause of poverty lay in unequal income distribution. The Johnson administration never committed itself to the redistribution of income or wealth. Spending on social welfare jumped from 7.7 percent of the gross national product in 1960 to 16 percent in 1974. But roughly three-quarters of social welfare payments went to the nonpoor. The largest sums went to Medicare, established by Congress in 1965 to provide basic health care for the aged, and to expanded Social Security payments and unemployment compensation. The major surge in federal spending on poor people resulted from the explosive growth of Aid to Families with Dependent Children (AFDC), a program begun during the New Deal. But the total cost of AFDC in the mid-1970s was only about $5 billion per year, compared with $65 billion annually for the roughly 30 million Americans receiving Social Security payments.

The War on Poverty, like the Great Society itself, became a forgotten dream. "More than five years after the passage of the Economic Opportunity Act," a 1970 study concluded, "the war on poverty has barely scratched the surface. Most poor people have had no contact with it, except perhaps to hear the promises of a better life to come." The OEO finally expired in 1974. Having made the largest commitment to federal spending on social welfare since the New Deal, Johnson could take pride in the gains scored in the War on Poverty. At

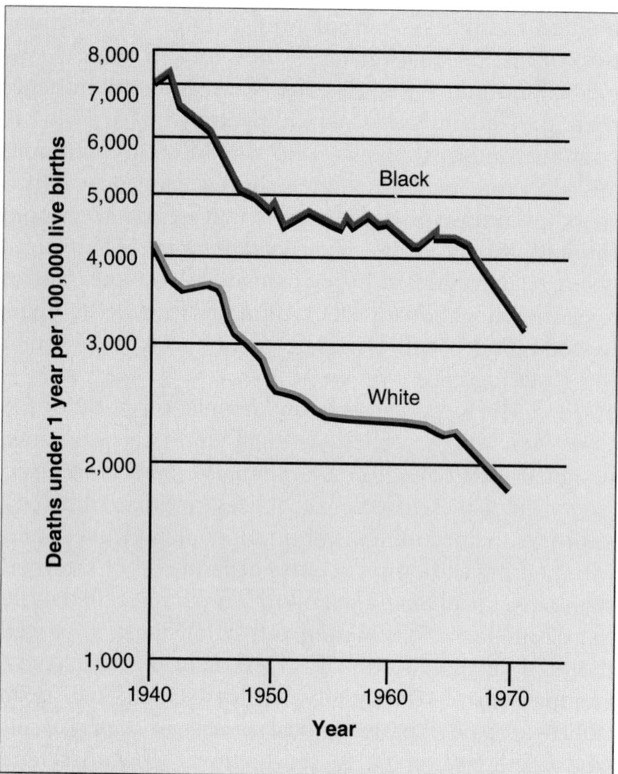

Comparative Figures on Infant Mortality by Race, 1940–1970 *The causes of infant mortality such as inadequate maternal diets, prenatal care, and medical services were all rooted in poverty, both rural and urban. Despite generally falling rates of infant mortality, nonwhite people continued to suffer the effects more than white people.*

the same time, he had raised expectations higher than could be reached without a more drastic redistribution of economic and political power. Even in the short run, the president could not sustain the welfare programs and simultaneously fight a lengthy and expensive war abroad.

Crisis in the Cities

As Harrington's *The Other America* pointed out, some of the nation's poorest communities were located in the Appalachian mountains and in the Deep South. But since World War II, urban areas had suffered disproportionally from a steady process of decay. "White flight"—the exodus of white people to the suburbs—had reduced the tax base for public services of all kinds, especially schools and recreational facilities. Johnson's War on Poverty scarcely addressed the problems plaguing the nation's metropolitan areas (defined by the U.S. Census as those with populations of 250,000 people or more). On the contrary, urban conditions grew worse.

With funds for new construction limited during the Great Depression and World War II, and the postwar boom taking place in the suburbs, the housing stock in the cities diminished and deteriorated. The Federal Housing Administration had encouraged this trend by insuring loans to support the building of new homes in suburban areas (see Chapter 27). The federal government also encouraged "redlining," which left people in poor neighborhoods without access to building loans. In these areas, the supply of adequate housing declined sharply. Slumlords took advantage of this situation, collecting high rents while allowing their properties to deteriorate. City officials meanwhile appealed for federal funds under Title I of the 1949 Housing Act to upgrade housing. Designed as a program of civic revitalization, these urban renewal projects more often than not sliced apart poor neighborhoods with new highways, demolished them in favor of new office complexes, or, as in Chicago's Uptown, favored new developments for the middle class rather than the poor. In 1968 a federal survey showed that 80 percent of those residents who had been displaced under this program were nonwhite, a finding that prompted civil rights leaders to call urban renewal programs "Negro removal." As a result, the inner city became not only increasingly crowded in the 1960s but more segregated.

Urban employment opportunities declined with the urban housing stock. The industries and corporations that had lured working men and women to the cities a century earlier either automated their plants, thus scaling back their workforces, or relocated to the suburbs or other regions, such as the South and Southwest, that promised lower corporate taxes and nonunion labor. Nationwide, military spending prompted by the escalation of the Vietnam War brought the unemployment rate down from 6 percent,

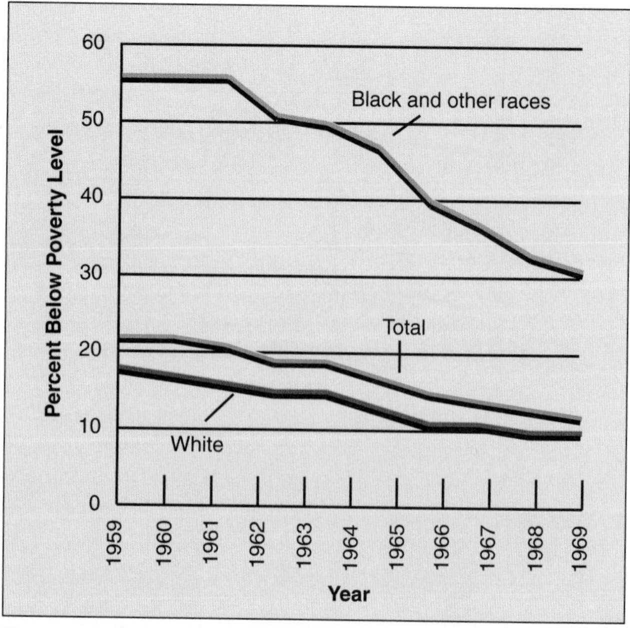

Percent of population below poverty level, by race, 1959–1969

Note: The poverty threshold for a nonfarm family of four was $3,743 in 1969 and $2,973 in 1959.

Source: *Congressional Quarterly, Civil Rights: A Progress Report*, 1971, p. 46.

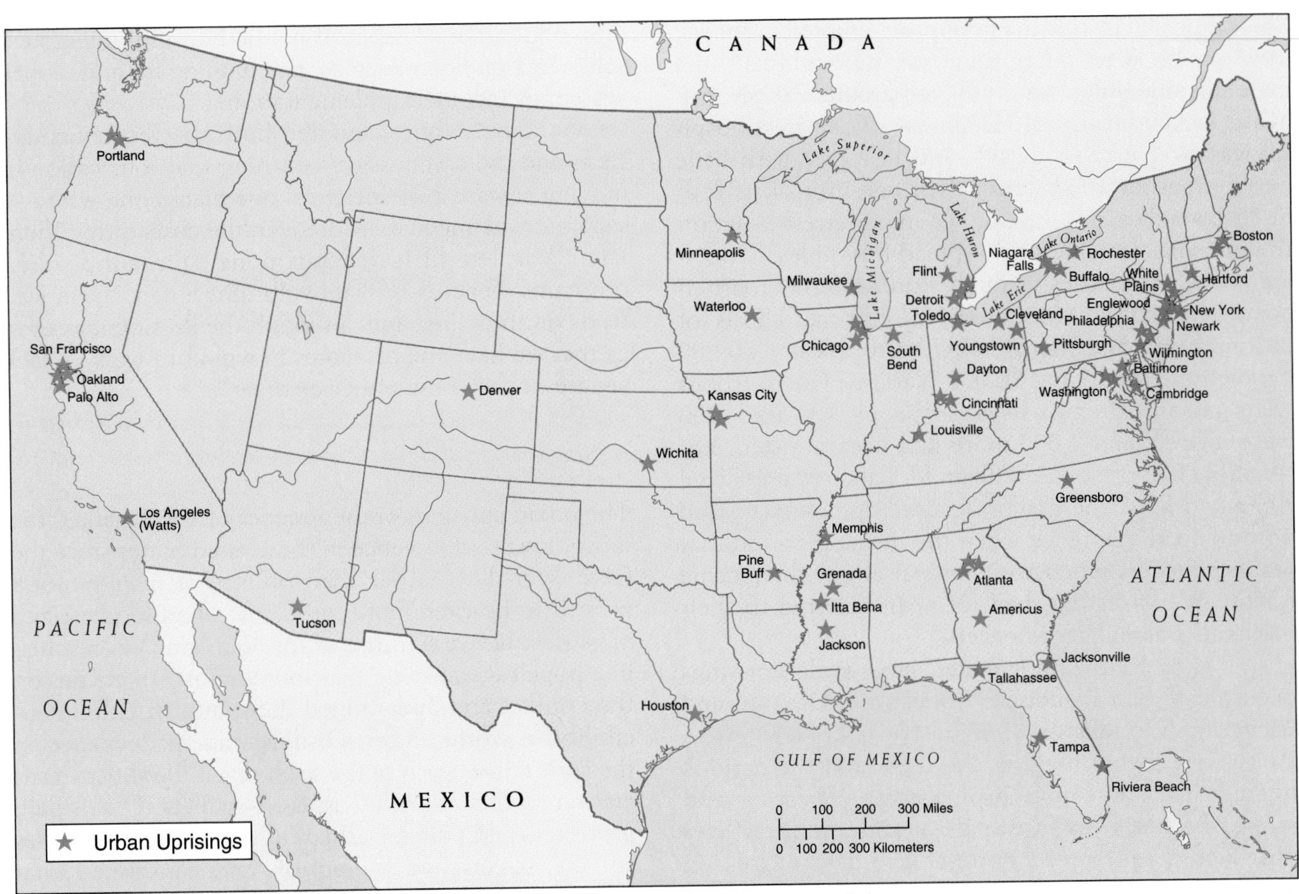

Urban Uprisings, 1965–1968 *After World War II urban uprisings precipitated by racial conflict increased in African American communities. In Watts in 1965 and in Detroit and Newark in 1967 rioters struck out at symbols of white control of their communities, such as white-owned businesses and residential properties.*

where it was in 1960, to 4 percent in 1966, where it remained until the end of the decade. Black unemployment, however, was nearly twice that of white unemployment. New jobs were concentrated in the defense-related industries in the South and Southwest. In northern cities, the proportion of the workforce employed in the higher-paying manufacturing jobs declined precipitously while the proportion working in minimum-wage service industries rose at a fast rate. In short, African Americans were losing good jobs and steadily falling further behind whites.

Pollution, which had long plagued traffic-congested cities like Los Angeles and industrial cities like steel-producing Pittsburgh, became an increasingly pervasive urban problem. Cities like Phoenix that once had clean air began to issue smog alerts. Pointing to high levels of lead in the blood of urban children, scientists warned of the long-term threat of pollution to public health.

Despite deteriorating conditions, millions of Americans continued to move to the cities, mainly African Americans from the Deep South, white people from the Appalachian mountains, and Latinos from Puerto Rico. By the mid-1960s African Americans had become near majorities in the nation's decaying inner cities. Since World War II nearly 3 million African Americans had left the South for northern cities. In that time, New York's black population had more than doubled, and Detroit's had tripled. The vast majority of these African Americans fled rural poverty only to find themselves earning minimum wages at best and living in miserable, racially segregated neighborhoods.

Urban Uprisings

These deteriorating conditions brought urban pressures to the boiling point in the mid-1960s. In the "long, hot summers" of 1964 to 1968 the nation was rocked by more than 100 urban uprisings. As poet Imamu Amiri Baraka (formerly LeRoi Jones) noted, these incidents were spontaneous rebellions against authority. Unlike the race riots of the 1920s and 1940s, when angry whites assaulted blacks, masses of African Americans now took revenge for the white domination of their communities and specifically for police abuse.

In 1964, waves of turbulence rippled through the black neighborhoods of Harlem, Rochester, and

Philadelphia. The first major uprising erupted in August 1965 in the Watts section of Los Angeles. Here, the male unemployment rate hovered around 30 percent. Watts lacked health care facilities—the nearest hospital was twelve miles away—and in a city with little public transportation, fewer than one-fifth of its residents owned cars. It took only a minor arrest to set off the uprising, which quickly spread fifty miles. Throwing rocks and bottles through store windows, participants reportedly shouted, "This is for Selma! This is for Birmingham!" and "Burn, baby, burn!" Nearly 50,000 people turned out, and 20,000 National Guard troops were sent in. After six days, 34 people lay dead, 900 were injured, and 4,000 more had been arrested. Los Angeles chief of police William H. Parker blamed civil rights workers, the mayor accused communists, and both feigned ignorance when the media reported that white police assigned to "charcoal alley," their name for the Watts district, had for years referred to their nightsticks as "nigger knockers."

The following summer, large-scale uprisings occurred in San Francisco, Milwaukee, Dayton, and Cleveland. On July 13, 1967, in Newark, New Jersey, a city with severe housing shortages and the nation's highest black unemployment rate, the beating and arrest of a black taxi driver by a white police officer provoked a widespread protest. Five days of looting and burning of white-owned buildings ended with twenty-five people killed by the bullets of police and the National Guard. One week later the Detroit "Great Rebellion" began. This time a vice squad of the Detroit police had raided a bar and arrested the after-hours patrons. One spectator called out, "Don't let them take our people away. . . . Let's get the bricks and bottles going." *Time* magazine later reported, "Detroit became the scene of the bloodiest uprising in a half century and the costliest in terms of property damage in U.S. history." Army tanks and paratroopers were brought in to quell the massive disturbance, which lasted a week and left 34 people dead and 7,000 under arrest.

The uprisings seemed at first to prompt badly needed reforms. After Watts, President Johnson set up a task force headed by Deputy Attorney General Ramsey Clark and allocated funds for a range of antipoverty programs. Several years later the Kerner Commission, headed by Governor Otto Kerner of Illinois, studied the riots and found that the participants in the uprisings were not the poorest or least-educated members of their communities. They suffered instead from heightened expectations sparked by the civil rights movement and Johnson's promise of a Great Society, expectations that were not to be realized. The Kerner Commission concluded its report by indicting "white racism" for creating an "explosive mixture" of poverty and police brutality and recommending a yet more extensive program of public housing, integrated schools, 2 million new jobs, and funding for a "national system of income supplementation."

But Congress ignored both the recommendations and the commission's warning that "our nation is moving toward two societies, one black, one white—separate and unequal." Moreover, the costs of the Vietnam War left little federal money for antipoverty programs. Senator William Fulbright noted, "Each war feeds on the other, and, although the President assures us that we have the resources to win both wars, in fact we are not winning either of them."

1968

The urban uprisings of the summer of 1967 marked the most drawn-out violence in the United States since the Civil War. But, rather than offering a respite, 1968 proved to be even more turbulent. The bloodiest and most destructive fighting of the Vietnam War resulted in a hopeless stalemate that soured most Americans on the conflict and undermined their faith in U.S. invincibility in world affairs. Disillusionment deepened in the spring when two of the most revered political leaders were struck down by assassins' bullets. Once again protesters and police clashed on the nation's campuses and city streets, and millions of Americans asked what was wrong with their country. Why was it so violent? A former graduate student at Columbia University, Mike Wallace, spoke for many when he later recalled, "1968 just cracked the universe open for me."

The Tet Offensive

On January 30, 1968, the North Vietnamese and their Vietcong allies launched the Tet Offensive (named for the Vietnamese lunar new year holiday), stunning the U.S. military command in South Vietnam. The Vietcong managed to push into the major cities and provincial capitals of the South, as far as the courtyard of the U.S. embassy in Saigon. U.S. troops ultimately halted the offensive, suffering comparatively modest casualties of 1,600 dead and 8,000 wounded. The North Vietnamese and Vietcong suffered more than 40,000 deaths, about one-fifth of the total forces. Civilian casualties ran to the hundreds of thousands. As many as 1 million South Vietnamese became refugees, their villages totally ruined.

The Tet Offensive, despite U.S. success in stopping it, shattered the credibility of American officials who had repeatedly claimed the enemy to be virtually beaten. Television and press coverage—including scenes of U.S. personnel shooting from the embassy windows in Saigon—dismayed the public. Americans saw the beautiful, ancient city of Hue devastated almost beyond recognition and heard a U.S. officer casually remark about a village in the Mekong delta, "We had to destroy

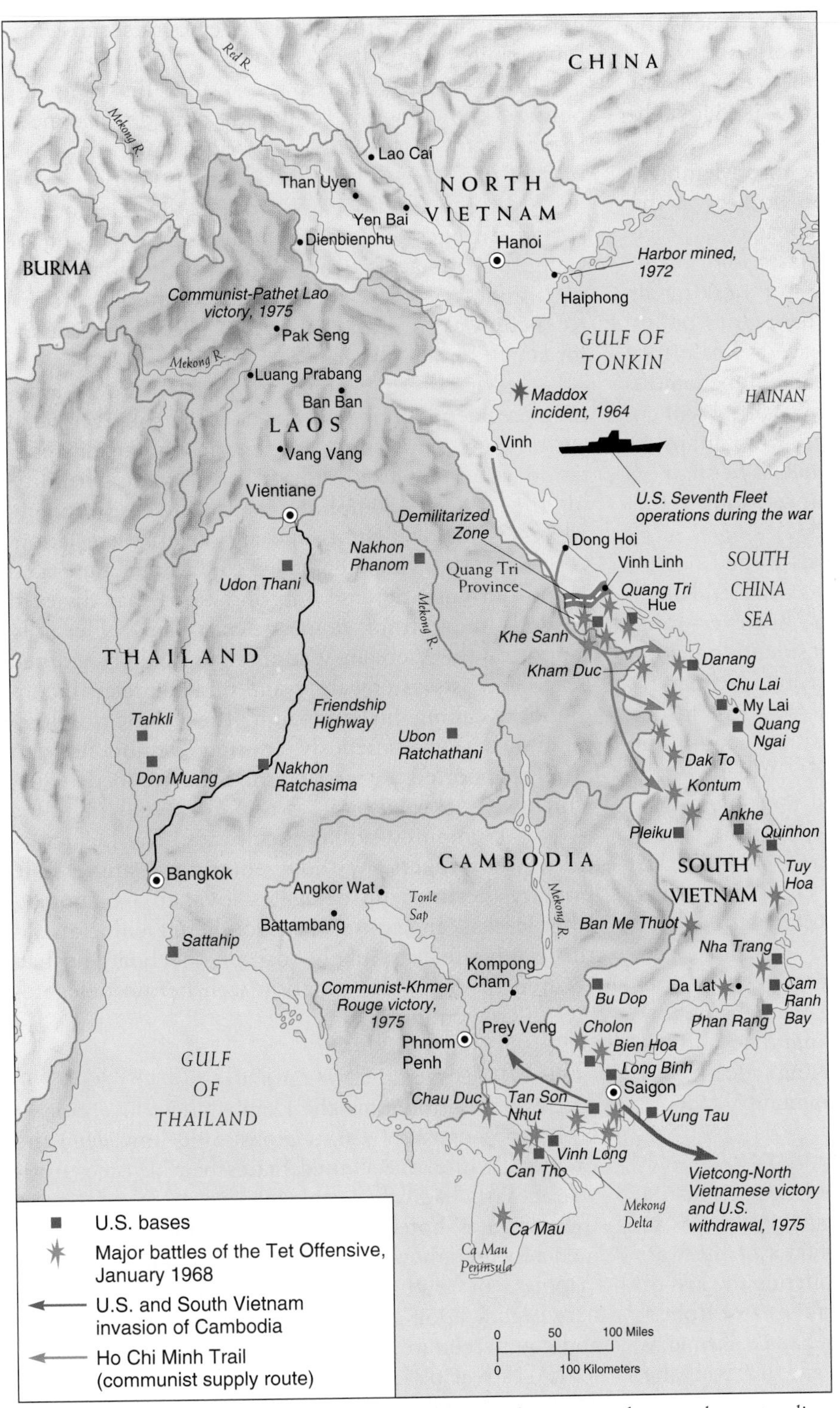

The Southeast Asian War *The Indo-Chinese subcontinent, home to long-standing regional conflict, became the center of a prolonged war with the United States.*

it, in order to save it." Television newscasters began to warn parents: "The following scenes might not be suitable viewing for children."

The United States had chalked up a major military victory during the Tet Offensive but lost the war at home. For the first time, polls showed strong opposition to the war, 49 percent concluding that the entire operation in Vietnam was a mistake. The majority believed that the stalemate was hopeless. Meanwhile, in Rome, Berlin, Paris, and London, students and others turned out in huge demonstrations to protest U.S. involvement in Vietnam. At home, sectors of the antiwar movement began to shift from resistance to open rebellion.

The Tet Offensive also opened a year of political drama at home. Congress resoundingly turned down a request for a general increase in troops issued by General Westmoreland. President Johnson, facing the 1968 election campaign, knew the odds were now against him. He watched as opinion polls showed his popularity plummet to an all-time low. After he squeaked to a narrow victory in the New Hampshire primary, Johnson decided to step down. On March 31 he announced he would not seek the Democratic Party's nomination. He also declared a bombing halt over North Vietnam and called Hanoi to peace talks, which began in Paris in May. Like Truman almost thirty years earlier, and despite his determination not to repeat that bit of history, Johnson had lost his presidency in Asia.

King, the War, and the Assassination

By 1968 the civil rights leadership stood firmly in opposition to the war, and Martin Luther King Jr. had reached a turning point in his life. The Federal Bureau of Investigation had been harassing King, tapping his telephones and spreading malicious rumors about him. Despite the threat from the FBI (Bureau chief J. Edgar Hoover had sworn to "destroy the burrhead"), King abandoned his customary caution in criticizing U.S. policy in Vietnam. In the fall of 1965 he began to connect domestic unrest with the war abroad, calling the U.S. government the "greatest purveyor of violence in the world today." As he became more militant in opposing the war, King lost the support of liberal Democrats who remained loyal to Johnson. King refused to compromise.

In the spring of 1968 King chose Memphis, Tennessee, home of striking sanitation workers, as the place to inaugurate a Poor People's Campaign for peace and justice. Noting that the United States was "much, much sicker" than when he had begun working in 1955, he nonetheless delivered, in what was to be his final speech, a message of hope. "I have a dream this afternoon that the brotherhood of man will become a reality," King told the crowd. "With this faith, I will go out and carve a tunnel of hope from a mountain of despair." The next evening, April 4, 1968, as he stepped out on the balcony of his motel, King was shot in the head by a lone assassin, James Earl Ray.

Throughout the world crowds turned out to mourn King's death. The *New York Times* declared King's murder "a national disaster." Cheers, however, rang through the regional FBI office. President Johnson, who had ordered the investigation of King, declined to attend the funeral, sending the vice president in his place. Student Nonviolent Coordinating Committee leader Stokely Carmichael stormed, "When white America killed Dr. King, she declared war on us."

Riots broke out in more than 100 cities. Chicago Mayor Richard Daley ordered his police to shoot to kill. In Washington, D.C., U.S. Army units set up machine guns outside the Capitol and the White House. By week's end, nearly 27,000 African Americans had been jailed. The physical scars of these riots remained for years, as banks redlined black neighborhoods and refused funds for rebuilding. The psychic scars survived even longer. With King's death, his vision of humanity as a "Beloved Community" faded.

The Democratic Campaign

The dramatic events of the first part of the year had a direct impact on the presidential campaign. For those liberals dissatisfied with Johnson's conduct of the war, and especially for African Americans suffering the loss of their greatest national leader, New York senator Robert F. Kennedy emerged as the candidate of choice. Kennedy enjoyed a strong record on civil rights, and, like King, he had begun to interpret the war as a mirror of injustice at home. Kennedy insisted during the Tet Offensive that "our nation must be told the truth about this war, in all its terrible reality." On this promise he began to build a campaign for the Democratic nomination.

Ironically, Kennedy faced an opponent who agreed with him, Minnesota senator Eugene McCarthy. The race for the Democratic nomination positioned McCarthy, the witty philosopher, against Kennedy, the charismatic campaigner. McCarthy garnered support from liberal Democrats and white suburbanites. On college campuses his popularity with idealistic students was so great that his campaign became known as the "children's crusade." Kennedy reached out successfully to African Americans and Latinos and won all but the Oregon primary.

Kennedy appeared to be the Democratic Party's strongest candidate as June 4, the day of the California primary, dawned. But as the final tabulation of his victory came in just past midnight, Robert Kennedy was struck down by the bullet of an assassin, Jordanian Sirhan Sirhan.

Vice President Hubert H. Humphrey, a longtime presidential hopeful, was now the sole Democrat with the credentials to succeed Johnson. But his reputation as a cold war Democrat had become a liability. In the 1950s Humphrey had delivered stirring addresses for civil rights and antipoverty legislation; yet he also sponsored repressive cold war measures and supported huge defense appropriations that diverted needed funds from domestic programs. He fully supported the Vietnam War and had publicly scorned peace activists as cowardly and un-American. Incongruously calling his campaign "the Politics of Joy," Humphrey simultaneously courted Democrats who grimly supported the war and the King-Kennedy wing, which was sickened by it.

Humphrey skillfully cultivated the Democratic power brokers. Without entering a single state primary, he lined up delegates loyal to city bosses, labor leaders, and conservative southern Democrats. As the candidate least likely to rock the boat, he had secured his party's nomination well before delegates met in convention.

"The Whole World Is Watching!"

The events surrounding the Democratic convention in Chicago, August 21–26, demonstrated how deep the divisions within the United States had become. Antiwar activists had called for a massive demonstration at the delegates' hotel and at the convention center. The media focused, however, on the plans announced by the "Yippies," or Youth International Party, a largely imaginary organization of politicized hippies led by jokester and counterculture guru Abbie Hoffman. Yippies called for a Festival of Life, including a "nude-in" on Lake Michigan beaches and the release of a greased pig—Pigasus, the Yippie candidate for president. Still reeling from the riots following King's assassination, Chicago's Mayor Richard Daley refused to issue parade permits. According to later accounts, he sent hundreds of undercover police into the crowds to encourage rock throwing and generally incite violence so that retaliation would appear necessary and reasonable.

Daley's strategy boomeranged when his officers staged what a presidential commission later termed a

The "police riot" in Chicago, August 1968, during the Democratic National Convention capped a spring and summer of violence. Mayor Richard Daley had prepared his city for the anticipated protest against the war by assembling more than 20,000 law enforcement officials, including police, National Guard, and U.S. Army troops carrying flame throwers and bazookas. Television cameras and photographers recorded the massive clubbing and teargassing of demonstrators as well as bystanders and news reporters.

"police riot," randomly assaulting demonstrators, casual passersby, and television crews filming the events. For one of the few times in American history, the media appeared to join a protest against civil authorities. Angered by the embarrassing publicity, Daley sent his agents to raid McCarthy's campaign headquarters, where Democrats opposed to the war had gathered.

Inside the convention hall, a raging debate over a peace resolution underscored the depth of the division within the party over the war. Representative Wayne Hays of Ohio lashed out at those who substituted "beards for brains . . . [and] pot [for] patriotism." When the resolution failed, McCarthy delegates put on black armbands and followed folk singer Theodore Bikel in singing "We Shall Overcome." Later, as tear gas used against the demonstrators outside turned the amphitheater air acrid, delegates heard the beaming Humphrey praise Mayor Daley and Johnson's conduct of the Vietnam War. When Senator Abraham Ribicoff of Connecticut addressed the convention and protested the "Gestapo tactics" of the police, television cameras focused on Mayor Daley saying, "You Jew son of a bitch . . ., go home!" The crowd outside chanted, "The whole world is watching! The whole world is watching!" Indeed, through satellite transmission, it was.

Protest and social strain spread worldwide. Across the United States the antiwar movement picked up steam. In Paris, students took over campuses and workers occupied factories. Young people scrawled on the walls such humorous and half-serious slogans as "Be Realistic, Demand the Impossible!" Similar protests against authority occurred in eastern Europe. In Prague, Czechoslovakia, students wearing blue jeans and singing Beatles songs threw rocks at Soviet tanks. Meanwhile, demonstrations in Japan, Italy, Ireland, Germany, and England all brought young people into the streets to demand democratic reforms in their own countries and an end to the war in Vietnam.

THE POLITICS OF IDENTITY

The tragic events of 1968 brought whole sectors of the counterculture into political activism. But, remember, hippie Tuli Kupferberg warned them, "the first revolution (but not of course the last) is in yr own head." Many young Americans seemed to hear his message, intensifying their protest against the war while at the same time expressing their own political grievances and promoting their own sense of collective identity. United in their opposition to "the Establishment"—that is, the politicians and business leaders who maintained the status quo—these baby boomers sought also to empower themselves and their communities in myriad smaller but vital movements.

With great media fanfare, gay liberation and women's liberation movements emerged in the late 1960s. By the early 1970s young Latinos, Asian Americans, and Indian peoples had pressed their own claims. In different ways, these groups drew their own lessons from the nationalist movement that formed in the wake of Malcolm X's death—Black Power. Soon, "Brown Power," "Yellow Power," and "Red Power" became the slogans of movements constituted distinctly as new communities of protest.

Black Power

In African American communities, when the Great Society programs failed to lessen poverty and black men began to die in disproportionate numbers in Vietnam, faith in the old ways lapsed. Impatient with the strategies of social change based on voting rights and integration, many younger activists spurned the tactics of civil disobedience of King's generation for direct action and militant self-defense. In 1966 Stokely Carmichael, who had helped turn SNCC into an all-black organization, began to advocate Black

PROTEST MOVEMENTS OF THE 1960S

Year	Organization/ Movement	Description
1962	Students for a Democratic Society (SDS)	Organization of college students that became the largest national organization of left-wing white students. Calling for "participatory democracy," SDS involved students in community-based campaigns against poverty and for citizens' control of neighborhoods. SDS played a prominent role in the campaign to end the war in Vietnam.
1964	Free Speech Movement	Formed at the University of California at Berkeley to protest the banning of on-campus political fund-raising. Decried the bureaucratic character of the "multiuniversity" and advocated an expansion of student rights.
1965	Anti-Vietnam War Movement	Advocated grass-roots opposition to U.S. involvement in Southeast Asia. By 1970 a national mobilization committee organized a demonstration of a half-million protesters in Washington, D.C.
1965	*La raza*	A movement of Chicano youth to advance the cultural and political self-determination of Mexican Americans. *La raza* included the Brown Berets, which addressed community issues, and regional civil rights groups such as the Crusade for Social Justice, formed in 1965.
1966	Black Power	Militant movement that emerged from the civil rights campaigns to advocate independent institutions for African Americans and pride in black culture and African heritage. The idea of Black Power, a term coined by Stokely Carmichael, inspired the formation of the paramilitary Black Panthers.
1968	American Indian Movement (AIM)	Organization formed to advance the self-determination of Indian peoples and challenge the authority of the Bureau of Indian Affairs. Its most effective tactic was occupation. In February, 1973, AIM insurgents protesting land and treaty violations occupied Wounded Knee, South Dakota, the location of an 1890 massacre, until the FBI and BIA agents drove them out.
1968	Women's Liberation	Movement of mainly young women that took shape following a protest at the Miss America Beauty Pageant. Impatient with the legislative reforms promoted by the National Organization for Women, founded in 1966, activists developed their own agenda shaped by the slogan "The Personal Is Political." Activities included the formation of "consciousness-raising" groups and the establishment of women's studies programs.
1968	Asian American Political Alliance (AAPA)	Formed at the University of California at Berkeley, the AAPA was one of the first pan-Asian political organizations to struggle against racial oppression. The AAPA encouraged Asian Americans to claim their own cultural identity and to protest the war against Asian peoples in Vietnam.
1969	Gay Liberation	Movement to protest discrimination against homosexuals and lesbians that emerged after the Stonewall Riots in New York City. Unlike earlier organizations such as the Mattachine Society, which focused on civil rights, Gay Liberationists sought to radically change American society and government, which they believed were corrupt.

Power as a means for African Americans to take control of their own communities.

Derived from a century-long tradition of black nationalism, the key tenets of Black Power were self-determination and self-sufficiency. National conferences of activists, held annually beginning in 1966, adopted separatist resolutions, including a plan to partition the United States into black and white nations. Black Power also promoted self-esteem by affirming the unique history and heritage of African peoples.

The movement's boldest expression was the Black Panther Party for Self-Defense, founded in Oakland, California, in 1966 by Huey P. Newton and Bobby Seale. "We want freedom," Newton demanded. "We want power. . . . We want full employment. . . . We want all black men to be exempt from military service. We want . . . an end to POLICE BRUTALITY. . . . We want land, bread, housing, education, clothing, and justice." Armed self-defense was the Panthers' strategy, and they adopted a paramilitary style—black leather jackets, shoes, black berets, and firearms—that infuriated local authorities. Monitoring local police, a practice Panthers termed "patrolling the pigs," was their major activity. In several communities, Panthers also ran free breakfast programs for schoolchildren, established medical clinics, and conducted educational classes. For a time the Panthers became folk heroes in the black community. Persecuted by local police and the FBI—there were more than thirty raids on Panther offices in eleven states during 1968 and 1969—the Panthers were arrested, prosecuted, and sentenced to long terms in jail that effectively destroyed the organization.

The war in Vietnam contributed to the growing racial militancy in the United States. African Americans served on the front lines in Vietnam in disproportionate numbers, and many came to view the conflict as a "white man's war."

Black Power nevertheless continued to grow during the late 1960s and became a multifaceted movement. The Reverend Jesse Jackson, for example, rallied African Americans in Chicago to boycott the A&P supermarket chain until the firm hired 700 black workers. A dynamic speaker and skillful organizer, Jackson encouraged African Americans to support their own businesses and services. "We are going to see to it," he explained in 1969, "that the resources of the ghetto are not siphoned off by outside groups. . . . If a building goes up in the black community, we're going to build it." His program, Operation Breadbasket, strengthened community control. By 1970 it had spread beyond Chicago to fifteen other cities.

Cultural nationalism became the most enduring component of Black Power. In their popular book *Black Power* (1967), Stokely Carmichael and Charles V. Hamilton urged African Americans "to assert their own definitions, to reclaim their history, their culture; to create their own sense of community and togetherness." Thousands of college students responded by calling for more scholarships and for more classes on African American history and culture. At San Francisco State University, students formed the Black Student Union and, with help from the Black Panthers, demanded the creation of a black studies department. After a series of failed negotiations with the administration, the black students called for a campuswide strike and in December 1968 shut down the university. In the end, 134 school days later, the administration agreed to fund a black studies department but also fired about 25 faculty members and refused to drop charges against 700 arrested campus activists. Strikes for "third world studies" soon broke out on other campuses, including the Newark campus of Rutgers University, the San Diego and Berkeley campuses of the University of California, and the University of Wisconsin at Madison, where the national guard was brought in to quell the protest.

Meanwhile, trend setters put aside Western dress for African-style dashikis and hairdos, and black parents gave their children African names. Many well-known African Americans such as Imamu Amiri Baraka (formerly LeRoi Jones), Muhammad Ali (formerly Cassius Clay), and Kwame Touré (formerly Stokely Carmichael) rejected their "slave names." The African

American holiday Kwanzaa began to replace Christmas as a seasonal family celebration. This deepening sense of racial pride and solidarity was summed up in the popular slogan "Black Is Beautiful."

Sisterhood Is Powerful

Betty Friedan's best-selling *Feminine Mystique* (1963) had swelled feelings of discontent among many middle-class white women who had come of age in the 1950s (see Chapter 27) and sparked the formation of the National Organization for Women (NOW) in 1966. NOW pledged itself "to take action to bring women into full participation in the mainstream of American society now." Members spearheaded campaigns for the enforcement of laws banning sex discrimination in work and in education, for maternity leaves for working mothers, and for government funding of day-care centers. NOW also came out for the Equal Rights Amendment, first introduced in Congress in 1923, and demanded the repeal of legislation that prohibited abortion or restricted birth control.

The second half of the decade produced a different kind of movement: women's liberation. Like Black Power, the women's liberation movement attracted especially women who had been active in civil rights, SDS, and campus antiwar movements. These women resented the sexist attitudes and behaviors of their fellow male activists. Women must come to understand, one angry woman wrote, that "they are not inferior—nor chicks, nor bunnies, nor quail, nor cows, nor bitches, nor ass, nor meat," but agents of their own destiny. Like Black Power, the women's liberation movement issued its own separatist plan.

In 1967 small groups of women broke off from male-led protest movements. They formed myriad all-women organizations such as Radical Women and Redstockings in New York, the Women's Liberation Union in Chicago, Berkeley, and Dayton, and Bread and Roses and Cell 16 in Boston. Impatient with the legislative reforms promoted by NOW, and angered by the sexism of SNCC and SDS, these women proclaimed "Sisterhood Is Powerful." "Women are an oppressed class. Our oppression is total, affecting every facet of our lives," read the Redstocking Manifesto of 1969. "We are exploited as sex objects, breeders, domestic servants, and cheap labor."

The women's liberation movement developed a scathing critique of patriarchy—that is, the power of men to dominate all institutions, from the family to business to the military to protest movements themselves. Patriarchy, they argued, was the prime cause of exploitation, racism, and war. Outraged and sometimes outrageous, radical feminists, as they called themselves, conducted "street theater" at the 1968 Miss America Beauty Pageant in Atlantic City, crowning a live sheep queen and "throwing implements of female torture" (bras, girdles, curlers, and copies of the *Ladies' Home Journal*) into a "freedom trash can." A few months later, the Women's International Terrorist Conspiracy from Hell (WITCH) struck in Lower Manhattan, putting a hex on the male-dominated New York Stock Exchange.

The media focused on the audacious acts and brazen pronouncements of radical feminists, but the majority involved in the women's liberation movement were less flamboyant women who were simply trying to rise above the limitations imposed on them because of their sex. Most of their activism took place outside the limelight in consciousness-raising (CR) groups. CR groups, which multiplied by the thousands in the late 1960s and early 1970s, brought women together to discuss the relationship between public events and private lives, particularly between politics and sexuality. Here women shared their most intimate feelings toward men or other women and established the constituency for the movement's most important belief, expressed in the aphorism "The personal is political." Believing that no aspect of life lacked a political dimension, women in these groups explored the power dynamics of the institutions of family and marriage as well as the workforce and government. "The small group has served as a place where thousands of us have learned to support each other," one participant reported, "where we have gained new feelings of self-respect and learned to speak about what we are thinking and to respect other women."

Participants in the women's liberation movement engaged in a wide range of activities. Some staged sit-ins at *Newsweek* to protest demeaning media depictions of women. Others established health clinics, day-care centers, rape crisis centers, and shelters for women fleeing abusive husbands or lovers. The women's liberation movement also had a significant educational impact. Feminist bookstores and publishing companies, such as the Feminist Press, reached out to eager readers. Scholarly books such as Kate Millett's *Sexual Politics* (1970) found a wide popular audience. By the early 1970s campus activists were demanding women's studies programs and women's centers. Like black studies, women's studies programs included traditional academic goals, such as the generation of new scholarship, but also encouraged personal change and self-esteem. Between 1970 and 1975, as many as 150 women's studies programs had been established. The movement continued to grow; by 1980 nearly 30,000 women's studies courses were offered at colleges and universities throughout the United States.

The women's liberation movement remained, however, a bastion of white middle-class women. The appeal to sisterhood did not unite women across race or class or even sexual orientation. Lesbians, who charged the early leaders of NOW with homophobia, found large pockets of "heterosexism" in the women's liberation movement and broke off to form their own organizations. Although some African American women were outraged at the posturing of Black Power leaders like Stokely Carmichael, who joked that "the only position for women in SNCC is prone," the majority remained wary of white women's appeals to sisterhood. African American women formed their own "womanist" movement to address their distinct cultural and political concerns. Similarly, by 1970 a Latina feminist movement had begun to address issues uniquely relevant to women of color in an Anglo-dominated society.

Although the women's liberation movement could not dispel ethnic or racial differences, it fostered a sense of community among many women. By August 1970 hundreds of thousands of women responded to NOW's call for a Women's Strike for Equality, a mass demonstration marking the fiftieth anniversary of the woman suffrage amendment and the largest turnout for women's rights in U.S. history.

Gay Liberation

The gay community had been generations in the making but gained visibility during World War II (see Chapter 25). By the mid-1950s two pioneering homophile organizations, the Mattachine Society and the Daughters of Bilitis, were campaigning to reduce discrimination against homosexuals in employment, the armed forces, and all areas of social and cultural life. Other groups, such as the Society for Individual Rights, rooted themselves in New York's Greenwich Village, San Francisco's North Beach, and other centers of gay night life. But it was during the tumultuous 1960s that gay and lesbian movements encouraged many men and women to proclaim publicly their sexual identity: "Say It Loud, Gay Is Proud."

The major event prompting gays to organize grew out of repeated police raids of gay bars and harassment of their patrons. In February 1966 New York City's popular liberal mayor John Lindsay announced a crackdown against "promenading perverts" and assigned police to patrol the bars between Times Square and Washington Square. The American Civil Liberties Union responded by pointing out that the mayor was "confusing deviant social behavior with criminal activity." Lindsay's police commissioner soon announced the end of the entrapment policy by which undercover police had been luring homosexuals into breaking the law, but various forms of individual harassment continued. Finally, on Friday, June 27, 1969, New York police raided the Stonewall Inn, a well-known gay bar in Greenwich Village, and provoked an uprising of angry homosexuals that lasted the entire night. The next day, "Gay Power" graffiti appeared on buildings and sidewalks throughout the neighborhood.

The Stonewall Riot, as it was called, sparked a new sense of collective identity among many gays and lesbians and touched off a new movement for both civil rights and liberation. Gay men and women in New York City formed the Gay Liberation Front (GLF), announcing themselves as "a revolutionary homosexual group of men and women formed with the realization that complete sexual liberation for all people cannot come about unless existing social institutions are abolished. We reject society's attempt to impose sexual roles and definitions of our nature. We are stepping outside these roles and simplistic myths. We are going to be who we are." The GLF also took a stand against the war in Vietnam and supported the Black Panthers. It quickly adopted the forms of public protest, such as street demonstrations and sit-ins, developed by the civil rights movement and given new direction by antiwar protesters.

Changes in public opinion and policies followed. As early as 1967 a group of Episcopal priests had urged church leaders to avoid taking a moral position against same-sex relationships. The San Francisco-based Council on Religion and Homosexuality established a network for clergy sympathetic to gay and lesbian parishioners. In 1973 the American Psychiatric Association, which since World War II had viewed homosexuality as a treatable mental illness, reclassified it as a normal sexual orientation. Meanwhile, there began a slow process of decriminalization of homosexual acts between consenting adults. In 1975 the U.S. Civil Service Commission ended its ban on the employment of homosexuals.

The founders of gay liberation encouraged not only legal changes and the establishment of supporting institutions but self-pride. "Gay Is Good" (like "Black Is Beautiful" and "Sisterhood Is Powerful") expressed the aspiration of a large hidden minority (estimated at 10 million or more people) to "come out" and demand public acceptance of their sexual identity. The Gay Activist Alliance, founded in 1970, demanded "freedom of expression of our dignity and value as human beings." By the mid-1970s Gay Pride marches held simultaneously in several cities were drawing nearly 500,000 participants.

The Chicano Rebellion

By the mid-1960s young Mexican Americans had created, according to one historian, a moral community founded on collectivist principles and a determination to resist Anglo domination. Mainly high school and college students, they adopted the slang term *Chicano*, in preference to Mexican American, to express a militant

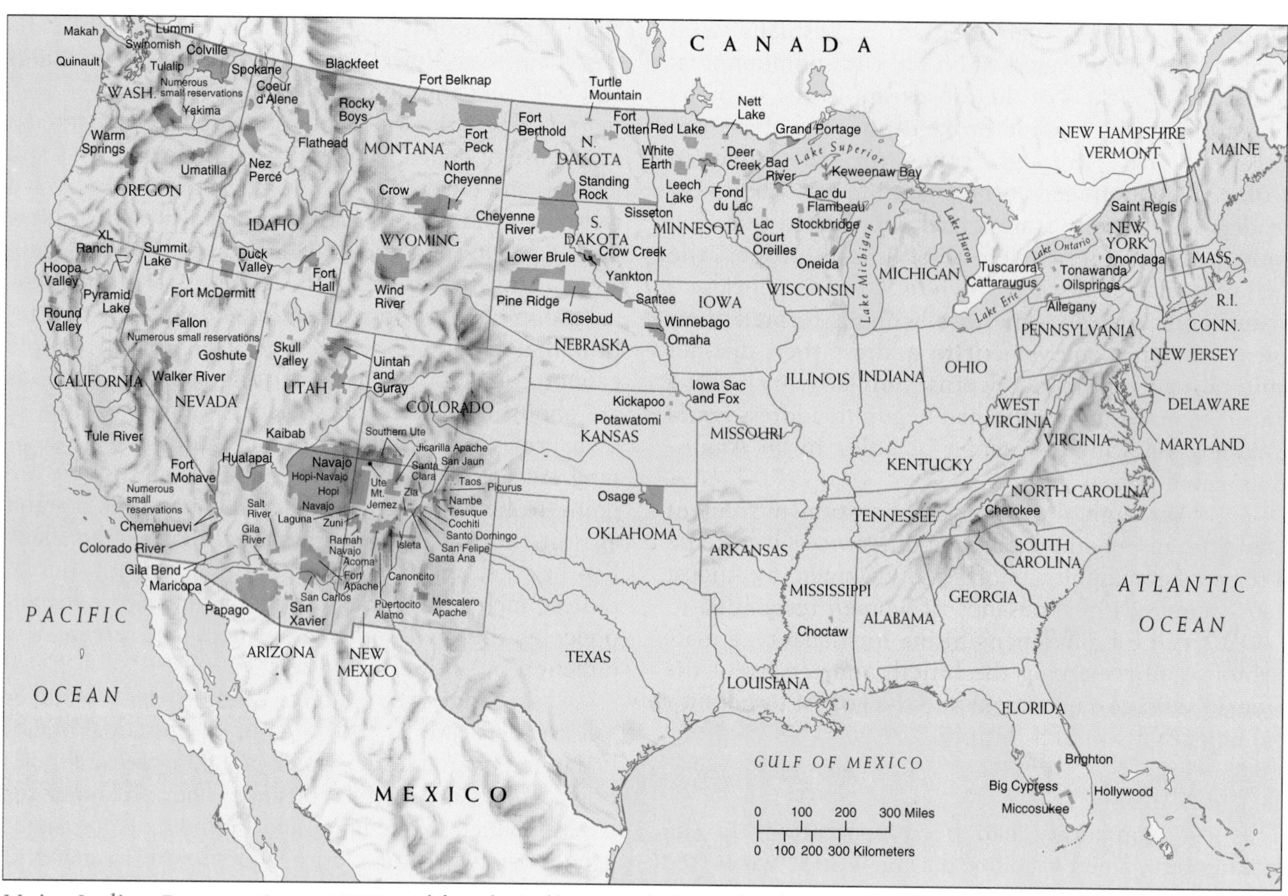

Major Indian Reservations, 1976 *Although sizable areas, designated Indian reservations represented only a small portion of territory occupied in earlier times.*

ethnic nationalism. Chicano militants demanded not only equality with white people but cultural and political self-determination. Tracing their roots to the heroic Aztecs, they identified *la raza* (the race or people) as the source of a common language, religion, and heritage.

Between 1965 and 1969 the Chicano movement reached its peak. Students staged "blowouts" or strikes in East Los Angeles high schools to demand educational reform and a curricular emphasis on the history, literature, art, and language of Mexican Americans. In 1968 President Johnson had signed the Bilingual Education Act, which reversed state laws that prohibited the teaching of classes in any language but English. Nevertheless, as Sal Castro, an East Los Angeles teacher, complained, "If a kid speaks in Spanish, he is criticized. If a kid has a Mexican accent, he is ridiculed. If a kid talks back, in any language, he is arrested. . . . We have a gun-point education. The school is a prison." Castro encouraged 15,000 students from five Los Angeles schools to strike against poor educational facilities. The police conducted a mass arrest of protesters, and within a short time students in San Antonio and Denver were conducting their own blowouts, holding placards reading "Teachers, Sí, Bigots, No!" By 1969, on September 16, Mexican Independence Day, high school students throughout the Southwest skipped classes in the First National Chicano Boycott. Meanwhile, students organized to demand Mexican American studies on their campuses. In 1969, a group staged a sit-in at the administrative offices of the University of California–Berkeley, which one commentator called "the first important public appearance of something called Brown Power."

In 1967 David Sanchez of East Los Angeles formed the Brown Berets, modeled on the Black Panthers, to address such community issues as housing and employment and generally to encourage teenagers to express *Chicanismo,* or pride in their Mexican American identity and heritage. By 1972, when the organization disbanded, the Brown Berets had organized twenty chapters, published a newspaper, *La Causa,* and run a successful health clinic. From college campuses spread a wider cultural movement that spawned literary journals in "Spanglish" (a mixture of English and Spanish), theatrical companies and music groups, and murals illustrating ethnic themes on buildings in Los Angeles and elsewhere.

Chicano nationalism inspired a variety of regional political movements in the late 1960s. Several organizations, such as Corky Gonzales's Crusade for Justice, formed in 1965 to protest the failure of the Great Society's antipoverty programs. A former boxer and popular poet, Gonzales was especially well liked by barrio youth and college students. He led important campaigns for greater job opportunities and land reform throughout the Southwest well into the 1970s. In Colorado and New Mexico, the *Alianza Federal de Mercedes,* formed in 1963 by Reies López Tijerina, fought to reclaim land fraudulently appropriated by white settlers. The Texas-based *La Raza Unida* Party (LRUP), meanwhile, increased Mexican American representation in local government and established social and cultural programs. The student-led Mexican American Youth Organization (MAYO) worked closely with the LRUP to help Mexican Americans take political power in Crystal City, Texas. The two organizations registered voters, ran candidates for office, and staged a massive boycott of Anglo-owned businesses.

Mexican American activists, even those who won local office, soon discovered that economic power remained out of community hands. Stifled by poverty, ordinary Mexican Americans had less confidence in the political process, and many fell back into apathy after early hopes of great, sudden change. Despite these setbacks, a sense of collective identity had been forged among many young people. A member of the Brown Berets summed up: "We're not in the melting pot sort of thing. Chicanos don't melt."

Red Power

Having battled government programs to terminate their tribal status (see Chapter 28), Indian peoples entered the 1960s determined to reassert themselves. The Civil Rights Act passed in 1968 restored the legitimacy of tribal laws on the reservations, and Lyndon Johnson personally promised a "new goal" that "erases old attitudes of paternalism." Although economic and social reforms were limited by a shortage of antipoverty and educational funds, a movement to build a sense of Indian identity spread widely among young people. In the 1970 census, many of the 800,000 respondents who identified themselves as Indians did so for the first time.

The American Indian Movement (AIM) was founded in 1968 by Chippewas George Mitchell and Dennis Banks. Like the Black Panthers and Brown Berets, AIM was organized for self-defense, to protect Indians in Minneapolis from police harassment and brutality. The group's activities soon expanded to include a direct challenge of the Bureau of Indian Affairs' guidance over tribal life. Affirming Indian dignity while calling for greater economic opportunities and an end to police harassment, AIM quickly inspired a plethora of new publications and local organizations. In 1969 the new militancy created national headlines when a group of young Indians occupied the deserted federal prison on Alcatraz Island in San Francisco Bay and demanded government funds for a cultural center and university. The federal government did not respond, however, and the Indians eventually pulled out.

The most dramatic series of events of the Red Power movement began in November 1972, when tribal members occupied the headquarters of the Bureau of Indian affairs for nearly a week. Soon AIM insurgents took over the site of the 1890 massacres at Wounded Knee, South Dakota, swearing to hold their position by force if necessary. Occupiers asked only that the federal government honor treaty rights. Instead, dozens of FBI agents invaded under shoot-to-kill orders, leaving two Indians dead and one federal marshal wounded. AIM

Members of the American Indian Movement (AIM) guard the door to the Bureau of Indian Affairs in Washington, D.C., during a week-long occupation in November 1972 meant to dramatize their grievances. Formed in 1968 to work for equal rights and better living conditions, AIM had led a march of Indian peoples along the "Trail of Broken Treaties" before occupying the BIA offices.

gained widespread support for its actions but alienated the more conservative leaders of various tribes.

Several tribes won in court, by legislation or by administrative fiat, small parts of what had earlier been taken from them. The sacred Blue Lake was returned to Pueblo Indians in Taos, New Mexico, and Alaskan natives were granted legal title to 40 million acres (and compensation of almost $1 billion). The Native American Rights Fund (NARF), established in 1971, gained additional thousands of acres in Atlantic coast states. Despite these victories, tribal lands continued to suffer from industrial and government dumping and other commercial uses. On reservations and in urban areas with heavy Indian concentrations, alcohol abuse and ill health remained serious problems.

The 1960s also marked the beginning of an "Indian Renaissance." New books like Vine Deloria Jr.'s *Custer Died for Your Sins* (1969), Dee Brown's *Bury My Heart at Wounded Knee* (1971), and the classic *Black Elk Speaks* (1961), reprinted from the 1930s, reached millions of readers inside and outside Indian communities. A wide variety of Indian novelists, historians, and essayists, such as Pulitzer Prize–winning N. Scott Momaday and Leslie Silko, followed up these successes, and fiction and nonfiction works about Indian life and lore continued to attract a large audience.

The Asian American Movement

Inspired by the Black Power movement, college students of Asian ancestry sought to unite fellow Asian Americans in a struggle against racial oppression "through the power of a consolidated yellow people." In 1968 students at the University of California at Berkeley founded the Asian American Political Alliance (AAPA), one of the first pan-Asian political organizations bringing together Chinese, Japanese, and Filipino American activists. Similar organizations soon appeared on campuses throughout California and spread quickly to the east coast and Midwest.

These groups took a strong stand against the war in Vietnam, condemning it as a violation of the national sovereignty of the small Asian country. They also protested the racism directed against the peoples of Southeast Asia, particularly the practice common among American soldiers of referring to the enemy as "Gooks." This racist epithet, first used to denigrate Filipinos during the Spanish-American War, implied that Asians were something less than human and therefore proper targets for slaughter. In response, Asian American activists rallied behind the people of Vietnam and proclaimed racial solidarity with their "Asian brothers and sisters."

The antiwar movement brought many young Asian Americans into political organizations such as the AAPA that encouraged them to claim their own cultural identity. In 1968 and 1969 students at San Francisco State College and the University of California at Berkeley, for example, rallied behind the slogan "Shut It Down!" and waged prolonged campus strikes to demand the establishment of ethnic studies programs. These students sought alternatives to the goal of assimilation into mainstream society, promoting instead a unique sense of ethnic identity, a pan-Asian counterculture. Berkeley students, for example, sponsored the "Asian American Experience in America—Yellow Power" conference, inviting their peers to learn about "Asian American history and destiny, and the need to express Asian American solidarity in a predominantly white society."

Between 1968 and 1973, major universities across the country introduced courses on Asian American studies, and a few, such as the City College of New York, set up interdisciplinary departments. Meanwhile, artists, writers, documentary filmmakers, oral historians, and anthropologists worked to recover the Asian American past. Writer Frank Chin, who advocated a language that "coheres the people into a community by organizing and codifying the symbols of the people's common experience," wrote the first Asian American drama, *The Year of the Dragon,* to be produced on national television. It was, however, Maxine Hong Kingston's *Woman Warrior: A Memoir of a Girlhood among Ghosts* (1976) that became the major best-seller.

Looking to the example of the Black Panthers, young Asian Americans also took their struggle into the community. In 1968, activists presented the San Francisco municipal government with a list of grievances about conditions in Chinatown, particularly the poor housing and medical facilities, and organized a protest march down the neighborhood's main street. They led a communitywide struggle to save San Francisco's International Hotel, a low-income residential facility for mainly Filipino and Chinese men, which was ultimately leveled for a new parking lot.

Community activists ranging from college students to neighborhood artists worked in a variety of campaigns to heighten public awareness. The Redress and Reparations Movement, initiated by Sansei (third-generation Japanese Americans), for example, encouraged students to ask their parents about their wartime experiences and prompted older civil rights organizations, such as the Japanese American Citizens League, to bring forward the issue of internment. At the same time, trade union organizers renewed labor organizing among new Asian workers, mainly in service industries such as hotel and restaurant work, and in clothing manufacturing. Other campaigns reflected the growing diversity of the Asian population. Filipinos, the fastest growing group, organized to protest the destructive role of

U.S.-backed Philippine dictator Ferdinand Marcos. Students from South Korea similarly denounced the repressive government in their homeland. Samoans sought to publicize the damage caused by nuclear testing in the Pacific Islands. Ultimately, however, in blurring intergroup differences, the Asian American movement failed to reach the growing populations of new immigrants, especially the numerous Southeast Asians fleeing their devastated homeland.

Despite its shortcomings, the politics of identity would continue to grow through the next two decades of mainly conservative rule, broadening the content of literature, film, television, popular music, and even the curriculum of the nation's schools. Collectively, the various movements for social change pushed issues of race, gender, and sexual orientation to the forefront of American politics and simultaneously spotlighted the nation's cultural diversity as a major resource.

THE NIXON PRESIDENCY

The sharp divisions among Americans in 1968, due to a large degree to President Johnson's policies in Vietnam, paved the way for the election of Richard Milhous Nixon. The new Republican president inherited not only an increasingly unpopular war but a nation riven by internal discord. Without specifying his plans, he promised a just and honorable peace in Southeast Asia and the restoration of law and order at home. Yet, once in office, Nixon puzzled both friends and foes. He ordered unprecedented illegal government action against private citizens while agreeing with Congress to enhance several welfare programs and improve environmental protection. He widened and intensified the war in Vietnam, yet made stunning moves toward détente with the People's Republic of China. An architect of the cold war in the 1950s, Nixon became the first president to foresee its end. Nixon worked hard in the White House, centralizing authority and reigning defiantly as an Imperial President—until he brought himself down.

The Southern Strategy

In 1968, Republican presidential contender Richard Nixon deftly built on voter hostility toward youthful protesters and the counterculture. He represented, he said, the "silent majority"—those Americans who worked, paid taxes, and did not demonstrate, picket, or protest loudly, "people who are not haters, people who love their country." Recovering from defeats in runs for the presidency in 1960 and the governorship of California in 1962, Nixon declared himself the one candidate who could restore law and order to the nation.

After signing the landmark Civil Rights Act of 1964, President Johnson said privately, "I think we just

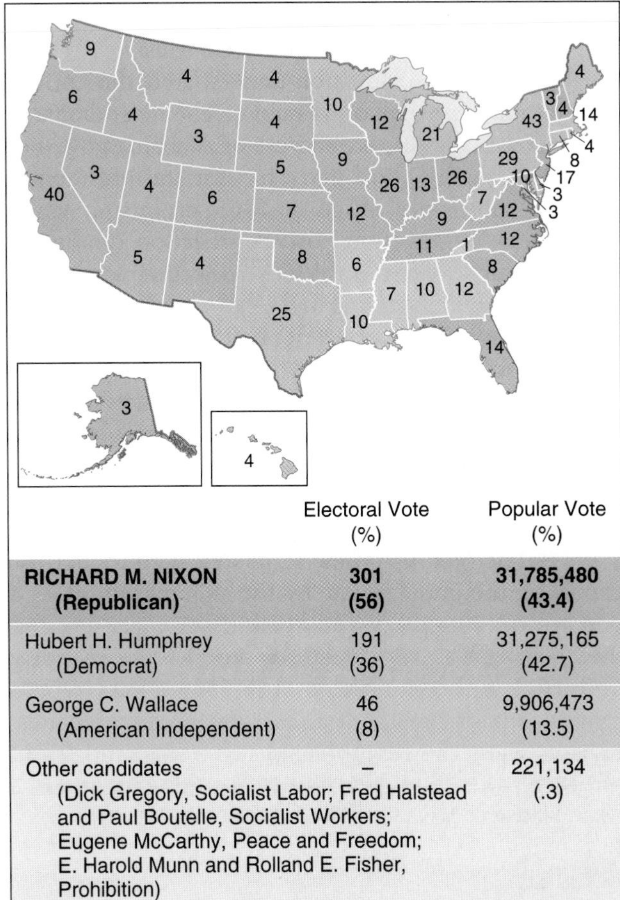

	Electoral Vote (%)	Popular Vote (%)
RICHARD M. NIXON (Republican)	**301 (56)**	**31,785,480 (43.4)**
Hubert H. Humphrey (Democrat)	191 (36)	31,275,165 (42.7)
George C. Wallace (American Independent)	46 (8)	9,906,473 (13.5)
Other candidates (Dick Gregory, Socialist Labor; Fred Halstead and Paul Boutelle, Socialist Workers; Eugene McCarthy, Peace and Freedom; E. Harold Munn and Rolland E. Fisher, Prohibition)	–	221,134 (.3)

The Election of 1968 *Although the Republican Nixon-Agnew team won the popular vote by only a small margin, the Democrats lost in most of the northern states that had voted Democratic since the days of FDR. Segregationist Governor George Wallace of Alabama polled more than 9 million votes.*

delivered the South to the Republicans for a long time to come." Republican strategists moved quickly to make this prediction come true. They also recognized the growing electoral importance of the Sunbelt, where populations grew with the rise of high-tech industries and retirement communities. A powerful conservatism dominated this region, home to many military bases, defense plants, and an increasingly influential Protestant evangelism. Nixon appealed directly to these voters by promising to appoint to federal courts judges who would undercut liberal interpretations of civil rights and be tough on crime. Nixon also promised to roll back the Great Society. "I say it's time," he announced, "to quit pouring billions of dollars into programs that have failed."

Nixon selected as his running mate Maryland governor Spiro T. Agnew, known for his vitriolic oratory. Agnew treated dissent as near treason. He courted the silent majority by attacking all critics of the war as "an effete corps of impudent snobs" and blasted liberal newscasters as "nattering nabobs of negativism."

Democratic nominee Hubert Humphrey chose as his running mate Maine senator Edmund Muskie.

The 1968 campaign underscored the antiliberal sentiment of the voting public. The most dramatic example was the relative success of Alabama governor George Wallace's third-party bid for the presidency. Wallace took state office in 1963 promising white Alabamans "Segregation now! Segregation tomorrow! Segregation forever!" In 1968 he waged a national campaign around a conservative hate list that included school busing, antiwar demonstrations, and urban uprisings. His running mate in the American Independent Party, retired air force general Curtis LeMay, proposed the use of nuclear weapons to "bomb the North Vietnamese back to the Stone Age." Winning only five southern states, Wallace nevertheless captured 13.5 percent of the popular vote.

The Nixon-Agnew team squeaked to victory, capturing the popular vote by the slim margin of 43.4 percent to Humphrey and Muskie's 42.7 percent but taking nearly all the West's electoral votes. Bitterly divided by the campaign, the Democrats would remain out of presidential contention for decades, except when the Republicans suffered scandal and disgrace. The Republicans in 1968 had inaugurated a new political era.

In view of the developments since we entered the fighting in Vietnam, do you think the United States made a mistake sending troops to fight in Vietnam?

Yes	52%
No	39
No opinion	9

Interviewing Date 1/22–28/1969, Survey #774-K, Question #6/Index #45

Public Opinion on the War in Vietnam *By 1969 Americans were sharply divided in their assessments of the progress of the war and peace negotiations. The American Institute of Public Opinion, founded in 1935 by George Gallup, charted a growing dissatisfaction with the war in Vietnam.*

Source: *The Gallup Poll: Public Opinion*, 1935–1974 (New York: Random House, 1974), p. 2189.

Nixon's War

Nixon promised to bring "peace with honor." Yet, despite this pledge, the Vietnam War raged for four more years before a peace settlement was reached.

Much of the responsibility for the prolonged conflict rested with Henry A. Kissinger. A dominating personality on the National Security Council, Kissinger insisted that the United States could not retain its global leadership by appearing weak to either allies or enemies. "However we got into Vietnam," he wrote in 1969, the United States "cannot accept a military defeat, or a change in the political structure of South Vietnam brought about by external military forces." Brilliant and ruthless, Kissinger helped Nixon centralize foreign policy making in the White House. Together, they overpowered those members of the State Department who had concluded that the majority of Americans no longer supported the war.

In public Nixon followed a policy of "Vietnamization." On May 14, 1969, he announced that the time was approaching "when the South Vietnamese . . . will be able to take over some of the fighting." During the next several months, he ordered the withdrawal of 60,000 U.S. troops. Hoping to placate public opinion, Nixon also intended to "demonstrate to Hanoi that we were serious in seeking a diplomatic settlement." In private, with Kissinger's guidance, Nixon mulled over the option of a "knockout blow" to the North Vietnamese.

On April 30, 1970, Nixon made one of the most controversial decisions of his presidency. Without seeking congressional approval, Nixon added Cambodia (through which North Vietnam had been ferrying troops and supplies south) to the war zone. Although Nixon had authorized secret bombing raids of Cambodia in 1969, he now ordered U.S. troops to invade the tiny nation. Nixon had hoped in this way to end North Vietnamese infiltration into the South, but he had also decided to live up to what he privately called his "wild man" or "mad bomber" reputation. The enemy would be unable to anticipate the location or severity of the next U.S. strike, Nixon reasoned, and would thus feel compelled to negotiate.

Nixon could not have predicted the outpouring of protest that followed the invasion of Cambodia. The largest series of demonstrations and police-student confrontations in the nation's history took place on campuses and in city streets. At Kent State University in Ohio, twenty-eight National Guardsmen apparently panicked. Shooting into an unarmed crowd of about 200 students, they killed four and wounded nine. Ten days later, on May 14, at Jackson State University, a black school in Mississippi, state troopers entered a campus dormitory and began shooting wildly, killing two students and wounding twelve others. Demonstrations broke out on 50 campuses.

The nation was shocked. Thirty-seven college and university presidents signed a letter calling on the president to end the war. A few weeks later the Senate adopted a bipartisan resolution outlawing the use of funds for U.S. military operations in Cambodia, starting July 1, 1970. Although the House rejected the resolution, Nixon saw the writing on the wall. He had planned to negotiate a simultaneous withdrawal of North Vietnamese and U.S. troops, but he could no longer afford to hold out for this condition.

The president, still goaded by Kissinger, did not accept defeat easily. In February 1971 Nixon directed the South Vietnamese army to invade Laos and cut supply lines, but the demoralized invading force suffered a quick and humiliating defeat. Faced with enemy occupation of more and more territory during a major offensive in April 1972, Nixon ordered the mining of North Vietnamese harbors and directed B-52s on massively destructive bombing missions in Cambodia and North Vietnam.

Nixon also sent Kissinger to Paris for secret negotiations with delegates from North Vietnam. They agreed to a cease-fire specifying the withdrawal of all U.S. troops and the return of all U.S. prisoners of war. Knowing these terms ensured defeat, South Vietnam's president refused to sign the agreement. On Christmas Day 1972, hoping for a better negotiating position, Nixon ordered one final wave of bomb attacks on North Vietnam's cities. To secure a halt to the bombing, the North Vietnamese offered to resume negotiations. But the terms of the Paris Peace Agreement, signed by North Vietnam and the United States in January 1973, differed little from the settlement Nixon could have procured in 1969, hundreds of thousands of deaths earlier. Beginning in March 1973, the withdrawal of U.S. troops left the outcome of the war a foregone conclusion. By December of that year only 50 American military personnel remained, and the government of South Vietnam had no future.

In April 1975 North Vietnamese troops took over Saigon, and the communist-led Democratic Republic of Vietnam soon united the small nation. The war was finally over. It had cost the United States 58,000 lives and $150 billion. The country had not only failed to achieve its stated war goal but had lost an important post in Southeast Asia. Equally important, the policy of containment introduced by Truman had proved impossible to sustain.

While Nixon was maneuvering to bring about "peace with honor," the chilling crimes of war had already begun to haunt Americans. In 1971 the army court-martialed a young lieutenant, William L. Calley Jr., for the murder of "at least" twenty-two Vietnamese civilians during a 1968 search-and-destroy mission subsequently known as the My Lai Massacre. Calley's platoon had destroyed a village and slaughtered more than 350 unarmed South Vietnamese, raping and beating many of the women before killing them. "My Lai was not an isolated incident," one veteran attested, but "only a minor step beyond the standard official United States policy in Indochina." Commander of the platoon at My Lai, Calley was first sentenced to life imprisonment before being given a reduced term of ten years. The secretary of the army paroled Calley after he served three years under house arrest in his apartment.

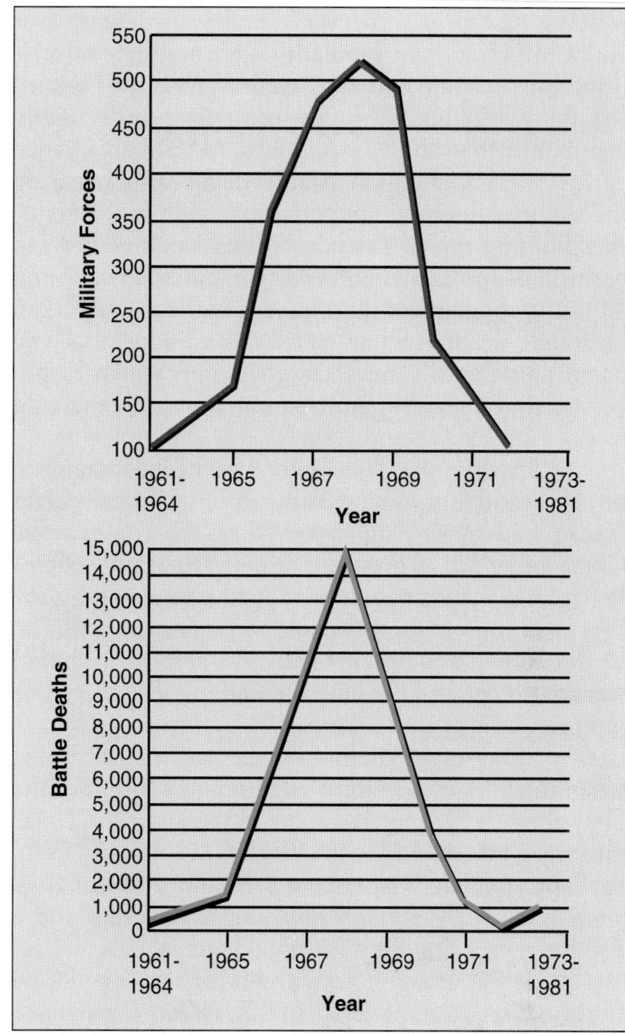

U.S. Military Forces in Vietnam and Casualties, 1961–1981 *The United States government estimated battle deaths between 1969 and 1973 for South Vietnamese troops at 107,504 and North Vietnamese and Vietcong at more than a half-million. Although the United States suffered fewer deaths, the cost was enormous.*

Source: U.S. Department of Defense, *Selected Manpower Statistics*, annual, and unpublished data; beginning 1981, National Archives and Records Service, "Combat Area Casualty File" (3-330-80-3).

"The China Card"

Apart from Vietnam, Nixon's foreign policy defied the expectations of liberals and conservatives alike. Actually, he followed traditions of previous Republican moderates such as Herbert Hoover and Dwight Eisenhower, who had so effectively "proved" their anticommunism that they could conciliate international foes without undermining their popularity at home. Nixon added a new page, however, a policy of détente that replaced U.S.-Soviet bipolarity with multilateral relations. Nixon could cultivate relations with the People's Republic of China, a rising world power more rigidly communist than the Soviet Union, to form an alliance against the Soviet Union. And he could easily persuade the Soviet Union to cooperate on trade agreements, thus limiting the two nations' ruthless competition to control governments in Asia, the Middle East, and Africa. Opponents of the Vietnam War accused Nixon of double dealing, while conservatives howled at any compromise with communist governments. But Nixon persisted in his plans, anticipating an end to the cold war on American terms.

Playing "the China card" was the most dramatic of the president's moves. Early in his political career Nixon had avidly supported the arch-conservative China lobby. But as president he considered the People's Republic of China too important to be isolated by the West and too obviously hostile to the Soviet Union to be discounted as a potential ally. "If there is anything I want to do before I die," he confided to a *Time* magazine reporter, "it is to go to China."

"Ping-pong diplomacy" began in April 1971, when the Chinese hosted a table tennis team from the United States. Henry Kissinger embarked on a secret mission a few months later. Finally, in February 1972, Richard and Pat Nixon flew to Beijing, where they were greeted by foreign minister Zhou Enlai and a band playing "The Star-Spangled Banner."

It was a momentous and surprising event, one that marked a new era in East-West diplomacy. Nixon claimed that he had succeeded in bridging "16,000 miles and twenty-two years of hostility." The president's move successfully increased diplomatic pressure on the Soviet Union but simultaneously weakened the Nationalist Chinese government in Taiwan, which now slipped into virtual diplomatic obscurity.

Next the president went to Moscow to negotiate with Soviet leader Leonid Brezhnev, who was anxious about U.S. involvement with China and eager for economic assistance. Declaring, "There must be room in this world for two great nations with different systems to live together and work together," Nixon offered to sell $1 billion of grain to the Soviets. Winning the favor of American wheat farmers, this deal simultaneously relieved U.S. trade deficits and crop surpluses. Afterward, the Soviet leader became visibly more cautious about supporting revolutions in the third world. Nixon also completed negotiations of the Strategic Arms Limitation Treaty (SALT, known later as SALT I). A limited measure, SALT I represented the first success at strategic arms control since the opening of the cold war and a major public relations victory for the leaders of the two superpowers.

Nixon's last major diplomatic foray proved far less effective. The president sent Kissinger on a two-year mission of "shuttle diplomacy" to mediate Israeli-Arab disputes, to ensure the continued flow of oil, and to increase lucrative U.S. arms sales to Arab countries. The Egyptians and Israelis agreed to a cease-fire in their October 1973 Yom Kippur War, but little progress toward peace in the area was achieved.

Domestic Policy

Nixon deeply desired to restore order in American society. "We live in a deeply troubled and profoundly unsettled time," he noted. "Drugs, crime, campus revolts, racial discord, draft resistance—on every hand we find old standards violated, old values discarded." Despite his hostility to liberalism, however, Nixon had some surprises for conservatives. Determined to win reelection in 1972, he supported new Social Security benefits and subsidized housing for the poor and oversaw the creation of the Environmental Protection Agency and the Occupational Safety and Health Administration. Most notable was his support, under the guidance of Democratic adviser Daniel P. Moynihan, for the Family Assistance Plan, which proposed a minimal income for the poor in place of welfare benefits. Conservatives judged the plan too generous while liberals found it inadequate. Moreover, the plan was expensive. Bipartisan opposition ultimately killed the bill.

Nixon also embraced a policy of fiscal liberalism. Early in 1971 he accepted the idea of deficit spending. Later that year he ordered a first: he took the nation off the gold standard. Subsequently, the dollar's value would float on the world market rather than being tied to the value of gold. His ninety-day freeze on wages, rents, and prices, designed to halt the inflation caused by massive spending on the Vietnam War, also closely resembled Democratic policies. Finally, Nixon's support of "black capitalism"—adjustments or quotas favoring minority contractors in construction projects—created an explosive precedent for set-aside programs later blamed on liberals.

Nixon lined up with conservatives, however, on most civil rights issues and thus enlarged southern Republican constituencies. He accepted the principle of school integration but rejected the busing programs required to implement racial balance. His nominees to the Supreme Court were far more conservative than those appointed by Eisenhower. Warren E. Burger, who replaced Chief Justice Earl Warren, steered the Court away from the liberal direction it had taken since the 1950s.

One of the most newsworthy events of Nixon's administration was a distant result of President Kennedy's determination to outshine the Soviets in outer space (see Chapter 27). On July 21, 1969, the lunar module of Apollo 11 descended to the moon's Sea of Tranquility. As millions watched on television, astronauts Neil Armstrong and Buzz Aldrin stepped out to plant an American flag and to bear the message, "We came in peace for all mankind."

WATERGATE

At times Richard Nixon expressed his yearning for approval in strange ways. A few days after the bombing of Cambodia in May 1970, he wandered out of the White House alone at 5:00 in the morning to talk to antiwar demonstrators. He tried to engage them in small talk about football and pleaded, "I know that probably most of you think I'm an SOB, but I want you to know I understand just how you feel." According to H. R. Haldeman, one of Nixon's closest advisers, the killings at Kent State deeply troubled the president.

Yet only a few months later Nixon ordered illegal wiretaps of news professionals. He also reaffirmed his support of Central Intelligence Agency (CIA) surveillance of U.S. citizens and organizations—a policy specifically forbidden by the CIA charter—and encouraged members of his administration to spy on Democrats planning for the 1972 election campaign. When news of these illegal activities surfaced, one of the most canny politicians in American history found himself the first president since Andrew Johnson to face the likelihood of impeachment proceedings.

Foreign Policy as Conspiracy

Nixon's conduct of foreign policy offered early clues into his political character. Although he had welcomed the publicity surrounding his historic moves toward détente with the Soviet Union and normalized relations with China, Nixon generally handled the nation's foreign affairs in surreptitious fashion. But as opposition to the Vietnam War mounted in Congress, he began to face hard questions about this practice. As early as 1970 Republicans as well as Democrats had condemned covert operations in foreign countries. In response, the president, the Department of State, and the CIA developed plans to tighten security even further. Nixon issued a tough mandate against all leaks of information by government personnel, news specialists, or politicians.

At the time, apart from the highly publicized tour to China, Nixon revealed little about his policy for other parts of the globe. Unknown to most Americans, he accelerated the delivery of arms supplies to foreign dictators, including the shah of Iran, Ferdinand Marcos of the Philippines, and the regime of Pieter William Botha in South Africa. His CIA assistants trained and aided SAVAK, the Iranian secret police force notorious for torturing political dissidents. They also stood behind the South African government in its effort to curtail the activities of the antiapartheid African National Congress. In Latin America, Nixon provided financial assistance and military aid to repressive regimes such as that of Anastasio Somoza of Nicaragua, notorious for its blatant corruption and repeated violations of human rights.

Still more controversial was Nixon's plan to overthrow the legally elected socialist government of Salvador Allende in Chile. With the assistance of nongovernment agencies, such as the AFL-CIO's American Institute for Free Labor Development, the CIA destabilized the regime by funding right-wing parties, launching demonstrations, and preparing the Chilean army for a coup. In September 1973, a military junta killed President Allende and captured, tortured, or murdered thousands of his supporters. Nixon and Kissinger warmly welcomed the new ruler, Augusto Pinochet, granting him financial assistance to restabilize the country.

Toward the end of Nixon's term, members of Congress who had been briefed on these policies began to break silence, and reports of clandestine operations flooded the media. Several former CIA agents issued anguished confessions of their activities in other countries. More troubling to Nixon, in spite of all his efforts the United States continued to lose ground as a superpower.

The Age of Dirty Tricks

As Nixon approached the 1972 reelection campaign, he tightened his inner circle of White House staff who assisted him in withholding information from the public, discrediting critics, and engaging in assorted "dirty tricks." Circle members solicited illegal contributions for the campaign and laundered the money through Mexican bank accounts. They also formed a secret squad, "the plumbers," to halt the troublesome leaks of information. This team, headed by former CIA agent E. Howard Hunt and former FBI agent G. Gordon Liddy, assisted in conspiracy at the highest levels of government.

The first person on the squad's "hit list" was Daniel Ellsberg, a former researcher with the Department of Defense, who in 1971 had turned over to the press secret documents outlining the military history of American involvement in Vietnam. The so-called Pentagon Papers exposed the role of presidents and military leaders in deceiving the public and Congress about the

Richard Nixon bid a final farewell to his White House staff as he left Washington, D.C., in August 1974. The first president to resign from office, Nixon had become so entangled in the Watergate scandal that his impeachment appeared certain. He was succeeded by Vice President Gerald Ford, who appears next to the helicopter on the right.

conduct of the United States in Southeast Asia. Nixon sought to bar publication by the *New York Times*, but the Supreme Court ruled in favor of the newspaper on the basis of the First Amendment. Within weeks, a complete version of the Pentagon Papers became a best-selling book, and in 1972 the *New York Times* won a Pulitzer Prize for the series of articles. Frustrated in his attempt to suppress the report, Nixon directed the Department of Justice to prosecute Ellsberg on charges of conspiracy, espionage, and theft. Meanwhile, Hunt and Liddy, seeking to discredit Ellsberg, broke into the office of his former psychiatrist. They found nothing that would make their target less heroic in the eyes of an increasingly skeptical public, and by 1973 the charges against Ellsberg were dropped after the Nixon administration itself stood guilty of misconduct.

At the same time, Nixon ran a skillful negative campaign charging George McGovern, the liberal Democrat who had won his party's nomination on the first ballot, with supporting "abortion, acid [LSD], and amnesty" for those who had resisted the draft or deserted the armed forces. The Republicans also informed the news media that McGovern's running mate, Senator Thomas Eagleton, had once undergone electric shock therapy for depression, thus forcing his resignation from the Democratic team. Voter turnout fell to an all-time low, and McGovern lost every state but Massachusetts. (Later, when Nixon faced disgrace, bumper stickers appeared reading, "Don't Blame Me, I'm from Massachusetts.")

The Committee to Re-Elect the President (CREEP) enjoyed a huge war chest and spent a good portion on dirty tricks designed to divide the Democrats and discredit them in the eyes of the voting public. The most ambitious plan—wiretapping the Democratic National Committee headquarters—backfired.

On June 17, 1972, a security team had tripped up a group of intruders hired by CREEP to install listening devices in the Washington, D.C., Watergate apartment and office complex where the Democrats were headquartered. The police arrested five men, who were later found guilty of conspiracy and burglary. Although Nixon disclaimed any knowledge of the plan, two *Washington Post* reporters, Bob Woodward and Carl Bernstein, followed a trail of evidence back to the nation's highest office.

CHRONOLOGY

1964 President Lyndon Johnson calls for "an unconditional war on poverty" in his state of the union address

Tonkin Gulf resolution

The Economic Opportunity Act establishes the Office of Economic Opportunity

Free speech movement gets under way at University of California at Berkeley

Johnson defeats conservative Barry Goldwater for president

1965 President Johnson authorizes Operation Rolling Thunder, the bombing of North Vietnam

Teach-ins begin on college campuses

First major march on Washington for peace is organized

Watts uprising begins a wave of rebellions in black communities

1966 J. William Fulbright publishes *The Arrogance of Power*

Black Panther Party is formed

National Organization for Women (NOW) is formed

1967 Antiwar rally in New York City draws 300,000

Vietnam Veterans against the War is formed

Uprisings in Newark, Detroit, and other cities

Hippie "Summer of Love"

1968 U.S. ground troops levels in Vietnam number 500,000

Tet Offensive in Vietnam, followed by international protests against U.S. policies

Martin Luther King Jr. is assassinated; riots break out in more than 100 cities

Vietnam peace talks begin in Paris

Robert Kennedy is assassinated

Democratic National Convention, held in Chicago, nominates Hubert Humphrey; "police riot" against protesters

Richard Nixon elected president

American Indian Movement (AIM) founded

1969 Woodstock music festival marks the high tide of the counterculture

Stonewall Riot in Greenwich Village sparks the gay liberation movement

Apollo 11 lands on the moon

1970 U.S. incursion into Cambodia sparks campus demonstrations; students killed at Kent State and Jackson State Universities

Women's Strike for Equality marks the fiftieth anniversary of the woman suffrage amendment

1971 Lieutenant William Calley Jr. court-martialed for My Lai Massacre

New York Times starts publishing the Pentagon Papers

1972 Nixon visits China and Soviet Union

SALT I limits offensive intercontinental ballistic missiles

Intruders attempting to "bug" Democratic headquarters in the Watergate complex are arrested

Nixon is reelected in a landslide

Nixon orders Christmas Day bombing of North Vietnam

1973 Paris Peace Agreement ends war in Vietnam

FBI seizes Indian occupants of Wounded Knee, South Dakota

Watergate burglars tried; congressional hearings on Watergate

CIA destabilizes elected Chilean government, which is overthrown

Vice President Spiro T. Agnew resigns

1974 House Judiciary Committee adopts articles of impeachment against Nixon

Nixon resigns the presidency

Televised Senate hearings opened to public view more than a pattern of presidential wrongdoing: they showed an attempt to impede investigations of the Watergate case. Testifying before the committee, a former Nixon aide revealed the existence of secret tape recordings of conversations held in the Oval Office. After special prosecutor Archibald Cox refused to allow Nixon to claim executive privilege and withhold the tapes, the president ordered Cox fired. This "Saturday Night Massacre," as it came to be called, further tarnished Nixon's reputation and swelled curiosity about the tapes. On June 24, 1974, the Supreme Court voted unanimously that Nixon had to release the tapes to a new special prosecutor, Leon Jaworski.

The Fall of the Executive

The case against the president gained strength. Although incomplete, the Watergate tapes proved damning. They documented Nixon's ravings against his enemies, including anti-Semitic slurs, and his conniving efforts to harass private citizens through federal agencies. The tapes also proved that Nixon had not only known about plans to cover up the Watergate break-in but had ordered it. The news media enjoyed a field day with the revelations. In July 1974, the House Judiciary Committee adopted three articles of impeachment, charging Nixon with obstructing justice.

Charges of executive criminality had clouded the Nixon administration since his vice president had resigned in disgrace. In 1972 Spiro Agnew had admitted accepting large kickbacks while governor of Maryland. Pleading no contest to this and to charges of federal income tax evasion, Agnew resigned from office in October 1973. Gerald Ford, a moderate Republican representative from Michigan, had replaced him and now stood in the wings while the president's drama unfolded.

Facing certain impeachment by the House of Representatives, Richard Nixon became, on August 9, 1974, the first U.S. president to resign from office.

CONCLUSION

The resignations of Richard Nixon and Spiro Agnew brought little to relieve the feeling of national exhaustion that attended the Vietnam War. U.S. troops had pulled out of Vietnam in 1973 and the war officially ended in 1975, but bitterness lingered over the unprecedented—and, for many, humiliating—defeat. Morover, confidence in the government's highest office was severely shaken. The passage of the War Powers Act in 1973, written to compel any future president to seek congressional approval for armed intervention abroad, dramatized both the widespread suspicion of presidential intentions and a yearning for peace. But the positive dream of community that had inspired Johnson, King, and a generaton of student activists could not be revived. No other vision took its place.

In 1968 seven prominent antiwar protesters had been brought to trial for allegedly conspiring to disrupt the Democratic National Convention in Chicago. Just a few years later, the majority of Americans had concluded that presidents Johnson and Nixon had conspired to do far worse. They had intentionally deceived the public about the nature and fortunes of the war. This moral failure signaled a collapse at the center of the American political system. Since Dwight Eisenhower left office warning of the potential danger embedded in "the military-industrial complex," no president had survived the presidency with his honor intact. Watergate, then, appeared to cap the politics of the cold war, its revelations only reinforcing futility and cynicism. The United States was left psychologically at war with itself.

REVIEW QUESTIONS

1. Discuss the events that led up to and contributed to U.S. involvement in Vietnam. How did U.S. involvement in the war affect domestic programs?
2. Discuss the reasons the protest movement against the Vietnam War started on college campuses. Describe how these movements were organized and how the opponents of the war differed from the supporters.
3. Discuss the programs sponsored by Johnson's plan for a Great Society. What was their impact on urban poverty in the late 1960s?
4. What was the impact of the assassinations of Martin Luther King Jr. and Robert Kennedy on the election of 1968? How were various communities affected?
5. How were the "politics of identity" movements different from earlier civil rights organizations? In what ways did the various movements resemble one another?
6. Why did Richard Nixon enjoy such a huge electoral victory in 1972? Discuss his foreign and domestic policies. What led to his sudden downfall?

RECOMMENDED READING

Terry H. Anderson, *The Movement and the Sixties* (1995). A richly detailed and highly readable account of the political and cultural movements of the 1960s, beginning with an overview of the significance of the cold war and ending with an assessment of the impact of the various movements, including the counterculture.

Loren Baritz, *Backfire: A History of How American Culture Led Us into Vietnam and Made Us Fight the Way We Did* (1985). A keen study of U.S. military policies and dissent within the military during the Vietnam War. Baritz shows how decisions for aggressive military policies in Vietnam divided poorer young men from middle- and upper-class men by sending to war those who did not or could not manage deferments. He analyzes the increasing bitterness toward the government and the military by the men who fought the war.

Alexander Bloom and Wini Breines, eds., *Takin' It to the Streets: A Sixties Reader* (1996). A useful and popular anthology of documents from the time that emphasizes the connections of political and cultural developments.

Mary C. Brennan, *Turning Right in the Sixties: The Conservative Capture of the GOP* (1995). Challenges the conventional depiction of the 1960s as a time when liberals and radicals flourished. Brennan discusses the rise of conservatives within the Republican party and their emergence as the dominant force in American politics by 1980. She focuses on grassroots organizations and their ability to appeal to discontented but generally apolitical Americans.

Susan J. Douglas, *Where the Girls Are: Growing Up Female with the Mass Media* (1994). A witty and perceptive interpretation of the images created for young women in the 1960s and the ways in which they responded.

Michael H. Hunt, *Lyndon Johnson's War: America's Cold War Crusade in Vietnam, 1945–1968* (1996). Tracks Johnson's decisions to wage all-out war in Vietnam. Hunt interprets Johnson's actions as consistent with the Cold War foreign policy that had prevailed since the Truman Administration and its pledge to "contain" communism.

Neil Sheehan, *A Bright Shining Lie: John Paul Vann and America in Vietnam* (1988). A study of U.S. government deception of the public, conducted with greater and greater intensity as losses in Vietnam increased. Sheehan especially emphasizes the ways in which prowar messages played on false images of a noble and committed South Vietnamese government and a military program always on the verge of defeating an unpopular enemy.

Fred Turner, *Echoes of Combat: The Vietnam War in American Memory* (1996). Examines the paradox of a war that many Americans hope to forget and the rise of a "memory industry" devoted to its preservation. Turner asks two main questions: What are Americans remembering? What are they trying to forget?

William L. Van Deburg, *New Day in Babylon: The Black Power Movement and American Culture, 1965–1975* (1992). A well-researched and lively study of the transformation of racial consciousness among African Americans.

Bob Woodward and Carl Bernstein, *The Final Days* (1976). Journalistic accounts of the Watergate cover-up by the news team that broke the first stories. The authors trace the series of events that led to the resignation of President Nixon.

Marilyn B. Young, *The Vietnam Wars, 1945–1990* (1991). An excellent overview of the involvement of the French and the American military and diplomatic forces in Vietnam from the 1910s to 1975, and of the various movements against them. Young presents a thematic continuity that highlights the nationalism of the Vietnamese as ultimately more powerful than the troops and weaponry of their opponents.

ADDITIONAL BIBLIOGRAPHY

Vietnam: America's Longest War

David L. Anderson, *Shadow on the White House: Presidents and the Vietnam War, 1945–1975* (1993)

Christian G. Appy, *Working-Class War: American Combat Soldiers in Vietnam* (1993)

Larry Berman, *Lyndon Johnson's War* (1989)

Robert Buzzanco, *Masters of War: Military Dissent and Politics in the Vietnam War Era* (1996)

David L. DiLeo, *George Ball, Vietnam, and the Rethinking of Containment* (1991)

Virginia Elwood-Akers, *Women War Correspondents in the Vietnam War, 1961–1975* (1988)

George C. Herring, *America's Longest War: The United States and Vietnam, 1950–1975*, 2d ed. (1986)

———, *LBJ and Vietnam: A Different Kind of War* (1994)

———, ed., *The Pentagon Papers*, abridged ed. (1993)

Martha Hess, *Then the Americans Came: Voices from Vietnam* (1993)

Arnold R. Isaacs, *Without Honor* (1983)

Richard Moser, *The New Winter Soldiers: GI and Veteran Dissent during the Vietnam Era* (1996)

Robert D. Schulzinger, *A Time for War: The United States and Vietnam, 1941–1975* (1997)
Randy Shilts, *Conduct Unbecoming: Lesbians and Gays in the U.S. Military, Vietnam to the Persian Gulf* (1993)
Dennis E. Showalter and John G. Albert, eds., *An American Dilemma: Vietnam, 1964–1973* (1993)
James E. Westheider, *Fighting on Two Fronts: African Americans and the Vietnam War* (1997)
James R. Wilson, *Landing Zones: Southern Veterans Remember Vietnam* (1990)
Clarence R. Wyatt, *Paper Soldiers: The American Press and the Vietnam War* (1993)

A Generation in Conflict

John Morton Blum, *Years of Discord* (1991)
Wini Breines, *Community and Organization in the New Left* (1982)
David Chalmers, *And the Crooked Places Made Straight: The Struggle for Social Change in the 1960s* (1991)
Charles DeBeneditti, *An American Ordeal: The Antiwar Movement of the Vietnam Era* (1990)
David Farber, *The Age of Great Dreams: America in the 1960s* (1994)
———, ed., *The Sixties: From Memory to History* (1994)
Ronald Fraser, et al., *1968: A Student Generation in Revolt* (1988)
Sherry Gottlieb, *Hell No, We Won't Go* (1991)
Kenneth Heineman, *Campus Wars: The Peace Movement at American State Universities in the Vietnam Era* (1993)
Paul Lyons, *New Left, New Right, and the Legacy of the Sixties* (1996)
Jim Miller, *"Democracy Is in the Streets"* (1987)
Timothy Miller, *The Hippies and American Values* (1991)
Edward P. Morgan, *The 60s Experience* (1991)
W. J. Rorabaugh, *Berkeley at War: The 1960s* (1989)
Sohnya Sayres, et al., ed., *The 60s without Apology* (1984)
David Steigerwald, *The Sixties and the End of Modern America* (1995)
Barbara L. Tischler, ed., *Sights on the Sixties* (1992)
Tom Wells, *The War Within: America's Battle over Vietnam* (1994)

The Politics of Identity

Barry D. Adam, *The Rise of a Gay and Lesbian Movement* (1987)
Elaine Brown, *A Taste of Power* (1993)
James Button, *Black Violence: Political Impact of the 1960s Riots* (1978)
Jack Campisi, *The Mashpee Indians* (1991)
Margaret Cruikshank, *The Gay and Lesbian Liberation Movement* (1992)
John D'Emilio, *Making Trouble: Essays on Gay History, Politics, and the University* (1992)
Martin Dubermen, *Stonewall* (1993)
Gerald Horne, *Fire This Time: The Watts Uprising and the 1960s* (1996)
Blance Linden-Ward, *American Women in the 1960s* (1992)
Manning Marable, *Race, Reform, and Rebellion* (1984)
Eric Marcus, *Making History: The Struggle for Gay and Lesbian Equal Rights, 1945–1990: An Oral History* (1992)
Marguerite V. Marin, *Social Protest in an Urban Barrio: A Study of the Chicano Movement, 1966–1972* (1991)
Peter Matthiessen, *In the Spirit of Crazy Horse* (1991)
Armando Navarro, *Mexican American Youth Organization: Avant-Garde of the Chicano Movement in Texas* (1995)
M. Rivka Polatnick, *Strategies for Women's Liberation: A Study of a Black and White Group of the 1960s* (1987)

The Nixon Presidency and Watergate

Carl Bernstein and Bob Woodward, *All the President's Men* (1974)
John Ehrlichman, *Witness to Power* (1982)
Lewis L. Gould, *1968: The Election That Changed America* (1993)
Jim Hougan, *Secret Agenda: Watergate, Deep Throat, and the CIA* (1984)
Diane Kunz, ed., *The Diplomacy of the Crucial Decade* (1994)
Michael Schudson, *Watergate in American History* (1992)

Biography

Stephen E. Ambrose, *Nixon*, 3 vols. (1987–91)
LeRoy Ashby and Rod Gramer, *Fighting the Odds: The Life of Senator Frank Church* (1994)
Elaine Brown, *A Taste of Power: A Black Woman's Story* (1992)
Paul Buhle and Edward Rice-Maximin, *William Appleman Williams: The Tragedy of Empire* (1995)
Jody Carlson, *George C. Wallace and the Politics of Powerlessness* (1981)
David T. Dellinger, *From Yale to Jail: A Memoir* (1993)
Brian Dooley, *Robert Kennedy: The Final Years* (1996)
Robert Alan Goldberg, *Barry Goldwater* (1995)
Elliot Gorn, ed., *Muhammed Ali: The People's Champ* (1996)
David Hilliard and Lewis Cole, *This Side of Glory: The Autobiography of David Hilliard and the Story of the Black Panther Party* (1993)
Joan Hoff, *Nixon Reconsidered* (1994)
Walter Isaacson, *Kissinger* (1992)
Jonah Raskin, *For the Hell of It: The Life and Times of Abbie Hoffman* (1996)
Herb Schandler, *The Unmaking of a President: Lyndon Johnson and Vietnam* (1977)
Arthur M. Schlesinger Jr., *Robert Kennedy and His Times* (1974)
Tom Wicker, *One of Us: Richard Nixon and the American Dream* (1991)
Randall Bennett Woods, *Fulbright: A Biography* (1995)

CHAPTER THIRTY

THE OVEREXTENDED SOCIETY

1974–1980

Wayne Thiebaud. *Urban Freeways*, 1979–80. Oil on canvas, 44 x 36 in. Allan Stone Gallery, New York.

CHAPTER OUTLINE

AMERICAN COMMUNITIES
Three Mile Island, Pennsylvania

On Wednesday, March 28, 1979, a series of mechanical problems and judgment errors at the nuclear generating facility at Three Mile Island (TMI), near Harrisburg, Pennsylvania, led to the loss of a reactor's protective blanket of water. As much as two-thirds of the nuclear core was uncovered, causing the formation of a dangerously explosive hydrogen bubble and a massive release of radioactive gas into the atmosphere and posing the danger of a catastrophic core meltdown. The plant director declared a site emergency and reported a "slight problem" to the governor at 7:40 A.M. By 9:00 A.M. President Jimmy Carter had been notified. The Associated Press issued a national news bulletin announcing a general emergency but stating (mistakenly) that no radiation had been released. Metropolitan Edison, which ran the TMI facility, denied the existence of any danger.

At 8:00 A.M. on Friday, when a higher-than-anticipated radiation level above a vent was recorded, staff at the Nuclear Regulatory Commission suggested an evacuation of people living near the plant. Fearing panic, the governor urged residents within ten miles of TMI to stay indoors with their windows shut. Only pregnant women and preschool children within five miles of the facility were advised to leave the area. Federal officials ordered the shipment to Pennsylvania of massive doses of potassium iodide, which, taken orally, saturates the thyroid gland and inhibits absorption of radiation. The mayor of nearby Middletown later recalled:

> Friday was the day. . . . A lot of the kids thought about dying and wrote their last wills and testaments. Fifth and sixth grade kids! People were concerned. You could tell they were afraid because a lot of people who left town left their doors wide open, unlocked. They just put anything in the car and took off. . . . I had a bus set up in front of City Hall for pregnant women. But heck, most of the people who were in that condition left themselves.

While nearly 150,000 residents fled their homes, President and Rosalynn Carter tried to reassure the stricken community by visiting the site.

Ten days later, on Monday, April 9, Pennsylvania governor Richard Thornburgh announced that the danger of a meltdown had passed. The Nuclear Regulatory Commission, equally eager to end the crisis, reported that the size of the hydrogen bubble had decreased. The situation was now stable, the officials agreed. There was no longer any danger of explosion.

What had seemed an isolated event in one community grew quickly into a regional phenomenon with international repercussions. The world waited, as one newscaster put it, while "the danger faced by man for tampering with natural forces, a theme familiar from the myth of Prometheus to the story of

Frankenstein, moved closer to fact from fantasy." During the crisis, millions of people living in eastern states downwind of TMI stayed glued to their televisions or radios. Ten days after the near meltdown, elevated levels of radioactivity were found in milk supplies several hundred miles away. People throughout the mid-Atlantic area worried for months about consuming contaminated dairy products, meat, vegetables, and even jams or jellies coming from the agricultural region of central Pennsylvania. Massive demonstrations against nuclear power followed the accident, concluding in a rally of more than 200,000 people in New York City.

Closer to TMI, more than 1,000 people eventually became involved in legal claims of mental or physical harm. Protests and lawsuits against the plant's reopening continued for years, and its owner, General Public Utilities, teetered toward bankruptcy. Although steadfast proponents of nuclear energy argued that the events at TMI demonstrated that safety had prevailed even at the moment of the greatest potential danger, the scales had been tipped toward opponents of nuclear power plants.

The events at Three Mile Island capped a wave of community-based mobilizations against nuclear power. In 1975, a less serious accident at Brown's Ferry, Alabama, heightened public concern about safety. Broad coalitions, with members ranging from conservatives to liberals, from rural landowners to urban renters, formed to keep their communities safe from danger. Community groups defeated referendums to fund new nuclear facilities or rallied around candidates who promised to shut down existing ones. If few communities wanted nuclear power plants, fewer still were eager to accept the radioactive wastes they generated.

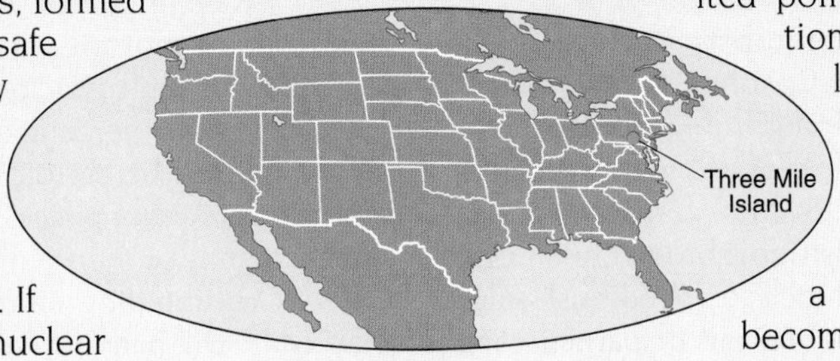

The economy itself helped slow the development of new plants. At the time of the TMI crisis, more than seventy generating plants had been built, producing altogether about 13 percent of the nation's electrical energy. Of the ninety-six still under construction and the thirty more planned, only a handful would ever be completed. The courts and regional authorities blocked the completed Shoreham plant on Long Island, New York, from going into operation. News of faulty construction and building-cost overruns sometimes topping 1,000 percent and amounting to hundreds of millions of dollars made local governments hesitant to back new projects.

The promoters of nuclear energy in the 1950s had billed it as a source of energy so cheap that utility companies would be able to "turn off the meter." Communities would bask in prosperity, enjoying the fruits of dramatic advances equal to those that followed the introduction of electricity itself seventy-five years earlier. As late as 1974 President Richard Nixon predicted that by 1980 nuclear power would free the United States of its dependence on foreign energy sources.

The end of the dream of unlimited, inexpensive, and safe nuclear energy was one of many disappointments in the 1970s that shattered the expectations of experts and ordinary citizens alike for a time of unsurpassed abundance. Faced with diminishing financial resources, environmental disasters, discredited political leaders, and international defeats, many Americans lowered their expectations. The cold war finally began to wind down, but international affairs remained turbulent. The Middle East, a major source of oil, was becoming the new battleground.

Key Topics

- The economics and politics of "stagflation"
- The Carter presidency
- Crisis in the cities and in the environment
- Community politics and the rise of the New Right
- The Iran hostage crisis
- The Republican presidential victory in 1980

STAGFLATION

In the 1970s Americans faced an unfamiliar combination of skyrocketing prices, rising unemployment, and low economic growth. Economists termed this novel condition "stagflation." The annual rate of economic growth slowed by almost one-quarter from its robust 3.2 percent average of the 1950s. By 1975 the unemployment rate had reached nearly 9 percent, its highest level since the Great Depression, and it remained close to 7 percent for most of the rest of the decade. Inflation, meanwhile, reached double-digit numbers.

The United States had reached a turning point in its economic history. Emerging from World War II as the most prosperous nation in the world and retaining this status through the 1960s, the country suddenly found itself falling behind western Europe and Japan. The standard of living in the United States dropped to fifth place, below that of Denmark, West Germany, Sweden, and Switzerland. Polls conducted at the end of the 1970s revealed that a majority of Americans believed that conditions would worsen. Faith in progress and prosperity, the hallmark of "the American Century," wore thin.

The Oil Crisis

In October 1973 American motorists received a big surprise at the gas pumps. Gasoline prices nearly doubled, in some regions jumping from forty to nearly seventy cents per gallon. Worse, many dealers suddenly ran out of supplies. In New Jersey, gas lines were up to four miles long. Fistfights broke out among frustrated motorists. Gas tank locks enjoyed brisk sales after thieves began to siphon fuel out of parked cars. Several states introduced rationing programs.

Although the oil crisis began suddenly, it had been in the making for decades. The United States, which used about 70 percent of all oil produced in the world, had been able to meet its demand from domestic supplies until the late 1950s. At that point, rising demand outstripped the capacity of national reserves and oil imports began to rise. By 1973 the nation was importing one-third of its total crude oil, mainly from the Middle East.

Although oil prices remained stable through most of the 1960s, rising political and military tensions in the Middle East threatened that stability. After Israel overwhelmed its Arab neighbors in the Six-Day War of 1967, the Arab nations became increasingly bitter toward the United States and other Western supporters of Israel. Then came the Yom Kippur War of 1973, so named because it began with an Arab attack on Israel on that Jewish holy day, which fell on October 6 that year.

On October 17, the Organization of Petroleum Exporting Countries (OPEC), a cartel of mainly Arab oil producers, announced an embargo on oil shipments to Israel's allies, including the United States, Japan, and other Western nations. American experts thought at first that the embargo would be short-lived. But although a cease-fire ended the Yom Kippur War on most fronts on October 25, the oil embargo continued until March 18, 1974, sending a shock wave through the United States. A few weeks after the embargo began, President Nixon, in a dramatic televised speech, announced "a very stark fact: We are heading toward the most acute shortage of energy since World War II." A newspaper headline pessimistically declared, "Things Will Get Worse before They Get Worse."

As oil prices continued to skyrocket through the 1970s, angry motorists usually blamed the Arabs, but some also looked suspiciously at U.S. oil companies. By 1978 almost 50 percent of those polled believed that they were "just being told" that there was a shortage as a pretext for raising prices. Skepticism grew as a congressional committee reported that American-owned Texaco Oil was withholding natural gas from the market and that Gulf Oil had overstated its crude oil costs and charged customers wildly inflated prices. Whatever the cause, whoever the scapegoat, the oil crisis played a major role in the economic downturn of 1974 and 1975, the worst since the Great Depression.

The Bill Comes Due

President Nixon quickly responded to the embargo. He appointed William E. Simon to the new position of "energy czar," paving the way for the creation of the Department of Energy in 1977. Nixon also imposed

Following the oil crisis of 1973, the supply of gasoline for automobiles remained tight. This photograph, taken in 1978, captured a scene that had become familiar to many motorists: cars lined up, bumper to bumper, outside a local filling station.

emergency energy conservation measures. He ordered a 10 percent reduction in air travel and appealed to Congress to lower speed limits on interstate highways to fifty-five miles per hour and to extend daylight saving time into the winter months. Many state governments introduced their own programs, turning down the thermostats in public buildings to sixty-eight degrees, reducing nonessential lighting, and restricting hours of service. Colleges and universities canceled midwinter sessions, and some factories voluntarily shortened their workday.

These conservation measures produced one unintended, positive result: a 23 percent reduction in highway deaths between 1973 and 1974 due to the lower speed limit. Meanwhile, however, children went to school in the dark, workers shivered in their offices, and the poor and elderly succumbed to hypothermia in cold apartments.

Virtually all energy prices rose following the Arab oil embargo, reversing a century-old trend. And with the rising costs of gasoline, home-heating fuel, and electricity, other prices jumped as well, from apartment rents to telephone bills to restaurant checks. In 1974 inflation was at 11 percent and polls showed it to have assumed first place among issues Americans were worried about. By 1980 inflation had reached 13.5 percent. The middle-class lifestyle that schoolteachers, secretaries, factory workers, and others had managed to create for themselves and their families on relatively modest incomes became harder to maintain; for young families it was often impossible to achieve. A San Francisco homemaker told a reporter, "I used to keep a budget, but it got so discouraging. I gave it up. The whole economic picture scares me. It's so unreal."

Falling Productivity

Many Americans had experienced the recessions of the 1950s, millions even remembered the Great Depression, but few were prepared to witness the death of entire sectors of basic industry. The problem, according to many experts, was not simply a result of dependence on foreign oil reserves. It had deeper roots in the failure of the United States to keep up with the rising industrial efficiency of western Europe and Japan. As long as American manufacturers faced scant competition from abroad, they had little incentive to update their machinery or to establish management techniques that took full advantage of the skills of younger, more educated employees. American companies could meet large production quotas, but they could not fabricate quality goods at low cost.

Asian, Latin American, and European manufacturers offered consumers cheaper and better alternatives. As a result, whereas the United States produced 60 percent of the world's steel in 1947, by 1975 it produced only 16 percent. Similar trends developed in related industries. Sales of foreign automobiles in the United States, negligible in 1960, topped 15 percent by the early 1970s and continued to grow. Meanwhile, sales of American-made autos dropped by 11 million in 1973 and another 8 million in 1974. In 1977 more American cars were recalled for defects than were produced in the same year. By the end of the decade foreign manufacturers had also shattered the near monopoly the United States once enjoyed in the production of precision machine tools. In high-tech electronics, the United States scarcely competed against Japanese-made televisions, radios, tape players, cameras, and computers.

Major American corporations began to devise their own strategies to combat falling profits. While General Motors lowered production costs by opening a new, highly automated plant in Lordstown, Ohio, other automakers turned to Mexico, Taiwan, South Korea, and the Philippines for cheaper labor. Many

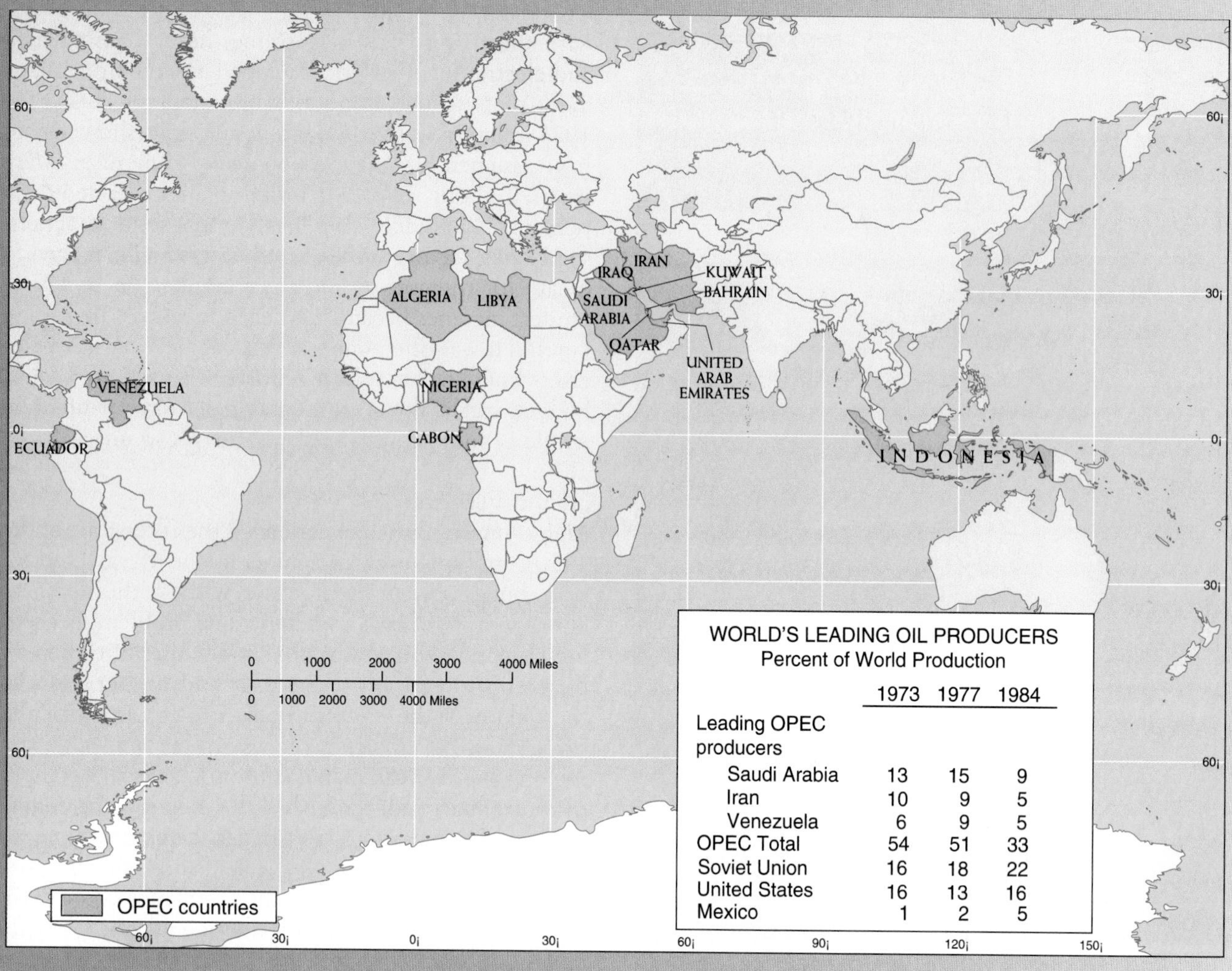

WORLD'S LEADING OIL PRODUCERS Percent of World Production	1973	1977	1984
Leading OPEC producers			
Saudi Arabia	13	15	9
Iran	10	9	5
Venezuela	6	9	5
OPEC Total	54	51	33
Soviet Union	16	18	22
United States	16	13	16
Mexico	1	2	5

parts of American automobiles were "outsourced"—that is, produced abroad and imported into the United States as semifinished materials (which were subject to a lower tariff than finished goods).

A few American corporations tried to improve their production capacities by adopting the model of labor-management relations developed by their foremost competitors. In many Japanese firms a system of benefits and rewards gave employees a sense of security and offered them incentives for helping to improve the quality and speed of production. However, in the United States "quality circles"—American versions of Japanese factory teams—were far less successful than their Japanese counterparts. Older workers feared the new management techniques would undermine their unions, and most new workers doubted the new techniques would bring them significant material benefits.

American industrial productivity continued to lag, increasing 1.4 percent between 1971 and 1975 and only 0.2 percent in the second half of the decade. The balance of trade tipped sharply toward the countries that manufactured and exported better and cheaper products than U.S. firms. An AFL-CIO leader complained that the United States was becoming "a nation of hamburger stands . . . a country stripped of industrial capacity and meaningful work . . . a service economy . . . a nation of citizens busily buying and selling cheeseburgers and root beer floats."

In agriculture the situation was equally grim. Ironically, a shortage of grain in the Soviet Union, Egypt, and the third world during the 1970s hiked up agricultural prices and encouraged American farmers to produce a bounty of crops for export. But the huge increase in oil prices translated into higher gasoline

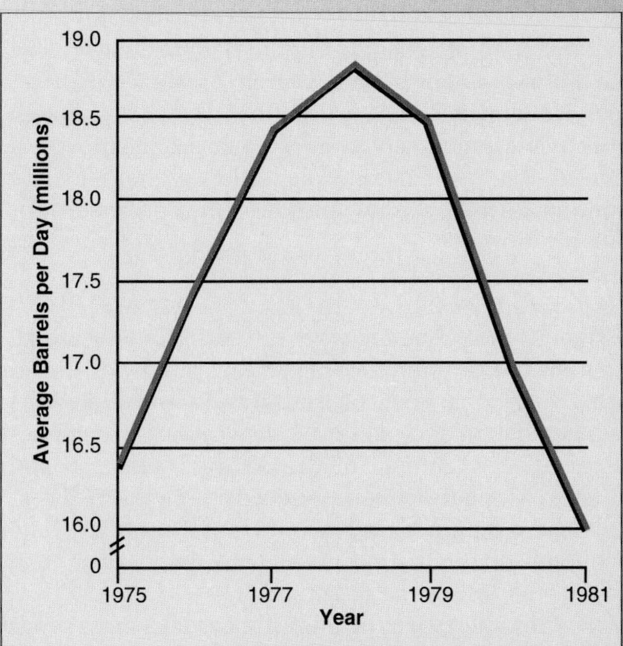

Decline of U.S. Oil Consumption, 1975–1981

Source: Department of Energy, *Monthly Energy Review*, June 1982.

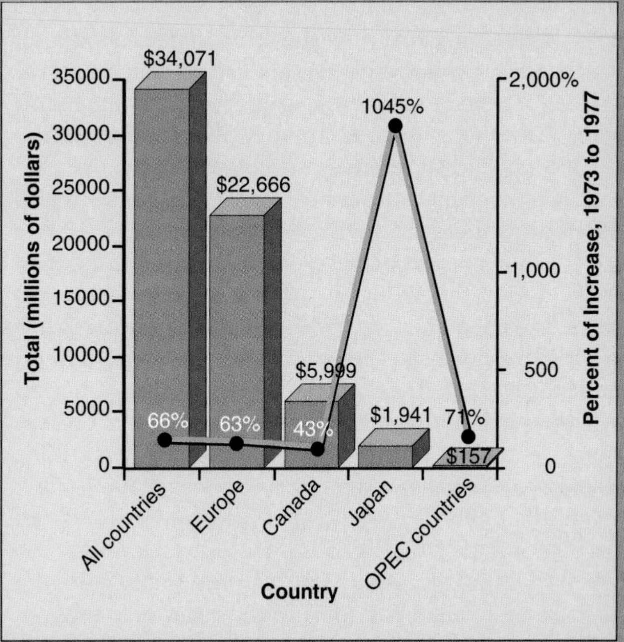

Foreign Direct Investment in the United States, 1977

Source: *Morgan Guaranty Survey*, September 1978.

1970s: *Oil Consumption*

OPEC (the Organization of Petroleum Exporting Countries), which is dominated by large Arab producers in the Middle East, began to use its control of much of the world's oil as a diplomatic lever and successfully increased the world price of crude oil during the 1970s. As a result, all energy prices rose sharply in the United States, leading to a previously unknown combination of inflation and recession that was dubbed "stagflation."

These developments had two dramatic and unanticipated consequences. One was a sharp decline in U.S. oil consumption after 1978. High prices and shortages induced Americans to drive fewer miles and to conserve energy. In some cases the energy squeeze forced factories and businesses to close. A second consequence was increased foreign investment in the United States and with it, increased foreign ownership of U.S. businesses. Despite the role of the oil crisis in triggering this shift, only a small percentage of outside investment came from OPEC entrepreneurs. Most of it came from Europe, Canada, and Japan. Japanese investment in the United States increased more than tenfold between 1973 and 1977.

and fertilizer costs, forcing farmers to borrow heavily from banks. Soon, the high interest rates on borrowed money put many farmers in a state of permanent indebtedness.

When overseas grain sales declined at the end of the 1970s, tens of thousands of farmers defaulted on loans and lost their farms to banks and credit companies. These failures often ended a way of life that was generations old. The remaining farmers often supplemented their income through part-time jobs in town. Many considered themselves fortunate if they could retire on the price offered by land developers who turned their farms into suburban housing. Continuing soil erosion, high costs, and unstable prices offered a gloomy prospect for all but the leaders in corporate-style agribusiness, the 12 percent of farmers who made 90 percent of all farm income.

Blue-collar Blues

In past decades, labor unions had typically responded to inflation by negotiating new contracts or, if necessary, striking for higher pay. When successful, these actions elevated living standards for millions of additional workers because nonunion employers often felt compelled to raise wages as well. But by the 1970s new legislation and legal decisions had changed labor-management relations. The National Labor Relations Board, created during the 1930s to ensure fair elections for union representation, now more frequently ruled in favor of management, making it increasingly difficult to form new union locals. Between 1970 and 1982 the AFL-CIO lost nearly 30 percent of its membership, and its political influence dipped accordingly. Labor-backed measures now routinely failed in Congress.

The only real growth in organized labor took place among public employees, including teachers, civil service workers, and health professionals. Their gains were, however, often less than expected. During the 1970s local and state budgets sagged because of inflation, lower revenues from business, and voters' unwillingness to shoulder a bigger tax burden.

The number of wage-earning women continued to rise during the 1970s. By 1980 more than half of all married women and nearly 60 percent of mothers with children between the ages of six and seventeen were in the labor force. It had become the norm for women to be employed, and most households depended on two wages. The two economic recessions during the last years of the Vietnam War—1969–70 and 1973–75—encouraged many married women to find jobs, as did the high inflation that followed the energy crisis.

Despite a higher rate of participation in the labor force, women had lost ground relative to men. In 1955 women earned 64 percent of the average wages paid to men; in 1980 they earned only 59 percent. The reason for this dip lay in the increasing concentration of women in a few, mostly nonunion occupations. More than 80 percent of employed women worked in only 20 of the 420 occupations listed by the U.S. Census Bureau. In 1973 less than 15 percent of all employed women were in professional occupations. The great majority were clustered in the clerical and service trades, where the lowest wages prevailed.

African American women made some gains. Through Title VII of the Civil Rights Act, which outlawed workplace discrimination by sex or race, and the establishment of the Equal Employment Opportunity Commission to enforce it, they managed to climb the lower levels of the job ladder. By 1980 black women's median earnings in the North were about 95 percent of white women's earnings. Proportionately, slightly more black women than white women were gainfully employed in technical, sales, and administrative jobs.

In contrast, Hispanic women, whose labor force participation leaped by 80 percent during the decade, were restricted to a very few, poorly paid occupations. Puerto Ricans found jobs in the garment industry of the Northeast; Mexican Americans more typically worked as domestics or agricultural laborers in the Southwest. Neither group earned much more than the minimum wage.

Several local organizations were formed in the 1970s to push for equality in the workplace. The most successful of these addressed office workers. In 1973 Boston's Nine to Five drew up an Office Workers' Bill of Rights calling for equal pay for equal work, maternity benefits, and promotion opportunities. California's WAGE (Women Act to Gain Equality) and Chicago's WU (Women United) pressured government agencies for stricter enforcement of antidiscrimination laws. The Coalition of Labor Union Women, organized in 1974, fought for greater rights within the AFL-CIO, although only two women served in national leadership positions in the organization. The leaders of the AFL-CIO continued to regard women as poor prospects for unionization.

Sunbelt/Snowbelt

Although the economic woes of the 1970s affected all sections of the country, some regions fared worse than others. The Snowbelt of the Midwest and Northeast lost population and political influence as its economies slumped. The Sunbelt of the South, Southwest, and West Coast, meanwhile, continued a growth trend that had begun during World War II (see Chapter 25). The economy of this region grew three times faster than that of the rest of the nation.

By the 1970s the Sunbelt boasted a gross product greater than that of many nations and more cars, television sets, houses, and even miles of paved roads than the rest of the United States. Large influxes of immigrants from Latin America, the Caribbean, and Asia combined with the shift of people from the depressed Northeast to boost the region's population. From 56 million people in 1940, the Sunbelt's population more than doubled to 118 million by 1980, just forty years later.

The Sunbelt states had gained enormously from cold war defense spending as well as the expenditure of Social Security and pension income by retirees. The number of residents over the age of sixty-five increased by 30 percent during the 1970s, reaching 26 million by 1980. Armed with retirement packages won decades earlier, "golden agers" created new communities in Florida, Arizona, and southern California, pumping $8 billion a year into the Florida economy alone.

The South witnessed extraordinary changes in its economy and population. High-profit agribusiness emerged to meet the growing demand for poultry, beef, and frozen foods. Giant processing plants like Perdue, Inc., of Salisbury, Maryland, marketed up to 2 million broiler chickens each week through a high-technology mix of computerized feedings, growth hormones, conveyor-belt packaging, and aggressive advertising. The South also gained in manufacturing, in older industries such as textiles, coal, and steel, but also in petrochemicals and automobile parts. As commerce flourished, southern cities began to reverse the century-long trend of African American out-migration. Of the "ten best cities for blacks" listed by *Ebony* magazine in 1978, five—Atlanta, Dallas, Houston, Baltimore, and Washington—were southern cities that had all been rigidly segregated only a few decades earlier. For the first time, African Americans returned south in large numbers.

The Southwest and West changed even more dramatically. With the help of air conditioning, public improvements, large-scale development, and its recreational attractions, California became the nation's most populous state; Texas moved to third, behind New York. Almost overnight farms and deserts were turned into huge suburban developments clogged with automobile traffic. The population of Phoenix grew from 664,000 in 1960 to 1,509,000 in 1980, that of Las Vegas from 127,000 to 463,000. Meanwhile, agribusiness giants turned entire California valleys to the production of a single crop, such as strawberries, lima beans, or artichokes.

The rapidly growing computer industry created California's Silicon Valley (named for the production of silicon chips) south of San Francisco, adding more than a half-million jobs and billions of dollars of profit during the 1970s in Santa Clara County alone. Even when the number of lucrative defense contracts dropped after the Vietnam War, military outlays in high technology increased, with spin-offs in research and development centered in the Los Angeles area.

On the downside, much of the surge in the Sunbelt's wealth tended to be temporary, producing a boom-and-bust economy. Corporate office buildings in cities like Houston emptied almost as fast as they filled. Likewise, textile and similarly labor-intensive industries that had earlier moved to the South for lower wages now relocated to Mexico, the Caribbean, or Asia. Even microchip processing, considered virtually a native Californian industry, gradually moved to Pacific islands and East Asia.

The Sunbelt's economic assets were also very unevenly distributed. Older Hispanic populations made only modest gains, while recent Mexican immigrants and Indian peoples survived on low incomes. Whereas eastern and midwestern states, traditionally dependent on urban political machines and liberal voters, spent significantly on public housing, education, and mass transit, the conservative Sunbelt states concentrated their tax and federal dollars on strengthening police

These newly built houses in Phoenix, Arizona, a popular retirement community as well as the state capital, helped accommodate a 55 percent rise in the city's population between 1970 and 1980. Like other burgeoning cities of the Mountain West, Phoenix experienced many urban tensions during this decade, including racial conflict, antagonism between affluent suburbs and the decaying downtown, air pollution, traffic congestion, and strained water supplies.

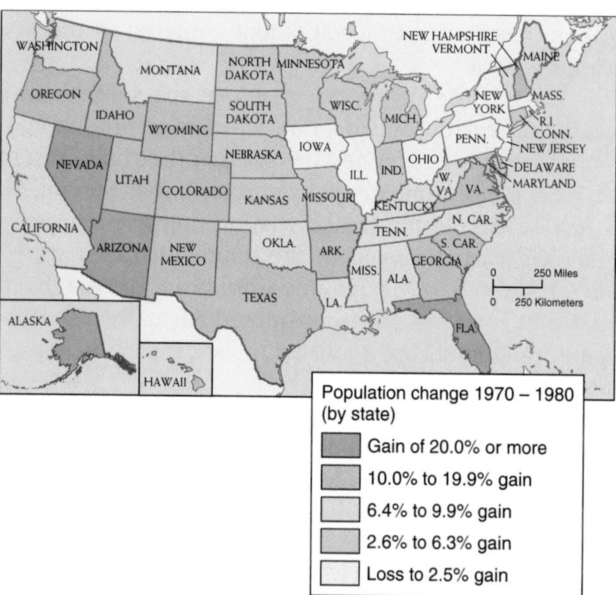

Population Shifts, 1970–1980 *Industrial decline in the Northeast coincided with an economic boom in the Sunbelt, encouraging millions of Americans to head for warmer climes and better jobs.*

forces, improving roads or sanitation systems for expanding suburbs, and creating budget surpluses.

Meanwhile, the Snowbelt (or "Rustbelt"), as the Northeast and upper Midwest came to be called, suffered population losses following a sharp decline in industry. Of the nineteen metropolitan areas that lost population during the 1970s, all were old manufacturing centers—topped by New York, Cleveland, Pittsburgh, Boston, Philadelphia, and Buffalo. Reduced federal outlays to city governments compounded municipal budget crises, accentuating a feeling of defeat that prevailed in these areas.

Philadelphia, once the nation's most important manufacturing center, was a case in point. From 1969 to 1981, the city lost 14 percent of its residents and 20 percent of its jobs, including 42 percent of its factory jobs. Only service employment grew, but in relatively small numbers (35,000 jobs gained versus more than 130,000 lost in all areas). Restored downtown neighborhoods with cobblestone streets dating to the eighteenth century bordered decayed neighborhoods and vacant commercial and industrial structures. Crime in the City of Brotherly Love increased by 200 percent, the municipal debt ballooned to $167 million, and the only city-owned hospital closed. Ranked fifty-seventh in terms of prosperity and service in a survey of sixty-five American cities, Philadelphia had nearly hit bottom.

New York City offered a still more spectacular example. A fiscal crisis in 1975 forced liberal mayor Abraham Beame to choose between wage freezes for public employees and devastating cuts and layoffs. Eventually, with the municipal government teetering on the brink of bankruptcy, he chose both. In response to cutbacks in mass transit and the deterioration of the city's public health system as well as municipal services generally, a large sector of the middle class left the city. At the same time, the proportion of poor people in the city's population rose from 15 percent in 1969 to nearly 25 percent fourteen years later.

"LEAN YEARS" PRESIDENTS

Gerald R. Ford and Jimmy Carter presided over a depressed economy and a nation of disillusioned citizens. Neither came up with a viable program to stimulate the economy. Carter contributed to voter apathy by admitting that he doubted that the government could solve the country's economic problems. After the 1968 election, voter participation began a two-decade decline, with only a little over half of eligible voters turning out for presidential elections. By the time Carter left office, a majority of those polled agreed that the "people running the country don't really care what happens to you."

"I'm a Ford, not a Lincoln"

When Gerald Ford replaced Nixon as president in August 1974 and Nelson Rockefeller became vice president, an overwhelming majority of Americans reported that they supported the new administration. But only a month after reassuring the public that "our long national nightmare is over," Ford turned around and pardoned Nixon for all the federal crimes he may have committed as president. Amid allegations that a deal had been struck, Ford irrevocably lost the nation's trust.

As president, Ford lacked a clear program and offered few initiatives to put the economy on the road to recovery. At best, he hoped to stimulate slow but steady growth by keeping interest rates stable, raising taxes to reduce federal deficits, and above all restraining federal spending. His voluntary anti-inflation program, Whip Inflation Now, publicized by big red-and-white lapel buttons emblazoned "WIN," failed to restore public confidence.

With inflation and unemployment soaring, the Democrats gained fifty-two seats in the House and four in the Senate in the 1974 midterm elections, eroding the Republican president's congressional support. Ford vetoed more major bills than any other president in the twentieth century, but Congress overrode him on most of them. Ford nevertheless swore to hold fast even against popular measures such as emergency job bills and education, health, and child nutrition programs. When New York City faced bankruptcy, Ford promised "to veto any bill that had as its purpose a federal bail-out." The *New York*

Daily News appeared the next day with the memorable headline "Ford to City: Drop Dead." When Congress united against him, the president relented.

Lyndon Johnson had once quipped: "The trouble with Jerry Ford is that he used to play football without a helmet." And indeed, the image Ford conveyed was that of a pleasant person of modest ability. The press often caught him stumbling or mixing up his ideas. He once claimed that "things are more like they are now than they have ever been."

First Lady Betty Ford, on the other hand, won the admiration of many Americans. Soon after she moved into the White House, she showed her personal courage by candidly discussing her mastectomy for breast cancer. "Lying in the hospital, thinking of all those women going for cancer checkups because of me," she later reported, "I'd come to recognize more clearly the power of the woman in the White House. Not my power, but the power of the position, a power which could be used to help." She soon broke ranks with other Republicans to champion the Equal Rights Amendment (ERA). She once told a television reporter that she supported abortion rights, would not scold her adult daughter for having premarital sex, and probably would have tried marijuana herself if it had been in vogue when she was growing up. Her popularity skyrocketed, and in 1975 *Newsweek* magazine chose her as Woman of the Year. Even after leaving the White House, Betty Ford remained in the spotlight when she openly discussed her dependency on drugs and alcohol.

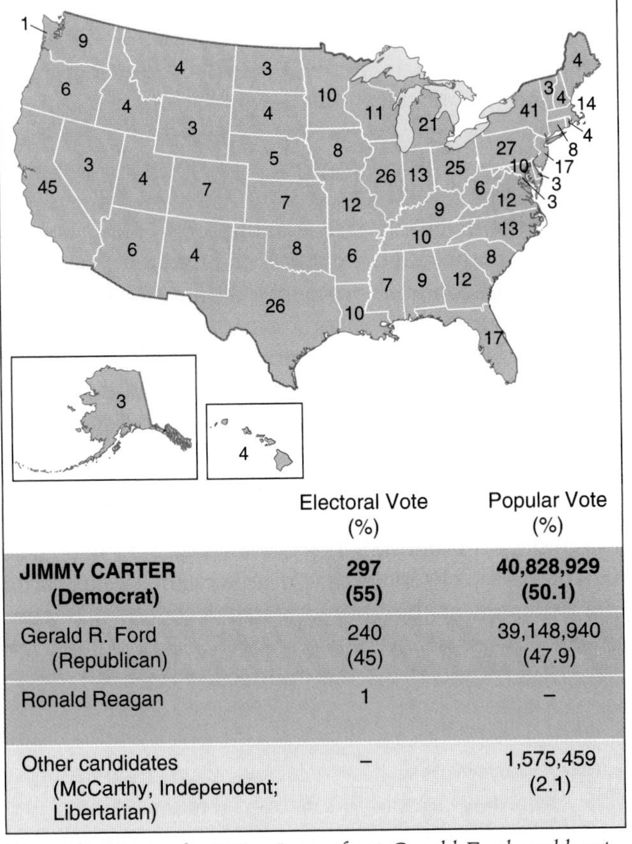

	Electoral Vote (%)	Popular Vote (%)
JIMMY CARTER (Democrat)	**297 (55)**	**40,828,929 (50.1)**
Gerald R. Ford (Republican)	240 (45)	39,148,940 (47.9)
Ronald Reagan	1	–
Other candidates (McCarthy, Independent; Libertarian)	–	1,575,459 (2.1)

The Election of 1976 *Incumbent Gerald Ford could not prevail over the disgrace brought to the Republican Party by Richard Nixon. The lingering pall of the Watergate scandal, especially Ford's pardon of Nixon, worked to the advantage of Jimmy Carter, who campaigned as an outsider to national politics. Although Carter and his running mate Walter Mondale won by only a narrow margin, the Democrats gained control of both the White House and Congress.*

The 1976 Election

Despite his flagging popularity, Gerald Ford banked on his incumbency and put himself forward in 1976 as the Republican candidate for president. His chief Republican opponent was Ronald Reagan, a film and television actor and a former governor of California who was widely known for his conservative views. Most Republicans feared, however, that a Reagan candidacy would push the party too far to the right and result in a landslide victory for the Democrats. Cautious in the aftermath of Watergate, the Republicans unenthusiastically nominated Ford, who named Senator Robert Dole of Kansas as his running mate.

On the Democratic side, the public's mistrust of government was the most important factor in the selection of a presidential candidate. Jimmy Carter, a former one-term governor of Georgia, depicted himself as an outsider, independent of the Washington establishment. (When Carter told his mother he was running for president, she reportedly asked, "President of what?") Trust and integrity were the chief planks of Carter's campaign for the nation's highest office. Promising to apply the "Golden Rule . . . in all public matters," he further pledged, "I will never lie to you."

A moderate Democrat, Carter appealed to conservative and southern voters by playing up his credentials as a born-again Christian. At the same time he made fairly liberal statements on domestic policy, including civil rights, and favored a strong national defense. Carter also capitalized on the Nixon pardon. His pointed references to the "Nixon-Ford administration," as well as the sagging economy, encouraged voters to try their luck with a Democrat. He entered the campaign with a 30 percent lead over Ford.

Carter and his running mate, Senator Walter Mondale of Minnesota, won the election with just over 50 percent of the popular vote and secured a 297-to-240 margin in the electoral college. Carter won more than 90 percent of the black vote, which provided his margin of victory in Pennsylvania, Ohio, and seven southern states. Apathy proved to be the most important factor, however. A record 46.7 percent of eligible voters, mainly the nation's poor, did not even bother to cast ballots.

The Carter Presidency

James Earl (Jimmy) Carter, the first president to come of age after World War II, was an enigma to most political analysts. As a professed outsider, he never gained the confidence of congressional Democrats, let alone Republicans, and could never command their votes. Uncertain and hesitant, he reflected the uneasiness that spread across the country in the late 1970s. Lacking an overarching political vision, Carter gradually shifted to the right, so much so that critics called him "a Democrat who often talks and thinks like a Republican."

The stalled economy resisted his best efforts, but Carter made his own mistakes. When he took office, he admitted that the nation's problems might require truly novel solutions but offered only a lackluster legislative program. His tax reform measure of 1977 did little to help the middle classes; his energy bill, enacted in 1978, appeared to benefit the oil companies as much as consumers; and the health reform measures promised during his campaign were never enacted.

Carter's style reflected his managerial outlook as well as his lack of experience as a politician. He generally abstained from the customary bargaining with legislators. Lacking leadership ability, he tended to seek technical solutions to the country's enormous social problems. On occasion he got caught up in trivial details, such as planning a players' schedule for the White House tennis courts. Overall, Carter relied on a small circle of advisers, mainly close friends from Georgia, and kept an unusually low profile for the nation's chief executive.

Carter's decisions nevertheless reflected his sense of political reality. Although he appointed a higher percentage of women, African Americans, and Latinos to full-time federal appointments than any previous president and created a "superfund" to clean up abandoned toxic waste sites, he broke ranks with liberal Democrats on important issues. Like many Southerners, Carter sought to reduce the scale of federal government as well as to lessen its control over the marketplace. He backed legislation that deregulated airlines, bringing fares down for millions of business and vacation travelers. He also backed the easing of congressional regulation of banks, a policy change that inadvertently encouraged fraud, the granting of questionable loans, and eventually a round of disastrous bank failures.

Carter made no effort to renew the social welfare initiatives of his Democratic predecessor, Lyndon B. Johnson. Under Carter's administration, inner-city schools and health and social services declined. The federal funds that might have gone to poverty programs instead bolstered military spending. The press, aided by whistle blowers working inside defense factories, found military spending loaded with fraud and abuse. Exposés of wasteful purchases—such as $50 screwdrivers—made Carter appear unable or unwilling to challenge dishonesty in government, despite his campaign promises.

Inflation proved to be his worst enemy. As older Americans could recognize, half of all the inflation since 1940 had occurred in just ten years. Interest rates rose, driving mortgages out of reach for many would-be home buyers. Rents in many locations doubled, sales of automobiles and other consumer products slumped, and many small businesses went under. Tuition costs skyrocketed along with unemployment, and many young men and women who could neither afford to go to college nor find a job moved back home. Carter could not deliver on his promise to turn the economy around.

Like Betty Ford, First Lady Rosalynn Carter played a prominent role in her husband's administration, which she described as a family affair. She promoted reforms in mental health care and policies for the elderly, and she served as a goodwill ambassador to South America. She also took a strong stand in support of the ERA. She never achieved Betty Ford's popularity, however. Many Americans believed Rosalynn Carter overstepped her role when she began to attend cabinet meetings.

THE NEW POVERTY

Despite the diversion of federal funds to military spending during the Vietnam War, the nation enjoyed a continuing economic prosperity during the 1960s that raised living standards for many. Income differences between black and white Americans—and between men and women—declined; segregation in schools, housing, and public facilities declined as well. By the mid-1970s, however, it had become clear that many of these gains were short-lived, reversed by a contracting economy and persistent racism. Michael Harrington, author of the highly influential *The Other America* (1962) (see Chapter 29), observed that nearly twenty years "after the President of the United States declared an 'unconditional' war on poverty, . . . we must deal . . . with a new poverty much more tenacious than the old."

A Two-tiered Society

During the 1970s Americans were healthier and living longer than at any time in history. Life expectancy had risen from sixty years in 1930 to seventy-three years, and gains were even greater for those who survived past the age of seventy-five. The majority of Americans also enjoyed greater wealth. Real personal income had doubled since the late 1930s, and by 1977 median family income had reached $15,000.

The gap between rich and poor, however, was starting to grow wider. By 1980 the wealthiest 20 percent

When Jimmy Carter took the oath of office in January 1977, he inherited an office dishonored by the Nixon-Ford administration. Hoping to dispel the political cynicism that had settled over the nation, he smiled broadly as he left the inaugural platform, bypassed his armored limousine, and walked hand-in-hand with Rosalynn Carter. Spectators cheered along the Pennsylvania Avenue parade route, greeting the new president's gesture as the symbolic end of an unhappy era.

of American families received about 40 percent of all income, whereas the poorest 20 percent received only about 5 percent. Nearly 26 million Americans—about 12 percent of the population—lived in poverty. Another 12 percent squeaked over the poverty line of $6,000 per family of four only because of welfare assistance. More than 11 million families were receiving welfare assistance from Aid to Families with Dependent Children (AFDC).

The widening gap between rich and poor was sharply defined by race. Although poor white people outnumbered poor black people by two to one, a disproportionate number of African Americans lived below the poverty line. Whereas 8.7 percent of white people lived in poverty in 1978, 30.6 percent of black and 21.6 percent of Hispanic people did (the rate was especially high among Puerto Ricans, low among Cuban Americans). The gains achieved by the civil rights movement and Great Society programs steadily eroded over the 1970s. Black family income, for example rose from 53 percent of white family income in 1954—the year of the *Brown v. Board of Education* decision—to 60 percent in 1969, peaked at 62 percent in 1975, then fell back to 57 percent in 1975. In most cities, residential segregation continued to increase.

Differences among African Americans also became more pronounced during the 1970s. The proportion of the African American population attending college peaked in 1976 at 9.3 percent, a 500 percent increase from 1960. Implementing federal affirmative action mandates, major corporations began to recruit black college graduates, and many African Americans found places in the ranks of professional, clerical, managerial, and technical workers. By the late 1970s one-third of all black workers had found white-collar employment.

But although 35 to 45 percent of African American families achieved middle-class status, others fell into poverty in nearly the same proportion. The sociologist William Julius Wilson confirmed "a deepening economic schism . . . in the black community." While middle-class black people were joining white people in the professional workplace and integrated suburbs, the poor stayed behind in increasingly segregated urban neighborhoods and in jobs that did not pay a living wage.

This trend affected the black community in dramatic ways. Until the 1970s the majority of African Americans had shared residential neighborhoods, institutions such as churches, and political outlooks. The growing income and residential disparity, which widened faster among black people than among white people, eventually produced sharp differences among African Americans on social, economic, and political issues as well.

Toward the end of the decade, opportunities for advancement into the middle class dwindled. By 1980 fewer black students attended integrated schools than in 1954, except in the South, where about half the black students did. The turnabout resulted in part from increasing opposition by white parents to court-ordered school busing, which had served since *Brown v. Board of Education* as the principal means of achieving racial balance in urban school systems where residential neighborhoods remained segregated by choice. In 1975 residents of a white neighborhood clashed with black children who had been sent to their school under a court-ordered busing plan. By the end of the decade the busing controversy had nearly disappeared, in part because federal judges hesitated to mandate such programs. But more important was the change in the racial composition of American cities. As a consequence of "white flight" to the suburbs, by 1980 big-city school systems served mainly African American and Latino children, making the issue of integration moot. By this time, the dropout rate of black teenagers had reached 50 percent in inner-city schools.

New legal rulings closed off important routes to employment in the professions. A 1978 U.S. Supreme Court decision dealt a sharp blow to affirmative action. To ensure acceptance of a minimum number of minority students, the University of California–Davis Medical School had established a quota system. In 1973 and 1974 the school denied admission to Allan Bakke, a white student. Bakke sued the university for "reverse discrimination," claiming his academic record was better than that of the sixteen minority students who were admitted. The California Supreme Court ruled in his favor in 1976, and, in a 5 to 4 decision, the Supreme Court upheld the California court's ruling, stating that the use of an "explicit racial classification" in situations where no earlier discrimination had been demonstrated violated the Equal Protection Clause of the Fourteenth Amendment. The Court ordered the University of California to admit Bakke to its medical school. Affirmative action programs could now operate only when "a legacy of unequal treatment" could be proved.

The Feminization of Poverty

Women as a group lost economic ground during the 1970s. The proportion of women in the labor force continued to grow, but most employed women earned less than a living wage. A rising divorce rate also left women—including employed women—at an economic disadvantage. Throughout the 1950s, the divorce rate averaged fifteen per thousand married women between the ages of fourteen and forty-four; by the time President Carter took office, the rate had more than doubled, reaching a new high of thirty-seven per thousand. At the same time, changes in divorce laws worked to men's financial advantage. For example, new no-fault divorce laws reduced or eliminated alimony payments to women. Most men, moreover, defaulted on child-support payments within one year after separation. Whereas divorced men enjoyed an average 42 percent increase in their standard of living, divorced women suffered a 73 percent decline.

During the 1970s the number of poor families headed by women increased nearly 70 percent. Divorce was the most important factor in this trend; more than 50 percent of female-headed families had divorced women as heads of the household, while 31 percent were headed by women separated from their husbands. Another factor was a sharp rise in pregnancy among unwed teenagers, although less than 20 percent of female-headed households were headed by an unwed mother. Unlike those of earlier generations, teenagers of the 1970s tended to keep their babies rather than put them up for adoption. Many dropped out of high school. Too young to have gained either the education or skills to secure more than minimum-wage jobs, unmarried mothers could rarely support themselves and their children.

Separated and divorced women and their children drifted downward into poverty, often from the relative security of the middle class. Even with AFDC payments and food stamps, it was nearly impossible for any single mother to keep her family's income above the poverty line. And with inflation, the real incomes of welfare recipients dropped in many states to a little over half their 1970 levels. In 1982 the National Advisory Council on Economic Opportunity issued a report predicting that, if these trends continued, by the turn of the century female heads of households and their children would account for just about all the poor people in the United States.

By the mid-1970s, the major organization promoting the rights of poor women had itself filed for bankruptcy. Between 1967 and 1975, the National Welfare Rights Organization (NWRO) had coordinated the work of various local welfare rights groups. Led mainly by African American women, the NWRO raised funds from churches and government poverty programs to enable welfare recipients to have a voice in policy decisions. They demanded adequate day-care facilities and job-training programs and insisted on the legitimacy of female-headed households. NWRO activists occasionally staged sit-ins at welfare agencies to secure benefits for their members. More often, they informed poor women of their existing rights and encouraged them to apply for benefits. By 1975, however, NWRO had exhausted itself fighting cutbacks in the federal welfare system.

"The Underclass"

"Behind the [ghetto's] crumbling walls," *Time* magazine announced in 1977, "lives a large group of people who are more intractable, more socially alien and more hostile than almost anyone had imagined. They are the unreachables: the American underclass. . . ." Although the majority of poor Americans lived in rural areas and small towns, with Missouri, South Dakota, and Texas accounting for the nation's largest pockets of poverty, *Time* and other news media spotlighted the inner cities. "The underclass," in their discussions, became a metaphor for the deteriorating conditions of urban America.

Most commentators focused on African Americans, the six out of ten who lived in central cities with rising unemployment rates. The economic boom during the Vietnam War and the expansion of public programs under Johnson's Great Society had built huge municipal payrolls, permitting many African Americans to secure jobs in the public sector. With the drastic cutbacks of the 1970s, many municipal workers were laid off. Jobs became scarcer than they had been at any time since the Great Depression. One unemployed worker in

Kansas City commented that despite the advances brought about by the civil rights movement, conditions appeared no better than they had been during the 1930s: "The truth is that black people ain't no closer to catching up with white than they were before."

The bleak prospects took an especially heavy toll on young African Americans. A black child was twice as likely as a white child to die before reaching his or her first birthday and four times more likely to be killed between the ages of one and four. Among black teenagers, the unemployment rate topped 40 percent; the few jobs available to them were among the lowest-paid in the economy. Despite the paucity of jobs for teenagers, the high school dropout rate skyrocketed during the 1970s. Among dropouts, illiteracy, frequent arrests, alcohol and drug abuse, and long-term reliance on public welfare were endemic.

The growth of teenage poverty also correlated positively with a rise in crime. Rates of violent crimes, such as aggravated assault, robbery, rape, and murder increased dramatically in poor communities throughout the country. The number of serious crimes, such as burglary, car theft, and murder, perpetrated by children between the ages of ten and seventeen increased at an alarming rate.

Although some policy experts attributed the emergence of an "underclass" to declining economic opportunities, the news media revived the "tangle of pathology" argument, which had been at the heart of Daniel Patrick Moynihan's *Negro Family: The Case for National Action* (1965). This report identified the major cause of disorder within the African American community as the prevalence of female-headed households, or what Moynihan called "the black matriarchy." At the time, many civil rights leaders and feminists objected to Moynihan's assessment, claiming that it shifted blame from the causes of poverty to its victims. Over a decade later, this argument still found favor in the news media and with many legislators who linked the emergence of "the underclass" to the increase of single mothers and welfare dependence.

Indian peoples remained the poorest and most disadvantaged of all racial or ethnic groups. They suffered from a high death rate—six times the national average from tuberculosis, and twenty-two times the national average from alcohol-related causes. Tribes continued to struggle for autonomy during the 1970s—that is, to gain authority over their reservations, including mineral and water resources—but often encountered resistance and competing claims from white neighbors. In 1978 the Supreme Court ruled in *United States v. Wheeler* that tribal sovereignty existed "only at the sufferance of Congress." Another case in the same year, *Oliphant v. Suquamish Indian Tribe,* added that tribes had no authority to arrest or punish trespassers who violated their laws. Meanwhile the federal government did little to help integrate Indian peoples who lived off the reservations—slightly less than half of the total Indian population—into mainstream society.

COMMUNITIES AND GRASS-ROOTS POLITICS

The mass demonstrations of the 1960s gave way in the 1970s to a style of political mobilization centered squarely in communities. Unlike national elections, which registered increasing voter apathy, local campaigns brought a great many people to the voting booth and into voluntary associations. "I didn't care so much about my neighborhood until I had children," one city dweller told a sociologist. "I wasn't aware of the various facets of the community. Then came a lot of other things that I began to do as the parent of a child in this neighborhood. We became committed to this area."

The New Urban Politics

In many cities, new groups came into political power. In several college towns, such as Berkeley, California, and Eugene, Oregon, both of which had been centers of antiwar activism during the 1960s, student coalitions were formed to secure seats for their candidates on city councils. In 1973 labor unions, college students, and community groups in Madison, Wisconsin, elected a former student activist to the first of three terms as mayor.

African American candidates scored impressive victories during the 1970s. The newly elected African American mayor of Atlanta, Maynard Johnson, concluded that "politics is the civil rights movement of the 1970s." By 1978, 2,733 African Americans held elected offices in the South, ten times the number a decade earlier. Mississippi, a state where the civil rights movement had encountered violent opposition, had more African American elected officials by 1980 than any other state in the union. Most of these elected officials served on city councils, county commissions, school boards, and law enforcement agencies. But voters also elected African American mayors in the South's premier cities, New Orleans and Atlanta. In other parts of the country, black mayors, such as Coleman Young in Detroit, Richard Hatcher in Gary, and Tom Bradley in Los Angeles, held power along with many minor black officials. Cities with black mayors spent more than other municipalities of similar size on education and social services. They worked hardest at improving community health services and to ensure equity in government employment.

Other racial or ethnic groups advanced more slowly, rarely in proportion to their actual numbers in the population. Mexican Americans had already won offices in Crystal City, Texas, and in 1978 took control

Geronimo, 1981, *by Victor Orozco Ochoa. During the 1970s public murals appeared in many cities, often giving distinctive expression to a community's racial or ethnic identity. The murals painted in the mid-1970s on the outside of the* Centro Cultural de la Raza, *in San Diego, were among the most striking. After vandals ruined one section, Ochoa, whose grandmother was Yaqui, replaced it with this enormous representation of Geronimo, surrounded by figures of contemporary Chicano cultural life.*

of a major city council, in San Antonio, for the first time. They also scored electoral victories in other parts of Texas and in New Mexico and developed strong neighborhood or ward organizations in southern California. Puerto Ricans elected a handful of local officials in New York, mostly in the Bronx. Asian Americans advanced in similar fashion in parts of Hawai'i.

The fiscal crises of the 1970s undercut these efforts to reform municipal government. Most of these new officials found themselves unable to make the sweeping changes they had promised during their campaigns. In tackling the problem of youth unemployment, they discovered that temporary job programs could not counteract the effects of factory shutdowns and the disappearance of industrial jobs. Moreover, affirmative action programs aroused cries of "reverse discrimination" from angered whites who felt that the progress of others was being made at their expense. But although support for them frequently dissipated when the cycle of poverty and violence could not be slowed, community-based mobilizations remained the political touchstone of the decade.

The City and the Neighborhood

The nation's cities inspired a range of responses from residents who chose to resist the pull of the suburbs and from those who simply could not afford to leave. For city dwellers, the city's hospitals, public libraries, symphony orchestras, museums, and art galleries became anchoring institutions requiring public support. Changes in federal policies also encouraged local initiative. The Community Development Act of 1974, signed by President Ford, combined federal grant programs for cities into a single program and put mayors and city managers directly in charge of spending. With grants totaling $8.4 billion over three years, city governments could allocate funds as they saw fit to public works, law enforcement, residential redevelopment, or even to salaries for public employees. These community development block grants encouraged citizens to take part in local planning. Communities Organized for Public Service (COPS) in San Antonio, Texas, and the Association of Community Organizations for Reform Now (ACORN) in Little Rock, Arkansas, were formed to advise public officials. In other cities, Save the City campaigns engaged residents in defining problems important to the community, such as traffic, sewerage, or stray dogs.

Groups of preservationists organized to save historic buildings and public spaces and formed land trusts to take over and refurbish old houses or to turn vacant lots into neighborhood parks. In Rhode Island, the Providence Preservation Society worked with city planners and individual donors to restore hundreds of houses, organized festival tours of neighborhoods to lure prospective buyers, and spurred the formation of similar societies in nearby towns.

Local and national foundations joined federal agencies in funding Community Development Corporations (CDCs) through a series of antipoverty agencies. By the end of the 1970s some 700 community-based economic development groups had been formed to infuse capital into neighborhood businesses and housing. These community groups promoted "development banks" that would facilitate "sweat equity"—that is, the granting of low-interest mortgage loans to buyers who were willing to rebuild or refurbish dilapidated housing. They also acted to prevent local banks from closing when a neighborhood became mainly black.

Those who guided the neighborhood campaigns often became known as "local heroes." They usually insisted that tensions between old and new neighborhood residents, problems of housing and schools, and the like could be solved face to face and cooperatively with the resources available to them. In San Francisco during the early 1970s, a law professor, Ray Schonholtz, launched "community boards," neighborhood arbitration centers that he described as "a new justice model . . . a neighborhood stabilization program . . . a volunteer service delivery system" with a "new philosophy about conflict, viewing it positively instead of negatively." Federal assistance proved crucial in maintaining most community-based programs, however, especially in the late 1970s when cities faced major fiscal crises.

In 1979 President Carter's National Commission on Neighborhoods compiled 200 specific recommendations to broaden and speed the development of local institutions. The long-range goal of such efforts, the commission suggested, should be "to reorganize our society . . . to a new democratic system of grassroots involvement." But local advocacy groups often found themselves enmeshed in projects that foundations and federal agencies, not the local groups, thought best for a neighborhood. As a leader of a Bronx advocacy group concluded, he and his fellow activists were "diverted from organizing" and "seen—rightly—as part of the establishment" when they found themselves administering large-scale, well-funded projects that they had not originally intended to create. And even when local preservationists succeeded in restoring entire urban districts to an earlier splendor, "gentrification" often followed, with poor residents displaced by middle-class professionals who craved the increasingly fashionable old homes.

The Endangered Environment

As at Three Mile Island, threats to the environment rallied whole communities. For example, the discovery of high rates of cancer and birth defects among the residents of Love Canal, a neighborhood of Niagara Falls, New York, offered compelling evidence of a growing danger to many American communities. Love Canal had been built over a site used by the Hooker Chemical Laboratory as a dump for toxic wastes, which began oozing into basements and backyards in the late 1970s. Homemaker Lois Gibbs organized a vigorous publicity campaign to draw attention to the grim situation. Residents demanded to be evacuated from the site and compensated for damages. Hooker and the city of Niagara Falls eventually paid a group of former homeowners more than $20,000,000. Many residents of southern Florida, meanwhile, were outraged to learn that modifications of water flow into the Everglades for sugar production and housing developments, undertaken decades earlier by the Army Corps of Engineers, had degraded thousands of acres of wilderness, eliminating natural filtration systems and killing millions of birds and other species. These and similar problems alerted communities nationwide to the perils of industrial and economic development unchecked by concern for their environmental consequences.

The roots of the modern environmental movement can be traced to the works of scientist Rachel Carson, especially *Silent Spring* (1962), which detailed the devastating effects of the then commonly used DDT and other pesticides. By the spring of 1970, opinion polls showed that the public was more concerned about the environment than any other domestic issue. Senator Gaylord Nelson of Wisconsin and Representative Paul "Pete" McCloskey of California invited Americans to devote an entire day—April 22, Earth Day—to discuss the environment. The response was overwhelming; nearly 20 million Americans gathered in local parks, high schools, and colleges and at the nation's capital. Many wore green peace symbols and sang "All we are saying is give earth a chance."

The residents of many communities began to reassess their priorities and even to make changes in the way they lived. Municipal governments introduced recycling programs, encouraging residents to save glass, plastic bottles, and newspapers for reuse. Many families changed their diets to reduce or eliminate beef, which was far more costly to produce than the grains fed to cattle. Backyard vegetable gardens became popular, as did grocers who stocked organic foods, which were grown without pesticides or chemical fertilizers. Nutritionist Frances Moore Lappe's popular *Diet for a Small Planet* (1971) sought to counter the logic of excess that had made Americans consumers of one third of the world's energy resources. Barry Commoner's *Closing*

Circle (1971) helped make the term "ecology" (the name of the branch of biology that deals with the relationship between organisms and their environment) into a synonym for environmental balance ("eco" means "home" in Greek).

The environmentalist movement grew stronger on college campuses and in a handful of long-standing organizations, such as the Audubon Society and the Wilderness Society. The Sierra Club, formed in 1892 as a small society of western mountain hikers, grew to 100,000 members in 1970 and a half-million over the next decade. New groups sprang up in response to the energy crisis, often devoted to developing renewable energy sources such as solar power. Some, like Greenpeace, sponsored direct action campaigns to halt practices that caused harm to the environment.

Environmentalism cut across social and geographic boundaries. The dangers of toxic wastes, the destruction of wetlands, the ruin of fishing industries, and other problems aroused concern even in such traditionally conservative areas as the Deep South (where bumper stickers read "Don't Dump It in Dixie!"). Sometimes campaigns succeeded in blocking massive construction projects, such as nuclear energy plants; more often they halted small-scale destruction—of a particular natural habitat or historic urban district, for example. Most important, all these campaigns made the public more aware of the consequences of private and government decisions about the environment. Responding to organized pressure groups, Congress passed scores of bills designed to protect endangered species, reduce pollution caused by automobile emissions, limit and ban the use of some pesticides, and control strip mining. The Environmental Protection Agency (EPA), established in 1970, grew to become the federal government's largest regulatory agency, employing more than 10,000 people by the end of the decade.

Environmentalists had only limited success, however, in effecting large-scale policy changes. Congress passed clean air mandates to reduce air pollution, but cities often avoided the mandates with petitions for lengthy extensions of the deadlines for meeting them. Despite the introduction of lead-free gasoline, the air in major metropolitan areas grew worse because of a rapid increase in automobile traffic. Environmentalists lost an important campaign when Nixon's secretary of the interior, former Alaska governor Walter Hickel, chose Earth Day to announce the approval of the Alaska pipeline, 800 miles of pipe connecting oil fields with refining facilities. Despite predictions of environmental destruction from leaks and other catastrophes, pipeline construction began in 1973. As White House adviser John Ehrlichman explained, "Conservation is not in the Republican ethic."

Small-town America

A host of unresolved problems, ranging from air pollution to rising crime rates to higher taxes, encouraged a massive exodus from the nation's cities. Between 1970 and 1975, for every 100 people relocating to metropolitan areas, 138 moved out. Newer residential communities in small towns and in semirural or formerly rural areas grew at a fast pace, attracting retirees and others seeking solace or security.

Government programs such as mortgage guarantees and low-interest financing on individual homes promoted these large "low-density" developments of single-family houses. In many regions, the countryside gradually disappeared into "exurbia," a trend that population experts Peter A. Morison and Judith P. Wheeler attributed to the American "wish to love one's neighbor but keep him at arm's length." Opinion poles suggested that many Americans wanted to live in a small town that was not a suburb but was still no more than thirty miles from a major city.

Soon even small towns developed their own suburbs, usually moderate-income tracts of ranch houses squeezed between older wood-frame colonial or Victorian farmhouses. Federal subsidies for the construction of sewage and water lines, originally intended to aid rural communities, now became springboards for further development. Ironically, shopping malls on former farmland drained commercial activity from the small-town centers, channeling the benefits of development to chain stores rather than to local merchants.

Some communities organized to oppose these trends. Following the publication of E. F. Schumacher's *Small Is Beautiful* (1973), groups of people began to question the advantages of "bigness." Seeking to rebuild communities on a smaller, more environmentally sound scale, they opposed new development, new highways, the construction of nuclear power plants, and the dumping of toxic waste. In Vermont, liberal "hippies" and "back-to-the-landers" joined traditionally conservative landowners to defeat a 1974 gubernatorial plan to attract developers. In other locales, such as the Berkshire Mountains, community land trusts were organized to encourage common ownership of the land. "From coast to coast," the *New York Times* reported, "environmental, economic and social pressures have impelled hundreds of cities and towns to adopt limitations on the size and character of their populations." To encourage public discussion of land-use issues, such as the use of open space or farms for commercial development, President Carter created the Small Community and Rural Development Policy group.

Some small towns, especially those without mild climates or nearby cities, did not prosper during

Archie (Carroll O'Connor) and Edith Bunker (Jean Stapleton) endowed television with a social and political complexity that previous situation comedies had scrupulously avoided. First broadcast in 1971, All in the Family *featured a working-class family living in Queens, New York, trying to sort out their differences with Archie, the highly bigoted but lovable center of the household. Producer Norman Lear explained that the show "holds a mirror up to our prejudices. . . . We laugh now, swallowing just the littlest bit of truth about ourselves, and it sits there for the unconscious to toss about later."*

the 1970s. In parts of Kansas, Iowa, and the Dakotas, where family farms failed at a high rate, other businesses also closed. A "snowball effect" resulted in rundown schools, inadequate medical care, and abandoned movie theaters and grocery stores. Only nursing homes and funeral parlors continued to thrive.

THE NEW CONSERVATISM

While many Americans concentrated their political energies in their communities, others organized to turn back the liberal Great Society programs. Many taxpayers resented having to pay for government programs that benefited minorities or provided expanded social services for the poor. In 1978 California voters staged a "taxpayers' revolt" and approved Proposition 13, which cut property taxes and government revenues for social programs and education. In other, mainly economically hard-pressed urban areas, white voters who resented the gains made by African Americans and Latinos formed a powerful backlash movement. Poles in Chicago, Irish in Boston, and Italians and Jews in Brooklyn, for example, organized to consolidate their political influence. By the end of the decade, the only substantial increase in voter participation was among conservatives.

The New Right

The political surge rightward in the 1970s united many traditionally probusiness conservatives with a new constituency of alienated lower-class white voters. This alliance gained strength from widespread bitterness about both the United States defeat in Vietnam and the growing regulatory powers of the federal government. It gained intellectual respectability from neoconservatives, former liberals who blamed the social movements of the 1960s for the demoralization of the nation. The American Enterprise Institute and the Heritage Foundation, richly funded by major corporations, established major research centers for conservative scholars. These and other foundations also funded campus publications attacking welfare programs, affirmative action, and environmentalism. Leaders of the New Right, as the movement was called, identified themselves with the defense of "family values" and sought to gain political power by influencing legislation and public policy, and most of all by winning elections.

The most sensational element of the New Right was its paramilitary wing, which was concentrated in rural districts of the upper Midwest and Southwest. Inspired by white supremicist author William Pierce's *Turner Diaries* (1978), a novel that predicted the revolt by white "Aryans" against people of color and the federal government, thousands of enthusiasts bolstered their apocalyptic vision by arming themselves with assault weapons and training surreptitiously for combat.

The largest New Right constituency, however, united behind major conservative religious and political leaders to preserve and promote what they viewed as traditional moral values. By decade's end more than 50 million Americans had joined the ranks of evangelical Christians, and Southern Baptists had become the nation's largest Protestant denomination. One year after Billy Graham published his fast-selling *How to Be Born Again* (1977), 40 percent of all Americans, including the nation's president, reported that they were indeed "born again." These evangelical Christians became the backbone of key organizations such as the National Conservative Political Action Committee and, most especially, Moral Majority. Together they raised the funds to wage well-publicized campaigns against abortion, the ERA, gay rights, and the busing of schoolchildren.

Phyllis Schlafly led the campaign to defeat ratification of the Equal Rights Amendment. She wrote widely and delivered speeches throughout the country denouncing women's liberation as a threat to the family. The Alton, Illinois, homemaker appears here on the steps of the Illinois State Capitol in 1978.

The New Right used sophisticated marketing techniques to build its constituency. Conservative political groups were among the first to use direct mail campaigns to mobilize followers and raise funds. In the 1970s approximately 100 conservative organizations each created lists of potential donors, traded or sold these lists, and kept in circulation millions of personally addressed letters requesting financial contributions in return for monthly newsletters, insignia buttons, bumper stickers, or even embossed Bibles.

"Televangelists" enjoyed even greater success in attracting a following. Evangelical programming emerged on the local level in the early days of television. By the late 1960s, several shows had achieved national syndication. Televangelists such as Pat Robertson and Jim Bakker frequently mixed conservative political messages with appeals to prayer. The *Old Time Gospel Hour,* featuring the Reverend Jerry Falwell, was broadcast on more than 200 television stations and 300 radio stations each week. Falwell told his listeners that Christians were morally compelled to support issues and candidates that punish "the enemies of God," including communists, supporters of abortion rights, and the "secular humanist" opponents of prayer in public schools. Christian broadcasters generally endorsed Falwell's faith that "the free-enterprise system is clearly outlined in the Book of Proverbs of the Bible." By the end of the 1970s more than 1,400 radio stations and 30 TV stations specialized in religious broadcasts that reached an audience of perhaps 20 million weekly.

Urging Americans to repent their sins and acknowledge God's authority or suffer terrible wrath, Falwell formed Moral Majority, Inc., as a political lobbying group to urge the rightful "place for biblical moral law in public policy." Moral Majority advocated tough laws against homosexuality and pornography, a reduction of government services, especially welfare payments to poor families, and increased spending for a stronger national defense. It promised campaign funds and votes for, as Falwell put it, "the mighty man . . . that man of war, that judge, that prophet, that preacher who is willing to call sin by its right name."

Jesse Helms was the first major politician to appeal directly to the New Right and to build his own impressive fund-raising empire with its help. A North Carolina journalist who had fought the integration of public schools and affirmative action programs and defended the Ku Klux Klan, Helms had often attacked Martin Luther King Jr. as a communist-influenced demagogue. Helms entered national politics as a Goldwater supporter in 1964 and ran for the Senate in 1972. Carried to victory with Richard Nixon's success in North Carolina, Helms immediately promoted a host of conservative bills. He introduced legislation to allow automobile owners or dealers to disconnect mandatory antipollution devices. He also defended the Watergate break-ins as necessary to offset the "traitorous conduct" of antiwar activists. By 1978 he had raised $8.1 million, the largest amount ever, for his successful reelection campaign. Helms won few victories in the Senate but built a powerful, loyal, and wealthy following.

Anti-ERA, Antiabortion

The New Right sponsored several important campaigns during the 1970s. Conservatives sought, without success, to pass a Balanced Budget Amendment to the Constitution and to return prayer to the public schools. They endorsed the Supreme Court's decision permitting the resumption of the death penalty in 1977. And in one of the New Right's best-funded campaigns, they sought to

Asked of those who said they had heard of or read about the Equal Rights Amendment: Do you favor or oppose this amendment?

Favor	58%
Oppose	24%
No opinion	18%
By Sex	
Male	
Favor	63%
Oppose	22%
No opinion	15%
Female	
Favor	54%
Oppose	25%
No opinion	21%

Interviewing Date 3/7–10/1975, Survey #925-K

Gallup Poll on the Equal Rights Amendment, 1975 *By 1973 thirty of the thirty-eight states required to ratify the ERA had done so. Although the amendment ultimately failed to achieve ratification and died in June 1982, public support was strong. In the 1976 presidential campaign, the platforms of both Democrats and Republicans included planks favoring its passage.*

Source: *The Gallup Poll: Public Opinion*, 1935–1974 (New York: Random House, 1974).

restore the "traditional family values" that, in their minds, the women's liberation movement had destroyed.

The defeat of the Equal Rights Amendment (ERA) stood at the top of the New Right agenda. Approved by Congress in March 1972, nearly fifty years after its introduction (see Chapter 22), the ERA stated: "Equality of rights under the law shall not be denied or abridged by the United States or by any State on account of sex." Endorsed by both the Democratic and Republican Parties, the amendment appeared likely to be ratified by the individual states. Nearly all mainstream women's organizations, including the Girl Scouts of America, endorsed the ERA. Even the AFL-CIO retracted its long-standing opposition and endorsed the amendment.

Responding to this groundswell of support in favor of the ERA, the New Right swung into action. Phyllis Schlafly, a self-described suburban housewife who had been active in Republican Party politics since the 1950s, headed the STOP ERA campaign. Schlafly described the amendment's supporters as "a bunch of bitter women seeking a constitutional cure for their personal problems." She warned that the ERA would deprive women of their true rights "such as the right of a wife to be supported by her husband" and that it would lead to unisex public toilets and homosexual marriages. As one woman wrote her senator, "Forced busing, forced mixing, forced housing. Now forced women. No thank you!" Hostile to "Big Government," antiratificationists believed that the ERA would allow the state to intrude further into the private domain of family by requiring massive changes in laws concerning marriage, divorce, and child custody.

The New Right mounted large, expensive campaigns in each swing state, overwhelming pro-ERA resources. By 1979, although thirty-five states had ratified the ERA, the amendment remained three votes short of passage. Despite a three-year extension, the ERA died in 1982.

As part of its counterattack against the women's liberation movement, the New Right also waged a steady campaign against abortion, which the women's movement had defined as a woman's right rather than a mere medical issue. In 1973 the Supreme Court had ruled in *Roe v. Wade* that state laws outlaw-

Would you favor or oppose a law that would permit a woman to go to a doctor to end pregnancy at any time during the first three months?

Favor	40%
Oppose	50%
No opinion	10%

Interviewing Date 11/12–17/1969, Survey #793-K, Question #4, Index #54

The United States Supreme Court has ruled that a woman may go to a doctor to end pregnancy at any time during the first three months of pregnancy. Do you favor or oppose this ruling?

Favor	47%
Oppose	44%
No opinion	9%

Interviewing Date 3/8–11; 3/15–18/1974, Survey #894-K; 895 -K

Gallup Polls on Abortion: 1969, 1974 *During the 1960s, numerous American women began to demand control over their own reproductive processes and the repeal of legislation in place in all fifty states rendering abortion illegal. The American Institute of Public Opinion surveyed Americans in 1969, when abortion was still illegal, and again in 1974, one year after* Roe v. Wade, *the Supreme Court ruling that struck down state laws prohibiting abortion during the first three months of pregnancy.*

Source: *The Gallup Poll: Public Opinion*, 1935–1974 (New York: Random House, 1974).

ing abortion during the first two trimesters of pregnancy were unconstitutional because they violated a woman's right to privacy. The decision in effect legalized abortion on demand. Opponents of *Roe* sought a constitutional amendment that would define conception as the beginning of life and outlaw abortion. They argued that the "rights of the unborn" supersede a woman's right to control her own body. The Roman Catholic Church organized the first antiabortion demonstrations after the Supreme Court's decision and sponsored the formation of the National Right to Life Committee, which claimed 11 million members by 1980. Many more groups organized, such as Concerned for Life, Life and Equality, Right to Life, and the American Life Lobby, all framing the issue in terms of a fundamental and sacred "right to life."

Abortion foes rallied behind the conservative representative from Illinois, Henry Hyde, who sponsored a legislative bill that severely restricted the use of Medicaid funds for abortions. Upheld by the Supreme Court in 1980, the Hyde Amendment affected mainly poor women. Antiabortion groups also picketed Planned Parenthood counseling centers and abortion clinics, humiliating and intimidating potential clients. They rallied against government-subsidized day-care centers and against sex education programs in public schools. A small minority turned to more extreme actions, including violence.

"The Me Decade"

During the 1970s many Americans disengaged themselves from politics altogether. In 1976 novelist Tom Wolfe coined the phrase "the Me Decade" to describe an era obsessed with personal well-being, happiness, and emotional security. Health foods and diet crazes, a mania for physical fitness, and a quest for happiness through therapy involved millions of middle-class Americans. The historian Christopher Lasch provided his own label for this enterprise in the title of his best-selling book *The Culture of Narcissism: American Life in an Age of Diminishing Expectations* (1978). "After the political turmoil of the sixties," he explained, "Americans have returned to purely personal preoccupations."

The rise of the "human potential movement" provided a vivid example of this trend. Its most successful manifestation was Erhard Seminars Training (EST), a self-help program that blended insights from psychology and mysticism. Founded by Werner Erhard (a former door-to-door seller of encyclopedias), the institute taught individuals to form images of themselves as successful and satisfied. Through sixty hours of intensive training involving playacting and humiliation, participants learned one major lesson: "You are the one and only source of your experience. You created it." In addition to emphasizing self-esteem, the seminars taught the value of "power relationships"—that is, the importance of selecting friends or business colleagues who are compatible with one's own goals and ambitions. Priced at $400 for a series of two weekend sessions, EST peaked at 6,000 participants per month, grossing $25 million in revenue in 1980. In the San Francisco Bay Area, where Erhard had established his headquarters, one of every nine college graduates enrolled in EST. Typically white, single, middle class, and between the ages of twenty and forty-five, EST participants appeared to find in therapy what previous generations and other contemporaries found in religion.

Other popular therapies encouraged clients to "live in the present" and to "get in touch with" their body signals rather than make abstract plans for the future. The record-breaking best-seller *Open Marriage: A New Life Style for Couples* (1972), by Nena O'Neill and George O'Neill, for example, urged husbands and wives to stress "personal growth" and to search for "the true ME." Transcendental meditation (TM) promised a shortcut to mental tranquility and found numerous advocates among Wall Street brokers, Pentagon officials, and star athletes. Techniques of TM were taught in more than 200 special centers and practiced by a reputed 350,000 devotees.

Religious cults also formed in relatively large numbers during the 1970s. The Unification Church, founded by the Korean Reverend Sun Myung Moon, extracted intense personal loyalty from its youthful disciples. The parents of many of these disciples, however, were horrified by church practices, which included mass marriage ceremonies of couples selected for pairing by church leaders. Some desperate parents hired private detectives to "kidnap" their own children from the "Moonies." According to a 1977 Gallup survey, the Reverend Moon "elicited one of the most overwhelmingly negative responses ever reported by a major national poll." Moon's financial empire, which included hundreds of retail businesses and the *Washington Times*, a conservative daily newspaper, nevertheless proved very lucrative and kept his church solvent despite numerous lawsuits. By contrast, Jim Jones's People's Temple, a liberal interracial movement organized in the California Bay Area, ended in a mass murder and suicide when Jones induced more than 900 of his followers to drink cyanide-laced Kool-Aid in Guyana in 1978.

Popular music expressed and reinforced the self-absorption of the 1970s. The songs of community and hope that had been common in the late 1960s gave way to songs of despair or nihilism. Bruce Springsteen, whose lyrics lamented the disappearance of the white working class, became the decade's most popular new rock artist. At the same time, heavy metal bands such as Kiss, as well as "punk" and "new wave" artists underscored themes of decadence and drew crowds of mainly young white men to their concerts. At the other end of the popular music scale, country and western music hit its peak with mainstream sales or "crossover" hits, charismatic stars, and numerous new all-country and western radio stations. The songs of Willie Nelson, who was invited to perform at the White House by President Carter, evoked a sense of loneliness and nostalgia that appealed to older, white, working-class Americans.

ADJUSTING TO A NEW WORLD

In April 1975 the North Vietnamese struck Saigon and easily captured the city as the South Vietnamese army fell apart without U.S. assistance. All fighting stopped within a few weeks, and Saigon was renamed Ho Chi Minh City. The Vietnamese had finally triumphed over the French and Americans, and the nation was reunited under a government dominated by communists. For many Americans, this outcome underscored the futility of U.S. involvement.

By the mid-1970s a new realism prevailed in U.S. diplomacy. Presidents Ford and Carter, as well as their chief advisers, acknowledged that the cost of fighting the Vietnam War had been high, speeding the decline of the United States as the world's reigning superpower. The "realists" shared with dissatisfied nationalists a single goal: "No More Vietnams."

A Thaw in the Cold War

The military defeat in Vietnam forced the makers of U.S. foreign policy to reassess priorities. The United States must continue to defend its "vital interests," declared Ford's secretary of state Henry Kissinger, but must also recognize that "Soviet-American relations are not designed for tests of manhood." Both nations had experienced a relative decline of power in world affairs. And both were suffering from the already enormous and relentlessly escalating costs of sustaining a prolonged cold war.

At the close of World War II, the United States could afford to allocate huge portions of its ample economic resources to maintaining and enlarging its global interests. Soon, however, military and defense expenses began to grow at a much faster rate than the economy itself. Whereas the Korean War cost around $69.5 billion, the Vietnam War cost $172.2 billion. But the expenses of military conflicts accounted for only one portion of the defense budget. Clandestine operations, alliance building, spending for the United Nations and NATO, and weapons production accounted for trillions of dollars more. The Voice of America's network of radio stations, which broadcast anticommunist propaganda abroad, cost $640 million in the 1970s alone.

Military spending at this level eventually took its toll on the American economy, especially as the federal government increasingly relied on deficit spending to cover the bill. The federal debt, which stood at $257 billion in 1950, had jumped to $908 billion by 1980, and an increasingly large part of the federal budget was devoted just to paying the interest on this debt. At the same time, military spending diverted funds from programs that could have strengthened the economy. The results were disastrous. While the United States endured falling productivity levels and rates of personal savings, rising high school dropout rates and a disappearing skilled workforce, other nations rushed ahead. In the 1970s, when Japan and West Germany had emerged as potent economic competitors, *Business Week* noted that the American "colossus" was "clearly facing a crisis of the decay of power."

Western European nations acted to nudge U.S. foreign policy away from its cold war premises.

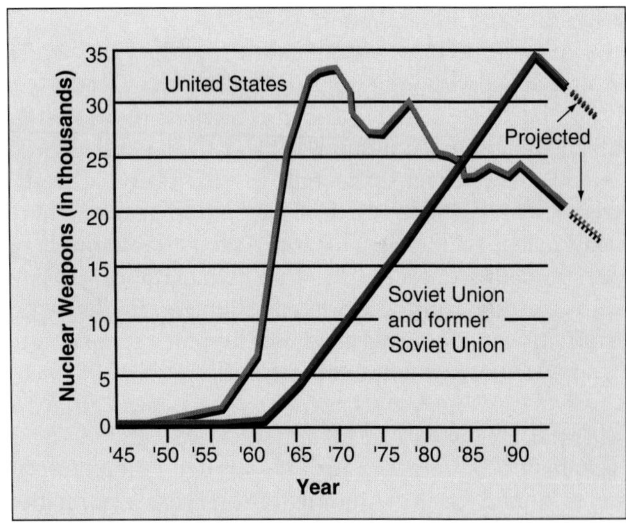

Nuclear Arsenals, the United States and the Soviet Union *During the cold war, both superpowers built up huge stockpiles of nuclear weapons, including sea and land missiles. President Lyndon Johnson began negotiations with the Soviet Union in an attempt to slow down the perilous nuclear arms race. In 1972, the Strategic Arms Limitation Treaty (SALT) set limits on offensive intercontinental ballistic missiles. SALT II, negotiated by President Carter in 1979, called for further reductions but failed to win approval in the U.S. Senate. Negotiations resumed under President Reagan and culminated in 1991 in the Strategic Arms Reduction Treaty (START), which included plans for the destruction of the stockpile of nuclear weapons.*

Source: James Sterngold, "Milestones of the Nuclear Era," *New York Times*, December 1, 1992, p. C10. Copyright © The New York Times Company; Illustrations by Rebecca Perry and Martha Hernandez; and the Bulletin of the Atomic Scientists.

In 1975, in Helsinki, Finland, representatives of thirty-five nations approved the national boundaries drawn in eastern and western Europe after World War II, and in return the Soviet Union agreed to enact a more liberal human rights policy, including the loosening of restrictions on the emigration of Soviet Jews. Recognizing that the Soviet Union no longer posed a military threat to their national sovereignty—if indeed it ever had—Western leaders also sought to strengthen economic relations between the two major blocs.

The Soviet Union, whose economy suffered even greater setbacks from defense spending, joined the United States in moving toward détente. The signing of SALT I, the first Strategic Arms Limitation Treaty, during Nixon's administration, followed by the U.S. withdrawal from Vietnam, encouraged new efforts to negotiate on strategic arms control. In November 1974 Ford and Soviet leader Leonid Brezhnev met in Vladivostok to set the terms of SALT II, and Carter secured the final agreement in 1979. The treaty failed to win confirmation from the Senate, however, when the Soviet Union invaded Afghanistan in December, 1979.

Although repeated conflicts in the third world continued to slow the pace toward détente, leaders in both the United States and the Soviet Union recognized that their economic well-being depended on a reduction in defense spending. However haltingly, steps toward reconciliation had to be taken. Many Americans, including business leaders, welcomed or accepted this change in policy as inevitable. "If you think you can run the world and then you find out you can't," the aged journalist Walter Lippmann explained, "you withdraw to what you can run."

Foreign Policy and "Moral Principles"

The historian Gaddis Smith has argued that "the four years of the Carter Administration were among the most significant in the history of American foreign policy in the twentieth century" because each of Carter's major decisions confronted long-entrenched diplomatic policy. In fresh approaches to Latin America and the Middle East in particular, Carter emphasized regional solutions and human rights over "gunboat diplomacy" and competition with the Soviet Union. By the end of the Carter years, however, the familiar U.S. strategies had returned with a vengeance.

In 1977, when Carter took office, he happily admitted his lack of experience in foreign affairs and viewed it as an asset. "We've seen a loss of morality," he noted, "and we're ashamed." His policy would demonstrate "the decency and generosity and common sense of our own people," its "soul" an "absolute" commitment to human rights. Carter condemned policies that had allowed the United States to support "right-wing monarchs and military dictators" in the name of anticommunism. In 1976 a powerful human rights lobby had pressured Congress to pass a bill that required the secretary of state to report annually on the status of human rights in all countries receiving aid from the United States and to cut off assistance to any country with a record of "gross violations." Carter's secretary of state, Cyrus R. Vance, and the assistant secretary for human rights and humanitarian affairs, Pat Derrian, worked to punish or at least to censure repressive military regimes in Brazil, Argentina, and Chile. For the first time, leading U.S. diplomats spoke out against the South African white supremacist "Apartheid" regime rather than commending or quietly supporting that government's avid anticommunism.

But when it came to troubled nations considered vital to U.S. interests, such as South Korea, the Philippines, and several countries in Central America, Carter put aside human rights principles to support brutally antidemocratic governments. Likewise, in restoring diplomatic relations with the People's Republic of China in January 1979, Carter overlooked that nation's imprisonment of dissidents. "The real problem," a U.S. diplomat observed, was that human rights was "not a policy but an attitude." Carter hoped to persuade others without paying any real price for his administration's efforts. The Soviet Union dismissed his initiative as mere propaganda, and many world leaders treated it as typical American political rhetoric.

Carter did attempt, however, to institute reforms at the Central Intelligence Agency (CIA), especially to halt the blatant intervention in the affairs of foreign governments that many Americans found embarrassing after the Vietnam misadventure. Carter appointed Admiral Stansfield Turner, a Rhodes scholar, as the agency's new director and ordered a purge of the "rogue elephants" who had pursued massive covert operations in Southeast Asia. "The CIA must operate within the law," Carter insisted, and restrict its activities mostly to the process of intelligence gathering. Neither Congress nor the president had the determination to press these reforms, however. Limited in their effect, they would be reversed in later years.

Carter scored his biggest moral victory in foreign affairs by paving the way for Panama to assume the ownership, operation, and defense of the Panama Canal Zone. Negotiations with Panama had begun during Lyndon Johnson's administration, following riots by Panamanians against U.S. territorial rule of their country. Carter pressured the Senate to ratify new treaties in 1978 (by a vote of 68 to 32) that would give the Canal over to Panamanian control by the year 2000.

President Carter signs the Middle East Peace Treaty with Egyptian President Anwar Sadat and Israeli Prime Minister Menachem Begin, in Washington, D.C., March 1979. President Carter had invited both leaders to Camp David, the presidential retreat in Maryland, where for two weeks he mediated between them on territorial rights to the West Bank and Gaza Strip. Considered Carter's greatest achievement in foreign policy, the negotiations, known as the Camp David Peace Accords, resulted in not only the historic peace treaty but the Nobel Peace Prize for Begin and Sadat.

The Camp David Accords

Carter nearly triumphed in the Middle East, where U.S. policies had historically balanced military and diplomatic support of Israel with the quest for Arab oil. Following the Israeli victory in the Yom Kippur War of 1973, Henry Kissinger devoted two years to "shuttle diplomacy" between various regimes but could not resolve regional problems. Carter himself had little knowledge of the Middle East before taking over the presidency, although as a born-again Christian he had strong feelings about the "Holy Land." Early in his administration, Carter met privately with Israeli prime minister Menachem Begin to encourage conciliation with Egypt. When negotiations between the two countries stalled in 1978, Carter brought Begin together with Egyptian president Anwar el-Sadat for a planned three-day retreat at Camp David, Maryland, which lasted thirteen days and resulted in unprecedented agreements.

The Camp David Accords, signed in September 1978, set the formal terms for peace in the region. Egypt became the earliest Arab country to recognize Israel's right to exist, the two nations establishing mutual diplomatic relations for the first time since the founding of Israel in 1948. In return, Egypt regained control of the Sinai Peninsula, including important oil fields and airfields. Israel, however, was the biggest winner: it secured a virtual permanent guarantee of greatly enhanced U.S. military support, including three new air force bases that cost several billion dollars. Later in 1979, Begin and Sadat shared the Nobel Prize for Peace.

But disappointment lay ahead. Carter staked his hopes for regional peace on the final achievement of statehood, or at least political autonomy, for Palestinians in a portion of their former lands now occupied by the Israelis. As specified in the new Israeli-Egyptian treaty, Israel would return eventually to its approximate borders of 1967. Begin, who had said "My right eye will fall out, my right hand will fall off, before I ever agree to the dismantling of a single Jewish settlement," did dismantle Israeli settlements in the Sinai—but otherwise refused to budge.

Carter nevertheless continued to believe that the Camp David Accords had set the peace process in motion. He repeatedly pressed Begin to issue promises of Palestinian autonomy within the "Occupied Territories" of the West Bank and Gaza. Begin, however, announced more and more government-sponsored Jewish settlements expropriating Palestinian holdings. The final status of the Palestinians remained in limbo, and so did that of Jerusalem, which many Christians and Muslims felt should be an autonomous holy city, free of any direct government control. Sadat, frustrated and unable to halt Begin, grew increasingly isolated within the Arab world. In 1981, he was assassinated by Islamic fundamentalists. Meanwhile, a new regional war threatened in Lebanon where tens of thousands of Palestinian refugees had relocated.

Carter was only the second American standing president ever to visit the Middle East. But his focus on the region exaggerated his foreign policy failures, and his expressed sympathy for the Palestinian plight weakened his support among some traditionally Democratic Jewish constituencies in his bid for reelection.

CARTER'S "CRISIS OF CONFIDENCE"

Carter's modest victories in Middle East negotiations, as it turned out, marked the final high point of his presidency. By 1979 it was clear that his domestic program for economic recovery had failed. To reassess his priorities, Carter withdrew with his staff to Camp David in July and emerged ten days later with a series of new energy proposals that Congress later rejected. But in his first public speech after the retreat, the president struck a nerve. The nation was experiencing a "crisis of confidence," he complained, and a feeling of "paralysis and stagnation and drift" hung like a dark cloud over the land. He called upon the people to change their attitude, to stop wallowing in personal problems, and to show more faith in their leaders.

Carter's "malaise speech," as it was called, backfired. His public approval rating hardly rose again from its low point of 26 percent. Many Americans resented the president for heaping blame on the public instead of taking responsibility for his own failures. News analysts attacked Carter with zeal, breaking stories of minor scandals in his administration and ridiculing the president in various ways. Far from pleasing the public, Carter lost its respect. His prospects for reelection therefore appeared to rest on his conduct of international affairs. If he could only put his human rights policy on a firm ground, move toward lasting peace in the Middle East, or strike a bargain with the Soviets on arms limitation, he might restore voter confidence. If not, his presidency would end after a single term.

(Mis)Handling the Unexpected

As Carter's first term came to a close, several crises erupted in foreign affairs, and long-standing divisions within the State Department drew the president first one way and then the other in response to them. Secretary of State Cyrus Vance recommended well-planned negotiations to soothe Soviet-U.S. relations and resolve disagreements with third world nations. National Security Adviser Zbigniew Brzezinski, a bitterly anticommunist Polish exile, adhered to a cold war view and interpreted events in even remote sections of Africa or South America as plays in a zero-sum game: wherever the United States lost influence, the Soviet Union gained, and vice versa. Mired in problems inherited from his predecessors, the president found himself disoriented by contradictory advice.

In 1979 the brutal Nicaraguan dictatorship of Anastasio Somoza, a long-time ally of the United States, was overthrown by the revolutionary Sandinista Liberation Front (which took its name from Augustino Sandino, a popular leader who had led the resistance against U.S. occupation forces in the 1920s and 1930s, see Chapter 23). The Sandinistas were not the kind of moderate successor to Somoza that Carter would have preferred. Nonetheless, when they asked for financial help, the president requested $75 million in aid for Nicaragua, but Congress turned him down. The Sandinistas aligned Nicaragua with Cuba and the Soviet Union and began to assist a revolutionary movement in El Salvador against a repressive anticommunist regime supported by the United States. Carter continued to back the Salvadoran government despite atrocities attributed to its ultraright partisans, including the assassination of Catholic archbishop Oscar Romero, who supported the revolutionaries. Following the rape and murder of four U.S. Catholic church women, apparently by members of the ultraright Salvadoran armed forces, who had been trained in the United States, peace activists and other Americans pleaded with Carter to withhold further military aid. Conservatives meanwhile demanded yet more funds to bolster the regime.

Africa posed similarly perplexing problems. Emerging from colonial rule, African nations vacillated between allying with the United States and courting the Soviet Union. In this tricky political territory, UN ambassador (and former civil rights leader) Andrew Young, the first major African American diplomat assigned to Africa, scored an important victory when he persuaded oil-rich Nigeria to resume economic relations with the United States. But Young could not persuade Carter to recognize the antiapartheid

Iranians demonstrate against the United States, burning an American flag and waving signs declaring "The U.S. Is Our Enemy." The Iran hostage crisis, which began November 4, 1979, when a mob of Iranians seized the U.S. embassy in Tehran, contributed to Carter's defeat at the polls the following year. Fifty-two embassy employees were held hostage for 444 days.

government of Angola, which had invited 20,000 Cuban troops to help in its fight against South Africa. Nor did Carter's and Young's verbal criticisms of the South African regime, unaccompanied by economic sanctions, satisfy black Africans. Then, suddenly, Young was forced from office because he had met privately with officials of the Palestine Liberation Organization (PLO). The PLO, although an opponent of apartheid, was also an enemy of Israel, and the meeting exposed Carter to bitter congressional criticism. Without Young, Carter proved even less effective in negotiating with antiapartheid leaders.

Carter had once advised Americans to put their "inordinate fear of Communism" behind them in order to focus more clearly on the pressing problems of the third world. By 1979, however, events in Central America and Africa gave the fear of communism a new twist and caused relations between the United States and the Soviet Union, which supported these revolutionary movements, to slide backward.

The Soviet invasion of neighboring Afghanistan produced a major stalemate. Two Afghan military coups during the 1970s had troubled the Soviets, who feared that the United States might forge an alliance with a new right-wing government and create yet another border fortified with U.S. missiles. After widespread rioting broke out, 30,000 Soviet troops invaded Afghanistan in December 1979 to prop up a communist government. The invasion precipitated a civil war between Islamic fundamentalist guerillas and the Soviet-backed government that was quickly labeled the "Russian Vietnam" by the American press. Despite their high-technology weapons, the Soviets were stymied by the guerillas, who were intimately familiar with their territory and armed by the United States. As the war bogged down, stories of disillusionment and drug use reminiscent of Vietnam emerged, but this time involving Soviet soldiers. The United States called for an immediate withdrawal of Soviet troops.

President Carter responded to these events with his own corollary to the Monroe Doctrine. The so-called Carter Doctrine asserted U.S. determination to protect its interests in yet another area of the world, the Persian Gulf. Carter acted on the advice of Brzezinski, who believed that the Soviet Union would soon try to secure for itself a warm-water port on the gulf, an area rich in oil and now vital to U.S. interests. The president backed up his policy by halting exports of grain and high technology to the Soviet Union, asking American athletes to boycott the 1980 Olympic Games in Moscow, reinstituting registration for the military draft in the United States, and beginning what would become a massive U.S. arms buildup during the 1980s.

By the end of Carter's term, the cold war had once again heated up. In his State of the Union Address in January 1980, Carter pledged that "the United States will remain the strongest of all nations." With the economy still hurting from the effects of cold war spending, Carter called for yet another increase in the military budget. He also signed Presidential Directive 59, which guaranteed the production of weapons necessary to win a prolonged nuclear war. The prospect of peace and détente dried up.

The Iran Hostage Crisis

On November 4, 1979, Iranian fundamentalists seized the U.S. embassy in Tehran; for the next 444 days they held fifty-two embassy employees hostage. This event made President Carter's previous problems seem small by comparison. "I-R-A-N," Rosalynn Carter later wrote. "Those four letters had become a curse to me."

For decades, U.S. foreign policy in the Middle East had depended on a friendly government in Iran. After the CIA had helped to overthrow the reformist, constitutional government of Prime Minister Mohammed Mossadegh and restored Shah Mohammed Reza Pahlavi to the throne in 1953, millions of U.S. dollars poured into the Iranian economy and the shah's armed forces. By the late 1970s, Iran had become the most Westernized society in the Middle East. President Carter toasted the shah for his "great leadership" and overlooked the rampant corruption in the Iranian government and a well-organized opposition led by the Islamic fundamentalist Ayatollah Ruholla Khomeini. Revolutionary unrest erupted in 1978, and in January 1979, the shah was forced to flee the country.

After Carter allowed the deposed shah to enter the United States to be treated for cancer in November, a group of Khomeini's followers retaliated by storming the U.S. embassy and taking the staff as hostages. Islamic fundamentalists paraded in the streets of Tehran waving placards with anti-American and anti-Carter slogans and calling the United States "the Great Satan."

Cyrus Vance assured Carter that only negotiations could free the Americans while Brzezinski lobbied for decisive action. Carter, beginning his reelection campaign, ordered a nighttime helicopter rescue mission, but decided to abort it when it encountered mechanical problems and a sandstorm. One helicopter crashed, leaving eight Americans dead; their burned corpses were displayed in television broadcasts by the enraged Iranians. Short of an all-out attack, which surely would have resulted in the hostages' death, the United States had used up its options.

The political and economic fallout was heavy. Cyrus Vance resigned, the first secretary of state in sixty-five years to leave office over a political difference with the president. By supporting the shah, whose secret police were notorious for their brutality, Carter had violated his own human rights policy, which was to have been his distinctive mark on U.S. foreign affairs. He had also failed in the one area he had pronounced to be central to the future of the United States—energy. During the hostage crisis, as the price of oil rose by 60 percent, inflation once again soared.

The 1980 Election

Jimmy Carter began his campaign for renomination and reelection in what seemed to be the worst possible light. The *Wall Street Journal* commented in August 1980 that "one continues to look in vain for anything beyond his own reflection that he wants to accomplish with the power of his office, for any consistent purpose or vision." Carter had no significant accomplishments to stand on, not even a program for the future. His Democratic rival from 1976, Washington Senator Henry Jackson, described him as "washed up."

One more surprise dogged Carter. During May, Fidel Castro invited thousands of Cubans, including political prisoners and petty criminals, to leave the island. Dubbed the *"Marielitos,"* (because they left the Cuban port of Mariel), these Cuban refugees landed in Florida and demanded asylum. Unable to convince them to leave and unwilling to deport them, Carter established camps that were, according to the inmates, inhumane. Many Americans meanwhile demanded the return of "the boat people" to Cuba. Unconvincingly, Carter answered, "We ought to be thankful we have a country that people want to come to."

Carter's bid for renomination depended more on his incumbency than on his popularity. Delegates at the Democratic National Convention unenthusiastically endorsed Carter along with his running mate Walter Mondale, a similarly uninspiring campaigner. The Republicans nominated former California governor Ronald Reagan, who had come close to displacing Gerald Ford in 1976. Former CIA director and Texas oil executive George Bush, more moderate than Reagan, became the Republican candidate for vice president. Moral Majority placed itself squarely in Reagan's camp, promising a "conservative revolu-

CHRONOLOGY

1973 *Roe v. Wade* legalizes abortion
Arab embargo sparks oil crisis in the United States
Construction of Alaska oil pipeline begins

1974 Richard Nixon resigns presidency; Gerald Ford takes office
President Ford pardons Nixon and introduces anti-inflation program
Community Development Act funds programs for urban improvement
Coalition of Labor Union Women is formed

1975 Unemployment rate reaches nearly 9 percent
South Vietnamese government falls to communists
Antibusing protests break out in Boston
New York City government declares itself bankrupt

1976 Percentage of African Americans attending college peaks at 9.3 percent and begins a decline
Hyde Amendment restricts use of Medicaid funds for abortions
Tom Wolfe declares "the Me Decade"
James Earl Carter is elected president

1977 President Carter announces human rights as major tenet in foreign policy
Department of Energy is established

1978 *Bakke v. University of California* decision places new limits on affirmative action programs
Senator Edward Kennedy calls attention to "a permanent underclass"
Panama Canal Treaties arrange for turning the canal over to Panama by 2000
Camp David meeting sets terms for Middle East Peace
California passes Proposition 13, cutting taxes and government social programs

1979 Three Mile Island nuclear accident threatens a meltdown
Moral Majority is formed
SALT II treaty is signed in Vienna but later stalls in the Senate
Nicaraguan Revolution overthrows Anastasio Somoza
Iranian fundamentalists seize the U.S. embassy in Tehran and hold hostages 444 days
Soviets invade Afghanistan
Equal Rights Amendment, three states short of ratification, gets a three-year extension but eventually dies anyway

1980 United States boycotts Olympic Games in Moscow
Inflation reaches 13.5 percent
Ronald Reagan is elected president

tion" to end legal abortion, reinstate school prayer, and bear down on communism. Senator Jesse Helms's Congressional Club contributed $4.6 million to the Reagan campaign and funded strident campaigns targeting senatorial liberals.

The Republican campaign made the most of Carter's mismanagement of both domestic and foreign affairs. Reagan repeatedly asked voters, "Are you better off now than you were four years ago?" Although critics questioned Reagan's competence, the attractive, soft-spoken actor shrugged off criticisms while spotlighting the many problems besetting the country.

The Republican ticket cruised to victory. Carter won only 41.2 percent of the popular vote to Reagan's 50.9 percent, 49 votes in the electoral college to Reagan's 489. Liberal Republican John Anderson, running as an independent, won nearly 6 million votes, or 6.6 percent of the popular vote. The Republicans won control of the Senate for the first time since 1952 and with the largest majority since 1928. Still, most Americans remained apathetic toward the electoral process. Barely half of the eligible voters turned out in the 1980 election, bringing Ronald Reagan into office with a thin mandate of 25 percent.

CONCLUSION

Gerald Ford's failure to set a new course either domestically or internationally had completed the Republican debacle of Richard Nixon's administration. Democrat Jimmy Carter, elected to office on a promise to restore public confidence in government, suffered repeated embarrassments and political defeats. Hopeful signs appeared mainly in local communities in the form of campaigns for better schools, neighborhoods, and protection from toxic wastes. Grass-roots activism cut across political lines. At the national level, an unprecedented number of voters disengaged from the process and seemed to suffer from a deep malaise about the machinations of government.

As Carter's tenure in office came to a close, the economic problems that concerned most Americans were exacerbated still further by military spending and dependence on foreign oil. The focus of U.S. foreign policy had begun to shift from the Soviet Union to the Middle East, where diplomatic maneuvers brought neither national security nor a fresh supply of low-cost crude oil. The erosion of America's industrial base meanwhile mirrored the nation's decline from unquestioned superpower status. Like the Soviet Union, the United States had paid too much for the cold war.

REVIEW QUESTIONS

1. Discuss the impact of the accident at the Three Mile Island nuclear plant on communities in the eastern states. How did fears generated by the near meltdown combine with anxieties provoked by the oil crisis?
2. Evaluate the significance of the major population shifts in the United States from the 1940s through the 1970s. How do these shifts relate to changes in the American economy? What was their impact on local and national politics?
3. Discuss the character of the "new poverty" of the 1970s. Why did the poor comprise mainly women and children?
4. Discuss the connections between the energy crisis and the rise of the environmental movement during the 1970s.
5. Why was the 1970s dubbed "the Me Decade"? Interpret the decline of liberalism and the rise of conservative political groups. How did these changes affect Carter's role as president and his chances for reelection?
6. Was the Iran hostage crisis a turning point in American politics or only a thorn in Carter's reelection campaign?

RECOMMENDED READING

Peter N. Carroll, *It Seemed Like Nothing Happened* (1983). A broad overview of the 1970s, including its political and cultural aspects. Carroll captures the everyday lives of Americans, especially their frustrations over their failure to achieve according to their expectations, and finds a bitter comedy in the blunders of the era's mediocre political leaders.

Susan M. Hartmann, *From Margin to Mainstream: American Women and Politics since 1960* (1989). An interpretation of women's growing role in American politics. Hartmann analyzes the important developments of the 1970s, most pointedly women's influence on the Democratic Party, and looks at the forces that pushed the Equal Rights Amendment through Congress but failed to see it ratified in the states.

Jerome L. Himmelstein, *To the Right: The Transformation of American Conservatism* (1990). The story of the decline of "Old Right" fiscal conservatives, isolationists, and Republican "centrists" during the 1970s and the rise of the "New Right" based in evangelical Protestantism. Himmelstein analyzes the New Right's ability to rally support for cold war foreign policy and the rollback of social welfare programs at both federal and state levels of government.

Michael B. Katz, *Improving Poor People: The Welfare State, the "Underclass," and Urban Schools as History* (1995). Provides a broad overview of the history of urban poverty, welfare policy, and public education. Katz examines the "underclass" debates of the 1970s as a function of the interaction between politics and economics within the postindustrial inner city.

William B. Quandt, *Camp David: Peacemaking and Politics* (1986). An insider's story of Jimmy Carter's greatest triumph. Quandt analyzes the Middle Eastern diplomacy as the centerpiece of Carter's otherwise unsuccessful program of world peace through negotiations and better understanding.

Edwin Schur, *The Awareness Trap: Self Absorption Instead of Social Change* (1977). A description of the various contemporary "awareness" movements. Schur includes detailed examples of how programs of self-improvement and religious mysticism appealed to people disoriented by social change and willing to pay money to find "meaning" in their lives.

James L. Sundquist, *The Decline and Resurgence of Congress* (1981). A close political study of changing relations between the two key branches of government. Sundquist underlines the revival of congressional strength after President Johnson's successful broadening of executive powers and the bipartisan tug of war that took place between Congress and its 1970s counterparts: the often haughty Nixon, the congressional-style "weak" president Gerald Ford, and the distant Jimmy Carter.

Andrew Szasz, *EcoPopulism: Toxic Waste and the Movement for Environmental Justice* (1994). A careful analysis of a turning point in federal regulation of toxic waste. Szasz shows how the prevention of pollution, previously considered a local issue, through strengthened state and federal regulations became a national issue and a springboard for the environmental movement.

Cyrus R. Vance, *Hard Choices: Critical Years of America's Foreign Policy* (1983). A former secretary of state's day-to-day recollections of his time in office during the Carter years. Vance, a career diplomat, reviews the crucial policy decisions concerning Afghanistan and the Middle East as well as the factors that caused him to resign from the Carter administration.

Winifred D. Wandersee, *On the Move: American Women in the 1970s* (1988). A highly readable overview of the changes that brought American women into political life but also kept them at the margins of power. This study includes a close description of the National Organization for Women as well as media personalities, such as Jane Fonda, who gave feminism a public face.

ADDITIONAL BIBLIOGRAPHY

Stagflation and the Oil Crisis

Michael A. Bernstein and David E. Adler, eds., *Understanding American Economic Decline* (1994)
Gordon L. Clark, *Unions and Communities under Siege* (1989)
Sara M. Evans and Barbara J. Nelson, *Wage Justice: Comparable Worth and the Paradox of Technocratic Reform* (1989)
Daniel F. Ford, *Three Mile Island: 30 Minutes to Meltdown* (1982)
Claudia Goldin, *Understanding the Gender Gap: An Economic History of American Women* (1990)
Burton I. Kaufman, *The Arab Middle East and the United States: Inter-Arab Rivalry and Superpower Diplomacy* (1996)
Robert Leppzer, *Voices from Three Mile Island* (1980)
Emma Rothschild, *Paradise Lost: The Decline of the Auto-Industrial Age* (1973)
Bruce J. Schulman, *From Cotton Belt to Sun Belt* (1990)
Richard Sherrill, *The Oil Follies of 1970–1980* (1983)
Jeffrey K. Stine, *Mixing the Waters: Environmental Politics and the Building of the Tennessee-Tombigbee Waterway* (1993)
Jon Teaford, *Cities of the Heartland: The Rise and Fall of the Industrial Midwest* (1993)

"Lean Year" Presidents

Richard J. Barnet, *The Lean Years* (1980)
George C. Edwards III, *At the Margins: Presidential Leadership of Congress* (1989)
Charles O. Jones, *The Trusteeship Presidency: Jimmy Carter and the United States Congress* (1988)
Burton I. Kaufman, *The Presidency of James Earl Carter, Jr.* (1993)
Alexander P. Lamis, *The Two-Party South*, 2d ed. (1990)
Gary Sick, *October Surprise* (1991)
Alan Ware, *The Breakdown of the Democratic Party Organization, 1940–1980* (1985)

The New Poverty

Chicago Tribune, *The American Millstone: An Examination of the Nation's Permanent Underclass* (1986)
James D. Cockcroft, *Outlaws in the Promised Land: Mexican Immigrant Workers and America's Future* (1986)
Barbara Ehrenreich, *Fear of Falling: The Inner Life of the Middle Class* (1989)
Jacqueline Jones, *The Dispossessed: America's Underclasses from the Civil War to the Present* (1992)
Michael B. Katz, ed., *The "Underclass" Debate* (1993)
Ruth Sidel, *The Plight of Poor Women in Affluent America* (1986)
Lenore J. Weitzman, *The Divorce Revolution: The Unexpected Social and Economic Consequences for Women and Children in America* (1985)
William Julius Wilson, *The Declining Significance of Race: Blacks and Changing American Institutions*, rev. ed. (1980)

Grass-roots Politics and the New Conservatism

Carl Abbott, *The New Urban America: Growth and Politics in the Sunbelt Cities* (1987)
Henry F. Bedford, *Seabrook Station: Citizen Politics and Nuclear Power* (1990)
Steve Bruce, *The Rise and Fall of the New Christian Right* (1988)
Pamela Johnston Conover and Virginia Gray, *Feminism and the New Right: Conflict over the American Family* (1983)
Craig Cox, *Storefront Revolution: Food Co-ops and the Counterculture* (1994)

Robert M. Entman, *Democracy without Citizens: Media and the Decay of American Politics* (1989)

Marian Faux, *Roe v. Wade* (1988)

Suzanne Garment, *Scandal: The Crisis of Mistrust in American Politics* (1991)

Joan Hoff-Wilson, ed., *Rights of Passage: The Past and Future of the ERA* (1986)

Rebecca Klatch, *Women of the New Right* (1987)

Michael C. D. MacDonald, *America's Cities: A Report on the Myth of the Urban Renaissance* (1984)

Nicol C. Rae, *The Decline and Fall of the Liberal Republicans* (1989)

Suzanne Staggenborg, *The Pro-Choice Movement: Organization and Activism in the Abortion Conflict* (1991)

Steven M. Tipton, *Getting Saved from the Sixties* (1982)

William Clyde Wilcox, *God's Warriors: The Christian Right in Twentieth-Century America* (1992)

Robert Wuthnow, *The Restructuring of American Religion* (1988)

Foreign Policy

Warren Christopher, et al., *American Hostages in Iran* (1985)

Walter LaFeber, *The Panama Canal* (1978, 1989)

Morris Morley, *Washington, Somoza and the Sandinistas: State and Regime in U.S. Policy toward Nicaragua, 1969–1981* (1994)

A. Glenn Mower Jr., *Human Rights and American Foreign Policy* (1987)

Nancy Peabody Newell and Richard S. Newell, *The Struggle for Afghanistan* (1981)

Robert A. Pastor, *Condemned to Repetition* (1987)

Lars Schoultz, *Human Rights and U.S. Policy toward Latin America* (1981)

Sandy Vogelgesang, *American Dream, Global Nightmare* (1980)

Biography

Peter Carroll, *Famous in America: Jane Fonda, George Wallace, and Phyllis Schlafly* (1986)

Jimmy Carter, *Keeping Faith: Memoirs of a President/Jimmy Carter* (1982, 1995)

Rosalynn Carter, *First Lady from Plains* (1984)

Betty Ford, with Chris Chase, *Betty, a Glad Awakening* (1987)

Ernest B. Furgurson, *The Hard Right: The Rise of Jesse Helms* (1986)

Carolyn G. Heilbrun, *The Education of a Woman: A Life of Gloria Steinem* (1995)

John C. Jeffries, *Justice Lewis F. Powell, Jr.* (1994)

David S. McLellan, *Cyrus Vance* (1985)

Kenneth E. Morris, *Jimmy Carter: American Moralist* (1996)

Richard Reeves, *A Ford and not a Lincoln* (1975)

Kenneth S. Stern, *Loud Hawk: The United States versus the American Indian Movement* (1994)

CHAPTER THIRTY-ONE

THE CONSERVATIVE ASCENDANCY

SINCE 1980

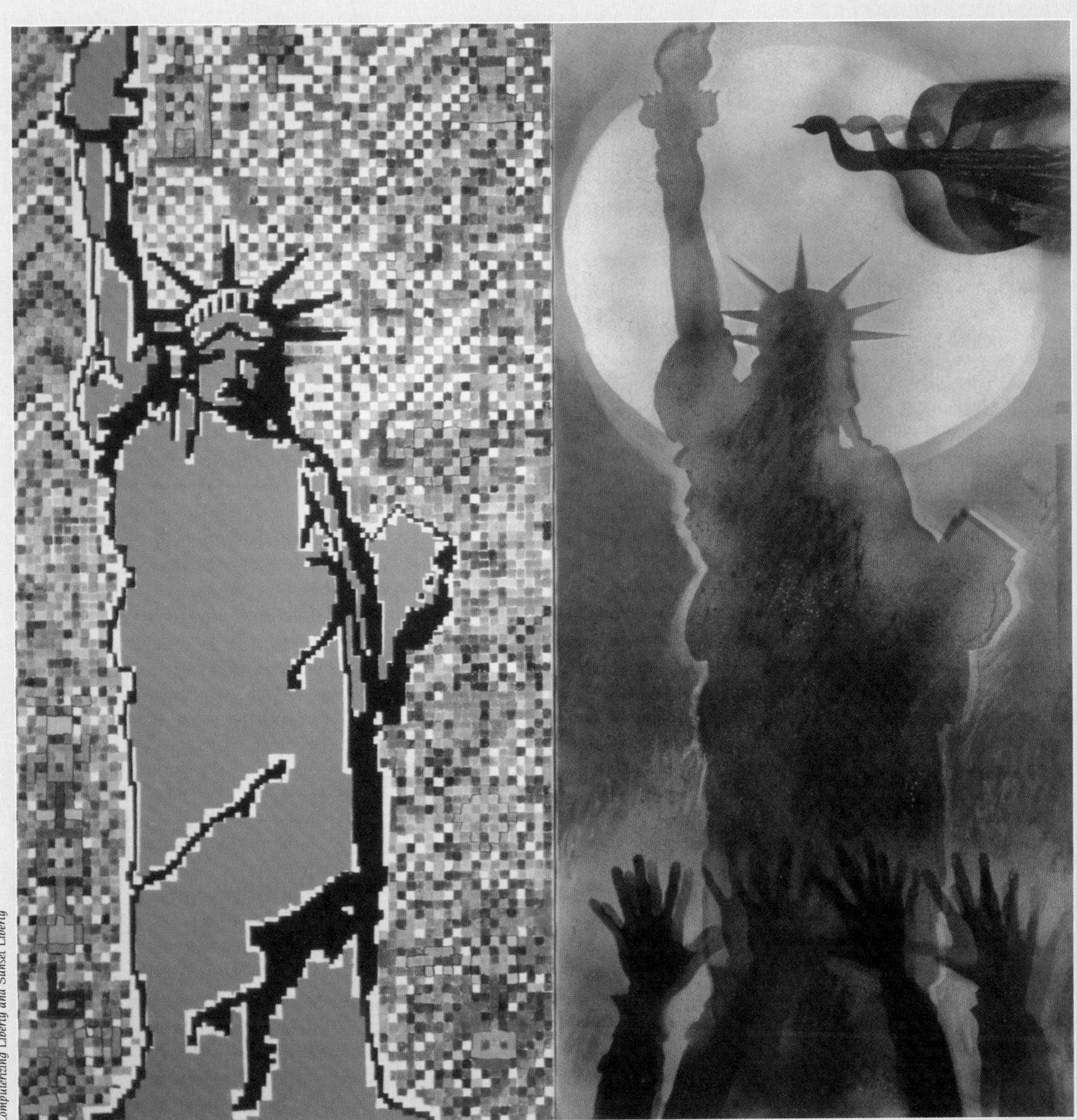

Computerizing Liberty and Sunset Liberty

Chapter Outline

AMERICAN COMMUNITIES
Virtual Communities on the Electronic Frontier

When the moving van carrying lawyer Mike Godwin's possessions across the country from Cambridge, Massachusetts, to Washington state caught fire, most of his belongings were destroyed. In a new city, with a new job, Godwin felt uprooted and alone. "I didn't know my new neighbors in Washington," he recalled, "but I knew who my cyberspace neighbors were." Godwin turned to his neighbors on the Whole Earth 'Lectronic Link (WELL), an electronic community of 8,000 based in Sausalito, California. Using his personal computer, Godwin posted news of his misfortune, including a list of books he had lost, books he had been collecting since his youth "And for the next six months," he reported, "not a day went by that I didn't get a book, or a box of books, in the mail."

Cyberspace is the conceptual region occupied by people linked through computers and communications networks. It began with ARPANET, the first computer network, which was created by the Department of Defense in the early 1970s. Computer enthusiasts known as "hackers" created unexpected grass-roots spin-offs from ARPANET, including electronic mail, computer conferencing, and computer bulletin board systems.

In the mid-1980s the boom in cheap personal computers capable of linking to the worldwide telecommunications network began a population explosion in cyberspace. By then tens of thousands of researchers and scholars at universities and in private industry were linked to the Internet—the U.S. government-sponsored successor to ARPANET—through their institutions' computer centers. "Virtual communities" emerged from the Internet (or Net) whenever a group of users with a common interest reached a critical mass.

By 1998 there were more than 40 million cybercitizens in a variety of thriving virtual communities that suggested both the democratic and exploitative possibilities of cyberspace. WELL, for example, began in 1985 as a spin-off of the Whole Earth Review, a magazine with deep roots in the counterculture and ecology movements of the 1960s. Among its original goals were to make it easier for people in the San Francisco Bay area to communicate with each other, to provide sophisticated computer conferencing services, and to provide users who wanted it with electronic mail. Users were charged a small monthly fee plus an hourly rate for the time they spent "online." WELL initially attracted adventurous Bay area computer professionals and journalists, many of whom were given free accounts in exchange for "hosting" conversations. Passionate fans of the rock group the Grateful Dead—known as "Deadheads"—provided another early base of users.

WELL's subscriber list soon grew to the thousands. "What it is is up to us," became the motto of this virtual community. In scores of "public conferences" members of the WELL exchanged information on a wide range of topics under headings such as arts and letters, recreation, parenting, social responsibility and politics, body-mind-health, computers, and, of course, the Grateful Dead. Admission to "private conferences," which covered an equally broad range of subjects, was restricted to those invited by conference hosts. WELL was unusual among virtual communities in that it had a strong geographic locus, the Bay Area, making it easy for members to meet "I.T.R.W."— in the real world—if they chose. "We rent a nice site under the Golden Gate Bridge once a month and sort of see what happens," said Gail Williams, WELL's conferencing manager. As many as 500 people showed up for these gatherings.

Anger, feuds, and "flaming" with abusive interchanges were not unknown among WELL subscribers. But the sense of communal support was strong. For many the virtual community replaced more traditional centers of community like neighborhood, church, and family. Those who faced illness or loss were consoled by "beams" from electronic well-wishers. Howard Rheingold, one WELL pioneer, attributed its appeal to "the hunger for community that grows in the breasts of people around the world as more and more informal public spaces disappear from our real lives." WELL also posed a challenge to corporate-dominated communications media, and it offered a model for revitalizing citizen-based democracy.

Other services, such as Prodigy, Compuserve, and America Online, provided powerful alternatives to the utopian WELL. These nationwide services evolved not from the grass roots but from corporate efforts to commercialize cyberspace. By the mid-1990s each counted between 500,000 and 2 million subscribers. Unlike WELL, they emphasized consumer services over interactive communication. Prodigy, a joint venture of IBM and Sears, cost nearly $1 billion to launch. For a flat monthly fee Prodigy users could play games, make airplane reservations, send electronic mail, and discuss issues in public forums. They also received a steady stream of advertising and had to agree to give Prodigy the right to edit public messages.

By blurring the lines between the public and private spheres, virtual communities created a whole new set of legal, political, and ethical issues that have yet to be fully resolved. In 1995 Congress passed the Communications Decency Act, which imposed jail terms and fines on those who created or solicited online material deemed "obscene, lewd, lascivious, filthy, or indecent." But in 1997 a unanimous Supreme Court found the act unconstitutional because it abridged the freedom of speech protected by the First Amendment. Noting that "the growth of the Internet has been and continues to be phenomenal," Justice John Paul Stevens' opinion argued that "we presume that governmental regulation of the content of speech is more likely to interfere with the free exchange of ideas than to encourage it." Those who worried about protecting children from "cyberporn" looked to new "gateway" technologies, which would allow parents to block out offensive material from their computers. But free speech advocates and the Internet industry continued to argue that no law can effectively monitor and regulate content on the global web without compromising fundamental freedoms.

Perhaps more ominous than the threat of legal restrictions on the internet is the Orwellian flip side of the utopian dream of virtual community. The same technology that permits citizens to communicate in new ways also opens them to government and corporate surveillance. As more and more intimate and private data about individuals moves into cyberspace, the potential for abuse of that information increases.

Virtual communities are still in their infancy. They will continue to evolve as more Americans join them, but the forms they take and the solutions to the problems they pose resist easy prediction. Can the democratic promise of cyberspace be fulfilled, for example, if poverty or lack of education bar a substantial part of the American population from access to computer technology? Even WELL experienced discontent and grumbling as growth created crowded, impersonal conferences and overloaded the system's technical infrastructure. In 1994 the nonprofit organization that founded WELL sold it to California businessman Bruce Katz, who had made a fortune manufacturing Rockport shoes. The relentless commercialization of cyberspace accelerated in the late 1990s as millions of businesses explored the profit potential of selling goods and services over the Internet. By 1998 there were some 320 million Web sites in the United States, representing everything from large corporations to fringe political groups to personal "home pages." At the close of the twentieth century, more and more Americans were finding—and inventing—versions of community on the electronic frontier of cyberspace.

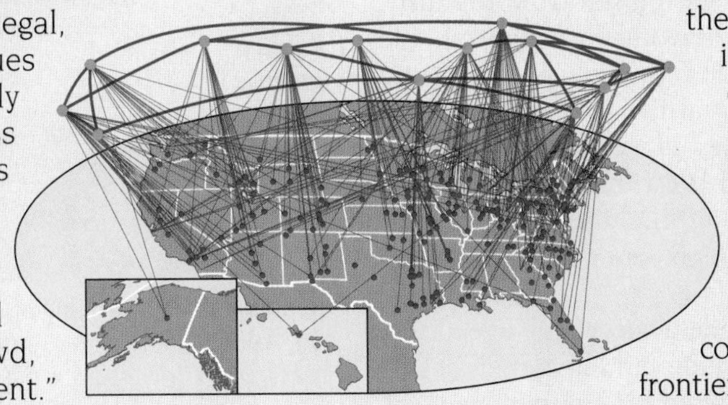

KEY TOPICS

- Domestic policies under the Reagan administration
- Reagan era foreign policy: Soviet Union, Central America, Middle East
- Structural shifts in the economy and culture of the 1980s
- The growth of inequality
- The new immigration
- Contradictions and difficulties attending America's role in world affairs
- The Clinton presidency and the resurgent right

THE REAGAN REVOLUTION

No other twentieth-century president except Franklin D. Roosevelt left as deep a personal imprint on American politics as Ronald Reagan. Ironically, Reagan himself began his political life as an ardent New Deal Democrat. Even after his transformation into a conservative Republican, Reagan regularly invoked the words and deeds of FDR. Reagan admired Roosevelt as an inspirational leader who had led the nation through depression and war. But by the time he entered the White House in 1981, Reagan had rejected the activist welfare state legacy of the New Deal era. Following his overwhelming electoral victories in 1980 and 1984, Reagan and his conservative allies tried to radically reshape the political and social landscape of the nation.

The Great Communicator

Ronald Reagan was born in 1911 and raised in the small town of Dixon, Illinois. His father, a salesman, was an alcoholic who had a tough time holding a job. His strong-willed mother was a fundamentalist Christian who kept the family together despite frequent moves. During the Great Depression his father obtained a Works Progress Administration (WPA) job that helped the family survive hard times. As a child, Reagan learned to disconnect himself from the difficult scenes at home, withdrawing into himself. He took refuge in his own world of imaginary stories and plays. He identified with real-life sports heroes like Babe Ruth and Jack Dempsey as well as with fictional figures, heroes of the Wild West. Encouraged by his mother, Reagan began acting in church plays and in productions at Eureka College, from which he graduated in 1932.

In 1937 Reagan made a successful screen test with the Warner Brothers studio in Hollywood, beginning an acting career that lasted for a quarter-century. He was never a big star, appearing in scores of mostly "B" movies, but he became a skilled actor. On screen, he was tall, handsome, and affable, and his characters usually projected an optimistic and sunny personality. In later years, Reagan cheerfully credited his political

Ronald and Nancy Reagan at the Inaugural Ball, January 20, 1981. The Reagans, supported by a circle of wealthy conservative friends from the business world and Hollywood, brought a lavish style to the White House that helped define the culture of the 1980s.

success to his acting experience. He told one interviewer: "An actor knows two important things—to be honest in what he's doing and to be in touch with the audience. That's not bad advice for a politician either. My actor's instincts simply told me to speak the truth as I saw it and felt it."

In Hollywood, Reagan became active in union affairs. While serving as president of the Screen Actors Guild from 1947 to 1952, he became a leader of the anticommunist forces in Hollywood and began to distance himself from New Deal liberalism. In 1954 Reagan became the host of a new national television program, *General Electric Theater,* and began a long stint as a national spokesman for GE. He toured GE plants and surrounding communities across the country, publicizing the TV show and making speeches on behalf of the company. These talks celebrated the achievements of corporate America and emphasized the dangers of big government, excessive liberalism, and radical trade unions.

Reagan's GE experience made him a significant public figure and allowed him to perfect a political style and a conservative message. He switched his party affiliation to the Republicans and became a popular fund-raiser and speaker for the California GOP. Reagan took a leading role in conservative Republican Barry Goldwater's 1964 presidential campaign. A televised address on Goldwater's behalf thrust Reagan himself to national prominence. By this time, Reagan had formulated a standard speech that hammered home his conservative message: antitax, anticommunism, antigovernment. The attack on big government was at the core of the Reagan message. He lashed out at the growing government bureaucracy and celebrated the achievements of entrepreneurs unfettered by governmental regulation or aid. He invoked the nation's founders, who, he claimed, knew "that outside of its legitimate functions, government does nothing as well or as economically as the private sector of the economy."

A group of wealthy, conservative southern Californians encouraged Reagan to run for office himself. These backers, most of whom had made fortunes in California real estate and the oil business, saw themselves as self-made men and shared a basic distrust of government intervention in the economy. With their financial and political support, Reagan defeated Democratic governor Edmund G. Brown in 1966 and won reelection in 1970. As governor, Reagan cut the state welfare rolls, placed limits on the number of state employees, and funneled a large share of state tax revenues back to local governments. He vigorously attacked student protesters and black militants, thereby tapping into the conservative backlash against the activism of the 1960s.

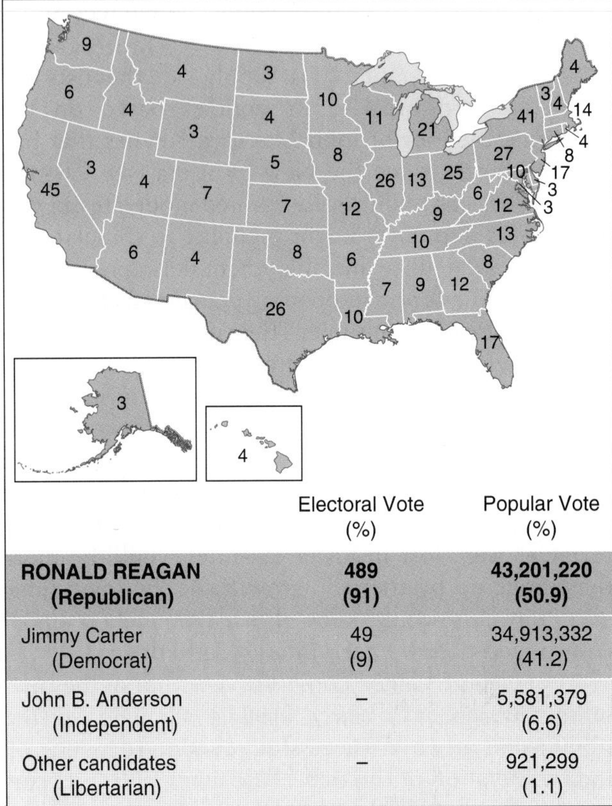

	Electoral Vote (%)	Popular Vote (%)
RONALD REAGAN (Republican)	**489 (91)**	**43,201,220 (50.9)**
Jimmy Carter (Democrat)	49 (9)	34,913,332 (41.2)
John B. Anderson (Independent)	–	5,581,379 (6.6)
Other candidates (Libertarian)	–	921,299 (1.1)

The Election of 1980 *Ronald Reagan won a landslide victory over incumbent Jimmy Carter, who managed to carry only six states and the District of Columbia. Reagan attracted millions of traditionally Democratic voters to the Republican camp.*

As governor, Reagan also perfected a laid-back style of governing that left most of the actual work to his aides and allowed him to concentrate on speech making and fund-raising. In 1980 he became the Republican candidate for president after failing to win the nomination in 1968 and 1976. Exploiting his strengths as an actor and salesman, he was an extremely likable and effective campaigner. The conservatism that had been forced to the backwaters of American politics in 1964 now reemerged as the mainstream. Jimmy Carter's political weakness also helped the Republicans to carry the Senate for the first time since 1952. When Reagan entered the White House in January 1981, his supporters confidently predicted that the "Reagan revolution" would usher in a new age in American political life.

Reaganomics

In the 1980 election Republicans successfully exploited popular discontent over the stagflation of the Carter years—an unprecedented combination of recession, high inflation, and the highest interest rates in American history. During the Reagan presidency, supply-side economic theory, dubbed "Reaganomics," dominated the administration's thinking and helped redirect American economic policy.

Since the mid-1970s, supply-side theorists had urged a sharp break with policies based on the economic theories of John Maynard Keynes that had been dominant since the New Deal era (see Chapter 24). Keynesians traditionally favored moderate tax cuts and increases in government spending to stimulate the economy and reduce unemployment during recessions. Putting more money in people's pockets, they argued, would increase consumer demand and stimulate economic expansion. By contrast, supply-siders called for simultaneous tax cuts and reductions in public spending. This combination, they claimed, would give private entrepreneurs and investors greater incentives to start businesses, take risks, invest capital—and thereby create new wealth and jobs. Whatever revenues were lost in lower tax rates would be more than made up by the new growth. At the same time, spending cuts would keep the federal deficit under control and thereby keep interest rates down.

George Gilder, conservative author of the best-selling *Wealth and Poverty* (1981), summarized the supply-side view: "A successful economy depends on the proliferation of the rich." Perceiving entrepreneurs as the heroes of the American economy, Gilder concluded, "To help the poor and middle classes, one must cut the taxes of the rich." On the political level, supply-siders looked to reward the most loyal Republican constituencies: the affluent and the business community. At the same time, they hoped to reduce the flow of federal dollars received by two core Democratic constituencies: the recipients and professional providers of health and welfare programs.

Reagan quickly won approval for two key pieces of legislation based on these ideas. The Economic Recovery Tax Act of 1981, passed by a very willing Congress, cut income and corporate taxes by $747 billion over five years. For individuals, the act cut taxes across the board by 5 percent in 1981, 10 percent in 1982, and another 10 percent in 1983. It also reduced the maximum tax on all income from 70 percent to 50 percent, lowered the maximum capital gains tax—the tax paid on profitable investments—from 28 percent to 20 percent, and eliminated the distinction between earned and unearned income. This last measure proved a boon to the small and richest fraction of the population, which derives most of its income from rent, dividends, and interest instead of from wages.

With the help of conservative southern and western Democrats in the House, the administration also pushed through a comprehensive program of spending cuts awkwardly known as the Omnibus Reconciliation Act of 1981. This bill mandated cuts of $136 billion in federal spending for the period 1982–84, affecting more than 200 social and cultural programs. The hardest-hit areas included federal appropriations for education, the environment, health, housing, urban aid, food stamps, research on synthetic fuels, and the arts. The conservative coalition in the House allowed only one vote on the entire package of spending cuts, a strategy that allowed conservatives to slash appropriations for a wide variety of domestic programs in one fell swoop. One leading House liberal, Democrat Leon Panetta of California, lamented: "We are dealing with over 250 programs with no committee consideration, no committee hearings, no debate and no opportunity to offer amendments."

The Reagan administration quickly created a chilly atmosphere for organized labor. In the summer of 1981 some 13,000 members of the Professional Air Traffic Controllers Organization (PATCO) went on strike. As federal employees, PATCO members had been bargaining with the government. The president retaliated against the strikers by firing them, and the Federal Aviation Administration started a crash program to replace them. Conservative appointees to the National Labor Relations Board and the federal courts set an anti-union tone throughout the government. The militantly antilabor mood in Washington, combined with the decline of the nation's manufacturing infrastructure, kept trade unions on the defensive. By 1990 fewer than 15 percent of American workers belonged to a labor union, the lowest proportion since before World War II.

Reagan appointed conservatives to head the Environmental Protection Agency, the Occupational Safety and Health Administration, and the Consumer Product Safety Commission. These individuals abolished or weakened hundreds of rules governing environmental protection, workplace safety, and consumer protection, all in the interest of increasing the efficiency and productivity of business. The deregulatory fever dominated cabinet departments as well. Secretary of the Interior James Watt typified the administration's desire to privatize the federal government, opening up formerly protected wilderness areas and wetlands to private developers. Secretary of Transportation Andrew L. "Drew" Lewis Jr. eliminated regulations passed in the 1970s aimed at reducing air pollution and improving fuel efficiency in cars and trucks.

The Reagan administration aggressively curbed the federal government's regulatory authority in the business sphere as well. Following the tenets of supply-side economics, Reagan weakened the Antitrust Division of the Justice Department, the Securities and Exchange Commission, and the Federal Home Loan Bank Board. Large corporations,

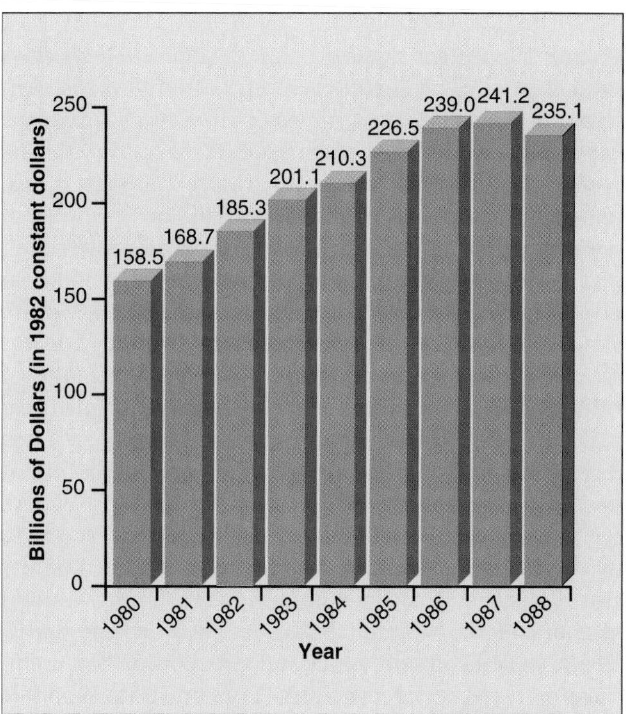

U.S. Military Spending, 1980–1988 *Measured in constant dollars, American military spending grew nearly 50 percent between 1981 and 1987.*

Source: Robert Griffith, ed., *Major Problems in American History since 1945* (Lexington, MA: D.C. Heath, 1992), p. 694. Statistics compiled by David Murphy.

Wall Street stock brokerages, investment banking houses, and the savings and loan industry were all allowed to operate with a much freer hand than ever before. By the late 1980s, the unfortunate consequences of this freedom would become apparent in a series of unprecedented scandals in the nation's financial markets and banking industry.

Military Buildup

During the 1980 election campaign, Reagan argued that American military capability had been seriously weakened since the Vietnam War. His calls to "restore America's defenses" helped reinforce the public perception that President Jimmy Carter had dealt ineffectively with the Iran hostage crisis. For Reagan, there was no contradiction between his campaign vows to cut the cost of government and his intention to increase defense spending. Reduced government spending and a strengthened military posture were both ideological linchpins of Reagan's world view. Military strength symbolized the power of the nation rather than the authority of government.

The Reagan administration greatly accelerated a sharp increase in defense spending that began during the last two years of the Carter presidency. The Pentagon's annual budget expanded from $169 billion in 1981 to $239 billion in 1986. Secretary of Defense Caspar Weinberger and Secretary of State Alexander Haig persistently lobbied Congress for a more potent nuclear arsenal, including the MX missile, based mostly in western states, and the deployment of Cruise and Pershing missiles in western Europe. In 1983, President Reagan proclaimed his Strategic Defense Initiative (SDI), an expensive space-based missile defense system popularly called "Star Wars." Overall, the Reagan budgets for military spending totaled $1.6 trillion over five years.

Defense contracts meant the difference between prosperity and recession for blue- and white-collar workers, merchants, developers, and bankers in scores of communities. The Pacific, Atlantic, and Gulf coast states were the chief beneficiaries. In 1983, California led all states with more than $26 billion in military contracts, followed by New York ($9.6 billion), Texas ($8.2 billion), and Virginia ($7.1 billion). The military buildup of the 1980s reflected a significant shift in federal budget priorities. In 1980, 28 percent of federal spending went to what the Office of Management and Budget calls "human resources" (excluding Social Security and Medicare): housing, education, and urban and social services. By 1987, federal outlays for human resources had declined to only 22 percent of the total. In the same period, defense spending rose from 23 percent to 28 percent of the federal budget.

Recession, Recovery, Fiscal Crisis

The Reagan administration's economic policies had mixed results. In 1982 a severe recession, the worst since the 1930s, gripped the nation. By the end of that year the official unemployment rate reached nearly 11 percent, or more than 11.5 million people. Another 3 million had been out of work so long they no longer actively looked for jobs and therefore were not counted in official statistics. Many communities, particularly in the industrial Midwest and Northeast, experienced depressionlike conditions. In January 1983, 20,000 people lined up for hours in subfreezing weather to apply for 200 jobs at a Milwaukee auto-frame factory. American steel plants operated at only about one-third of capacity.

By the middle of 1983 the economy had begun to recover. During that year unemployment dropped to about 8 percent, and inflation fell below 5 percent. The economy as a whole grew 3.6 percent, the biggest increase since the mid-1970s. Unemployment remained relatively low, and the stock market boomed, pushing the Dow Jones industrial average from 776 in August 1982 to an all-time high of 2,722 in August 1987. Inflation averaged just over 3 percent from 1982 to 1986. The administration took credit for the turnaround, hailing the supply-side fiscal policies that had drastically cut taxes and domestic spending. But critics pointed to other factors: the Federal Reserve Board's tight-money policies, an energy glut and consequent sharp drop in energy prices, and the billions of dollars pumped into the economy for defense spending.

The economic recovery affected the nation's regions, industries, and social classes unequally. It produced over 13 million new jobs between 1981 and 1986, but half of these paid less than $11,661, the federally defined poverty level for a family of four. Real family income rose nearly 11 percent from 1982 to 1986, but with average hourly earnings stagnant, most of this gain came from families adding a second paycheck. While certain industries—computers, electronics, real estate, financial services—boomed, others experienced painful shrinkage—automobiles, steel, rubber, machine tools, and textiles—and the communities they supported thrived or suffered accordingly.

The supply-side formula also intensified an ominous fiscal crisis. Although President Reagan had promised to balance the federal budget, his policies had the opposite effect. The 1981 tax cuts, which shrank the government's revenue base, along with the massive increase in military spending, produced chronic annual budget deficits and a mushrooming federal debt. Before the 1980s, the largest single-year budget deficit in U.S. history had been $66 billion; in 1986 the deficit reached $221 billion. The national debt grew from $907 billion in 1980 to over $2 trillion in 1986, more than the federal government had accumulated in its entire previous history. Expenditures for paying just the interest on the national debt reached 14 percent of the annual budget in 1988, double the percentage set aside for that purpose in 1974.

Deficit spending and a large national debt predated the 1980s, but in the Reagan years they took on proportions that threatened to become a structural problem with newly disturbing and perhaps permanent implications for the American economy. Interest rates rose as the government borrowed the money it needed to pay its own bills. Foreign investors, attracted by high interest rates on government securities, pushed up the value of the dollar in relation to foreign currencies. The overvalued dollar made American products expensive abroad and foreign products cheaper for American consumers. Basic American industries—steel, autos, textiles—thus found it difficult to compete abroad and at home. In 1980, the United States still enjoyed a trade surplus of $166 billion. By 1987 the nation owed foreigners $340 billion. The nation that had been the world's leading creditor since World War I had become, by the mid-1980s, its biggest debtor.

The Election of 1984

As the 1984 election approached, several Democrats vied for the opportunity to challenge President Reagan. They believed he was politically vulnerable, especially on the economic issue of recession and the weakening of social programs. Many Americans also expressed fears over the nuclear weapons buildup of the early 1980s, concerned that such arms spending not only fueled deficits but also made a nuclear confrontation more likely. Polls showed that more than 70 percent of Americans favored a nuclear freeze with the Soviet Union. In June 1982, three-quarters of a million people—the largest political rally in American history—demonstrated in New York City for a halt to spending on and deployment of nuclear weapons.

By early 1984, Walter Mondale had emerged as the leading candidate for the Democratic nomination. As a senator from Minnesota and Jimmy Carter's vice president, Mondale had close ties with the party's liberal establishment, which helped win him the nomination. At the Democratic convention, Mondale named Representative Geraldine Ferraro of New York as his running mate, a first for women in American politics. Charismatic speakers such as the Reverend Jesse Jackson, a dynamic disciple of Martin Luther King Jr., and Governor Mario Cuomo of New York stirred the delegates and many television viewers with their appeals to compassion, fairness, and brotherhood. Opinion polls showed Mondale running even with Reagan. But the president's enormous personal popularity, bolstered by the now-booming economy, overwhelmed the Democratic ticket. While Mondale emphasized the growing deficit and called attention to Americans who were left out of prosperity, Reagan cruised above it all. It was "morning again in America," his campaign ads claimed. The nation was strong, united, and prosperous, a far cry from the dark years of the Carter administration.

As *Newsweek* put it, Reagan embodied "America as it imagined itself to be—the bearer of the traditional Main Street values of family and neighborhood, of thrift, industry, and charity instead of government intervention where self-reliance failed." Reagan, despite his close association with the rich and powerful, remained what one journalist called a "cultural democrat," the affable, friendly, neighborly citizen he had portrayed as a movie actor. Mondale's effort to revive the New Deal coalition failed. In one of the biggest landslides in American history, Reagan won 59 percent of the popular vote and carried every state but Minnesota and the District of Columbia. A quarter of registered Democrats, more than 60 percent of independents, and a majority of blue-collar voters cast their ballots for the president, as

The Reverend Jesse Jackson won wide support from black voters and poor people in the 1984 and 1988 Democratic presidential primaries. His Rainbow Coalition registered thousands of new voters in the South and the inner cities. Jackson's inspiring oratory emphasized the "common ground" shared by Americans of all races and classes.

did 54 percent of women, despite Ferraro's presence on the Democratic ticket. No wonder Republicans believed they now had a chance to replace the Democrats as the nation's majority party.

REAGAN'S FOREIGN POLICY

Against the stark imagery of the Iran hostage crisis, Ronald Reagan campaigned to restore American leadership in world affairs. As president, he revived cold war patriotism and championed American interventionism in the third world, especially the Caribbean. The unprecedented military buildup during the Reagan years would have enormous consequences for the domestic economy as well as for America's international stance. Yet along with its hard-line exhortations against the Soviet Union and international terrorism, the Reagan administration also pursued a less ideological, more pragmatic approach in key foreign policy decisions. Most important, sweeping and unanticipated internal changes within the Soviet Union made the entire cold war framework of American foreign policy largely irrelevant by the late 1980s.

The Evil Empire

Part of Reagan's success in the 1980 campaign lay in appeals to restoring America's will to assert itself in the post–Vietnam era. In the early 1980s the Reagan administration made vigorous anticommunist rhetoric the centerpiece of its foreign policy. In sharp contrast to President Carter's focus on human rights and President Nixon's pursuit of détente, Reagan brought a return to the cold war mode of the 1950s and early 1960s. In a March 1983 speech to the National Association of Evangelicals, Reagan described the Soviet Union as "an evil empire . . . the focus of evil in the modern world." The president denounced the growing movement for a nuclear freeze, arguing that "we must find peace through strength."

Administration officials asserted that the nation's military strength had fallen dangerously behind that of the Soviet Union during the 1970s. Critics disputed this assertion, pointing out that the Soviet advantage in intercontinental ballistic missiles (ICBMs) was offset by American superiority in submarine-based forces and strategic aircraft. When asked at a congressional hearing whether he would exchange forces with his Soviet counterpart, General John Vessey, chairman of the Joint Chiefs of Staff, replied, "Not on your life." Nonetheless, the administration proceeded with plans designed to enlarge America's nuclear strike force. These included placing multiple-warhead MX missiles in fixed silos in the American West; deploying Cruise and Pershing II missiles in western Europe, a short distance from the Soviet Union; and pressing for 100 new B-1 long-range bombers.

Reagan's call for the Strategic Defense Initiative (SDI) introduced an unsettling new element into relations between the superpowers. The president claimed, though few scientists agreed, that satellites and lasers could create an impregnable shield against nuclear attack. The project eventually grew into a $17 billion research and development program. From the Soviet perspective, SDI looked like a potentially offensive weapon that would enhance U.S. first-strike capability. Not only the Soviets but millions of Europeans and Americans worried about the administration's routine acceptance of the possibility of nuclear war. A National Security Council directive outlined how the United States might "prevail" in a "protracted" nuclear conflict. The Federal Emergency Management Agency published detailed plans for the evacuation of major cities in the event of such a war.

Attempts at meaningful arms control stalled in this atmosphere, and U.S.-Soviet relations deteriorated.

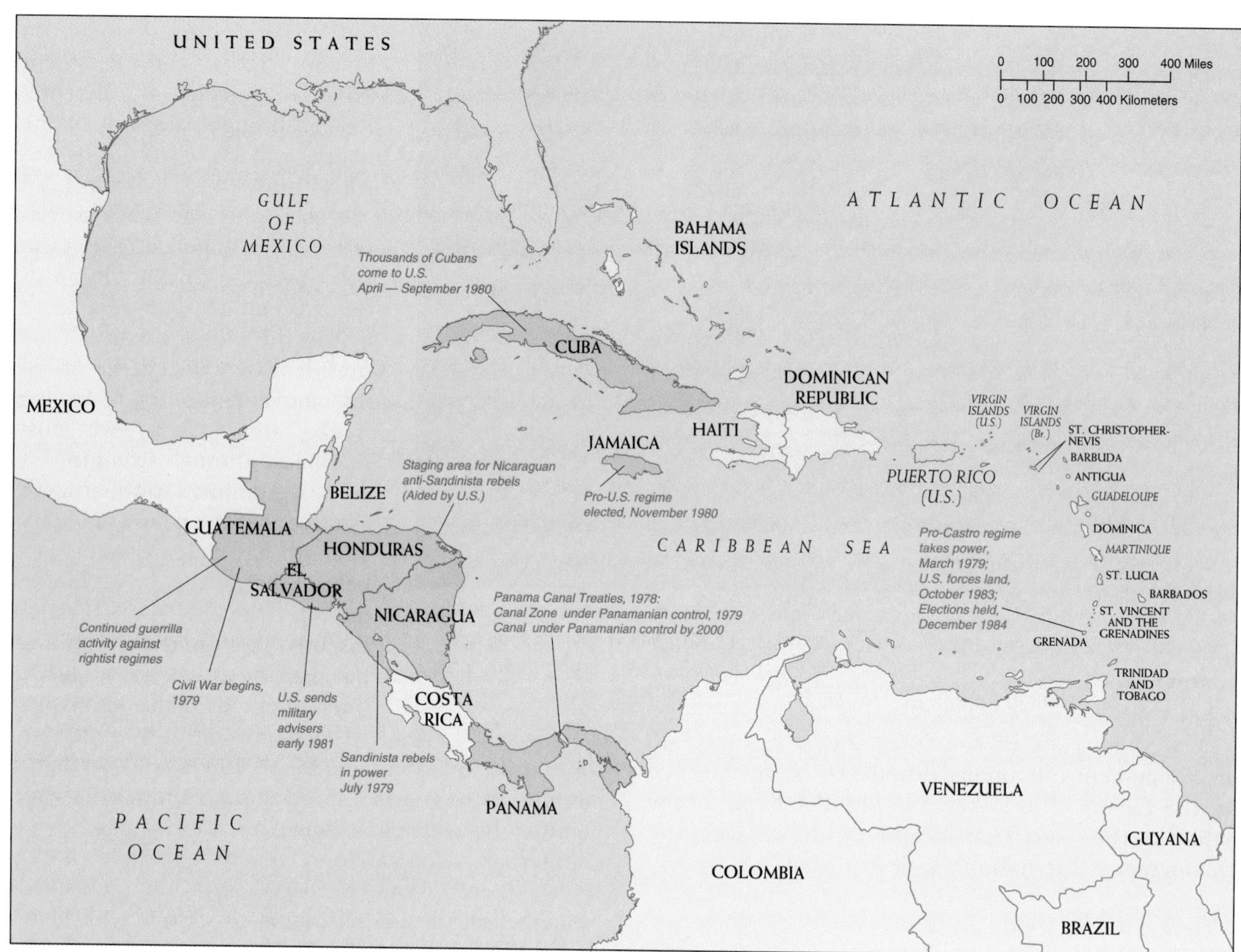

The United States in Central America, 1978–1990 *U.S. intervention in Central America reached a new level of intensity with the so-called Reagan Doctrine. The bulk of U.S. aid came in the form of military support for the government of El Salvador and the Contra rebels in Nicaragua.*

In the fall of 1983, the Soviets shot down a Korean airliner that had strayed over Soviet airspace, killing 269 people. Soviet military officials, believing the plane to be on a spy mission, acted at best in a confused and incompetent manner. President Reagan immediately denounced the act as a deliberate "crime against humanity," and a wave of anti-Soviet sentiment swept the country. The Soviet Union and its eastern European allies boycotted the 1984 Olympic Games in Los Angeles, partly in response to the American boycott of the 1980 Moscow games. While Reagan transformed images of enthusiastic Americans chanting "USA! USA!" and "We're number one!" into an effective backdrop for his reelection campaign, the American-Soviet relationship seemed to have fallen to a new low.

Central America

Declaring the "Vietnam syndrome" over, the president confidently reasserted America's right to intervene anywhere in the world to fight communist insurgency. The Reagan Doctrine, as this declaration was later called, offered a corollary to the notion of the "evil empire." It assumed that social revolution anywhere in the world was directed and controlled by the Soviet Union and its allies. The Reagan Doctrine found its most important expression in Central America, where the United States hoped to reestablish its historical control over the Caribbean basin. In early 1981 the U.S. ambassador to the United Nations, Jean Kirkpatrick, declared, "Central America is the most important place in the world for the United States today."

On the economic front, the Caribbean Basin Initiative (CBI) promised to revitalize friendly nations through $350 million in U.S. aid and what Reagan called "the magic of the marketplace." The idea was to stimulate the Caribbean economy by encouraging the growth of corporations and a freer flow of capital. Yet Congress refused to play by the rules of free trade, placing stiff tariffs and quotas on imports of shoes, leather goods, and sugar that might compete with U.S. products. Many Latin American business people opposed key parts of CBI, such as generous tax breaks for foreign investors. They feared that once large multinational corporations entered their markets, CBI would strengthen the kind of chronic economic dependency that had shaped so much of the region's past.

The administration's policy toward Central America, however, was little influenced by any understanding of the region's history, its internal political struggles, or the grinding poverty of most of its inhabitants. The administration believed, as National Security Adviser Richard Allen argued, that Central America's problems stemmed from "Fidel Castro's Soviet directed, armed, and financed marauders," and required an essentially military solution. Between 1980 and 1983 the United States poured more military aid into Central America than it had during the previous thirty years. In October 1983, American marines landed on the tiny island of Grenada, population 110,000, and quickly ousted its anti-American Marxist regime. The administration claimed that Grenada had become a base for the Cuban military and therefore posed a dangerous threat to the hemisphere. The easy triumph proved popular with most Grenadans and Americans. But in the larger and more complicated nations of El Salvador and Nicaragua, this sort of unilateral military action proved politically and strategically more difficult to carry out.

Unencumbered by the concern for human rights that President Carter had sought, however inconsistently, to incorporate in foreign policy, the Reagan administration stepped up U.S. support for El Salvador's repressive regime in its struggle against a coalition of rebel groups. Salvadoran soldiers received special training in North American camps and from U.S. advisers sent to El Salvador. U.S. military aid to El Salvador jumped from $6 million in 1980 to $82 million in 1982, and economic aid exceeded that to any other Latin American country. Right-wing death squads, backed by representatives of the military in the regime, operated with increasing impunity. In 1980 they had murdered Roman Catholic archbishop Oscar Romero; by 1983, they had tortured and assassinated thousands more opposition leaders. The election in 1984 of centrist president José Napoleón Duarte failed to end the bloody civil war. Some 53,000 Salvadorans, more than one out of every hundred, lost their lives in the conflict. As many as 300,000 Salvadoran refugees entered the United States illegally between 1979 and 1985.

In Nicaragua, the Reagan administration claimed that the revolutionary Sandinista government—which had come to power in 1979 after overthrowing the dictatorial regime of the Somoza family—posed "an unusual and extraordinary threat to the national security." U.S. officials accused the Sandinistas of shipping arms to antigovernment rebels in El Salvador. In December 1981 Reagan approved a Central Intelligence Agency (CIA) plan to spend $19 million arming and organizing the Contras—anti-Sandinista Nicaraguan exiles—to fight against the Sandinista government. Reagan described the Contras, made up mostly of former members of the overthrown Somoza regime's National Guard, as "freedom fighters" and "the moral equivalent of the Founding Fathers." As Reagan escalated this undeclared war, the aim became not merely the cutting of Nicaraguan aid to Salvadoran rebels but the overthrow of Nicaragua's Sandinista regime itself.

Toward this end the CIA used neighboring Honduras as a sanctuary and training base for the Contras. In 1984 the CIA secretly mined Nicaraguan harbors. When Nicaragua won a judgment against the United States in the World Court over this violation of its sovereignty, the Reagan administration refused to recognize the court's jurisdiction in the case and ignored the verdict. Predictably, the U.S. covert war pushed the Sandinistas closer to Cuba and the Soviet bloc. Meanwhile, in the United States, grass-roots opposition to Contra aid grew more vocal and widespread. A number of American communities set up sister city projects offering humanitarian and technical assistance to Nicaraguan communities. Scores of U.S. churches offered sanctuary to political refugees from Central America.

In 1984 Congress reined in the covert war by passing the Boland Amendment, forbidding government agencies from supporting "directly or indirectly military or paramilitary operations" in Nicaragua. Denied funding by Congress, President Reagan turned to the National Security Council to find a way to keep the Contra war going. Between 1984 and 1986 the NSC staff secretly ran the Contra assistance effort, raising $37 million in aid from foreign countries and private contributors. In 1987, the revelation of this unconstitutional scheme exploded before the public as part of the Iran-Contra affair. This led to the most damaging political scandal of the Reagan years.

Glasnost and Arms Control

Meanwhile, momentous political changes within the Soviet Union set in motion a reduction in East-West tensions and ultimately the end of the cold war. Soviet premier Leonid Brezhnev, in power since 1964, died toward the end of 1982. His successors, Yuri Andropov and Konstantin Chernenko, both died after brief terms in office. But in 1985 a new, reform-minded leader, Mikhail Gorbachev, won election as general secretary of the Soviet Communist Party. A lifelong communist and a pure product of Soviet education and politics, Gorbachev represented a new generation of disenchanted party members. He initiated a radical new program of economic and political reform under the rubrics of *glasnost* (openness) and *perestroika* (restructuring). Gorbachev's "new thinking" focused on modernizing the rigid Soviet economy, democratizing its politics, and transforming its relations with the rest of the world.

Gorbachev and his advisers opened up political discussion and encouraged internal critiques of the Soviet economy and political culture. There was much to criticize. Inefficiency and chronic shortages plagued Soviet production of such staples as meat, grain, clothing, and housing. Even when consumer goods were available, high prices often put them beyond the means of the average Soviet family. The government released long-time dissidents like Andrei Sakharov from prison and took the first halting steps toward profit-based, private initiatives in the economy. The "new thinking" inspired an unprecedented wave of diverse, often critical perspectives in Soviet art, literature, journalism, and scholarship.

In Gorbachev's view, improving the economic performance of the Soviet system depended first on halting the arms race. A large slice of the Soviet gross national product went to defense spending, while the majority of its citizens still struggled to find even the most basic consumer items in shops. Gorbachev thus took the lead in negotiating a halt to the arms race with the United States. The historical ironies were stunning. Reagan had made militant anticommunism the centerpiece of his political life. He staunchly resisted arms control initiatives and presided over the greatest military buildup in American history. But between 1985 and 1988 Reagan had four separate summit meetings with the new Soviet leader. In October 1986 Reagan and Gorbachev met in Reykjavík, Iceland. Gorbachev proposed a startling 50 percent cut in all strategic nuclear weapons. He also suggested a policy known as "zero option" for intermediate-range nuclear forces (INF), with the Soviets giving up their predominance in missiles in the European theater in exchange for the removal by the United States of its Pershing missiles. But the Iceland summit bogged down over the issue of SDI. Reagan refused to abandon his plan for a space-based defensive umbrella. Gorbachev insisted that the plan violated the 1972 Strategic Arms Limitation Treaty (SALT I) and that SDI might eventually allow the United States to make an all-out attack.

After another year of tough negotiating, the two sides agreed to a modest INF Treaty providing for the elimination of a total of 2,611 medium- and short-range nuclear missiles. This was a small dent in the combined arsenals of the two superpowers, covering less than 4 percent of total nuclear warheads. However, the INF Treaty also called for comprehensive, mutual, on-site inspections, and it provided an important psychological breakthrough. Reagan himself visited Moscow in 1988, a remarkable reversal from the days when he had thundered against the "evil empire." At one of the summits a Soviet leader humorously announced, "We are going to do something terrible to you Americans—we are going to deprive you of an enemy."

The Iran-Contra Scandal

With Gorbachev clearing the way for scaling back the cold war, the Soviet Union no longer presented itself as the overarching foe that had shaped American foreign policy for more than four decades. Yet the gift of glasnost did not eliminate cold war thinking entirely, especially in the continuing covert war in Central America. Nor could it resolve long-standing and complex international disputes in regions like the Middle East. In 1987 the revelations of the Iran-Contra affair laid bare the continuing contradictions and difficulties attending America's role in world affairs. The affair also demonstrated how overzealous and secretive government officials subverted the Constitution and compromised presidential authority under the guise of patriotism.

The Middle East presented the Reagan administration with its most frustrating foreign policy dilemmas. In Afghanistan, the administration expanded military aid, begun under President Carter, to the forces resisting the Soviet-backed regime. In June 1982 Israel invaded Lebanon in an attempt to destroy the Palestine Liberation Organization (PLO). Hoping to shore up a weak Lebanese government threatened by a brutal civil war, President Reagan dispatched marines to Beirut. In October 1983, however, a terrorist bombing in the marine barracks killed 241 American servicemen, and the administration pulled the marines out of Lebanon, shying away from a long-term commitment of U.S. forces in the Middle East.

Terrorist acts, including the seizing of Western hostages and the bombing of commercial airplanes and cruise ships, redefined the politics of the region. These were desperate attempts by small, essentially powerless sects, many of them splinter groups associated with the Palestinian cause or Islamic fundamentalism. In trying to force the Western world to pay attention to their grievances, they succeeded mostly in provoking outrage and anger. The Reagan administration insisted that behind international terrorism lay the sinister influence and money of the Soviet bloc, the

Ayatollah Khomeini of Iran, and Libyan leader Muammar Qaddafi. In the spring of 1986 the president, eager to demonstrate his antiterrorist resolve, ordered the bombing of Tripoli in a failed effort to kill Qaddafi.

Although administration officials railed against "state-sponsored terrorism," they had little luck in capturing terrorists or gaining the release of Western hostages. During the fierce and prolonged war between Iran and Iraq (1980–1988), the administration tilted publicly toward Iraq to please the Arab states around the Persian Gulf. But in 1986 the administration began secret negotiations with the revolutionary Iranian government. In exchange for help in securing the release of Americans held hostage by radical Islamic groups in Lebanon, the United States offered to supply Iran with sophisticated weapons for use against Iraq. A Lebanese magazine broke the story of the arms-for-hostages deal in November 1986, igniting a firestorm of criticism in Congress and the press. The president, it appeared, had broken his oft repeated promise that he would "never negotiate with terrorists."

Subsequent disclosures elevated the story into a major scandal. Some of the money from the arms deal had been secretly diverted into covert aid for the Nicaraguan Contras. The American public soon learned the sordid details from investigative journalists and through televised congressional hearings held during the summer of 1987. In order to escape congressional oversight of the CIA, Reagan and CIA director William Casey had essentially turned the National Security Council, previously a policy-coordinating body, into an operational agency. Under the direction of National Security Advisers Robert McFarlane and later Admiral John Poindexter, the NSC sold TOW and HAWK missiles to the Iranians, using Israel as a go-between. Millions of dollars from these sales were then given to the Contras in blatant and illegal disregard of the Boland Amendment.

In the hearings, NSC staffer and marine lieutenant colonel Oliver North emerged as the figure running what he euphemistically referred to as "the Enterprise." North defiantly defended his actions in the name of patriotism. Some Americans saw the

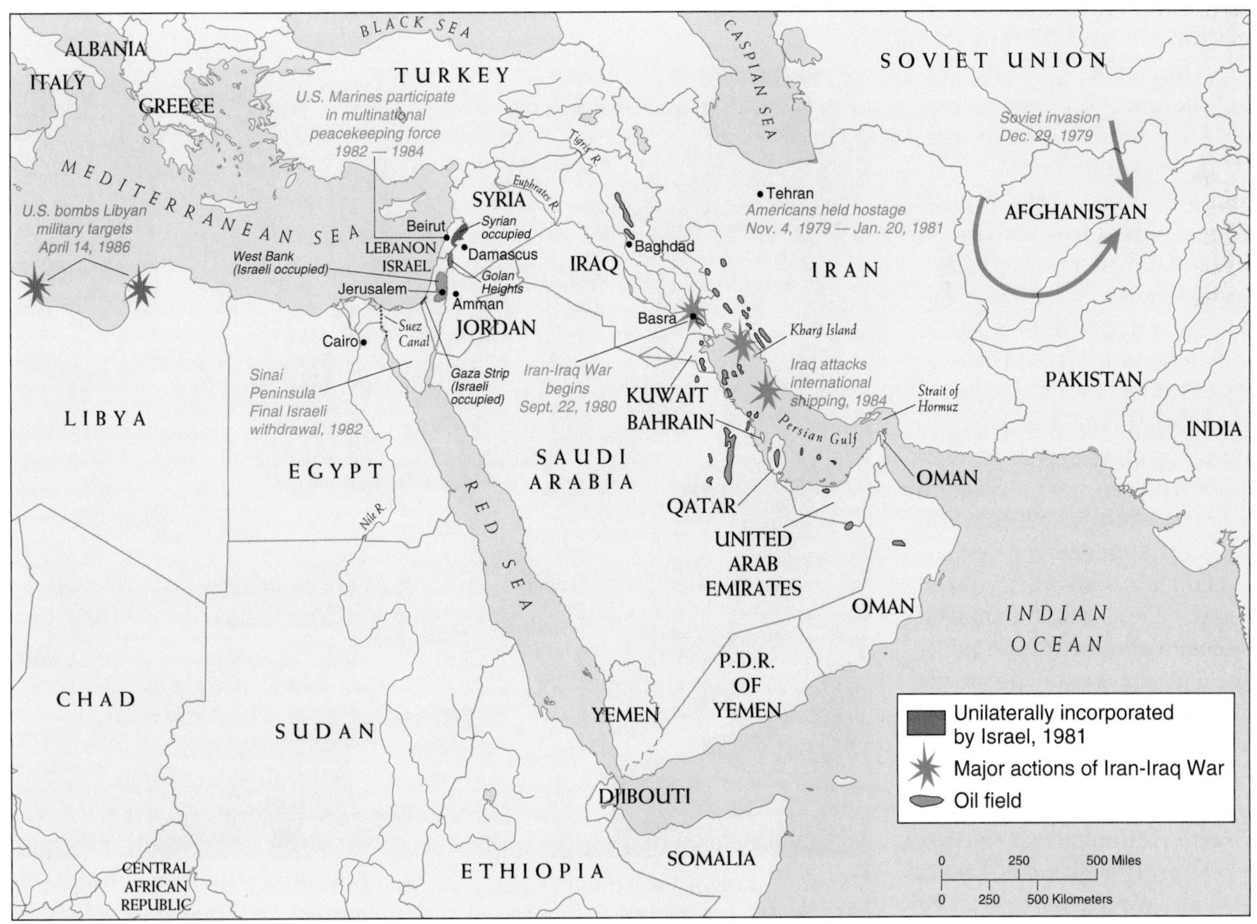

The United States in the Middle East in the 1980s *The volatile combination of ancient religious and ethnic rivalries, oil, and emerging Islamic fundamentalism made peace and stability elusive in the Middle East.*

handsome and dashing North as a hero, but most were appalled by his and Poindexter's blithe admissions that they had lied to Congress, shredded evidence, and refused to inform the president of details in order to guarantee his "plausible deniability." A blue-ribbon commission led by former senator John Tower concluded that Reagan himself "did not seem to be aware" of the policy or its consequences. But the Tower report offered a stunning portrait of a president who was at best confused and far removed from critical policy-making responsibilities. The joint congressional committee investigating the "profoundly sad" story concluded: "The common ingredients of the Iran and Contra policies were secrecy, deception, and disdain for the law. A small group of senior officials believed that they alone knew what was right."

Ultimately, the Iran-Contra investigation raised more questions than it answered. The full role of CIA director Casey, who died in 1987—particularly his relationships with North and the president—remained murky. The role of Vice President George Bush remained mysterious as well, and it would surface as an issue in the 1992 presidential election. Both North and Poindexter were convicted of felonies, including lying to Congress and falsifying official documents, but their convictions were overturned by higher courts on technical grounds. Like Watergate, the scandal had mesmerized a national television audience. But Iran-Contra produced no equivalent movement for impeachment. Unlike Richard Nixon, Ronald Reagan did not defiantly stonewall congressional investigators. Instead, he pleaded ignorance. When pressed on what had happened, he repeatedly claimed, "I'm still trying to find out." The scandal damaged the Reagan administration politically, but the genial president remained personally popular and was protected by his reputation for not being in charge.

In December 1992, after his own election defeat and six years after the scandal broke, President George Bush granted pardons to six key players in the Iran-Contra affair. Among those pardoned was former secretary of defense Caspar Weinberger, who was scheduled to be tried on four felony counts, including perjury. Bush asserted that the officials had been motivated by "patriotism," and he attacked Special Prosecutor Lawrence Walsh for the "criminalization of policy differences." Yet critics argued that the Bush pardons suggested that government officials might violate the law as long as they believed their actions were good for the country. The Bush pardons made it unlikely that the full truth about the arms-for-hostages affair would ever be known.

BEST OF TIMES, WORST OF TIMES

During the 1980s, American communities experienced economic and social change in profoundly diverse ways. However they judged the economic policies of the Reagan era, all observers agreed that the reality of recession and recovery varied enormously across the nation's regions, cities, and industries. On a deeper structural level, the decade witnessed the rapid expansion of relatively new industries such as microelectronics, biotechnology, robotics, and computers. Simultaneously, old standbys such as steel and auto manufacturing declined

Marine Lieutenant Colonel Oliver North, the key figure in the Iran-Contra affair, being sworn in to testify before the special Senate committee investigating the scandal, July 7, 1987. A joint congressional investigation later found that when North and his compatriots were threatened with exposure, "they destroyed official documents and lied to Cabinet officials, to the public, and to elected representatives in Congress."

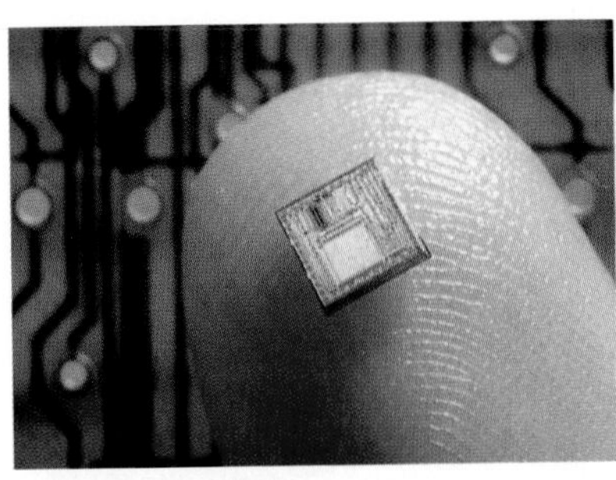

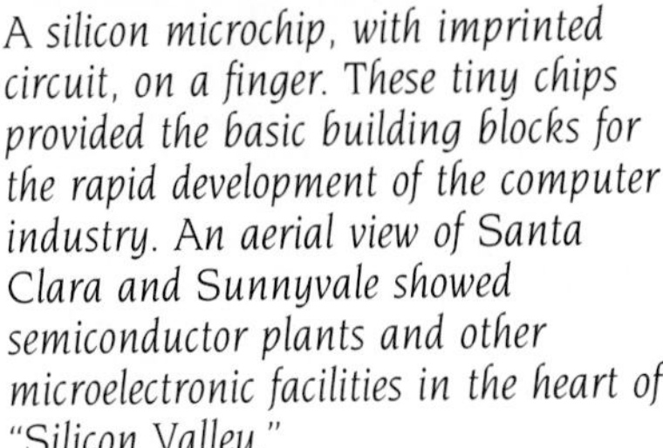

A silicon microchip, with imprinted circuit, on a finger. These tiny chips provided the basic building blocks for the rapid development of the computer industry. An aerial view of Santa Clara and Sunnyvale showed semiconductor plants and other microelectronic facilities in the heart of "Silicon Valley."

more quickly than many could have imagined. Communities that had long depended on industry and manufacturing for their livelihood now struggled to create alternative job bases around newer service- and information-based enterprises.

Silicon Valley

In the early 1980s, a thirty-by-ten-mile strip of Santa Clara County, California, emerged as both the real and symbolic capital of the most important new industry in America. Silicon Valley achieved a special place in the American economy and imagination as the center of the microelectronics industry. As recently as the 1950s, the valley was largely uninhabited range land and fruit orchards. Now two dozen cities, each with about 100,000 people, formed a continuous suburban sprawl between San Francisco and San Jose. None of the cities had real centers, unless shopping malls could be considered the heart of a community. Silicon Valley was a suburb of nowhere.

The name "Silicon Valley" referred to the semiconductor chips, made of silicon, that provided the foundation for local high-technology firms. Semiconductors containing complex integrated circuits formed the brains of computers and the basic building blocks of modern electronics. The nucleus for Silicon Valley was formed in the 1950s in Stanford Research Park, a development on previously unused land in Palo Alto that Stanford University started leasing to electronics firms as a way to earn money. Firms such as Hewlett-Packard and Fairchild Semiconductor wanted the advantages of being close to a major research university. Military contracts played a crucial role in the business during the 1950s and 1960s, but in the 1970s a consumer electronics revolution fueled an explosive new wave of growth. Silicon Valley firms gave birth to pocket calculators, video games, home computers, cordless telephones, digital watches, and almost every other new development in electronics.

Silicon Valley flourished thanks to its unique combination of research facilities, investment capital, attractive environment, and a large pool of highly educated people. By 1980 it was home to some 1,700 high-tech firms that engaged in gathering, processing, or distributing information or in manufacturing information technology. Companies like Atari, Apple, and Intel achieved enormous international success and became household names. Silicon Valley boasted the greatest concentration of new wealth in the United States, and it attracted widespread coverage in trade magazines, business periodicals, and the popular press, which documented the amazing success stories of young entrepreneurs such as Steve Jobs of Apple and Nolan Bushnell of Atari. These tales reinforced the powerful popular image of Silicon Valley as a place where technological breakthroughs and great fortunes emerged from a unique culture of youth, inventiveness, and entrepreneurship.

Silicon Valley became increasingly divided along geographic and class lines. The affluent managers and engineers, nearly all of whom were white males, tended to live in North County communities such as Palo Alto, Mountain View, and Sunnyvale. Manual workers on assembly lines and in low-paying service jobs clustered in San Jose and Gilroy. Most of these were Latino, black, Vietnamese, Chinese, and Filipino men and women. The majority of Silicon Valley workers did not see or enjoy the affluent lifestyle publicized in the mass media; they constituted a cheap, nonunionized labor pool with an extremely high turnover rate. Public services in South County—schools, welfare, police and fire protection—were poor; among Latino public school students in Santa Clara County, the dropout rate reached 50 percent in the mid-1980s.

By the early 1990s the Silicon Valley economy had matured; its rate of growth slowed, as did the infusion of new venture capital. Stiff competition from computer companies in Japan, Korea, and Malaysia made it much more difficult for young entrepreneurs to start successful new companies. And the leap from small, start-up company to large corporation was becoming more and more difficult. The computer industry had diffused around the whole Pacific Rim, of which Silicon Valley was only one part. The crowds, traffic jams, and inflated cost of living led many companies and individuals to move out of the area. The mature Silicon Valley was so well developed and dense that it still had a critical mass of technological and business talent, but the boom-town atmosphere of the early years had faded.

Monongahela Valley

Across the continent, in western Pennsylvania, a different kind of economic transformation reshaped the industrial cities along the Monongahela River Valley. Since the late nineteenth century, the "Mon Valley" had proudly stood as the steelmaking center of the nation and much of the world. The very way of life in cities like Pittsburgh, Homestead, and Clairton revolved around manufacturing jobs at companies like U.S. Steel, Bethlehem, and smaller firms in the area. In the 1980s, however, the American steel industry declined. Part of the problem was the overvalued dollar, which raised the price of American goods relative to imports. As a result, steel companies lost sales, both directly to cheaper imported steel and indirectly as their domestic customers in steel-intensive industries (automobiles, machine tools) also lost sales to imports.

But much of the problem stemmed from the long-term failure of big steel companies to invest in modernizing their operations. Instead they used their profits to diversify into other industries, buying chemical firms, shopping malls, and oil companies. In 1984, U.S. Steel's sales from steel accounted for just 34 percent of its total revenues and only 9 percent of its total operating income. It paid $6 billion to acquire Marathon Oil of Ohio. At the same time, U.S. Steel increased its investments in overseas mining and mineral processing companies, some of which worked closely with foreign steelmakers. This policy of disinvestment had a devastating impact on the people and communities who had helped build the nation's basic production industries.

Demolished blast furnaces at Pittsburgh's Jones and Laughlin Steel Company testified to the decline of the American steel industry. The permanent loss of high-paying jobs in the manufacturing sector devastated scores of American communities in the 1980s.

Overall employment in the American steel industry dropped from 400,000 in 1980 to 167,000 in 1987. In Mon Valley, U.S. Steel employed 26,500 people in 1979, but just 4,000 by 1990. The company's steelmaking capacity plunged from 8.5 million tons to 2.3 million tons a year in that period. Its Homestead Steel Works, where 15,000 people once made the steel for the Empire State Building, the Golden Gate Bridge, and the Sears Tower, closed for good in 1986. During the 1980s the valley lost 30,000 people, or 10 percent of its population. Those who stayed behind were often middle-aged steelworkers unable to find jobs or sell their homes. A survey of nearly 30,000 laid-off workers found that a majority of those over forty remained either unemployed or underemployed in part-time, low-paying jobs. Many were haunted by mental and physical problems and an overall sense of resignation.

The community of Clairton epitomized these conditions. Situated on a hill about fifteen miles south of Pittsburgh, Clairton was once a bustling small city, with active Slavic, Italian, and Irish communities. At the end of World War II its coke works were the largest in the world, and its by-products division made components for thousands of different products, including fertilizer, resin, and dyes. By the mid-1980s, however, Clairton was suffering a permanent unemployment rate of about 35 percent, and it was bankrupt. The taxes once paid to the city by U.S. Steel dropped from $805,000 in 1980 to $331,000 in 1985. The entire thirteen-member police force had to be laid off. A state-appointed trustee handled Clairton's financial affairs. Several thousand residents have moved out since 1980; others remain trapped and dependent on charity and food banks.

Some Mon Valley communities have made strides toward rebuilding around "postindustrial" enterprises. One plan called for demolishing steel mills to make way for the area's first interstate highway. Another project would turn the valley's steelmaking past into a tourist attraction, transforming the remnants of the Homestead Works into a museum run by the National Park Service. In Pittsburgh, on the former site of Jones and Laughlin Steel, state government, business, and local universities pooled resources to create a high-tech industrial park. Commercial tenants include new ventures born of university research into biotechnology, robotics, and computer software. UPARC (University of Pittsburgh Applied Research Center) has also attracted industrial and academic tenants. Pittsburgh's assets now include the world's largest robotics institute and the biggest research program on industrial uses of artificial intelligence. This modest boom may point the way toward a future in which the old steelmaking center becomes a knowledge-based community.

Indian Country

During the 1970s and 1980s Indians won a series of legal and political victories that cumulatively bolstered the principle of what the Supreme Court in *United States v. Wheeler* (1978) called "unique and limited" sovereignty. The federal government recognized tribal sovereignty except where limited by treaty or Congress. A series of court decisions defined precisely what those limits were. Tribes, for example, could tax corporations located on reservations, were exempted from paying state income taxes, and won greater powers for their own courts. In *United States v. John* (1978), the Court ruled that Indian tribes are essentially self-defined and can only be dissolved by their members, thus negating the policy of termination (see Chapter 28). The 1983 Tribal Government Tax Status Act authorized tribes to be treated like states for certain purposes.

But this strengthening of the principle of self-determination had only a limited impact on the lives of most Indians. The postwar trends toward urbanization and assimilation continued. By the 1980s more than half of the nation's Indian population lived in urban areas, with the largest communities in Los Angeles, Tulsa, Oklahoma City, and Phoenix. More than 50 percent of all Americans identifying themselves as Indians were married to non-Indians. On reservations, most tribes lacked the independence or authority of state governments since they continued to rely on federal funding.

This continued dependence on Washington was underscored in 1981 when the Reagan administration cut appropriations for Indians by a third. As Indians experienced the greatest per capita cut in federal programs of any American citizens, reservations saw a dramatic increase in unemployment and poverty. By the mid-1980s, for example, Navajo per capita income was $1,700, compared to $9,000 for the United States as a whole. In Arizona, a state with a large reservation population, more than a third of reservation Indians lived below the poverty line. On the Pine Ridge Reservation in South Dakota, some 18,000 Oglala Sioux lived amid corrosive poverty and an unemployment rate that averaged well above 50 percent. On Wyoming's Wind River Reservation about 8,000 Northern Arapaho and Eastern Shoshone Indians lived on land without any functioning economy except a few trading posts that brought in tourist dollars.

By the late 1980s a new source of income and economic power emerged for Indian tribes—gambling. An outgrowth of the drive for sovereignty rights, the Indian Gaming Regulatory Act of 1988 allowed tribes to operate any sort of gambling establishment that is legal in their state. Thus, if a church or social club can hold a "Las Vegas night," a tribe can run a casino. Within a few years, at least seventy-five tribes in eighteen states had signed agreements with states to open reservation casinos.

For some tribes, the results proved spectacular. In Ledyard, Connecticut, the Mashantucket

Gamblers crowded around card games and dice tables at the Foxwoods High Stakes Bingo and Casino, on the Ledyard, Connecticut, reservation of the Mashantucket Pequots, 1993. The success of Foxwoods made it one of the biggest employers in southeast Connecticut. It also spurred a host of Indian nations and municipalities across the nation, all eager to rake in profits and create new jobs, to propose plans for more gambling casinos.

Pequots built Foxwoods, a full-scale gambling casino and hotel complex that not only brought riches to the tribe but also reshaped the economic landscape of surrounding communities. To build Foxwoods, the Mashantuckets borrowed $55 million from a Malaysian company that operated hotels and casinos in Asia. Under an agreement between Connecticut and the tribe, state agencies regulated the casino. All profits remained with the tribe after it reimbursed the state for money spent on regulation. The Mashantuckets paid no taxes to the state or federal governments.

Some people in the adjacent community of Ledyard, a traditional New England village of 15,000, worried about traffic congestion, pollution, and crime. Others expressed concern over the human tragedies caused by compulsive gambling. But the potential for Foxwoods to reverse southeastern Connecticut's disastrous economic decline dominated all discussion. A 1990 state study estimated that New London County stood to lose anywhere from 13,000 to 27,000 jobs over the next five years as a result of cutbacks in military spending. Out of 110,000 jobs in the county, 66,000 depended directly on the Pentagon. General Dynamics' Electric Boat Division alone employed 23,000 people building Seawolf submarines, a program scheduled for cancellation. Forty percent of all households in Ledyard had at least one person in a military-related job. No wonder, then, that more than 25,000 people applied for the 2,300 job openings at Foxwoods. At $3.75 an hour plus tips, dealers and cocktail waitresses would earn as much as $30,000 a year.

By 1998 Foxwoods was the single most profitable gambling casino in the United States. An average of fifty thousand visitors each day brought an estimated annual profit of more than $200 million on gross revenues of more than $400 million. Since 1993, in exchange for permission to install slot machines and a promise from the state not to legalize gambling off the reservation, the Pequots have contributed $100 million a year to Connecticut's treasury. The tribe could now guarantee college tuition for all its children, world travel for its elders, and new homes for its 250 members. It hired its own archaeologist to help recover evidence of lost tribal history. Steady expansion resulted in 1200 hotel rooms, 300,000 square feet of casino space, and a new $135 million Mashantucket Pequot Museum and Research Center.

Foxwoods's success inspired other Indian peoples across the nation. In California the once impoverished Cabayan Mission Indians, who had built the first reservation casino in the early 1980s, constructed a 950-unit housing development and a new power plant and guaranteed universal employment, health care, and education for tribal members. In New Mexico, $16 million in annual gambling profits helped the 600-year-old Sandia tribe reinvigorate its culture and helped revive the economy in Albuquerque.

Not all these ventures were bonanzas. The Wisconsin Winnebago tribe almost went bankrupt when its casinos were mismanaged by a corrupt businessman who had bribed tribal officials to win a lucrative contract to run them. Some Indians opposed casino gambling on philosophical and spiritual grounds, leading to intratribal conflicts. But most shared the view of Reid A. Walker, an executive with the National Indian Gaming Association, who argued that reservation gambling had "brought us new hope. It's a renaissance for Indian country, giving us power to start our own programs in health care, infrastructure, education and more."

An Electronic Culture

Important technological developments helped reconfigure American cultural life during the 1980s. Revolutions in computers and telecommunications merged telephones, televisions, computers, cable, and satellites into a single differentiated system. The new information technologies of the 1980s changed the way people worked and played. They made the nation's cultural life more homogeneous, and they played a greater role than ever in shaping politics. The new world of "compunications" (referring to the merging of computer and communications technologies) speeded the growth of what many analysts call postindustrial society. In this view, the creation, processing, and sale of information and services have replaced the manufacturing and distribution of material goods as society's most important and dynamic wealth-producing activities.

The twin arrivals of cable and the videocassette recorder (VCR) expanded and redefined the power of television. By the end of the 1980s pay cable services and VCRs had penetrated roughly two-thirds of American homes. Cable offered television viewers scores of new programming choices, especially sports events and movies. For the first time ever, the mass audience for traditional network programming declined as "narrowcasting"—the targeting of specialized audiences—competed with broadcasting. The VCR revolutionized the way people used their sets, allowing them to organize program watching around their own schedules. People also used their televisions to play video games. Hollywood studios began releasing movies on videotape and the rental and sale of movies for home viewing quickly outstripped ticket sales at theaters as the main profit source for filmmakers. The VCR thus radically changed the economics of the entertainment business.

The intensification of television's power could be measured in many ways. In 1981, a new cable channel called MTV (for Music Television) began airing videos of popular music stars performing their work. The intent was to boost sales of the stars' audio recordings, but the music video soon became a new art form in itself. MTV redefined popular music by placing as much emphasis on image as on sound, and it revived dance as a popular performance art as well. Artists who best exploited music video, such as Madonna and Michael Jackson, achieved international superstar status. MTV also transformed smaller, cult musical forms, such as rap and heavy metal, into giant mass-market phenomena. MTV pioneered an imaginative visual style, featuring rapid cutting, animation, and the sophisticated

Pioneer female rappers Salt 'N' Pepa, shown here at the 1995 American Music Awards in Los Angeles. Among the most popular rap groups of the 1980s and '90s, their music and videos celebrated individuality, sexual freedom, and self-confidence for young women.

fusion of sound and image. Television producers, filmmakers, advertisers, and political consultants quickly adapted MTV techniques to just about every kind of image making.

More than ever, television drove the key strategies and tactics defining American political life. Politicians and their advisers focused on shaping a candidate's television image, producing slick campaign commercials, and raising the enormous amounts of money needed to get them on TV. Issues, positions, and debate all paled alongside the key question: How did it look on television? Even Ronald Reagan's harshest critics conceded that the former actor had mastered the art of television-based politics. Fewer citizens voted or took an active role in campaigns, and most relied on television coverage to make their choices. Thus creating an effective television "character" emerged as perhaps the most crucial form of political discourse. Evangelical preachers also discovered that they could use televised appeals to religious faith to make money and gain political power. "Televangelists" like Pat Robertson, Jimmy Swaggart, and Jim and Tammy Bakker attracted large audiences and built lucrative empires by preaching versions of fundamentalist Protestantism over cable networks.

The dominant themes in popular culture were money, status, and power—the values embraced by the Reagan administration. The newly elected president himself set the tone when he responded to a reporter's question asking him what was best about America. "What I want to see above all," Reagan replied, "is that this remains a country where someone can always get rich." Certainly there were many thousands of Americans who made fortunes in the expansive and lucrative sectors of the economy: stock trading, real estate, business services, defense contracting, and high-tech industries. A step below the new rich were the "yuppies" (young upwardly mobile professionals). The term, coined in 1984, gained influence as a tool for the advertising and marketing worlds, a shorthand description of those people most likely to define themselves by their upscale consumer behavior. Yuppies ate gourmet foods, wore designer clothes, drove expensive automobiles, and lived in "gentrified" neighborhoods. They were not necessarily rich, but they patterned their lifestyle after that of the wealthy.

Popular culture reflected and reinforced an obsession with getting rich and living well. Novelist Tom Wolfe called this phenomenon "plutography"—"graphic depictions of the acts of the rich." Hit TV series like *Dallas* and *Dynasty* (and their imitators) focused on the family wars and business intrigues of oil tycoons and fashion queens. Shows such as *Lifestyles of the Rich and Famous* and *Entertainment Tonight* offered vicarious pleasures by taking viewers into the homes and on the shopping sprees of wealthy celebrities. Movies like *Risky Business* (1983), *Ghostbusters* (1984), and *Working Girl* (1988) that reveled in moneymaking and the entrepreneurial spirit attracted huge audiences. So, too, did films that combined spectacular special effects and science fiction with the comforting verities of so-called traditional family values: *ET: The Extraterrestrial* (1982), *Return of the Jedi* (1983), and *Back to the Future* (1985).

The marketing of marketing drove American culture, as exposure through the mass media became more crucial than ever for business success. Tie-ins proliferated among films, television shows, advertising, newspapers and magazines, popular music, and politicians. A growing concentration of ownership among television networks, movie studios, publishers, and cable companies accelerated this trend. New media forms—the newspaper *USA Today*, the news channel Cable News Network (CNN), the weekly magazine *People*—intensified the national culture of celebrity. On a deeper level, demographic analysis created the most important "communities" in American life—communities of consumer choice. Polls, graphs, and charts increasingly located and divided Americans by race, gender, ethnicity, education, income, and religion so that advertisers, manufacturers, book publishers, moviemakers, television producers, and political candidates—anyone looking to sell a product or provide a service—could define and target the right demographic community.

Epidemics: Drugs, AIDS, Homelessness

The scourge of drug addiction and drug trafficking took on frightening new dimensions in the early 1980s. The arrival of crack, a cheap, smokable, and highly addictive form of cocaine, made that drug affordable to the urban poor. As crack addiction spread, the drug trade assumed alarming new proportions both domestically and internationally. Crack ruined hundreds of thousands of lives and led to a dramatic increase in crime rates. Studies showed that over half the men arrested in the nation's largest cities tested positive for cocaine. The crack trade spawned a new generation of young drug dealers who were willing to risk jail and death for enormous profits. In city after city, drug wars over turf took the lives of dealers and innocents, both caught in the escalating violence. Many ghetto youths looked at the drug trade as the only real business enterprise open to them.

Well-financed and carefully organized groups like the Medellin cartel in Colombia linked coca plant farmers in Bolivia, money launderers in Panama, and smugglers in Mexico and the United States. Drug money corrupted many public officials in all of these countries. By the end of the 1980s, opinion polls revealed that Americans identified drugs as the nation's number one problem. The Reagan administration declared a highly publicized "war on drugs" to bring the traffic under control. This multibillion-dollar campaign focused on stopping the flow of illegal drugs into the United States, destroying cocaine-producing labs in Bolivia, and stiffening the penalties for those convicted of violating federal drug statutes. Critics charged that the war on drugs needed to focus less on the supply of drugs from abroad and more closely on the demand for them at home. They urged more federal money for drug education, treatment, and rehabilitation. Drug addiction and drug use, they argued, were primarily health problems, not law enforcement issues.

The AIDS Quilt in Washington, D.C., October 1992. The quilt project united thousands of individual memorials to AIDS victims into one powerful statement expressing the national sense of loss from the disease. Mourners were thus able to transcend their personal grief and connect with the larger movement to fight AIDS.

In 1981 doctors in Los Angeles, San Francisco, and New York began encountering a puzzling new medical phenomenon. Young homosexual men were dying suddenly from rare types of pneumonia and cancer. The underlying cause was found to be a mysterious new viral disease that destroyed the body's natural defenses against illness, making its victims susceptible to a host of opportunistic infections. Researchers at the U.S. Public Health Service's Centers for Disease Control (CDC) in Atlanta called the new disease acquired immune deficiency syndrome (AIDS). The virus that causes AIDS (the human immunodeficiency virus, or HIV) is transmitted primarily in semen and blood, but it can be years before a person exposed to HIV develops full-blown AIDS. Thus one could infect others without knowing one had the disease. Although tests emerged to determine whether one carried HIV, there was no effective treatment for AIDS in these early years. Because the preponderance of early AIDS victims were homosexual men who had been infected through sexual contact, many Americans perceived AIDS as a disease of homosexuals.

As more and more gay men fell victim to the disease, AIDS aroused fear, anguish, and anger. It also brought an upsurge of organization and political involvement. The Gay Men's Health Crisis, formed in New York in 1981, drew thousands of volunteers to care for the sick, raised millions of dollars for education and research, and lobbied vigorously for federal funding of research toward finding a cure. In city after city, gay communities responded to the AIDS crisis with energy and determination. Most gay men changed their sexual habits, practicing "safe sex" to reduce the chances of infection. The Reagan administration, playing to antihomosexual prejudices, largely ignored the epidemic. One important exception was Surgeon General C. Everett Koop, who urged a comprehensive sex education program in the nation's schools, including information about condoms. Individual American communities became bitterly divided over whether school boards and other local agencies ought to take on these responsibilities.

By the 1990s the AIDS epidemic had spread far beyond gay men. The fastest-growing group of AIDS victims were intravenous drug users, their sex partners (including many heterosexuals), and their babies. The AIDS epidemic spread rapidly among African Americans and Latinos as well. Revelations that well-known public figures such as actor Rock Hudson and athletes Magic Johnson and Arthur Ashe were infected helped remove some of the stigma and increased AIDS awareness in the public. More important were the continuing political and educational efforts mounted by groups like the AIDS Coalition to Unleash Power (ACT-UP), Women's Health Action Mobilization (WHAM), and the AIDS Quilt Project, which stitched together a moving tribute to victims out of thousands of individual memorial quilts. In 1994 Congress passed the Comprehensive AIDS Revenue Emergency Act, which pumped hundreds of millions of federal dollars into AIDS research and prevention programs.

By 1997, some 612,000 Americans had contracted AIDS, of whom 379,000 had died. About 900,000 Americans (1 in 300) was infected with the HIV virus. But although the HIV infection rate remained steady, the death rate from AIDS began to drop by 1995. A variety of new drug treatments, such as AZT and protease inhibitors, proved effective in slowing the disease's progress and in relieving some symptoms. For those patients with access to the new drugs, AIDS became a long-term chronic condition rather than an automatic death sentence. But these treatments were enormously expensive and required difficult regimens for patients, thus limiting their effectiveness against the epidemic.

Another chronic social problem plagued America during the 1980s. In cities throughout the country, citizens could not help noticing the disturbing presence of homeless people. Often disoriented, shoeless, and forlorn, growing numbers of "street people" slept over heating grates, on subways, and in parks. Homeless people wandered city sidewalks panhandling and struggling to find scraps of food. Winters proved especially difficult. In the early 1980s, the Department of Housing and Urban Development placed the number of the nation's homeless at between 250,000 and 350,000. But advocates for the homeless estimated that the number was as high as 3 million.

Who were the homeless? Analysts agreed that at least a third were mental patients who had been discharged from hospitals during the 1970s as the result of a large-scale policy of deinstitutionalization. That policy was in part a response to charges that institutionalization violated patients' right. But without adequate community mental health centers to ease their transition, deinstitutionalization proved a disaster for many thousands of the mentally ill. Alcoholics and drug addicts unable to hold jobs also contributed to the growing homeless problem, but the ranks of the homeless also included female-headed families, battered women, Vietnam veterans, AIDS victims, and elderly people with no place to go. Some critics pointed to the decline in decent housing for poor people and the deterioration of the nation's health-care system as a cause of homelessness. Some communities made strong efforts to place their homeless residents in city-run shelters, but violence and theft in the shelters scared away many people. No matter how large and what its components, the permanent class of American homeless reflected the desperate situation of America's poor.

Economic Woes

The government had only mixed success in trying to curb the excesses of economic development in the 1980s. Congress sought to check burgeoning deficits, which had topped $200 billion in the annual budget for 1984. In late 1985, amid great fanfare, Congress enacted the Balanced Budget and Emergency Deficit Reduction Act, more popularly known as Gramm-Rudman after its principal authors, Senators Phil Gramm and Warren Rudman. It mandated automatic spending cuts if the government failed to meet fixed deficit reduction goals. Under the plan, congressional and presidential budget officials would forecast whether target reductions would be met. If not, the General Accounting Office would compile a list of across-the-board reductions, evenly divided between domestic and military programs. Although Gramm-Rudman targeted a deficit of $172 billion for 1986, with further reductions leading to a balanced budget by 1991, the deficit for 1986 reached $238 billion, some $66 billion over the target. In fact, the actual deficit was $283 billion. Congress and the president masked the true size of the deficit by taking the $45 billion surplus from Social Security and other trust funds and spending it on government programs. This tactic of diverting trust funds to reduce the deficit became standard during the 1980s. Congress revised the Gramm-Rudman targets in 1987, but once again the numbers did not add up. The 1989 deficit wound up at $153 billion instead of the promised $136 billion. The 1991 deficit set a record at $269 billion; if the Social Security surplus was subtracted from government spending books, the real deficit totaled $321 billion.

On Wall Street, the bull market of the 1980s ended abruptly in the fall of 1987. The Dow-Jones average of thirty leading industrial stocks had reached an all-time high of 2,722 at the end of August. There followed a gradual slide over the next few weeks and then a resounding crash. On October 19, the Dow lost an incredible 508 points in one day, almost 23 percent of its value. Analysts blamed the decline on computerized program trading, which automatically instructed money managers to sell stock-index futures when prices on the New York Stock Exchange fell below certain levels. The panic on the trading floors recalled the pandemonium set off by the stock market crash of 1929. Millions of Americans now feared that the 1987 crash would signal the onset of a great recession or even a depression.

In late 1986, the Securities and Exchange Commission (SEC) uncovered the biggest stock scandal in history, in the process revealing the inner workings of high finance in the 1980s. Ivan Boesky, one of the nation's leading stock speculators, admitted to using confidential information about upcoming corporate takeovers to trade stocks illegally. Just two years earlier the dapper Boesky had made more than $100 million on two deals. "Greed is all right," he told a cheering University of California Business School audience in 1985. "Everybody should be a little bit greedy. . . . You shouldn't feel guilty."

Now Boesky agreed to pay the U.S. government $100 million to settle civil charges, and he cooperated with SEC investigators. The biggest fish caught in their net was Michael Milken, a Boesky ally and the most successful businessman of the era. An investment banker for Drexel Burnham Lambert, Milken perfected the art of corporate raiding through creative manipulation of debt. He showed how enormous profits could be earned from weak firms that offered tempting targets for takeovers and mergers. Their debt could be used as tax write-offs; less efficient units could be sold off piecemeal; and more profitable units could be retained, merged, or sold again to form new entities. Instead of borrowing from banks, Milken financed his deals by underwriting high-yield, risky "junk bonds" for companies rated below investment grade. Investors in turn reaped huge profits by selling these junk bonds to hostile-takeover dealers.

Milken and other corporate raiders reshaped the financial world, setting off the greatest wave of buying and selling in American business history. During the 1980s corporate America undertook 25,000 mergers, takeovers, and restructuring deals, cumulatively valued at more than $2 trillion. Between 1984 and 1987, there were twenty-one such deals involving over a billion dollars each. Milken himself made a staggering $550 million in one year alone. Just before filing for bankruptcy in 1990, Drexel Burnham Lambert paid its executives $350 million in bonuses—almost as much as it owed its creditors. Milken was eventually convicted of insider trading and stock fraud and sent to prison. Critics both within and outside the Wall Street world questioned the economic benefits of this "paper entrepreneurialism." Many American businesses enjoyed rising profits and cash flow, but these depended as much on debt manipulation and corporate restructuring as on investment in research and development or the creation of new products.

Growing Inequality

The celebration of wealth, moneymaking, and entrepreneurship dominated much of popular culture, politics, and intellectual life in the 1980s. But grimmer realities lay under the surface. A variety of measures strongly suggested that the nation had moved toward greater inequality, that the middle class was shrinking, and that poverty was on the rise. Analysts disagreed over the causes of these trends. No doubt some reflected structural changes in the American economy and a rapidly changing global marketplace. After eight years of tax cuts, defense buildup, growing budget deficits, and record trade imbalances, the economic future looked uncertain at best. Two of the most cherished basic assumptions about America—that life would improve for most people and their children, and that a comfortable middle-class existence was available to all who worked for it—looked shaky by the early 1990s.

The very wealthy did extremely well during the 1980s. In 1989 the richest 1 percent of American households accounted for 37 percent of the nation's private wealth—up from 31 percent in 1983, a jump of almost 20 percent. This top 1 percent, consisting of 834,000 households with about $5.7 trillion of net worth, owned more than the bottom 90 percent of Americans, the remaining 84 million households, whose total net worth was about $4.8 trillion. The top 1 percent owned a disproportionate share of many types of assets: 78 percent of bonds and trusts, 62

Percentage Share of Aggregate Family Income, 1980–1992

	1980	1992
Top 5 Percent	15.3%	17.6%
Highest Fifth	41.6	44.6
Fourth Fifth	24.3	24.0
Third Fifth	17.5	16.5
Second Fifth	11.6	10.5
Lowest Fifth	5.1	4.4

Source: U.S. Bureau of the Census, Current Population Reports: Consumer Incomes, Series P-60, Nos. 167 and 184, 1990, 1993. U.S. federal data compiled by Ed Royce, Rollins College.

Share of Total Net Worth of American Families

	1983	1989
Richest 1 percent of families	31%	37%
Next richest 9 percent	35	31
Remaining 90 percent	33	32

Source: *New York Times*, April 21, 1992, from Federal Reserve Survey of Consumer Finances.

percent of business assets, 49 percent of publicly held stock, and 45 percent of nonresidential real estate. The average wealth of the Fortune 500 (the wealthiest individuals in America) jumped from $230 million in 1982 to $682 million in 1990. The total net worth of this group rose from $92 billion to $273 billion over the same period, and the number of billionaires jumped from thirteen to sixty-six.

The most affluent Americans made the biggest gains in family income as well. In 1980 the top 5 percent of families earned 15.3 percent of the nation's total income. By 1992 their share had grown to 17.6 percent, an increase of 15 percent; their average income was $156,000 a year. In 1980 the top 20 percent of families earned 41.6 percent of the nation's total. By 1992 their share had grown to 44.6 percent, an increase of about 7 percent, with an average income of $99,000 a year. In contrast, the bottom 40 percent of families had 16.7 percent of aggregate income in 1980. By 1992 their share had declined to 14.9 percent, a drop of nearly 11 percent, with an average income of about $16,500 a year.

The average weekly earnings of American workers declined from $373 in 1980 to $339 in 1992, and average hourly wages dropped from $10.59 to $9.87 (in 1990 dollars). Both these figures reflected that most of the new jobs created during the 1980s were in low-paying service and manufacturing sectors. Of the roughly 12 million (net) new jobs created between 1979 and 1987, 50.4 percent paid less than the $11,611 poverty-level income for a family of four. Only 12 percent were high-wage jobs paying over $46,445. Millions of families now needed two wage earners to maintain middle-class status where formerly one would have sufficed.

The number and percentage of Americans in poverty grew alarmingly during the decade. In 1979 the government classified about 26.1 million people as poor, 11.7 percent of the total population. By 1992 the number of poor had reached 36.9 million, or 14.5 percent of the population. This represented an increase of more than 23 percent in the nation's poverty rate. In 1992 nearly 22 percent of all American children under eighteen lived in poverty, including 47 percent of all black children and 40 percent of all Hispanic children. Thirty-three percent of all African Americans lived in poverty, as did 29 percent of Hispanics. Female-headed

Measures of Average Earnings, 1980–1992 (in 1990 Dollars)

Year	Average Weekly Earnings	Average Hourly Earnings
1980	$373.81	$10.59
1985	363.30	10.41
1992	339.37	9.87

Source: U.S. House of Representatives, Committee on Ways and Means, *Overview of Entitlement Programs* (Washington, D.C.: GPO, 1993), table 35, p. 557. U.S. federal data compiled by Ed Royce, Rollins College.

Number of Poor, Rate of Poverty, and Poverty Line, 1979–1992

	1979	1992
Millions of poor	26.1	36.9
Rate of poverty	11.7%	14.5%
Poverty line (family of four)	$7,412	$14,335

Source: U.S. Bureau of the Census, Current Population Reports: Consumer Income, Series P-60, Nos. 161 and 185, 1988, 1993. U.S. federal data compiled by Ed Royce, Rollins College.

NET NEW JOB CREATION BY WAGE LEVEL, 1979–1987

	Number of Net New Jobs Created	Percentage of Net New Jobs Created
Low-wage Jobs (less than $11,611)	5,955,000	50.4%
Middle-wage Jobs ($11,612 to $46,444)	4,448,000	31.7%
High-wage Jobs ($46,445 and above)	1,405,000	11.9%

Source: U.S. Senate, Committee on the Budget, *Wages of American Workers in the* 1980s (Washington, D.C.: GPO, 1988). U.S. federal data compiled by Ed Royce, Rollins College.

MEDIAN FAMILY INCOME AND RATIO TO WHITE, BY RACE AND HISPANIC ORIGIN, 1980–1992 (IN 1992 DOLLARS)

Year	All Races	White	Black	Hispanic
1980	$35,839	$37,341	$21,606 (58%)	$25,087 (67%)
1985	36,164	38,011	21,887 (58%)	25,596 (67%)
1992	36,812	38,909	21,161 (54%)	23,901 (61%)

Source: U.S. Bureau of the Census, Current Population Reports, Series P-60, No. 184, 1993. U.S. federal data compiled by Ed Royce, Rollins College.

households, comprising 13.7 million people, accounted for 37 percent of the poor.

END OF AN ERA?

As Americans approached the end of the twentieth century, they faced dramatic changes around the world and at home. The fall of world communism promised to reshape the fundamental premises of the nation's foreign policy. Economic competition with the nations of the Pacific Rim and Europe would replace the ideological rivalry between Marxism-Leninism and capitalism. But capitalism was hardly triumphant. Global economic struggles forced a reassessment of the core beliefs in growth and abundance that had dominated the nation's political and cultural life since World War II. The limits of military power to solve complex political and economic disputes became clear in the aftermath of victory in the Persian Gulf War. Economic inequality and racial divisions continued to plague many American communities. In 1992 Democrats recaptured the White House for the first time since 1976, riding a wave of desire for change. But in 1994 a resurgent and more right-wing Republican Party won control of both houses of Congress for the first time in forty years.

The Election of 1988

For the 1988 campaign, the Republicans nominated Vice President George Bush. Bush embodied the eastern establishment, with a few twists. The son of an investment banker and senator from Connecticut, educated at Yale, he had moved to Texas after serving in World War II as a fighter pilot. Bush made money in the oil business and entered Texas Republican politics. His detractors dismissed him as a "wimp" and "the resume candidate." He had held a string of appointive offices under three presidents—head of the National Republican Committee, UN ambassador, envoy to China, director of the CIA—before being elected vice president. In his campaign for the presidency, Bush promised to continue the policies of his patron, Ronald Reagan.

The Democratic nominee, Governor Michael Dukakis of Massachusetts, stressed competence over ideology and took credit for his state's economic boom. With Reagan retiring, the Democrats believed they had a good chance to recapture the White House in 1988. At first Dukakis led Bush in the polls. But Republican strategists, led by Lee Atwater and Roger Ailes, created and ran a cynical and effective negative campaign that painted Dukakis as outside the mainstream of "American values." They attacked

Dukakis for vetoing a law requiring students to pledge allegiance to the flag; for opposing the death penalty and mandatory school prayer; and for being a "card-carrying member" of the American Civil Liberties Union. Most damaging was an ad campaign accusing Dukakis of being soft on crime by authorizing weekend furloughs for some Massachusetts prison inmates. One TV spot focused on Willie Horton, a black man serving time for rape and assault, who had escaped during a furlough and committed another rape. The gut-level appeal to racist stereotypes was shocking and potent. "If I can make Willie Horton a household name," said Lee Atwater, "we'll win the election."

The Bush campaign succeeded in creating a negative image of Dukakis, especially among undecided voters. While Bush excoriated liberalism, wrapped himself in the flag, and made thinly veiled racist and nativist appeals, Dukakis distanced himself from the campaign and the Democratic Party's liberal tradition. The 1988 election intensified the importance of image over substance in the nation's politics. The creation of daily "sound bites" for the evening news, along with carefully calculated "spin control" by campaign aides, seemed far more crucial than debate over issues. Even during televised debates, the candidates appeared unwilling and incapable of discussing such pressing concerns as the political upheaval in the Soviet Union, the environmental crisis, and the globalization of the world economy. Bush and his running mate, Dan Quayle, won the popular vote by 54 to 46 percent and carried the electoral votes of forty out of fifty states. Above all, the election of 1988 signaled that more sophisticated levels of media manipulation and image making were the keys to success in presidential politics.

The New Immigration

Figures from the 1990 census confirmed what many Americans had observed over the previous decade in their communities and workplaces. The face of the nation was perceptibly changing. The Census Bureau estimated that 6 million legal and 2 million undocumented immigrants entered the country during the 1980s, second only to the 8.8 million foreign immigrants who had arrived between 1900 and 1910. More than a third of the nation's population growth over the decade—from 227 million to 248 million—came from immigration, a greater proportion than in any decade since 1910–1920, when immigration accounted for 40 percent of population growth. Seven states, headed by California, New York, Texas, and Florida, received 75 percent of the newcomers.

Hispanics and Asians led the accelerated trend toward cultural diversity. The Hispanic population

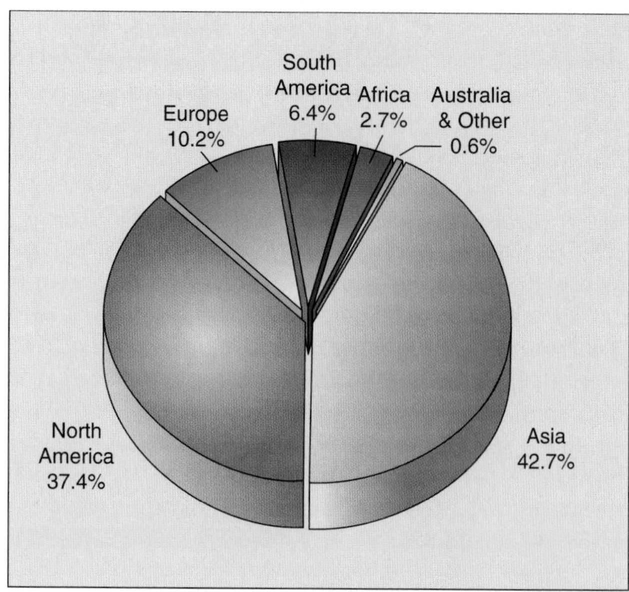

Continent of Birth for Immigrants, 1981–1989

increased by more than 50 percent, from 14.6 million to 22.4 million. One out of every five immigrants living in the United States was Mexican-born, and Mexican Americans accounted for more than 60 percent of the Hispanic population identified in the 1990 census. Hispanics formed over a third of the population of New Mexico, a quarter of the population of Texas, and over 10 percent of the populations of California, Arizona, and Colorado. Nearly a million Mexican Americans lived in Los Angeles alone. Large Hispanic communities, including Cuban, Puerto Rican, Dominican, and Salvadoran Americans, also grew in New York City, Miami, and Chicago. Demographers predicted that by the middle of the next century Hispanics would replace African Americans as the largest minority group in the nation.

The decline of oil prices had a devastating impact on the Mexican economy, worsening poverty and unemployment and spurring more people to seek a better life in North America. Most Mexican Americans struggled in low-paying jobs and fought to hold on to their distinctive cultural heritage. They worked on farms, in garment sweatshops and high-tech assembly plants, and as gardeners and domestics. Through education and business success, many joined the middle class. But almost 20 percent of Mexican Americans lived below the poverty line.

The number of Asian Americans more than doubled, from 3.5 million to 7.3 million. Nearly two out of every five Asian Americans lived in California. The population of Koreatown in Los Angeles approached 300,000. Like earlier immigrant groups, new Americans from Korea, Vietnam, and the Philippines tended to cluster in their own communities and maintain a durable group identity. As a whole, Asian

Americans made mobility through education a priority, along with pooling family capital and labor to support small businesses. Newcomers selected communities with job opportunities or where family members and friends had settled previously. This "chain migration" is illustrated by the large numbers of Hmongs, a tribal group from Laos, living in Minneapolis and St. Paul. The stream of Hmongs began with church-sponsored refugee programs, then gained momentum as more and more family members followed. Minnesota's total Asian population tripled, increasing during the 1980s from 26,000 to 78,000.

The Immigration and Nationality Act of 1965 had eliminated quotas based on national origin. It also gave preferential treatment to highly educated foreigners seeking professional opportunities. The 1965 act set limits of 120,000 immigrants per year from the Western Hemisphere and 170,000 from countries outside the Western Hemisphere. However, many more immigrants entered the nation illegally. By the mid-1980s, growing concern over "illegal aliens" had become a hotly debated political issue, particularly in the Southwest. The Immigration Reform and Control Act of 1986 addressed the concerns of Anglos worried about "illegals" and the increasingly influential Mexican American community. It required employers to vouch for the legal status of their employees. At the same time, it offered an amnesty to all undocumented workers who had entered the country before 1982. The law, critics charged, led to discrimination in hiring. And no matter what Congress did, the desperate economic realities in Mexico and Central America continued to enlarge the flow of illegal immigrants.

Anti-immigrant sentiment re-emerged as a potent political force during the 1990s. Proposition 187, a referendum on California's ballot in 1994, proved a lightning rod for anti-immigrant sentiment. The proposition called for making all undocumented aliens ineligible for any welfare services, schooling, and non-emergency medical care, and it required teachers and clinic doctors to report illegals to the police. Proponents, such as Republican Governor Pete Wilson, argued that illegals created a crushing burden on state and local welfare agencies and school systems. They also hoped the measure would force federal action to stem the flow of illegals. A spokesman for Americans Against Illegal Immigration, a pro-187 Southern California group, asserted, "Enough is enough. We're going broke in this state. . . . It's insanity, it doesn't make sense and the average guy in this country is not going to buy into it anymore." A deep and lingering economic recession during the early 1990s no doubt contributed to the state's increasingly anti-immigrant political mood.

Proposition 187 passed by a 3–2 margin, but it was immediately challenged in the streets and in the courts. In Los Angeles more than 70,000 people marched to protest its passage and the City Council voted not to enforce it. In 1998, after several years of legal wrangling, a Los Angeles federal district court judge ruled that Proposition 187 unconstitutionally usurped federal authority over immigration policy. But the national debate over immigration policy, in which economic issues and racial fears were deeply entangled, continued unabated. As one Stanford law professor who had worked to overturn Proposition 187 put it: "Some people genuinely worry about the problem of too many immigrants in a stagnant economy. But for most, economics is a diversion. Underneath it is race."

The Collapse of Communism

At the end of the 1980s, Americans watched with amazement as the political structures that had defined postwar eastern Europe disintegrated. In the Soviet Union, the political reforms initiated by Mikhail Gorbachev in the mid-1980s ultimately led to the dissolution of the Soviet state. By calling for a greater openness and a new spirit of democracy, Gorbachev had boldly challenged the Communist Party establishment that had dominated Soviet life for three-quarters of a century. He had also inspired open opposition to communist rule throughout eastern Europe. The outright revolt against communist rule gathered strength first in eastern European nations, then hit home in Moscow with stunning swiftness.

In June 1989 Poland held its first free elections since the communists took power after World War II, bringing an overwhelming victory for the Solidarity movement. Solidarity leader Tadeusz Mazowiecki became prime minister, forming a government that shared power with, but was no longer dominated by, communists. In Hungary, the Communist Party changed its name and called for a multiparty system, which in 1990 resulted in the election of a center-right government. In the fall of 1989 angry prodemocracy demonstrations forced out long-time Communist Party leaders in Czechoslovakia, Bulgaria, and Romania.

Most dramatic of all were the events in East Germany. First Hungary opened its border with Austria, allowing the exit of East Germans gathered at the West German Embassy in Budapest. Then huge protests broke out during official celebrations of East Germany's fortieth anniversary, and thousands of refugees flooded routes to the West. The Berlin Wall had suddenly been rendered irrelevant. The wall, which for thirty years had loomed as the ultimate symbol of cold war division, was torn down by gleeful protesters. Revelations of corruption forced East Germany's Communist Party leaders out of power and paved the way for German reunification the next year.

In the Soviet Union political change had progressed more slowly. In 1987, on the seventieth anniversary of the Russian Revolution, Gorbachev had denounced Josef Stalin, helping to legitimize growing criticism of censorship and organs of political repression, including the secret police, or KGB. In March 1989, the Soviet Union held its first free elections since 1917 as a new Congress of People's Deputies replaced the old Communist Party–dominated Supreme Soviet. Hundreds of party officials went down to defeat. In early 1990, over the fierce objections of hard-liners, the Central Committee agreed to Gorbachev's plan to end the Communist Party's constitutional monopoly of power. In elections held in March 1990, prodemocracy groups in Russia, Ukraine, and Byelorussia achieved major gains, and the Communist Party lost control of the local governments in Moscow, Leningrad, and other cities. By the middle of 1991, most of the fifteen republics that constituted the Soviet Union had announced plans to break away from Moscow's control.

German demonstrators defiantly tearing down the Berlin Wall, November 1989. For three decades the wall dividing East and West Berlin had embodied the political divisions of the cold war. Images such as these underscored the passing of an era.

The party's hard-liners made one final attempt to prevent the dissolution of the Soviet Union. In August 1991, they attempted a coup by placing Gorbachev under house arrest at his vacation home in the Crimea, reasserting control of the press, and banning street demonstrations. Boris Yeltsin, president of the Russian Republic, denounced Gorbachev's removal and urged thousands of Muscovites gathered outside the Parliament building to resist. The coup failed when Soviet army troops refused orders to attack the Russian parliament building. Upon his return from the Crimea, Gorbachev resigned as head of the Communist Party and then banned it. As leader of Russia, the largest of the republics, Yeltsin now emerged as the most powerful political leader. At the end of 1991 Russia proclaimed its independence and, along with Ukraine and Byelorussia (now Belarus), formed the Commonwealth of Independent States. Eight more republics quickly joined the new commonwealth, and on Christmas Day 1991 a weary and bitter Gorbachev resigned as president of the Soviet Union and recognized the Commonwealth of Independent States.

In the end, Gorbachev's zeal to reform politics had outrun his ability to reform the economy. As one sympathetic editorial in *Pravda* put it: "Gorbachev was unable to change the living standards of the people, but he changed the people." Attempts to move toward a more open free-market economy had been stymied by resistance of the entrenched and privileged Communist Party apparatchiks. A severe shortage of capital had also hampered plans to shift the economy toward greater production of consumer goods. Promises of economic investment and technical aid from the United States and the European Economic Community ran far behind the actual delivery of assistance. Violent ethnic conflict and a weak economy threatened the future of the new commonwealth. The sticky question of who controlled the enormous nuclear and military might of the former Soviet Union remained unresolved. Gorbachev and the movement he had inspired had wrought revolutionary changes. But the 280 million people of the former Soviet Union faced a very uncertain future.

The Persian Gulf War

Like most Americans, President George Bush greeted the momentous changes in the Soviet Union and eastern Europe with a sense of hope. A consensus emerged among the nation's citizens and elected officials that the cold war was over. The collapse of the Soviet Union meant the end of the great superpower rivalry that had shaped American foreign policy and domestic politics since World War II. What, if anything, would take its place? Bush spoke optimistically of an emerging "new world order" for the post–cold war era, "freer from the threat of terror, stronger in the pursuit of justice, and more secure in the quest for peace, an era in which the nations of the world, East and West, North and South, can prosper and live in harmony." But the first great post–cold war international crisis demonstrated how new kinds of conflicts might now define global politics. Economic competition, ethnic hatreds, and regional struggles for power seemed to replace the old ideological divide between the United States and the Soviet Union as the fulcrum of international conflict.

On August 2, 1990, 120,000 Iraqi troops backed by 850 tanks swept into neighboring Kuwait and quickly seized control of that tiny country. The motives of Saddam Hussein, Iraq's military dictator, were mixed. Like most Iraqis, Saddam believed that oil-rich Kuwait was actually an ancient province of Iraq that had been illegally carved away by British imperial agents in the 1920s as part of the dismemberment of the Ottoman Empire. Control of Kuwait would give Saddam control of its huge oil reserves, as well as Persian Gulf ports for his landlocked country. Rivalry within the Organization of Petroleum Exporting Countries (OPEC) was a factor as well. Iraq, just emerging from an exhausting and inconclusive eight-year war with Iran, bitterly resented Kuwait's production of oil beyond OPEC quotas, which had helped send the world price of oil plummeting from the highs of the 1970s and early 1980s.

The United States responded swiftly to news of the invasion. Its first concern was that Saddam also might attack Saudi Arabia, which the United States had defined as vital to its interests as far back as 1943. On August 15, President Bush ordered U.S. forces to Saudi Arabia and the Persian Gulf, calling the action Operation Desert Shield. The president stressed the importance of oil supplies. "Our jobs, our way of life, our own freedom, and the freedom of friendly countries around the world will suffer if control of the world's great oil reserves fall in the hands of that one man, Saddam Hussein." The United States also led a broad coalition in the United Nations that condemned the Iraqi invasion of Kuwait and declared strict economic sanctions against Iraq if it did not withdraw. By the middle of October, some 230,000 American troops had been sent to the Persian Gulf.

In early November, President Bush announced a change in policy to what he called "an offensive military option," and the U.S. troop deployment quickly doubled to more than 400,000, reaching 580,000 by January 1991. The president also shifted to the moral high ground in justifying the biggest U.S. troop buildup since the Vietnam War. "The fight isn't about oil," he insisted. "The fight is about naked aggression that will not stand." Bush administration officials now demonized Saddam as another Adolf Hitler and warned that he controlled a formidable fighting machine of over a million men. The UN sanctions failed to budge Saddam from Kuwait, and the drift to war now looked inevitable. In January 1991, the Senate and House of Representatives vigorously debated a joint resolution authorizing the president to use military force. Opponents urged the president to give the economic sanctions more time to force Iraq out of Kuwait, and they warned of the bloody cost of a drawn-out ground war against Saddam. They also pointed out that only recently the United States had supported Saddam in his war with Iran by providing economic aid, wheat exports, and arms sales. Supporters argued that if war came, it would be both morally just and in the nation's strategic economic interest. The resolution passed narrowly in the Senate (52 to 47) and more comfortably in the House (250 to 183).

U.S. *Marines swept into Kuwait City, March 1991. After six weeks of intensive bombing and less than five days after the start of a massive ground offensive,* U.S. *and allied forces overwhelmed the Iraqi army and ended Saddam Hussein's occupation of Kuwait.*

A last-minute UN peace mission failed to break the deadlock. On January 16, 1991, President Bush announced the start of Operation Desert Storm. U.S. and Allied air forces began forty-two days of massive bombing of Iraqi positions in Kuwait, as well as Baghdad and other Iraqi cities. They dropped 142,000 tons of bombs on Iraq and Kuwait, roughly

Looters struggled to make off with their booty during the Los Angeles riots of April 1992. Most of the 12,000 people arrested during the riots were from the most economically marginal elements of the L.A. population, including a large number of recent immigrants from Central America and Mexico.

six times the equivalent of the atomic bomb dropped on Nagasaki in World War II. The ground war began on February 24, taking only 100 hours to force Saddam out of Kuwait. Iraqi troops, most of whom were poor conscripts reluctant to fight, surrendered in droves. Saddam's vaunted military machine turned out to be far weaker than advertised. U.S. forces lost only 184 dead, compared with nearly 100,000 Iraqi deaths, mostly from bombing.

At home, the vast majority of Americans supported Operation Desert Storm; the scattered antiwar protests around the nation received scant media coverage. Almost every community in the country had sent men and women to the Gulf either as part of regular armed forces units or as National Guard support personnel. Millions placed yellow ribbons outside their doors as a show of support for American forces. Unlike what occurred during the Vietnam War, television coverage showed virtually no blood or death. The Pentagon required "military escorts" to accompany all reporters, giving army commanders unprecedented control over the press. The Pentagon carefully regulated the release of silent film footage documenting precision bombing runs. On television these looked more like video games than bombing attacks. American military officials insisted that the bombing had been limited to Iraqi military targets. But subsequent investigations revealed the devastation of Iraq's electrical and communications systems, waterways, bridges, factories, and highways—in short, the nation's entire infrastructure.

Politically, the Persian Gulf War marked the high point of President Bush's popularity. Along with General Norman Schwarzkopf and General Colin Powell, chairman of the Joint Chiefs of Staff, Bush enjoyed enormous acclaim in the afterglow of the swift victory. To most Americans, the war seemed a welcome reassertion of the nation's military prowess and world leadership. Bush received a hero's welcome from a joint session of Congress in March. His approval rating with the public reached nearly 90 percent, higher than President Franklin Roosevelt's during World War II.

Yet nagging questions remained. Saddam himself survived, and the United States abandoned Iraqi opposition forces and the Kurds of northern Iraq after encouraging them to rebel. The United States had succeeded in restoring the government of

Kuwait to power, but that government was itself an undemocratic feudal monarchy. The ecological damage in the Gulf region, mainly due to the torching of Kuwaiti oil wells by Iraqi troops, was extensive. The massive bombing of Iraq led to a severe public health crisis and destroyed the country's economy. Human rights groups reported an appalling toll among civilians. Congressman Jim McDermott (D-Washington), who visited Iraq during the summer after the war, testified before a House committee on the misery he saw and the ethical dilemma posed by American policy. "The Iraqi people did not vote for Saddam Hussein, yet hundreds of thousands of Iraqis, most of them children, are hungry, sick, and dying because of Saddam's intransigence and our commitment to oust Hussein at all cost." The war brought an intense spirit of triumph to the people of the United States. But for the 18 million people of Iraq, heavily bombed and left with Saddam in power, it produced the worst possible outcome.

Multicultural Riot in Los Angeles

In the spring of 1992 a devastating riot in Los Angeles offered the starkest evidence of how racial tensions and desperate poverty continued to plague many American communities. The spark that ignited the worst riot of the century was black outrage over police brutality. Rodney King, a black motorist, had been severely beaten by four white police officers after being stopped and pulled from his vehicle in 1991. An amateur videotape of the incident made by an onlooker was aired widely on television news shows, and it seemed to confirm long-standing charges by minority groups that many Los Angeles police officers were racist.

The four white officers were charged with eleven counts of assault, but they were tried in the white middle-class suburb of Simi Valley. When the jury acquitted them of all but one charge, minority communities erupted in outrage. For three days, rioters swept through South Central Los Angeles and nearby Koreatown, looting and burning businesses. Fifty-one people were killed, more than $750 million in damage was reported, and about 500 buildings were destroyed before L.A. police and National Guard troops managed to restore order. More than 12,000 people were arrested for looting, arson, and violations of curfew. Journalists were quick to make comparisons with the Watts riot of 1965, in which thirty-four people died. But the 1992 riot was different. Not only was it more deadly and more destructive, it was also more complex. The riot was not simply a black-versus-white affair. It was a multicultural riot that involved the large Korean and Latino populations of Los Angeles as well.

A Sheriff's Department analysis of riot-related arrests revealed that 45 percent of those arrested were Latino, 41 percent African American, and 12 percent Anglo. Sixty percent lacked prior criminal records. They included a large number of poor, non-English-speaking recent immigrants from Mexico, El Salvador, and Nicaragua, many of whom were undocumented. These rioters represented the most desperate and marginal people in Los Angeles. They were generally confined to minimum wage jobs as laborers, busboys, domestics, and factory workers, and their unemployment rate had tripled during two years of economic recession. Thousands lived in homeless colonies near the MacArthur Park neighborhood and in the concrete bed of the Los Angeles River. Those who engaged in looting appeared more interested in clothing and food than in televisions or other consumer durables.

The city's large Korean community suffered enormous economic and psychological damage in the riot. Almost 2,000 Korean businesses, mostly liquor stores, groceries, and discount "swap meets," were destroyed. Koreans angrily accused the police of making no effort to defend their stores, and many hired armed guards to patrol their property. Animosity between Korean store owners and African American customers ran deep. Black people had been outraged by the recent acquittal of a Korean grocer who had shot and killed an African American girl she thought was stealing a bottle of orange juice. Black people also complained about the large number of Korean-owned liquor stores in South Central. They resented the success of Korean businesses in black neighborhoods, where very few Koreans lived. The Korean community, generally ambitious and hardworking, questioned why it had been singled out for attack and wondered if the American dream was dead.

For most African Americans, the situation in Los Angeles seemed more desperate than ever, reflecting many of the larger trends in American society over the previous decade. The poverty rate in South Los Angeles was 30.3 percent, over twice the national average. The unemployment rate for adult black males hovered around 40 percent, and a quarter of the population was on welfare. Los Angeles had lost 100,000 manufacturing jobs in the three years before the riot. In 1978, the passage of the statewide Proposition 13 tax cut had led to a sharp reduction in public investment in the inner-city educational system. Drug dealing and gang warfare had escalated, reflecting the sense of despair among young people. The riot exposed the festering ethnic and racial divisions within Los Angeles. "We are all quite isolated in our own communities," a resident of Westwood, a mostly white middle-class neighborhood, explained. "We don't know and don't care about the problems in the inner cities. Driving to work every day most of us don't even know where South Central is—except many of us saw the fires from that direction when we were stuck in traffic."

The Election of 1992

As President Bush's popularity soared after the Persian Gulf War, most political analysts believed that he would win reelection easily. But the glow of military victory faded, and so did Bush's political fortunes. A harsh and lingering recession in 1991 and 1992 dominated the presidential election campaign. The recession was different from other post–World War II slumps in several ways. Although interest rates were low and theoretically should have encouraged investment, business continued to shrink rather than expand. The nation's manufacturers faced stiffer competition than ever, especially from Japan, Korea, and the industrialized nations of Europe. As unemployment climbed above 8 percent, consumer confidence and retail sales plummeted. The effect of previous recessions had been hardest on blue-collar workers, but this one hit white-collar workers severely as well, leaving many in the declining real estate, financial, and computer industries unemployed.

The paradoxes of the Reagan-Bush years became apparent. Conservatives took credit for forcing the fall of communism and reviving America's military strength. Yet the fundamental international problem facing the country seemed to be the erosion of American economic competitiveness and the decline in real wages. In communities devastated by the loss of key industries, millions wondered whether the structural changes transforming the world economy meant an irreversible decline in the American standard of living. Conservatives had made cutting government spending a central premise of their appeal. But after twelve years of Republican rule the national debt stood at an astronomical $4 trillion and threatened to undermine the

Republican President George Bush, Democrat Bill Clinton, and independent H. Ross Perot debated the issues on television three times during the 1992 presidential campaign. Bush emphasized the "character" issue by hammering away at Clinton's failure to serve during the Vietnam War. Clinton focused on the plight of the "forgotten middle class," many of whom had deserted the Democratic Party. Perot made the national debt the centerpiece of his campaign, and he appealed to voter frustration with the two major parties.

nation's economic future. Perhaps the clearest success for Reagan and Bush came in remaking the courts; by 1992, 65 percent of all federal judges and a majority of Supreme Court justices were their appointees. Conservative courts rewrote criminal procedure and allowed states to limit women's access to abortion.

During the primary elections President Bush faced a challenge from the right with the insurgent candidacy of conservative commentator Patrick Buchanan. A former aide to Presidents Nixon and Reagan, Buchanan espoused a conservate ideology that emphasized "traditional values": opposition to abortion and gay rights; celebration of the nuclear family above all others; attacks on government social programs, welfare recipients, and the poor; and a tough stance on crime. Buchanan failed to win any primaries, but his campaign forced the president to shore up his conservative flank. At the Republican National Convention Buchanan and the Reverend Pat Robertson, a conservative fundamentalist, tried to frame the upcoming election as a "cultural war," and in the process they alienated many moderate voters.

After a vigorous primary season the Democrats nominated Governor Bill Clinton of Arkansas. Clinton had begun his political life as a liberal, anti-Vietnam War Democrat. But after suffering defeat in his quest for a second term as governor of Arkansas, he had remade himself politically as a centrist. Clinton's campaign for the nomination effectively adopted many of the conservative themes that had proved so popular for Republicans over the past twelve years. He called for "responsibility" on the part of recipients of social programs, spoke of the importance of stable families, promised to be tough on crime and bureaucracy, and stressed the need for encouraging private investment to create new jobs. Clinton also promised to reform the nation's ailing health care system.

A wild-card element in the 1992 election was the independent campaign of Texas billionaire H. Ross Perot. Perot had made a fortune with a data-processing company that had computerized Social Security and Medicare records in the 1960s and 1970s. He promoted his candidacy through appearances on television talk shows, hoping to bypass traditional media outlets and reach voters directly. With his folksy, East Texas twang, Perot appealed to the deep distrust and anger that millions of people felt toward the two major parties. He made the national debt his central issue, and he argued that a successful businessman like him was better qualified to solve the nation's economic woes than Washington insiders. Perot spent millions of dollars of his own money funding "volunteer" organizations in the fifty states. In July, with polls showing him running nearly even with Bush and Clinton, he abruptly announced that he was quitting the race. His reasoning was unclear. Two months later, in an effort to restore his damaged reputation, he reentered the race.

All the candidates' campaigns featured sophisticated new media strategies. Clinton, Bush, and Perot appeared frequently on call-in television and radio talk shows in an effort to circumvent the power of professional journalists and connect more directly with voters. Perot spent millions of dollars on half-hour "infomercials" broadcast over the major networks. Clinton made a special effort to reach younger voters by appearing on MTV and youth-oriented programs. As the first baby-boomer candidate, the forty-six-year-old Clinton stressed the theme of generational change.

On election day, the Democrats recaptured the White House after twelve years of Republican control. Clinton won big, beating Bush 43 percent to 38 percent in the popular vote and 370 to 168 in the electoral vote. Although he carried no states, Perot garnered 19 percent of the popular vote, the strongest showing by a third-party candidate since Theodore Roosevelt in 1912. Clinton ran especially strong in the Northeast, the industrial Midwest, and the West, where he became the first Democratic presidential candidate to capture California since Lyndon Johnson in 1964. Clinton won back many of the Reagan Democrats, and his campaign also broke the long Republican grip on the states of the trans-Mississippi West.

"The Era of Big Government Is Over"

With a solidly Democratic House and Senate, President Clinton called for an "American renewal" as he began his first term. A self-styled "new Democrat," he tempered his commitment to activist government with a strategy sensitive to widespread cynicism about Washington politics and "big government" in general. Although his party also controlled Congress, Clinton sought to distance himself from its liberal core. On several key domestic and foreign policy issues Clinton thus found himself fighting with Democrats nearly as much as with Republicans.

As part of a campaign strategy that promised a new government attentiveness to the "forgotten middle class," Clinton pledged a sweeping reform of the nation's health-care system. Nearly 40 million Americans had no health insurance at all. Many simply could not afford it, and others were denied coverage by private insurers because of preexisting conditions such as AIDS and heart disease. Sudden illness or long-term hospital care could wipe out the savings of the uninsured and underinsured. For millions of others, health insurance was tied to the workplace; and a loss or change of jobs threatened

U. S. Secretary of State Madeleine Albright and United Nations Secretary General Kofi Annan begin a session of the Security Council on Africa at UN headquarters, September 25, 1997. Albright, the first woman Secretary of State in American history, embodied President Bill Clinton's commitment to appointing more women to high offices in his administration.

their coverage. National spending on health care had skyrocketed from roughly $200 billion in 1980 to more than $800 billion in 1992, constituting about one-seventh of the entire domestic economy.

Once in office Clinton appointed his wife, Hillary Rodham Clinton, to head a task force charged with preparing a sweeping legislative overhaul of health care. The task force sought a political middle ground between conservative approaches, which stressed fine tuning the system by making private insurance available to all, and more liberal approaches, which would have the federal government guarantee health care as a right. Indeed, nearly 100 House Democrats supported a "single payer plan" modeled on the Canadian system of government-run, universal health care.

The complex plan that emerged from the task force in the fall of 1993 was difficult to understand and impossible to sell politically. Under this "managed competition" proposal, most Americans would obtain coverage through large purchasing groups called health-care alliances. Employers would be mandated to pay at least 80 percent of their employees' insurance premiums. Private insurance companies would remain at the center of the system.

Powerful forces attacked the Clinton administration's health-care plan immediately. The Chamber of Commerce and National Association of Manufacturers opposed the employer mandate provision. Republicans and conservative Democrats called for greater reliance on "market forces" and criticized the "big government" approach. Many of these members of Congress had received large campaign donations from political action committees associated with the pharmaceutical industry, insurance companies, and the American Medical Association. One of the most powerful of these special interest groups, the Health Insurance Association of America, spent millions of dollars on a series of television advertisements designed to spread doubts about the administration's plan. After a year of congressional wrangling, no plan was approved and the president was forced to abandon his reform effort.

In foreign affairs Clinton focused on improving America's international trade position as the key to national economic growth. He pushed two important trade agreements through Congress, both of which built on efforts by the Reagan and Bush administrations to expand markets and encourage "free trade." Approved in late 1993, the North American Free Trade Agreement (NAFTA) eased the international flow of goods, services, and investments among the United States, Mexico, and Canada by eliminating tariffs and other trade barriers. Supplemental agreements called for cooperation on environmental and labor concerns. The broad goal of NAFTA was to improve productivity and living standards through a freer flow of commerce in North America. It created the largest free trade zone in the world, comprising 360 million people and an annual gross national product of $6 trillion. In 1994 Congress also approved the General Agreement on Tariffs and Trade (GATT), which slashed tariffs on thousands of goods throughout the world and phased out import quotas imposed by the United States and other industrialized nations. It also established the World Trade Organization to mediate commercial disputes among 117 nations. GATT supporters argued that the agreement would encourage global competition, thereby boosting American export industries and creating new high-wage jobs for American workers.

But NAFTA and GATT barely won approval after bruising congressional fights, and both found their strongest champions among Republicans. Many Democrats in Congress, especially those from traditionally liberal

districts in the Northeast and Midwest, bitterly opposed the agreements, creating a strain within the party. Critics of GATT questioned the rosy predictions of a net gain in high-wage jobs. Increases in imports, they pointed out, would threaten hundreds of thousands of high-paying jobs in American industries such as automobiles and textiles. Opponents of NAFTA feared that the free trade agreements would mean an exodus of millions of jobs to Mexico because industries would be attracted there by its low wages and lax enforcement of workers' rights. They worried, too, that the environmental sections of the agreement were too weak to prevent Mexico from becoming a haven for corporate polluters.

In the first few years after the passage of NAFTA and GATT many of these fears seemed confirmed. Free trade with the United States was supposed to bring prosperity to Mexico, but instead the peso collapsed and the Mexican economy slipped into a serious depression. From 1994 to 1997 the wages of the average Mexican worker fell from $1.45 per hour to only 78 cents. Trade did boom between the two countries, but a 1997 study conducted by the Department of Labor estimated that some 142,000 U.S. and Canadian jobs had been lost as a direct result of NAFTA. Moreover, the report admitted, many American employers were using the threat of moving plants or facilities to Mexico as a weapon in wage negotiations with workers. There was also increasing evidence that environmental conditions along the U.S.-Mexico border were growing worse, not better, and there were several episodes in which tainted Mexican fruit and vegetables caused local epidemics in American communities.

The failure of health-care reform and the debate over NAFTA revealed a Democratic Party deeply divided against itself. President Clinton's political position was also weakened by publicity attending his personal life. Paula Jones, a former Arkansas state employee, filed a sexual harassment suit against him. Nagging questions arose about real estate deals in which Clinton and his wife were involved while he was still governor of Arkansas—a scandal that became known as Whitewater. Responding to Republican charges that a former business partner of Clinton's had received favorable insider treatment in connection with a failed savings and loan company, the Attorney General eventually appointed an independent counsel, former judge Kenneth Starr.

Reacting to doubts about Clinton's character and leadership, voters in the 1994 congressional elections rewarded Republicans with control of both the House and Senate for the first time in forty years—a disaster of historic proportions for Clinton and the Democratic Party. Congress was now dominated by a new breed of younger, ideologically more conservative Republicans. Their leader was the new House Speaker, Newt Gingrich of Georgia. First elected to Congress in 1978, Gingrich had quickly won a reputation as a formidable polemicist for the Republican Party's far right. A brilliant organizer and fund raiser, he had moved from the margins to the center of his party's power structure. With his scathing denunciations of big government, attacks on the counterculture of the 1960s, and celebration of entrepreneurship, Gingrich captured the heart of the Republican Party and emerged as potentially the most influential House Speaker in this century.

The Republicans exploited prevailing social conditions. As more and more working-class and middle-class voters expressed fear for their jobs and economic security in the new global economy, race and immigration loomed as effective "hot button" issues for political candidates. With attacks on welfare, affirmative action, and federal initiatives to aid education and the inner cities, conservatives exploited a continuing white backlash against the limited economic and political gains African Americans had achieved in the previous decades. No candidates addressed the deepening poverty and economic inequality that put one of every seven Americans, and one of every five children, below the poverty line.

The Republican victory at the polls allowed Gingrich to challenge Clinton as the key figure setting the nation's political agenda. His priorities were expressed in a set of proposals labeled the "Contract with America." Invoking the "hundred days" of Franklin D. Roosevelt's New Deal in 1933 (Chapter 24), Gingrich promised to bring all these proposals to a vote in the House within 100 days. The House did indeed pass much of the Contract, including a large tax cut, an increase in military spending, cutbacks in federal regulatory power in the environment and at the workplace, a tough anticrime bill, and a sharp reduction in federal welfare programs. Differences with the Senate, however, and the threat of presidential veto thwarted Gingrich's plans and created conditions that allowed President Clinton to make a political comeback.

In December of 1995 the Republican-controlled Congress forced a shutdown of the federal government rather than accede to President Clinton's demand for changes in their proposed budget. The result was a public relations disaster for the Republicans. Gingrich's reputation plummeted, and after little more than a year as Speaker he had become one of the most unpopular figures in American politics.

The Election of 1996 and Clinton's Second Term

Meanwhile, Clinton undercut the Republicans by adapting many of their positions to his own. He endorsed the goal of a balanced federal budget and

The era of divided government at century's end meant that Democrats controlled the White House while Republicans dominated the Congress. Here President Bill Clinton talked to Senate Majority Leader Trent Lott (R-MS), as House Speaker Newt Gingrich (R-GA) looked on, during a White House meeting to discuss combating terrorism, July 29, 1996.

declared, in his January 1996 State of the Union message, that "the era of big government is over." With such deft maneuvers, the president set the theme for his 1996 reelection campaign, portraying himself as a reasonable conservative and the Republicans in Congress as conservative radicals. In a blitz of effective television ads, Democrats portrayed Republicans as reckless extremists bent on destroying the safety net of Social Security and Medicare and inattentive to the educational needs of children.

Leading Republicans, meanwhile, attacked each other as they fought to win their party's presidential nomination. In the state primaries leading up to the national convention, Robert Dole of Kansas, Majority Leader of the Senate, was forced to move to his right to counter more conservative opponents such as commentator Patrick Buchanan and wealthy publisher Steve Forbes, who advocated replacing the income tax with a so-called "flat tax." Dole had the nomination locked up by June, but the bruising primary battles cost him the support of many voters who worried that Dole's positions were cut from the same cloth as Gingrich's "Contract with America."

Dole waged an inept campaign for president, Clinton a brilliant one. A veteran of the Senate, Dole was at home in the halls of Congress but extremely uncomfortable on the campaign trail. Seventy-three years old and a poor public speaker, he proved a pale contrast to Clinton—young, vigorous, and surely one of the most adroit politicians of the century. Sensing Dole's weakness, Ross Perot once again threw his hat into the ring as the candidate of his own Reform Party, siphoning off many potential Dole supporters.

Pursuing a strategy his advisers called "triangulation," the president successfully positioned himself above and between the interests of warring Democrats and Republicans. Welfare reform provided a prominent example of this strategy in action. Despite his attacks on the Republicans as radicals, Clinton opposed his own party's efforts to block a Republican plan to dismantle the federal welfare system in place since the New Deal. The new legislation—the Welfare Reform Act—abolished the sixty-year-old Aid to Families with Dependent Children program (AFDC). Poor mothers with dependent children would now have access to aid for only a limited period and only if they were preparing for or seeking work. When Congress passed the act in August of 1996, Clinton held a public signing ceremony and declared "an end to welfare as we know it."

Clinton's greatest strength was a resurgent American economy. The recession that had plagued George Bush's presidency bottomed out in 1994, followed over the next two years by strong economic growth, a dramatic rise in the stock market, and a sharp decline in unemployment. Some economists began to talk of a "third industrial revolution," led by high-technology companies, that would produce an extended boom. Others went so far as to suggest that the new, technology-driven global economy might end the historic business cycle of boom and bust. Such claims easily could be dismissed as wildly optimistic speculation—but the political credit for the newly robust economy went largely to President Clinton.

Confounding the predictions of political pundits, who had pronounced his political death after the Republican congressional sweep of 1994, President Bill Clinton won a resounding reelection victory in

November of 1996. But it was a victory without coattails; the Republicans retained control of both houses of Congress. The era of big government may have ended, as Clinton had proclaimed, but the era of divided government would continue.

The 1996 campaign had been the most expensive in history. The Democrats spent $250 million, the Republicans $400 million, a total that was more than twice the amount spent in 1992. Both parties created fund-raising machines of enormous ingenuity and dubious legality. In 1997 Republicans organized congressional hearings that exposed Democratic campaign finance abuses, such as soliciting funds in the White House. But with Congress unable to agree on campaign finance reform, the revelations served only to deepen popular cynicism about the electoral process.

The conflict between the Democratic president and the Republican Congress reached historic proportions in 1998. Although the sexual harassment lawsuit brought by Paula Jones was thrown out of court that year, it indirectly led to the deepest crisis of the Clinton presidency. In the summer of 1998, independent counsel Kenneth Starr delivered an explosive report of his investigation to the House Judiciary Committee. The Starr report focused entirely on an extramarital affair the president had conducted with a young White House intern, Monica Lewinsky. Starr claimed his office had discovered evidence of the affair while reviewing depositions from the Paula Jones lawsuit. The report outlined several potentially impeachable offenses, allegedly committed by the president in the course of trying to keep his affair with Lewinsky secret. These included lying under oath, witness tampering, and obstruction of justice.

After agreeing to testify before a grand jury empanelled by Starr—a first for an American president—Clinton made an extraordinary television address to the nation in which he defended his legal position and attacked the Starr inquiry as politically motivated. The Congress and the American people at large fiercely debated the nature of the charges against the president: Were they truly impeachable—"high crimes and misdemeanors" as the Constitution put it—or merely part of a partisan political effort to overturn the election of 1996? In October 1998, the House of Representatives voted along largely partisan lines to begin a full-scale, open-ended inquiry into possible grounds for the impeachment of President Clinton. It was only the third time in American history that the House had taken such action.

Republicans expected the Lewinsky scandal and the impeachment inquiry to bolster their fortunes in the election of 1998, augmenting the gains the party out of power in the White House can traditionally expect in a midterm election. Indeed all summer and fall, virtually every professional pollster and media commentator predicted big Republican gains in the House and Senate. Instead, for the first time since 1934, the President's party added seats in a midterm election. The Democrats gained five seats in the House, cutting the Republican majority from 228–206 in the 105th Congress to 223–211 in the 106th. In the Senate, Republicans were unable to increase their 55–45 majority.

Voters no doubt had more on their minds than President Clinton's sex life. Democratic candidates benefited from continued strength in the economy, and they made effective appeals on a range of issues, from preserving Social Security and Medicare to protecting a woman's right to choose an abortion. Higher than expected turnout from such core constituencies as union members and African Americans (especially in the South) also contributed to the unexpectedly strong Democratic showing. The election also brought a shakeup in the Republican leadership. Newt Gingrich, under pressure from Republican colleagues angry about a campaign strategy that had narrowly focused on Clinton's impeachment problem, announced his resignation as Speaker of the House and from his seat in Congress. Ironically Gingrich, who had led the Republican resurgence in the 1990s, now appeared to be the first political victim of the Lewinsky scandal.

In the aftermath of the 1998 election, most politicians and analysts, and indeed most Americans, believed the impeachment inquiry to be at a dead end. But the House Judiciary Committee, after raucous televised debate, voted to bring four articles of impeachment—charging President Clinton with perjury, obstruction of justice, witness tampering, and abuse of power—to the full House. But unlike the bipartisan case the Judiciary Committee brought against Richard Nixon in 1974 (see Chapter 29), this time the votes were all along strictly party lines. Neither the 1998 election results, nor polls showing a large majority of Americans opposed to removing the President, curbed the Republican determination to push impeachment through the House. On December 19, 1998, for only the second time in American history, the full House voted to impeach a sitting president, passing articles charging Clinton with perjury and obstruction of justice along party lines and sending them to the Senate for trial. The impeachment drive could be understood as the culmination of divided government and the bitterly partisan turn American politics had taken since 1980.

Changing American Communities

The 1990 census showed that for the first time in U.S. history a majority of Americans lived within large metropolitan areas. The census defined a metropolitan area as "one or more counties including a large population nucleus and nearby communities that have a high degree of interaction." The census divided these areas into two groups: those with populations above 1 million and those with smaller populations. It revealed that nearly 125 million people out of a total population of 249 million lived within the thirty-nine large (over 1 million) metropolitan centers. Greater New York City, with more than 18 million people, was the largest of these areas, followed by Greater Los Angeles, with 14.5 million residents. The nation's fastest-growing large metropolitan areas were all in the West and South. These included Orlando, which grew by 53 percent in the 1980s, Phoenix (40 percent), Sacramento (34 percent), San Diego (34 percent), Dallas-Fort Worth (32 percent), Atlanta (32 percent), and Los Angeles (26 percent).

This historic statistical shift stemmed directly from the expansion of the economy's service sector. The nation's postindustrial economy relied heavily on the growth of management, research and development, marketing, and distribution activities. These required the critical mass of educated people and services that could be found only in metropolitan areas. The proportion of the population with at least a college degree grew disproportionately in those areas, to 22.5 percent, compared with 13 percent in nonmetropolitan areas.

An enormous range of differences could be found both between and within metropolitan area communities. Recent immigrants brought a striking new multiculturalism to many coastal and Sunbelt "port of entry" communities, while smaller communities in the Midwest remained relatively unchanged. In Greater Los Angeles, for example, half the population was Hispanic, black, or Asian, and 27 percent of the residents were foreign-born. But the community that many demographers called typical was Indianapolis, where less than 15 percent of the population was Hispanic, black, or Asian and less than 2 percent of the residents were foreign-born. A larger percentage of people lived in expanding metropolitan areas, but a larger proportion of metropolitan people lived in the suburbs. Metropolitan expansion created huge semiurban sprawls, which erased the old boundaries between many towns. Population and job growth were concentrated at the geographic edges of metropolitan areas.

The suburban city of Plano, Texas, offered a harbinger of the future for many American communities. Part of the Dallas-Fort Worth metropolitan area, Plano's population jumped from 72,000 to 128,000 during the 1980s, an increase of 78 percent. Plano was one of five suburban cities with populations of more than 100,000 in the Dallas-Fort Worth area. The others included Arlington, Garland, Irving, and Mesquite. Altogether, these five suburban cities grew almost twice as much as Dallas and Fort Worth during the 1980s. Whereas the traditional American city was built around a central business district, newer suburban cities grew up around a principal business or economic activity: a collection of computer companies, a large regional medical center, or a sports complex. Plano's economic life revolved around Legacy Park, a huge office development housing one of the world's largest data-processing centers, along with the headquarters of five major corporations. Two large fiber optic communications stations kept Legacy Park plugged into the global economy. A nearby complex of telecommunications manufacturing plants provided another new source of jobs.

Every rush hour, traffic moved in both directions as commuters drove to and from Plano for jobs in office buildings, factories, warehouses, and shopping malls. During the 1980s, Plano began to display many attributes associated with large urban centers. Thai, Chinese, and other ethnic restaurants opened up. A quaint downtown featured antique and crafts shops in storefronts where cotton farmers used to buy supplies. The city boasted its own small chamber music ensemble. Yet the rapid growth of suburban cities like Plano also exposed and reinforced the deepening economic and racial divisions in American society. Plano had a very small immigrant and minority population, and nearly 90 percent of its public school students were white. In Dallas, by contrast, the 1990 census showed that for the first time a majority of the city's population was African American or Latino.

Suburban cities have become even more economically specialized than the industrial centers of the nineteenth century. Yet their gains often meant losses for older cities. As core cities like Fort Worth lost jobs and part of their tax base to suburban cities like Plano, it became more difficult for them to pay the costs of maintaining infrastructure and caring for the elderly, poor, and sick. While suburban cities like Plano often suffered from labor shortages, unemployment increased in the core cities, especially among African Americans and Latinos. Lack of adequate transportation and low-cost housing made it difficult for central-city residents to take advantage of new job opportunities in the suburban city.

CONCLUSION

In the late 1980s and early 1990s, as the nation faced competition from a tougher, more dynamic global economy, citizens, politicians, and business leaders had to rethink some of their most basic assumptions about the American way of life. American society became more stratified along lines of race and income. New immigrant groups, especially from Asia and Latin America, changed the face of the nation's neighborhoods, schools, and workplaces. New epidemics and spreading poverty threatened the public health of whole communities. New media technologies made cultural life more homogenized and caused the manipulation of image to become more crucial than ever in both politics and entertainment.

During these decades the very notion of community itself, once defined entirely in terms of

CHRONOLOGY

1980	Ronald Reagan is elected president
1981	Reagan administration initiates major cuts in taxes and domestic spending
	Military buildup accelerates
	AIDS is recognized and named
	MTV and CNN start broadcasting as cable channels
1982	Economic recession grips the nation
	Nuclear freeze rally attracts 750,000 in New York City
1983	Reagan announces the Strategic Defense Initiative, labeled "Star Wars" by critics
	241 marines are killed in Beirut terrorist bombing
	Marines land on Grenada and oust anti-American Marxist regime
1984	Reagan is reelected overwhelmingly
1985	Mikhail Gorbachev initiates reforms—*glasnost* and *perestroika*—in the Soviet Union
1986	Immigration Reform and Control Act addresses concerns about illegal aliens
	Democrats regain control of the Senate
1987	Iran-Contra hearings before Congress reveal arms-for-hostages deal and funds secretly, and illegally, diverted to Nicaraguan rebels
	Stock market crashes
	Reagan and Gorbachev sign INF Treaty
1988	George Bush is elected president
1989	Communist authority collapses in eastern Europe
1990	August: Iraqi invasion of Kuwait leads to massive U.S. military presence in the Persian Gulf
1991	January–February: Operation Desert Storm forces Iraq out of Kuwait
	Soviet Union dissolves into Commonwealth of Independent States
1992	Rodney King verdict sparks rioting in Los Angeles
	Bill Clinton is elected president
1993	Clinton administration introduces comprehensive health-care reform, but it fails to win passage in Congress
	Congress approves the North American Free Trade Agreement
1994	Republicans win control of Senate and House for first time in forty years
	Congress approves the General Agreement on Tariffs and Trade
	Congress passes the Comprehensive AIDS Revenue Emergency Act
1996	Congress passes Welfare Reform Act
	President Bill Clinton is reelected

space, increasingly became a function of demographics. The proliferation of computer-based communication technologies made it easier to create communities based on the demographic categories of income, profession, education level, and consumption preferences. The mass media, advertisers, and political professionals all intensified their reliance on sophisticated marketing and polling techniques. Thus American culture defined and addressed its citizens less as whole human beings and more as the sums of statistical characteristics. At the same time, new technologies created "virtual communities" with the potential for new kinds of human relationships not defined by corporate values or even by physical familiarity. As American communities continue to evolve in response to a more global, service-oriented, and high-tech economy, they will no doubt be forced to seek both regional and international solutions to the problems posed by the twenty-first century.

REVIEW QUESTIONS

1. Describe the central philosophical assumptions behind "Reaganomics." What were the key policies by which it was implemented? To what extent were these policies a break with previous economic approaches?
2. Evaluate Reagan-Bush era foreign policy. What successes and failures stand out? Which problems from those years remain central and/or unsolved for today's policy makers?
3. Analyze the key structural factors underlying recent changes in American economic and cultural life. Do you see any political solutions for the growth of poverty and inequality?
4. Assess the growing political appeal of conservatism in American life. How would you explain its successes? What future do you see for the liberal and radical traditions?
5. Is the United States entering a "new era" at the turn of the twenty-first century? What effects have the globalized economy and the fall of the Soviet Union had on American life?

RECOMMENDED READING

Donald Barlett and James B. Steele, *America: What Went Wrong* (1992). An expansion of the authors' series in the *Philadelphia Inquirer.* This book offers a mass of interesting data documenting the declining fortunes of the American middle class in the 1980s.

Sidney Blumenthal and Thomas B. Edsall, eds., *The Reagan Legacy* (1988). A collection of critical essays assessing the impact of Reagan's presidency on American society and culture.

Colin Campbell and Bert A. Rockman, eds., *The Clinton Presidency: First Appraisals* (1996). A wide-ranging collection of essays assessing the political and historical significance of the Clinton administration.

Haynes Johnson, *Sleepwalking through History* (1991). A readable, journalistic narrative of the Reagan presidency.

Michael T. Klare and Peter Kornbluh, eds., *Low Intensity Warfare* (1988). A valuable set of essays offering case studies of counterinsurgency and antiterrorist tactics during the 1980s.

Robert Lekachman, *Visions and Nightmares* (1987). An economist's view of Reagan's legacy, emphasizing the long-range impact of military spending, tax cuts, and the shrinking of social programs.

Nicolaus Mills, *Culture in an Age of Money* (1990). An acerbic account of the impact of corporate power and big money on the cultural life of the nation during the 1980s.

New York Times, The Downsizing of America (1996). A well-researched account detailing the devastating impact of corporate "downsizing" on American communities and families.

Kevin Phillips, *The Politics of Rich and Poor* (1990). A fascinating, superbly documented, and often brilliant analysis of the growth in economic inequality that characterized the 1980s. Phillips, a prominent Republican strategist, makes historical comparisons with the 1920s and the late nineteenth century to bolster his argument.

Howard Rheingold, *The Virtual Community* (1994). Very thoughtful examination of the promises and problems posed by the new computer-based technologies associated with "virtual communities."

Micah L. Sifry and Christopher Cerf, eds., *The Gulf War Reader* (1991). An excellent collection of historical essays, government documents, and political addresses that provides a comprehensive overview of the Persian Gulf War.

James B. Stewart, *Den of Thieves* (1991). A well-documented inside look at the people and events at the center of Wall Street's insider trader scandal. Stewart offers a detailed account of the shady financial practices of the 1980s.

ADDITIONAL BIBLIOGRAPHY

The Reagan Revolution

Ryan Barilleaux, *The Post-Modern Presidency* (1988)

Lou Cannon, *President Reagan: The Role of a Lifetime* (1991)

Rowland Evans and Robert Novak, *The Reagan Revolution* (1991)

Dilys Hill et al., *The Reagan Presidency* (1990)

Michael Schaller, *Reckoning with Reagan* (1992)

C. Brant Short, *Ronald Reagan and the Public Lands* (1989)

David Stockman, *The Triumph of Politics* (1986)

Susan Tolchin and Martin Tolchin, *Dismantling America: The Rush to Deregulate* (1983)

Garry Wills, *Reagan's America* (1987)

Reagan's Foreign Policy

Raymond Bonner, *Weakness and Deceit: U.S. Policy and El Salvador* (1984)
William J. Broad, *Teller's War: The Top-Secret Story behind the Star Wars Deception* (1992)
William E. Brock and Robert D. Hormats, eds., *The Global Economy* (1990)
Thomas Crothers, *In the Name of Democracy: U.S. Foreign Policy toward Latin America in the Reagan Years* (1991)
Theodore Draper, *A Very Thin Line: The Iran-Contra Affairs* (1991)
John L. Gaddis, *The United States and the End of the Cold War* (1992)
Stephen R. Graubard, *Mr. Bush's War* (1992)
Roy Gutman, *Banana Diplomacy* (1988)
Jonathan Kwitny, *Endless Enemies* (1984)
David E. Kyvig, ed., *Reagan and the World* (1990)
Walter LaFeber, *Inevitable Revolutions*, 2d ed. (1984)
Michael Mandelbaum, *Reagan and Gorbachev* (1987)
Bob Woodward, *Veil: The Secret Wars of the CIA* (1987)

Best of Times, Worst of Times

Michael A. Bernstein and David A. Adler, eds., *Understanding American Economic Decline* (1994)
Barbara Ehrenreich, *Fear of Falling: The Inner Life of the Middle Class* (1989)
Elizabeth Fee and Daniel M. Fox, eds., *AIDS: The Making of a Chronic Disease* (1992)
Bennet Harrison and Barry Bluestone, *The Great U Turn: Corporate Restructuring and the Polarizing of America* (1988)
James D. Hunter, *Culture Wars: The Struggle to Define America* (1991)
Daniel Ichbiah, *The Making of Microsoft* (1991)
Martin Lowy, *High Rollers: Inside the Savings and Loan Debacle* (1991)
Everett M. Rogers and Judith K. Larsen, *Silicon Valley Fever* (1984)
William Serrin, *Homestead* (1991)
Randy Shilts, *And the Band Played On* (1986)
Richard White, *Rude Awakenings: What the Homeless Crisis Tells Us* (1992)
William Julius Wilson, *The Truly Disadvantaged: The Inner City, the Underclass, and Public Policy* (1987)
Edward N. Wolff, *Top Heavy* (1995)

End of an Era?

Michael R. Beschloss and Strobe Talbott, *At the Highest Levels: The Inside Story of the End of the Cold War* (1994)
Mike Davis, *City of Quartz: Excavating the Future in Los Angeles* (1990)
Michael Duffy, *Marching in Place: The Status Quo Presidency of George Bush* (1992)
Susan Faludi, *Backlash: The Undeclared War against American Women* (1991)
Andrew Hacker, *Two Nations: Black and White, Separate, Hostile, and Unequal* (1992)
Richard Hallion, *Storm over Iraq* (1992)
Denis Lynn Daly Heyck, ed., *Barrios and Borderlands: Cultures of Latinos and Latinas in the United States* (1993)
Bill Ong Hing, *Making and Remaking Asian America through Immigration Policy, 1850–1990* (1993)
Juliet B. Schor, *The Overworked American* (1991)
James B. Stewart, *Blood Sport: The President and His Adversaries* (1996)
Reed Ueda, *Postwar Immigrant America* (1994)
Bob Woodward, *The Agenda: Inside the Clinton White House* (1994)

Biography

Charles F. Allen, *The Comeback Kid: The Life and Career of Bill Clinton* (1992)
Ken Gross, *Ross Perot: The Man behind the Myth* (1992)
Harry Hurt, *The Lost Tycoon: The Many Lives of Donald J. Trump* (1993)
Kitty Kelley, *Nancy Reagan* (1991)
Nicholas King, *George Bush* (1980)
David Maraniss, *First in His Class: A Biography of Bill Clinton* (1995)
Roger Morris, *Partners in Power: The Clintons and Their America* (1996)
Michael Rogin, *Ronald Reagan* (1987)

IMMIGRATION & COMMUNITY

The Changing Face of Ethnicity in America

SINCE 1930

During the last three quarters of the twentieth century, the character and sources of immigration to the United States changed radically. With America's growing power and prominence in the international arena, the laws governing immigration became increasingly tools of foreign policy. The social devastation of World War II and the ideological battles of the Cold War created whole new categories of immigrant, such as that of political refugee. Recent immigration has also reflected the dynamic transformations in the economies of the United States and of the rest of the world. The national quotas established in the 1920s severely limited the flow of immigrants from Europe. But lawmakers, responding to the labor needs of industry and agriculture, had placed no barriers to newcomers from the Western Hemisphere. Thus, Canadians and Mexicans grew into the two largest national immigrant groups. Circular migration shaped the experience of these peoples; they were *transborder peoples*, going frequently back and forth between their homelands and the United States. Dividing their political and cultural loyalties between the United States and their homelands, Mexicans and Canadians developed an ambiguous identity. As a result, they were slower to adopt U.S. citizenship than were other immigrants.

Some 1.4 million Canadians arrived in the United States between 1920 and 1960, with three quarters from British Canada (Ontario, Nova Scotia, New Brunswick) and one quarter from French Canada (Quebec). They settled close to the border, primarily in New England cities, such as Boston, Lowell, Nashua, and Holyoke, as well as in the Great Lakes region. During the same period, more than 840,000 Mexicans arrived as permanent settlers and 4.7 million more as temporary guest workers. They headed mainly for the rich agricultural areas of southern California and the lower Rio Grande Valley of Texas. Many, however, looking for factory work, settled in big Midwestern industrial centers such as Chicago, Detroit, and Kansas City. In the Southwest, Mexicans tended to cluster in isolated *barrios*. In the midwest, in contrast, following the pattern of older European immigrant communities in big cities, they tended to assimilate more.

Perhaps more than any other group, Mexican immigrants were subject to the vagaries of the U.S. economy. The Great Depression drastically reduced the need for their labor and spurred a mass reverse migration. As many as half a million Mexicans were repatriated during the 1930s, often at the urging of local American officials who did not want Mexican aliens on public relief rolls. The onset of World War II brought a new demand for Mexican labor in agriculture and transportation. In 1942 the U.S. and Mexican governments revived the guest worker program of World War I. The *bracero* ("farmhand") program admitted agricultural workers on short-term contracts; they were classified as foreign laborers, not immigrants. By 1947, some 200,000 *braceros* worked in twenty-one states, including 100,000 in California. Congress renewed the program after the war ended. By 1960 Mexicans made up more than one quarter of the nation's farm labor force.

Puerto Ricans, the third largest group of immigrants to the U.S. mainland from the Western Hemisphere, were a special case because, as U.S. citizens since 1917, they could come and go without restriction. Like Canadians and Mexicans, they helped fill the labor demand caused by the restriction of European immigration. Between 1945 and 1965 the Puerto Rican-born population jumped from 100,000 to roughly 1 million. The majority headed for New York City and surrounding communities.

Another growing class of immigrants consisted of refugees uprooted by World War II and the emergence of Communist regimes in Eastern Europe. A series of laws combined the historical notion of America as a haven for the world's oppressed with the new reality of Cold War power politics. The Displaced Persons Act of 1948 was the first law in American history to set refugee policy as opposed to immigration policy. It provided 202,000 visas over a two-year period, allowing permanent settlement in the United States for refugees from fascist and Communist regimes. A 1950 amendment upped the number of visas to 341,000 annually. The Refugee Relief Act of 1953 authorized admission of 205,000 "nonquota" refugees, but limited these to people fleeing persecution from Communist regimes. In practice, this policy gave priority to refugees from the Baltic states and Eastern European Communist nations; only a minority admitted under the act were Jews or other victims of Hitler. Indeed, hundreds of former Nazis, including many scientists, were allowed in under the act in the interest of "national security."

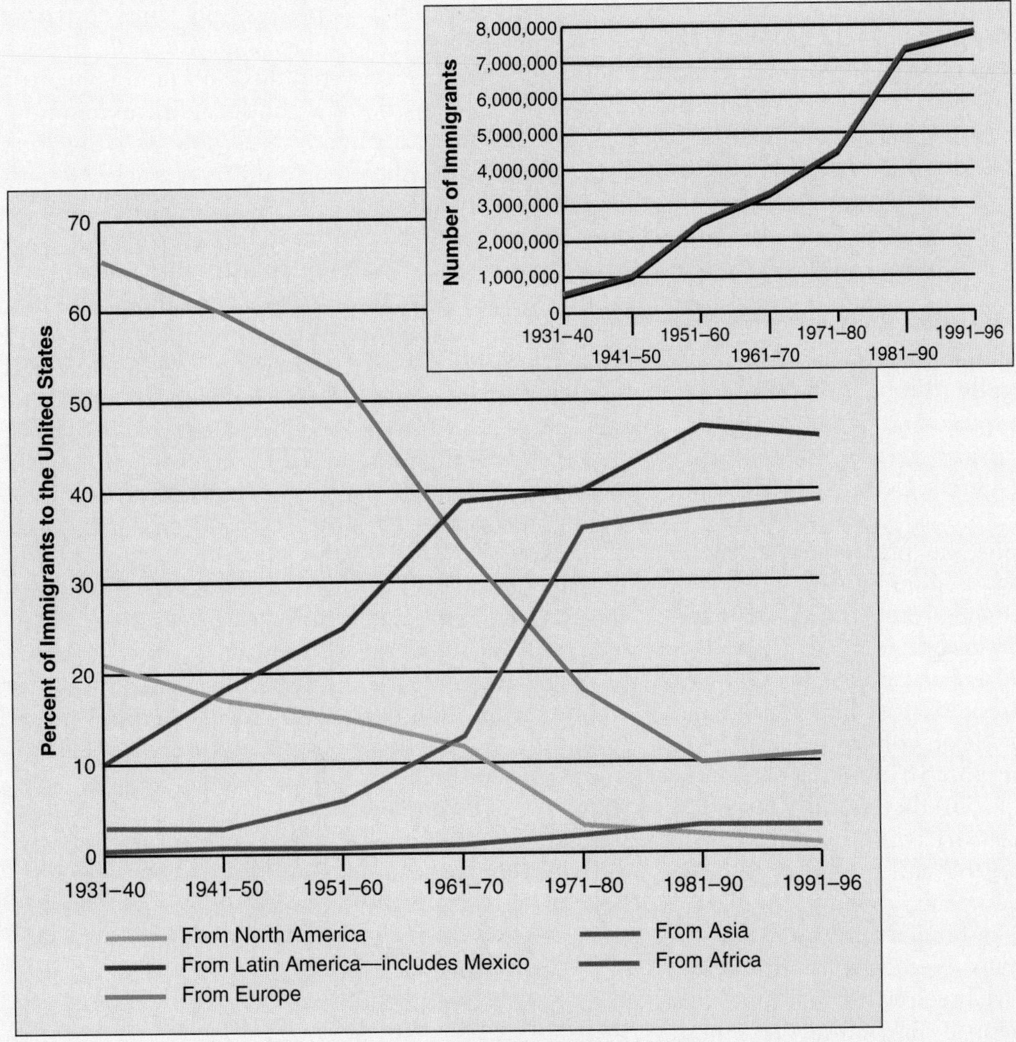

Immigration to the United States, by Decade, 1930–1996

In 1952, as a conservative counterpoint to the growth of refugee legislation, Congress passed the McCarran-Walter Act. Reaffirming the 1920s principle of discriminatory quotas based on national origin, the act specified that 85 percent of those admitted annually were to come from Northern and Western European countries. Yet McCarran-Walter also contained some important liberal innovations. It revoked the denial of admission based on race, and it allowed for small, token quotas for immigrants from China and Japan, ending the long-standing policy of Asian exclusion.

The Immigration Act of 1965, passed almost unnoticed in the context of the egalitarian political climate created by the Civil Rights movement, had revolutionary consequences, some of them unintended. The act abolished the discriminatory national origins quotas that had been in place since the 1920s. But it also limited immigration from the Western Hemisphere for the first time, allowing 120,000 annual visas from that region, compared to 170,000 from the Eastern Hemisphere. It continued the policy of selective admissions, but with important exceptions. Exempted from numerical quotas were immigrants seeking family reunification with American citizens or resident aliens. In addition, preferences to those with specialized job skills and training were extended to people from the nations of the Eastern Hemisphere.

The high priority given family reunification greatly increased the *chain migration* of people seeking to join relatives already in the United States. After 1965, Asian immigrants made up the fastest growing ethnic groups, with more than 1.5 million arriving during the 1970s, as opposed to roughly 800,000 from Europe. The new Asian migration included many professionals and well-educated technical workers. For example, immigrants from the Philippines and India included a high number of health care professionals, and many Chinese and Korean immigrants found work in professional and managerial occupations. At the same time, low-skilled and impoverished Asians poured into the "Chinatowns" and "Koreatowns" of cities like New York and Los Angeles, seeking work in restaurants, hotels, and garment manufacturing. The end of the Indochina War brought new refugees from Cambodia, Laos, and Vietnam. The 1965 act also created conditions that increased undocumented immigration from Latin America. The new limits on Western Hemisphere migration, along with simultaneous ending of the *bracero* program, tempted many thousands to enter the United States illegally. The Immigration and Naturalization Service arrested and deported 500,000 illegal aliens each year in the decade following the act, most of them from Mexico, Central America, and the Caribbean.

During the 1980s the rate of immigration accelerated. The estimated 6 million legal and 2 million undocumented immigrants who entered the United States during that decade was second only to the 8.8 million who had arrived between 1900 and 1910. By 1990, one out of every five immigrants living in the United States was Mexican-born, and Mexican Americans accounted for more than 60 percent of all Hispanics. Demographers predicted that by 2050 Hispanics would replace African Americans as the largest minority group in the nation.The number of Asian Americans more than doubled during the 1980s, from 3.5 million to 7.3 million. Nearly two out of every five Asian Americans lived in California, with 300,000 in Los Angeles' "Koreatown." Among recent immigrant groups, Asians—Vietnamese, Filipinos, Koreans, and Chinese—gained naturalization (citizenship) at the fastest rate. Asians totaled nearly 50 percent of all people naturalized in the 1980s. Unlike early-twentieth-century Asian migrants, the post-1965 newcomers were mostly intent on settling here permanently, and they migrated in family units. The new Asian immigrants also remade the small ethnic enclaves from earlier migrations, reinvigorating them with new energy, new capital, and a more explicit ethnic consciousness.

By the mid-1980s, growing concern over "illegal aliens" had become a hotly debated political issue, particularly in the Southwest. The Immigration Reform and Control Act of 1986 marked a break with past attempts to address this problem. Instead of mass deportation programs, the law offered an amnesty to all undocumented workers who had entered the country since 1982. Although opening the "front door" of admissions wider, the law also tried to shut the "back door" by imposing sanctions on employers who knowingly hired or recruited undocumented aliens. Yet no matter what Congress did, the desperate economic realities in Mexico and Central America continued to enlarge the flow of undocumented aliens. At the century's end, both American immigration policy and the immigrants now arriving look radically different than they did 75 years ago. Nativist sentiment and calls for greater immigration restriction are still powerful voices on the political scene, especially during economic downturns and within those states absorbing the bulk of new immigrants. Thus, in 1994, California voters, by a 3–2 margin, approved Proposition 187, which declared all undocumented immigrants ineligible for any welfare services, public schooling, and nonemergency medical care. But in 1998 a federal court ruled that Proposition 187 unconstitutionally usurped federal authority over immigration policy. Nativist appeals and campaigns will likely remain part of the American political landscape—but they have been defeated by the fundamental idea that immigration has ultimately strengthened America's economy, culture, and society. At the dawn of the new millennium, a glance at almost any American city, school, or workplace reinforces that point clearly.

IN THEIR OWN WORDS

Born in a small Estonian town in 1939, Anton Tamsarre and his family lived in camps for displaced persons after World War II. They were allowed entry into the United States under the Displaced Persons Act. Private agencies were responsible for placement, and the Tamsaares were sent by a Norwegian Lutheran Church agency to Fargo, North Dakota, in February of 1949.

> We came by boat. I remember it sailing into New York. [Laughs.] My father woke me up and showed me the Statue of Liberty. It was kind of nice! And then we took a train across the country. We were met in Fargo by some people from the Lutheran agency. We were taken to a little place with a population of one hundred or so—Arthur, North Dakota—where they had an old-folks home. My father's job was to be a caretaker there, and that's where we ended up for a while....
>
> I had a relatively conventional kind of midwestern American upbringing insofar as school life was concerned. At home, it was still quite foreign. We spoke Estonian, still do when I go home, but it's not a place noted for any immigrant culture. There are no ghettos. People kind of forget that you've come recently. You live just like everyone else....

No one ever made fun of me for being different. I suppose that was helped a little bit because I was a very good student. There was another interesting factor. My parents were very eager for me to succeed. This is not uncommon, I'm sure, with immigrant families, but there was an understanding that I was supposed to be number one in what I chose to do. I did manage to succeed there. I was valedictorian of the high school and of the college and straight A's all the way through. I took a great deal of pleasure in this. This was the way I made my identity.

Let me say just a couple of other things which occur to me as being important. One is this dislocation that occurred, which is so strong with my parents. Going from being upper middle class to lower middle class, this hurt them a great deal. They've dealt with this now. But this is an absolutely overpowering sort of theme. This change of status and then an attempt to gain respectability and wealth in some limited way. That is why they were very careful and very eager to have me do as well as I possibly could, and I'm sure it's also been in the back of my mind.[1]

Duong Van Minh came to the United States in 1975 at age twenty-five. A Catholic, he was raised in Saigon, earned a graduate degree in economics, and worked for the South Vietnamese government. He was one of the 130,000 Vietnamese refugees allowed to enter the United States at the end of the Indochina War.

I had a very wonderful sponsor in El Paso, Texas. The Ashbury United Methodist Church sponsor my family with three persons. They provide everything—house, transportation, food, health, clothing. The minister of the church asked the people to help the Vietnamese. The church was ready to sponsor a family with eight people, but nobody like to come to El Paso. They want to live in a big city with Americans, not to live in El Paso, with about 70 percent Mexican. And they want better weather and sometimes it's 110 degrees there. I'm a person who doesn't mind about that point....I just want people who will help me and show me how to rent an apartment, to get a job.

We go to El Paso. Church prepare everything for us. They have a house belong to church. They repaint that, bring in some furniture and clothing for us. Some people take care of painting, some take care of furniture like committees. One committee for transportation, one for food, one for health and one for education....They give us some money and also show me how to get a high school equivalency diploma. I have a Master Degree in Economics, but I try to forget about that. I get an equivalency diploma and start college. I go for two semesters to University of Texas and work part-time in the library....

I save my money and I send to my parents in Vietnam through France. They get the money and contact some people and they plan to get a ship. They give the money, but still the Communists come and take the ship and we lose the money.

After we settle in El Paso we try to be in touch with friends and relatives from Vietnam. We know some people left but we do not know where they are. So I write note in the newspaper....My sister had a friend from Vietnam and we know he is in the Western United States but not where exactly. She wrote a letter in the paper and he answered from Albuquerque, New Mexico....

Soon my sister's friend came from Albuquerque every week to see her. First he has a low pay job because of English barrier. But he works hard. I see he is a good worker, try very hard to make success and he will take good care of my sister. About ten months after we come to El Paso they want to get married. My parents not here so I think about it and give my permission. Now they both work and he gets steady upgrade. Very good.[2]

In 1984 Rosa Maria Urbina, a thirty-one-year-old widow from Juarez, Mexico, crossed the Rio Grande River looking for work as a housecleaner in El Paso. She had hoped to earn enough money to take her three children out of an orphanage. José Luis, a Juarez farm worker, moved to El Paso permanently in 1981 at the age of twenty-two. The two married and made their life among El Paso's fifty thousand illegal immigrants, known in Mexican slang as *"mojados,"* or "wets," the river people.

West Indian-American Day Parade, Brooklyn New York, 1991

José: The majority of the people in our apartment building have the same problem as my family. All of us are in El Paso without legal papers. I have been living here since 1981.

Rosa: I came in 1984, to find work. After José and I were married and we found a place to live, I brought my children from my previous marriage. We lived across the river in Juárez. But I was born further south, in Zacatecas.

José: My hometown is Juárez. Since I was nine years old, I've been coming to El Paso to work. At first I did gardening in people's yards, but I have stayed in El Paso constantly since 1981, going out to the fields to do farm work. I used to go to Juárez to visit my relatives at least one day each month. But in the last year, I haven't gone, because of the immigration law. To visit Juarez I have to swim across the river. I can't cross the bridge or the "*migra*" [Border Patrol officers] can catch me right there....

Rosa: When I was a teenager, I worked as a hairdresser in a beauty salon, cutting hair. My first husband was a mechanic, fixing cars. We made a good living. But my husband spent the money he made drinking in the *cantinas.* And after a while, he wouldn't let me work, because I had young children to take care of. When he died in 1984, he left me with nothing at all....My children were nine, seven, and three years old. I had to find a way to pay rent and feed them.

At that time, the economy in Mexico had become horrible. Inflation was going crazy. The peso jumped to 500 per dollar. Today it is still climbing at 1,000 per dollar. I found a job working on an assembly line at a factory. We produced rubber gloves for hospitals and medical supplies like caps for syringes. I would go into work at 4:30 in the afternoon and stay until 2:00 A.M. I was paid only 7,000 pesos [$14] each week. That was not enough to feed my kids. And I didn't have any relatives or friends to watch the kids while I worked. So I had no other choice but to put them in a special institution, like an orphanage, for children without parents. This upset me very much. But with my husband dead, and no other form of support, there was nothing I could do.

My only hope was to cross the river to the United States. If I could find a job that paid enough money, my children could join me. I wanted them to have an education and a proper life...to be someone....

Before I met José, I crossed back and forth across the river five days each week to my housekeeping jobs in El Paso. On weekends, I took my children out of the orphanage. Then I had to reluctantly return them to the orphanage on Sunday evenings and prepare to go back across the river.

For a while I traveled alone, which can be dangerous. But after I met José Luis, we crossed together. There are men who carry people across the river on their shoulders. The water is kind of rough, but that's what these men do to make a living. They charge passengers, 1,500 to 2,000 pesos [$1.50 to $2.50]. The water is up to their chests, but they manage to hold us up on their shoulders so we can get to work dry....

José: Farm-labor jobs are not very steady. We just grab whatever is open at the moment. I accept anything, any time, as long as it is work. But suppose I take a job that only pays me $12 a day. It would only be enough to cover my transportation and meals in the field. I must find jobs that pay enough to feed my family.

In order to make $25, I must pick seventy-two buckets of chili peppers. That could take me four or five hours; it depends on how fast my hands are. The total amount of buckets we pick depends upon the amount contracted by the big companies in California. For a big contract, we work as long as necessary to complete the order. But the most I can earn in a day is $35....

Rosa: We would like an ordinary life, but our problems with the *migra* are nothing new. If they catch me again and send me back to Juarez, I will just come back across the river.[3]

Wing Ng, a Cantonese woman born into a poor family, emigrated to California in 1975 at the age of twenty-three. She came alone, but had the sponsorship of her sister's friend in Los Angeles, as well as financial help from the YMCA for the airfare from Hong Kong. She soon relocated to New York's Chinatown.

The reason I wanted to come to the United States is that I heard it is really freedom. That's the first thing. And the second was the education. It's hard to get an education in China. Only the United States can support you to get a good education and a good life. My childhood was not happy. Too many children. Poor. I don't want that again. I graduated from high school but nothing can get you into college. Even though you have good grades and a good record you can never get into college in China. I don't know how it is now but in my experience, when I was young, during the Cultural Revolution, there were no colleges to get into. Every student

Chinese parents reading with their children.

who graduated from high school in 1968, 1970, around that time, was sent to work in the countryside, to become a farmer....

I came first to California. Los Angeles. Then I came here to New York. I had some friends. They told me there were more opportunities to find a good job in New York. To learn English. In Los Angeles everything is far away. You have to drive in a car for hours to get anywhere. There's not that much chance to get an education, to go to school, because of the distance between places. I stayed there just two weeks and then I came to New York.

When I got here I worked as a babysitter. I had a green card and I could have gotten another kind of job but I wanted to learn English. Even though you go to school, you are just listening a lot of the time, and I wanted a job where I could talk English. So I found a job with an American family. They talked to me and corrected me. Told me how to do things. I took care of their little boy. He was seven years old and very easy to take care of. I took him to the park on his bicycle or to the museum. For me it was very interesting....

In February 1978, I started at City University, New York City Community College. There are many Chinese people there, many different races. Many, many. I have helped about twenty people go there myself. Told them it was a very good college, especially for data processing. I promised myself I will go on to a four-year college when I graduate but I do not know how long it will take. First I will get a job and then ask the boss to help me with my education....That first year back in college was very difficult for me. I had to take any kind of job, just to get money. Type. Work in a restaurant. Whatever I could find.[4]

Questions

1. To what extent were different immigrant experiences shaped by post-World War II changes in United States immigration laws?
2. How do the immigrants' narratives reflect their encounters with new gender roles and possibilities in American life?
3. Discuss the importance of educational opportunities for immigrants. Why were these critical for some and not for others?
4. For many immigrants, the trip to the United States was only one of several migrations. What other kinds of migrations shaped their lives before they arrived here?
5. What do the immigrants' stories reveal about the role of economic instability in their decision to emigrate?

Sources

1. June Namias, *First Generation: In the Words of Twentieth Century American Immigrants* (Boston: Beacon Press, 1978), 142–144. Copyright © 1978 by June Namias. Reprinted with the permission of Beacon Press, Boston.
2. Thomas Kessner and Betty Boyd Caroli, *Today's Immigrants/Their Stories: A New Look at the Newest Americans* (New York: Oxford University Press, 1981), 49–51. Copyright © 1981 by Thomas Kessner and Betty Boyd Caroli. Reprinted with the permission of Oxford University Press, Inc.
3. Al Santoli, *New Americans: An Oral History* (New York: Viking/Penguin, 1988), 306–308. Copyright © 1988 by Al Santoli. Reprinted with the permission of Viking Penguin, a division of Penguin Putnam, Inc.
4. Thomas Kessner and Betty Boyd Caroli, *Today's Immigrants/Their Stories: A New Look at the Newest Americans* (New York: Oxford University Press, 1981), 252–254. © 1981 by Thomas Kessner and Betty Boyd Caroli. Reprinted with the permission of Oxford University Press, Inc.

APPENDIX

THE DECLARATION OF INDEPENDENCE

When in the course of human events it becomes necessary for one people to dissolve the political bands which have connected them with another and to assume, among the powers of the earth, the separate and equal station to which the laws of nature and of nature's God entitle them, a decent respect to the opinions of mankind requires that they should declare the causes which impel them to the separation.

We hold these truths to be self-evident, that all men are created equal; that they are endowed by their Creator with certain unalienable rights; that among these are life, liberty, and the pursuit of happiness. That, to secure these rights, governments are instituted among men, deriving their just powers from the consent of the governed; that, whenever any form of government becomes destructive of these ends, it is the right of the people to alter or to abolish it, and to institute a new government, laying its foundation on such principles, and organizing its powers in such form, as to them shall seem most likely to effect their safety and happiness. Prudence, indeed, will dictate that governments long established should not be changed for light and transient causes; and, accordingly, all experience hath shown that mankind are more disposed to suffer, while evils are sufferable, than to right themselves by abolishing the forms to which they are accustomed. But when a long train of abuses and usurpations, pursuing invariably the same object, evinces a design to reduce them under absolute despotism, it is their right, it is their duty, to throw off such government and to provide new guards for their future security. Such has been the patient sufferance of these colonies, and such is now the necessity which constrains them to alter their former systems of government. The history of the present King of Great Britain is a history of repeated injuries and usurpations, all having, in direct object, the establishment of an absolute tyranny over these States. To prove this, let facts be submitted to a candid world:

He has refused his assent to laws the most wholesome and necessary for the public good.

He has forbidden his governors to pass laws of immediate and pressing importance, unless suspended in their operation till his assent should be obtained; and, when so suspended, he has utterly neglected to attend to them.

He has refused to pass other laws for the accommodation of large districts of people, unless those people would relinquish the right of representation in the legislature, a right inestimable to them and formidable to tyrants only.

He has called together legislative bodies at places unusual, uncomfortable, and distant from the depository of their public records, for the sole purpose of fatiguing them into compliance with his measures.

He has dissolved representative houses, repeatedly for opposing, with manly firmness, his invasions on the rights of the people.

He has refused, for a long time after such dissolutions, to cause others to be elected; whereby the legislative powers, incapable of annihilation, have returned to the people at large for their exercise; the state remaining, in the meantime, exposed to all the danger of invasion from without and convulsions within.

He has endeavored to prevent the population of these States; for that purpose, obstructing the laws for naturalization of foreigners, refusing to pass others to encourage their migration hither, and raising the conditions of new appropriations of lands.

He has obstructed the administration of justice by refusing his assent to laws for establishing judiciary powers.

He has made judges dependent on his will alone for the tenure of their offices and the amount and payment of their salaries.

He has erected a multitude of new offices and sent hither swarms of officers to harass our people and eat out their substance.

He has kept among us, in time of peace, standing armies, without the consent of our legislatures.

He has affected to render the military independent of, and superior to, the civil power.

He has combined with others to subject us to a jurisdiction foreign to our Constitution and unacknowledged by our laws, giving his assent to their acts of pretended legislation—

For quartering large bodies of armed troops among us;

For protecting them, by mock trial, from punishment for any murders which they should commit on the inhabitants of these States;

For cutting off our trade with all parts of the world;

For imposing taxes on us without our consent;

For depriving us, in many cases, of the benefit of trial by jury;

For transporting us beyond seas to be tried for pretended offences;

For abolishing the free system of English laws in a neighboring province, establishing therein an arbitrary government, and enlarging its boundaries, so as to render it at once an example and fit instrument for introducing the same absolute rule into these colonies;

For taking away our charters, abolishing our most valuable laws, and altering, fundamentally, the powers of our governments.

For suspending our own legislatures and declaring themselves invested with power to legislate for us in all cases whatsoever.

He has abdicated government here by declaring us out of his protection and waging war against us.

He has plundered our seas, ravaged our coasts, burnt our towns, and destroyed the lives of our people.

He is, at this time, transporting large armies of foreign mercenaries to complete the works of death, desolation, and tyranny already begun with circumstances of cruelty and perfidy scarcely paralleled in the most barbarous ages, and totally unworthy the head of a civilized nation.

He has constrained our fellow citizens, taken captive on the high seas, to bear arms against their country, to become the executioners of their friends and brethren, or to fall themselves by their hands.

He has excited domestic insurrections amongst us and has endeavored to bring on the inhabitants of our frontiers, the merciless Indian savages, whose known rule of warfare is an undistinguished destruction of all ages, sexes, and conditions.

In every stage of these oppressions, we have petitioned for redress in the most humble terms; our repeated petitions have been answered only by repeated injury. A prince whose character is thus marked by every act which may define a tyrant is unfit to be the ruler of a free people.

Nor have we been wanting in attention to our British brethren. We have warned them, from time to time, of attempts made by their legislature to extend an unwarrantable jurisdiction over us. We have reminded them of the circumstances of our emigration and settlement here. We have appealed to their native justice and magnanimity, and we have conjured them, by the ties of our common kindred, to disavow these usurpations, which would inevitably interrupt our connections and correspondence. They, too, have been deaf to the voice of justice and consanguinity. We must, therefore, acquiesce in the necessity which denounces our separation, and hold them, as we hold the rest of mankind, enemies in war, in peace, friends.

We, therefore, the representatives of the United States of America, in general Congress assembled, appealing to the Supreme Judge of the world for the rectitude of our intentions, do, in the name and by the authority of the good people of these colonies, solemnly publish and declare, that these united colonies are, and of right ought to be, free and independent states: that they are absolved from all allegiance to the British Crown, and that all political connection between them and the state of Great Britain is, and ought to be, totally dissolved; and that, as free and independent states, they have full power to levy war, conclude peace, contract alliances, establish commerce, and to do all other acts and things which independent states may of right do. And, for the support of this declaration, with a firm reliance on the protection of Divine Providence, we mutually pledge to each other our lives, our fortunes, and our sacred honor.

THE CONSTITUTION OF THE UNITED STATES OF AMERICA

We the people of the United States, in order to form a more perfect union, establish justice, insure domestic tranquillity, provide for the common defense, promote the general welfare, and secure the blessings of liberty to ourselves and our posterity, do ordain and establish this Constitution for the United States of America.

Article I

Section 1. All legislative powers herein granted shall be vested in a Congress of the United States, which shall consist of a Senate and House of Representatives.

Section 2. 1. The House of Representatives shall be composed of members chosen every second year by the people of the several States, and the electors in each State shall have the qualifications requisite for electors of the most numerous branch of the State legislature.

2. No person shall be a representative who shall not have attained to the age of twenty-five years, and been seven years a citizen of the United States, and who shall not, when elected, be an inhabitant of that State in which he shall be chosen.

3. Representatives and direct taxes[1] shall be apportioned among the several States which may be included within this Union, according to their respective numbers, which shall be determined by adding to the whole number of free persons, including those bound to service for a term of years, and excluding Indians not taxed, three fifths of all other persons.[2] The actual enumeration shall be made within three years after the first meeting of the Congress of the United States, and within every subsequent term of ten years, in such manner as they shall by law direct. The number of representatives shall not exceed one for every thirty thousand, but each State shall have at least one representative; and until such enumeration shall be made, the State of New Hampshire shall be entitled to choose three, Massachusetts eight, Rhode Island and Providence Plantations one, Connecticut five, New York six, New Jersey four, Pennsylvania eight, Delaware one, Maryland six, Virginia ten, North Carolina five, South Carolina five, and Georgia three.

4. When vacancies happen in the representation from any State, the executive authority thereof shall issue writs of election to fill such vacancies.

5. The House of Representatives shall choose their speaker and other officers; and shall have the sole power of impeachment.

Section 3. 1. The Senate of the United States shall be composed of two senators from each State, chosen by the legislature thereof,[3] for six years; and each senator shall have one vote.

2. Immediately after they shall be assembled in consequence of the first election, they shall be divided as equally as may be into three classes. The seats of the senators of the first class shall be vacated at the expiration of the second year, of the second class at the expiration of the fourth year, and of the third class at the expiration of the sixth year, so that one third may be chosen every second year; and if vacancies happen by resignation, or otherwise, during the recess of the legislature of any State, the executive thereof may make temporary appointments until the next meeting of the legislature, which shall then fill such vacancies.[4]

3. No person shall be a senator who shall not have attained to the age of thirty years, and been nine years a citizen of the United States, and who shall not, when elected, be an inhabitant of that State for which he shall be chosen.

4. The Vice President of the United States shall be President of the Senate, but shall have no vote, unless they be equally divided.

5. The Senate shall choose their other officers, and also a president pro tempore, in the absence of the Vice President, or when he shall exercise the office of the President of the United States.

6. The Senate shall have the sole power to try all impeachments. When sitting for that purpose, they shall be on oath or affirmation. When the President of the United States is tried, the chief justice shall preside: and no person shall be convicted without the concurrence of two thirds of the members present.

7. Judgment in cases of impeachment shall not extend further than to removal from office, and disqualification to hold and enjoy any office of honor, trust or profit under the United States: but the party convicted shall nevertheless be liable and subject to indictment, trial, judgment and punishment, according to law.

Section 4. 1. The times, places, and manner of holding elections for senators and representatives, shall be prescribed in each State by the legislature thereof; but the Congress may at any time by law make or alter such regulations, except as to the places of choosing senators.

2. The Congress shall assemble at least once in every year, and such meeting shall be on the first Monday in December, unless they shall by law appoint a different day.

Section 5. 1. Each House shall be the judge of the elections, returns and qualifications of its own members, and a majority of each shall constitute a quorum to do business; but a smaller number may adjourn from day to day, and may be authorized to compel the attendance of absent members, in such manner, and under such penalties as each House may provide.

2. Each House may determine the rules of its proceedings, punish its members for disorderly behavior, and, with the concurrence of two thirds, expel a member.

3. Each House shall keep a journal of its proceedings, and from time to time publish the same, excepting such parts as may in their judgment require secrecy; and the yeas and nays of the members of either House on any ques-

[1]See the Sixteenth Amendment.

[2]See the Fourteenth Amendment.

[3]See the Seventeenth Amendment.

[4]See the Seventeenth Amendment.

tion shall, at the desire of one fifth of those present, be entered on the journal.

4. Neither House, during the session of Congress, shall, without the consent of the other, adjourn for more than three days, nor to any other place than that in which the two Houses shall be sitting.

Section 6. 1. The senators and representatives shall receive a compensation for their services, to be ascertained by law, and paid out of the Treasury of the United States. They shall in all cases, except treason, felony, and breach of the peace, be privileged from arrest during their attendance at the session of their respective Houses, and in going to and returning from the same; and for any speech or debate in either House, they shall not be questioned in any other place.

2. No senator or representative shall, during the time for which he was elected, be appointed to any civil office under the authority of the United States, which shall have been created, or the emoluments whereof shall have been increased, during such time; and no person holding any office under the United States shall be a member of either House during his continuance in office.

Section 7. 1. All bills for raising revenue shall originate in the House of Representatives; but the Senate may propose or concur with amendments as on other bills.

2. Every bill which shall have passed the House of Representatives and the Senate, shall, before it become a law, be presented to the President of the United States; If he approves he shall sign it, but if not he shall return it, with his objections, to that House in which it shall have originated, who shall enter the objections at large on their journal, and proceed to reconsider it. If after such reconsideration two thirds of that House shall agree to pass the bill, it shall be sent, together with the objections, to the other House, by which it shall likewise be reconsidered, and if approved by two thirds of that House, it shall become a law. But in all such cases the votes of both Houses shall be determined by yeas and nays, and the names of the persons voting for and against the bill shall be entered on the journal of each House respectively. If any bill shall not be returned by the President within ten days (Sundays excepted) after it shall have been presented to him, the same shall be a law, in like manner as if he had signed it, unless the Congress by their adjournment prevent its return, in which case it shall not be a law.

3. Every order, resolution, or vote to which the concurrence of the Senate and the House of Representatives may be necessary (except on a question of adjournment) shall be presented to the President of the United States; and before the same shall take effect, shall be approved by him, or being disapproved by him, shall be repassed by two thirds of the Senate and House of Representatives, according to the rules and limitations prescribed in the case of a bill.

Section 8. The Congress shall have the power

1. To lay and collect taxes, duties, imposts, and excises, to pay the debts and provide for the common defense and general welfare of the United States; but all duties, imposts, and excises shall be uniform throughout the United States.

2. To borrow money on the credit of the United States;

3. To regulate commerce with foreign nations, and among the several States, and with the Indian tribes;

4. To establish a uniform rule of naturalization, and uniform laws on the subject of bankruptcies throughout the United States;

5. To coin money, regulate the value thereof, and of foreign coin, and fix the standard of weights and measures;

6. To provide for the punishment of counterfeiting the securities and current coin of the United States;

7. To establish post offices and post roads;

8. To promote the progress of science and useful arts, by securing for limited times to authors and inventors the exclusive right to their respective writings and discoveries;

9. To constitute tribunals inferior to the Supreme Court;

10. To define and punish piracies and felonies committed on the high seas, and offenses against the law of nations;

11. To declare war, grant letters of marque and reprisal, and make rules concerning captures on land and water;

12. To raise and support armies, but no appropriation of money to that use shall be for a longer term than two years;

13. To provide and maintain a navy;

14. To make rules for the government and regulation of the land and naval forces;

15. To provide for calling forth the militia to execute the laws of the Union, suppress insurrections and repel invasions;

16. To provide for organizing, arming, and disciplining the militia, and for governing such part of them as may be employed in the service of the United States, reserving to the States respectively, the appointment of the officers, and the authority of training the militia according to the discipline prescribed by Congress;

17. To exercise exclusive legislation in all cases whatsoever, over such district (not exceeding ten miles square) as may, by cession of particular States, and the acceptance of Congress, become the seat of the government of the United States, and to exercise like authority over all places purchased by the consent of the legislature of the State in which the same shall be, for the erection of forts, magazines, arsenals, dockyards, and other needful buildings; and

18. To make all laws which shall be necessary and proper for carrying into execution the foregoing powers, and all other powers vested by this Constitution in the government of the United States, or any department or officer thereof.

Section 9. 1. The migration or importation of such persons as any of the States now existing shall think proper to admit, shall not be prohibited by the Congress prior to the year one thousand eight hundred and eight, but a tax or duty may be imposed on such importation, not exceeding ten dollars for each person.

2. The privilege of the writ of habeas corpus shall not be suspended, unless when in cases of rebellion or invasion the public safety may require it.

3. No bill of attainder or ex post facto law shall be passed.

4. No capitation, or other direct, tax shall be laid, unless in proportion to the census or enumeration hereinbefore directed to be taken.[5]

5. No tax or duty shall be laid on articles exported from any State.

6. No preference shall be given by any regulation of commerce or revenue to the ports of one State over those of another: nor shall vessels bound to, or from, one State be obliged to enter, clear, or pay duties in another.

7. No money shall be drawn from the treasury, but in consequence of appropriations made by law; and a regular statement and account of the receipts and expenditures of all public money shall be published from time to time.

8. No title of nobility shall be granted by the United States: and no person holding any office of profit or trust under them, shall, without the consent of the Congress, accept of any present, emolument, office, or title, of any kind whatever, from any king, price, or foreign State.

Section 10. 1. No State shall enter into any treaty, alliance, or confederation; grant letters of marque and reprisal; coin money; emit bills of credit; make any thing but gold and silver coin a tender in payment of debts; pass any bill of attainder, ex post facto law, or law impairing the obligation of contracts, or grant, any title of nobility.

2. No State shall, without the consent of the Congress, lay any imposts or duties on imports or exports, except what may be absolutely necessary for executing its inspection laws: and the net produce of all duties and imposts laid by any State on imports or exports, shall be for the use of the treasury of the United States; and all such laws shall be subject to the revision and control of the Congress.

3. No State shall, without the consent of the Congress, lay any duty of tonnage, keep troops, or ships of war in time of peace, enter into any agreement or compact with another State, or with a foreign power, or engage in war, unless actually invaded, or in such imminent danger as will not admit of delay.

Article II

Section 1. 1. The executive power shall be vested in a President of the United States of America. He shall hold his office during the term of four years, and, together with the Vice President, chosen for the same term, be elected, as follows:

2. Each State shall appoint, in such manner as the legislature thereof may direct, a number of electors, equal to the whole number of senators and representatives to which the State may be entitled in the Congress: but no senator or representative, or person holding any office of trust or profit under the United States, shall be appointed an elector.

The electors shall meet in their respective States, and vote by ballot for two persons, of whom one at least shall not be an inhabitant of the same State with themselves. And they shall make a list of all the persons voted for, and of the number of votes for each; which list they shall sign and certify, and transmit sealed to the seat of the government of the United States, directed to the president of the Senate. The president of the Senate shall, in the presence of the Senate and House of Representatives, open all the certificates, and the votes shall then be counted. The person having the greatest number of votes shall be the President, if such number be a majority of the whole number of electors appointed; and if there be more than one who have such majority, and have an equal number of votes, then the House of Representatives shall immediately choose by ballot one of them for President; and if no person have a majority, then from the five highest on the list the said House shall in like manner choose the President. But in choosing the President, the votes shall be taken by States, the representation from each State having one vote; a quorum for this purpose shall consist of a member or members from two thirds of the States, and a majority of all the States shall be necessary to a choice. In every case after the choice of the President, the person having the greatest number of votes of the electors shall be the Vice President. But if there should remain two or more who have equal votes, the Senate shall choose from them by ballot the Vice President.[6]

3. The Congress may determine the time of choosing the electors, and the day on which they shall give their votes; which day shall be the same throughout the United States.

4. No person except a natural born citizen, or a citizen of the United States, at the time of the adoption of this Constitution, shall be eligible to the office of President; neither shall any person be eligible to the office who shall not have attained to the age of thirty-five years, and been fourteen years a resident within the United States.

5. In case of the removal of the President from office, or of his death, resignation, or inability to discharge the powers and duties of the said office, the same shall devolve on the Vice President, and the congress may by law provide for the case of removal, death, resignation or inability, both of the President and Vice President, declaring what officer shall then act as President, and such officer shall act accordingly until the disability be removed, or a President shall be elected.

6. The President shall, at stated times, receive for his services a compensation which shall neither be increased nor diminished during the period for which he shall have been elected, and he shall not receive within that period any other emolument from the United States, or any of them.

7. Before he enter on the execution of his office, he shall take the following oath or affirmation:—"I do

[5]See the Sixteenth Amendment.

[6]Superseded by the Twelfth Amendment.

solemnly swear (or affirm) that I will faithfully execute the office of President of the United States, and will to the best of my ability, preserve, protect and defend the Constitution of the United States."

Section 2. 1. The President shall be commander in chief of the army and navy of the United States, and of the militia of the several States, when called into the actual service of the United States; he may require the opinion in writing, of the principal officer in each of the executive departments, upon any subject relating to the duties of their respective offices, and he shall have power to grant reprieves and pardons for offenses against the United States, except in cases of impeachment.

2. He shall have power, by and with the advice and consent of the Senate, to make treaties, provided two thirds of the senators present concur; and he shall nominate, and by and with the advice and consent of the Senate, shall appoint ambassadors, other public ministers and consuls, judges of the Supreme Court, and all other officers of the United States, whose appointments are not herein otherwise provided for, and which shall be established by law; but the Congress may by law vest the appointment of such inferior officers, as they think proper, in the President alone, in the courts of laws, or in the heads of departments.

3. The President shall have power to fill up all vacancies that may happen during the recess of the Senate, by granting commissions which shall expire at the end of their next session.

Section 3. He shall from time to time give to the Congress information of the state of the Union, and recommend to their consideration such measures as he shall judge necessary and expedient; he may, on extraordinary occasions, convene both Houses, or either of them, and in case of disagreement between them with respect to the time of adjournment, he may adjourn them to such time as he shall think proper; he shall receive ambassadors and other public ministers; he shall take care that the laws be faithfully executed, and shall commission all the officers of the United States.

Section 4. The President, Vice President, and all civil officers of the United States, shall be removed from office on impeachment for, and conviction of, treason, bribery, or other high crimes and misdemeanors.

Article III

Section 1. The judicial power of the United States shall be vested in one Supreme Court, and in such inferior courts as the Congress may from time to time ordain and establish. The judges, both of the Supreme and inferior courts, shall hold their offices during good behavior, and shall, at stated times, receive for their services, a compensation, which shall not be diminished during their continuance in office.

Section 2. 1. The judicial power shall extend to all cases, in law and equity, arising under this Constitution, the laws of the United States, and treaties made, or which shall be made, under their authority;—to all cases of admiralty and maritime jurisdiction;—to controversies to which the United States shall be a party;[7]—to controversies between two or more States;—between a State and citizens of another State;—between citizens of different States;—between citizens of the same State claiming lands under grants of different States, and between a State, or the citizens thereof, and foreign States, citizens or subjects.

2. In all cases affecting ambassadors, other public ministers and consuls, and those in which a State shall be party, the Supreme Court shall have original jurisdiction. In all the other cases before mentioned, the Supreme Court shall have appellate jurisdiction, both as to law and fact, with such exceptions, and under such regulations as the Congress shall make.

3. The trial of all crimes, except in cases of impeachment, shall be by jury; and such trial shall be held in the State where the said crimes shall have been committed; but when not committed within any State, the trial shall be such place or places as the congress may by law have directed.

Section 3. 1. Treason against the United States shall consist only in levying war against them, or in adhering to their enemies, giving them aid and comfort. No person shall be convicted of treason unless on the testimony of two witnesses to the same overt act, or on confession in open court.

2. The Congress shall have power to declare the punishment of treason, but no attainder of treason shall work corruption of blood, or forfeiture except during the life of the person attained.

Article IV

Section 1. Full faith and credit shall be given in each State to the public acts, records, and judicial proceedings of every other State. And the Congress may by general laws prescribe the manner in which such acts, records and proceedings shall be proved, and the effect thereof.

Section 2. 1. The citizens of each State shall be entitled to all privileges and immunities of citizens in the several States.[8]

2. A person charged in any State with treason, felony, or other crime, who shall flee from justice, and be found in another State, shall on demand of the executive authority of the State from which he fled, be delivered up to be removed to the State having jurisdiction of the crime.

3. No person held to service or labor in one State under the laws thereof, escaping into another, shall, in consequence of any law or regulation therein, be discharged from such service or labor, but shall be delivered up on claim of the party to whom such service or labor may be due.[9]

Section 3. 1. New States may be admitted by the Congress into this Union; but no new State shall be formed or erected within the jurisdiction of any other State, nor any State be formed by the junction of two or more States, or parts of States, without the consent of the legislatures of the States concerned as well as of the Congress.

[7]See the Eleventh Amendment.

[8]See the Fourteenth Amendment, Sec. 1.

[9]See the Thirteenth Amendment.

2. The Congress shall have power to dispose of and make all needful rules and regulations respecting the territory or other property belonging to the United States; and nothing in this Constitution shall be so construed as to prejudice any claims of the United States, or of any particular State.

Section 4. The United States shall guarantee to every State in this Union a republican form of government, and shall protect each of them against invasion; and on application of the legislature, or of the executive (when the legislature cannot be convened) against domestic violence.

Article V

The Congress, whenever two thirds of both Houses shall deem it necessary, shall propose amendments to this Constitution, or, on the application of the legislatures of two thirds of the several States, shall call a convention for proposing amendments, which in either case shall be valid to all intents and purposes, as part of this Constitution, when ratified by the legislatures of three fourths of the several States, or by conventions in three fourths thereof, as the one or the other mode of ratification may be proposed by the Congress; Provided that no amendment which may be made prior to the year one thousand eight hundred and eight shall in any manner affect the first and fourth clauses in the ninth section of the first article; and that no State, without its consent, shall be deprived of its equal suffrage in the Senate.

Article VI

1. All debts contracted and engagements entered into, before the adoption of this Constitution, shall be as valid against the United States under this Constitution, as under the Confederation.[10]

2. This Constitution, and the laws of the United States which shall be made in pursuance thereof; and all treaties made, or which shall be made, under the authority of the United States, shall be the supreme law of the land; and the judges in every State shall be bound thereby, any thing in the Constitution or laws of any State to the contrary notwithstanding.

3. The senators and representatives before mentioned, and the members of the several State legislatures, and all executive and judicial officers, both of the United States and of the several States, shall be bound by oath or affirmation to support this Constitution; but no religious test shall ever be required as a qualification to any office or public trust under the United States.

Article VII

The ratification of the conventions of nine States shall be sufficient for the establishment of this Constitution between the States so ratifying the same.

Done in Convention by the unanimous consent of the States present the seventeenth day of September in the year of our Lord one thousand seven hundred and eighty-seven, and of the independence of the United States of America the twelfth. In witness whereof we have hereunto subscribed our names.

[Names omitted]

* * *

Articles in addition to, and amendment of, the Constitution of the United States of America, proposed by Congress, and ratified by the legislatures of the several States, pursuant to the fifth article of the original Constitution.

Amendment I [First ten amendments ratified December 15, 1791]

Congress shall make no law respecting an establishment of religion, or prohibiting the free exercise thereof; or abridging the freedom of speech, or of the press; or the right of the people peaceably to assemble, and to petition the government for a redress of grievances.

Amendment II

A well regulated militia, being necessary to the security of a free State, the right of the people to keep and bear arms, shall not be infringed.

Amendment III

No soldier shall, in time of peace be quartered in any house, without the consent of the owner, nor in time of war, but in a manner to be prescribed by law.

Amendment IV

The right of the people to be secure in their persons, houses, papers, and effects, against unreasonable searches and seizures, shall not be violated, and no warrants shall issue, but upon probable cause, supported by oath or affirmation, and particularly describing the place to be searched, and the persons or things to be seized.

Amendment V

No person shall be held to answer for a capital or otherwise infamous crime, unless on a presentment or indictment of a grand jury, except in cases arising in the land or naval forces, or in the militia, when in actual service in time of war or public danger; nor shall any person be subject for the same offense to be twice put in jeopardy of life or limb; nor shall be compelled in any criminal case to be a witness against himself, nor be deprived of life, liberty, or property, without due process of law; nor shall private property be taken for public use, without just compensation.

Amendment VI

In all criminal prosecutions, the accused shall enjoy the right to a speedy and public trial, by an impartial jury of the State and district wherein the crime shall have been committed, which district shall have been previously ascertained by law, and to be informed of the nature and cause of the accusation; to be confronted with the witnesses against him; to have compulsory process for obtaining witnesses in his favor, and to have the assistance of counsel for his defense.

[10]See the Fourteenth Amendment, Sec. 4.

Amendment VII

In suits at common law, where the value in controversy shall exceed twenty dollars, the right of trial by jury shall be preserved, and no fact tried by a jury shall be otherwise reexamined in any court of the United States, than according to the rules of the common law.

Amendment VIII

Excessive bail shall not be required, nor excessive fines imposed, nor cruel and unusual punishments inflicted.

Amendment IX

The enumeration in the Constitution of certain rights shall not be construed to deny or disparage others retained by the people.

Amendment X

The powers not delegated to the United States by the Constitution, nor prohibited by it to the States, are reserved to the States respectively, or to the people.

Amendment XI [January 8, 1798]

The judicial power of the United States shall not be construed to extend to any suit in law or equity, commended or prosecuted against one of the United States by citizens of another State, or by citizens or subjects of any foreign State.

Amendment XII [September 25, 1804]

The electors shall meet in their respective States, and vote by ballot for President and Vice President, one of whom, at least, shall not be an inhabitant of the same State with themselves; they shall name in their ballots the person voted for as President, and in distinct ballots, the person voted for as Vice President, and they shall make distinct lists of all persons voted for as President and of all persons voted for as Vice President, and of the number of votes for each, which lists they shall sign and certify, and transmit sealed to the seat of the government of the United States, directed to the President of the Senate;—The President of the Senate shall, in the presence of the Senate and House of Representatives, open all the certificates and the votes shall then be counted;—The person having the greatest number of votes for President, shall be the President, if such number be a majority of the whole number of electors appointed; and if no person have such majority, then from the persons having the highest numbers not exceeding three on the list of those voted for as President, the House of Representatives shall choose immediately, by ballot, the President. But in choosing the President, the votes shall be taken by States, the representation from each State having one vote; a quorum for this purpose shall consist of a member or members from two thirds of the States, and a majority of all the States shall be necessary to a choice. And if the House of Representatives shall not choose a President whenever the right of choice shall devolve upon them, before the fourth day of March next following, then the Vice President shall act as President, as in the case of the death or other constitutional disability of the President.

The person having the greatest number of votes as Vice President shall be the Vice President, if such number be a majority of the whole number of electors appointed, and if no person have a majority, then from the two highest numbers on the list, the Senate shall choose the Vice President; a quorum for the purpose shall consist of two thirds of the whole number of Senators, and a majority of the whole number shall be necessary to a choice. But no person constitutionally ineligible to the office of President shall be eligible to that of Vice President of the United States.

Amendment XIII [December 18, 1865]

Section 1. Neither slavery nor involuntary servitude, except as a punishment for crime whereof the party shall have been duly convicted, shall exist within the United States, or any place subject to their jurisdiction.

Section 2. Congress shall have power to enforce this article by appropriate legislation.

Amendment XIV [July 28, 1868]

Section 1. All persons born or naturalized in the United States, and subject to the jurisdiction thereof, are citizens of the United States and of the State wherein they reside. No State shall make or enforce any law which shall abridge the privileges or immunities of citizens of the United States; nor shall any State deprive any person of life, liberty, or property, without due process of law; nor deny to any person within its jurisdiction the equal protection of the laws.

Section 2. Representatives shall be apportioned among the several States according to their respective numbers, counting the whole number of persons in each State, excluding Indians not taxed. But when the right to vote at any election for the choice of electors for President and Vice President of the United States, representatives in Congress, the executive and judicial officers of a State, or the members of the legislature thereof, is denied to any of the male inhabitants of such State, being twenty-one years of age, and citizens of the United States, or in any way abridged, except for participating in rebellion, or other crime, the basis of representation there shall be reduced in the proportion which the number of such male citizens shall bear to the whole number of male citizens twenty-one years of age in such State.

Section 3. No person shall be a senator or representative in Congress, or elector of President and Vice President, or hold any office, civil or military, under the United States, or under any State, who having previously taken an oath, as a member of Congress, or as an officer of the United States, or as a member of any State legislature, or as an executive or judicial officer of any State, to support the Constitution of the United States, shall have engaged in insurrection or rebellion against the same, or given aid or comfort to the enemies thereof. But Congress may by a vote of two thirds of each House, remove such disability.

Section 4. The validity of the public debt of the United States, authorized by law, including debts incurred for payment of pensions and bounties for services in suppressing insurrection or rebellion, shall not be questioned.

But neither the United States nor any State shall assume or pay any debt or obligation incurred in aid of insurrection or rebellion against the United States, or any claim for the loss or emancipation of any slave; but all such debts, obligations, and claims shall be held illegal and void.

Section 5. The Congress shall have the power to enforce, by appropriate legislation, the provisions of this article.

Amendment XV [March 30, 1870]

Section 1. The right of citizens of the United States to vote shall not be denied or abridged by the United States or by any State on account of race, color, or previous condition of servitude.

Section 2. The Congress shall have power to enforce this article by appropriate legislation.

Amendment XVI [February 25, 1913]

The Congress shall have power to lay and collect taxes on incomes, from whatever source derived, without apportionment among the several States, and without regard to any census or enumeration.

Amendment XVII [May 31, 1913]

The Senate of the United States shall be composed of two senators from each State, elected by the people thereof, for six years; and each senator shall have one vote. The electors in each State shall have the qualifications requisite for electors of the most numerous branch of the State legislature.

When vacancies happen in the representation of any State in the Senate, the executive authority of such State shall issue writs of election to fill such vacancies: *Provided,* That the legislature of any State may empower the executive thereof to make temporary appointments until the people fill the vacancies by election as the legislature may direct.

This amendment shall not be so construed as to affect the election or term of any senator chosen before it becomes valid as part of the Constitution.

Amendment XVIII[11] [January 29, 1919]

After one year from the ratification of this article, the manufacture, sale, or transportation of intoxicating liquors within, the importation thereof into, or the exportation thereof from the United States and all territory subject to the jurisdiction thereof for beverage purposes is thereby prohibited.

The Congress and the several States shall have concurrent power to enforce this article by appropriate legislation.

This article shall be inoperative unless it shall have been ratified as an amendment to the Constitution by the legislatures of the several States, as provided in the constitution, within seven years from the date of the submission hereof to the States by Congress.

[11]Repealed by the Twenty-first Amendment.

Amendment XIX [August 26, 1920]

The right of citizens of the United States to vote shall not be denied or abridged by the United States or by any State on account of sex.

Congress shall have the power to enforce this article by appropriate legislation.

Amendment XX [January 23, 1933]

Section 1. The terms of the President and Vice President shall end at noon on the 20th day of January and the terms of Senators and Representatives at noon on the 3d day of January, of the years in which such terms would have ended if this article had not been ratified; and the terms of their successors shall then begin.

Section 2. The Congress shall assemble at least once in every year, and such meeting shall begin at noon on the 3d day of January, unless they shall by law appoint a different day.

Section 3. If, at the time fixed for the beginning of the term of President, the President-elect shall have died, the Vice President-elect shall become President. If a President shall not have been chosen before the time fixed for the beginning of his term, or if the President-elect shall have failed to qualify, then the Vice President-elect shall act as President until a President shall have qualified; and the Congress may by law provide for the case wherein neither a President-elect nor a Vice President-elect shall have qualified, declaring who shall then act as President, or the manner in which one who is to act shall be selected, and such person shall act accordingly until a President or Vice President shall have qualified.

Section 4. The Congress may by law provide for the case of the death of any of the persons from whom, the House of Representatives may choose a President whenever the right of choice shall have devolved upon them, and for the case of the death of any of the persons from whom the Senate may choose a Vice President whenever the right of choice shall have devolved upon them.

Section 5. Sections 1 and 2 shall take effect on the 15th day of October following the ratification of this article.

Section 6. This article shall be inoperative unless it shall have been ratified as an amendment to the Constitution by the legislatures of three-fourths of the several States within seven years from the date of its submission.

Amendment XXI [December 5, 1933]

Section 1. The Eighteenth Article of amendment to the Constitution of the United States is hereby repealed.

Section 2. The transportation or importation into any State, Territory, or possession of the United States for delivery or use therein of intoxicating liquors in violation of the laws thereof, is hereby prohibited.

Section 3. This article shall be inoperative unless it shall have been ratified as an amendment to the Constitution by conventions in the several States, as provided in the Constitution, within seven years from the date of the submission thereof to the States by the Congress.

Amendment XXII [March 1, 1951]

No person shall be elected to the office of the President more than twice, and no person who has held the office of President, or acted as President, for more than two years of a term to which some other person was elected President shall be elected to the office of the President more than once.

But this article shall not apply to any person holding the office of President when this article was proposed by the Congress, and shall not prevent any person who may be holding the office of President, or acting as President, during the term within which this article becomes operative from holding the office of President or acting as President during the remainder of such term.

This article shall be inoperative unless it shall have been ratified as an amendment to the Constitution by the legislatures of three-fourths of the several States within seven years from the date of its submission to the States by the Congress.

Amendment XXIII [March 29, 1961]

Section 1. The District constituting the seat of Government of the United States shall appoint in such manner as the Congress may direct.

A number of electors of President and Vice President equal to the whole number of Senators and Representatives in Congress to which the District would be entitled if it were a State, but in no event more than the least populous State; they shall be in addition to those appointed by the States, but they shall be considered, for the purposes of the election of President and Vice President, to be electors appointed by a State; and they shall meet in the District and perform such duties as provided by the twelfth article of amendment.

Section 2. The Congress shall have power to enforce this article by appropriate legislation.

Amendment XXIV [January 23, 1964]

Section 1. The right of citizens of the United States to vote in any primary or other election for President or Vice President, for electors for President or Vice President, or for Senator or Representative in Congress, shall not be denied or abridged by the United States or any State by reason of failure to pay any poll tax or other tax.

Section 2. The Congress shall have power to enforce this article by appropriate legislation.

Amendment XXV [February 10, 1967]

Section 1. In case of the removal of the President from office or of his death or resignation, the Vice President shall become President.

Section 2. Whenever there is a vacancy in the office of the Vice President, the President shall nominate a Vice President who shall take office upon confirmation by a majority of both Houses of Congress.

Section 3. Whenever the President transmits to the President pro tempore of the Senate and the Speaker of the House of Representatives his written declaration that he is unable to discharge the powers and duties of his office, and until he transmits to them a written declaration to the contrary, such powers and duties shall be discharged by the Vice President as Acting President.

Section 4. Whenever the Vice president and a majority of either the principal officers of the executive departments or of such other body as Congress may by law provide, transmit to the President pro tempore of the Senate and the Speaker of the House of Representatives their written declaration that the President is unable to discharge the powers and duties of his office, the Vice President shall immediately assume the powers and duties of the office as Acting President.

Thereafter, when the President transmits to the President pro tempore of the Senate and the Speaker of the House of Representatives his written declaration that no inability exists, he shall resume the powers and duties of his office unless the Vice President and a majority of either the principal officers of the executive departments or of such other body as Congress may by law provide, transmit within four days to the President pro tempore of the Senate and the Speaker of the House of Representatives their written declaration that the President is unable to discharge the powers and duties of his office. Thereupon Congress shall decide the issue, assembling within forty-eight hours for that purpose if not in session. If the Congress, within twenty-one days after receipt of the latter written declaration, or, if Congress is not in session, within twenty-one days after Congress is required to assemble, determines by two-thirds vote of both Houses that the President is unable to discharge the powers and duties of his office, the Vice President shall continue to discharge the same as Acting President; otherwise, the President shall resume the powers and duties of his office.

Amendment XXVI [June 30, 1971]

Section 1. The right of citizens of the United States who are eighteen years of age or older to vote shall not be denied or abridged by the United States or by any State on account of age.

Section 2. The Congress shall have power to enforce this article by appropriate legislation.

Amendment XXVII[12] [May 7, 1992]

No law, varying the compensation for services of the Senators and Representatives, shall take effect until an election of Representatives shall have intervened.

[12]James Madison proposed this amendment in 1789 together with the ten amendments that were adopted as the Bill of Rights, but it failed to win ratification at the time. Congress, however, had set no deadline for its ratification, and over the years—particularly in the 1980s and 1990s—many states voted to add it to the Constitution. With the ratification of Michigan in 1992 it passed the threshold of 3/4ths of the states required for adoption, but because the process took more than 200 years, its validity remains in doubt.

PRESIDENTS AND VICE PRESIDENTS

1. George Washington (1789)
   John Adams (1789)
2. John Adams (1797)
   Thomas Jefferson (1797)
3. Thomas Jefferson (1801)
   Aaron Burr (1801)
   George Clinton (1805)
4. James Madison (1809)
   George Clinton (1809)
   Elbridge Gerry (1813)
5. James Monroe (1817)
   Daniel D. Thompkins (1817)
6. John Quincy Adams (1825)
   John C. Calhoun (1825)
7. Andrew Jackson (1829)
   John C. Calhoun (1829)
   Martin Van Buren (1833)
8. Martin Van Buren (1837)
   Richard M. Johnson (1837)
9. William H. Harrison (1841)
   John Tyler (1841)
10. John Tyler (1841)
11. James K. Polk (1845)
    George M. Dallas (1845)
12. Zachary Taylor (1849)
    Millard Fillmore (1849)
13. Millard Fillmore (1850)
14. Franklin Pierce (1853)
    William R. King (1853)
15. James Buchanan (1857)
    John C. Breckinridge (1857)
16. Abraham Lincoln (1861)
    Hannibal Hamlin (1861)
    Andrew Johnson (1865)
17. Andrew Johnson (1865)
18. Ulysses S. Grant (1869)
    Schuyler Colfax (1869)
    Henry Wilson (1873)
19. Rutherford B. Hayes (1877)
    William A. Wheeler (1877)
20. James A. Garfield (1881)
    Chester A. Arthur (1881)
21. Chester A. Arthur (1881)
22. Grover Cleveland (1885)
    T. A. Hendricks (1885)
23. Benjamin Harrison (1889)
    Levi P. Morgan (1889)
24. Grover Cleveland (1893)
    Adlai E. Stevenson (1893)
25. William McKinley (1897)
    Garret A. Hobart (1897)
    Theodore Roosevelt (1901)
26. Theodore Roosevelt (1901)
    Charles Fairbanks (1905)
27. William H. Taft (1909)
    James S. Sherman (1909)
28. Woodrow Wilson (1913)
    Thomas R. Marshall (1913)
29. Warren G. Harding (1921)
    Calvin Coolidge (1921)
30. Calvin Coolidge (1923)
    Charles G. Dawes (1925)
31. Herbert C. Hoover (1929)
    Charles Curtis (1929)
32. Franklin D. Roosevelt (1933)
    John Nance Garner (1933)
    Henry A. Wallace (1941)
    Harry S. Truman (1945)
33. Harry S. Truman (1945)
    Alben W. Barkley (1949)
34. Dwight D. Eisenhower (1953)
    Richard M. Nixon (1953)
35. John F. Kennedy (1961)
    Lyndon B. Johnson (1961)
36. Lyndon B. Johnson (1963)
    Hubert H. Humphrey (1965)
37. Richard M. Nixon (1969)
    Spiro T. Agnew (1969)
    Gerald R. Ford (1973)
38. Gerald R. Ford (1974)
    Nelson A. Rockefeller (1974)
39. James E. Carter Jr. (1977)
    Walter F. Mondale (1977)
40. Ronald W. Reagan (1981)
    George H. Bush (1981)
41. George H. Bush (1989)
    James D. Quayle III (1989)
42. William J. Clinton (1993)
    Albert Gore (1993)

PRESIDENTIAL ELECTIONS

Year	Number of States	Candidates	Party	Popular Vote*	Electoral Vote†	Percentage of Popular Vote
1789	11	GEORGE WASHINGTON	No party designations		69	
		John Adams			34	
		Other Candidates			35	
1792	15	GEORGE WASHINGTON	No party designations		132	
		John Adams			77	
		George Clinton			50	
		Other Candidates			5	
1796	16	JOHN ADAMS	Federalist		71	
		Thomas Jefferson	Democratic-Republican		68	
		Thomas Pinckney	Federalist		59	
		Aaron Burr	Democratic-Republican		30	
		Other Candidates			48	
1800	16	THOMAS JEFFERSON	Democratic-Republican		73	
		Aaron Burr	Democratic-Republican		73	
		John Adams	Federalist		65	
		Charles C. Pinckney	Federalist		64	
		John Jay	Federalist		1	
1804	17	THOMAS JEFFERSON	Democratic-Republican		162	
		Charles C. Pinckney	Federalist		14	
1808	17	JAMES MADISON	Democratic-Republican		122	
		Charles C. Pinckney	Federalist		47	
		George Clinton	Democratic-Republican		6	
1812	18	JAMES MADISON	Democratic-Republican		128	
		DeWitt Clinton	Federalist		89	
1816	19	JAMES MONROE	Democratic-Republican		183	
		Rufus King	Federalist		34	
1820	24	JAMES MONROE	Democratic-Republican		231	
		John Quincy Adams	Democratic-Republican		1	
1824	24	JOHN QUINCY ADAMS	Democratic-Republican	108,740	84	30.5
		Andrew Jackson	Democratic-Republican	153,544	99	43.1
		William H. Crawford	Democratic-Republican	46,618	41	13.1
		Henry Clay	Democratic-Republican	47,136	37	13.2
1828	24	ANDREW JACKSON	Democrat	647,286	178	56.0
		John Quincy Adams	National-Republican	508,064	83	44.0
1832	24	ANDREW JACKSON	Democrat	687,502	219	55.0
		Henry Clay	National-Republican	530,189	49	42.4
		William Wirt	Anti-Masonic	33,108	7	2.6
		John Floyd	National-Republican		11	

*Percentage of popular vote given for any election year may not total 100 percent because candidates receiving less than 1 percent of the popular vote have been omitted.

†Prior to the passage of the Twelfth Amendment in 1904, the electoral college voted for two presidential candidates; the runner-up became Vice-President. Data from *Historical Statistics of the United States, Colonial Times to 1957* (1961), pp. 682–683, and *The World Almanac.*

PRESIDENTIAL ELECTIONS
(continued)

Year	Number of States	Candidates	Party	Popular Vote	Electoral Vote	Percentage of Popular Vote
1836	26	MARTIN VAN BUREN	Democrat	765,483	170	50.9
		William H. Harrison	Whig	739,795	73	49.1
		Hugh L. White	Whig		26	
		Daniel Webster	Whig		14	
		W. P. Mangum	Whig		11	
1840	26	WILLIAM H. HARRISON	Whig	1,274,624	234	53.1
		Martin Van Buren	Democrat	1,127,781	60	46.9
1844	26	JAMES K. POLK	Democrat	1,338,464	170	49.6
		Henry Clay	Whig	1,300,097	105	48.1
		James G. Birney	Liberty	62,300		2.3
1848	30	ZACHARY TAYLOR	Whig	1,360,967	163	47.4
		Lewis Cass	Democrat	1,222,342	127	42.5
		Martin Van Buren	Free-Soil	291,263		10.1
1852	31	FRANKLIN PIERCE	Democrat	1,601,117	254	50.9
		Winfield Scott	Whig	1,385,453	42	44.1
		John P. Hale	Free-Soil	155,825		5.0
1856	31	JAMES BUCHANAN	Democrat	1,832,955	174	45.3
		John C. Frémont	Republican	1,339,932	114	33.1
		Millard Fillmore	American ("Know Nothing")	871,731	8	21.6
1860	33	ABRAHAM LINCOLN	Republican	1,865,593	180	39.8
		Stephen A. Douglas	Democrat	1,382,713	12	29.5
		John C. Breckinridge	Democrat	848,356	72	18.1
		John Bell	Constitutional Union	592,906	39	12.6
1864	36	ABRAHAM LINCOLN	Republican	2,206,938	212	55.0
		George B. McClellan	Democrat	1,803,787	21	45.0
1868	37	ULYSSES S. GRANT	Republican	3,013,421	214	52.7
		Horatio Seymour	Democrat	2,706,829	80	47.3
1872	37	ULYSSES S. GRANT	Republican	3,596,745	286	55.6
		Horace Greeley	Democrat	2,843,446	*	43.9
1876	38	RUTHERFORD B. HAYES	Republican	4,036,572	185	48.0
		Samuel J. Tilden	Democrat	4,284,020	184	51.0
1880	38	JAMES A. GARFIELD	Republican	4,453,295	214	48.5
		Winfield S. Hancock	Democrat	4,414,082	155	48.1
		James B. Weaver	Greenback-Labor	308,578		3.4
1884	38	GROVER CLEVELAND	Democrat	4,879,507	219	48.5
		James G. Blaine	Republican	4,850,293	182	48.2
		Benjamin F. Butler	Greenback-Labor	175,370		1.8
		John P. St. John	Prohibition	150,369		1.5
1888	38	BENJAMIN HARRISON	Republican	5,447,129	233	47.9
		Grover Cleveland	Democrat	5,537,857	168	48.6
		Clinton B. Fisk	Prohibition	249,506		2.2
		Anson J. Streeter	Union Labor	146,935		1.3

*Because of the death of Greeley, Democratic electors scattered their votes.

PRESIDENTIAL ELECTIONS
(continued)

Year	Number of States	Candidates	Party	Popular Vote	Electoral Vote	Percentage of Popular Vote
1892	44	GROVER CLEVELAND	Democrat	5,555,426	277	46.1
		Benjamin Harrison	Republican	5,182,690	145	43.0
		James B. Weaver	People's	1,029,846	22	8.5
		John Bidwell	Prohibition	264,133		2.2
1896	45	WILLIAM MCKINLEY	Republican	7,102,246	271	51.1
		William J. Bryan	Democrat	6,492,559	176	47.7
1900	45	WILLIAM MCKINLEY	Republican	7,218,491	292	51.7
		William J. Bryan	Democrat; Populist	6,356,734	155	45.5
		John C. Woolley	Prohibition	208,914		1.5
1904	45	THEODORE ROOSEVELT	Republican	7,628,461	336	57.4
		Alton B. Parker	Democrat	5,084,223	140	37.6
		Eugene V. Debs	Socialist	402,283		3.0
		Silas C. Swallow	Prohibition	258,536		1.9
1908	46	WILLIAM H. TAFT	Republican	7,675,320	321	51.6
		William J. Bryan	Democrat	6,412,294	162	43.1
		Eugene V. Debs	Socialist	420,793		2.8
		Eugene W. Chafin	Prohibition	253,840		1.7
1912	48	WOODROW WILSON	Democrat	6,296,547	435	41.9
		Theodore Roosevelt	Progressive	4,118,571	88	27.4
		William H. Taft	Republican	3,486,720	8	23.2
		Eugene V. Debs	Socialist	900,672		6.0
		Eugene W. Chafin	Prohibition	206,275		1.4
1916	48	WOODROW WILSON	Democrat	9,127,695	277	49.4
		Charles E. Hughes	Republican	8,533,507	254	46.2
		A. L. Benson	Socialist	585,113		3.2
		J. Frank Hanly	Prohibition	220,506		1.2
1920	48	WARREN G. HARDING	Republican	16,143,407	404	60.4
		James M. Cox	Democrat	9,130,328	127	34.2
		Eugene V. Debs	Socialist	919,799		3.4
		P. P. Christensen	Farmer-Labor	265,411		1.0
1924	48	CALVIN COOLIDGE	Republican	15,718,211	382	54.0
		John W. Davis	Democrat	8,385,283	136	28.8
		Robert M. La Follette	Progressive	4,831,289	13	16.6
1928	48	HERBERT C. HOOVER	Republican	21,391,993	444	58.2
		Alfred E. Smith	Democrat	15,016,169	87	40.9
1932	48	FRANKLIN D. ROOSEVELT	Democrat	22,809,638	472	57.4
		Herbert C. Hoover	Republican	15,758,901	59	39.7
		Norman Thomas	Socialist	881,951		2.2
1936	48	FRANKLIN D. ROOSEVELT	Democrat	27,752,869	523	60.8
		Alfred M. Landon	Republican	16,674,665	8	36.5
		William Lemke	Union	882,479		1.9
1940	48	FRANKLIN D. ROOSEVELT	Democrat	27,307,819	449	54.8
		Wendell L. Willkie	Republican	22,321,018	82	44.8
1944	48	FRANKLIN D. ROOSEVELT	Democrat	25,606,585	432	53.5
		Thomas E. Dewey	Republican	22,014,745	99	46.0

PRESIDENTIAL ELECTIONS
(continued)

Year	Number of States	Candidates	Party	Popular Vote	Electoral Vote	Percentage of Popular Vote
1948	48	HARRY S. TRUMAN	Democrat	24,105,812	303	49.5
		Thomas E. Dewey	Republican	21,970,065	189	45.1
		J. Strom Thurmond	States' Rights	1,169,063	39	2.4
		Henry A. Wallace	Progressive	1,157,172		2.4
1952	48	DWIGHT D. EISENHOWER	Republican	33,936,234	442	55.1
		Adlai E. Stevenson	Democrat	27,314,992	89	44.4
1956	48	DWIGHT D. EISENHOWER	Republican	35,590,472	457*	57.6
		Adlai E. Stevenson	Democrat	26,022,752	73	42.1
1960	50	JOHN F. KENNEDY	Democrat	34,227,096	303†	49.9
		Richard M. Nixon	Republican	34,108,546	219	49.6
1964	50	LYNDON B. JOHNSON	Democrat	42,676,220	486	61.3
		Barry M. Goldwater	Republican	26,860,314	52	38.5
1968	50	RICHARD M. NIXON	Republican	31,785,480	301	43.4
		Hubert H. Humphrey	Democrat	31,275,165	191	42.7
		George C. Wallace	American Independent	9,906,473	46	13.5
1972	50	RICHARD M. NIXON‡	Republican	47,165,234	520	60.6
		George S. McGovern	Democrat	29,168,110	17	37.5
1976	50	JIMMY CARTER	Democrat	40,828,929	297	50.1
		Gerald R. Ford	Republican	39,148,940	240	47.9
		Eugene McCarthy	Independent	739,256		
1980	50	RONALD REAGAN	Republican	43,201,220	489	50.9
		Jimmy Carter	Democrat	34,913,332	49	41.2
		John B. Anderson	Independent	5,581,379		
1984	50	RONALD REAGAN	Republican	53,428,357	525	59.0
		Walter F. Mondale	Democrat	36,930,923	13	41.0
1988	50	GEORGE BUSH	Republican	48,901,046	426	53.4
		Michael Dukakis	Democrat	41,809,030	111	45.6
1992	50	BILL CLINTON	Democrat	43,728,275	370	43.2
		George Bush	Republican	38,167,416	168	37.7
		H. Ross Perot	United We Stand, America	19,237,247		19.0
1996	50	BILL CLINTON	Democrat	45,590,703	379	49.0
		Robert Dole	Republican	37,816,307	159	41.0
		H. Ross Perot	Reform	7,874,283		8.0

*Walter B. Jones received 1 electoral vote.

†Harry F. Byrd received 15 electoral votes.

‡Resigned August 9, 1974: Vice President Gerald R. Ford became President.

ADMISSION OF STATES INTO THE UNION

State	Date of Admission	State	Date of Admission
1. Delaware	December 7, 1787	26. Michigan	January 26, 1837
2. Pennsylvania	December 12, 1787	27. Florida	March 3, 1845
3. New Jersey	December 18, 1787	28. Texas	December 29, 1845
4. Georgia	January 2, 1788	29. Iowa	December 28, 1846
5. Connecticut	January 9, 1788	30. Wisconsin	May 29, 1848
6. Massachusetts	February 6, 1788	31. California	September 9, 1850
7. Maryland	April 28, 1788	32. Minnesota	May 11, 1858
8. South Carolina	May 23, 1788	33. Oregon	February 14, 1859
9. New Hampshire	June 21, 1788	34. Kansas	January 29, 1861
10. Virginia	June 25, 1788	35. West Virginia	June 20, 1863
11. New York	July 26, 1788	36. Nevada	October 31, 1864
12. North Carolina	November 21, 1789	37. Nebraska	March 1, 1867
13. Rhode Island	May 29, 1790	38. Colorado	August 1, 1876
14. Vermont	March 4, 1791	39. North Dakota	November 2, 1889
15. Kentucky	June 1, 1792	40. South Dakota	November 2, 1889
16. Tennessee	June 1, 1796	41. Montana	November 8, 1889
17. Ohio	March 1, 1803	42. Washington	November 11, 1889
18. Louisiana	April 30, 1812	43. Idaho	July 3, 1890
19. Indiana	December 11, 1816	44. Wyoming	July 10, 1890
20. Mississippi	December 10, 1817	45. Utah	January 4, 1896
21. Illinois	December 3, 1818	46. Oklahoma	November 16, 1907
22. Alabama	December 14, 1819	47. New Mexico	January 6, 1912
23. Maine	March 15, 1820	48. Arizona	February 14, 1912
24. Missouri	August 10, 1821	49. Alaska	January 3, 1959
25. Arkansas	June 15, 1836	50. Hawaii	August 21, 1959

DEMOGRAPHICS OF THE UNITED STATES

POPULATION GROWTH

Year	Population	Percent Increase
1630	4,600	
1640	26,600	478.3
1650	50,400	90.8
1660	75,100	49.0
1670	111,900	49.0
1680	151,500	35.4
1690	210,400	38.9
1700	250,900	19.2
1710	331,700	32.2
1720	466,200	40.5
1730	629,400	35.0
1740	905,600	43.9
1750	1,170,800	29.3
1760	1,593,600	36.1
1770	2,148,100	34.8
1780	2,780,400	29.4
1790	3,929,214	41.3
1800	5,308,483	35.1
1810	7,239,881	36.4
1820	9,638,453	33.1
1830	12,866,020	33.5
1840	17,069,453	32.7
1850	23,191,876	35.9
1860	31,443,321	35.6
1870	39,818,449	26.6
1880	50,155,783	26.0
1890	62,947,714	25.5
1900	75,994,575	20.7
1910	91,972,266	21.0
1920	105,710,620	14.9
1930	122,775,046	16.1
1940	131,669,275	7.2
1950	150,697,361	14.5
1960	179,323,175	19.0
1970	203,235,298	13.3
1980	226,545,805	11.5
1990	248,709,873	9.8
1996	265,557,000	6.8

Source: *Historical Statistics of the United States* (1975); *Statistical Abstract by the United States* (1991, 1997).

Note: Figures for 1630–1780 include British colonies within limits of present United States only; Native American population included only in 1930 and thereafter.

WORKFORCE

Year	Total Number Workers (1000s)	Farmers as % of Total	Women as % of Total	% Workers in Unions
1810	2,330	84	(NA)	(NA)
1840	5,660	75	(NA)	(NA)
1860	11,110	53	(NA)	(NA)
1870	12,506	53	15	(NA)
1880	17,392	52	15	(NA)
1890	23,318	43	17	(NA)
1900	29,073	40	18	3
1910	38,167	31	21	6
1920	41,614	26	21	12
1930	48,830	22	22	7
1940	53,011	17	24	27
1950	59,643	12	28	25
1960	69,877	8	32	26
1970	82,049	4	37	25
1980	108,544	3	42	23
1990	117,914	3	45	16
1995	124,900	3	46	15

Source: *Historical Statistics of the United States* (1975); *Statistical Abstract of the United States* (1991, 1996).

VITAL STATISTICS
(per thousands)

Year	Births	Deaths	Marriages	Divorces
1800	55	(NA)	(NA)	(NA)
1810	54.3	(NA)	(NA)	(NA)
1820	55.2	(NA)	(NA)	(NA)
1830	51.4	(NA)	(NA)	(NA)
1840	51.8	(NA)	(NA)	(NA)
1850	43.3	(NA)	(NA)	(NA)
1860	44.3	(NA)	(NA)	(NA)
1870	38.3	(NA)	9.6 (1867)	0.3 (1867)
1880	39.8	(NA)	9.1 (1875)	0.3 (1875)
1890	31.5	(NA)	9.0	0.5
1900	32.3	17.2	9.3	0.7
1910	30.1	14.7	10.3	0.9
1920	27.7	13.0	12.0	1.6
1930	21.3	11.3	9.2	1.6
1940	19.4	10.8	12.1	2.0
1950	24.1	9.6	11.1	2.6
1960	23.7	9.5	8.5	2.2
1970	18.4	9.5	10.6	3.5
1980	15.9	8.8	10.6	5.2
1990	16.7	8.6	9.8	4.7
1994	15.0	8.8	9.1	4.6

Source: *Historical Statistics of the United States* (1975); *Statistical Abstract of the United States* (1991, 1997).

RACIAL COMPOSITION OF THE POPULATION
(in thousands)

Year	White	Black	Indian	Hispanic	Asian
1790	3,172	757	(NA)	(NA)	(NA)
1800	4,306	1,002	(NA)	(NA)	(NA)
1820	7,867	1,772	(NA)	(NA)	(NA)
1840	14,196	2,874	(NA)	(NA)	(NA)
1860	26,923	4,442	(NA)	(NA)	(NA)
1880	43,403	6,581	(NA)	(NA)	(NA)
1900	66,809	8,834	(NA)	(NA)	(NA)
1910	81,732	9,828	(NA)	(NA)	(NA)
1920	94,821	10,463	(NA)	(NA)	(NA)
1930	110,287	11,891	(NA)	(NA)	(NA)
1940	118,215	12,866	(NA)	(NA)	(NA)
1950	134,942	15,042	(NA)	(NA)	(NA)
1960	158,832	18,872	(NA)	(NA)	(NA)
1970	178,098	22,581	(NA)	(NA)	(NA)
1980	194,713	26,683	1,420	14,609	3,729
1990	205,710	30,486	2,065	22,354	7,458
1996	219,749	30,503	2,288	28,269	9,743

Source: U.S. Bureau of the Census, *U.S. Census of Population: 1940*, vol. II, part 1, and vol. IV, part 1; *1950*, vol. II, part 1; *1960*, vol. I, part 1; *1970*, vol. I, part B; and *Current Population Reports*, P25-1095 and P25-1104; *Statistical Abstract of the United States* (1997); and unpublished data.

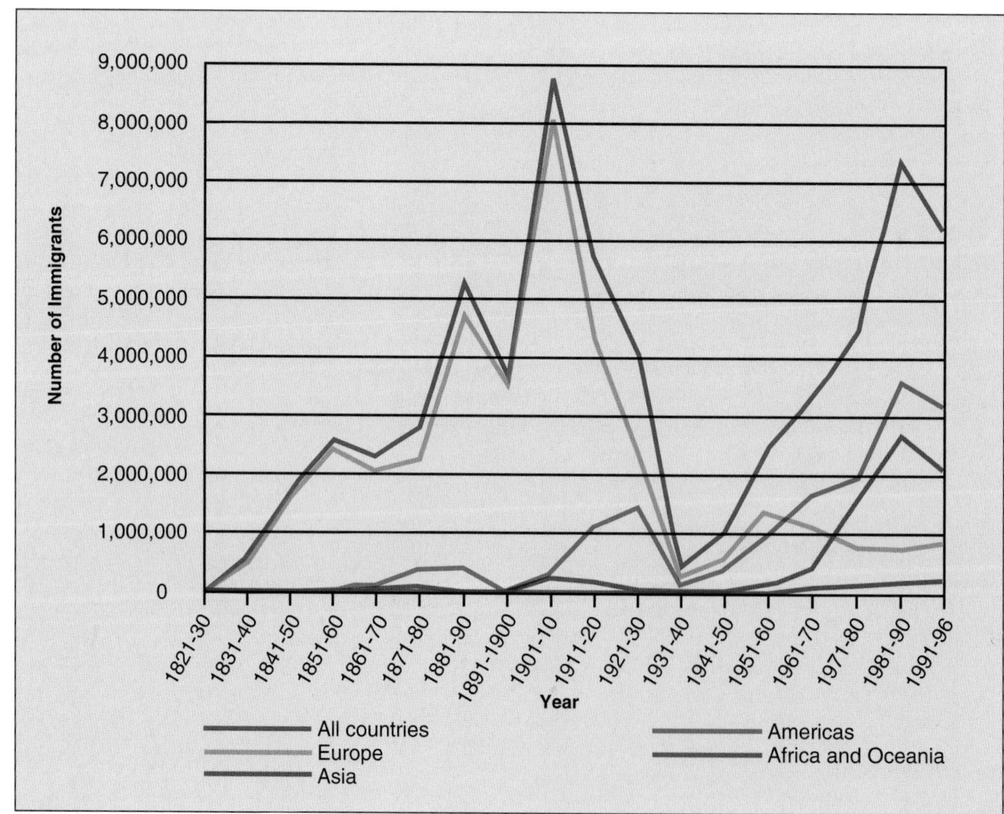

Immigration to the United States since 1820

Source: *Statistical Yearbook of the Immigration and Naturalization Service*, 1996.

Photo and Text Credits

Chapter 1: Photos: Cahokia Mounds State Historic Site, xxxii (vols. I, II, A, B, C)/xlviii (combined edition); Jerry Jacka/Arizona State Museum, University of Arizona, 6; Denver Museum of Natural History, 7; American Museum of Natural History, 11; National Museum of the American Indian/Smithsonian Institution, 13; Helga Teiwes, Arizona State Museum, 13; David Hiser/David Muench Photography, Inc., 14; George Gerster/Comstock, 15; Rota/American Museum of Natural History, 20 Text: "Emergence Song" (excerpt) from William Brandon, *The Magic World: American Indian Songs and Poems*. Copyright © 1971 by William Brandon. Reprinted with the permission of William Morrow and Company, Inc., 5; Winnebago song, "This Newly Created World," from the Winnebago Medicine Rite as recorded in Raul Radin, *The Road to Life and Death: A Ritual Drama of the American Indians* (Bollinger Series V), p. 254. Copyright 1945 and © renewed 1972 by Princeton University Press. Reprinted with the permission of the publishers., 10

Chapter 2: Photos: The Granger Collection, 25; Art Resource, Musee Conde, Chantilly/Giraudon, Art Resource, NY, 29; From THE SHIP, AN ILLUSTRATED HISTORY by Bjorn Landstrom, Copyright © 1961 by Bokforlaget Forum AB. Used by permission of Doubleday, a division of Bantam Doubleday Dell Publishing Group, Inc., 31; The Granger Collection, 32; The British Library, 34; Library of Congress, 35; The British Library, 36; Jacques Le Moyne, "Rene de Loudonniere and Chief Athore," 1564, watercolor, The New York Public Library, NY, 41; Capitaine de la Nation, *Codex Canadienses*, artist Louis Nicolas, from the collection of Gilcrease Museum, Tulsa, OK, 42; The Bridgeman Art Library, 43; The Granger Collection, 44 Text: "The African, Indian and European Population of the Americas" from Colin McEvedy and Richard Jones, *Atlas of World Population History*. Copyright © 1978 by Colin McEvedy and Richard Jones. Reprinted with the permission of Penguin Putnam, Inc., 39

Chapter 3: Photos: Jerry Jacka Photography, 49; New York Public Library, 53; (left) "Princeton University Library," Manuscripts Division. Department of Rare Books and Special Collections. Princeton University Library, 55; Library of Congress, 55; Library of Congress, 56; Library of Congress, 60; The John Carter Brown Library, at Brown University, 61; The Fine Arts Museum of San Francisco, 62; The New York Historical Society, 65; The Historical Society of Pennsylvania, 66; Courtesy, American Antiquarian Society, 68

Chapter 4: Photos: The British Library, 73; Library of Congress, 77; The Bridgeman Art Library, 79; Library of Congress, 81; The Granger Collection, New York, 82; American Antiquarian Society, 83; The Maryland Historical Society, 85; Carolina Art Association/Gibbes Museum of Art, 86; Colonial Williamsburg Foundation, 90; The Philbrook Museum of Art, 91; Michael Holford/The Victoria and Albert Museum, 93; The Saint Louis Art Museum, 96; Virginia Museum of Fine Arts, 99 Text: "Estimated Number of Africans Imported to British North America," from R.C. Simmons, *The American Colonies: From Settlement to Independence* (London:Longman, 1976). Copyright © 1976 by R.C. Simmons. Reprinted with the permission of The Peters Fraser and Dunlop Group Limited, 80

Chapter 5: Photos: Colonial Williamsburg Foundation, 103; The Historical Society of Pennsylvania, 106; Jack W. Dykinga & Associates, 110; United States Geological Survey, 112; William Johnson/Stock, Boston, 113; Henry Glassie, Pattern in the Material Folk Culture of the Eastern United States, 114; (left) Courtesy, American Antiquarian Society, 118; Library of Congress, 118; Schalkwijk/Art Resource, NY, 121; American Antiquarian Society, 124; John Carter Brown Library, Brown University, 127 Text: "Distribution of Assessed Taxable Wealth in Eighteenth-Century Chester County, Pennsylvania," Copyright © 1968 by Peter N. Stearns. Reprinted with the permission of the publishers. 122; "Wealth Held by Richest 10 Percent of the Population: Northern and Southern Colonies Compared, 1770," Copyright © by Princeton University Press, renewed 1993 by Jackson Turner Main. Reprinted with the permission of Princeton University Press, 122

Chapter 6: Photos: The Granger Collection, 132; National Gallery of Canada, 138; Treaty, dated 13 July 1765, between Sir William Johnson and representatives of the Delaware, Shawnee, and Mingo nations. On parchment, 16" x 24.5". Photo by Carmelo Guadagno. Photograph courtesy of National Museum of the American Indian/Smithsonian Institution. Neg. 39369, 140; Massachusetts Historical Society, 142; Museum of Fine Arts, Boston, 144; Library of Congress, 145; The Granger Collection, 146; Library of Congress, 147; Library of Congress, 149; Christie's Images, 150; Connecticut Historical Society, 154; The Granger Collection, 156; The Granger Collection, 158

Chapter 7: Photos: Sam Holland, South Carolina State House, 162; Anne S. K. Brown Military Collection, Brown University Library, 166; Museum of Fine Arts, Boston, 167; The Granger Collection, 168; (top) Gilbert Stuart. "The Mohawk Chief Joseph Brant," 1786. Oil on canvas, 30" x 25". New York State Historical Association, Cooperstown, NY, 172; The Bostonian Society/Old State House, 172; Library of Congress, 176; Data available from U.S. Geological Survey, EROS Data Center, Sioux Falls, SD, 181; Corbis-Bettmann, 185; Library of Congress, 186; Art Resource, NY, 189

Chapter 8: Photos: The Granger Collection, 193; Print and Picture Collection, The Free Library of Philadelphia, 197; Collection of The New York Historical Society, 200; "The Republican Court," 1861, by Daniel P. Huntington. Oil on canvas. Gift of the Crescent Boys' Club. Brooklyn Museum of Art, 201; Indiana Historical Society Library (negative no. C2584), 205; "General George Washington Reviewing the Western Army...," by Francis Kemmelmeyer, after 1794. Oil on paper backed with linen. Dimensions 18 1/8" x 23 1/8". Courtesy of Winterthur Museum, 206; Collection of The New York Historical Society, 210; The Granger Collection, 212; Pennsylvania Academy of the Fine Arts, 213; Library of Congress, 214; Courtesy of American Antiquarian Society, 216; Library Company of Philadelphia, 217 Text: "Housing Values," Copyright © 1985 by Social Science History Association. Reprinted with the permission of Duke University Press, 215

Immigration & Community, to 1800: Photos: The Granger Collection, 225; The Granger Collection, 226 Text: "The Ancestry of the British Colonial Population" from Thomas L. Purvis, "The European Ancestry of the United States Population" in *William and Mary Quarterly*, 61 (1984): 85–101. Copyright © 1984 by the Institute of Early American History and Culture. Reprinted with the permission of the publishers., 223

Chapter 9: Photos: Henry Ford Museum & Greenfield Village, 228; Friedrich H. von Kittlitz, A View of the Russian Capital, 1827, from F.P. Litke. Alaska and Polar Regions, Department, Elmer E. Rasmusen Library Rare books, University of Alaska, Fairbanks, 232; Launching of ship "Fame" from Becket's Shipyard, Essex, Massachusetts, 1802, oil on canvas, by George Ropes. Mark Sexton, Peabody Essex Museum, 236; top, Library of Congress, 237; Library of Congress, 237; Museum of Early Southern Decorative Arts, 238; Thomas Gilcrease Institute of American History and Art, 243; Field Musuem of Natural History, 245; Library of Congress, 245; Library of Congress, 249; Library of Congress, 250; The New York Historical Society, 253

Chapter 10: Photos: NationsBank, 261; Walters Art Gallery, 268; Library of Congress, 270; The Maryland Historical Society, 273; Munson-Williams-Proctor Institute, 275; Chicago Historical Society, 277; Museum of the City of New York, 282; Library of Congress, 285; "Collection of the

Boston Athenaeum," 289; New York Public Library, 290 Text: "The Impact of the Erie Canal on Household Textile Manufacture" from Arthur Harrison Cole, The American Wool Manufacture. Copyright 1926 by the President and Fellows of Harvard College. Reprinted with the permission of Harvard University Press, 274

Chapter 11: Photos: Chicago Historical Society, 294; Library of Congress, 298; Wilson S. Armistead, University of Michigan Press, 299; Library of Congress, 307; The Historic New Orleans Collection, 308; Sophia Smith Collection, Smith College, 309; Library of Congress, 310; American Numismatic Society of New York, (left and right), 311; Daughters of the Republic of Texas, Yanaguana Society Collection, 312; The Historic New Orleans Collection, 315; National Archives, 317; Library of Congress, 319

Chapter 12: Photos: American Textile History Museum, 324; Abby Aldrich Rockefeller Folk Art Center, Williamsburg, VA, 328; Museum of Fine Arts, Boston, 329; Library of Congress, 332; Rhode Island Historical Society, 333; James L. Amos, National Geographic Society, (top & bottom) 336; High-Pressure Steamboat Mayflower, 1855, color lithograph by N. Currier. The Bettmann Archive. Corbis-Bettmann, 338; Baker Library, Graduate School of Business Administration, Harvard University, 340; Musuem of Fine Arts, Boston, 343; Mathew Brady/Brown Brothers, 344; The New York Historical Society, 346; Library of Congress, 347

Chapter 13: Photos: The New York Historical Society, 351; The Granger Collection, 358; Library of Congress, 360; Zelsa P. Mackay Collection, Courtesy George Eastman House, 362; "Seabury Champlin's June 3, 1791 Certificate of Membership in NY Mechanic Society," Abraham Godwin, print. Courtesy Winterthur Museum, 363; Frank and Marie-Therese Wood Print Collections, The Picture Bank, 364; The Schlesinger Library, Radcliffe College, 367; Library of Congress, 369; Hannah Harrison, Hancock Shaker Village, 371; Library of Congress (left & right), 373; Sophia Smith Collection, Smith College, 374; Lynn Historical Society, 376

Immigration & Community, 1800–1860: Photos: Dover Publications, Inc., 383; Museum of the City of New York, 384

Chapter 14: Photos: San Jacinto Museum of History Association, 386; Walters Art Gallery, 390; Henry E. Huntington Library and Art Gallery, 395; American Antiquarian Society, 397; The Walters Art Gallery, Baltimore, 398; Art Resource, NY, 399; Brown University Library, 404; National Gallery of Art, 406; The New York Historical Society, 408; California State Library, 409; Bigelow Collection, Museum of Fine Arts, Boston, 410; Steven Laschever/Museum of American Political Life/University of Hartford, 413 Text: "Overland Emigration to Oregon, California, and Utah, 1840-1860" from John Unruh, Jr., *The Plains Across: The Overland Emigrants and the Trans-Mississippi West, 1840-60*. Copyright © 1979 by the Board of Trustees of the University of Illinois. Reprinted with the permission of the University of Illinois Press., 396; "California in the Gold Rush," from Warren A. Beck and Ynez D. Haase, *Historical Atlas of California*. Copyright © 1974 by the University of Oklahoma Press. Reprinted with the permission of the publishers., 407

Chapter 15: Photos: The Granger Collection, 417; Harriet Beecher Stowe Center, Hartford, CT, Stowe-Day Foundation, 422; Courtesy American Antiquarian Society, 423; Library of Congress, 424; The Granger Collection, 431; Corbis-Bettmann, 432; New York Public Library, 434; Library of Congress, 435; Museum of the City of New York, 436; The Granger Collection, 437; Library of Congress, 440; United States Senate, 443

Chapter 16: Photos: Armen Shamalian Photographers, Art Resource, NY, 447; Courtesy Museum of Fine Arts, Boston, 451; The Picture Bank, 455; Alexander Gardner, National Archives, 456; Library of Congress, 458; Valentine Museum Library, (left) 459; Library of Congress, 459; Reproduced from Pauli Murray, *Proud Shoes: The Story of an American Family*, HarperCollins Publishers, Inc., 1987, 466; Center of Military History, U.S. Army, 468; The Metropolitan Museum of Art, 469; Culvery Pictures, Inc., 471; Thomas C. Roche, Library of Congress, 475; Army Military History Institute, 476; Library of Congress, 477

Chapter 17: Photos: The Metropolitan Museum of Art, 481; National Archives, 485; Chicago Historical Society, 486; The Granger Collection, 488; The Susan B. Anthony House, Rochester, NY, 492; The Picture Bank/Harper's Weekly, 495; Library of Congress, 498; Library of Congress, 499; The University of North Carolina, (left) 501; Rutherford B. Hayes Presidential Center, 501; The Granger Collection, New York, 505; The Picture Bank, Frank and Marie-Therese Wood Print Collection, 507

Chapter 18: Photos: Christie's Images, 513; National Anthropological Archives, 518; Marion Koogler McNay Art Museum, 519; Timothy O'Sullivan, Amon Carter Museum, 522; Witte Museum, 525; Harper's Weekly, 527; Nebraska State Historical Society, Solomon D. Butcher Collection, 531; Library of Congress, 532; The Metropolitan Museum of Art, 537; Library of Congress, 538; Photo courtesy of State Historical Society of Iowa, Iowa City, 541; Edward Truman/The Denver Public Library, Western History Collection, 542 Text: "Oklahoma Territory" from John W. Morrois, Charles R. Goins, and Edwin C. McReynolds, *Historical Atlas of Oklahoma*, Third Edition. Copyright © 1965, 1976, 1986 by the University of Oklahoma Press. Reprinted with the permission of the publishers., 515; History and the Land feature and "Ethnic Composition of North Dakota, 1900," from John R. Shortridge, "The Great Plains" in Mary Kupiec Cayton, Elliott J. Gorn, and Peter W. Williams, *Encyclopedia of American Social History II*. Copyright © 1993 by Charles Scribner's Sons. Reprinted with the permission of Scribner's, an imprint of Simon & Schuster Macmillan. 528–529

Chapter 19: Photos: The Granger Collection, 547; U.S. Department of the Interior, National Park Service, Edison National Historic Site, 551 Chicago Historical Society, 553; Color engraving by J. Keppler from Puck, February 23, 1881, Collection of The New York Historical Society, New York City, 554; The Denver Public Library, Western History Collection, 556; Museum of the City of New York, 563; National Archives, 565; Terra Museum of American Art, 568; The Granger Collection, 570; Rhode Island School of Design, 573 Text: "U.S. Economy, 1873-1900" from Bernard Bailyn et al., *The Great Republic*, Third Edition. Copyright © 1985 by D.D. Heath and Company. Reprinted with the permission of Houghton Mifflin Company., 557

Chapter 20: Photos: Vermont State House, 578; Sally Anderson-Bruce/Museum of American Political Life, 583; Library of Congress, 585; Library of Congress, 588; Library of Congress, 590; The Granger Collection, New York, 594; National Archives, 596; Library of Congress, 601; Library of Congress, 603; Library of Congress, 604

Chapter 21: Photos: San Diego Museum of Art, 609; Lewis W. Hine/George Eastman House, 614; Henry Street Settlement, 615; Museum of the City of New York, 618;The Toledo Museum of Art, 622; Brown Brothers, 624; UPI/Corbis-Bettmann, 626; Collection of The American Labor Museum, Botto House National Landmark, 629; Planned Parenthood ® Federation of America, Inc. At, 810 Seventh Avenue, New York, NY, 10019., 631; Schomburg Center for Research in Black Culture, 632; California Historical Society, 635; Theodore Roosevelt Collection, Harvard College Library/The Houghton Library, Harvard University, 636

Chapter 22: Photos: Corbis-Bettmann, 642; The Granger Collection, 646; Culver Pictures, Inc., 649; Wallace Kirkland Papers, Jane Addams Memorial Collection, Special Collections, The University Library, University of Illinois at Chicago, 651; The Granger Collection; 652; Library of Congress, 653; National Archives, 654; National Archives, 655; Virginia War Museum/War Memorial Museum of Virginia, 659; Library of Congress, 661; Stock Montage Inc./ Historial Pictures Collection, 665;

Pemco Webster & Stevens Collection, Museum of History and Industry, Seattle, WA, 666; Art Resource, NY 667

Chapter 23: Photos: The Equitable Life Assurance Society of the United States, 673; A&P Food Stores, LTD, 678; Brown Brothers, 679; Ford Motor Company, Detroit, 680; Culver Pictures, Inc., 683; Gaslight Advertising Archives, Inc., Commack, NY, 685; The Granger Collection, 688; Corbis-Bettmann, 689; Bracken Library, Ball State University Libraries, Archives and Special Collections, W.A. Swift Photo Collection, 695; AP/Wide World Photos, 696; Library of Congress, 699; Reiss, Winold. Portrait of Langston Hughes (1902-1967 Poet) © 1925. National Portrait Gallery, Washington, DC, USA, Art Resource, NY, 701; "Copyright, 1928, Los Angeles Times. Reprinted by permission." Los Angeles Times Syndicate International, 702

Immigration & Community, 1860–1930: Photos: UPI/Lewis W. Hine, Corbis-Bettmann, 711; Jacob A. Riss/Museum of the City of New York, 713

Chapter 24: Photos: SuperStock, Inc., 714; Brown Brothers, 718; Dorothea Lange/The Oakland Museum, 720; Whitney Museum of American Art, 721; Cartoon by Covarrubias from *Vanity Fair* depicting Franklin D. Roosevelt's first-term inauguration on March 4, 1933. Conde Nast/Franklin D. Roosevelt Library, Hyde Park, NY, 724; Terry Dintenfass Gallery, 730; The Granger Collection, 732; Library of Congress, 736; Walker Evans/Library of Congress, 738; Whitney Museum of American Art, 739; Frank Driggs Collection, 741; UPI/Corbis-Bettmann, 743

Chapter 25: Photos: Christie's Images, 748; National Archives, 754; Franklin D. Roosevelt Library, 755; The Granger Collection, 759; Corbis-Bettmann, 761; Japanese American National Museum, 763; Graydon Wood/Philadelphia Museum of Art, 764; AP/Wide World Photos, 765; National Archives, 769; Center of Military History, U.S. Army, 771; Robert Capa/Corbis-Bettmann, 776; Imperial War Museum, London, 779; Corbis-Bettmann, 780 Text: "Gallup Polls: European War and World War I, 1938-1940" from *The Gallup Poll: Public Opinion, 1935-1974*. Reprinted with the permission of Random House, Inc., 753; "Effects of War Spending, 1940-1945" from Robert L. Heilbroner, *The Economic Transformation of America*. Copyright © 1977 by Harcourt Brace and Company. Reprinted with the permission of the publisher., 757; Langston Hughes, "Beaumont to Detroit: 1943" from *The Collected Poems of Langston Hughes*, edited by Arnold Rampersad and David Roessel. Originally published in *Common Ground* (Autumn 1943). Copyright © 1994 by the Estate of Langston Hughes. Reprinted with the permission of Alfred A. Knopf, Inc. and Harold Ober Associates, Inc., 764

Chapter 26: Photos: Michael Barson, 785; UPI/Corbis-Bettmann, 789; Brown Brothers, 793; AP/Wide World Photos, 797; UPI/Corbis-Bettmann, 799; Michael Barson/Archive Photos, 803; Hank Walker/Time Life Syndication, 804; Corbis-Bettmann, 806; National Archives, 809; AP/Wide World Photos, 812

Chapter 27: Photos: Saatchi Collection, London/A.K.G., Berlin/SuperStock, Inc., 817; Bernard Hoffman/*Life Magazine*/© 1950 Time Ind., Time Life Syndication, 821; Williger, FPG International LLC, 822; UPI/Corbis-Bettmann, 826; Archive Photos, 828; Motorola, Inc., 831; Globe Photos, Inc., 832; A. Wagg/FPG International LLC, 834; AP/Wide World Photos, 838; Corbis-Bettmann, 839; NASA Headquarters, 841; Photo. No. ST-A26-18-62 in the John F. Kennedy Library, 843; AP/Wide World Photos, 844 Text: Allen Ginsberg, "Howl" (excerpt) from *Collected Poems, 1947-1980*. Copyright © 1955, 1958, and renewed 1983, 1986 by Allen Ginsberg. Reprinted with the permission of HarperCollins Publishers, Inc., 833

Chapter 28: Photos: Romare Bearden Foundation/Licensed by VAGA, New York, NY, 848; Frank Driggs Collection,852; Dan McCoy/Black Star, (left) 853; Corbis-Bettmann, 853; UPI/Corbis-Bettmann, 856; John G. Moebes/Greensboro New & Record, 857; UPI/Corbis-Bettmann, 860; Bill Hudson/AP/Wide World Photos, 863; AP/Wide World Photos, 864; George Ballis/Take Stock, 867; John Launois/Black Star, 868; Matt Herron/Media Image Resource Alliance, 869; Benson Latin American Collection, University of Texas at Austin, 872; Corbis-Bettmann, 873

Chapter 29: Photos: Library of Congress, 878; Philip Jones Griffiths/Magnum Photos, Inc., 883; Jeffrey Blankfort/Jeroboam, Inc., 884; Bernie Boston, 885; Archive Photos, 888; Jeffrey Blankfort/Jeroboam, Inc., 895; Matt Herron/Media Image Resource Alliance, 897; Corbis-Bettmann, 901; Corbis-Bettmann, 908 Text: Bob Dylan, "The Times They are a-Changin'" (excerpt). Copyright © 1963, 1964 by Warner Bros. Music, renewed 1991 by Special Rider Music. All rights reserved. International copyright secured. Reprinted with the permission of Special Rider Music., 885

Chapter 30: Photos: Robert McElroy/Woodfin Camp & Associates, 917; Guido Alberto Rossi/The Image Bank, 921; Corbis-Bettmann, 925; Centro Cultural de la Raza, 928; Everett Collection, Inc., 931; AP/Wide World Photos, 932; Corbis-Bettmann, 937; SIPA Press, 939

Chapter 31: Photos: Tsing-Fang Chen/SuperStock, Inc., 945; Dennis Brack/Black Star, 948; Dennis Brack/ Black Star, 953; Corbis-Bettmann, 958; (left) Photo Network for Michael Philip Manheim, 959; Alberto Guido Rossi/The Image Bank, 959; Lynn Johnson/Black Star, 960; Joyce Dopkeen/*The New York Times*, January 31, 1993, 962; A. Berliner/Liaison Agency, Inc., 963; Lisa Quinones/Black Star, 965; Peter Turnley/Black Star, 972; Patrick Downs/Los Angeles Times Syndicate, 973; Lloyd Francis, Jr./Black Star, 1992, San Jose Mercury News/Black Star, 974; Sygma, 976; Reuters/Mike Segar/Archive Photos, 978; Joe Marquette/AP/Wide World Photos, 980

Immigration & Community, since 1930: Photos: Ed Bohon/The Stock Market, 989; Charles Gupton/The Stock Market, 991

INDEX

B

D

F

G

H

M

T

U

V

X

Y

Z